Tasmania

Paul Smitz

W9-AUK-395

LONELY PLANET PUBLICATIONS
Melbourne • Oakland • London • Paris

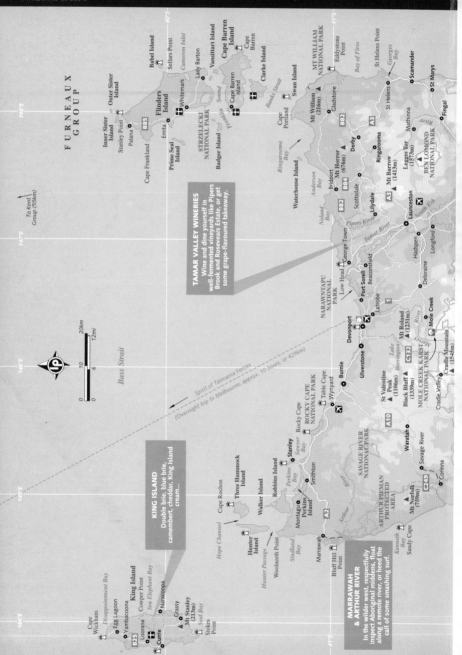

FURNEAUX GROUP

Bass Strait

To Kent Group (55km)

TAMAR VALLEY WINERIES
Wine and dine yourself in well-fermented vineyards like Pipers Brook and Rosevears Estate, or get some grape-flavoured takeaway.

KING ISLAND
Double brie, blue brie, camembert, cheddar, King Island cream...

MARRAWAH & ARTHUR RIVER
In the wilder west, respectfully inspect Aboriginal middens, float along a remote river, or heed the call of some smashing surf.

Spirit of Tasmania Ferries
(Overnight trip to Melbourne, approx. 10 hours, or 429km)

King Island
Currie
Naracoopa
Grassy
Mt Stanley (213m)
Stokes Point
Seal Bay
Sea Elephant Bay
Cowper Point
Egg Lagoon
Yambacoona
Disappointment Bay
Cape Wickham
Loorana
B25

Hope Channel
Cape Rochon
Three Hummock Island
Walker Island
Robbins Island
Hunter Island
Hunter Passage
Woolnorth Point
Perkins Island
Montagu
Smithton
Stanley
Sawyer Bay
Rocky Cape
ROCKY CAPE NATIONAL PARK
Table Cape
Wynyard
Burnie
Ulverstone
Devonport
Latrobe
Port Sorell
Beaconsfield
Low Head
George Town
Tamar River
Launceston
Longford
Hadspen
Deloraine
Mole Creek
MOLE CREEK KARST NATIONAL PARK
Cradle Mountain (1545m)
Cradle Valley
Lake Barrington
Black Bluff (1339m)
St Valentine Peak (1106m)
Waratah
Savage River
SAVAGE RIVER NATIONAL PARK
ARTHUR PIEMAN PROTECTED AREA
Corinna
C249
Mt Norfolk (759m)
Kenneth Bay
Sandy Cape
Marrawah
Bluff Hill Point
Sundland Bay
A2
A10

NARAWNTAPU NATIONAL PARK
Mole Creek
Mt Roland (1231m)
C132
South Esk
Mathinna
A3
Ben Lomond National Park
Legges Tor (1573m)
Mt Barrow (1413m)
A3
Lilydale
Scottsdale
Derby
B2
Mt Horror (676m)
B4
Bridport
Waterhouse Island
Anderson Bay
Ringarooma Bay
Cape Portland
Eddystone Point
Bay of Fires
St Helens
St Helens Point
Georges Bay
Scamander
St Marys
Fingal
Mt William (216m)
MT WILLIAM NATIONAL PARK
Gladstone
B2
Ringarooma
Noland Bay
Pipers River
Low Head

Inner Sister Island
Outer Sister Island
Stanley Point
Palana
B85
Emita
Whitemark
Flinders Island
STRZELECKI NATIONAL PARK
Badger Island
Prime Seal Island
Cape Frankland
Babel Island
Sellars Point
Cameron Inlet
Lady Barton
Vansittart Island
Franklin Sound
Cape Barren Island
Cape Barren
Clarke Island
Swan Island
Banks Strait

Bass Strait

20km
12ml

2 Contents – Text

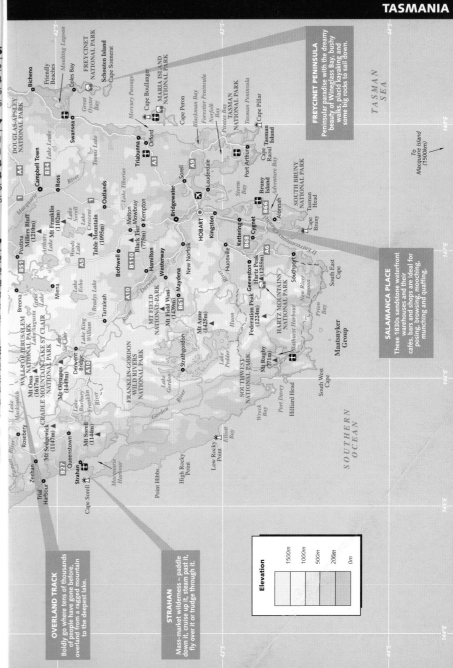

TASMAN SEA

To Macquarie Island (1500m)

FREYCINET PENINSULA
Peninsular paradise with the dreamy beauty of Wineglass Bay, bushy walks, placid kayaking and some big rocks to sail down.

SALAMANCA PLACE
These 1830s sandstone waterfront warehouses and their cafés, bars and shops are ideal for posing, browsing, mooching, munching and quaffing.

SOUTHERN OCEAN

OVERLAND TRACK
Boldly go where tens of thousands of people have gone before, overland from a ragged mountain to the deepest lake.

STRAHAN
Mass-market wilderness – paddle down it, cruise up it, steam past it, fly over it or trudge through it.

Elevation
1500m 1000m 500m 200m 0m

Tasmania
3rd edition – October 2002
First published – September 1996

Published by
Lonely Planet Publications Pty Ltd ABN 36 005 607 983
90 Maribyrnong St, Footscray, Victoria 3011, Australia

Lonely Planet offices
Australia Locked Bag 1, Footscray, Victoria 3011
USA 150 Linden St, Oakland, CA 94607
UK 10a Spring Place, London NW5 3BH
France 1 rue du Dahomey, 75011 Paris

Photographs
Many of the images in this guide are available for licensing from
Lonely Planet Images.
w www.lonelyplanetimages.com

Front cover photograph
Valley mist at dawn, Southwest National Park (Grant Dixon)

ISBN 1 74059 230 1

text & maps © Lonely Planet Publications Pty Ltd 2002
photos © photographers as indicated 2002

Printed through Colorcraft Ltd, Hong Kong
Printed in China

Contents – Text

THE NORTH   231

THE NORTHWEST   254

THE WEST   277

MT FIELD & THE SOUTHWEST   306

BASS STRAIT ISLANDS   314

THANKS   326

INDEX   330

MAP LEGEND   back page

METRIC CONVERSION   inside back cover

Contents – Maps

MAP INDEX

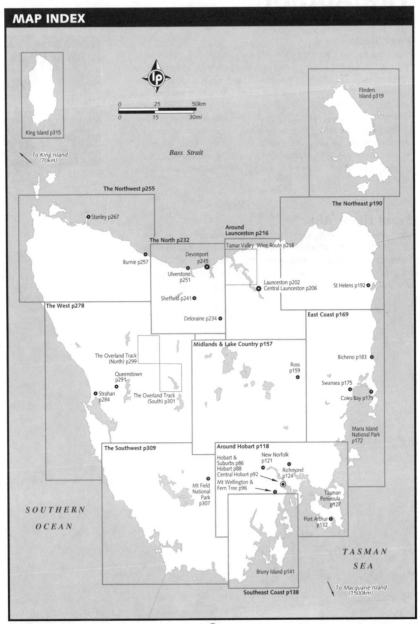

0   25   50km
0   15   30mi

The Author

Paul Smitz

According to Paul's lemon juice–soaked resume, he escaped from a test tube in Canberra and in some early wanderings collected gold bullion in Mexico, cruised the Panama Canal, tottered around Europe, and navigated Africa's west coast (he was only six at the time but reckoned it still counted). After other travels, he left Canberra for a round-Oz odyssey but ran out of petrol in Melbourne, where he joined Lonely Planet and ruined lives as an editor, map publishing manager and Web writer. He lives just outside Melbourne with an enigmatic woman who has an unfortunate spiritual connection with Ute Lemper. Paul has also worked on Lonely Planet's *Australia* and *Prague* guidebooks.

From the Author

Thank you to the people across the island and offshore on even smaller islands who gave me information, opinions and many good-humoured moments, including those that were entirely unintentional. Ta also to people closer to home and at LP for their help and support – you know who you are, and if you don't, it's time to contact a genealogy service.

This Book

This edition of *Tasmania* was written by Paul Smitz, who built on the work of John & Monica Chapman in the 1st edition and Lyn McGaurr in the 2nd.

From the Publisher

This edition of *Tasmania* was produced in Lonely Planet's Melbourne office. Kyla Gillzan and Rebecca Hobbs coordinated the editing with text reformatting by Ilana Sharp, and Sarah Sloane, Kusnandar, Clare Capell and Karen Fry did the mapping with assistance from Anthony Phelan. John Shippick coordinated the layout and design with help from Nick Stebbing. The cover was designed by Maria Vallianos. Kusnandar compiled the climate charts. Thanks to Karen Fry for last-minute sea-kayaking advice and to Mark Germanchis for Quark support through layout. Thanks also to Corinne Waddell, Jane Thompson, Adriana Mammarella, Bridget Blair and Errol Hunt for keeping the whole thing shipshape.

THANKS
Many thanks to the travellers who used the last edition and wrote to us with helpful hints, advice and interesting anecdotes. Your names appear in the back of this book.

Foreword

ABOUT LONELY PLANET GUIDEBOOKS

The story begins with a classic travel adventure: Tony and Maureen Wheeler's 1972 journey across Europe and Asia to Australia. There was no useful information about the overland trail then, so Tony and Maureen published the first Lonely Planet guidebook to meet a growing need.

From a kitchen table, Lonely Planet has grown to become the largest independent travel publisher in the world, with offices in Melbourne (Australia), Oakland (USA), London (UK) and Paris (France).

Today Lonely Planet guidebooks cover the globe. There is an ever-growing list of books and information in a variety of media. Some things haven't changed. The main aim is still to make it possible for adventurous travellers to get out there – to explore and better understand the world.

At Lonely Planet we believe travellers can make a positive contribution to the countries they visit – if they respect their host communities and spend their money wisely. Since 1986 a percentage of the income from each book has been donated to aid projects and human rights campaigns, and, more recently, to wildlife conservation.

Although inclusion in a guidebook usually implies a recommendation, we cannot list every good place. Exclusion does not necessarily imply criticism. In fact there are a number of reasons why we might exclude a place – sometimes it is simply inappropriate to encourage an influx of travellers.

UPDATES & READER FEEDBACK

Things change – prices go up, schedules change, good places go bad and bad places go bankrupt. Nothing stays the same. So, if you find things better or worse, recently opened or long-since closed, please tell us and help make the next edition even more accurate and useful.

Lonely Planet thoroughly updates each guidebook as often as possible – usually every two years, although for some destinations the gap can be longer. Between editions, up-to-date information is available in our free, quarterly *Planet Talk* newsletter and monthly email bulletin *Comet*. The *Scoop* section of our website covers news and current affairs relevant to travellers. Lastly, the *Thorn Tree* bulletin board and *Postcards* section carry unverified, but fascinating, reports from travellers.

Tell us about it! We genuinely value your feedback. A well-travelled team at Lonely Planet reads and acknowledges every email and letter we receive and ensures that every morsel of information finds its way to the relevant authors, editors and cartographers.

Everyone who writes to us will find their name listed in the next edition of the appropriate guidebook, and will receive the latest issue of *Comet* or *Planet Talk*. The very best contributions will be rewarded with a free guidebook.

We may edit, reproduce and incorporate your comments in Lonely Planet products such as guidebooks, websites and digital products, so let us know if you don't want your comments reproduced or your name acknowledged.

How to contact Lonely Planet:
Online: **e** talk2us@lonelyplanet.com.au, **w** www.lonelyplanet.com
Australia: Locked Bag 1, Footscray, Victoria 3011
UK: 10a Spring Place, London NW5 3BH
USA: 150 Linden St, Oakland, CA 94607

Introduction

Referred to locally as 'Tassie', Tasmania is Australia's smallest state and this down-under country's only island state. It's nature's verdant holiday house, a place of enormously diverse inland and coastal wilderness areas that range from the wildest of ocean dunes and satellite islets to near-impenetrable rainforest, rugged mountain ranges, soaring sea cliffs and serenely fragile alpine moorlands. One quarter of this outlandishly beautiful island is made up of wildlife-saturated national parks, with most of that awarded the status of World Heritage Area.

Tasmania is also an exuberant human habitat. The main cities might be engaged in a cosmopolitan face-off across the length of the island, but smaller settlements are also getting in on the act, continually adding to their urban inventories with a mixture of plush new accommodation, cruisy hostels, sit-back-and-relax cafes, artsy shops, festive occasions, and restaurants that prepare the splendid local seafood, game and produce with creative culinary fervour, digestively aided by superb local wines. Bucolic rural retreats are also multiplying, with many small-town bed and breakfasts seducing weary nerves across the state.

Tasmania was originally known as Van Diemen's Land, notorious as a British penal colony and the place where Aboriginal people, the land's traditional owners, were brutally subjugated during the 19th century. There are fascinating Tasmanian Aborigine–owned sites all over the island, while evocative architectural remnants of the convict era can be explored in the ruins of the penal settlement at Port Arthur, the many convict-built midlands bridges, and beautifully preserved Georgian sandstone buildings in more than 20 historic towns.

Don't be lulled by tourist brochures and their persuasively compact itineraries into thinking that Tasmania is merely a series of 'attractions' to speed between, with little of interest along the way. The exact opposite is true. So take your time, have a long look around, talk to the locals, and above all, discover the place for yourself.

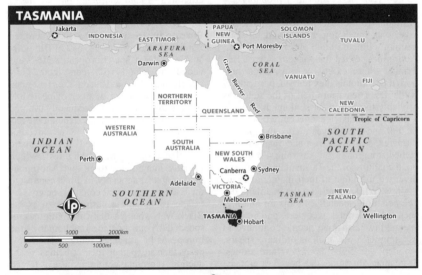

9

Facts about Tasmania

HISTORY
Tasmanian Aborigines

Since European settlement, the story of the Tasmanian Aborigines has had a terribly unhappy theme. The Aboriginal people were subjected to an attempted genocide, during which they were dispossessed of their land so quickly and thoroughly that it's remarkable any trace of their history, culture or language survives. Survive they do though, in the form of carvings and paintings in the rocky caves they once inhabited, coastal middens comprising the remnants of shells that yielded meals, quarries where stone tools were fashioned, and, most importantly, in the form of the Tasmanian Aborigines themselves and their persisting cultural identity and reasserted sovereignty.

Some Tasmanian Aborigines use the word Palawa (First Man) as a collective noun for their people.

Early History The land mass now called Tasmania was settled by Aborigines at least 35,000 years ago, when they probably migrated across the land bridge that joined Tasmania to the rest of Australia. The sea level was much lower then and the Tasmanian climate much drier and colder. Aborigines settled the western side of Tasmania, where extensive grasslands supported the animals they hunted, particularly wallabies. The eastern half of the state was probably too barren for settlement.

When the last ice age ended between 18,000 and 12,000 years ago, the glaciers retreated, sea levels rose and Tasmania detached from mainland Australia. From then on, the culture of the Tasmanian Aborigines diverged from that of their mainland counterparts. While people on the mainland developed more specialised tools for hunting, such as boomerangs, woomeras and pronged spears, the Tasmanian people continued to use simpler tools, such as ordinary spears, wooden war clubs *(waddies)* and stones. Tasmanian Aborigines did, however, produce

boats of a design more sophisticated than those created on the mainland and used them to hunt seals and mutton birds on and around the offshore islands.

As the climate changed after the ice age, the vegetation in the western half of the island altered, enabling tall forests to become established, while in the east rainfall increased and extensive grasslands developed. Most of the Aborigines abandoned their caves and shelters and followed the animals they hunted to the more open eastern tracts of land. Those who remained in the west lived primarily on the coast.

Tasmanian Aborigines fed themselves by hunting, fishing and gathering, and sheltered in bark lean-tos. They protected themselves from the island's cold weather by rubbing a mixture of ochre, charcoal and fat on their skin. It's estimated there were between 5000 and 10,000 Aborigines in Tasmania when Europeans arrived. They were organised into 'bands' of around 50 people, with each band claiming rights over a specific area of land and being part of one of the nine main language groups.

European Invasion The first recorded European landing was in 1642 at Bruny Island's Fluted Cape. European settlers invaded the island 161 years later. They established a base at Risdon after first massacring an unknown number of peaceable Aboriginal people and subsequently usurped traditional hunting grounds, fencing the fertile ground into farms. In 1816, Governor Thomas Davey produced his idealistic 'Proclamation to the Aborigines', which visually imagined settlers and Aborigines living together amicably, in direct contrast to the realities of a brutal colonial society.

The 1820s saw a period known as the Black War, when Tasmanian Aborigines responded to being treated as subhuman by the Europeans by attacking settlers. The Europeans then stepped up their atrocities by abducting Aboriginal children to use as forced

Truganini

Truganini's name is often mentioned in historical accounts of the European invasion and its consequences for Tasmanian Aborigines. She was born on Bruny Island in 1812, a daughter of Mangana, the chief of the Nuennone Tribe. Along with her husband, Woureddy, she left her island home to travel with George Robinson on his island-wide expeditions to win the confidence of the remaining Aboriginal people and during this three-year period twice saved his life. Truganini then lived with fellow Tasmanian Aborigines in the derelict environment of Wybalenna on Flinders Island and afterwards at Oyster Cove.

After living out her final years in Hobart, Truganini died on 8 May 1876. For many years, her skeleton was displayed as a public curio in the Tasmanian capital. One hundred years after her death, her wishes were granted when her ashes were finally scattered in the channel beside her beloved Bruny Island.

labour, raping and torturing Aboriginal women, giving poisoned flour to friendly tribes and laying steel traps in the bush.

The Black Line In 1828, martial law was proclaimed by Lieutenant-Governor Arthur in Tasmania's central districts, giving soldiers the right to arrest or shoot on sight any Aboriginal person found in an area of European settlement. In 1830, in an attempt to flush out all Aborigines and corner them on the Tasman Peninsula, a human chain of about 2200 men, known as the Black Line, was formed by settlers and soldiers. This line moved for three weeks through the settled areas of the state. Three weeks later, the farcical manoeuvre had succeeded in capturing only an old man and a boy, and confirmed settlers' fears that they couldn't defeat the Aborigines by force of arms.

Lieutenant-Governor Arthur then consented to missionary George Augustus Robinson's plan to 'conciliate' the remaining Aborigines. During the next three years, Robinson travelled throughout most of the

state and persuaded (through a mixture of encouragement and force) virtually all of the Aborigines in mainland Tasmania to lay down their arms and accompany him to new settlements. Robinson may have actually believed that his actions were ultimately in the best interests of the Aborigines, but even as he was mounting his final expeditions, the Europeans were virtually abandoning the west coast. Historian Lyndall Ryan argues in *The Aboriginal Tasmanians* that 'the western Aborigines would probably have survived if Robinson had not captured them'.

There is strong historical evidence that the Aborigines were enticed to follow Robinson to a succession of settlements in the Furneaux Islands with promises of sanctuary and land. Instead, they were subjected to European attempts to 'civilise' and 'Christianise' them and made to work for the government. After enduring a number of moves to places such as Sarah Island on the west coast, they were finally settled at Wybalenna (Black Man's Houses) on Flinders Island, where one by one they began dying from a potent mixture of despair, homesickness, poor food and respiratory disease.

Oyster Bay Community In 1847, the surviving residents petitioned Queen Victoria, complaining of their treatment and referring to the 'agreement' they thought Robinson had made with Lieutenant-Governor Arthur on their behalf. Wybalenna was eventually abandoned and the survivors transferred to mainland Tasmania. Of the 135 who had been sent to Flinders Island, only 47 survived to make the journey to Oyster Cove south of Hobart. Their new accommodation proved to be substandard and the Aborigines once again experienced the criminal neglect of the European authorities, and growing demoralisation. Within a decade, half of them were dead. Truganini, the last of the Oyster Cove community, died in 1876 (see the boxed text on this page).

Furneaux Islands Community European sealers had been working in Bass Strait since 1798 and they raided tribes along the coast, kidnapping Aboriginal women as sexual partners and workers. The sealers were disinterested in Aboriginal land and eventually formed a reciprocal trade relationship with the Aborigines, whereby the sealers traded dogs and other items for accompaniment back to their islands by Aboriginal women, and occasionally men. A disapproving Tasmanian establishment contemptuously termed the descendants of sealers and Aboriginal women 'half-castes', and even though Cape Barren was designated an Aboriginal reserve in the 1880s, there was continual pressure on the Islanders to adopt European farming ways and assimilate with mainlanders.

Today Tasmanian Aborigines continue to claim rights to land and compensation for past injustices. Acknowledgement of the genocidal treatment meted out to Aborigines by Europeans has resulted in the recognition of native titles to land. In 1995, the state government returned 12 sites to the Tasmanian Aboriginal community, including Oyster Cove, Kutikina Cave and Steep Island. Wybalenna was added to this list in 1999.

European Discovery
Known history records that the first European to see Tasmania was the Dutch navigator Abel Tasman, who arrived in 1642 and promptly called it Van Diemen's Land, after the governor of the Dutch East Indies. Between 1770 and 1790, Tasmania was sighted and visited by a series of other European sailors, including captains Tobias Furneaux, James Cook and William Bligh. They all visited Adventure Bay on Bruny Island and believed it to be part of the Australian mainland rather than an island off Van Diemen's Land. In 1792, Admiral Bruni D'Entrecasteaux explored the southeastern coastline more thoroughly, mapping and naming many of its features. Most major landmarks still bear names bequeathed by this expedition.

European contact with the Tasmanian coast became more frequent after the soldiers and convicts of the First Fleet settled at Sydney Cove in 1788, mainly because ships heading to the colony of New South Wales (NSW) from the west had to sail around the island.

In 1798, Lieutenant Matthew Flinders circumnavigated Van Diemen's Land and proved that it was an island. He named the rough stretch of sea between the island and the mainland Bass Strait, after George Bass, the ship's surgeon. The European discovery of Bass Strait shortened the journey to Sydney from India or Africa's Cape of Good Hope by a week.

Founding of Hobart
In the late 1790s, Governor King of NSW decided to establish a second settlement in Australia, south of Sydney Cove. Port Phillip Bay in Victoria was initially considered, but the site was rejected due to a lack of water on the Mornington Peninsula and, in 1803, Tasmania's Risdon Cove was chosen. One year later, the settlement was moved to the present site of Hobart. The threat of other nations gaining a foothold on the island by starting settlements prompted expansion, and in 1804 the first settlement on the Tamar River was established at George Town.

Convicts
Although convicts were shipped out with the first settlers, penal colonies weren't built until later when free settlers demanded social demarcation. Meeting the criteria that it had to be inhospitable and as far away as possible, Macquarie Harbour on the harsh west coast hosted the first penal colony in 1822. The actual site was on small Sarah Island and the prisoners sent there were those who had committed further crimes after arriving in Australia. Their punishment was the severe manual labour of cutting down Huon pines in the rainforest. It's believed conditions were so dreadful here that some prisoners actually committed murder in order to be sent to Hobart for trial and execution.

The number of prisoners sent to Van Diemen's Land increased. In 1825, the year the island was constituted a colony independent of NSW, another penal settlement was established, this one on the east coast of Maria Island, where prisoners were treated more humanely. In 1830, a third penal colony was established at Port Arthur on the Tasman Peninsula. Shortly after its construction, the other two penal colonies closed – Maria Island in 1832 and Macquarie Harbour in 1833.

Punishments meted out to convicts at Port Arthur, which like its predecessors was considered escape-proof, included weeks of solitary confinement, sometimes in total darkness and silence. The worst prisoners were sent to work in the coal mines of nearby Saltwater River, where they were housed in miserably damp underground cells.

In 1840, convict transportation to NSW ceased, resulting in an increase in the number of people being sent to Van Diemen's Land; there was a peak of 5329 new arrivals in 1842. In 1844, control of the Norfolk Island penal settlement was transferred from NSW to Van Diemen's Land, and by 1848 the colony was the only place in the British Empire to which convicts were still being transported.

Vociferous opposition to the continued transportation of convicts came from free settlers, who in 1850 formed the Anti-Transportation League to successfully lobby for change. The last convicts transported to the colony arrived in 1853.

Van Diemen's Land had been the most feared destination for British prisoners for more than three decades. During those years a total of 74,000 convicts had been transported to the island. The majority of these people had served out their sentences and settled in the colony, yet so terrible was its reputation that in 1856 – the year it achieved responsible self-government – it changed its name to Tasmania in an attempt to free its image once and for all from the shackles of its past.

Exploration & Expansion

The establishment of Hobart Town and George Town attracted new settlers, resulting in a demand for more land. Settlers initially spread along the southern coast towards Port Arthur, along the east coast and around the Launceston area. By 1807 an overland route from Hobart to Launceston had been forged. The earliest buildings were rough timber huts, but as towns developed, settlers with stone masonry skills arrived. Stone was readily available for construction work and many early stone buildings have survived.

To the Europeans Tasmania's big unknown was its rugged hinterland, where difficult, mountainous country barred the way. The first Europeans to cross the island were escapees from Macquarie Harbour; many escaped, but only a few survived the journey across to Hobart Town. A significant though highly controversial early explorer was George Robinson, who in 1830 set out to entice and cajole the Tasmanian Aborigines into leaving their traditional lands, and so became the first European to walk across much of the state.

In 1828 George Frankland was appointed Tasmania's surveyor-general. Determined to map the entire state, he sent many surveyors on long, arduous journeys during the 1830s, often accompanying them. By 1845, when Frankland died, most of the state was roughly mapped and catalogued.

Building roads across the mountainous west was difficult, and many were surveyed across all sorts of difficult landscapes before being abandoned. But in 1932, the Lyell Hwy from Hobart to Queenstown was finally opened for business, linking the west coast to Hobart.

Mining

In the 1870s gold was discovered near the Tamar River and tin in the northeast. These discoveries prompted a deluge of international prospectors. In the northeast a number of Chinese miners arrived, bringing their culture with them.

Mining was a tough way of life and most people didn't make their fortune. Individual prospectors grabbed the rich, easily found surface deposits, but once these were gone the miners had to form larger groups and companies to mine deeper deposits, until eventually these either ran out or became unprofitable to work. Remains of the mine workings at Derby and Beaconsfield can still be visited today.

Once it was realised that there was mineral wealth to be found, prospectors randomly explored most of the state. On the west coast, discoveries of large deposits of silver and lead resulted in a boom in the 1880s and an associated rush at Zeehan. In fact, so rich in minerals was the area that it ultimately supported mines significant enough to create the towns of Rosebery, Tullah and Queenstown. Geological exploitation went unchecked, however, and by the 1920s copper mining at Queenstown had gashed holes in the surrounding hills, while logging, pollution, fires and heavy rain stripped the terrain of its vegetation and topsoil. The environment has only begun repairing itself over the past few decades.

The rich belt of land from Queenstown to the northern coast is still being mined in several places, but this is now being done with a little more environmental consideration and less-visible effects than in the past. New finds will undoubtedly occur in this mineral-rich belt. At the time of writing, for instance, the establishment of a large magnesite mine in the northwest was a distinct possibility (magnesite is refined into magnesium, which is used by the car industry in the production of lighter and more economical vehicles), though for the moment it has been postponed due to a slump in world magnesite prices.

The Last Century

Tasmania officially became a state when Australia's Federation took place in 1901. For Tasmanians, as for mainlanders in the new Commonwealth of Australia, the first half of the 20th century was dominated by war, beginning with the dispatch of a contingent of 80 Tasmanian soldiers to South Africa to fight in the Boer War (which began in October 1899), through the Great War and WWII, with the Depression of the late 1920s thrown in for bad measure.

The state's post-WWII economy was reassuringly buoyant, with industrial success embodied by Bell Bay's aluminium refinery and the ongoing developments of the powerful Hydro-Electric Commission. However, by the 1980s it had suffered a worrisome decline – subsequent years have seen social reflections of economic unease in climbing 'emigration' levels and falling birth rates.

GEOGRAPHY

Tasmania is the smallest Australian state and the only one that is an island. It's 240km south of Victoria, across stormy Bass Strait. To its east is the Tasman Sea, which separates Australia and New Zealand, while to its west and south is the Southern Ocean, which keeps Australia from bumping into Antarctica. It's 296km from north to south and 315km from east to west – including its lesser islands, it has an area of 68,049 sq km.

Although Tasmania's highest mountain, Mt Ossa, is only 1617m (5300 feet) high, much of the island's interior is extremely rugged. One indication of the dearth of flat land is the proximity of the centres of its two largest cities, Hobart and Launceston, to extremely steep hills. The only large, relatively flat area is the broad, undulating plain extending from Launceston towards Hobart.

The coastline is beautiful, with a multitude of coves and beaches, shallow bays and broad estuaries, the result of river valleys being flooded by rising sea levels after the last ice age. By contrast, the Central Plateau, which was covered by a single ice sheet during the last ice age, is a bleak, harsh environment unsuitable for farming; Australia's deepest natural freshwater lake, Lake St Clair, is up here.

Most of the island's western half is a maze of mountainous ranges and ridges bearing signs of recent glaciation. The climate here is inhospitable and the annual rainfall a discouraging 3m or more, and for much of the year uncompromising seas batter the coast. Yet the cliffs, lakes, rainforests and wild rivers of this magnificent region are among Tasmania's greatest attractions, drawing walkers, adventurers and photographers (see the World Heritage Area entry in the special section 'Flora, Fauna, National Parks & Reserves').

CLIMATE

Australia's seasons oppose those of the northern hemisphere: here, midsummer is in January and midwinter is in July.

Tasmania is in the path of the Roaring Forties, a notorious band of wind that encircles the globe and produces very changeable weather. It's not surprising, then, that the west and southwest can be blasted by strong winds and drenched by heavy rain. Nevertheless, because the state is small and also an island, it does enjoy a maritime climate, which means that it's rarely extremely cold or extremely hot.

The prevailing airflow is westerly, creating a rain shadow that results in the west receiving much more rain than the east: while the annual rainfall in the west is 3m or more, the east receives only about 1m. The east coast is nearly always warmer and milder than anywhere else in the state, and the Bureau of Meteorology in Tasmania (actually classified as the Tasmania &

Antarctica Regional Office, much to the chagrin of some tourist operators who despair at the impression of the state's climate this gives visitors) claims that towns such as Swansea and Bicheno receive more hours of sunshine than other major Australian coastal resorts. Hobart is Australia's second-driest capital after Adelaide.

Tasmania has four distinct seasons, although storms can deposit wintry conditions any time of year. In summer the days are generally warm rather than hot, and the nights mild. This is the most pleasant time of year, and conditions often improve right up until March, after which temperatures drop. The rest of autumn is generally characterised by cool, sunny days and the occasional frosty night.

Winter is wet, cold and stormy, particularly in the west. Overcast days are common in the east, despite its lower rainfall. Snow falls on the higher peaks but usually isn't deep enough for skiing: the two ski resorts operate spasmodically.

Spring is windy. Storms sweep the island in a winter pattern, but in-between the sun shines and gradually warmth returns to the state. In some years, however, stormy spring weather has continued well into summer.

ECOLOGY & ENVIRONMENT

Despite a long history of bad, and often atrocious, environmental management, Tasmania is famous for its pristine wilderness areas. Both the air and water in parts of the state are claimed to be the purest on the planet, while its Tasmanian Wilderness World Heritage Area, which covers approximately 20% of the island, is internationally renowned. Yet, ironically, the preservation of much of the environment that Tasmania is proud of has been achieved only by protracted campaigns on rivers and in forests, streets, the media, parliaments and courts.

In the late 1960s and early 1970s, the efforts of bushwalkers and conservationists to stop Lake Pedder in the southwest from being flooded for the purposes of electricity production resulted in the formation of what's believed to be the first Green political party in the world. Although that

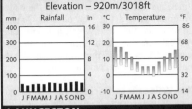

campaign was ultimately unsuccessful, the lessons learnt during the fight were crucial in enabling a new generation of activists to plan and execute a vastly more sophisticated campaign a decade later, one that saved the Franklin River – one of the finest wild rivers on the planet – from being flooded for similar purposes. The Franklin River campaign saw the conservation movement mature as a political force and gain acceptance as an influential player in the policy-making process. (For more information see the Mt Field & The Southwest chapter later.)

A successful campaign in the late 1980s to prevent the construction of a new pulp mill in the northwest saw the formation of a party of Green independents, led by Bob Brown, and the subsequent election of five of its members to parliament. The Greens held the balance of power in the Tasmanian parliament from 1989 to 1998.

Changes to the number of state parliamentarians, however, resulted in three of the four sitting Tasmanian Greens members losing their seats in the 1998 state election (see the Government & Politics section later) and a significant muting of the Greens' voice in parliament. In the 2002 election the Greens once again increased their representation in parliament to four seats.

Conservation Groups

Tasmanian Conservation Trust The Tasmanian Conservation Trust *(TCT; ☎ 6234 3552; W www.tct.org.au; 102 Bathurst St, Hobart)* is the state's primary nongovernmental conservation organisation. In addition to managing its own campaigns, the TCT hosts the Tasmanian offices of two other Australian environmental organisations: the National Threatened Species Network, which undertakes public education programmes aimed at students, landholders and the wider community; and the Marine and Coastal Community Network, which has particular interests in the establishment of no-take marine reserves and the promotion of safe marine waste-management practices.

The Wilderness Society The Wilderness Society in Tasmania *(☎ 6234 9366; W www .wilderness.org.au; 130 Davey St, Hobart)* is presently concentrating on ensuring the preservation of several important areas: the Styx Valley, which contains the tallest hardwood eucalypt forests on Earth, with specimens reaching in excess of 90m in what's been dubbed the Valley of the Giants; the Tarkine Wilderness, 3500 sq km of wilderness between the Arthur and Pieman Rivers that includes a staggering 2000 sq km of

Bob Brown

Robert James Brown is undoubtedly the most famous figure in Australia's conservation movement. He is a qualified doctor who became a strong wilderness advocate in 1976 after rafting down the Franklin River. He was an unsuccessful state senate candidate in 1975 for the United Tasmania Group, the world's first Greens party, which formed during the struggle to save Lake Pedder. Together with friends, he also made films about the Franklin and soon became a public figure.

He became the Wilderness Society's director in 1979 and a leading figure in the battle to save the Franklin. At the height of the Franklin River Blockade in 1983 he was arrested and imprisoned for protesting. In a strange twist of fate he went directly from jail to parliament because, with the resignation of Green independent Dr Norm Saunders, the seat passed to the runner-up at the previous election – Bob Brown.

In state parliament he was a strong but solitary voice as an independent. He eventually formed his own political party and by 1989 his Green independents held five of the 35 seats in parliament and had become a significant political force. In 1992 he played a key role in the formation of the Australian Greens party. He resigned from state parliament in 1993 and then followed his mentor, Dr Norm Saunders, and stood as an Australian Greens candidate for Federal Parliament in 1996. He won his seat by a handful of votes, joining other Green independents (not members of Bob's party) in the upper house of parliament.

cool-temperate rainforest (the largest single area of such forest in Australia), over 70% of which is unprotected and threatened by logging and mining; and the Great Western Tiers (also known by its Aboriginal name of Kooparoona Niara, meaning Mountain of Spirits), where long battles over the Mother Cummings Peak area have been engaged, if not in the total protection of the area, then at least regarding the use of far more sensitive logging practices. The Wilderness Society is also developing a continent-wide environmental management plan called WildCountry – see its website for details.

Marine Issues

In 1999 the federal government established the Tasmanian Seamounts Marine Reserve, a 370-sq-km deep-sea reserve 170km south of Hobart that is home to many unique animals and plants, not to mention 70 submerged and extinct volcanoes.

CCAMLR The Hobart-based Commission for the Conservation of Antarctic Marine Living Resources (CCAMLR) meets in Hobart every spring and is responsible for managing the ecologically sustainable exploitation of the living marine resources of the Southern Ocean.

Patagonian Toothfish & Albatrosses A major concern in recent times has been the illegal fishing of the Patagonian toothfish, an endangered bottom-dwelling fish found around sub-Antarctic islands. The toothfish is caught on longlines that can also cause the deaths of vast numbers of albatrosses, which take baits intended for the fish and are hooked and drowned as a result. Licensed fishing boats are ordered to take measures that aim to minimise these deaths, but solely self-interested pirate vessels are thought to be responsible for both the overfishing of the toothfish itself and the destruction of as many as 100,000 sea birds a year. In an encouraging display of cooperation, private fishing companies licensed to trawl for Patagonian toothfish got together with Australian conservation groups after a CCAMLR meeting in 1997 to form Isolfich

(the International Southern Oceans Longline Fisheries Information Clearing House), a nongovernmental organisation that collects and disseminates information on longline fishing in the southern oceans.

Introduced Pests

In mid-2001, Tasmania received some of the worst environmental news imaginable: a fox had been spotted near Longford in the state's north. Fox predation puts nearly 80 of the island's indigenous land species at enormous risk because of their vulnerability to attack from an animal against which they have no defence. Just as horrifying as the original sighting and subsequent reports of the European red fox in other parts of the state, including the Tasman Peninsula, is the revelation that the foxes were deliberately introduced to Tasmania, probably for the purposes of hunting. A full-time fox taskforce has been set up by the state government, though it may be too late to eradicate the threat to Tasmania's biodiversity that the animal poses.

The second-biggest entrenched threat to native wildlife in Tasmania is the cat (unless the speed-obsessed automobile drivers responsible for killing incalculable numbers of native animals on the state's roads count as introduced pests). The cat has established itself throughout the state, including on the Overland Track and Macquarie Island.

While feral dogs, goats and pigs can be found in Tasmania, they are not nearly so widespread as on the mainland. Even rabbits, which are a problem in rural areas, have had trouble penetrating the state's natural forests; this is just as well, because it appears that one of science's most touted weapons against the animal – calicivirus – is not particularly effective in cool, wet areas.

European carp, which are now flourishing in Lake Crescent, are a major headache for Inland Fisheries because of the impact they have on trout stocks and native fish. And the trout themselves, so prized by recreational fishers, pose a threat to such important species as *Pedder galaxias* (see the Threatened Species entry in the special section 'Flora, Fauna, National Parks & Reserves').

The European wasp is arguably more of a nuisance than anything else, although it is a threat to native bees, which it will kill. It's disheartening to hear reports that it has been spotted even in such remote areas as the Franklin River.

The root rot phytophthora and weeds such as willow and gorse are the major introduced threats to Tasmanian flora: two new species of phytophthora are thought to be responsible for the massive destruction of pencil pines near Pine Lake on the Central Plateau. This area is currently still under quarantine.

Energy

Energy production in Tasmania was controversial during the later years of 'hydro-industrialisation' (see the start of the Ecology & Environment section earlier). Today, however, further dam building for electricity production doesn't appear to be a viable economic or political option, and the government is looking elsewhere for new power supplies. The most significant (and still controversial) new venture is a proposed $500 million project called Basslink, which will connect Tasmania to the mainland electricity grid via an underwater cable stretching from a Victorian power station along the floor of Bass Strait to Bell Bay at the mouth of the Tamar River.

GOVERNMENT & POLITICS

Australia has a federal system of government with elements of both the US and Westminster systems. The federal government controls areas of national importance such as defence and foreign affairs. It collects income tax and shares a portion of this revenue with the states. The state government controls most internal affairs within the state. If there's a dispute between the two levels of government, then the high court studies the problem and the constitution and makes a ruling.

Tasmanian state elections are held every four years. The lower house is the House of Assembly, which has 25 members – five from each of the five electorates. The majority party in this house forms government, and its leader becomes premier. Members are elected by a system of proportional representation: candidates must achieve a quota of votes to gain a seat. In the past, this system resulted in smaller parties and independent candidates being well represented in parliament. However, at the 1998 election, the number of members in each electorate was reduced from seven to five; as a result,

Lake Johnston Nature Reserve

In 1987, an exceptional stand of Huon pine was discovered among a patch of deciduous beech at Lake Johnston on Tasmania's west coast by Forestry Tasmania forester Mike Peterson. Unusually, the stand has been found to be exclusively male, which means it must be reproducing itself vegetatively rather than sexually. Further tests have revealed very limited genetic diversity within the trees of the area, suggesting that the hundred or so existing specimens are all descended from remarkably few individuals.

According to Parks and Wildlife Service (PWS) botanist Jayne Balmer (commenting on the work of former PWS botanist Alison Shapcott), all the trees in the main stand are likely to be clones of a single ancestor. This lack of diversity in the trees' DNA and the absence of females indicate that the stand is extremely old, possibly dating from the last deglaciation 10,000 years ago. As such, it is of enormous importance, both botanically and for the contribution it has made to a 5000-year record of climate change. For this reason, the PWS-managed, 1.4-sq-km Lake Johnston Nature Reserve, 8km south of Rosebery, has been excised from the mining lease of which the stand was originally a part.

The area is highly sensitive and the issue of access has already been the subject of a legal case involving the Tasmanian Conservation Trust and the state government, the latter wanting to allow commercial tourism and the former wanting to prevent it. Nonetheless, at the time of writing, one operator had begun conducting short tours to the reserve (see the Rosebery section in The West chapter).

the number of votes required to meet a quota increased, and this has made it much harder for candidates who are not members of one of the two major parties to be elected. Only one of the four sitting Greens members was re-elected in the 1998 election, which saw the government change from Liberal to Labor. Labor, headed by Premier Jim Bacon, was returned to term in 2002, and the Greens won four seats, increasing their presence in parliament.

The upper house is the Legislative Council, members of which review government legislation.

ECONOMY

Tasmania's economy is based primarily on mining and agriculture. There are only a couple of heavy industries and they employ only a small proportion of the population. Tasmania has difficulty encouraging large industry because the major markets are on the Australian mainland and Bass Strait is an expensive obstacle to negotiate.

Mineral production has always been an important part of the economy, although the fortunes of particular mines have fluctuated alarmingly in recent times. The other main earner has been agricultural products, and Tasmania's economy remains susceptible to price trends of the competitive world market. In the 1960s, Tasmania was the primary supplier of apples to Europe, but then prices plummeted and the economy suffered. Having learnt from this, farmers now produce a diverse range of high-quality products like cheese, pickled onions, fruit and lavender.

Tasmania has some of the cleanest air and water in the world and exports pollution-free, bottled rainwater, while clean ocean waters support a healthy fishing industry. An industry that's now a major export earner is fish farming – Atlantic salmon from these farms is sold around the world. Dairying is another major industry, with King Island cheese being world-famous. Vegetables and potatoes are major crops in the north, with the produce mainly being sold to mainland Australia.

Last, but certainly not least, is tourism, which makes an enormous contribution to the economy. Tasmania (or at least its local entrepreneurs and tourism industry officials) has come to realise that it has a certain rarity in abundance: huge, undeveloped areas that are wild and beautiful. The industry has a fair proportion of small, family-style businesses that offer good value for money, as well as friendly personal service. That said, it remains to be seen how the current disastrous public liability situation will, if unaddressed, affect smaller businesses (see the boxed text 'Public Liability' in the Activities chapter).

POPULATION & PEOPLE

According to the last Australian census, conducted in August 2001, Tasmania's population was 472,931 – this figure reveals a 0.7% decrease in the state's population, continuing a recent pattern of decline. Tasmania also has the second-highest median age of any Australian state or territory (37 years). The greater Hobart area has a population of around 200,000, while about 100,000 people live in greater Launceston.

Around 15,000 people of Aboriginal descent live in Tasmania. No Tasmanian Aboriginal languages remain in use, although they are still remembered by Elders of Aboriginal communities and words of the Palawa Kani language have recently been incorporated into school curricula for Aboriginal children.

Most Tasmanians have a British background – there are fewer non-British migrants here per head of population than in any other Australian state. Tasmanians living outside Hobart and Launceston can sometimes seem parochial to 'mainlanders' and other visitors, though travellers who simply assume this will be the case are in reality the ones being stereotypically narrow-minded.

EDUCATION

The University of Tasmania is particularly strong in the fields of geology and Antarctic science and policy. At Franklin, south of Hobart, the skills of wooden boatbuilding are taught at the highly regarded Shipwright's Point School of Wooden Boatbuilding. The Australian School of Fine Furniture is based in Launceston, while at Beauty Point in the Tamar Valley north of Launceston is the

Australian Maritime College, which trains students in the techniques of fishing and navigation.

SCIENCE

Hobart is a centre for the study of marine science, climate change, geology and Antarctic science: the Australian Antarctic Division has its headquarters on the outskirts of nearby Kingston; the Commonwealth Scientific and Industrial Research Organisation (CSIRO) Division of Marine Research has its chief office and one of its three marine laboratories in Castray Esplanade, next to Princes Wharf; and a national cooperative research centre, the Antarctic CRC, is located on the campus of the University of Tasmania. The Antarctic Division's research and resupply vessel the *Aurora Australis* and the CSIRO's research vessels the *Southern Surveyor* and the MV *Franklin* can often be seen docked at the wharfs, as can a number of international research vessels.

At the University of Tasmania is the Centre for Ore Deposit Research, a national research centre with close links to the School of Earth Sciences at the university.

ARTS
Aboriginal Arts & Crafts

The traditional arts, crafts and culture of the Tasmanian Aborigines includes rock engravings (petroglyphs), body decoration, bark painting, basketry and shell necklace-making.

Tiagarra *(Tasmanian Aboriginal Culture Centre; ☎ 6424 8250)*, in Devonport, was set up to preserve the art and culture of the Tasmanian Aborigines. It has artefact exhibits, a rare collection of more than 250 rock engravings, and contemporary craftwork that is for sale.

Literature

Tasmania's unique culture and landscape and its unpalatable historical treatment of Tasmanian Aborigines and convicts have inspired and burdened writers of both fiction and nonfiction.

Marcus Clarke, a prolific writer who was born in London but spent most of his life in Australia, visited Tasmania in the 1870s and wrote *For the Term of His Natural Life,* an epic novel about convict life.

Queensland-born poet Gwen Harwood lived in Tasmania from 1945 until her death in 1996, and much of her work, such as *The Lion's Bride* (1981) and *Bone Scan* (1988), explores the island's natural beauty and the history of its Aboriginal population.

Robert Drewe's novel *The Savage Crows* (1976) also explores the oppression of Tasmanian Aborigines by the Europeans, while Hal Porter's *The Tilted Cross* (1961) is a novel set in old Hobart Town.

Christopher Koch is a Hobart-born author. His novels include *The Boys in the Island* (1958), an account of growing up in Tasmania; *The Year of Living Dangerously* (1978), which was made into a high-profile film; and *Out of Ireland* (1999), worked around the journal of a revolutionary Irishman who finds himself exiled in Van Diemen's Land.

Carmel Bird, born in Launceston but now living in Melbourne, is known for the quirky black humour of her stories and novels, including *The Bluebird Cafe* (1990), set in a fictional Tasmanian mining ghost town, and *Red Shoes* (1998), short-listed for the prestigious Miles Franklin award.

The seven novels of James McQueen, who died in 1998, include *Hook's Mountain* (1982), which has as a subplot the struggle to save Tasmania's forests.

Down Home: Revisiting Australia (1988), by academic Peter Conrad, is an evocative recollection of the author's childhood in Tasmania. It describes the island's cultural isolation and the ensuing sense of displacement of its people.

Tasmanian Amanda Lohrey's novels include *Morality of Gentlemen* (1984), set against the backdrop of Tasmania's waterfront disputes, and *Camille's Bread* (1995).

Hobart author Richard Flanagan's award-winning novel *Death of a River Guide* (1995) weaves together Tasmanian history and myths in a story set on the Franklin River – it makes an excellent introduction to Tasmanian history and life. His next novel, *The Sound of One Hand Clapping* (1997), won a national literary award, while the film of the same name was also well received (see the Films section in the Facts for the Visitor chapter). Most recently Flanagan wrote an enigmatic fictional account of Sarah Island in *Gould's Book of Fish* (2002).

In 1999 Tom Gilling published *The Sooterkin,* an idiosyncratic novel about a highly unusual child set in Hobart Town in the early 1800s, while Julia Leigh came up with the compelling, clinical tale of a man pursuing a living thylacine in *The Hunter*.

Matthew Kneale was short-listed for a Booker Prize for the historical fiction *English Passengers* (1999), a witty stew of multiple narratives telling the interwoven stories of a mid-19th-century expedition to Van Diemen's Land and the trials of the Tasmanian Aborigines.

Tasmania has a thriving literary scene, with annual events such as the annual Tasmanian Readers and Writers Festival (March) and the Tasmanian Poetry Festival (Launceston, in October) providing opportunities for discussion and readings. For details, contact the **Tasmanian Writers' Centre** (☎ 6224 0029; **w** *www.fearless.org .au/taswriters*). Local writers' work is published in the literary magazine *Island*. The biennial $40,000 Tasmania Pacific Region Prize is awarded to the best novel written by a resident of Australia, New Zealand or Melanesia.

Painting & Sculpture

Tasmania's art scene flourished from colonial times, particularly in the early 19th century under the governorship of Sir John Franklin and the patronage of his wife, Lady Jane Franklin. One of the first artists to successfully capture the Australian landscape's distinctive forms and colours was John Glover, an English artist who migrated to Tasmania in 1830. The English sculptor Benjamin Law also arrived in Tasmania in the 1830s, and he sculpted busts of two of the better-known Tasmanian Aborigines, Truganini and Woureddy.

Benjamin Duterrau is best known for his somewhat coarse paintings of Tasmanian Aborigines, including *The Conciliation,* which commemorated George Robinson's pursuit of the Aborigines. Successful convict artists included portraitists TG Wainewright (a convicted forger and reputed poisoner), Thomas Bock, and WB Gould, who executed charmingly naive still lifes.

Hobart-born William Piguenit has been called 'the first Australian-born professional painter'. He painted romantic Tasmanian landscapes, including Lake St Clair and Lake Pedder in the 1870s, and his works were among the first exhibited by the Art Society of Tasmania, founded in 1884. Other early exhibitors were J Haughton Forrest, who painted 'chocolate-box' landscapes and maritime subjects, and Belgian-born modernist Lucien Dechaineux, who also founded the art department at Hobart Technical College.

Major mainland Australian artists who visited Tasmania for inspiration early last century included Tom Roberts, Arthur Streeton and Frederick McCubbin.

In 1938 the Tasmanian Group of Painters was founded to foster the work of local artists. Founding members included Joseph Connor, a Hobart-born landscape watercolourist who was one of the early Australian modernists. Other innovators of the time were the under-recognised women artists Edith Holmes and Dorothy Stoner.

Since the 1940s a strong landscape watercolour school has developed in Tasmania, with artists such as Max Angus and Patricia Giles among the best known.

Launceston-born artist and teacher Jack Carington Smith won Australia's coveted Archibald Prize for portraiture in 1963. Tasmanian sculptor Stephen Walker has produced many bronze works that adorn Hobart's public spaces – he was also responsible for a sculptural tribute to the Midlands at The Steppes, near Great Lake. Renowned Australian landscape painter Lloyd Rees spent his final years living and working in Tasmania. During this time he was also involved in the Tasmanian conservation movement.

Notable contemporary artists include Bea Maddock, whose serialised images incorporate painting and photography, and Bob and Lorraine Jenyns, both sculptors and ceramicists. Since the early 1980s Tasmania's art culture has been revitalised and the new wave includes printmaker Ray Arnold, painter David Keeling, photographer David Stephenson and video-maker Leigh Hobbs.

The **Tasmanian Museum & Art Gallery** (☎ 6211 4177; W www.tmag.tas.gov.au) in Hobart has a good collection of Tasmanian colonial art and exhibits relating to Tasmanian Aboriginal culture. Also worth visiting are the Inveresk site of the Queen Victoria Museum & Art Gallery in Launceston, Burnie's Regional Art Gallery and Devonport's Gallery & Arts Centre. On your travels around the island, you'll also find plenty of smaller contemporary galleries to enjoy.

Crafts

A strong crafts movement has existed in Tasmania since the turn of the century. Studio potters Maude Poynter and Mylie Peppin were active in the 1940s and furniture-making has been particularly important, with cedar pieces from colonial times highly prized today. Contemporary furniture designers such as Leslie Wright, John Smith, Gay Hawkes and Peter Costello are nationally recognised for their highly refined and often sculptural use of Tasmania's superb native timbers, such as Huon pine and sassafras.

The **Design Centre of Tasmania** (☎ 6331 5506) – the full, official, jaw-stretching name of which is the Design Centre of Tasmania featuring the Wood Design Collection – in Launceston displays and sells work by Tasmanian artisans. The galleries, shops and craft market at Hobart's Salamanca Place also show and sell crafts, while regional craftspeople advertise their creative efforts throughout the state.

Performing Arts

The Tasmanian Symphony Orchestra is highly regarded and tours nationally and internationally. It gives regular performances at Hobart's Federation Concert Hall, its home venue, and in Launceston's Princess Theatre.

Tasmania's professional contemporary dance company is Tasdance, which is based in Launceston and tours statewide and interstate. It performs dance and dance-theatre, and often collaborates with artists in other fields. Another innovative company is IHOS Opera in Hobart, which is an experimental music and theatre troupe.

The Terrapin Puppet Theatre is a leading Australian contemporary performing arts company that has created puppetry productions for audiences of all ages both locally and internationally. Its works combine a variety of theatrical styles, including object theatre, black theatre, shadow puppetry and mobile interactive performances.

For detailed information on Tasmania's performing arts scene, visit W www.theatrewise.com.au.

Facts for the Visitor

HIGHLIGHTS

Tasmania's diversity and relatively small size make it a great holiday destination. In the space of a week, you can walk to views of dazzling coastal scenery, pamper yourself in a high-class resort, eat your way through some of the best seafood in the country, and still have time to visit Hobart's Salamanca Market and spend a day wine tasting in and around the Tamar Valley. But though you can see a lot in a short space of time, resist the urge to zoom around cramming absolutely everything in – as they say, stop to smell the roses, or in Tasmania's case, the fresh air, forests, cheeses, wines…

The historically rich legacy of Tasmania's abject convict era is evident throughout the state, but particularly in places such as Port Arthur and Richmond in the south and Ross in the Midlands. The 1830s warehouses of Hobart's waterfront are brimming with arts and crafts shops, cafés and restaurants, while many of the historic cottages in the northwestern fishing town of Stanley have been reborn as B&Bs, making it a charming place to stay overnight. Elsewhere, grand houses classified by the National Trust repose in the countryside and are open for inspection.

The east of the state is justly popular for its beaches and diving, but it's the more remote northeast that boasts some of the most stunning combinations of bleached sand and blue-green seas.

The spectacular cliffs of the Tasman Peninsula attract ocean kayakers, abseilers and divers, while completing the famous Overland Track in Cradle Mountain-Lake St Clair National Park is the single objective of many visiting bushwalkers. The wild Franklin River in the west draws rafters from around the world and the tourist enclave of Strahan attracts those who prefer the more sedate (but much more crowded) option of cruising the famous Gordon River.

Those with a yen for either the great outdoors, fine food, accommodating locals or a complex social and architectural history, but especially all of the above, will be hardpressed to find a more rewarding destination than Australia's island state of Tasmania.

SUGGESTED ITINERARIES

Because of the sheer range of landscapes and activities that are available, it's impossible to come up with generic itineraries to satisfy all tastes and desires. But here are some suggestions to start you thinking.

One Week

If arriving in Devonport or Launceston, consider a day cruising around the Tamar Valley, with a side-trip to the wine-ridden Pipers River. You could spend another day taking in the historic sights south at Evandale and Westbury, before drifting further west to Deloraine and to Mole Creek's subterranean attractions. Cradle Mountain could be your next full-day stop or you could head back east and hit the beach at Bicheno. From there, wander south to marvellous Freycinet Peninsula, well worth an extended look, before winding carefully down the east coast to the rocky Tasman Peninsula and Port Arthur. Hobart will beckon, but drop in to Richmond on the way or perhaps detour south to wonderful Bruny Island. After a leisurely meal and some beers/wines/coffees down on Hobart's cosmopolitan waterfront, you'll be ready to stroll onto your waiting plane. Obviously if you're flying in to Hobart, you can try this trip in reverse.

Two Weeks

Assuming you've undertaken the Launceston to Hobart route, take a closer look at the southeast coast, including Bruny Island if you haven't been there, and then inland to the Tahune Forest Reserve. Retracing your steps, head northwest to Mt Field, from where the highway will take you north to the beautiful walks at Lake St Clair. Keep going west to the remarkably sparse landscape of Queenstown and act the hobo (albeit a paying one) on the Abt Wilderness Railway. Strahan, on the west coast, will gobble up a day with a Gordon River cruise and a harbour-side meal. Coast north to some old mining towns and then to the north coast, with a lengthy Cradle Mountain detour possible on the way. Reaching the coast, you can go west to relaxing Boat Harbour and on to The Nut, or eastwards to connect with your boat or plane.

One Month

Just use your imagination; there's plenty more to see at all points of the compass: from Mt William and the Bay of Fires in the northeast to Arthur River and Marrawah's surf in the northwest, and from Maria Island off the east coast to the indomitable wilderness of the southwest, not to mention the lake-splattered Central Plateau in between.

PLANNING
When to Go

Tasmania is most popular during summer, when it's warm enough for swimming and it's great to be outdoors. Most days are fine in the major towns and cities, though in the southwest and west regions only about half the days are fine – the other half are often rainy and cloudy.

December, January and February are therefore the busiest times for tourism. Accommodation is heavily booked (and often more expensive) and the popular venues and restaurants are more crowded, but as compensation you can expect to see quite a variety of sporting events, including the finish of the Sydney to Hobart Yacht Race.

The winter months are generally cold, wet and cloudy, but winter days are capable of bucking this trend and are sometimes clear, crisp and sunny – ideal for sightseeing and short bushwalks. The great advantage of visiting in winter is that tourist numbers and prices are low, and it can seem as if you have parts of the island to yourself. In addition, the peaks and ranges you pass in your travels are likely to be all the more attractive for being covered in snow (when they're not hidden by cloud, that is).

Spring is the windiest time in Tasmania. Temperatures in early September are quite cold, the weather can be changeable and snowfalls can still occur. Daffodils, tulips and lavender bloom in the north of the state – the *Blooming Tasmania* brochure, available from visitor information centres, outlines the floral festivals and horticultural events that take place over spring.

Autumn is often pleasant, with mild temperatures, and is the season in which many festivals are held (see the Public Holidays & Special Events section later in this chapter for more information). Briefly between late April and early May, the deciduous beech changes colour from mid-green to a glorious gold and red. It can be seen in Mt Field and Cradle Mountain-Lake St Clair National Parks. Towards the end of autumn, the days (even sunny ones) are usually quite cold and windy.

The other major consideration when travelling is school holidays. Australian families take to the road (and air) en masse at these times, so many places are booked out, prices rise and things generally get a bit crazy. Holidays vary from year to year, but the main leisure period is from mid-December to late January; the other two-week periods are roughly early to mid-April, late June to mid-July, and late September to early October. Tasmanians are predisposed to holidaying in their own state and camping in national parks is particularly popular at such times.

Maps

The selection of maps available is wide, but many are of average quality. The best road map of the whole state (1:500,000) is produced by the **Royal Automobile Club of Tasmania** *(RACT;* ☎ *13 27 22;* **w** *www.ract .com.au)* and is on sale in the organisation's offices around the island. This sheet map includes detail of main city centres.

For more detail, including contours, the maps (1:250,000) published by the state government's Department of Primary Industries, Water & Environment (DPIWE), more specifically its map publication arm TASMAP, are recommended. The state is covered in four sheets, which are available from map retailers.

The *Tasmanian Towns Street Atlas* ($25.50) is also published by the DPIWE and contains reasonably clear and certainly detailed maps of every significant town. It's available from various newsagencies, bookshops and visitor information centres, at **Service Tasmania** (☎ *1300 135 513;* W *www .servicetasmania.tas.gov.au; 134 Macquarie St, Hobart)* and the **Tasmanian Map Centre** *(☎ 6231 9043; www.map-centre.com.au; 96 Elizabeth St, Hobart).*

DPIWE also produces topographic sheets appropriate for bushwalking, ski-touring and other activities requiring large-scale maps. Many of the more popular sheets, including day walks and bushwalks in national parks, are available over the counter at shops specialising in bushwalking gear and outdoor equipment, and also at urban and national park visitor information centres, Service Tasmania or the Tasmanian Map Centre.

You'll also find reliable small-scale Tasmania maps (1:1,250,000) in Lonely Planet's *Australia Road Atlas,* which includes a central Hobart map.

What to Bring

Tasmanians are generally casual dressers (shorts or jeans and T-shirts are common) and neat, informal clothes are standard in most hotels and restaurants. Casinos and more expensive restaurants may require long trousers, a neat shirt and shoes for men (ties and jackets are rarely needed).

You'll definitely need a warm jumper (pullover, sweater) or jacket, as well as something wind-proof and waterproof, no matter what time of the year you visit Tasmania. In autumn, spring and early summer you'll often be quite warm during those times in the day when the sun is shining and there's no wind, but the moment it becomes cloudy, the wind rises or you stand in the shade, you'll need another layer of clothing.

UV radiation in Tasmania is dangerously potent, which means that a good sunscreen (15+) or zinc cream, a hat and sunglasses are essential.

If you're intending to bushwalk, you should bring a sturdy, comfortable pair of boots. The ubiquitous rubber sandals known as thongs (easily purchased here and known as jandals or flip-flops elsewhere) are suitable beach or casual wear, but aren't allowed in most pubs and restaurants and are not good for sightseeing or walking long distances.

RESPONSIBLE TOURISM

Tasmania's 'disease-free' status is one of the things that makes its produce attractive to buyers and the state government has stringent rules in place to ensure the island maintains this agricultural advantage. To this end, plants, fruit and vegetables cannot be brought into the state without certification. Essentially, this means tourists must discard all such items prior to their arrival.

Live fish that can breed in Tasmanian waters cannot be brought into the state – the dire carp infestation in Lake Crescent is an example of what happens when this regulation is flouted. Anglers must not bring live bait into Tasmania and, in order to prevent the introduction of disease into native and recreational fisheries and aquaculture industries, they should also wash, disinfect and dry their gear before packing it for their trip.

Phytophthora is a root rot that's spread in soil and is devastating flora in parts of the state. Always clean dirt off your shoes and equipment before and after you spend time in the bush. For more information about responsible bushwalking, see the Bushwalking section in the Activities chapter.

For information on responsible 4WD touring, read *Cruisin' Without Bruisin',* a free brochure available at most visitor information centres. And whether you're travelling in a 4WD on bush tracks or in a conventional vehicle on a highway, watch out for wildlife on the road and try to avoid driving at dusk, which is when many animals become more active and harder to see – it's not uncommon to see more dead animals on the road than live ones in the bush.

Finally, be sure never to disturb or remove items from sites significant to Tasmanian Aborigines.

TOURIST OFFICES
Local Tourist Offices

Tasmania's **visitor information centres**, sometimes referred to as TTICs (Tasmanian Tourist Information Centres), are privately run. The key ones are located in Hobart

(☎ 6230 8233; 20 Davey St), Launceston (☎ 6336 3133; cnr St John & Paterson Sts), Devonport (☎ 6424 8176; 92 Formby Rd) and Burnie (☎ 6434 6111; Little Alexander St). As well as supplying brochures, price lists, maps and other information, they will often book transport, tours and accommodation too. They are generally open from around 8.30am or 9am to 5pm or 5.30pm weekdays and slightly shorter hours weekends.

Other centres belonging to the Tasmanian Visitor Information Network are scattered in many smaller towns across the island. The standard of service provided varies enormously from place to place. The centres at Kettering, Oatlands and Geeveston, for example, are very efficient, while others are staffed by volunteers who can alternately prove to be excellent sources of information or well intentioned but vague. Opening hours for the volunteer-staffed centres are often irregular.

The state government–run Tourism Tasmania publishes an invaluable bimonthly newspaper called *Tasmanian Travelways,* which is available at all information centres around the state. It's packed with information, including comprehensive listings of accommodation, tourist activities, public transport, connecting transport facilities and vehicle hire, all with an indication of current costs throughout the state; best of all, it's free.

The information centres also stock a host of other free tourist literature, including *This Week in Tasmania* (which must specialise in time travel, as it's actually published seasonally), the monthly *Treasure Island* and the annual *Tasmania: The Visitors Guide.*

Interstate Tourist Offices
On the mainland, there are state government–run **Tasmanian Travel Centres** (☎ 1800 808 776; W www.tastravel.com.au) in Sydney (60 Carrington St), on the corner of Wynyard St, and Melbourne (259 Collins St). These centres have information on all things Tasmanian and can also book accommodation, tours and airline, boat and bus tickets.

Tourist Offices Abroad
The **Australian Tourist Commission** (ATC; W www.australia.com) is the government body that informs potential visitors about the country. It's strictly an external marketing operator – within the country, tourist promotion is handled by state or local tourist offices – but is still handy for pre-trip research.

ATC agents have a useful free periodical called *Australia Travellers Guide,* which details relevant information and things of interest for visitors to Australia.

The ATC also publishes a number of handy fact sheets on topics such as camping, fishing, skiing, disabled travel and national parks, and provides a handy map of the country for a small fee. This literature is only distributed overseas, but you should be able to print the information from the ATC website.

VISAS & DOCUMENTS
Visas
All visitors to Australia need a visa. Only New Zealand nationals are partially exempt and even they receive a 'special category' visa on arrival. Visa application forms are available from Australian diplomatic missions overseas, travel agents or the website of the **Department of Immigration & Multicultural & Indigenous Affairs** (☎ 13 18 81; W www.immi.gov.au). There are several visa types.

Tourist Visas Electronic Travel Authority (ETA; see next section) has basically replaced tourist visas, but if you're from a country not covered by the ETA or you want to stay longer than three months, you have to apply for a visa. Standard visas allow one (in some cases multiple) entry, stays of up to three months, are valid for use within 12 months of issue, and cost $60. Depending on the circumstances, you can also apply for long-stay (12-month) visas.

Electronic Travel Authority (ETA)
Many visitors can get a free ETA through any International Air Transport Association (IATA)-registered travel agent or overseas airline, who make the application direct

when you buy a ticket and issue the ETA, which replaces the usual visa stamped in your passport. This system operates in over 30 countries. If booking online and not through a travel agent, make an online ETA application at **w** www.eta.immi.gov.au (service charge A$20).

Working Holiday Maker (WHM) Visas
Young, single visitors from the UK, Canada, Korea, the Netherlands, Malta, Ireland, Japan, Germany, Sweden, Norway, Finland and Denmark are eligible for a WHM visa. This allows a visit for up to 12 months and casual employment. 'Young' is defined as between 18 and 30 years of age.

The emphasis of this visa is on casual and not full-time employment, so you're only supposed to work for any one employer for a maximum of three months. This visa can only be applied for in Australian diplomatic missions abroad (citizens of Japan, Korea, Malta and Germany must apply in their home) and you can't change from a tourist visa to a WHM visa once you're in Australia.

You can apply for this visa up to a year in advance, which is worthwhile, as there's a limit on the number issued each year. Conditions include having a return air ticket or A$5000 in the bank and an application fee of $155 is charged.

See the Work section later in this chapter for details of what sort of work is available.

Visa Extensions The maximum stay allowed to visitors in Australia is one year, including extensions. Visa extensions are made through the Department of Immigration & Multicultural & Indigenous Affairs and you should apply at least two to three weeks before your visa expires. The application fee is $155 – it's nonrefundable, even if your application is rejected.

Travel Insurance
A travel insurance policy to cover theft, loss and medical problems is a good idea. Some policies offer lower and higher medical-expense options; the higher ones are chiefly for countries such as the USA, which have extremely high medical costs. There is a wide variety of policies available, so check the small print.

Some policies specifically exclude 'dangerous activities', which can include scuba diving, motorcycling and even bushwalking. A locally acquired motorcycle licence is not valid under some policies.

You may prefer a policy that pays doctors or hospitals directly rather than your having to pay on the spot and claim later. If you have to claim later, make sure you keep all documentation. Some policies ask you to call back (reverse charges) to a centre in your home country where an immediate assessment of your problem is made. Check that the policy covers ambulances or an emergency flight home.

Medicare Card
Under reciprocal arrangements, residents of the UK, New Zealand, the Netherlands, Finland, Ireland, Malta and Italy are entitled to free or subsidised medical treatment under **Medicare** (☎ 13 20 11), Australia's compulsory national health-insurance scheme. To enrol in the system – recommended if you plan to stay a while – go to any Medicare office and show your passport and home-country health-care card or certificate.

A Medicare card entitles you to free, necessary public hospital treatment. Visits to a private doctor's practice are partially claimable, though claim methods vary between doctors and you may have to pay the bill first and then make a claim yourself from Medicare. You also need to find out how much the doctor's consultation fee is, as Medicare only covers you for a certain amount and you'll need to pay the balance. Clinics that advertise 'bulk billing' are the easiest to use as they charge Medicare direct.

Driving Licence
You can use your own country's driving licence in Australia, as long as it's in English (if it's not, a certified translation must be carried) and has an identifying photograph.

Copies
All important documents (passport, credit cards, travel insurance, air/bus/train tickets,

driving licence etc) should be photocopied before you leave home. Leave one copy with someone at home and keep another with you, separate from the originals.

EMBASSIES & CONSULATES
Australian Embassies & Consulates

Australian diplomatic offices located overseas include:

Canada (☎ 613-236 0841, **W** www.ahc-ottawa .org) Suite 710, 50 O'Connor St, Ottawa, Ontario K1P 6L2; also in Toronto and Vancouver
France (☎ 01-40 59 33 00, **W** www.austgov.fr) 4 Rue Jean Rey, 75724 Cedex 15, Paris
Germany (☎ 030-880 0880, **W** www.austral ianembassy.de) Friedrichstrasse 200, 10117 Berlin; also in Frankfurt
Indonesia (☎ 021-2550 5555, **W** www.austem bjak.or.id) Jalan HR Rasuna Said Kav C15-16, Kuningan, Jakarta Selatan 12940; also in Bali and Medan (Sumatra)
Ireland (☎ 01-676 1517, **W** www.australianem bassy.ie) Fitzwilton House, Wilton Terrace, Dublin 2
Japan (☎ 03-5232 4111, **W** www.australia.or.jp) 2-1-14 Mita Minato-Ku, Tokyo 108-8361; also in Osaka, Nagoya, Sendai, Sapporo and Fukuoka City
Netherlands (☎ 070-310 82 00, **W** www.aus tralian-embassy.nl) Carnegielaan 4, The Hague 2517 KH
New Zealand (☎ 04-473 6411, **W** www.australia .org.nz) 72–78 Hobson St, Thorndon, Wellington; (☎ 09-303 2429, fax 377 0798) Union House, 132–138 Quay St, Auckland
Singapore (☎ 6836 4100, **W** www.singapore .embassy.gov.au) 25 Napier Rd, Singapore 258507
Thailand (☎ 02-287 2680, **W** www.austembassy .or.th) 37 Sth Sathorn Rd, Bangkok 10120; also in Chiang Mai
UK (☎ 020-7379 4334, **W** www.australia.org.uk) Australia House, The Strand, London WC2B 4LA; also in Edinburgh
USA (☎ 202-797 3000, **W** www.austemb.org) 1601 Massachusetts Ave NW, Washington DC 20036; also in Los Angeles and New York

Embassies & Consulates in Australia

The principal diplomatic representations to Australia are in Canberra. There are also representatives in other major cities, particularly from countries which have strong links with Australia like the USA, the UK and New Zealand.

Consulates in Hobart include the following. For a complete listing, look in the Tasmanian *Yellow Pages* (**W** www.yellowpages .com.au).

Germany (☎ 6223 1814) 348 Sandy Bay Rd
Japan (☎ 6211 6666) 31 Davey St
Netherlands (☎ 6225 3951) 8a Willowdene Ave, Sandy Bay

It's important to realise what your own embassy – the embassy of the country of which you are a citizen – can and can't do to help you if you get into trouble. Generally speaking, it won't be much help in emergencies if the trouble you're in is remotely your own fault. Remember that you are bound by the laws of the country you're in. Your embassy will not be sympathetic if you end up in jail after committing a crime locally, even if such actions are legal in your own country.

In genuine emergencies you might get some assistance, but only if other channels have been exhausted. For example, if you need to get home urgently, a free ticket home is exceedingly unlikely – the embassy would expect you to have insurance. If you have all your money and documents stolen, it might assist with getting a new passport, but a loan for onward travel is out of the question.

CUSTOMS

When entering Australia you can bring most articles in free of duty provided that Customs is satisfied they're for personal use and that you'll be taking them back out again. There's also the usual duty-free quota per person of 1125mL of alcohol, 250 cigarettes and dutiable goods up to the value of A$400.

With regard to prohibited goods, problem/ target number one is drugs. Australian Customs can be extremely efficient when it comes to finding them, so unless you want to make a first-hand inspection of an Australian jail, don't bring illegal drugs with you.

Problem/target two involves animal and plant quarantine. You'll be asked to declare and show all goods of animal or vegetable origin – wooden spoons, straw hats, the lot. The authorities are naturally keen to prevent weeds, pests or diseases getting into the country. Flowers are also unpopular, as is fresh food, particularly meat, cheese, fruit and vegetables. There are also restrictions on transporting fruit and vegetables between states.

Weapons and firearms are either prohibited or require a permit and safety testing. Other restricted goods include products made from protected wildlife species (such as ivory), unapproved telecommunications devices and live animals.

MONEY
Currency
Australia's currency is the Australian dollar, which comprises 100 cents. There are 5c, 10c, 20c, 50c, $1 and $2 coins, and $5, $10, $20, $50 and $100 notes.

Although the smallest coin in circulation is 5c, prices are often still marked in single cents and then rounded to the nearest 5c when you come to pay.

There are no notable restrictions on importing or exporting travellers cheques, but cash amounts in excess of A$5000 (in any currency) must be declared on arrival and departure.

Exchange Rates
The Australian dollar fluctuates markedly against the US dollar, but has been particularly weak in recent years – this has been a disaster for Australians travelling overseas but a bonus for inbound visitors.

country	unit		A$
Canada	C$1	=	1.16
euro zone	€1	=	1.75
Japan	¥100	=	1.50
New Zealand	NZ$1	=	0.86
UK	UK£l	=	2.74
USA	US$1	=	1.77

Exchanging Money
Changing foreign currency or travellers cheques is usually no problem at most banks throughout Australia or licensed moneychangers in the main cities.

Travellers Cheques If your stay is short, then travellers cheques are safe and generally enjoy a better exchange rate than foreign cash. They can also be readily replaced if stolen. On the downside, there's a fee for purchasing travellers cheques (usually 1% of the total amount) and there may be fees when you exchange them.

AmEx, Thomas Cook and other well-known international brands of travellers cheques are widely used in Australia. A passport is required for identification when cashing the cheques.

Fees per transaction for changing foreign-currency travellers cheques vary from bank to bank. Of the 'big four' banks, the National Australia Bank charges $5, ANZ charges $6.50, Westpac charges $7.50 and the Commonwealth a hefty $15. You're clearly better off using the main exchange bureaus.

Buying travellers cheques in Australian dollars is an option worth considering. These can be exchanged immediately at banks without being converted from a foreign currency or incurring commissions, fees and exchange-rate fluctuations.

Bank Accounts, ATMs & Eftpos Banks exist in most sizeable Tasmanian towns, but in the smaller centres are often open only two or three days a week. Post offices act as agents for the Commonwealth Bank, although like banks, post offices in many of the smaller towns are open only restricted weekday hours. Even the 24-hour ATMs, most of which accept cards from other banks and can be used to withdraw up to $1000 a day (cash amount varies depending on the bank), can be few and far between outside the state's largest centres. However, there's usually at least one pub, general store, petrol station or newsagent in town that offers an Electronic Funds Transfer at Point Of Sale (Eftpos) service. This means that you can use your credit or debit card to pay for purchases and, in the case of debit cards, simultaneously make small cash withdrawals; again, you'll need your PIN at hand.

Opening a Bank Account If you're planning to stay in Australia a while, consider opening a local bank account. It's fairly straightforward if done within six weeks of arrival – just present the bank with your passport and a postal address and they'll open the account and send you an ATM card.

After six weeks, though, a points system operates and you need to score a minimum of 100 points before being given the privilege of letting the bank take your money. Passports or birth certificates are worth 70 points, an international driving licence with photo gets 40 points, and minor IDs like credit cards get you 20 points.

If you don't have an Australian Tax File Number, interest earned from your funds will be taxed at the rate of 47% (see the Work section later in this chapter).

Credit & Debit Cards Credit cards are arguably the best way to carry your cash in Australia, providing an alternative to carrying large numbers of travellers cheques. Visa and MasterCard are widely accepted, while Diners Club and AmEx are not so widely accepted.

Credit cards can also be used to get cash advances over the counter and from many automatic teller machines (ATMs; see following), depending on the card. If you're planning to rent cars while travelling around Tasmania, a credit card is basically essential in lieu of a large deposit.

To avoid blowing your credit card limit and incurring a large debt and interest charges, consider using a debit card, which you can use to withdraw money from your home-country bank account via ATMs or Eftpos (see following). Any card connected to the international banking network – Cirrus, Maestro, Plus and Eurocard – should work provided you remember your Personal Identification Number (PIN).

Costs

Travellers from the USA, Canada and continental Europe will find Australia generally cheap to travel around, particularly in regard to food and accommodation, though ultimately this depends on the exact exchange rate, of course. But manufactured goods, like clothes and cars, tend to be relatively expensive: if they're imported, they are burdened with the additional costs of transport and duties, and if they're locally manufactured they suffer from the extra costs entailed in making things in comparatively small quantities.

The biggest expense in visiting Tasmania is transport, both in terms of getting there – your options are restricted to planes and ferries – and getting around.

How much you should budget depends on what sort of traveller you are and your itinerary. You could get by on about $40 per day if you budget fiercely and *always* take the cheapest option, while $60 per day will allow you to actually enjoy yourself. Travel that revolves around better-standard accommodation and restaurant meals will generally entail $80 to $100 per day, though you can easily spend more by regularly taking tours and staying in top-end guesthouses. Staying in places for longer periods and/or travelling in a group will lower your costs.

Tipping

In Australia, tipping isn't entrenched the way it is in the USA, though it's a common occurrence in everything from mid-range cafés to upmarket restaurants, particularly in cities – the higher the bill, the greater the expectation of a tip, but ultimately it's up to you. If the service has been good and you decide to leave a tip, 5% to 10% of the bill is the usual amount. Taxi drivers don't expect tips, but they'll frown if you don't at least round up the fare to the nearest dollar.

POST & COMMUNICATIONS
Postal Rates

Australia's postal services are efficient and reasonably cheap. It costs 45c to send a standard letter or postcard within Australia.

Australia Post has divided international destinations into two regions: Asia-Pacific and Rest of the World. Airmail letters cost $1/1.50 to the former/latter, while postcards cost $1 across the board (up to 20g).

The rates for posting parcels abroad from Tasmania are calculated according to five international zones. For the two zones that include Europe/South Africa and the

Flora, Fauna, National Parks & Reserves

Title Page: Cradle Mountain and Dove Lake, Cradle Mountain-Lake St Clair National Park. (Photograph by Richard I'Anson.)

Top: Cushion plant and alpine vegetation, Southwest National Park. This is Tasmania's largest national park and has a diverse range of flora.

Middle: The Tasmanian Devil is a marsupial found only in Tasmania. It's nocturnal and was named by early European settlers because of its eerie growl, which starts as a kind of whistle and ends in a bark.

Bottom: A rapid river surrounded by lush vegetation in the Tarkine Wilderness.

USA/Canada respectively, it costs $14/26 per 1/2kg by sluggish seamail and around $18/30 per 1/2kg by economy airmail. Airmail is the only option for the other zones, comprising Asia-Pacific nations ($14/26 per 1/2kg economy) and also including New Zealand ($10.50/18.50 per 1/2kg economy).

Sending & Receiving Mail

Post offices are usually open from 9am to 5pm Monday to Friday (slightly longer in Hobart and Launceston). There are also many post office agencies lurking within general stores and newsagencies. In larger towns and cities, these are usually open from 9am to 5pm and on Saturday morning, but in the small towns they may only be open for a few hours a day or in some cases a few days a week. You can often buy stamps from newsagencies and local shops.

All post offices hold mail for visitors. The poste restante service at Hobart's main post office is particularly good but also particularly busy – it will hold your mail for one month before returning it to the sender, or you can pay a monthly fee ($7 for the first month, $5 for subsequent months) to have your mail forwarded to you within Australia. If you own an AmEx card or buy AmEx travellers cheques, you can have mail sent to you care of **American Express Travel** *(☎ 6234 3711; 74a Liverpool St, Hobart 7000)*.

Telephone

The Australian telecommunications industry is deregulated and there are a number of providers offering various services. Private phones are serviced by the two main companies, Telstra and Optus, but it's in the mobile (cell) phone and payphone markets where companies like Vodafone, Orange and AAPT are operating that you'll find the most competition.

Payphones & Phonecards Lonely Planet's ekno global communication service provides low-cost international calls – for local calls you're usually better off with a local phonecard. ekno also offers free messaging services, email, travel information and an online travel vault, where you can securely store all your important documents. You can join online at **w** www.ekno.lonely planet.com, where you will find the local-access numbers for the 24-hour customer-service centre. Once you've joined, always check the ekno website for the latest access numbers for each country and updates on new features.

There are a number of local and international phonecards issued by the various telecommunications companies, which can be bought from newsagents and post offices and used in any public cardphone or from a private phone by dialling a toll-free access number and then the relevant PIN. Charges vary from company to company so compare the costs.

Some public phones conveniently accept credit cards, though you need to keep an eye on how much the call is costing as it can quickly mount up.

Local Calls From public phones local calls cost 40c and from private phones they cost 25c; either way, you can talk for an unlimited amount of time. Calls to mobile phones are timed and the rates are much higher.

Long-Distance Calls & Area Codes It's also possible to make long-distance Subscriber Trunk Dialling (STD) calls from virtually any public phone. These calls are cheaper during off-peak hours (usually 7pm to 7am) and different service providers charge different rates.

All standard Tasmanian telephone numbers have eight digits. The area code across the entire state is ☎ 03, which is the same code as Victoria. When calling from one area of Tasmania to another, there's no need to dial ☎ 03 before the local number. Local numbers start with the digits 62 in Hobart and southern Tasmania, 63 in Launceston and the northeast, and 64 in the west and northwest.

There are three other Australian area codes: ☎ 02 covers New South Wales (NSW) and the Australian Capital Territory (ACT), ☎ 07 covers Queensland, and ☎ 08 covers South Australia (SA), Western Australia (WA) and the Northern Territory (NT).

International Calls From most payphones you can also make International Subscriber Dialling (ISD) calls, which connect you quickly to overseas numbers and, if your call is brief, need not cost very much. Note that the international dialling code will vary depending on which provider you use.

International calls from Australia are very cheap and there are often specials that lower the rates more. Contact **Telstra** (☎ *1800 113 011;* W *www.telstra.com.au)* for more details.

Country Direct is a service that gives travellers in Australia direct access to operators in nearly 60 countries, to make reverse-charge (collect) or credit-card calls. For a full list of the countries hooked into this system, check any local *White Pages* telephone book or W www.whitepages.com.au.

To call overseas, dial the international access code (☎ 0011 or ☎ 0018), the country code and the area code (drop the initial '0').

Toll-Free Calls Many businesses and some government departments operate a toll-free service (prefix 1800), so no matter where you're ringing from within the country, it's a free call. Other companies, such as the airlines, have six-digit numbers beginning with 13 or 1300, and these are charged at the rate of a local call. Calls to these services still attract higher charges if you're calling from a mobile phone.

To make a reverse-charge call from any public or private phone, just dial ☎ 1800 REVERSE (1800 738 3773).

Information Calls Other odd numbers you may come across are those starting with 1900. These numbers, usually recorded information services and the like, are provided by private companies, and your call is charged at anything from 35c to $5 or more per minute (more from mobile and payphones).

Mobile (Cell) Phones Australia has two mobile networks: digital and the digitally based CDMA. The networks are compatible with GSM 900 and 1800 (used in Europe) but not compatible with US or Japanese systems. Ask the carrier you use in your home country whether your mobile phone will operate in Australia.

Although these networks cover 90% of the population, they cover a much smaller percentage of the country's land area. In Tasmania's case, coverage outside main towns is poor to nonexistent.

Phone numbers with the prefix 04 are mobile phones. The main network operators are the mostly government-owned **Telstra** (W *www.telstra.com.au)* and two private companies, **Optus** (W *www.optus.com.au)* and **Vodafone** (W *www.vodafone.com.au).* Calls to and from mobile numbers are subject to mobile phone rates.

All three network operators have prepaid mobile systems allowing quick and relatively inexpensive short-term connection. Compare the starter kits and deals offered by these companies as their products differ.

Email & Internet Access

Whether you use Internet cafés or bring along your own computer, it's very easy to get connected in Tasmania. You'll find cybercafés in the main cities and a few (but not many) smaller towns, and Internet kiosks or terminals at many hostels and hotels. Costs range from 15c per minute to $1/9 per 5/60 minutes.

The most convenient way to send and receive email from cybercafés is to open an account with a free, Web-based email service such as **ekno** (W *www.ekno.lonelyplanet.com),* **Yahoo!** (W *www.yahoo.com),* **Excite** (W *www.excite.com)* or the advertising-riddled **MSN Hotmail** (W *www.hotmail.com).*

As part of a government-funded telecommunications scheme, online access centres have been set up in around 65 of the state's towns. They are intended primarily for rural Tasmanians, but also provide Internet access for visitors. For a complete listing of these centres, which charge reasonable rates and are located primarily (but not exclusively) in libraries and schools, pick up the *Tasmanian Communities Online* brochure at any visitor information centre, or visit the scheme's website (W *www.tco.asn.au).*

[Continued on page 44]

FLORA, FAUNA, NATIONAL PARKS & RESERVES

JOHN BANAGAN

ROB BLAKERS

Tasmania's diverse flora ranges from the dry forests of the east through the alpine moorlands of the centre, to the rainforests of the west. Many of the state's plants are unlike those found in the rest of Australia and have ties with species that grew millions of years ago, when the southern continents were joined as Gondwanaland; similar plants are found in South America and fossilised in Antarctica.

Tasmania's fauna is not as varied as that of the rest of Australia and it has relatively few large mammals. Its best-known marsupial, the Tasmanian tiger, which resembled a large dog or wolf and had dark stripes and a stiff tail, has been extinct for nearly 70 years (see the boxed text 'A Tiger's Tale').

FLORA

Many of Tasmania's trees are unique to the state, with its native pines being particularly distinctive. Perhaps the best known is the Huon pine, which can live for thousands of years (see the Huon Pine section later), but there are other slow-growing Tasmanian pines, including **King Billy pines**, **celery-top pines** and **pencil pines**, all of which are commonly found in the higher regions and live for about 500 years. Some pencil pines on the Central Plateau have grown to be 1000 years old, but they are especially vulnerable to fire – one-third of the plateau's pencil pine population has been burnt out in the past 200 years.

The dominant tree of the wetter forests is **myrtle beech**, which is similar to the beeches of Europe.

One of Tasmania's many flowering trees is the **leatherwood**, which is nondescript most of the year but can be positively eye-catching in summer, when it's covered with a mass of white and pale pink flowers that yield a unique and fragrant honey prized by apiarists.

While many of Tasmania's eucalyptus trees also grow on the mainland, its own are often extremely tall. The **swamp gum** (*Eucalyptus regnans*, known as mountain ash on the mainland) can grow to 100m in height and is the tallest flowering plant in the world. It's readily seen in the forests of the southeast, where you'll also find the state's floral emblem, the **Tasmanian blue gum** (*Eucalyptus globulus*).

In autumn you might see the **deciduous beech**, the only truly deciduous native plant in Australia. It usually grows as a fairly straggly bush with bright green leaves. In autumn, however, the leaves become golden and sometimes red, adding a bright splash of colour to the forests. The best places to look for this plant are Cradle Mountain and Mt Field.

A notable component of the understorey in Tasmanian forests is the infamous horizontal scrub (see the Horizontal Scrub section later), a plant that can make life hell for bushwalkers attempting to avoid established tracks. More familiar to bushwalkers, but also considerably more benign, is **buttongrass**. Growing in thick clumps up to 2m high, this unique Tasmanian grass prefers broad, swampy areas like the

Inset: Cradle Mountain (Photograph by Richard I'Anson)

many flat-bottomed valleys pressed out by ice ages. Buttongrass plains are usually so muddy and unpleasant to walk over that in many places the Parks and Wildlife Service (PWS) has found it necessary to incorporate sections of elevated boardwalk into tracks crossing such areas, for both walker comfort and protection of the environment.

Another interesting specimen is the **cushion plant**, which is found in alpine areas and at first sight resembles a green rock. In fact, it's an extremely tough, short plant that grows into thick mats ideally suited to helping it cope with its severe living conditions.

Huon Pine

This is perhaps the most famous of Tasmania's native flora. The water-repellent qualities of its oily yellow wood are responsible for its reputation as an exceptional boatbuilding timber, but it's also prized by furniture-makers and woodturners. It grows very slowly and so barely survived the widespread logging undertaken in the colony's early years, when its timber was premium shipbuilding material. Some older trees remain, however, and one 2500-year-old specimen can be viewed during a cruise on the Gordon River. (See the boxed text 'Lake Johnston Nature Reserve' in the Facts about Tasmania chapter.)

King's Lomatia

This endemic Tasmanian plant, which is a member of the Proteaceae family and has flowers similar to those of the grevillea, only grows in the wild in one small area of the Tasmanian Wilderness World Heritage Area. Studies of the plant's chromosomes have revealed that it's incapable of reproducing sexually, which is why it must rely on sending up shoots to create new plants. Further research has shown that there's absolutely no genetic diversity within the population, which means that every King's lomatia in existence is a clone. The plant is believed to be the oldest known clone in the world and is thought to have been around for at least 43,600 years.

MARTIN HARRIS

Left: Tasmania's famous Huon pine

Horizontal Scrub

This slender plant *(Anodopetalum biglandulosum)* is a feature of the undergrowth in many parts of Tasmania's southwest. It grows by sending up thin, vigorous stems whenever an opening appears in the forest canopy. The old branches soon become heavy and fall, after which they put up shoots of their own. This continual process of growth and collapse creates dense, tangled thickets that are a notorious obstacle to bushwalkers venturing off the beaten track.

You can see some good examples of this tangled plant on nature walks in the southwest and in the Hartz Mountains. One adventurer to record his experience of horizontal scrub was Alex Sklenica, who walked from Lake Pedder to the Gordon River by way of the Olga River valley in 1959 and described crawling on top of it like a monkey, bending tea trees down over it to cushion his hands and knees, and occasionally even slipping down a couple of feet into it under the weight of his pack.

FAUNA

The distinctive mammals of mainland Australia, the marsupials and monotremes, are also found in Tasmania. **Marsupials**, including wallabies and pademelons, give birth to partially developed young that they then protect and suckle in a pouch. **Monotremes** (platypuses and echidnas) lay eggs but also suckle their young. Most are nocturnal and the best time to see them in the wild is around dusk. The smaller mammals can be very difficult to find in the bush, but there are plenty of wildlife parks around the state where they can be seen.

Kangaroos & Wallabies

The kangaroo and wallaby species found in Tasmania are related to those found on the mainland, but are usually smaller. The largest marsupial is the **Forester kangaroo**, which at one stage looked like becoming extinct because it favoured farmland for grazing. The Narawntapu and Mt William National Parks have been set aside to preserve this kangaroo.

The **Bennett's wallaby** thrives in colder climes and this is the animal you're most likely to see begging for food at the Cradle Mountain-Lake St Clair National Park. Don't feed them though, as the animals are meant to be wild and must feed themselves – also, giving them processed foods like bread causes a fatal disease called 'lumpy jaw'. Bennett's wallabies stand just over 1m in height and seem very friendly, but be careful, as these and other native animals are not tame and can sometimes be aggressive.

If you spy any shorter, rounder wallabies hiding in the forest, then you'll have seen either a **rufous wallaby** or a **pademelon**. These smaller species are shyer than their larger relatives.

FLORA, FAUNA, NATIONAL PARKS & RESERVES

A Tiger's Tail

The story of the Tasmanian tiger (*Thylacinus cynocephalus* or thylacine), a striped carnivore once widespread in Tasmania, currently has two different endings.

Version one has it that thylacines were hunted to extinction by European settlers in the 19th and early 20th centuries, and that the last tiger died in miserable captivity in Hobart's Beaumaris Zoo in 1936. Those who put their faith in the thylacine's extinction point out that no living specimen has been conclusively discovered since then, regardless of hundreds of alleged 'sightings'.

Version two maintains that thylacines continue a furtive existence deep in the Tasmanian wilderness. Advocates of this theory deny they live in a state of fanciful denial over the tiger's demise, curiously preferring to believe that the more unsubstantiated tiger encounters get reported, the more likelihood of a substantiated one.

The physical mystique of a large nocturnal hunter that carried its young in a pouch and had a yawn bigger than Mick Jagger's (a jaw-dropping 120 degrees), combined with the conveniently perpetuated enigma of its existence, has made the tiger prime corporate fodder. Oblivious to the irony of using a long-dead animal to promote the relevance of their products, companies have plastered the animal's picture on everything from beer bottles (Cascade) to television network promos (Southern Cross Television). Even Tourism Tasmania has invested in the myth, implying on its website that the thylacine is likely still alive, and offering tips on how to spot one.

In mid-2000, scientists at Sydney's Australia Museum began scripting another possible ending to the tiger saga. Kicking off version three, biologists managed to scrape some high-quality DNA from a thylacine pup preserved in alcohol since 1866. Under the auspices of an $80 million programme, they now hope to use the DNA to synthesise artificial chromosomes and, ultimately, to clone new living tigers. The scientists face years of research and a low potential for success, not to mention criticism from those who would rather see the money spent on helping current endangered species. But they seem intent on adding a new twist to the tiger's tale.

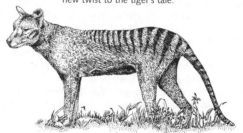

MARTIN HARRIS

Tasmanian Devils

This scavenging marsupial's diet consists mainly of carrion, insects and small birds and mammals, and it can often be seen at night feasting on roadkill, a habit that unfortunately leads to it becoming roadkill itself. Its bad temper and unpleasant odour are among its most distinctive features. It is about 75cm long and has a short, stocky body covered in black fur with a white stripe across its chest. You'll see it in plenty of wildlife parks around the state.

MARTIN HARRIS

Possums

There are several varieties of possums in the state, one of which is the **sugar glider**, which has developed webs between its legs, enabling it to glide from tree to tree. The most common and boldest is the **brushtail possum**. They live and sleep in trees, but will come down to the ground in search of food. Possums show little fear of humans and regularly do late-night food 'shopping' at camping grounds. A shyer relation is the smaller **ringtail possum**.

Wombats

These are very solid, powerfully built marsupials with broad heads and short stumpy legs – they often reach around 40kg. They live in underground burrows that they excavate, and are usually very casual, slow-moving animals, partly because they don't have any natural predators to worry about.

Platypuses & Echidnas

The platypus and the echidna are the only living monotremes. Monotremes are often regarded as living fossils, and although they display some intriguing features from reptile ancestors, such as laying eggs, they are now recognised as a distinct mammalian lineage rather than a primitive stage in mammalian evolution. Although they lay eggs, they suckle their young on milk secreted from mammary glands.

The platypus lives in water and has a duck-like bill, webbed feet and a beaver-like body. You're most likely to see one in a stream or lake, searching out food in the form of crustaceans, worms and tadpoles with its electro-sensitive bill.

Top: The Tasmanian devil is renowned for its bad temper.

Echidnas are totally different and look similar to porcupines, being covered in sharp spikes. They primarily eat ants and have powerful claws for unearthing their food and digging into the dirt to protect themselves when threatened. They are common in Tasmania but if you approach one, all you're likely to see up close is a brown, spiky ball. However, if you keep quiet and don't move, you might be lucky: they have poor eyesight and will sometimes walk right past your feet.

Southern Right Whales

These majestic creatures migrate annually from Antarctica to southern Australia to give birth to their calves in shallow waters. So named because they were the 'right' whales to kill, they were hunted to the point of extinction. They are sometimes seen off the Tasmanian coast and occasionally beach themselves.

Rare Birds

Some extremely rare birds are found in Tasmania; one of the best known is the **orange-bellied parrot**, of which only a small number survive on the buttongrass plains of the southwest. They winter on the mainland and make the treacherous crossing of Bass Strait to reach their breeding grounds in southwest Tasmania. More common, but also threatened with extinction, is the **ground parrot**. To see it you'll need to fly to Melaleuca in the southwest and wait in the specially constructed bird-hide.

Many birdwatchers visit the eastern side of Tasmania to try to catch a glimpse of the very rare **forty-spotted pardalote**, mainly found on Bruny Island and in Mt William National Park. This bird prefers dry sclerophyll forest as its residence.

Black Currawongs

The black currawong, found only in Tasmania, lives primarily on plant matter and insects, but will sometimes kill small mammals or infant birds. You'll often see this large, black, fearless bird around picnic areas.

Mutton Birds

The interesting mutton bird (a name derived after a marine officer on Norfolk Island nicknamed a closely related bird 'flying sheep') is more correctly called the short-tailed shearwater. It lives in burrows in sand dunes and migrates annually to the northern hemisphere. These small birds

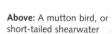

MARTIN HARRIS

provide spectacular displays as they fly back to their burrows in their thousands at dusk. They are still hunted by some Tasmanians and you'll occasionally see cooked mutton bird advertised for sale.

Above: A mutton bird, or short-tailed shearwater

Penguins

The little (fairy) penguin is the smallest penguin in the world and lives in burrows in the sand dunes. There are plenty of penguin rookeries around Tasmania where you can see them waddle from the ocean to their nests just after sunset. Bruny Island, Burnie, Stanley, Bicheno, Penguin and King Island all have rookeries you can visit to see these birds.

Other Birds

There's a very wide variety of **sea birds**, **parrots**, **cockatoos**, **honeyeaters** and **wrens**. Birds of prey such as **falcons** and **eagles** are also readily seen. There are many excellent publications available on Australian birds, both in the form of field guides and large-format picture books (see Flora & Fauna in the Books section in the Facts for the Visitor chapter).

Snakes & Spiders

There are only three types of snake found in Tasmania and they're all poisonous. The largest and most dangerous is the **tiger snake**, which will sometimes attack, particularly in late summer. The other snakes are the **copperhead** and the smaller **white-lipped whipsnake**. Bites are very rare, as most snakes are generally shy and try to avoid humans. If you do get bitten, don't try to catch the snake, as there's a common antivenin for all three – instead, get to hospital for treatment. Also see the Dangers & Annoyances section in the Facts for the Visitor chapter.

The eight-legged critter with the longest reach (up to 18cm) on the island is the **Tasmanian cave spider**, which spins horizontal mesh-webs on the ceiling of a cave, just inside the entrance, to catch insects like cave crickets.

Threatened Species

Since Europeans arrived, Tasmania has lost over 30 species of plants and animals – currently, over 600 types of flora and fauna are listed under the state's Threatened Species Protection Act.

Among Tasmania's threatened birds are the **forty-spotted pardalote**, the **orange-bellied parrot** and the **wedge-tailed eagle**. Tasmania is also home to the largest invertebrate in the world, the giant **freshwater crayfish**, whose numbers have been so depleted by recreational fishing and habitat destruction that it's now illegal to take any specimens from their natural habitat.

Pedder galaxias is a small, extremely rare fish discovered shortly before the inundation of Lake Pedder, which appears to have been its only natural habitat. It has since become virtually extinct in the enlarged lake and its feeder streams – Inland Fisheries has been unable to locate any specimens for a number of years – but attempts to establish a viable population in another lake in the southwest have been successful.

NATIONAL PARKS & RESERVES

About one-quarter of Tasmania comprises dedicated parks and re-serves. Comprehensive information on all the state's national parks, conservation areas and reserves is available on the website of the **PWS** (☎ 6233 6191; Ⓦ *www.dpiwe.tas.gov.au).*

National Parks

There are 19 national parks in the state, including two in Bass Strait, and they're worth visiting to walk on their trails, sit on their peaks, or just breathe in the awesome diversity of their environments. Many of the parks are easily accessed by vehicle.

Park Fees National parks are managed by the PWS and visitors fees apply to them all, even when there's no ranger's office. A permit system was proposed a few years ago, which would apply to overnight bushwalkers, but at the time of writing there was still no indication of when it might be introduced.

There are two types of fees: per vehicle and per person. For vehicles with up to eight people the charge for 24 hours is $10; a two-month holiday pass (all parks) is $33; and an annual pass is $46 for all parks and $20 for one park. For individuals arriving by bus, bicycle, motor-bike or boat, entry fees are $3 for 24 hours and $13 for two months.

The longer term passes are better if you're staying in Tasmania for a while or visiting more than a few parks – for most visitors, the holiday pass is the best value. Passes are available at most park entrances, at many visitors centres and at the offices of **Service Tasmania** *(☎ 1300 135 513; 134 Macquarie St, Hobart).*

The Parks This A–Z (or rather B–W) of Tasmania's national parks begins with **Ben Lomond National Park**, a 165-sq-km park arranged around a glacial plateau filled with wondrous alpine flora, which doubles as the state's main ski field in the years when Mother Nature orders Father Nature into the environmental kitchen to whip up some snow. **Cradle Mountain-Lake St Clair National Park** needs little introduction, a sublime area dotted with moorlands and mountain peaks, and thread-ed by the Overland Track – the jagged remnants of Cradle Mountain dominate the north, while the deepest freshwater lake in the country, Lake St Clair, fills out the south. On the east coast is **Douglas-Apsley National Park**, a rugged protectorate for one of the state's last undis-turbed swathes of dry eucalypt forest, while on the opposite side of the island is **Franklin-Gordon Wild Rivers National Park**, dedicated to two grand wilderness watercourses. South of Douglas-Apsley are the abun-dant walks and striking coastal scenery of **Freycinet Peninsula National Park**, its entrance guarded by the enormous granite Hazards.

The remote dolerite ridge of **Hartz Mountains National Park** shields fan-tastic alpine heath, rainforest and glacial lakes, and allows unforgettable

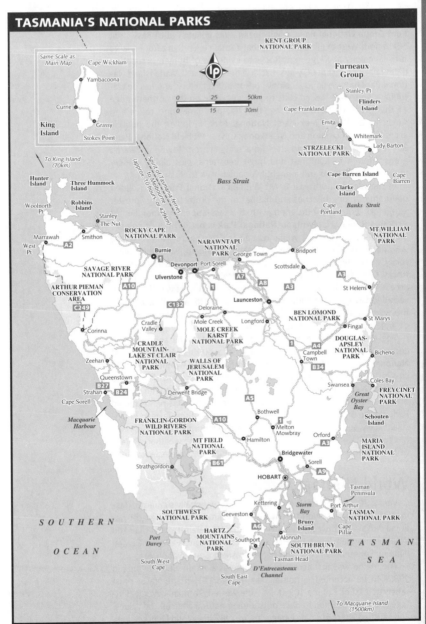

TASMANIA'S NATIONAL PARKS

Same Scale as Main Map

Cape Wickham

Yambacoona

Currie

King Island

Grassy

Stokes Point

To King Island (70km)

Hunter Island

Three Hummock Island

Woolnorth Pt

Robbins Island

Stanley
The Nut

Marrawah

West Pt

A2

Smithton

ROCKY CAPE NATIONAL PARK

Burnie

SAVAGE RIVER NATIONAL PARK

Devonport   Port Sorell

Ulverstone

1

ARTHUR PIEMAN CONSERVATION AREA

A10

C249

C132

Corinna

Cradle Valley

Deloraine

Mole Creek

CRADLE MOUNTAIN– LAKE ST CLAIR NATIONAL PARK

Zeehan

MOLE CREEK KARST NATIONAL PARK

WALLS OF JERUSALEM NATIONAL PARK

Queenstown

Strahan

B27   B24

Cape Sorell

Derwent Bridge

A5

Macquarie Harbour

FRANKLIN–GORDON WILD RIVERS NATIONAL PARK

A10

MT FIELD NATIONAL PARK

Strathgordon

B61

Bothwell

Hamilton

1

Melton Mowbray

KENT GROUP NATIONAL PARK

Furneaux Group

Stanley Pt

Flinders Island

Cape Frankland

Emita

Whitemark   Lady Barton

STRZELECKI NATIONAL PARK

Cape Barren Island   Cape Barren

Clarke Island

Cape Portland   *Banks Strait*

Bass Strait

NARAWNTAPU NATIONAL PARK

George Town   Bridport

A7   A8   A3

Scottsdale

A3

St Helens

MT WILLIAM NATIONAL PARK

Launceston

Longford

1

BEN LOMOND NATIONAL PARK

Fingal

St Marys

A4

Campbell Town

B34

DOUGLAS– APSLEY NATIONAL PARK

Bicheno

Swansea

Coles Bay

Great Oyster Bay

FREYCINET NATIONAL PARK

Schouten Island

Orford

A3

MARIA ISLAND NATIONAL PARK

Bridgewater

Sorell

A9

HOBART

Kettering

Storm Bay

Port Arthur

Tasman Peninsula

TASMAN NATIONAL PARK

Cape Pillar

S O U T H E R N

O C E A N

SOUTHWEST NATIONAL PARK

Geeveston

Port Davey

HARTZ MOUNTAINS NATIONAL PARK

Southport

A6

Bruny Island

Alonnah

SOUTH BRUNY NATIONAL PARK

Tasman Head

T A S M A N

S E A

South West Cape

D'Entrecasteaux Channel

South East Cape

To Macquarie Island (1500km)

0   25   50km
0   15   30mi

Spirit of Tasmania ferries to Melbourne (approx 10 hours, or 429km)

views of the massive southwest wilderness. Tasmania's newest park is **Kent Group National Park**, a half-dozen islets poking out of Bass Strait 55km northwest of Flinders Island, that contain everything from a large fur seal colony at Judgement Rocks to evidence of human occupation dating back at least 8000 years. Back on the east coast, **Maria Island National Park** has served as a colonial prison and a factory, and has peaceful bays and fossil-loaded cliffs to explore, while on the northern edge of the Great Western Tiers are the 200-plus limestone caves and sinkholes of **Mole Creek Karst National Park**, including the publicly accessible King Solomon and Marakoopa Caves. **Mt Field National Park**, 80km northwest of Hobart, has flora ranging from towering swamp gums through to rainforest and huge tree ferns, plus alpine scenery around Lake Dobson and a mightily popular walk to Russell Falls.

In the island's northeast is **Mt William National Park**, an isolated panorama of long beaches and habitat of the protected grey Forester kangaroo. Formerly burdened with the less-appealing moniker of Asbestos Range, **Narawntapu National Park** is packed full of navigable north-coast lagoons, wetlands and tea tree mazes, and is dense with native wildlife. West of Narawntapu are the appealing bushland, rocky quartzite headlands and exceptional marine environment of **Rocky Cape National Park**. Keeping to itself thanks to a lack of road access in the middle of the sprawling Tarkine Wilderness is the utterly secluded **Savage River National Park**. South of Hobart is Bruny Island, the wild southern cliffs, beaches and heathlands of which have been designated **South Bruny National Park**.

The enormous, multi-peaked wilderness that is the southwestern corner of Tasmania is protected within the 6000-sq-km **Southwest National Park**, one of the world's most pristine natural wonders. Over 40 sq km in the southwestern corner of Flinders Island are devoted to **Strzelecki National Park**, a mountainous slice of islandscape with numerous rare flora and fauna, while within the confines of **Tasman National Park** are the dramatic sea cliffs, islands and forests of the Tasman Peninsula. Finally, secreted in spectacular alpine and mountain wilderness east of Cradle Mountain, where it's regularly beset by harsh weather, is **Walls of Jerusalem National Park**, a solitude-seeking bushwalker's favourite.

World Heritage Areas

Covering 20% of the state, the huge and internationally significant **Tasmanian Wilderness World Heritage Area** contains its four largest national parks – Southwest, Wild Rivers, Cradle Mountain-Lake St Clair and Walls of Jerusalem – plus the Hartz Mountains National Park, the Central Plateau Conservation Area and the Adamsfield Conservation Area.

The region was first accepted for listing as a World Heritage area in 1982. To be accepted, a nomination for World Heritage status must satisfy at least one of the 10 criteria – the western Tasmania World Heritage Area was deemed to have outstanding natural and cultural values, and satisfied a record seven categories. In 1989 the World Heritage area was enlarged to 13,800 sq km and renominated as the Tasmanian Wilderness World Heritage Area.

The area is managed by the PWS, the same government agency that runs the national parks. Most of the area is managed as a publicly accessible wilderness, but being so large, most of it is accessible only to bushwalkers who can carry at least one week's food. One way to get a quick look at the area is to take one of the scenic flights operating from Strahan and Hobart (see those sections for details).

In December 1997, the **Macquarie Island World Heritage Area** was proclaimed, though the outstanding geological and faunal significance of this site will be difficult for visitors to appreciate, as Macquarie Island is a sub-Antarctic island located 1500km southeast of Tasmania.

Other Protected Areas

The PWS also manages a set of conservation areas and state reserves around the island, such as the Arthur-Pieman Conservation Area in the state's northwest. These reserves are usually established around one significant feature that is to be protected – often wildlife – but allow activities such as mining, farming, forestry and tourism development. Many of these places are very small and include caves, waterfalls, historic sites and some coastal regions. Usually there are no entry fees to these areas, except those where the government has actively restored or developed the area.

Forest Reserves

These are small areas that have been given some protection inside larger regions of state forests. They are on crown land and their primary purpose is for timber production. Many of the waterfalls and picnic areas on the state's scenic forest drives are in this type of reserve, which doesn't have real protection from future alterations. During weekdays some forestry roads are closed to private vehicles; if the roads are open, drive slowly and give way to logging trucks. There are no entry fees to the forests.

Marine Reserves

Tasmania is becoming increasingly aware of the significance and vulnerability of its marine environment. Marine reserves aim to protect fragile ecosystems, and fishing or the collection of living or dead material within their boundaries is illegal. There are marine reserves at Tinderbox near Hobart, at Ninepin Point near Verona Sands south of Hobart, in the waters around the northern part of Maria Island, and around Governor Island off the coast at Bicheno.

In May 1999, the federal government established a 370-sq-km marine reserve 170km south of Hobart. The Tasmanian Seamounts Marine Reserve is a deep-sea reserve in which any activities that could threaten its population of rare animals and plants have been outlawed, including mining and trawling (though fishing can still occur down to 500m).

[Continued from page 32]

Plugging Yourself In The notebook or palmtop computer you're planning to bring with you may not be compatible with the local power supply (220–240V AC, 50Hz), in which case you'll have to invest in a universal AC adaptor that will enable you to plug it in without frying the innards. Australia uses RJ-45 telephone plugs and Telstra EXI-160 four-pin plugs, neither universal; local electronics shops can help you out. You'll also need a plug adaptor – it's often easiest to buy these before you leave home.

Your PC-card modem may not work in Australia. The safest option is to buy a reputable 'global' modem before you leave home, or buy a local PC-card modem once you get to Australia.

There are a number of options for connecting to a local Internet Service Provider (ISP) – just make sure you're equipped with a list of all the relevant dial-in numbers. Major ISPs servicing Tasmania include:

America Online (AOL; ☎ 1800 265 265, **w** www.aol.com.au)
CompuServe (for local log-in numbers ☎ 1300 555 520, **w** www.compuserve.com.au)
OzEmail (☎ 13 28 84, **w** www.ozemail.com.au)
Primus (☎ 1300 858 585, **w** www.iprimus.com.au)
Telstra BigPond (☎ 13 12 82, **w** www.bigpond.com)

DIGITAL RESOURCES

The World Wide Web is a rich resource for travellers. You can research your trip, hunt down bargain air fares, book hotels, check on weather conditions or chat with locals and other travellers about the best places to visit (or avoid).

There's no better place to start your Web explorations than the website of **Lonely Planet** (**w** *www.lonelyplanet.com*). Here you will find succinct summaries on travelling to most places on earth, postcards from other travellers and the Thorn Tree bulletin board, where you can ask questions before you go or dispense advice when you get back. You can also find travel news and the subWWWay section, which links you to the most useful travel resources elsewhere on the Web.

Other sites providing a range of information on Tasmania include:

ABC News Online (**w** www.abc.net.au/news/default.htm) See the 'Australia/Local' section of this site for a good summary of the latest news stories in Tasmania and other Australian states.
Discover Tasmania (**w** www.discovertasmania.com.au) The official site of Tourism Tasmania has comprehensive details of the state's key destinations, festivals, tours and accommodation, but be warned that its search engine is highly temperamental and can be extremely frustrating to use.
Parks & Wildlife (**w** www.dpiwe.tas.gov.au) Visit this site for introductory information on Tasmania's national parks, World Heritage area, flora and fauna.

Other useful website addresses are listed throughout the text.

BOOKS

Most books are published in different editions by different publishers in different countries. Thus, a book might be a hardcover rarity in one country while it's readily available in paperback in another. Fortunately, bookshops and libraries search by title or author, so your local bookshop or library is best placed to advise you on the availability of the following recommendations.

Lonely Planet

Lonely Planet publishes a number of books you may want to refer to when planning your trip to Tasmania.

Walking in Australia has information on walks in Tasmania that will complement the briefer walk descriptions outlined in this book, while the Pisces guide *Diving & Snorkeling Australia: Southeast Coast & Tasmania* is a must for those interested in underwater explorations around the island. Those touring by bicycle should consider getting their hands on a copy of *Cycling Australia*. Finally, anyone intending to use Hobart as a departure point for a visit to Antarctica should check out our fascinating and comprehensive *Antarctica* guide by Jeff Rubin.

Guidebooks

In Hobart and Launceston bookshops and visitor information centres you'll find a host of general travel guides, many of which will give a brief overview of the state while focusing on a specific aspect of travel such as colonial accommodation, vineyards or guesthouses. For details about guides to particular activities (cycling, bushwalking, etc) see the Activities chapter.

Travel

The *Australian Geographic Book of Tasmania* by Lindsay Simpson (photographs by Bruce Miller) is the author's personal account of her travels around the state and features her partner's excellent photographs. It includes a useful lift-out map and some travel information.

The Ribbon and the Ragged Square by Linda Christmas is an intelligent, sober account of a nine-month investigatory trip around Australia by a *Guardian* journalist.

Down Home: Revisiting Tasmania, by Tasmanian-born academic, journalist and critic Peter Conrad, combines autobiography and history in a penetrating account of his return to the island after a 20-year absence. This is a contemplative book that will appeal particularly to those with a love of language.

For something less weighty, you might consider *Travelling Tales* by journalist and former Tasmanian resident Charles Wooley, whose affection for his home state finds expression in chapters on such subjects as Lake Pedder and fly-fishing on the Meander River.

Bill Bryson, the American humorist travel writer, takes his usual well-rehearsed and statistically supported potshots in *Down Under*.

History

For a comprehensive and accessible history lesson, read *A Short History of Tasmania,* Michael Roe's updated edition of the classic Lloyd Robson book.

Manning Clark's *A Short History of Australia* and Robert Hughes' bestselling account of the convict era, *The Fatal Shore,* are a good introduction to general Australian history.

Geoffrey Blainey's book *The Peaks of Lyell* gives a compelling account of the Mt Lyell Mining and Railway Company and a century of mining in western Tasmania. It's a great introduction to Queenstown for those with an interest in that intriguing community.

A number of books documenting Port Arthur's recent history and the aftermath of the 1996 massacre are available, notably *Port Arthur: A Story of Strength and Courage* by Margaret Scott. For more on this terrible event, see the Port Arthur section in the Around Hobart chapter.

King of the Wilderness: the Life of Deny King by Christobel Mattingley sacrifices objectivity for at-times melodramatic hero worship, but details the nonetheless interesting history of a man who made the southwest wilderness his home.

Books about Aboriginal and environmental history are listed under Aboriginal People and Environment respectively.

Aboriginal People

There are many books on the history of Tasmania's Aborigines. Lonely Planet's *Aboriginal Australia & the Torres Strait Islands* is a comprehensive, practical guidebook covering Aboriginal history, culture and places of interest.

The Aboriginal Tasmanians by Lyndall Ryan is a well-researched and presented argument against what the author calls the myth of the 'last Tasmanian'. Other authoritative and questioning tomes are *Blood on the Wattle* by Bruce Elder, and the works of Brian Plomley.

In *Fate of a Free People,* Henry Reynolds re-examines history from an Aboriginal perspective and puts a case for Tasmanian Aboriginal land rights. Cassandra Pybus' book *Community of Thieves* considers the fate of the Nuennone people of southeastern Tasmania from her perspective as a descendant of Richard Pybus, a European who took up a large land grant on Bruny Island, the traditional home of the Nuennone.

Flora & Fauna

Among the many guides to Tasmania's fauna are *The Fauna of Tasmania: Birds* and *The Fauna of Tasmania: Mammals* by RH Green, and *Tasmanian Mammals – A Field Guide* by Dave Watts. Lonely Planet's *Watching Wildlife: Australia* is a comprehensive guide to Australia's fauna, parks and habitats.

If you're interested in the now extinct Tasmanian tiger, browse *Thylacine: The Tragedy of the Tasmanian Tiger* by Eric Guiler. It's a very dry book, but the author draws together a diverse array of scientific knowledge and anecdotal evidence about the marsupial carnivore to argue that one of the greatest tragedies of its sorry history is that nobody bothered to study it thoroughly when they had the chance.

Among guides to Tasmania's flora are *Native Trees of Tasmania* by JB Kirkpatrick & Sue Backhouse; and a number of pocket-sized plant identi-kits by Phil Collier, including *Alpine Flowers of Tasmania, Orchids of Tasmania,* and *Wildflowers of Mt Wellington.* The Launceston Field Naturalists Club is now up to the 3rd edition of its excellent *A Guide to Flowers & Plants in Tasmania.*

Environment

For a summary of the legacy of early European exploration, read *Trampled Wilderness* by Ralph & Kathleen Gowlland.

The Australian Conservation Foundation's *The South West Book* has a plethora of information about the southwest, from scientific debate to reproductions of newspaper articles and posters printed at times of conflict over the region's future. Published in 1978, this book is already something of a historical document itself and can be viewed in Hobart's main libraries or in the library of the **Tasmanian Environment Centre** (☎ *6234 5566; 102 Bathurst St, Hobart).*

The Rest of the World is Watching, edited by Richard Flanagan & Cassandra Pybus, covers the history to 1990 of the groundbreaking Tasmanian Green movement.

Anyone who wants to know about the original Lake Pedder should take the time to visit the **State Library of Tasmania** (☎ *6233 7529; 91 Murray St, Hobart;* **w** *www.statelibrary.tas.gov.au)* and view the magnificent collection of photographs compiled by Bob Brown in the large-format publication simply entitled *Lake Pedder.* The accompanying article 'I saw my Temple Ransacked', written by Kevin Kiernan (and reprinted in an abridged form in *The Rest of the World is Watching),* is a first-hand account of the Pedder campaign including a brief but harrowing description of the drowning lake that will remain with you long after you've finished reading the book.

Among the photographers featured in *Lake Pedder* is Olegas Truchanas, an adventurer and conservationist whose exceptional images of Pedder were wielded by conservationists during their fight to try and save the lake. If you like his work, you may also be interested in the more extensive collection of his wilderness photographs compiled by Max Angus in *The World of Olegas Truchanas.*

Truchanas died photographing the Gordon River in 1972, the year Lake Pedder was flooded, but his protégé, Peter Dombrovskis, continued in his footsteps, producing work of a similarly high standard now ubiquitous in Tasmania on postcards, greeting cards, posters and calendars. *Wild Rivers* by Bob Brown contains photographs of the Franklin taken by Dombrovskis during his three full-length trips down its course and is accompanied by the author's account of his own experiences on that river.

Like his mentor, Dombrovskis died in the pursuit of his art. *On the Mountain,* published after his death in the Western Arthur Range in 1996, is a selection of images of Mt Wellington, which was his home for the greater part of 50 years. This book also contains a personal reflection on the mountain and its significance by Richard Flanagan and an account of its natural history by academic Jamie Kirkpatrick.

Fiction

Christopher Koch uses Tasmania as the setting for large sections of many of his novels, including *The Doubleman, Highways to a War* and *The Boys in the Island.* Richard Flanagan's novels *Death of a River Guide* and *The Sound of One Hand*

Clapping, and Amanda Lohrey's novel *Morality of Gentlemen* are also set in the state. For more information about these authors and their works, see the Arts section in the Facts about Tasmania chapter.

The Potato Factory by Bryce Courtenay is a fictionalised account of the life of Tasmanian convict Ikey Solomon.

Souvenir Books

Bruce Miller's photographs in Lindsay Simpson's *The Australian Geographic Book of Tasmania* (mentioned under Travel earlier in this section) make this glossy, soft-cover book an appealing keepsake. For pictures of the World Heritage area, buy a coffee-table book like *South West Tasmania* by Richard Bennett or *The Mountains of Paradise* by Les Southwell. The Wilderness Shop always has a good range of books on the Franklin River, the Styx Valley and the Tarkine Wilderness.

FILMS

Richard Flanagan's harrowing *The Sound of One Hand Clapping,* released in 1998 and shot in Tasmania, traces the impact on successive generations of war, displacement and abandonment by recounting the story of a single family of European migrants from the time their grief finally becomes unendurable in a remote construction camp in the Tasmanian highlands.

Another Tasmanian film for which the highlands provide a grim setting is *The Tale of Ruby Rose* (1986), the story of a woman brought up in harsh isolation who has to come to terms with her marriage to a reclusive trapper.

Two documentaries that consider Tasmanian Aboriginal history and experience are *The Last Tasmanian* (1978) and *Black Man's Houses* (1992). The former was widely acclaimed when it was first released, but the version of history it provides has been refuted by successive historians and Tasmanian Aborigines. The latter documents racial tensions on Flinders Island, where the graves of members of the Wybalenna Aboriginal settlement of the 1830s (see the History section in the Facts about Tasmania chapter) were desecrated shortly after they had been restored by the island's present-day Aboriginal community.

NEWSPAPERS & MAGAZINES

In Hobart and the south, the main newspaper daily is the *Mercury;* in Launceston and the northeast, it's the *Examiner;* and in Burnie and the northwest, it's the *Advocate.* All are tabloids covering local, national and international news, with a headline-shouting emphasis on the local. Larger newsagents in both Hobart and Launceston stock major mainland dailies.

40° South is a glossy quarterly magazine packed with articles about the state, many of which will be of interest to travellers. With a price tag approaching $10, though, it's not for light reading.

If you're interested in Tasmanian culture, particularly performing and visual arts (plus liberal doses of smug urbanity), look out for the monthly booklet *getout* ($3).

Good Australian outdoor and adventure magazines that regularly include articles about Tasmania are the quarterly *Wild* and *Outdoor Australia,* and the monthly *Rock.*

About every two years the Hobart Walking Club publishes *Tasmanian Tramp,* a journal of various trips undertaken by club members containing valuable information on out-of-the-way walks and articles on conservation, history and humorous episodes. Back issues are held in the State Reference Library and as a collection are a fascinating record of how the experiences available to bushwalkers in the southwest have been altered by the construction of successive dams.

RADIO & TV

The national advertising-free TV and radio network is the Australian Broadcasting Corporation (ABC).

In major centres there are usually a number of radio stations, both AM and FM, featuring everything from rock to talkback to the euphemistic 'easy-listening music'. Triple J is the ABC's youth FM radio station; broadcast nationally, it generally plays non-mainstream Australian and international music, though of late it has tended towards heavier and at times not-so 'alternative' sounds. ABC Classic FM plays classical music, while Radio National is an Australiawide service featuring current affairs and information. All three can be received in larger Tasmanian towns, though reception of Triple J and Classic FM may be poor in Queenstown and on parts of the east coast.

If it's TV you're looking for, ABC, Southern Cross and WIN Television (the state's two commercial stations), and SBS (a federal government–sponsored multicultural service) are all available in Hobart and Launceston. Tasmania's numerous hills, however, can often block reception of the commercial stations and SBS; several remoter towns receive only the ABC. Sports events broadcast via satellite Pay TV are a regular fixture at many pubs and clubs.

VIDEO SYSTEMS

Australia uses the PAL system, and so prerecorded videos purchased in Australia may be incompatible with overseas systems. Check this before you buy.

PHOTOGRAPHY & VIDEO

Australian film prices are not too far out of line with those of the rest of the Western world. A roll of 36-exposure Kodachrome 64 or Fujichrome 100 slide film costs around $25 to $30 including developing, or $11 to $15 for film only.

There are several camera shops in Hobart and Launceston with high camera service and developing standards. Many places offer one-hour developing of print film. **Photoforce** (☎ 6234 6234; 178 Campbell St) is one of Hobart's higher-quality labs and can develop slide film within a day.

The best photographs are obtained early in the morning and late in the afternoon. As the sun gets higher, colours begin to appear washed out. You must also allow for the intensity of reflected light when taking shots at coastal locations. Especially in the summer, allow for temperature extremes and do your best to keep film as cool as possible, particularly after exposure.

Lonely Planet's *Travel Photography: A Guide to Taking Better Pictures* by Richard I'Anson is a comprehensive guide to technical and creative travel photography.

As in any country, politeness goes a long way when taking photographs; ask before taking pictures of people. Note that many Tasmanian Aborigines do not like to have their photographs taken, even from a distance.

If you come from a country that uses a video system other than PAL and you wish to buy a camera in Australia to record your holiday, you should shop for this in Melbourne or Sydney if possible, as it's very difficult to find such equipment in Tasmanian retail outlets.

TIME

Australia is divided into three time zones: Western Standard Time (GMT/UTC plus eight hours) applies in WA; Central Standard Time (plus 9½ hours) covers the NT and SA; and Eastern Standard Time (plus 10 hours) covers Tasmania, Victoria, NSW and Queensland. When it's noon in WA it's 1.30pm in the NT and SA and 2pm in the rest of the country.

During the summer things get slightly screwed up, as daylight saving time (when clocks are put forward an hour) does not operate in WA, Queensland or the NT, and in Tasmania it starts a month earlier and finishes up to a month later than in the other states.

ELECTRICITY

Electrical supply is 220–240V AC, 50Hz, and the plugs are three-pin, but not the same as British three-pin plugs. Users of electric shavers or hairdryers should note that, apart from in fancy hotels, it's difficult to find converters to take either US flat two-pin plugs or the European round two-pin plugs. Adaptors for British and European plugs can be found in good hardware shops, chemists and travel agents.

WEIGHTS & MEASURES

Australia uses the metric system. Petrol and milk are sold by the litre, apples and potatoes by the kilogram, distance is measured by the metre or kilometre, and speed limits are in kilometres per hour (km/h).

If you need help converting metric to imperial, there's a conversion table at the back of this book.

HEALTH

Australia is a remarkably healthy country in which to travel, with upset stomachs and unapologetic hangovers among the worst-case scenarios. If you do happen to fall ill, the standard of medical care in Australia is high.

Predeparture Planning

Immunisations No vaccinations are required for entry to Australia unless you're arriving from a country infected with yellow fever, in which case you'll need proof of vaccination.

Health Insurance Make sure that you have adequate health insurance. See the Travel Insurance entry in the Visas & Documents section earlier in this chapter.

Other Preparations Make sure you're healthy before you start travelling. If you are going on a long trip make sure your teeth are OK. If you wear glasses take a spare pair and your prescription.

If you require a particular medication take an adequate supply, as it may not be available locally. Take part of the packaging showing the generic name rather than the brand, which will make getting replacements easier. To avoid any problems, it's a good idea to have a legible prescription or letter from your doctor to show that you legally use the medication.

A well-stocked medical kit is a good idea when travelling into more remote areas, where there can be a dearth of hospitals and doctors (see the boxed text 'Medical Kit Check List' on this page).

Water

Tap water is safe to drink in towns and cities throughout the state (though travellers are advised to boil water in Queenstown). Always be wary of taking drinking water direct from waterways, as it may have been

---

Medical Kit Check List

Following is a list of items you should consider including in your medical kit – consult your pharmacist for brands available in your country.

☐ **Aspirin or paracetamol (acetaminophen in the USA)** – for pain or fever

☐ **Antihistamine** – for allergies, eg, hay fever; to ease the itch from insect bites or stings; and to prevent motion sickness

☐ **Cold and flu tablets, throat lozenges and nasal decongestant**

☐ **Multivitamins** – consider for long trips, when dietary vitamin intake may be inadequate

☐ **Antibiotics** – consider including these if you're travelling well off the beaten track; see your doctor, as they must be prescribed, and carry the prescription with you

☐ **Loperamide or diphenoxylate** – 'blockers' for diarrhoea

☐ **Prochlorperazine or metaclopramide** – for nausea and vomiting

☐ **Rehydration mixture** – to prevent dehydration, which may occur, for example, during bouts of diarrhoea; particularly important when travelling with children

☐ **Insect repellent, sunscreen, lip balm and eye drops**

☐ **Calamine lotion, sting relief spray or aloe vera** – to ease irritation from sunburn and insect bites or stings

☐ **Antifungal cream or powder** – for fungal skin infections and thrush

☐ **Antiseptic (such as povidone-iodine)** – for cuts and grazes

☐ **Bandages, Band-Aids (plasters) and other wound dressings**

☐ **Water purification tablets or iodine**

☐ **Scissors, tweezers and a thermometer** – note that mercury thermometers are prohibited by airlines

---

infected by stock or wildlife – if there's any doubt, boil the water for 10 minutes.

Environmental Hazards

Hypothermia If you're hiking in the colder climes of Tasmania, you should always be prepared for cold, wet or windy conditions.

Hypothermia occurs when the body loses heat faster than it can produce it and the core temperature of the body falls. It's surprisingly easy to progress from being very cold to being dangerously cold due to a combination of wind, wet clothing, fatigue and hunger, even if the air temperature is above freezing. It's best to dress in layers; silk, wool and some of the new artificial fibres are all good insulating materials. A hat is important, as a lot of heat is lost through the head. A strong, waterproof outer layer (and a 'space' blanket for emergencies) is essential. Carry basic supplies, including food containing simple sugars to generate heat quickly, and fluid to drink.

Symptoms of hypothermia are exhaustion, numb skin (particularly toes and fingers), shivering, slurred speech, irrational or violent behaviour, lethargy, stumbling, dizzy spells, muscle cramps and violent bursts of energy. Irrationality may take the form of sufferers claiming they are warm and trying to take off their clothes.

To treat mild hypothermia, first get the person out of the wind and/or rain, remove their clothing if it's wet and replace it with dry, warm clothing. Give them hot liquids – not alcohol – and some high-energy, easily digestible food. Do not rub victims: instead, allow them to slowly warm themselves. This should be enough to treat the early stages of hypothermia.

Motion Sickness Eating lightly before and during a trip will reduce the chances of motion sickness. If you're prone to motion sickness, try to find a place that minimises movement – near a wing on aircrafts, close to midships on boats, near the centre on buses. Fresh air usually helps; reading and cigarette smoke don't. Commercial motion-sickness preparations, which can cause drowsiness, have to be taken before the trip commences. Ginger (available in capsule form) and peppermint (including mint-flavoured sweets) are natural preventatives.

Sunburn You can get sunburnt surprisingly quickly in Tasmania, even through cloud. Use a high-factor sunscreen, a hat and a barrier cream (zinc) for your nose and lips. Calamine lotion or a commercial after-sun preparation are good for mild sunburn. Protect your eyes with good quality sunglasses, particularly if you will be near water, sand or snow.

Infectious Diseases

HIV/AIDS Infection with the human immunodeficiency virus (HIV) may lead to acquired immune deficiency syndrome (AIDS), which is a fatal disease. Any exposure to blood, blood products or body fluids may put the individual at risk. The disease is often transmitted through sexual contact or dirty syringes.

Sexually Transmitted Diseases (STDs) STDs include gonorrhoea, herpes and syphilis; sores, blisters or rashes around the genitals and discharges or pain when urinating are common symptoms. With some STDs, such as wart virus or chlamydia, symptoms may be less marked or not observed at all, especially in women. Chlamydia infection can cause infertility in men and women before any symptoms have been noticed. Syphilis symptoms eventually disappear completely but the disease continues and can cause severe problems in later years. While abstinence from sexual contact is the only 100% effective prevention, using condoms is also effective. The treatment of gonorrhoea and syphilis is with antibiotics.

Cuts, Bites & Stings

Wash well and treat any cut with an antiseptic such as povidone-iodine. Apply a breathable waterproof dressing such as Cutifilm or Tegaderm.

Bee and wasp stings are usually painful rather than dangerous. Calamine lotion or a sting-relief spray will give some relief and ice packs can be used to reduce the pain and swelling. People who are allergic to these stings, however, may have severe breathing difficulties and require urgent medical care. There are some spiders with dangerous bites but antivenins are usually available.

Women's Health
The contraceptive pill is available on prescription only, so a visit to a doctor is necessary. Doctors are listed in the *Yellow Pages* phone book or online at **w** www.yellowpages.com.au.

Gynaecological Problems Antibiotic use, synthetic underwear, sweating and contraceptive pills can lead to fungal vaginal infections, especially when travelling in hot climates. Fungal infections are characterised by a rash, itch and discharge and are usually treated with nystatin, miconazole or clotrimazole pessaries. Maintaining good personal hygiene and wearing loose-fitting clothes and cotton underwear may help prevent these infections.

Sexually transmitted diseases are a major cause of vaginal problems. Symptoms include a smelly discharge, painful intercourse and sometimes a burning sensation when urinating. Medical attention should be sought and male sexual partners must also be treated. Besides abstinence, the best thing is to practise safer sex using condoms.

Pregnancy Miscarriages occur during the first three months of pregnancy and can occasionally lead to severe bleeding. The last three months of pregnancy should also be spent within reasonable distance of good medical care. A baby born as early as 24 weeks stands a good chance of survival, but only in a modern hospital. Pregnant women should take additional care to prevent illness and particular attention should be paid to diet and nutrition – alcohol and nicotine, for example, should be avoided.

WOMEN TRAVELLERS
Tasmania is generally a safe place for women travellers, although it's probably best to avoid walking alone late at night in major towns, particularly in the vicinity of pubs and bars at closing time. Sexual harassment is an ongoing problem, be it via an aggressive cosmopolitan male or a rural bloke living a less-than-enlightened proforma bush existence.

Female hitchhikers should exercise care at all times (see the Hitchhiking section in the Getting Around chapter). A contact in a time of need is the **Sexual Assault Support Service** (☎ *6231 1811*) in Hobart.

GAY & LESBIAN TRAVELLERS
On 1 May 1997, after a nine-year law-reform campaign, the Tasmanian parliament repealed Tasmania's anti-gay laws, thereby complying with the 1994 United Nations ruling on this issue and eliminating Australia's only remaining state law banning same-sex relations. Tasmania is now considered by gay- and lesbian-rights groups to have greater equality in the criminal law for homosexual and heterosexual people than most of the other Australian states.

The **Gay and Lesbian Community Centre** (*GLC Centre;* ☎ *0500 808 031;* **w** *www.gaytas .org),* based in Hobart but with Tasmania-wide links, is a good source of information on issues and events involving the gay and lesbian community. It publishes the free, annual *Tasmanian Gay & Lesbian Business & Service Directory* and a monthly newsletter called *CentreLines* ($2).

SENIOR TRAVELLERS
The majority of attractions listed in this book have reduced rates for senior citizens, so make sure you ask whether a discount is available whenever you purchase a ticket. You'll usually need to show some authoritative identification, such as a pensioner concession card, to qualify for the discount. Discounts are also often available for senior travellers using public transport.

TRAVEL WITH CHILDREN
Tasmania is a place where kids can't complain about a lack of nature-based activities, because there's always a forest, national park trail, beach or guided tour (eg, a cruise) in the immediate vicinity. There's also plenty to involve them indoors, in the form of historic building interiors, museums and attractions that cater specifically to the child-like, though this will usually mean a bit more financial expenditure from parents. Nearly all tourist attractions offer

Disabled Travellers in Tasmania

Tasmania has a rapidly improving awareness of disability issues. Most of the state's key attractions provide the requisite access and a good number of tour operators also have the appropriate facilities – it's still a good idea, though, to call ahead and confirm this. There are also a number of local agencies that provide information and/or assistance to disabled travellers.

Information

Tourism Tasmania (☎ 1800 808 776; W www.discovertasmania.com.au) has information on disability-friendly accommodation, attractions and services. Accessible Youth Hostels Association (YHA) hostels are listed in its annual YHA Accommodation & Discounts Guide booklet or at W www .yha.org.au.

The **Royal Automobile Club of Tasmania** (RACT; ☎ 13 27 22; W www.ract.com.au) also has some information for travellers with disabilities. The **Paraplegic & Quadriplegic Association** (☎ 6272 8816) is a key information source with accommodation, accessible toilets, mobility maps and attractions, and can help with specific requests from travellers. You can also contact the **Australian Council for Rehabilitation of the Disabled** (ACROD; ☎ 6223 6086) and **The Aged & Disability Care Information Service** (☎ 6234 7448; W www.adcis.org.au). Another organisation to get in touch with is the **Royal Tasmanian Society for the Blind & Deaf** (☎ 6232 1299).

Attractions & Accommodation

The **Parks and Wildlife Service** (PWS; ☎ 6233 6191; W www.dpiwe.tas.gov.au) publishes Tasmania's National Parks, Forests & Waterways – A Visitors' Guide, which indicates accessible facilities. **Mt Field National Park** (☎ 6288 1149) has an accessible 500m-long bitumen track leading to spectacular Russell Falls, while Cape Tourville in Freycinet National Park has a similarly accessible boardwalk yielding great views.

The **Port Arthur Historical Site** (☎ 1800 659 101; W www.portarthur.org.au), one of the most significant attractions in Tasmania, has a full complement of accessible facilities and tours, including the ferry that plies the harbour. Buggies are also available to transport visitors with disabilities around the site.

At Cradle Mountain-Lake St Clair National Park, **Cradle Mountain Lodge** (☎ 6492 1303, 1800 737 678) has several accessible self-catering chalets. The **Cradle Mountain visitors centre** (☎ 6492 1110) has an accessible toilet and, nearby, a short boardwalk comprising the circular Rainforest Walk.

Transport

Transport options are limited so it's best to take your own vehicle on one of the **TT-Line** ferries (☎ 1800 634 906; W www.tt-line.com.au) that sail between Melbourne and Devonport. Several cabins on each ferry are accessible with the 'flood step' removed, a wheel-in shower and grab-rails. TT-Line staff will drive your vehicle on and off the vessel for you. The airports at Hobart and Launceston are not equipped with air bridges, so wheelchair passengers are boarded and disembarked using forklifts.

For wheelchair-accessible maxi-cabs in Hobart, try **Hobart & Southern Maxi-Taxis** (☎ 6227 9577, 0418 126 515); book 24 hours in advance if possible. **AVIS** (☎ 13 63 33; W www.avis.com) provides hand-controlled vehicles at Hobart and Launceston. You can pick up a copy of the Hobart CBD Mobility Map at the **Hobart Travel & Information Centre** (☎ 6230 8233). The **Devonport Visitor Centre** (☎ 6424 8176) can also supply a mobility map. Easy Access Australia has lots of detailed information on Tasmania and can be ordered online at W www.easyaccessaustralia.com.au.

significant discounts for children, with the very young often admitted free.

In Launceston there's Cataract Gorge and the Queen Victoria Museum & Art Gallery; in Beaconsfield there's the Grubb Shaft Gold & Heritage Museum; in the Mole Creek and Hastings areas there are grand caves to explore; near Lake Barrington is an extensive maze; between Queenstown and Strahan is the Abt Wilderness Railway; and in Hobart there's the Cadbury chocolate factory and Antarctic Adventure. These are just a few of the many places of interest to children, full details of which are given later in this book.

Most motel and hotel accommodation, and the better-equipped caravan parks and odd guesthouse, will be able to supply cots and baby baths – many also have playgrounds, games rooms or swimming pools. Cafés and restaurants in larger towns can often provide high chairs and kids' meals. Pubs are not the ideal place for kids but they often have a children's menu, which can be handy if you have no other culinary options.

USEFUL ORGANISATIONS

Most key organisations operating in Tasmania have their head offices in Hobart. For details of a particular group, check in the *Yellow Pages* under 'Organisations' or at ⓦ www.yellowpages.com.au.

Royal Automobile Club of Tasmania (RACT)

The RACT (☎ 13 27 22; ⓦ www.ract.com .au; cnr Patrick & Murray Sts) in Hobart, provides an emergency breakdown service and has reciprocal arrangements with services in other Australian states and some from overseas. It also provides literature, excellent maps and detailed guides to accommodation and camping grounds.

National Trust

The National Trust is dedicated to preserving historic buildings and important natural features throughout Australia. It owns and manages many properties, opening most of them to the public. The National Trust also 'classifies' sites to ensure their preservation.

The National Trust produces some excellent literature, including a fine series of walking-tour guides. These guides are often available from local tourist offices or from National Trust offices and are usually free.

Membership to the National Trust entitles you to free entry to most of the properties it manages. Annual membership costs $49.50 for individuals, $27.50 for concession and $77 for families, and includes a monthly or quarterly newsletter put out by the state organisation that you join; there's also a first-year joining fee of $38.50. The state head office (☎ 6344 6233; ⓦ www.tased.edu.au/ tasonline/nattrust; 413 Hobart Rd, Launceston) is in Franklin House, while the organisation's southern regional office (☎ 6223 5200; cnr Brisbane & Campbell Sts, Hobart) is at the Penitentiary Chapel Historic Site.

DANGERS & ANNOYANCES
Snakes

The best-known danger in the Australian bush, and the one that captures visitors' imagination the most, is snakes. Although all snakes in Tasmania are venomous, they are not aggressive and, unless you have the bad fortune to stand on one, it's unlikely you'll be bitten. The tiger snake, however, will sometimes attack if alarmed. February is the month when snakes are at their most active in Tasmania.

To minimise your chances of being bitten, always wear boots, socks and long trousers when walking through undergrowth where snakes may be present. Don't put your hands into holes and crevices, and be careful when collecting firewood. Most importantly, if you see a snake, leave it alone.

Snake bites do not cause instantaneous death and antivenins are usually available. Immediately wrap the bitten limb tightly, as you would a sprained ankle, and then attach a splint to immobilise it. Keep the victim still and seek medical help, if possible with the dead snake for identification. Don't attempt to catch the snake if there's a possibility of being bitten again. Tourniquets and sucking out the poison are now comprehensively discredited.

Flies & Mosquitoes

March flies are large, very persistent and will bite any uncovered area, leaving behind large, red lumps (similar to leech bites). They are prevalent in the summer months and are attracted to blue clothing, so you're better off wearing other colours. Insect repellents go some way to deterring these pests, and calamine lotion can soothe the bites, but it's best to just cover up.

Just when you think the flies have gone (around sunset) and it's safe to come out, the 'mossies' appear. Insect repellents usually keep them at bay.

Leeches

Leeches may be present in damp rainforest conditions; they attach themselves to your skin to suck your blood. Trekkers often get them on their legs or in their boots. Salt or a lighted cigarette end will make them fall off. Do not pull them off, as the bite is then more likely to become infected. Clean and apply pressure if the point of attachment is bleeding. An insect repellent may keep them away.

Bushfires & Blizzards

Bushfires occur almost every year in Tasmania, even with the state's higher-than-average rainfalls. Don't be the mug who starts one. In hot, dry, windy weather, be extremely careful with any naked flame – that means no cigarette butts out car windows. On a total fire ban day (listen to the radio or watch the billboards on country roads), it's forbidden to use even a camping stove in the open. The locals will not be amused if they catch you breaking this particular law; they'll happily dob you in, and the penalties are severe.

Bushwalkers should take local advice before setting out. On a day of total fire ban, delay your trip until the weather has changed. Chances are that it will be so unpleasantly hot and windy, you'll be far better off in an air-conditioned pub sipping a cool beer. If you're out in the bush and you see smoke, even at a great distance, take it seriously. Go to the nearest open space, downhill if possible. A forested ridge is the most dangerous place to be. Bushfires move very quickly and change direction with the wind.

At the other end of the elemental scale, blizzards can occur in Tasmania's mountains at any time of year. Some summer storms have been severe enough to deposit snow on the Lyell and Murchison Hwys. Bushwalkers need to be prepared for such freezing eventualities, particularly in remote areas. Take warm clothing like thermals and jackets, plus wind-proof and waterproof garments, and be sure to eat, drink and rest regularly. Carry a high-quality tent suitable for snow camping and carry enough food for two extra days, in case you get held up by bad weather. See also the Hypothermia entry in the Health section earlier in this chapter.

EMERGENCIES

In the case of a life-threatening situation dial ☎ 000. This call is free from any phone and the operator will connect you with either the police, ambulance or fire brigade. To dial any of these services direct, check the inside front cover of any local telephone book.

For other telephone crisis and personal counselling services (such as sexual assault, poisons information or alcohol and drug problems), check the Community pages of the local telephone book.

BUSINESS HOURS

Most shops close at 5pm or 6pm on weekdays (sometimes at 9pm on Friday), and either noon or 5pm on Saturday. At the time of writing, Sunday trading was still limited to a number of small shops, but the state government had signalled its intention to deregulate Tasmania's trading hours. Places that regularly stay open late and over the whole weekend include milk bars, convenience stores, small supermarkets, delis and city bookshops.

Banks are open from 9.30am to 4pm from Monday to Thursday, and until 5pm on Friday. The exception is in small towns where they may open only one or two days a week.

PUBLIC HOLIDAYS & SPECIAL EVENTS

The Christmas holiday season, from mid-December to late January, is part of the summer school vacation and is the time when accommodation often books out and there are long queues at attractions. There are three shorter school holiday periods during the year, but they vary by a week or two from year to year, falling from early to mid-April, late June to mid-July, and late September to early October.

Public holidays are as follows:

New Year's Day	1 January
Australia Day	26 January
Regatta Day	2nd Tuesday in February (southern Tasmania)
Launceston Cup	last Wednesday in February (Launceston only)
Eight Hour Day	1st Monday in March
King Island Show	1st Tuesday in March (King Island only)
Easter	March/April (Good Friday to Easter Monday inclusive)
Bank Holiday	Tuesday following Easter Monday
Anzac Day	25 April
Queen's Birthday	2nd Monday in June
Burnie Show	1st Friday in October (Burnie only)
Launceston Show	2nd Thursday in October (Launceston only)
Hobart Show	3rd Thursday in October (southern Tasmania)
Flinders Island Show	3rd Friday in October (Flinders Island only)
Recreation Day	1st Monday in November (northern Tasmania)
Christmas Day	25 December
Boxing Day	26 December

Major annual festivals and events include the following:

January

Sydney to Hobart Yacht Race The arrival (29 December to 2 January) in Hobart of the yachts competing in this annual New Year race is celebrated with lots of noise and colour.

Melbourne to Hobart Yacht Race The competitors for this race arrive on the same days as those competing in the Sydney to Hobart Yacht Race.

Hobart Summer Festival This festival starts around the time of the completion of the yacht races and stretches until the end of February, incorporating numerous festivities along the way, including Taste of Tasmania, a week-long food and drink celebration.

Australia Day This national holiday, commemorating the arrival of the First Fleet in 1788, is observed on 26 January.

February

Royal Hobart Regatta This large aquatic carnival is held over three days, with boat races and other activities.

Festivale Launceston residents and visitors indulge themselves over three days with plenty of food, drink and entertainment.

National Penny Farthing Championships Evandale hosts some decidedly anachronistic but fun races involving these tall bikes, with plenty of spills and other entertainment.

Cradle Mountain Overland Run A group of people attempt to run the entire 80.5km of the Overland Track in one day, thereby ignoring the purpose of the track, which is to allow people time to appreciate some wonderful landscapes.

March

Fingal Valley Festival The small town of Fingal hosts this unusual festival, which comprises unusual events like roof bolting and coal shovelling.

Taste of the Huon This is a two-day festival in mid-March celebrating the food, wine, music and crafts of the Huon Valley and Bruny Island.

Ten Days on the Island Held for the first time in 2001, this biennial event, which runs from late March until early April, is Tasmania's premier cultural festival, a state-wide celebration of local and international 'island culture'.

April

Anzac Day This national public holiday, on 25 April, commemorates the landing of Anzac troops at Gallipoli in 1915. Memorial marches by returned world war soldiers and the veterans of Korea and Vietnam are held all over the country.

Three Peaks Race This is an event where competitors have to sail their yachts and also run up three of Tasmania's higher mountains. It starts from Beauty Point north of Launceston.

Targa Tasmania This is a six-day rally for exotic cars that runs around the entire state (see the boxed text 'The Targa Tradition' later).

June

Suncoast Jazz Festival The east-coast haven of St Helens is the venue for this outstanding jazz festival, held during the last weekend in June.

The Targa Tradition

Targa Tasmania, a classic-car race that sees up to 300 competitors zooming along 2000km of the island's sealed roads, has been running for over a decade. But the Sicilian predecessor after which it was named, the famous Targa Florio, was run almost every year from 1906 until its demise in 1973.

Created and sponsored by the Marsala wine- and tuna-canning Florio family, and with first prize a copy of the family plate (*targa* in Italian), the Targa Florio was contested on the twisting roads of the Madonie mountains in Sicily, lined with what must have been every inhabitant of the region. In 1970 it was abundantly clear that Sicilian schoolteacher Nino Vaccarella, moonlighting as a Ferrari racing-car driver, was the hometown favourite. V-A-C-C-A-R-E-L-L-A was graffitied across every blank expanse of wall around the 72km length of the circuit, and at every corner (there were over 700 of them!) crowds of Sicilians leaned dangerously out on to the track to watch for the arrival of the local hero.

During its life the Targa Florio was run on a variety of circuits before settling down on the Piccolo Madonie circuit, winding along the coast from the town of Campofelice di Roccella then climbing up into the mountains through Cerda, Caltavuturo, Scillato and Collesano before dropping back down to the coast. Revived after WWII, the Targa Florio continued as a major event through the 1950s and into the 1960s, and in its last few years became a straight fight between the smaller, more agile Porsches and Alfa Romeos and the powerful Ferraris, of which one in particular was cheered on by the roars of the partisan crowd. In the late 1960s, motor racing faced greater demands for increased safety and the prospect of cars capable of over 300km/h (200 miles/h) hurtling along stone-walled straights and into tiny villages, where spectators stood unprotected on the circuit perimeter, became completely intolerable. The Targa Florio was doomed.

Nino Vaccarella never made it in the big league of Formula One racing, but in Sicily his knowledge of the local roads guaranteed that he would always challenge for the lead. As for the Targa Florio itself, it has been 30 years since a racing V12 Ferrari 512 hurtled through Campofelice, but the memory of the race survives in the annual Targa Tasmania rally.

Perhaps it was meant to be. There is, after all, a small town called Targa on the road between Launceston and Scottsdale, though any connection seems purely coincidental.

Tony Wheeler

September

Blooming Tasmania Lasting at least three months, this is more of a coordinated set of festivals and displays rather than a single event. A special brochure is produced every year detailing when each festival and garden is open to the public.

October

Royal Shows The royal agricultural and horticultural shows of Hobart, Burnie, Flinders Island and Launceston are held during this month.

Herald Sun Tour This is a major two-week professional bicycle race around Victoria and Tasmania. The local section is mainly through tough hilly sections on the northern coast.

Wynyard Tulip Festival At this time of year the tulips are in colourful flower; you can also visit the tulip farm at nearby Table Cape.

Derby River Derby Several thousand people cram into this old mining town to watch a ramshackle fleet raft down the river. There are no race rules,

which usually means everyone gets wet and has a great time.

Tasmanian Craft Fair This four-day event is held in Deloraine, always ending on the first Monday in November. It is claimed to be Australia's largest working craft fair.

November

Melbourne Cup The first Tuesday in November, the whole country comes to a virtual standstill (well, not really) for the three minutes or so when Australia's premier horse race is run in Melbourne.

Melbourne to Stanley Yacht Race Yachts dash across Bass Strait in early November.

December

Carols by Candlelight Evening services are held in both Hobart and Launceston before Christmas.

Latrobe Wheel & Latrobe Gift These are professional bicycle races held when most other towns are having Christmas meals.

WORK

If you come to Australia on a 12-month working-holiday visa (see the Visas & Documents section earlier in this chapter), there are plenty of opportunities for casual work. Working on a regular tourist visa, however, is strictly forbidden and you risk expulsion from the country if you're caught.

Casual work is often easy to find in the high season (summer) at the major tourist centres – prospects include cleaning or reception work at hostels (in exchange for board), factory work and labouring, bar work, waiting on tables or washing dishes, childcare and collecting for charities.

Seasonal fruit picking is another prime possibility, though be warned that it's a tough way to earn a few dollars and pay is proportional to the quantity and quality of fruits picked – many pickers struggle to earn enough to pay for their accommodation. In Tasmania the main harvest times for this type of casual work are February to May in the Huon Valley and on the Tasman Peninsula (apples, pears), and December to January in the Huon Valley and Kingston (soft fruit). Grape-picking jobs are sometimes available in late autumn and early winter, as a number of wineries still hand-pick their crops.

If you're coming to Tasmania with the intention of working, make sure you have enough funds to cover your stay, or have a contingency plan if the work is not forthcoming. Jobs can be hard to find here and there's a lot of competition from locals. And as with all short-term jobs, be wary of being ripped off with low pay or unfair conditions.

Information

Hostels, newspaper classifieds and backpacker magazines are usually good sources of information on potential casual work. **Australian Job Search** (w *www.jobsearch .gov.au*) is a Commonwealth government agency with a website that's worth checking out. For leads on fruit picking work, ring **Harvest Hotline** (☎ *1300 720 126),* run by the Australia-wide recruiting company **Employment National** (w *www.employment national.com.au).*

Tax File Number

It's important to apply for a Tax File Number (TFN) if you plan to work in Australia, because without it tax will be deducted from any wages you receive at the maximum rate (which is currently 47%!). To get a TFN, contact the Tasmanian branch of the **Australian Taxation Office** (☎ *13 28 61;* w *www.ato.gov.au; 200 Collins St, Hobart)* for a form. It's a straightforward procedure, but you'll have to supply adequate identification, such as your passport and driver's licence, and a valid working-holiday visa. The issue of a TFN takes about four weeks.

Paying Tax

Yes, it's one of the certainties in life! If you have supplied your employer with a TFN, tax will be deducted from your wages at the rate of 29% if your weekly income is below $383. As your income increases, so does the tax rate, with the maximum being 47% for weekly incomes over $961. For nonresident visitors, tax is payable from the first dollar you earn, unlike residents who have a tax-free threshold.

For this reason, if you have had tax deducted at the correct rate as you earn, it's unlikely you'll be entitled to a tax refund when you leave. But if you've had tax deducted at 47% because you have not submitted a TFN, chances are you'll be entitled to a partial refund of the tax paid. Once you lodge a tax return, you'll be refunded the extra tax you have paid. Before you can lodge a tax return, however, you must have a TFN. And the tax return must include a copy of the Group Certificate (financial summary) all employers issue to salaried workers at the end of the financial year, or on the last day of a job if they've received 14 days' notice.

ACCOMMODATION

Tasmania has a wide range of hostels, caravan/cabin parks with camping grounds, motels, hotels, self-contained units and bed & breakfasts (B&Bs). But despite the variety of places to stay, Tasmania's main tourist centres are often fully booked in summer, at Easter and during other public holidays, so it's wise to book ahead at these times.

For comprehensive listings, the RACT has a statewide directory (updated annually) listing accommodation to suit all budgets in almost every town. It's available from the club for a nominal charge if you're a member. Alternatively, check the listings in the bimonthly *Tasmanian Travelways*.

Prices

Accommodation prices quoted throughout this edition are high-season prices obtained at the time of writing. Use our prices as a guide and remember that stand-by (walk-in) rates and low-season rates (not to mention weekend specials and the like) will usually be significantly lower than anything quoted in this book. Walk-in rates are best queried late in the day.

We've received reports of a handful of accommodation operators apparently abusing the credit-card booking system, with travellers finding that their 'deposits' have been accessed weeks before their arrival, or in some cases weeks after a valid cancellation. If you encounter this or any other *serious* problem, you should write a letter of complaint and address it to 'Tourism Tasmania, Customer Feedback, GPO Box 399, Hobart 7001'.

Heating

If you're travelling around Tasmania in the cooler months, you may occasionally find your accommodation very cold when you arrive, particularly if you are staying in a cottage or self-contained unit heated by a wood heater. Always ask about heating when you make your booking, and if you know your arrival time, ask your hosts to light a fire in advance.

The heating in cheap hotel rooms, cabins and hostels can sometimes be plain inadequate; if you have your own transport and intend to stay in such accommodation, consider packing a small heater of your own as a back-up.

The important thing to remember is that if you feel the cold, you should always ask how a room is heated before making a booking.

Camping & Caravans

There's an abundance of places on the island where you can camp for free, many magical in their serenity. For details of the reserves, conservation areas, roadside bays and other bits of turf where you can lay your sleeping bag, check out *The Guide to Free-Camping in Tasmania* by S & S Collis.

Camping in most national parks requires you to purchase a park pass and then pay a small site fee (up to $6/4 per adult/child), but quite a few parks don't have site fees – though of course, this often means minimal facilities.

Tasmania has a large number of camping and caravan parks (sometimes calling themselves 'tourist parks') that generally comprise the state's cheapest form of accommodation, with nightly costs for two campers being anywhere between $10 and $16, slightly more for a powered site. Most cities and large towns in Tasmania have camping and caravan parks conveniently close to the city centre. In general, Tasmanian caravan parks are well maintained and very good value. Most have on-site vans that you can rent for the night, though there is a trend to phase these out in favour of on-site cabins. The cabins usually have one bedroom, or at least an area that can be screened off from the rest of the unit – just the thing if you have kids. The price difference is not always that great, say $40 for an on-site van and $55 to $60 for a cabin.

YHA Hostels

The Youth Hostels Association *(YHA;* ⓦ *www.yha.com.au)* is part of the International Youth Hostel Federation (IYHF, also known as Hostelling International or HI). If you're already a member of the YHA in your own country, your membership entitles you to use the hostels in Australia.

The annual *YHA Accommodation & Discounts Guide* booklet is available from any Australian YHA office and from some offices overseas, and gives details of all the YHA hostels in Australia, including prices. The Tasmanian YHA office (☎ *6234 9617; 28 Criterion St, Hobart)* hands out information to travellers and also conducts an

Australia-wide hostel-to-hostel booking service. If you wish to use the hostel at Freycinet National Park, you must book it here.

YHA hostels are sited in buildings that range from tiny to huge. They provide basic accommodation, usually in small dormitories (bunk rooms), although more and more are providing twin rooms. The nightly charges are anywhere between $12 and $21 per person. Most YHAs take non-YHA members for an additional nightly fee of $3 to $3.50 per person.

An HI card (for visitors to Australia) costs $32 for 12 months. Australian residents can become full YHA members for $52/84 per one/two years. You can join at the main office in Hobart or at any youth hostel. YHA members are also entitled to a number of handy discounts around the country – on things such as car hire, activities, accommodation etc – and these are detailed in the *YHA Accommodation & Discounts Guide* mentioned earlier.

To stay in a hostel you must have bed linen – for hygiene reasons, a regular sleeping bag will not do. If you haven't got sheets they can be rented at many hostels (usually for around $3). YHA offices and some larger hostels sell the official YHA sheet bag.

Most hostels have 24-hour access and cooking and laundry facilities, and there's usually a communal area where you can sit and talk or watch TV. Many have informative noticeboards and lots of brochures.

Other Hostels

Tasmania has plenty of independent hostels. The standard of these can vary enormously, with some amounting to little more than rough-edged inner-city hotels trying to fill empty rooms, and others having transformed themselves from a motel, so each unit (typically with four to six beds) will have a fridge, TV and bathroom. Lots of good, new independent places have erected themselves around the island over the past few years, particularly in the main cities.

Prices at the independents often parallel those charged at YHA hostels or are slightly higher, and many offer discount rates for stays of several nights or more.

Colleges

During the summer university vacations (from November to February) you can also stay at university colleges. These places can be relatively cheap and comfortable, and typically cost from about $30 to $45 per person for B&B.

Pubs

Not every pub has rooms to rent, although many still do – often the only way to find out is to ask over the bar. Pub rooms are invariably cheap, upstairs, small, older in style and plain. That said, plenty of aging hotels have been renovated in recent times and a few even retain an attractive, down-to-earth character. In cities, this accommodation will always be among the most centrally located.

Pubs will usually have rooms for around $40 to $60 a double. Breakfast is often included in the price and may be continental or cooked; ask about breakfast when inquiring about a room.

Hotels & Motels

Real hotels, often high-rises, tend to dot the central cityscapes and are usually fully equipped for weekenders and business-people – that means on-site restaurants and bars, fitness and business centres, and the contents of a small apartment in each room (TV, minibar, en suite, writing desk etc).

Motels tend to be squat structures that congregate just outside the CBD or on the highways at the edge of town. These will normally prove to be the best bet for mid-range accommodation, with rooms equipped with similar (though not as stylish) mod-cons as the hotels costing between $50 and $100.

Guesthouses & B&Bs

Tasmania is like a giant incubator for guesthouses, so numerous are these places across the island. New hospitable abodes are opening up all the time and the options include everything from restored convict-built cottages and renovated, rambling old guesthouses to suburban bedrooms and upmarket country manors.

Only in the cheapest B&Bs are you likely to have to share bathrooms and toilets – sometimes the lack of an en suite simply means exclusive use of a separate bathroom across the hall. Breakfast can either be cooked or continental (sometimes 'hearty continental' if an operator provides something in-between, or they just want to sound more upmarket) and is often supplied in the form of provisions that you must cook or serve yourself. Smokers note that the vast majority of B&Bs have outlawed cigarettes on their premises.

Prices are between about $60 and $120 a double. However, there's a lack of B&B accommodation at the lower end of this price range. This is unfortunate, because cheaper B&Bs would be an excellent alternative to often bland, impersonal hotel accommodation.

Self-Contained Units & Cottages

Holiday units are predominantly self-contained, with many rented on either a daily or weekly basis. They often have two or more bedrooms, making them cost-effective for groups. A two-bedroom holiday unit is typically priced at about 1½ times the cost of a comparable single-bedroom unit. The prices given in this guide are for single-night stays and are mostly in the range of about $65 to $90 a double – the larger units (which are often referred to as 'villas' or 'chalets') regularly cost over $100 per double, while historic cottages can be anything up to about $150 a double, higher in the pricier parts of Hobart. Unlike prices for holiday units, prices for historic cottages usually include breakfast.

Other Accommodation

There are lots of less-conventional accommodation possibilities. Farmers may be willing to rent out a room in exchange for some labour, or just to supplement a meagre income. If you want to spend longer in Tasmania, the first place to look for a shared flat or a room is in the classifieds of a daily newspaper – Wednesday and Saturday are usually best days for these ads. Noticeboards in universities, hostels and cafés are also good places to look for flats/houses to share or rooms to rent.

FOOD

Tasmania has a reputation for genuine culinary delights, which foodies will find are a highlight of a visit to the island. There are many fine restaurants and cafés offering a wide variety of innovative food, and innumerable farms and smaller enterprises supplying fresh, local produce – on King Island, for example, are fine quality meats, cheeses and creams. Tasmania is renowned for its superb range of seafood: fish like blue-eye and striped trumpeter are delicious, as is the local salmon. Rock lobster, crayfish and oysters are among the crustaceans and shellfish available.

The cities have a selection of cafés and restaurants serving food that can be termed 'modern Australian'. These are dishes that borrow from a wide range of foreign cuisines but have a definite local flavour. At some places, seemingly anything goes, so you might find Asian-inspired curries sharing a menu with European- or Mediterranean-inspired dishes.

Vegetarians are adequately catered for in the parts of the state where the local pub isn't the only eatery. While there are few dedicated vegetarian restaurants, most modern cafés and restaurants have vegetarian dishes on the menu, while others don't advertise specific vegetarian meals but will happily oblige a non-meaty customer.

Smoking is now illegal in Tasmania in enclosed public spaces, including indoor cafés, restaurants and pub dining areas.

Restaurants & Cafés

The best Tasmanian eateries serve food as exciting and as innovative as anything you can find anywhere, and it need not cost a fortune. Best value are the modern cafés, where you can get an excellent meal for less than $20, or a full-on breakfast for around $10. Such places are not confined to cities either, with an increasing number of modern, replenishing places opening up in rural and coastal towns. That said, be prepared for large servings of the predictable and unexciting in out-of-the way places. Mid-range restaurants usually charge between $15 and $20 a main course, while upmarket restaurants charge upwards of $20.

All over the state, you'll find restaurants advertising themselves as BYO, which stands for 'Bring Your Own'. This means that you're permitted to bring your own alcohol, which will work out cheaper than buying it at restaurant prices. There will normally be a small corkage charge for your 'imported' wine or beer.

Pubs

Most pubs serve two types of meals: bistro meals, which are usually in the $10 to $18 range and are served in the dining room or lounge bar; and bar (or counter) meals, which are filling, no-frills meals eaten in the public bar and costing around $5 to $10.

The quality of pub food varies enormously – upmarket city pubs will vary their menus as much as mid-range restaurants, while standard corner pubs will stick to the tried and true meals like schnitzels, roasts and basic seafood. The usual meal times are from noon to 2pm and 6pm to 8pm.

DRINKS

The maximum permissible blood-alcohol concentration level for drivers in Tasmania is 0.05%. If you blow a higher reading during one of the ubiquitous random breath tests or after being pulled over, you'll face a large fine and the loss of your licence.

Beer

Australian beer will be fairly familiar to North Americans and to lager enthusiasts from the UK. It may taste like lemonade to the European real-ale addict, but full-strength beer can still pack a punch. It's invariably chilled before drinking, even in winter.

In terms of breweries, there's Cascade Brewery in the state's south and Boag's Brewery in the north, with both having a core of loyal drinkers. Cascade is near Hobart and produces Cascade Premium Lager and Pale Ale. Visitors tend to ask for 'Cascade' expecting to get the bottle with the distinctive label bearing a Tasmanian tiger,

but you're unlikely to get Premium unless you ask specifically for it – you'll probably get Cascade Draught. Boag's is located in Launceston and produces similar-style beers to the Cascade brews such as James Boag's Premium Lager and Boag's Draught. See the Hobart and Launceston & Around chapters for details of tours of the Cascade and Boag's Breweries respectively.

Standard beer generally contains around 5% alcohol, while low-alcohol (light) beer contains between 2% and 3.5%.

Wine

The local wine industry was started by a few pioneers in the mid-1950s and has gained international recognition for producing quality wines. Tasmanian wines are characterised by their full, fruity flavour, along with the high acidity expected of cool, temperate wine regions.

Grapes are grown all over the state, with the largest wine-growing regions being at Pipers River in the northeast, the Tamar Valley in the north and the Huon Valley in the south. There are also wineries dotted down the east coast from Bicheno to Dunalley, and in the Derwent River valley.

Tasmania's wines are expensive compared to similar mainland wines, though you'll save money by buying your preferred drop at the cellar door. For information on visiting the state's vineyards, see the Touring Vineyards section in the Activities chapter.

ENTERTAINMENT
Live Music

Many suburban pubs have live music (mostly free) and these are often great places for catching bands, either nationally well-known names or up-and-coming performers trying to make a name for themselves. Most of Australia's popular bands cut their teeth on the pub circuit. The best way to find out about the local scene is to get to know some locals, or travellers who have spent some time in the place. Otherwise there are detailed listings in local newspapers.

The University of Tasmania Student Union building and the Derwent Entertainment

Centre are the venues used by the more famous visiting artists.

Nightclubs

These are confined to the cities. Clubs range from small chill-out affairs to barn-sized commercial emporiums where anyone who wants to spend money is welcomed with open arms. Admission charges range from around $8 to $20.

Some places have certain dress standards, but it's generally left to the discretion of the people at the door – if they don't like the look of you, bad luck. The more 'up-market' nightclubs attract an older, allegedly more sophisticated and affluent crowd, and often have stricter dress codes, smarter decor and higher prices. Some of these nightclubs double as wine bars and cafés earlier in the evening.

Cinemas

You'll find singular representatives of major commercial cinema chains in Hobart and the cities of the north coast. Hobart also has the independent State Cinema, which thankfully provides some alternatives to *American Pie* sequels (see the Hobart, Launceston, Burnie and Devonport sections for details). Smaller towns usually have a sole cinema that opens intermittently, sometimes set in a grand old building.

Seeing a new-release mainstream film costs around $12 ($8.50 for children under 15) in Hobart and Launceston. The price is often less certain nights or in country areas.

Gambling

In Hobart, the Wrest Point Casino is on the shores of Sandy Bay and will admit you as long as you are dressed neatly – this complex also has several gaming lounges and numerous bars, clubs and live shows. A similar minimal standard of dress applies to the Country Club Casino on the southern outskirts of Launceston.

Throughout the state, small hotels have embraced poker machines and TasKeno, the latter a 'game' where you pick up to 15 numbers and pray they match the random numbers appearing on a television screen (a

new game occurs every few minutes, testimony to either its mindless popularity or the maximising of profits by the system's managers).

SPECTATOR SPORTS

If you're an armchair (wooden-bench, or stand-up) sports fan, Tasmania has much to offer. The football season runs from about March to September and when it ends, it's simply time for the cricket season to begin.

Tickets for most major events, be they sporting occasions, theatre or concerts, can be obtained through **Centertainment** (☎ 6234 5998) or the national **Ticketmaster7** (☎ 13 61 00; W *www.ticketmaster7 .com.au*), as well as the places mentioned in the following entries.

Australian Rules (Footy)

Australian (Aussie) Rules is a unique form of football – only Gaelic football is anything like it. It's played by two teams of 18 players on an oval field with an oval ball that can be kicked, caught, hit with the hand or carried and bounced. There are four posts at either end of the oval. You get six points for kicking the ball between two central posts (a goal) and one point for kicking it between a central post and a side post (a behind). There are four quarters of around 20 minutes each, plus 'time on'. Fast, tactical, skilful, rough and athletic, it can produce gripping finishes where the outcome hangs on the very last kick.

Tasmania has two football leagues: the Northern Tasmania Football League (NTFL) and the Southern Football League (SFL), the latter divided into the Premier and Regional Leagues. Squads from either end of the state occasionally play an intra-state match.

Cricket

Cricket is played during the other (non-football) half of the year. To many casual observers, the longer (five-day) matches lack intensity and are useful only if you're fighting insomnia, but fans claim there's a lot of skill and tactical manoeuvring involved. Tasmania held its first international test in Hobart in 1995, though one-day matches had been played at Bellerive Oval in the past. Tasmania takes part in the interstate Pura Milk Cup (formerly the Sheffield Shield) competition and also has district cricket matches. Tasmania has never won the Pura Milk Cup, but has produced two outstanding Australian Test side batsmen: David Boon and Ricky Ponting. Contact the **Tasmanian Cricket Association** (☎ *6211 4000;* **W** *www.tascricket.com.au)* for tickets and match fixtures.

Horse Racing
Major Tasmanian race meetings include the Hobart Cup Carnival at Elwick in early February, the Launceston Cup in February and the Devonport Cup in January. Regular meetings are held about once every month at the Elwick racecourse in Hobart. You can't book tickets; just go along to the course. Most towns have a horse-racing track or a Totalisator Agency Board (TAB) betting office where you can bet on the races.

Yachting
Hobart is the finishing line of the famous Sydney to Hobart yacht race and the lesser-known Melbourne to Hobart race at New Year. Other sailing events subsequently take place on the Derwent River (as part of the ongoing Hobart Summer Festival) and spectators can get reasonable views from the hills – this includes the Royal Hobart Regatta in early February.

The Three Peaks race in April combines sailing with mountainous marathon running.

Tennis
The tennis courts at the Domain in Hobart are the venue for the Tasmanian Women's International Tennis tournament in early January and the state championships in March, the former being a warm-up tournament for the Australian Open. For bookings, contact the **Domain Tennis Centre** (☎ *6234 4805).*

SHOPPING
Most shops close at 5pm or 6pm on weekdays (sometimes at 9pm on Friday), and either noon or 5pm on Saturday. Sunday trading is limited to a number of small shops. As this book goes to press Tasmania is in the throes of deciding whether to deregulate shop trading hours, but the unanswered question seems to be 'when' rather than 'if'.

Australiana
Overseas visitors looking for gifts for the friends, aunts and uncles, nieces and nephews, and other sundry bods back home will stumble across plenty of inexpensive souvenirs in their travels. The cheapest, usually produced *en masse* and with little to distinguish them, are known collectively by the euphemism 'Australiana' – they are supposedly representative of Australia and its culture, but in reality are just lowest-common-denominator trinkets. Speaking of authenticity, far too many of these supposedly Australian items are actually made in Asia, so if you're going to buy any, check the label to see where it was manufactured.

Arts & Crafts
You'll find local arts and crafts displayed everywhere you travel, not just in galleries but also in souvenir emporiums, wood-turning and pottery studios, and home workshops. The varied output of Tasmanian artisans, which often reflects their immediate environment, includes ceramics, weaving, jewellery, clothing, sculpture and painting.

Many woodworkers have taken to producing carvings and wood turnings, some of it magnificent, from the local Huon pine. Good examples can be found at the Design Centre of Tasmania in Launceston, the Forest & Heritage Centre in Geeveston, stores in Richmond and Stanley, the craft stalls at Salamanca Market and sundry galleries around the state. Items locally produced from other unique, richly coloured Tasmanian timbers such as blackwood and myrtle should also be considered.

Killiecrankie Diamonds
These beautiful stones aren't real diamonds but are actually samples of topaz – a semi-precious stone that comes in pale blue, pale pink and white varieties – and can be

bought on Flinders Island. Killiecrankie Enterprises (the general store in Killiecrankie) can show you a selection of 'diamonds'. See the Flinders Island section of the Bass Strait Islands chapter for more details.

Blundstones

These heavy-duty boots are made in Tasmania, wear well and are reasonably priced considering their usually long life span. Intended for use on construction sites, they became adopted by inner-city folk as a generic fashion item many years ago and are still popular footwear. To get a pair, check out hardware stores or mainstream boot retailers.

Antiques

Antique stores exist all over the state, some selling wares that qualify as little more than browse-worthy bric-a-brac and others specialising in well-aged articles of jewellery, artworks, furniture and other domestic artefacts. The wealth of colonial antiquities is a result of the large number of settlers who migrated here from Europe in the 19th century and brought their furniture with them. However, the fact that something is old does not mean it's good quality or worth a high price – before buying antiques, do some research into what constitutes a genuine piece and good value.

Dealers from around Australia display their antique wares during the annual Tasmania Antiques Fair, held over four days in early June at Launceston's Albert Hall. For listings of many of the state's antiques and collectibles dealers, track down a copy of the exhaustively titled directory *The Buyer's Guide to Tasmania's Best Antiques & Collectibles Stores & Galleries* – you should be able to find it in the city information centres.

Food & Drink

What better way to memorialise the huge number of satisfying meals and tipsy afternoons that you're bound to enjoy around Tasmania than to snap up some local produce to re-create the experience back home. The island's produce can also make a fine, inexpensive last-minute gift for anyone with a set of operational taste buds.

Consider buying delicious King Island cheeses, the dairy produce of the Lactos factory in Burnie, or the clothbound and flavoured cheddars of Pyengana. Jams, preserves and sauces are the specialist domain of many small farms and factories – these are scattered from the Huon Valley to the east-coast towns of Swansea and Scamander, and regularly open their doors to sweet-seeking passers-by. Leatherwood honey is one of a number of potent local honey varieties and is harvested in a number of places including Mole Creek; more honey bounty can be found in nearby Chudleigh. For a summary of the island's many outstanding local wines, see the Touring Vineyards section in the Activities chapter.

Aboriginal Art & Artefacts

The handiwork of Tasmanian Aborigines can make a wonderful reminder of your trip. Though not prevalent in Tasmania, be warned that there's a lot of unauthentic Aboriginal art around and that purchasing it undermines the pursuit of cultural and economic development by local Aboriginal people and communities. In mid-2000, anticipating a flood of fake items swamping Australia before the Sydney Olympic Games, the National Indigenous Arts Advocacy Association launched the 'Label of Authenticity' to protect the copyright and intellectual property of Aboriginal artists. Look for the tag on any merchandise you're considering buying.

In Devonport, **Tiagarra** *(Tasmanian Aboriginal Culture Centre;* ☎ *6424 8250)* sells modern-day Aboriginal craftwork.

Books & Calendars

There are plenty of photographic calendars and coffee-table books about Tasmania, many of them displaying the wilderness areas. (See Books earlier in this chapter for some recommendations.)

Victoria Dock and Mt Wellington, Hobart

GRANT DIXON

JOHN HAY

Cascade is Australia's oldest brewery, Hobart

Town crier at Salamanca Market, Hobart

GLENN BEANLAND

Crowds throng to Hobart's Salamanca Place on market day

LINDSAY BROWN

JOHN HAY

Historic Richmond Bridge was built by convicts in 1823

ROB BLAKERS

Maria Island National Park rocks

LINDSAY BROWN

Convict church at the Port Arthur historic site

ROB BLAKERS

Rugged coastline of Maria Island National Park

Activities

However much you might enjoy wandering the streets of historic towns and lazing about in cafés, you haven't fully experienced Tasmania until you've ventured into the mountains and onto the rivers, oceans and cliffs that are this beautiful island's greatest attractions.

The bushwalks you can do here are among the best (and at times the most taxing and treacherous) in Australia: try tackling Federation Peak or the Western Arthurs if you really want to test your endurance. White-water rafting on the Franklin River has acquired a deserved reputation for environmental grandeur and excitement, while abseiling and rock climbing on the Tasman and Freycinet Peninsulas is also literally thrilling.

For those who want less physically demanding activities, there's boating on the Arthur and Pieman Rivers in the northwest, sea kayaking on the waters around Port Arthur in the southeast and caving at Hastings in the south.

If you have a yacht, or can afford to charter one, you can spend lazy days exploring the bays and inlets of the D'Entrecasteaux Channel, while if you're a trout fisher with a desire for seclusion, you'll find plenty of remote Central Plateau lakes well stocked with fish.

For information on the offerings of assorted Tasmanian outdoor-activity companies, visit the website of **Networking Tasmanian Adventures** (W *www.tasmanianadventures.com.au*) or pick up one of its price lists from a visitor information centre.

THE TASMANIAN TRAIL

The Tasmanian Trail is a 480km route from Devonport to Dover, intended for walkers, horse riders and cyclists. Most of the trail is on forestry roads, fire trails or country roads. It passes towns, pastoral land and forests, and there are camping spots about every 30km. All the information you need to follow the trail is in the *Tasmanian Trail Guidebook,* now in its 2nd edition, costing around $22 and available in bookshops, outdoor-equipment shops and visitor information centres.

BUSHWALKING

Tasmania's glorious trail-riddled environment attracts walkers from all over the world. Its most famous track is undoubtedly the superb Overland Track in Cradle Mountain-Lake St Clair National Park. In fact, most of the state's great walks are in national parks, which you can read more about in the special section 'Flora, Fauna, National Parks & Reserves' and other relevant chapters throughout this book.

Public Liability

At the time of writing, the rapidly rising cost or unavailability of public liability insurance in Tasmania was forcing the scaling back of numerous tours and organised outdoor activities like horse riding and rock climbing, and threatening the viability of many small businesses, including budget accommodation operators. Also at risk were volunteer-run community events, which could not get affordable insurance.

The exorbitant insurance costs faced by small businesses and volunteer organisations are being blamed on a vast range of issues: the recent collapse of several major Australian insurance companies, insurance industry greed, some ridiculously high legal pay-outs awarded to people for minor incidents, a growing culture of litigation, substandard safety standards, and ambulance-chasing lawyers seeking the biggest pay-outs possible.

Various solutions have been proposed, including exempting certain events and capping pay-outs. But unfortunately, unless these are effectively implemented soon, many more businesses may go to the wall by the time you read this.

Bushwalking Gear

There are heaps of Tasmanian shops selling outdoor gear. **Paddy Pallin** (☎ *6231 0777; 119 Elizabeth St, Hobart* • ☎ *6331 4240; 110 George St, Launceston)*, **Mountain Designs** (☎ *6234 3900; 111 Elizabeth St, Hobart)*, **Snowgum** (☎ *6234 7877; 104 Elizabeth St, Hobart)*, **Allgoods** (☎ *6331 3644; cnr York & St John Sts, Launceston)* and the **Backpacker's Barn** (☎ *6424 3628; 10-12 Edward St, Devonport)* all sell a good range of bushwalking gear and also offer invaluable advice. Snowgum, the Backpackers Barn and the **Launceston City Youth Hostel** (☎/*fax 6344 9779; 36 Thistle St, Launceston)* have plenty of bushwalking equipment for hire.

Maps

The Department of Primary Industries, Water & Environment (DPIWE) produces an excellent series of topographic maps, available at visitors centres, **Service Tasmania** (☎ *1300 135 513;* **w** *www.servicetas mania.tas.gov.au; 134 Macquarie St, Hobart)*, the **Tasmanian Map Centre** (☎ *6231 9043;* **w** *www.map-centre.com.au; 96 Elizabeth St, Hobart)* and some shops specialising in bushwalking gear and outdoor equipment.

Books

Lonely Planet's *Walking in Australia* describes Tasmanian walks of varying length and difficulty. These include short jaunts through Mt Field National Park and around Maria Island, as well as the Overland Track and more difficult walks such as the three-day circuit of Mt Anne and a seven-day excursion along the South Coast Track.

If you prefer shorter walks (one day or less), the books by Jan Hardy & Bert Elson are worth finding. Two of these cover the Hobart area, one covers Launceston and the northeast, and a fourth covers the northwest. Other writers also produce small books on specific areas, such as the Tasman Peninsula and the mines of the west coast. One very popular book of shorter walks throughout the state is *A Visitor's Guide to Tasmania's National Parks* by Greg Buckman. If those aren't compact enough,

information on 30 of the best Tasmanian short walks is detailed in the government-produced *Tasmania's Great Short Walks* brochure that's freely available at visitors centres.

Well worth getting is *100 Walks in Tasmania* by Tyrone Thomas, which covers a wide variety of short and multi-day walks. There are also many detailed guides to specific walks or areas, including *South West Tasmania* by John Chapman and *Cradle Mountain-Lake St Clair & Walls of Jerusalem National Parks* by John Chapman & John Siseman.

National Park Passes

Entry fees apply to all Tasmanian national parks. See the National Parks section of the special section 'Flora, Fauna, National Parks & Reserves' for details.

Guided Walks

There are plenty of companies offering guided walks that range from one-day excursions to multi-day trips involving accommodation in everything from tents to upmarket lodges, plus trips that blend foot power with time on a bike, in a bus or in a canoe.

Some well-established companies offering trips along the Overland Track, to Walls of Jerusalem and other popular destinations are **Craclair** (☎ *6424 7833;* **w** *www.south com.com.au/~craclair)* and **Tasmanian Expeditions** (☎ *6334 3477, 1800 030 230;* **w** *www.tas-ex.com)*. Also hitting trails in the Cradle Mountain area is **Tasman Bush Tours** (☎ *6423 2335;* **w** *www.tasmanbush tours.com)*, which operates out of Tasman House Backpackers in Devonport. **Cradle Mountain Huts** (☎ *6331 2006;* **w** *www .cradlehuts.com.au)* does a guided walk along the Overland Track where you spend the night in privately owned huts (for more details see the Cradle Mountain-Lake St Clair National Park section in The West chapter).

Cradle Mountain Huts also does a four-day, three-night walk along the magnificent **Bay of Fires** (**w** *www.bayoffires.com.au)*, the last two nights of which are spent in a comfy, isolated lodge (see the boxed text 'Fire Walking' in The Northeast chapter). **Freycinet Experience** (☎ 6223 7565, 1800 506 003; W www.freycinet.com.au) does a fully catered four-day stroll down that famous peninsula (see the Coles Bay & Freycinet National Park section in the East Coast chapter).

There are plenty of smaller companies, such as **Taswalks** (☎ 6363 6112; Sorell St, Chudleigh), which provide more personal service for small bushwalking groups.

Code of Ethics & Safety Precautions

The **Parks and Wildlife Service** (PWS; ☎ 6233 6191; W www.dpiwe.tas.gov.au) publishes a booklet called *Tasmania's Wilderness World Heritage Area – Essential Bushwalking Guide & Trip Planner*, which has sections on planning, minimal impact bushwalking, first aid and what gear you need to bring to cope with Tasmania's notoriously changeable weather. You can also pick up PWS literature at **Service Tasmania** (☎ 1300 135 513; W www.servicetasmania .tas.gov.au; 134 Macquarie St, Hobart), at any national park visitors centre or ranger station, or download them from the DPIWE website.

The Tasmanian Wilderness World Heritage Area and Freycinet National Park are 'fuel stove only' areas. A brochure outlining regulations relating to these and other areas under this classification is available from the PWS.

In Tasmania (particularly in the west and southwest), a fine day can quickly become cold and stormy at any time of year, so it's essential that you *always* carry warm clothing, waterproof gear and a compass. In addition, you should never rely on finding a bed in a hut; always carry a tent, particularly on popular walks such as the Overland Track.

On all extended walks, you must carry extra food in case you have to sit out a few days of especially bad weather. This is a very important point, as the PWS routinely hears of walkers running out of food in such instances and relying on the goodwill of

better-prepared people they meet along the way to supplement their supplies. In the worst of circumstances, such lack of preparation and disregard for others puts lives at risk: if the bad weather continues for long enough, everyone suffers.

Tasmanian walks are famous for their mud, so be prepared: waterproof your boots, wear gaiters and watch where you're putting your feet. Even on the Overland Track, long sections of which are covered by boardwalk, you can sometimes find yourself up to your hips in mud if you're not careful.

- Bushwalkers should stay on established trails, avoid cutting corners and taking short-cuts, and stay on hard ground where possible.
- Before tackling a long or remote walk, tell someone responsible about your plans and arrange to contact them when you return. Make sure you sign a PWS register at the start and finish of your walk.
- Keep bushwalking parties small.
- Where possible, visit popular areas at low-season times.
- When camping, always use designated camping grounds where provided. When bush camping, try to find a natural clearing to set up your tent.
- When driving, stay on existing tracks or roads.
- Don't harm native birds or animals; these are protected by law.
- Don't feed native animals.
- Carry all your rubbish out with you; don't burn or bury it.
- Avoid polluting lakes and streams; don't wash yourself or your dishes in them, and keep soap and detergent at least 50m away.
- Use toilets provided; otherwise bury human waste at least 100m from waterways.
- Boil all water for 10 minutes before drinking it, or use water-purifying tablets.
- Don't take pets into national parks.
- Don't light fires in the Tasmanian Wilderness World Heritage Area or Freycinet Peninsula National Park; use only fuel stoves for cooking. In other areas, don't light open fires unless absolutely necessary; if you do, keep the fires small, burn only dead fallen wood and use an existing fireplace. Make sure any fire that you light is completely extinguished before moving on.
- On days of total fire ban, don't light any fire whatsoever, including fuel stoves.

Sample Walks

Mt Wellington (half a day) Many visiting walkers ignore Mt Wellington because of its proximity to Hobart. But by doing so, they deprive themselves of some dramatic views. If scenery is your objective, take the level Organ Pipes Walk from the Chalet to its junction with the Zig Zag Track and follow that track to the summit. The Organ Pipes Walk takes you along the base of these majestic cliffs. There are expansive views of the city and river from both sections of the walk, and on the upper reaches of the Zig Zag Track you really can hear the wind moan through the Organ Pipes like mournful music. See the Mt Wellington section in the Hobart chapter for information about the mountain and a map of these tracks.

Hartz Peak (half a day) This good day walk is a shortish drive from Hobart. The views from the peak are panoramic, but because the mountain is so often in cloud, you should wait for a forecast of clear skies before setting off. See the Southeast Coast chapter for details of Hartz Mountains National Park.

Tarn Shelf (one day) This is a wonderful walk at any time of year, but particularly in fine weather when there are still patches of snow about the crags and tarns adorning the shelf. You can drive to Mt Field National Park from Hobart, complete the walk and return to Hobart in one long day, but to make the most of the experience you should stay in the area for a night or two. See the Mt Field National Park section in the Mt Field & The Southwest chapter for details of this and other walks in the area.

Peninsula Walks The **Freycinet Peninsula Circuit** (two days) takes walkers past the reddish granite peaks of the Hazards to some gorgeous white-sand beaches, including **Wineglass Bay**, which makes for a stunning day walk in itself. Freycinet has some of the best weather in the state, another reason for putting this walk at the top of your list. See the East Coast chapter for more information.

The **Tasman Peninsula Walk** (four days) from Devils Kitchen to Waterfall Bay, Fortescue Bay, Cape Hauy, Cape Pillar and back to Fortescue Rd is famous for its views of magnificent coastal cliffs and rock formations. See the Tasman Peninsula section of the Around Hobart chapter for details of other shorter walks in this area.

Both these walks are reasonably easy and are in popular national parks well served by public transport.

Walls of Jerusalem (one or more days) Many Tasmanian bushwalkers who value solitude regard the Walls of Jerusalem National Park as the most beautiful park in the state. The 'Walls' surround a central basin entered through a pass known as Herods Gate. Inside, the various peaks that comprise the Walls tower grandly above lakes, tarns and valleys. Once you've reached the park, you can camp and take day walks to various features. See the Walls of Jerusalem National Park section of The North chapter for details of road access and public transport to the start of the three- to four-hour walk into the park. It's also possible to walk to the Walls from Cradle Mountain-Lake St Clair National Park. Note that this park is very exposed and so can be highly dangerous in extreme weather conditions.

Frenchmans Cap (three to five days) Part of the reason this walk is so enticing is that Frenchmans Cap can be seen to great advantage from the Lyell Hwy between Hobart and Queenstown. However, steep climbing is required to reach the peak and the track can be formidably muddy. See the Franklin-Gordon Wild Rivers National Park section of The West chapter for details of bus services to the start of the walk.

Overland Track (five to six days) This is the most popular long bushwalk in Tasmania, drawing between 6000 and 7000 walkers a year. It extends 80.5km between Cradle Mountain and Lake St Clair and features craggy mountains, beautiful lakes and tarns, extensive forests and moorlands, and side walks to waterfalls, valleys and still more mountainous peaks, including Mt Ossa (1617m), the highest mountain in Tasmania. Because it is adequately served by public transport, well managed and signposted for its entire length, the Overland Track is suitable for those who are undertaking their first long-distance walk, provided they are reasonably fit and properly equipped. Track notes are provided in the Cradle Mountain-Lake St Clair section in The West chapter.

This is such a popular walk that gregarious trekkers are likely to have as much fun socialising in the huts at night as they have walking the track during the day.

South Coast Track (seven days) This is a relatively undemanding long track by Tasmanian standards but should still only be undertaken by walkers who have experience hiking in dreadful weather. The track extends from Cockle Creek to Port Davey and is renowned for its remoteness and views of magnificent beaches. Public transport is available to Cockle Creek from December until mid-April (see the Cockle Creek section of the Southeast Coast chapter) but the only transport from Port Davey is light plane or boat.

Difficult Walks The **Western Arthurs Skyline Traverse**, **Frankland Traverse** and **Federation Peak** are difficult long walks in Tasmania's rugged and remote southwest that will take up to 12 days to complete and should only be attempted by highly experienced walkers. Some writers claim that Federation Peak is the most difficult walk in Australia.

All three walks feature spectacular scenery, but the weather in this region is notoriously unpredictable and often appalling. Before Lake Pedder was inundated, it was possible to walk down to its once-famous beach from the Frankland Traverse. Today, however, the waters of the flooded lake are so extensive that there's no way to escape the track when the weather turns foul: all you can do is return to the beginning, continue to the end, or huddle in your tent until conditions improve.

CYCLING

Brake Out Cycling Tours (☎ 6239 1080) does a great Mt Wellington descent for $45. **Tasmanian Expeditions** (☎ 6334 3477, 1800 030 230; w www.tas-ex.com) has overnight and extended cycling tours available, and also offers statewide cycling, canoeing, rafting and/or walking combination packages.

If you intend to cycle between Hobart and Launceston via either coast, count on the trip taking 10 to 14 days. For a full circuit of the island, allow 14 to 28 days. If you're planning a circuit, consider following the Giro Tasmania, detailed on the excellent 'Giro Tasmania' page of the website of **Bicycle Tasmania** (w www.netspace.net .au/~dmurphy/giro.htm). For more information on Tasmanian cycling routes, check out Lonely Planet's *Cycling in Australia*.

In Hobart, **Derwent Bike Hire** (☎ 0407 342 918) charges from $7/20 per hour/ day (price includes helmet). **Rent-A-Cycle** (☎ 6344 9779; 36 Thistle St, Launceston) at the Launceston City Youth Hostel hires touring bikes ($10/70 per day/week) and mountain bikes ($15/110), plus all the requisite equipment.

Also see the Bicycle section in the Getting Around chapter.

Long lunch for one

SKIING

There are two small ski resorts in Tasmania: Ben Lomond, 60km southeast of Launceston, and Mt Mawson in Mt Field National Park, 80km northwest of Hobart. Both offer cheaper, though much less-developed, ski facilities than the main resorts in Victoria and New South Wales (NSW); for example, rope tows are still used on some runs. Despite the state's southerly latitude, snowfalls tend to be light and unreliable. For more information, see the Ben Lomond National Park section in the Launceston & Around chapter and the Mt Field National Park section in the Mt Field & The Southwest chapter.

SWIMMING

The north and east coasts have plenty of sheltered beaches that are excellent for swimming, although the water is (to understate it) rather cold. There are also pleasant beaches near Hobart, such as Bellerive and Sandy Bay, but these tend to receive some urban pollution, so it's better to head further south towards Kingston and Blackmans Bay, or east to Seven Mile Beach for safe swimming. On the west coast, the surf can be ferocious and the beaches are not patrolled.

SURFING

Tasmania has plenty of good surf beaches. Close to Hobart, the best spots are Clifton Beach and the surf beach en route to South Arm. The southern beaches of Bruny Island, particularly at Cloudy Bay, can be good when a southerly swell is rolling, while the area around Eaglehawk Neck on the Tasman Peninsula is also worth checking out. The east coast from Ironhouse Point south to Spring and Shelly Beaches near Orford has some fine surf. King Island also gets its share of big waves.

The greatest spot of all is Marrawah on the west coast, where the waves are often huge, as the ocean here is uninterrupted all the way to South America. It's far removed from urban centres and there's no public transport there, but this isolation just adds to its appeal. See the Marrawah section of The Northwest chapter for more information.

SCUBA DIVING & SNORKELLING

There are some excellent scuba-diving opportunities on the east coast, around Rocky Cape on the north coast, and around King and Flinders Islands. In addition, there are underwater trails marked at Tinderbox near Hobart and off Maria Island.

Diving equipment is rented to licensed divers in Hobart, Launceston, Wynyard and all along the east coast from Binalong Bay to Eaglehawk Neck. If you want to learn to dive, go on a diving course: they're considerably cheaper here than on the mainland. In Hobart, courses are run by **Southern Tasmanian Divers** (☎ 6234 7243; 212 Elizabeth St) and **The Dive Shop** (☎ 6234 3428; 42 Bathurst St). Other courses are run on the Tasman Peninsula and in Bicheno, St Helens and Wynyard; see the relevant chapters for details.

SAILING

Tassie's many harbours are well utilised by keen local sailors and those floating in from more distant land masses. Fleets of white sails often dot the Derwent River in the sailing season, while many Hobart residents own yachts and consider the city's sailing opportunities among its greatest attractions. The D'Entrecasteaux Channel is wide, deep and exceptionally beautiful. Its waters are sheltered by Bruny Island, although conditions can be difficult south of Gordon.

There are many good anchorages in the channel where you can spend a night or two, but it's best not to anchor overnight in the Derwent River between North Bruny and the Tasman Bridge except in Ralph's

MARTIN HARRIS

Built from local Huon pine, the *Olive May* is Australia's oldest working vessel and is now used primarily for cruises

Bay; moor at one of the yacht clubs or the city docks instead. A berth at the **Royal Yacht Club of Tasmania** (☎ 6223 4599; Ⓦ www .ryct.org.au) is $30 a night for vessels under 15m long; the organisation also publishes an excellent guide to circumnavigating the state. The **Hobart Ports Corporation** (☎ 6235 1000; Ⓦ www.hpc.com.au) charges $9/44 per day/week for vessels up to 13m long, and $13/54 per day/week for boats 13m to 20m long. North of the bridge, you can anchor in Cornelian Bay or New Town Bay. There's a good marina at Kettering, in the Channel south of Hobart, but it's usually crowded so finding a mooring isn't always easy. A very helpful organisation to get in touch with in Hobart is the **Cruising Yacht Club of Tasmania** (☎ 6273 4192).

If you're a capable sailor, you can hire a Beneteau Oceanis 361 or 411 from **Yachting Holidays** (☎ 6224 3195; Ⓦ www.yachting holidays.com.au). The 361/411 costs $500/ 650 per day, with reduced daily rates for sails of two or more days. The company's charter base is adjacent to Constitution Dock in Hobart.

If you don't possess a little cap, sea legs and a nautical-mile stare, take a cruise on the *Olive May* (☎ 6298 1062; Ⓦ www .dover.tco.asn.au/olivem.htm), an old Huon-pine boat. Tours from Dover are run from September to May.

CANOEING, KAYAKING & RAFTING

Tasmania is famous for its white-water rafting on the wild Franklin River, but it has many other rivers that are popular for both rafting and boating. The Arthur and Pieman Rivers in the northwest and Ansons River in the northeast are great for a long, lazy paddle through picturesque scenery. For medium-paced rides on the Arthur, you can set off from Kanunnah Bridge or Tayatea Bridge for downriver trips of two or four days respectively. Rivers popular with rafters and kayakers, and closer to population centres, are the Picton, Huon, Weld, Leven, Mersey and North Esk, all of which are well served by plenty of rafting companies.

You can hire canoes at Arthur River (see the Arthur River section in The Northwest chapter). In Hobart, you can hire kayaks from **Snowgum** (☎ 6234 7877; 104 Elizabeth St).

The most challenging river to raft is the Franklin. Most rafting trips are now run by commercial companies like **Tasmanian Expeditions** (☎ 6334 3477, 1800 030 230; Ⓦ www.tas-ex.com), **Tasmanian Wild River Adventures** (☎ 0409 977 506; Ⓦ www .wildrivers.com.au) and **Rafting Tasmania** (☎ 6239 1080; Ⓔ raftingtas@ozemail.com .au), as it takes a big effort to organise your own trip. (See the Franklin-Gordon Wild Rivers National Park section in The West chapter for more details, and note that companies tackling the Franklin usually offer trips on other rivers too.)

Aardvark Adventures Tasmania (☎ 6249 4098, 0408 127 714) offers white-water rafting trips on the Mersey River; tours depart from Devonport.

Sea kayaking is a popular activity at Kettering with **The Roaring 40's Ocean Kayaking Company** (☎ 6267 5000; Ⓦ www .roaring40skayaking.com.au), on the Freycinet Peninsula with **Freycinet Adventures** (☎ 6257 0500; Ⓦ www.freycinetadventures .com) and near Port Arthur with **Blackaby's** (☎ 6267 1508; Ⓦ www.blackabyseakayaks .com.au). For more details, see the relevant chapters.

Hypothermia can be a serious risk if you end up in the water when it's really cold. Always be aware of rapidly rising river levels, particularly when rafting on the Franklin, as waters can reach flood height at any time of year. You should also be careful when water levels are low, as there are plenty of logs, rocks and other potential entrapments at such times. The information on rafting in the Franklin River section of the PWS website (Ⓦwww.dpiwe.tas.gov.au) is invaluable for anyone considering rafting anywhere in the state.

FISHING

Brown trout were introduced into Tasmania's Plenty River in 1866 and into Lake Sorell between 1867 and 1870. Since then, innumerable lakes and rivers have been stocked, including many of the artificial lakes built by Hydro Tasmania for hydro-electricity production. Needless to say, the fish have thrived, and today, national and international anglers make the most of the state's abundant and often beautiful inland fisheries. The Tamar River is another great fishing area and recently had a series of 10 fishing and mooring pontoons (accessible by disabled fishers) established on it between Launceston and George Town – the area around George Town is particularly good for both freshwater and saltwater fishing.

A licence is required to fish in Tasmania's inland waters and there are bag, season and size limits on most fish. Licence costs vary from $15 for one day to $52 for the full season and are available from sports stores, post offices, visitors centres and some country shops and petrol stations.

In general, inland waters open for fishing on the Saturday closest to 1 August and close on the Sunday nearest 30 April; the best fishing is between October and April. Different dates apply to some special places and these (plus other essential bits of information) are all detailed in the *Fishing Code* brochure you'll be given when you buy your licence. The lakes in the centre of the state are some of the best-known spots for both brown and rainbow trout: Arthurs Lake, Great Lake, Little Pine Lagoon (fly-fishing only), Western Lakes (including Lake St Clair), Lake Sorell and Lake Pedder. On some parts of the Great Lake you're only allowed to use artificial lures. You are also not allowed to fish in any of the streams flowing into that lake.

One of the best books available on trout fishing in Tasmania is *Tasmanian Trout Waters* by Greg French. Also worth a look is the bimonthly publication *Tasmanian Fishing News* ($3.50). In Hobart, a good place to stock up on lures and information is **Spot On Fishing Tackle** (☎ 6234 4880; 89 Harrington St). For lots of up-to-date information on recreational freshwater fishing in Tasmania, have a look at the website of the **Inland Fisheries Service** (W www.ifc.tas.gov.au).

Tasmanian trout (brown and rainbow) can be difficult to catch as they're fickle about what they eat; the right lures are needed in the right season. If you find you just can't hook them yourself, there are experts who can take you to good fishing spots and teach you the local tricks. Rates at **Premier Guides** (☎ 6259 8295; W www.flyfishtasmania.com.au) start from $680 for one person, $340 per person for two people and $290 per person for three people, and include transport, lunch and (if required) fishing gear. The **Tasmanian Fly Fishing School & Guiding Service** (☎ 6362 3441; W www.vision.net.au/~tasflyfish) runs guided trips starting at $275 per person (maximum two people per guide) out of Deloraine; it also has a base at Brady's Lake.

Alluring Trout Tours (☎ 6260 2431; W www.southcom.com.au/~alltrout) operates out of Richmond and offers single- and multi-day tours year-round starting at $400 for one person and $280 per person for two people. Among the many other operators around the state are the Hobart-based **Dragonfly Trout Adventures** (☎ 6228 2264) and, in Kingston, **Red Tag Trout Tours** (☎ 6229 5896; W www.redtagtrout.com).

London Lakes Fly Fishers Lodge (☎ 6289 1159; W www.londonlakes.com.au) at Bronte Park is a private, luxury trout-fishing resort that offers various all-inclusive packages to interstate and international fishing folk (not just the guys either – according to its website, the lodge warmly welcomes 'lady anglers'). **Bronte Park Highland Village** (☎ 6289 1126; W www.bronteparkhighlandvillage.com.au) is a much cheaper accommodation-only option for fishers (see the Cradle Mountain-Lake St Clair National Park section of The West chapter for details).

Rod fishing in saltwater is allowed year-round without a permit, but size restrictions and bag limits apply. Recreational sea fishing licences are required if you're diving for abalone, rock lobsters or scallops, or fishing with a net – these are available from post offices, Service Tasmania or online at W rec.fishing.tas.gov.au. There are on-the-spot fines for breaches of fishing regulations.

For information on sea fishing around the state, see the DPIWE website W www .dpiwe.tas.gov.au.

ROCK CLIMBING & ABSEILING

Due to the public liability situation at the time of writing (see the boxed text 'Public Liability' at the start of this chapter), a number of outfits had indefinitely postponed their rock climbing excursions. The insurance issues may have been resolved and tours rescheduled by the time this book is published, but double-check the availability of such activities with the relevant companies.

Although dry weather is desirable for rock climbing and Tasmania's weather is often wet, the sport is nonetheless regularly conducted around the state, as is the sport of abseiling.

Some excellent cliffs have been adapted for rock climbing, particularly along the east coast where the weather is usually best. The Organ Pipes on Mt Wellington, the Hazards at Coles Bay and the cliffs on Mt Killiecrankie on Flinders Island provide excellent climbing on firm rock. Many enthusiasts see images of the magnificent rock formations on the Tasman Peninsula and head straight for that region, but while the coastal cliffs there are indeed spectacular, it may be impossible to climb them at certain times if the swell is too big. At Adamsfield, on the road to Strathgordon, there are lots of bolted, steep, overhanging climbs on conglomerate rock, plus opportunities for bouldering. Really keen climbers drag all their gear onto the huge cliffs of Frenchmans Cap and wait for a break in the rain. The inexperienced, on the other hand, can hone their skills at places like the beaches at Kingston and Blackmans Bay, close to Hobart, or at the indoor climbing venue **The Climbing Edge** (☎ 6234 3575; 54 Bathurst St, Hobart). Adults are $9.50 and children $6.50; equipment rental is extra.

If you want to climb or abseil with an experienced instructor, try **Aardvark Adventures Tasmania** (☎ 6249 4098, 0408 127 714; Grove Rd, Glenorchy, Hobart); **Freycinet Adventures** (☎ 6257 0500; W www.freycinet adventures.com; cnr Coles Bay Esplanade & Freycinet Dr, Coles Bay); the **Tasmanian Climbing Company** (☎ 6234 3575; 54 Bathurst St, Hobart) at The Climbing Edge; or **Summit Sports** (☎ 0418 362 210; W www .summitsports.southcom.com.au; 40 Hiern Rd, Blackman's Bay).

HORSE RIDING

Horse riding is allowed in some national parks and all protected areas. Several companies organise horse rides that range from hour-long trips to multi-day treks across the Central Plateau. Rates start from around $15 per hour for short rides to around $150 per person for overnight rides (including food) on guided treks. **Central Highlands Trail Rides** (☎ 6369 5298) and **Saddle Tramp Horseback Tours** (☎ 6254 6196) both offer short rides and overnight trips through different areas of the state.

The public liability situation outlined in the boxed text 'Public Liability' at the start of this chapter was affecting the viability of a number of horse riding companies at the time of writing.

CAVING

Tasmania's caves are regarded as being among the most impressive in Australia. The caves at Mole Creek, Gunns Plains and Hastings are open to the public daily, but gems such as the Kubla Khan and Croesus caves (near Mole Creek) and the extremely large Exit Cave are only accessible to experienced cavers. Permits are needed to enter these caves; they are not places for the inexperienced and most are locked. Apply through a speleological club or association in your own state or country for permits.

You can visit an undeveloped (wild) cave with **Wild Cave Tours** (☎ 6367 8142; W www .wildcavetours.com); see the Mole Creek section of The North chapter. At the time of writing, the Hastings Cave visitors centre was considering running tours of Mystery Creek Cave (see the Hastings section of the Southeast Coast chapter). Expect to get wet and muddy, as these caves have no walkways or ladders and often have to be entered through streams

BIRD-WATCHING

Bird-watchers flock to all parts of the state, but it's the eastern and southeastern regions that are their most popular destinations because the forest cover is thinner and birds are easier to see. Bruny Island Neck in the south and the Mt William National Park in the northeast are excellent places for finding the rare spotted pardalote and for general ornithological visions. If you want to see the orange-bellied parrot, one of the world's rarest birds, fly to Melaleuca in the southwest, where you might be able to catch a glimpse of one from the special bird-hide near the airstrip. Another excellent spot for the dedicated enthusiast is the Moulting Lagoon wetlands on the road to Freycinet Peninsula National Park.

Penguin viewing at dusk is also popular at many locations on Tasmania's north and east coasts, including Bruny Island Neck, Stanley, Burnie and George Town (see the relevant chapters for details).

SCENIC FLIGHTS

Scenic flights in four- and six-seat planes are popular and generally range from one hour to a day in length. In fine weather they're a great way to see the state's wilder regions.

Par Avion (☎ 6248 5390; ⓦ www.paravion .com.au) is based at Cambridge aerodrome, near Hobart airport, and runs scenic flights and some interesting trips into Southwest National Park. You can spend a day in the wilderness with a flight into the southwest and a cruise around Bathurst Harbour from $295 per person including lunch; there are flights daily from May to September. The company also has a fully catered camp at Port Davey, where you can spend two days and two nights for $815 per person.

Tasair (☎ 6248 5088; ⓦ www.tasair.com .au) also operates from Cambridge aerodrome, flying to the southwest, Freycinet Peninsula and Tasman Peninsula. **Tasmanian Seaplanes** (☎ 6227 8808, 0419 147 755; ⓦ www.tas-seaplane.com), based at a pontoon at Wrest Point, flies everything from 20-minute Hobart tours ($80/40 per adult/child) to half-day tours to Port Arthur

($260/120 per adult/child) and charters from $480 per hour.

Other scenic flights are available from most airports around the state. For example, from Cradle Mountain or Burnie/Wynyard airport you can fly over the Cradle Mountain region (see The Northwest and The West chapters respectively).

SEAL-WATCHING

Seals tend to congregate in 'haul-outs' (non-breeding sites) at various spots on Tasmania's north, east and southeast coasts. According to the PWS, they can be observed by kayak, yacht or power boat, but it may be more sensible to take an organised tour. Sharks often swim with seals, so you should only dive in their presence in a shark-proof cage. The PWS publishes a useful brochure about observing seals, available at **Service Tasmania** (☎ 1300 135 513; ⓦ www.ser vicetasmania.tas.gov.au; 134 Macquarie St, Hobart), visitors centres and also from the DPIWE website ⓦ www.dpiwe.tas.gov.au.

There are regular seal-watching tours at places like Stanley, Bruny Island, George Town, Freycinet Peninsula and Triabunna (see those sections for details).

TOURING VINEYARDS

Tasmania puts on a liquid smorgasbord of fine vintages for you to sample on your travels or back in the privacy of your own home. The state's key wine-producing regions are the Tamar Valley and Pipers River in the north, and the Coal River Valley, Derwent Valley, Huon Valley and Tasman Peninsula in the south. Notable vineyards in these areas include the likes of Pipers Brook, St Matthias, Meadowbank and Coombend, but there are also many smaller vineyards quietly going about the business of fine wine-making. Tasmania's wines are expensive compared to similar mainland wines – you'll fork out more than $20 for an acceptable bottle of wine – but the best of them are simply superb.

Wineries are dotted down the east coast from Bicheno to Dunalley, including the well-respected Freycinet Vineyard, and farther south to the Huon Valley area where, among others, you'll find Hartzview Vineyard. Major producers in the Derwent River Valley include Moorilla, established in 1958, making it the oldest vineyard in southern Tasmania (the island's first winery was established in New Town, Hobart, in 1821). To get an idea of the number of grape-wreathed properties around the island, pick up copies of the two *Tasmanian Wine Route* brochures (one each for the south and the north) from any visitors centre, though keep in mind that this list is nowhere near comprehensive.

The most enjoyable way to start educating your palate is to indulge in wine tastings right at the cellar door, where you can also pick up bottles of your preferred drops more cheaply than in retail outlets. Many wineries have such tastings; some of them are free but most charge a small fee (usually a few dollars), which is refundable if you purchase any wine. Bear in mind that the key word here is 'tasting', not 'guzzling' – you won't get to quaff endless glasses of the vineyard's finest, just enough in the bottom of a glass to whet your appetite.

Wine often isn't the only thing on offer in the bigger wineries, many of which also have fine modern dining facilities with excellent upmarket menu choices. Places serving good food as well as wine include Home Hill Vineyard near Huonville, Pipers Brook and Ninth Island wineries near Pipers River, Moorilla Estate on the northern outskirts of Hobart, and Meadowbank, formerly at Bushy Park but now relocated to the road between Richmond and Cambridge. Moorilla and Cambridge also host arts events and live music.

Details of the wineries mentioned here and numerous others are given throughout this book.

Getting There & Away

AIR

Air fares to Tasmania are constantly changing and you can get some good deals, especially if you book well in advance or if you're planning a wintertime trip. Discounts aren't uniform, though, with advertised bargains dependant on the route, day of the week and time.

Airlines

The airlines flying to Tasmania from the Australian mainland are **Qantas** (☎ 13 13 13; W www.qantas.com.au), including its subsidiary regional airlines, which collectively fly under the banner QantasLink; **Virgin Blue** (☎ 13 67 89; W www.virginblue .com.au); **Island Airlines Tasmania** (☎ 6359 2266, 1800 645 875); and **King Island Airlines** (☎ 9580 3777). Also servicing Tasmania at the time of writing was a new airline, **Regional Express** (☎ 13 17 13; W www.regionalexpress.com.au), which had

---

> ### Warning
>
> The information in this chapter is particularly vulnerable to change: Prices for international travel are volatile, routes are introduced and cancelled, schedules change, special deals come and go, and rules and visa requirements are amended. Airlines and governments seem to take a perverse pleasure in making price structures and regulations as complicated as possible. You should check directly with the airline or a travel agent to make sure you understand how a fare (and ticket you may buy) works. In addition, the travel industry is highly competitive and there are many lurks and perks.
>
> The upshot of this is that you should get opinions, quotes and advice from as many airlines and travel agents as possible before you part with your hard-earned cash. The details given in this chapter should be regarded as pointers and are not a substitute for your own careful, up-to-date research.

---

taken over from Kendell and Hazelton airlines.

Qantas flies direct to Launceston and Hobart from both Melbourne and Sydney, and to Burnie/Wynyard and Devonport from Melbourne – you can fly to Tasmania with Qantas from other cities across the country but these flights will link with flights from either Sydney or Melbourne for the final leg.

Virgin Blue flies from cities around Australia to Melbourne and then to both Hobart and Launceston. Regional Express flies from Melbourne to Devonport, Burnie/Wynyard and King Island.

Island Airlines Tasmania flies from Traralgon in Victoria's Latrobe Valley via Melbourne's Essendon airport to Flinders Island, and then on to Launceston. King Island Airlines flies between Melbourne and King Island. The two smaller airlines use Melbourne's second-string airports (Essendon and Moorabbin) and have lower base rates, but generally offer fewer discounts.

Hobart

To fly economy with Qantas from Melbourne to Hobart during the high season, booking at least 14 days in advance, costs from $230/ 250 one way/return. From Sydney, the similar fare will be $330/460.

To fly from Melbourne to Hobart with budget carrier Virgin Blue at its cheapest rate will cost $110/220 – to get this rate you need to book as far ahead as possible, otherwise you could end up paying as much as $220/440.

Launceston

To fly economy with Qantas from Melbourne to Launceston during the high season, booking at least 14 days in advance, costs from $220/290 one way/return; from Sydney, the cost is $320/440.

The cheapest fare for flying Melbourne to Launceston with Virgin Blue is $95/190 – again, book as far ahead as possible or risk paying as much as $190/380.

Island Airlines Tasmania's full economy fare from Traralgon, in country Victoria, to Launceston (via Melbourne's Essendon airport and Flinders Island) is $245/490.

Devonport & Burnie/Wynyard

Burnie/Wynyard airport is officially known as Burnie airport but is actually located 20km west of Burnie at the town of Wynyard. Due to the fact that some Tasmanians call the airport 'Burnie' and others call it 'Wynyard', we refer to the airport throughout this book as 'Burnie/Wynyard'.

Qantas flies from Melbourne to both Devonport and Burnie/Wynyard during the high season for $220/290 one way/return; these are 14-day advance-purchase fares. The 14-day advance fares offered by Regional Express from Melbourne are $155/300 to Devonport or Burnie/Wynyard.

King & Flinders Islands

King Island Airlines flies to King Island from Melbourne's Moorabbin airport, with full economy fares from $150/295 one way/ return; booking at least seven days in advance will reduce the return fare by as much as $50. Regional Express' 14-day advance fare from Melbourne to King Island is $135/260.

Island Airlines Tasmania flies to Flinders Island from Traralgon in Victoria (via Essendon airport in Melbourne) for $180/360 – to board the flight at Essendon costs an extra $20 for the one-way fare (extra $40 return).

Some discounts are available, but as you'll need to book accommodation and hire a car, the best deal is to buy a fly, drive and accommodation package (see the Package Deals section later).

Travellers with Specific Needs

If they're warned early enough, airlines usually make special arrangements for travellers such as wheelchair assistance at airports or vegetarian meals on the flight. Children under two years often travel for 10% of the standard fare or for free, as long as they don't occupy a seat; they don't get a baggage allowance. 'Skycots', baby food and nappies should be provided by the air-

line if requested in advance. Children aged between two and 12 can usually occupy a seat for half to two-thirds of the full economy fare, and do get a baggage allowance.

SEA

Bass Strait is known as one of the roughest shipping channels in the world, so travellers prone to seasickness should prepare themselves just in case.

Ferry

The two brand-new, high-speed *Spirit of Tasmania* ferries operated by **TT-Line** (☎ *13 20 10*; **w** *www.tt-line.com.au*), which cruise between Melbourne and Devonport, can each accommodate 1400 passengers and around 650 vehicles. With their restaurants, bars and games facilities, each vessel more closely resembles a floating hotel than a ferry. The public areas of the ships have been designed to cater for wheelchair access, as have a handful of on-board cabins.

At 9pm nightly year-round, one ferry departs from Melbourne's Station Pier and the other departs from the terminal on the Esplanade in Devonport, with both arriving at their destinations across Bass Strait at approximately 7am the next morning. Additional sailings are scheduled on weekends from mid-December through April and at other peak times as required – these day sailings depart at 9am and arrive at 6pm.

Fares depend on whether you're travelling in the high season (early December to late January, and Easter), shoulder season (late January to late April, and September to early December) or low season (late April to August). One-way adult fares in the shoulder/high season cost from $180/200 for a berth in a three- or four-bunk 'inside' cabin (no portholes), to $215/256 for a twin cabin with portholes, to $305/365 for a deluxe cabin, with several variations in-between. The cheapest overnight passage involves a cruise seat (think airline chair), which costs $100/125. Fees charged for day sailings are identical to the cost of a cruise seat. Child, student, pensioner and senior discounts apply to all accommodation except for deluxe cabins (only student and child discounts are given for cruise seats or day sail rates). Unlike the previous single-ferry service, fares do not include meals, which are purchasable from either a buffet or à la carte restaurant.

The cost for accompanied vehicles depends on the size of the vehicle and is subsidised by a federal government rebate. The standard size is up to 5m long and 2m wide, and the one-way rate is $40/55 low/high season. Motorcycles cost $30/38 and bicycles $21/27.

The **Southern Shipping Company** (☎ 6356 1753) operates a small passenger and car ferry once a month from Port Welshpool in Victoria to Bridport in Tasmania's northeast via Flinders Island. The full one-way trip across Bass Strait costs $60 per person ($580 for a car and its driver) and including the Flinders stopover takes about 2½ days.

Yacht

Every year hopeful adventurers head to Sydney to try to find a berth on a yacht in the Sydney to Hobart Yacht Race, but they nearly always luck out, as the yachts use their regular crews. You'll have far more luck crewing a boat from Hobart back to its home port after the race has been completed, when many of the regular crew fly home.

Cruise Ship

Just about the only way to see firsthand the spectacular diversity of wildlife on remote, sub-Antarctic Macquarie Island, which was proclaimed Tasmania's second World Heritage area in 1997 (see the special section 'Flora, Fauna, National Parks & Reserves'), is to take one of the sub-Antarctic islands cruises scheduled by New Zealand–based **Heritage Expeditions** (☎ 1800 143 585; W www.heritage-expeditions.com).

These cruises usually take place once a year, last up to two weeks, and incorporate two days on Macquarie Island. Prices per person can range from US$4400 for twin share to US$5800 for a 'suite', plus US$250 for landing fees.

PACKAGE DEALS

Tourist agencies offer various package deals to Tasmania – including transport there, accommodation and car hire – which are often considerably cheaper than purchasing each component separately. As you would expect, the biggest discounts apply in the quieter periods of autumn, winter and spring, whereas in summer the deals rise in price. Most package deals have conditions attached to them, of which the most common is twin share (two people), and sometimes an itinerary is fixed at booking.

Qantas (☎ 13 13 15; W www.qantas.com .au) offers fly, drive and accommodation packages from Melbourne, where you can pre-book to stay in motel chains, hotels, historic cottages or a mixture of each. The packages also allow you to alter your itinerary and fly in and out of different airports. You should be able to get the best deals from travel agents in your home town/city or by contacting Qantas directly.

If you're visiting King or Flinders Islands, consider saving money through a package deal. Car hire on both islands is around $75 per day with no discounting. High-season packages from Melbourne to King Island through **King Island Airlines** (☎ 9580 3777), with air fares and two nights accommodation, start at around $330 per person.

Island Airlines Tasmania (☎ 6359 2266, 1800 645 875) offers high-season air fare, accommodation and car-hire packages for Flinders Island starting from around $500 per person for two nights.

Getting Around

Tasmania is decentralised and its population very small. While transport is adequate between larger towns and popular tourist destinations, visiting more remote sights in the state might prove a tad frustrating due to irregular or, in some cases, non-existent services. There are, however, plenty of car-rental companies offering decent rates for early-model vehicles, an option you should seriously consider when planning your itinerary, particularly if your time is limited and the places you want to visit are far-flung.

AIR

At present, aerial choices within Tasmania are limited to three flight providers: **Tasair** (☎ 6248 5088, 1800 062 900; W *www.tasair.com.au*), **Island Airlines Tasmania** (☎ 6359 2266, 1800 645 875) and **Par Avion** (☎ 6248 5390; W *www.paravion.com.au*).

Tasair flies between Devonport and King Island (via Burnie/Wynyard if flights have been booked from that airport as well) twice daily from Monday to Friday and once on Saturday and Sunday ($165 one way, one to 1¼ hours) – it's also $165 from Burnie/Wynyard to King Island. Tasair also flies regularly from Hobart to King Island ($330, two hours), again with a brief Burnie/Wynyard stop depending on bookings. Recently, the airline began flights between Hobart and Burnie/Wynyard, operating twice a day Monday to Friday ($165).

Island Airlines Tasmania flies between Launceston and Flinders Island two to three times a day from Monday to Friday, and once on Saturday and on Sunday ($140, 35 minutes).

Par Avion flies daily from Hobart to Melaleuca ($155, 45 minutes).

BUS

Tasmania has a good bus network connecting all major towns and centres, but weekend services are infrequent and this can be inconvenient for the traveller with limited time. More buses ply the state's roads in summer than in winter.

The two main bus companies are **Redline Coaches** (☎ 6336 1446, 1300 360 000; W *www.tasredline.com.au*) and **TassieLink** (☎ 6272 7300, 1300 300 520; W *www.tigerline.com.au*), and between them they cover most of the state. TassieLink is owned by Tasmanian Tours & Travel, which also has a tours/charters arm called **Tigerline Coaches** (☎ 6272 6611, 1300 653 633).

TassieLink has a 7/10/14/21-day Explorer Pass that must be used within 10/15/20/30 days and costs $160/190/220/260. The pass is valid on all scheduled services for unlimited kilometres and can be bought from mainland Tasmanian Travel Centres, YHA and STA Travel offices, most other travel agents, or directly from TassieLink.

TASMANIAN AIR FARES

MELBOURNE

VICTORIA
Traralgon
To Sydney

150
110-230
220
180
Currie
220 245 320
95-220
165 Flinders Island
King Island 165 Whitemark
330 140 330
Burnie
Devonport
Launceston
TASMANIA
165

HOBART
155
Melaleuca

All fares in Australian dollars
One-way economy air fares

Explorer Pass holders are also entitled to discounts for Tigerline sightseeing tours from Hobart and Launceston. If you intend to buy a Explorer Pass, ask for TassieLink's timetables in advance or check its website and plan your itinerary carefully before making your purchase – this is the best way to ensure you'll be able to get where you want to go within the life of the pass. The free newspaper *Tasmanian Travelways* (available at visitors centres within and outside the state) has timetables and fares for major routes, but you're better off using one of the company's own printed timetables.

Buses run along most major highways year-round. TassieLink runs from both Hobart and Launceston to the state's west (Cradle Mountain, Strahan, Queenstown, Lake St Clair) and to the east coast (St Helens, Bicheno, Coles Bay), from Hobart to Port Arthur, and south from Hobart down the Huon Valley. It also runs express services that connect Bass Strait ferry arrivals/departures in Devonport to Launceston, Hobart and Burnie, with connecting services from Burnie on to Queenstown and Strahan.

Redline services the Midland Hwy between Hobart and Launceston, the north coast between Launceston and Smithton, and the east coast. Additionally, **Hobart Coaches** (☎ 6233 4232, 13 22 01) runs regular services from the capital south as far as Woodbridge and Cygnet, and north to Richmond and New Norfolk; its parent operator Metro also runs a service between Hobart and Bothwell. See the relevant chapters for details of these and other regional services.

To give you an idea of main-route costs and travel times, a one-way trip between Hobart and Launceston costs $23.40 and takes around three hours; between Hobart and Queenstown costs $44.70 and takes five hours; and between Launceston and Bicheno costs $22.70 and takes 2½ hours.

Over summer, TassieLink buses also run along numerous minor roads to popular bushwalking destinations. Special fares that enable you to be dropped off at the start of a walk and picked up at the end are offered. National Park passes can be also purchased from TassieLink. Buses take the link road from Devonport past Cradle Mountain to the Lyell Hwy, and the direct route from Launceston past the Great Lake to Derwent Bridge and Cynthia Bay. Buses also run from Hobart past Maydena to Scotts Peak, and from Hobart past Dover to Cockle Creek in the south. See these destinations in the relevant chapters for more information.

Note that all bus fares and conditions quoted throughout this book are subject to change and should be used as a guide only.

JOHN BANAGAN

A Tasmanian road winds through a landscape rich in textures and stunning views

TRAIN

For economic reasons there are no longer any passenger rail services in Tasmania, which probably accounts for the number of model railways and train exhibitions throughout the state.

TAXI

Taxis are available in all major towns and can be a handy way of getting to places otherwise not easily reached. However, that's not to suggest you should seriously consider using a taxi to get around the state, which would be an obscenely expensive exercise.

CAR

Driving around Tasmania is the easiest, most flexible way to see the state. If you do drive, don't make the mistake of drawing up exhaustive itineraries with carefully calculated driving times between each and every destination. Though this is sometimes necessary to catch a particular tour on a particular day or to check in at a pre-booked B&B, it runs contrary to the real idea behind driving around Tasmania – that you can stop for a spontaneous photo or a leisurely browse, or divert down a side-road to explore the unfamiliar whenever you feel like it.

Road Rules

Australia has countrywide road rules, the main one dictating you drive on the left-hand side of the road. Another important rule is 'give way to the right': if an intersection is unmarked (unusual), you must give way to vehicles entering the intersection from your right. Exceptions include that when turning left, you have right of way over any vehicles turning right, and at T-junctions the through road has right of way over all traffic on the approaching road.

In towns and cities, the general speed limit is 50km/h, while on the open road the general limit is 100km/h, although on major highways such as the Midlands it's 110km/h. For provisional licence holders, the speed limit is 80km/h. Speed cameras operate in Tasmania and are usually carefully hidden.

Australia was one of the first countries to make wearing seat belts compulsory – if you don't wear one, expect to be fined if you're pulled over by the police. The other main law applies to drinking and driving: a strict limit of 0.05% blood alcohol content applies. Heavy penalties apply if you break this law – your licence will be cancelled and jail sentences are imposed on offenders with multiple convictions. Random breath tests are also regularly conducted by police. All in all, the best policy is not to get behind the wheel if you've been drinking.

Overseas licences are acceptable in Australia for genuine overseas visitors. If you are staying for more than 12 months you'll need to obtain a local licence; apply at any police station.

On the Road

Watch out for wildlife while you're driving around the island – the huge number of carcasses lining main roads is sad testimony to the fact that many drivers don't use enough caution. Many local animals are nocturnal and often cross roads around dusk, so try to avoid driving in rural areas when darkness falls; if it's unavoidable, then slow down. And be warned that hitting a wombat not only kills the unfortunate animal, but can also make a mess of your car.

Many roads, including some highways, are fairly narrow with many sharp bends and occasionally one-lane bridges that aren't clearly signposted. Cycling is popular on some roads (particularly on the east coast) and when encountering bicycles you should wait until you can pass safely. It's wise to drive a little more slowly and allow more time to react to these hazards. Distances in Tasmania are short, so there's no need to speed.

Anyone considering travelling on 4WD tracks should read the free publication *Cruisin' Without Bruisin'*, available in the Parks and Wildlife Service (PWS) section of **Service Tasmania** (☎ 1300 135 513; ⓦ www .servicetasmania.tas.gov.au; 134 Macquarie St, Hobart), from the DPIWE website ⓦ www .dpiwe.tas.gov.au and at visitors centres around the state. It details over 20 tracks and explains how to minimise your impact on the regions you drive through.

Fuel Petrol is available in most towns across the state. In small towns there's often just a pump outside the general store, while the larger towns and cities have conventional service stations and garages. Most are open from 8am to 6pm on weekdays, but fewer are open on weekends, and fewer still are open late at night or 24 hours a day, something to keep in mind if you intend travelling long distances at night.

Rental

Although you can bring cars from the mainland to Tasmania, renting may be cheaper, particularly for shorter trips. Tasmania has many international, national and local car-rental agencies, and rates are considerably lower here than on the mainland. The free *Tasmanian Travelways* magazine lists many of the rental options.

Before you decide on a company, ask about any kilometre limitations and find out what the insurance covers – ensure there are no hidden seasonal adjustments. It is, however, quite normal for smaller rental companies to ask for a bond of upwards of $300. Also remember that the insurance offered by most companies does not cover accidents that occur on unsealed roads, which is a considerable disadvantage in a state where so many of the best destinations can only be visited using such routes.

Larger firms such as Avis (☎ 6248 5424; ⓦ www.avis.com), Budget (☎ 6234 5222, 1800 030 035; ⓦ www.budget.com.au), AutoRent-Hertz (☎ 6335 1111, 1800 067 222; ⓦ www.autorent.com.au), Thrifty (☎ 6234 1341, 1800 030 730; ⓦ www.thrifty.com.au) and Europcar (☎ 1800 030 118; ⓦ www .deltaeuropcar.com.au) have standard rates from about $70 to $80 for high-season, multi-day hire of a small car – the deal should include unlimited kilometres and no bond. By booking in advance and choosing smaller cars, rates can be as low as $60 per day for one week's hire (outside the high season). These big companies usually have branches in all the main cities and also at the airports.

Smaller local firms such as **Advance** (☎ 6231 1077, 1800 030 118), **Selective Car Rentals** (☎ 6234 3311), **Range/Rent-A-Bug** (☎ 6231 0678 for Range, 6231 0300 for Rent-A-Bug) and **Lo-Cost Auto Rent** (☎ 6231 0550, 1800 647 060) rent older cars for as little as $40 a day, depending on the length of time and season. The smaller companies don't normally have desks at arrival points but can usually arrange for your car to be picked up at airports and the ferry terminal in Devonport.

Another popular option is to invest in an accommodation and car-rental package. These can be arranged on the mainland or in Tasmania by travel agents or Tasmanian visitors centres and often work out to be very economical. And for backpackers who don't want to walk too far, there's the Tasmania Adventure Freedom Pass available from the **YHA** office (☎ 6234 9617; 28 Criterion St) in Hobart, which offers various combinations of YHA hostel accommodation and rental of a Nissan Pulsar or Toyota Camry including insurance (with a large excess) and unlimited kilometres. Seven nights accommodation and seven days rental of a Nissan Pulsar, for example, is $320; the same package over 21 days costs $900. If you opt for a bus ride instead of car rental, the prices become $300/680 per 7/21 days.

Tasmanian Travelways also has a listing of campervan rental companies. **AutoRent-Hertz** (☎ 1800 030 500; ⓦ www.autorent .com.au) has campervans from around $1300 a week for five people in the low season or $1600 a week in the high season. Savings can be made by going to the smaller operators but these should be weighed against the rental conditions and general condition of the vehicle; make sure you're familiar and confident with both before you sign.

BICYCLE

Tasmania's compact size makes it a tempting place to cycle around. It's a great way to get close to nature (not to mention, it has to be said, to log trucks, rain and roadkill), and provided you're prepared for steep climbs and strong headwinds in certain sections, you should enjoy the experience immensely. If you're planning an extended ride, it's worth considering buying a bike and reselling it at the end.

To bring a bike over on one of the *Spirit of Tasmania* ferries costs $27 each way in the high season. By air, Qantas charges $17; however, you should be aware that your bicycle may be off-loaded at the last minute if there's too much other freight to be carried.

While the same road rules that apply to cars also apply to bicycles, riders should also follow another rule – if in doubt either give way or get out of the way. Even if you're in the right, you will almost certainly come off second best in any collision. When cycling on the state's many narrow, winding roads, always keep your eyes and ears open for traffic. Also watch out for wooden bridges with gaps between the slats that can trap bicycle wheels, and remember to always wear a helmet (it's compulsory) and try not to cycle at night. Full notes and lots of practical advice for cycling around the state can be found in *Bicycling Tasmania* by Ian Terry & Rob Beedham.

See the Cycling section of the Activities chapter for more information.

Cycling in Tassie is a great way to get close to nature...and do your shopping!

HITCHING

Travel by thumb in Tassie is generally good, but wrap up in winter and keep a raincoat handy. Many of the state's minor roads are still unsurfaced and traffic on them can be very light, so although some of these roads lead to interesting places, you'll probably have to give them a miss if you're hitching.

Hitching is never entirely safe in any country in the world and we don't recommend it. Travellers who decide to hitch should understand that they're taking a small but potentially serious risk. People who do choose to hitch will be safer if they travel in pairs and let someone know where they are planning to go.

FERRY

A car ferry runs at least eight times a day from Kettering to Bruny Island. To effectively explore this rather long island, you'll need a car or bicycle. See the Bruny Island section of the Southeast Coast chapter for details.

Another ferry runs from the east coast (a few kilometres north of Orford) to small Maria Island, which is a national park. This ferry also operates daily, carrying only passengers and bicycles, as vehicles aren't allowed on the island. See the Maria Island section of the East Coast chapter for details.

The **Southern Shipping Company** (☎ *6356 1753*) operates a small passenger-and-car ferry once a week from Bridport in Tasmania's northeast to Flinders Island; once a month, the ferry continues on to Port Welshpool in Victoria. A return trip to Flinders Island costs $80 per person ($690 for a car and its driver). The journey is sometimes only eight hours, but three out of every four trips involve a refuelling stop at Bell Bay, making your total travel time 24 hours. For details of the trip to Port Welshpool, see the Sea section in the Getting There & Away chapter

ORGANISED TOURS

There are many companies offering tours of Tasmania and you should check in the magazine *Tasmanian Travelways* if you have a particular type of tour in mind.

One tour company that provides transport and lunches, but not accommodation, is

Under Down Under (☎ 6369 5555). It offers a five-day state tour for $415 (high season), that departs from Devonport, Hobart or Launceston; a seven-day high-season tour is $600 per person.

Another option available is **Bottom Bits Bus** (☎ 6234 5093, 1800 777 103; **w** www.bottombitsbus.com). It has a vast array of tours to choose from, including day trips from $70, three-day tours from $285 and a seven-day tour for $630.

Adventure Tours Australia (☎ 08-8309 2299, 1300 654 604; **w** www.adventuretours.com.au) runs a hop-on/hop-off minibus service around much of the state, including to isolated locales like Cockle Creek in the south and Arthur River in the northwest. To use this guide-accompanied service you need to buy an Adventure Tours Pass, which is valid for three months, costs $395, and can be purchased from travel agents, hostels and some of the cheaper hotels. The pass allows you to start from either Hobart, Devonport or Launceston – minibuses pick up from budget accommodation mainstays in each city at least four times a week – and travel in an anticlockwise direction around the state. You can get off as often and for as long as you like anywhere along the bus route – the only limitations are the life of the pass and the requirement to travel in the one direction.

For information on organised tours of King Island and Flinders Island, see the Bass Strait Islands chapter.

Hobart

☎ 03 • postcode 7000 • pop 126,120

Hobart is Australia's second-oldest city and its southernmost capital. Straddling the mouth of the Derwent River and backed by the towering bulk of Mt Wellington, Hobart has embellished its rich colonial heritage and splendid natural beauty with the youthful, lively atmosphere of numerous festivals and inner-city bars and eateries. Its attractive Georgian buildings, busy harbour, relaxed populace and serene surrounding districts make Hobart one of Australia's most stress-free and engaging cities.

HISTORY

The Tasmanian Aborigines who originally lived here were the Mouheneenner band of the South East Tribe, who called the area Nibberloonne. The first European colony in Tasmania was founded in 1803 at Risdon Cove, but a year later Lieutenant-Colonel David Collins, governor of the new settlement in Van Diemen's Land, sailed down the Derwent River and decided that a cove 10km below Risdon and on the opposite shore was a better place to settle. The site of Tasmania's future capital city thus began as a village of tents and wattle-and-daub huts with a population of 262 Europeans (178 of whom were convicts).

Hobart Town, as it was known until 1881, was proclaimed a city in 1842. The deep-water harbour of the Derwent River estuary was important to its development, as many merchants made their fortunes from the whaling trade, shipbuilding and the export of products such as merino wool and corn.

ORIENTATION

Hobart is sandwiched between the steep hills of Mt Wellington and the wide Derwent River. Blessed with little flat land, the city proper has spread along the riverbank and is about 20km long, though very narrow. The urban development has climbed into the hills and you'll find many western streets challengingly steep.

Highlights

- Eating, drinking and posing in waterfront restaurants and bars
- Ransacking stalls for creative buys at Salamanca Market
- Walking beneath the majestic Organ Pipes on Mt Wellington
- Going floral in the Royal Tasmanian Botanical Gardens
- Strolling by historic facades along the streets of Battery Point

The city centre is fairly small and pretty easy to navigate, with its streets arranged in a simple grid pattern around the Elizabeth St Mall – the main shopping area extends west from here. City authorities have regulated traffic in their narrow streets by making them one-way: so before you drive, study a map.

Salamanca Place, the famous row of Georgian warehouses, is along the waterfront, while behind its historic facade is the café- and bar-lined expanse of Salamanca Square. Just south of this is Battery Point, Hobart's delightful, well-preserved, early colonial district. If you follow the river around from

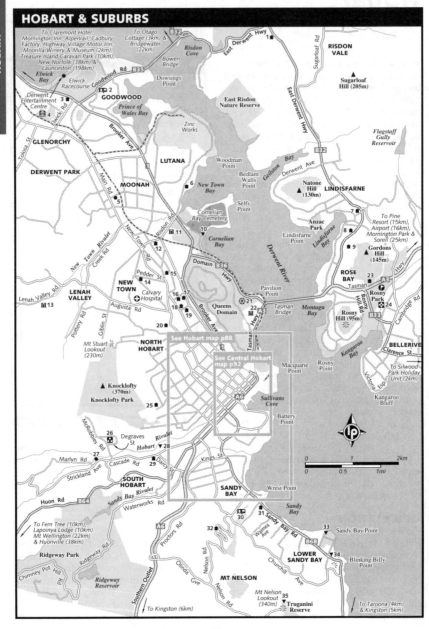

HOBART & SUBURBS

To Claremont Hotel,
Mornington Inn, Alpenrail, Cadbury
Factory, Highway Village Motor Inn,
Moorilla Winery & Museum (2km),
Treasure Island Caravan Park (10km),
New Norfolk (38km) &
Launceston' (198km)

To Otago
Cottage (3km) &
Bridgewater
(22km)

To Claremont Hotel

Risdon
Cove

Bowen
Bridge

East Derwent Hwy

RISDON
VALE

Sugarloaf
Hill (205m)

Elwick
Bay

Elwick Racecourse

Derwent
Entertainment
Centre

GOODWOOD

Dowsings
Point

Prince of
Wales Bay

East Risdon
Nature Reserve

Zinc
Works

Flagstaff
Gully
Reservoir

GLENORCHY

DERWENT PARK

LUTANA

MOONAH

Woodman
Point

Gellson

Bay

Bedlam
Walls
Point

Derwent Ave

Natone
Hill
(130m)

LINDISFARNE

New Town
Bay

Selfs
Point

Cornelian
Bay Cemetery

Cornelian
Bay

Anzac
Park

Lindisfarne
Point

Lindisfarne
Bay

To Pine
Resort (15km),
Airport (16km),
Mornington Park &
Sorell (25km)

Gordons
Hill
(145m)

LENAH
VALLEY

NEW
TOWN

Pedder St

Calvary
Hospital

Augusta Rd

Domain Hwy

Derwent River

Pavilion
Point

ROSE
BAY

Tasman

Rosny
Park

Mt Stuart
Lookout
(230m)

NORTH
HOBART

Queens
Domain

Tasman
Bridge

Montagu
Bay

Rosny
Hill
(95m)

BELLERIVE

Clarence St

Knocklofty
(370m)

Knocklofty Park

See Hobart map p88

See Central Hobart
map p92

Macquarie
Point

Rosny
Point

Kangaroo
Bay

To Silwood
Park Holiday
Unit (2km)

Kangaroo
Bluff

Sullivans
Cove

Battery
Point

Degraves
St

Hobart

Rivulet

Marlyn Rd

Cascade Rd

Strickland Ave

SOUTH
HOBART

Sandy Bay

Rivulet

Kings St

Wrest Point

To Fern Tree (10km),
Lapoinya Lodge (10km),
Mt Wellington (22km)
& Huonville (38km)

Huon Rd

Waterworks Rd

Sandy Bay Rd

Sandy
Bay

Sandy Bay Point

SANDY
BAY

Ridgeway Park

Chimney Pot
Hill

Ridgeway
Reservoir

Southern Outlet

Olinda Gve

Nelson Rd

Proctors Rd

Waimea Ave

Churchill Ave

LOWER
SANDY
BAY

Blinking Billy
Point

To Kingston (6km)

MT NELSON

Mt Nelson
Lookout
(340m)

Truganini
Reserve

To Taroona (4km)
& Kingston (5km)

0   1   2km
0   0.5   1mi

Battery Point you'll come to Sandy Bay and its yacht clubs, Hobart's university and the circular tower of Wrest Point – a hotel/casino and one of Hobart's main landmarks.

The northern side of the city centre is bounded by the recreation area known as the Domain (short for Queen's Domain), which includes the Royal Tasmanian Botanic Gardens and the Derwent River. From here the Tasman Bridge crosses the river to the eastern suburbs and the airport. North of the Domain, the suburbs continue beside the Derwent River almost all the way to Bridgewater.

There are very few large local industries and the ones that exist are well out of the main city area, generally beside the Derwent a fair way upstream.

Maps

The best maps of Hobart are the *Hobart Street Directory* and the capital maps in the *Tasmanian Towns Street Atlas,* both of which are available at various newsagents, bookshops, **Service Tasmania** (☎ 1300 135 513; ⓦ www.servicetasmania.tas.gov.au; 134 Macquarie St) and the **Tasmanian Map Centre** (☎ 6231 9043; ⓦ www.map-centre.com.au; 96 Elizabeth St), which also has a range of maps to guide your bushwalking exploits. Disabled travellers should get a copy of the useful *Hobart CBD Mobility Map* from the Hobart Travel & Information Centre; it's a guide to the relevant facilities and access.

INFORMATION
Tourist Offices

The **Hobart Travel & Information Centre** (☎ 6230 8233; 20 Davey St; open 8.30am-6pm Mon-Fri, 9am-6pm Sat, Sun & public holidays) is on the corner of Elizabeth St. You can also get information from many accommodation and tourist establishments. The city council stages its own website (ⓦ www.hobartcity.com.au).

Useful Organisations

The Tasmanian **YHA** (☎ 6234 9617; ⓦ www .yha.com.au; 28 Criterion St; open 9am-5pm Mon-Fri) has an office in Hobart. For information about driving around the state, contact the **Royal Auto Club of Tasmania** (RACT; ☎ 6232 6300, 13 27 22; ⓦ www .ract.com.au; cnr Murray & Patrick Sts). The **Wilderness Society** (☎ 6234 9366; ⓦ www .wilderness.org.au; 130 Davey St) has its head office on the outskirts of the city centre and its shop in The Galleria, Salamanca Place. The **Tasmanian Environment Centre** (☎ 6234 5566; 102 Bathurst St) is a community resource centre containing a range of environmental publications in its library.

Money

Banks are open for business from 9.30am to 4pm Monday to Thursday and from 9.30am to 5pm Friday. Automated teller machines (ATMs) can be used at any time and are installed at banks in the city centre and many

HOBART & SUBURBS

PLACES TO STAY
1   Bowen Park
2   Elwick Cabin & Tourist Park
3   Northside Holiday Villas
6   Waterfront Lodge Motel
7   Orana House
8   Lindisfarne Motor Inn
9   Roseneath
12 Wendover
14 Thirlmere Manor
15 Graham Court Apartments
16 Adelphi Court
17 Hobart Tower Motel
18 Argyle Motor Lodge
19 Rydges Hobart

20 Elms of Hobart
23 City View Motel
25 Bay View Villas
29 Cascade Hotel
30 Sandy Bay Caravan Park
31 Sandy Bay Motor Inn
32 Crawfords B&B

PLACES TO EAT
10 Cornelian Bay Boathouse
28 Le Provencal
33 Prosser's on the Beach
34 Beach House Hotel C afe Bar
35 Mount Nelson Signal Station
    Restaurant; Old Signal Station

OTHER
4   Tasmanian Transport
    Museum
5   Moonah Arts
    Centre
11 Runnymede
13 Lady Franklin Gallery
21 Royal Tasmanian Botanic
    Gardens; Botanical Discovery
    Centre
22 Government House
24 Eastlands Shopping
    Centre
26 Female Factory
27 Cascade Brewery

HOBART

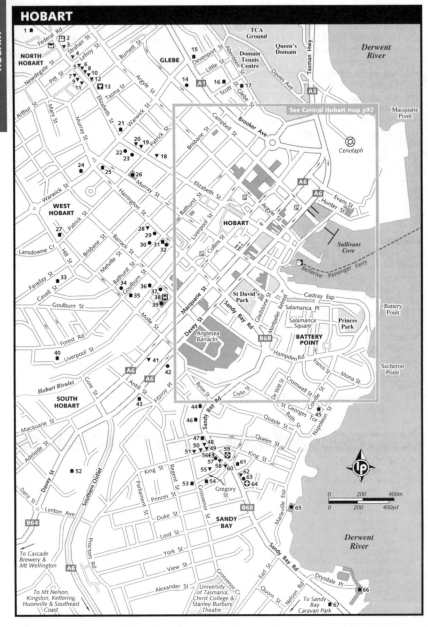

HOBART

See Central Hobart map p92

HOBART

PLACES TO STAY
1 Allport's
15 Trinity House
16 Wellington Lodge
17 Corinda's Cottages
21 Lodge on Elizabeth
24 Warwick Cottage
25 Waratah Hotel
27 Marquis of Hastings Hotel
31 Corus Hotel Hobart
33 Motel Mayfair
35 Narrara Backpackers
36 The Pickled Frog
40 Crows Nest B&B
43 Globe Hotel
44 Woolmers Inn
45 Cromwell Cottage
46 Dr Syntax Hotel
47 Bay Arcade Holiday Units;
   La Bella Pizza
52 Jane Franklin Hall
53 Grosvenor Court
54 Merre Be's
61 Mayfair Plaza Motel
66 Wrest Point; The Point
   Revolving Restaurant; The
   Asian Restaurant; Regines
   Nite Club; Casino
67 Amberley House

PLACES TO EAT
3 Dede
4 Vanidol's
5 Sen's Asian Sensation
6 Amigos
7 Marti Zucco
8 Anatolia
9 Dave's Noodle Box
10 La Porchetta
11 Concetta's
12 Annapurna
18 Rozzini's
19 Trattoria Casablanca
20 Kaos Cafe
28 Squid Roe
41 Flourishing Court
48 Mykonos
49 The Fish Bar
50 Solo Pasta
51 Poseidons
55 Tasmanian Coffee Roasters
58 Banjo's
60 Tonic
62 Bangkok Wok

OTHER
2 State Cinema
13 Republic Bar & Cafe
14 Woolworths Supermarket
22 Mundy & Sons
23 Southern Tasmanian
   Divers
26 RACT
29 AutoRent–Hertz
30 Birchalls
32 Europcar
34 Westside Laundromat
37 Lo-Cost Auto Rent
38 Transit Centre; Redline,
   TassieLink & Tigerline
   Coaches; Transit Centre
   Backpackers
39 Tasmanian Wine Centre
42 Wilderness Society Head
   Office
56 Commonwealth Bank &
   ATM; Sandy Bay
   Post Office
57 Sandy Bay Newsagency &
   Bookshop
59 Magnet Court Shopping
   Centre; Golden Tulip
   Patisserie
63 Coles Supermarket
64 Travellers Medical &
   Vaccination Centre
65 Royal Hobart Yacht Club of
   Tasmania

suburban branches. All major banks have their offices near the Elizabeth St Mall. There are multibank ATMs at Watermans Dock, the airport, in Salamanca Place and at Antarctic Adventure in Salamanca Square.

Post & Communications

The city's **main post office** (cnr Elizabeth & Macquarie Sts; open 8.30am-5.30pm Mon-Fri) is across from the Town Hall. Further out of the city centre is the **Sandy Bay post office** (cnr Sandy Bay Rd & King St; open 9am-5pm Mon-Fri).

Hobart's STD area telephone code is the same as the rest of southeastern Australia: ☎ 03. All numbers for the Hobart region begin with 62 and calls within the city are classed as local. Calls from Hobart to country regions are charged at STD rates, even when they begin with 62; rates depend on the distance involved. If you hear three pips at the start of a call, then STD rates are being charged and you should get ready to insert coins if you're using a payphone. Local calls from payphones are 40c for unlimited time.

You can log on at the following places: **Drifters Internet Cafe** (☎ 6224 6286; The Galleria, 33 Salamanca Place; open 10am-6pm Mon-Sat, 11am-6pm Sun), charging $1/5/9 for 5/30/60 minutes; **Pelican Loft** (☎ 6234 2225; 35a Elizabeth St; open 9am-9pm Mon-Fri, 9.30am-4.30pm Sat), next door to Noobar and charging $1/1.50/8 for 5/10/60 minutes; and **Access on Macquarie** (☎ 6231 6848; 157 Macquarie St; open 10am-9pm daily summer, 10am-6pm Mon-Sat, 10am-5pm Sun winter), found below the Astor Grill, and charging 13c per minute.

Bookshops

Fullers Bookshop (☎ 6224 2488; 140 Collins St; open 9am-5.30pm Mon-Fri, 9am-5pm Sat, 10am-4pm Sun) has a great range of literature and travel guides, plus a café. The **Sandy Bay Newsagency & Bookshop** (☎ 6223 6955; 197 Sandy Bay Rd; open

7am-7pm Mon-Sat, 9am-5.30pm Sun) and the **Hobart Bookshop** (☎ 6223 1803; 22 Salamanca Square) have quality literature and travel sections. Hobart Bookshop also has lots of second-hand titles, as does the **Imperial Bookshop** (☎ 6223 1663; 138 Collins St), beneath Central City Backpackers. **Ellison Hawker** (☎ 6234 2322; 90 Liverpool St), **Angus & Robertson Bookworld** (☎ 6234 4288; 96 Collins St) and **Birchalls** (☎ 6234 2122; 147 Bathurst St) are good general bookshops.

The **Wilderness Society Shop** (☎ 6234 9370; The Galleria, 33 Salamanca Place; open 9.15am-5.30pm Mon-Fri, 9.15am-4pm Sat, 11am-4pm Sun) has a range of environmental publications, wildlife posters, videos and calendars. The **Tasmanian Map Centre** (☎ 6231 9043; 96 Elizabeth St) has a reasonable range of travel books.

Libraries

True bookworms can visit the **State Library of Tasmania** (☎ 6233 7529; 91 Murray St; W www.statelibrary.tas.gov.au; lending library open 9.30am-6pm Mon-Thur, 9.30am-8pm Fri, 9.30am-12.30pm Sat).

Universities

The **University of Tasmania** (W www.utas .edu.au; Churchill Ave, Sandy Bay) has a theatre, gallery, bookshop, newsagency, Commonwealth Bank, multibank ATM and café, and is often a venue for visiting bands.

Laundry

The **Westside Laundromat** (cnr Goulburn & Molle Sts; open 6.30am-9.30pm daily) is reasonably central. Apparently it's cool to do your laundry, at least at **Machine Laundry Café** (☎ 6224 9922; 12 Salamanca Square; open 8am-6pm daily), a café and laundry rolled into one (see Cafés & Wine Bars in Places to Eat later).

There are also laundrettes at Magnet Court in Sandy Bay and in the Elizabeth St shopping centre in North Hobart.

Medical Services

The **Travellers Medical & Vaccination Centre** (☎ 6223 7577; 270 Sandy Bay Rd; open 9am-noon & 2pm-5pm Wed-Fri), in Sandy Bay, has consultations by appointment only. There are a number of chemists near the corner of Harrington and Macquarie Sts that are open long hours daily.

Emergency

The **Royal Hobart Hospital** (☎ 6222 8308; 48 Liverpool St) has an emergency section, as does **St Helen's Private Hospital** (☎ 6221 6444; 186 Macquarie St) and **Calvary Hospital** (☎ 13 22 05; 49 Augusta Rd, Lenah Valley).

In the event of a fire, or to contact the police or an ambulance in an emergency, dial ☎ 000.

TASMANIAN MUSEUM & ART GALLERY

The rewarding Tasmanian Museum & Art Gallery (☎ 6211 4177; W www.tmag.tas .gov.au; 40 Macquarie St; admission free; open 10am-5pm daily) complex is situated in the precinct where Hobart Town was established in 1804 and incorporates the city's oldest building, the 1808 Commissariat Store. The museum section features a display on the Tasmanian Aborigines and relics from the state's colonial heritage, while the gallery has a good collection of Tasmanian colonial art. Free 50-minute guided tours depart from the foyer at 2.30pm from Wednesday to Sunday. Wheelchairs are available at reception.

OTHER MUSEUMS & GALLERIES

The **Allport Library & Museum of Fine Arts** (☎ 6233 7484; 91 Murray St; admission free; open 9.30am-5pm Mon-Fri) is based in the State Library. It has a collection of rare books on Australasia and the Pacific region, colonial paintings, and antiques that it displays several times a year.

The **Maritime Museum of Tasmania** (☎ 6234 1427; W www.maritimetas.org; 16 Argyle St; adult/child $6.60/4; open 10am-5pm daily) is set up in the historic Carnegie Building, built by a philanthropic Scottish-American millionaire in the early 1900s to serve as Tasmania's first public library. The building is now home to an interesting, salt-encrusted collection of photos, paintings, models and relics that highlight Tasmania's strong shipping past. Upstairs from the museum is the city council–run **Carnegie Gallery** (admission free; open 10am-5pm daily), which exhibits mainly Tasmanian art and photography.

Narryna Heritage Museum (☎ 6234 2791; 103 Hampden Rd, Battery Point; adult/child $5/2; open 10.30am-5pm Tues-Fri, 2pm-5pm Sat & Sun Aug-June) is a fine Georgian sandstone mansion built in 1836, set amid beautiful grounds and containing a colonial treasure-trove of domestic artefacts. These include the Drawing Room's adjustable fire screen ('to protect ladies faces'), the old lace-maker in the Morning Room, and the old smith and coach house out back.

At the northeastern end of Macquarie St is the old Gasworks complex, part of which now houses the **Tasmanian Distillery** (☎ 6231 0588; W www.tasdistillery.com.au; 2 Macquarie St; open 9am-7pm daily Oct-Mar, 10am-5pm daily Apr-Sept), an operation that brewed its first drop of whisky on a nearby site in 1822. Besides getting into the spirit of the place with a shot of single malt, you can take a tour of the distillery and its museum for $5.50/2.20 per adult/child.

Continuing the boozy theme is **The Lark Distillery** (☎ 6231 9088; W www.larkdistillery.com.au; 14 Davey St; open 10am-5pm daily), which opened in 1992 to produce various liqueurs and schnapps; it has free tastings and a café.

Train rides are available on the first and third Sundays of each month at the **Tasmanian Transport Museum** (☎ 6272 7721; Anfield St, Glenorchy; adult/child $3/1.50; open 1pm-4.30pm Sat & Sun). When the trains run, admission increases to $5/2 per adult/child. Take bus No X1 from stop F on Elizabeth St: it's a short walk from Glenorchy bus station.

For more railway amusement, head north to **Alpenrail** (☎ 6249 3748; 82 Abbotsfield Rd, Claremont; adult/child $9.50/4.50; open 9.30am-4.30pm daily) to see its remarkably detailed, miniature recreation of a train-littered Swiss Alps, which took 20 years to complete; diehard train buffs can also buy video footage of international

railways. Take bus No 42 from Elizabeth St to the Abbotsfield sto

The modernistic lines of the **M Museum** (☎ 6249 7988; W www.moo .com.au; 655 Main Rd, Berriedale; admissio free; open 10am-4pm Wed-Sun), at Moorilla Estate vineyard, hide a wealth of antiquities brought together from private collections. Besides some floored Roman mosaics and African and Central American artefacts, there are excellent numismatic and Egyptian sections, the latter featuring a mummy case dating from around 600 BC. Free music and poetry recitals are often held here and there's a good on-site restaurant. Catch bus No X1 from stop F on Elizabeth St.

Lady Franklin Gallery (☎ 6228 2662; Lenah Valley Rd; admission free; open 1.30pm-5pm Sat & Sun), in a colonnaded 1842 sandstone building called Ancanthe (Greek for 'Vale of Flowers'), displays work by Tasmanian artists. Take bus No 6, 7, 8, 9 or 10 to the Lenah Valley terminus from stop G on Elizabeth St.

The **Moonah Arts Centre** (☎ 6274 0318; 65 Hopkins St, Moonah; admission free; open 12.30pm-5pm Mon-Fri) is a community arts centre involved in staging everything from Indigenous arts exhibitions and concerts to workshops and short-film screenings – it's 10 years old and going strong. All buses departing stop E on Elizabeth St go to Moonah.

HISTORIC BUILDINGS

One thing that makes Hobart so exceptional among Australian cities is its wealth of remarkably well-preserved old buildings. More than 90 buildings in Hobart are classified by the National Trust, with 60 of these – featuring some of Hobart's best Georgian architecture – on Macquarie and Davey Sts. More information is available at the local office of the **National Trust** (☎ 6223 5200; cnr Brisbane & Campbell Sts; open 9am-1pm Mon-Fri).

Close to the city centre is **St David's Park**, which has some lovely old trees, and gravestones dating from the earliest days of the colony. There's also **Parliament House** (Murray St), built in 1835 and originally used as a customs house; there is still a

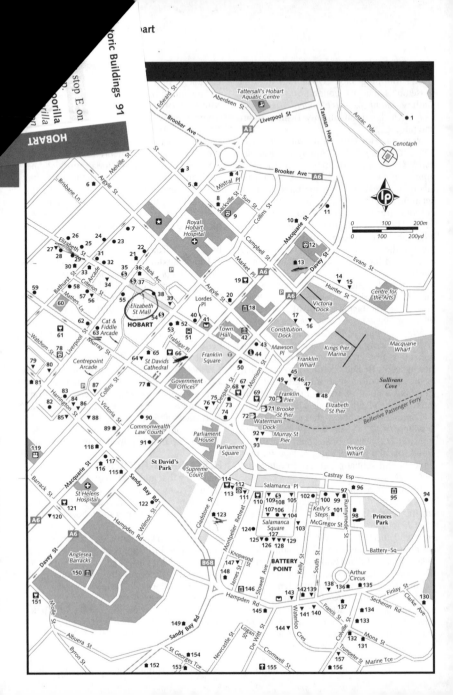

CENTRAL HOBART

HOBART

PLACES TO STAY

3 Royal Exchange Hotel
4 Fountainside Motor Inn
5 Hollydene House
6 Ocean Child Hotel
8 Theatre Royal Hotel
10 The Old Woolstore
13 Hotel Grand Chancellor; Meehan's Restaurant; The Cove
20 Montgomery's
21 Brunswick Hotel
30 New Sydney Hotel
33 Hobart Mid City Hotel
36 Alabama Hotel
48 Oakford on the Pier
52 Savoy Hobart; Savoy Baths
65 Central City Backpackers; Imperial Bookshop
73 Quest Waterfront
74 Customs House Hotel
77 Hadleys Hotel
81 Harringtons of Hobart
89 Hotel Astor; Astor Grill; Access on Macquarie (Internet)
96 Oakford on Salamanca
97 Salamanca Terraces
98 Lenna of Hobart; Alexander's Restaurant
101 Battery Point Guesthouse
115 Welcome Stranger Hotel
116 Macquarie Manor
118 Hobart Macquarie Motor Inn
123 Salamanca Inn
130 Jarem Waterfront B&B
131 Tantallon Lodge
132 Colville Cottage
133 Ascot of Battery Point
134 Avon Court Holiday Apartments
135 Battery Point Boutique Accommodation
136 The Grand Old Duke
137 Coopers Cottage
142 Prince of Wales Hotel
143 Barton Cottage
148 Portsea Terrace
149 Gattonside
152 Blue Hill Motel
153 Crelin Lodge
154 St Ives Motel
156 Battery Point Manor

PLACES TO EAT

14 Riviera Ristorante Italiano
15 Drunken Admiral
16 Mures Fish Centre; Upper Deck; Lower Deck; The Sushi Bar
17 Floating Seafood Stalls
27 Golden Bamboo
34 Thai Hut
39 Noobar; Pelican Loft (Internet)
45 Fish Frenzy
46 T-42°
47 A Splash of Paris
49 Pashas
56 Cumquat
64 Afterword Cafe; Fullers Bookshop
67 Rockerfellers
75 Elbow Room
76 L'Artisan
79 Tandoor & Curry House
80 Vanny's
84 Cafe Toulouse
85 Little Bali; Little Salama
86 Little India
87 Forture Court
88 Gusto Italiano
92 Sisco's; Blue Skies
93 Sticky Fingers
99 Mikaku; Mummaluka; Ball & Chain Grill
103 Mr Wooby's
104 Sal's
105 Vietnamese Kitchen
107 Bar Celona
109 Maldini
111 Retro Cafe
113 Zum Cafe
120 Flavour of India
125 Salamanca Bakehouse
127 Toshi's Kitchen
128 Sugo
129 Machine Laundry Café
138 Magic Curries
139 Da Angelo Ristorante
140 Restaurant Gondwana
141 Z's
143 Jackman & McRoss
144 Mummy's
147 Kelleys Seafood Restaurant
157 Shipwright's Arms Hotel

OTHER

1 Derwent Bike Hire
2 National Trust; Penitentiary Chapel & Criminal Courts
7 The Dive Shop
9 Theatre Royal; Backspace Theatre
11 Tasmanian Distillery
12 Federation Concert Hall
18 Tasmanian Museum & Art Gallery
19 Hope & Anchor Tavern
22 Auto Miniatures
23 The Climbing Edge; Tasmanian Climbing Company
24 Selective Car Rentals
25 Paddy Pallin
26 Tradeware
28 Snowgum
29 Tasmanian Map Centre
31 Mountain Designs
22 Jolly Swagman's
35 Commonwealth Bank & ATM
37 National Australia Bank & ATM
38 Qantas Office
40 The Antiques Market
41 Main Post Office; Metro Office
42 Maritime Museum of Tasmania; Carnegie Gallery
43 The Lark Distillery
44 Hobart Travel & Information Centre
49 Hobart City Council Offices
51 Metro City Bus Station
53 Angus & Robertson Bookworld
54 ANZ Bank & ATM
55 Ellison Hawker
57 Tasmanian YHA Office
58 Tasmanian Environment Centre
59 Rent-A-Bug
60 State Library of Tasmania; Allport Library & Museum of Fine Arts
61 Cow
62 Experience Tasmania
63 The Tasmania Shop
66 Temple Place
68 Brooke St Bar & Cafe
69 Isobar
70 Captain Fell's Historic Ferries
71 Port Arthur Cruises
72 Roche O'May Cruises; The Cruise Company; Multibank ATM
78 Odeon Theatre
82 Budget
83 Spot On Fishing Tackle
90 Service Tasmania; Parks & Wildlife Service Information Desk; Tasmap Sales
91 Royal Tennis Court
94 CSIRO Marine Laboratories
95 Despard Gallery
100 Tasmanian Woollen Company
102 Salamanca Arts Centre; Peacock Theatre; Foyer Espresso Bar
106 Hobart Bookshop
108 ANZ Bank ATM
110 Knopwood's Retreat; Round Midnight; Syrup
112 Galleria; Drifters Internet Cafe; Wilderness Society Shop; Tea House Restaurant
114 Irish Murphy's
117 Chemist
119 Village Cinemas
121 Bakers; lalaland
122 Conservatorium Recital Hall
124 Antarctic Adventure
126 Say Cheese
146 Narryna Heritage Museum
149 Military Museum of Tasmania
151 Bridie O'Reilly's
155 St George's Anglican Church

tunnel between it and the Customs House Hotel opposite, though the reason for the tunnel is unclear. Hobart's prestigious **Theatre Royal** *(29 Campbell St)* was designed by the architect of the Cascade Brewery. Built in 1837 and originally called the Victoria Theatre, it's the oldest theatre in Australia.

On Davey St is a **royal tennis court**, which you can visit on the Hobart Historic Walk – see the Walking Tours section later. Royal, or 'real', tennis is an ancient form of the highly-strung game played in a four-walled indoor court.

The court rooms, cells, tunnels and gallows of the **Penitentiary Chapel & Criminal Courts** *(☎ 6231 0911; 6 Brisbane St)* can be explored via the excellent National Trust–run tours that take place at 10am, 11.30am, 1pm and 2.30pm daily: the 90-minute rounds cost $7.70 per person. Ghost tours (adult/child $8.80/5.50) are run most nights at 8pm; they are popular so bookings (☎ 0417 361 392) are essential.

Runnymede *(☎ 6278 1269; 61 Bay Rd, New Town; adult/child $7.70/free; open 10am-4.30pm Mon-Fri, noon-4.30pm Sat & Sun)* is a gracious 1840 residence built for Robert Pitcairn, the first lawyer to qualify in Tasmania, and named by a later owner, Captain Charles Bayley, after his favourite ship. It's now managed by the National Trust. To get there take bus No 15 or 20 from Stop H on Elizabeth St and alight at the Old New Town station.

CASCADE BREWERY & FEMALE FACTORY

Australia's oldest brewery, Cascade *(☎ 6221 8300; 140 Cascade Rd)*, began its frothy production in 1832 and continues to produce fine beer for nationwide consumption. It's an imposing, photogenic sight from the approach road, and its neighbouring gardens are good for a wander. Two-hour brewery tours depart at 9.30am and 1pm from Monday to Friday except public holidays, costing $11/4.50 per adult/child and involving plenty of stair climbing. Bookings are recommended and visitors should wear flat, closed shoes.

Near the brewery, a few signposted turns off Cascade Rd, is the site of Australia's first purpose-built female factory *(Degraves St)*, or prison, which operated from 1828 to 1877. Major archaeological work is now being conducted here, funded by an on-site **fudge factory** *(shop open 8am-4pm Mon-Fri)*. You can take a 1¼-hour guided tour of both the historic site's diggings and the confectionary factory at 10.30am Monday to Friday that costs $6.60/3.30 per adult/child; for bookings call ☎ 6223 3233. Descendants of Willy Wonka welcome.

The brewery is on the southwestern edge of the city centre. Bus Nos 43, 44, 46 and 49 leave from the Elizabeth St side of Franklin Square and go right by it; alight at stop 17.

THE WATERFRONT

Hobart's busy waterfront area, centred on **Franklin Wharf**, is a great place for a stroll. At **Constitution Dock** are several floating takeaway seafood stalls – it's an obligatory holiday activity to sit in the sun munching fresh fish and chips while watching the busy harbour. At the finish of the annual Sydney to Hobart Yacht Race around New Year, and during the Royal Hobart Regatta in February, Constitution Dock is swamped by boat crews and spectators. The docks also have some fine restaurants if you prefer something more formal.

Nearby **Hunter St** has a row of fine Georgian warehouses. They're in a similar condition to those on Salamanca Place before they were restored, but haven't – yet – been developed as a tourist attraction.

The whole Hobart wharf area is actually reclaimed land. When the town was first settled, Davey St ran along the edge of the sea and the Hunter St area was an island used to safely store food and other goods. Subsequent projects filled in the shallow waters and provided land upon which the warehouses of Hunter St and Salamanca Place were constructed. On Hunter St itself, there are markers indicating the position of the original causeway, which was built in 1820 to link Hunter Island with Sullivans Cove.

SALAMANCA PLACE

The row of beautiful sandstone warehouses on the harbour front at Salamanca Place is a prime example of Australian colonial architecture. Dating back to the whaling days of the 1830s, these warehouses were the centre of Hobart Town's trade and commerce. Only 30 years ago, many of these buildings were in a derelict state and under threat of demolition. But they were tastefully developed and now house galleries, restaurants, nightspots and shops selling everything from vegetables to antiques.

The eastern side of Salamanca Place has been the subject of some major developments in recent years, with four old silos being converted into luxury apartment towers and a glut of upmarket accommodation being set up behind them. Ensuing years will likely see the conversion of more of the area's real estate into top-end residences.

Every Saturday morning sees the popular, open-air **Salamanca Market** *(Salamanca Place; open 8.30am-3pm)*, with its hundreds of arts-and-crafts stalls and hordes of local and visiting browsers. There are the generic goods you'll find at any large market, but there's a fair proportion of quality items like organic vegetables, handmade accessories, creative woodwork and ceramics, and the odd attention-getting curio or collectible.

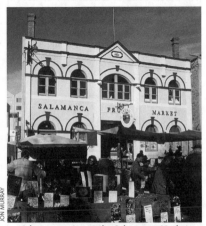

JON MURRAY

A busy morning at the Salamanca Market

Buskers and the intoxicating smell of vigorous lunchtime cooking from nearby cafés add to the atmosphere.

To reach Battery Point from Salamanca Place you can climb up **Kelly's Steps**, which are wedged between two of the warehouses about halfway along the main block of buildings.

Nearby **Antarctic Adventure** *(☎ 6220 8220; W www.antarctic.com.au; 2 Salamanca Square; adult/child $16/8; open 10am-5pm daily)* is a combination theme park and interactive science centre with lots to see. Admission is steep, but enables all-day access. There are heaps of displays on ecology and icy exploration, and kids will particularly enjoy the night-time views in the planetarium and the three-minute Blizzard ride.

BATTERY POINT

Behind Princes Wharf and Salamanca Place is the historic core of Hobart, the old port area known as Battery Point. Its name comes from the gun battery that stood on the promontory by the guardhouse. Built in 1818, the guardhouse is now the district's oldest building. The guns were never used in battle and the only damage they inflicted was on nearby windowpanes when fired during practice.

During colonial times, this area was a colourful maritime village, home to master mariners, shipwrights, sailors, fishers, coopers and merchants. The houses reflect their varying lifestyles, ranging from tiny one- and two-room houses, such as those around Arthur Circus, to mansions. While most houses are still occupied by locals, many are now guesthouses where you can stay and experience the area's unique village atmosphere. Battery Point's pubs, churches, conjoined houses and narrow winding streets have all been lovingly preserved and are a delight to wander around, especially when you get glimpses of the harbour between the buildings. Highlights of the area include **Arthur Circus**, a small circle of quaint little cottages built around a village green, and **St George's Anglican Church**.

Anglesea Barracks was built in Battery Point in 1811. Still used by the army, this is the oldest military establishment in Australia. It houses the volunteer-staffed **Military Museum of Tasmania** *(☎ 6237 7160; Davey St; adult/child $2/1; open 9am-2pm Tues, other times by appointment);* guided tours of the restored buildings and grounds begin at 11am.

Drivers with lead feet should note that the speed limit in Battery Point is now 40km/h.

QUEEN'S DOMAIN

When Hobart was originally settled, the high hill on the city's northern side was reserved for use by the governor, preventing development of any housing. Today the area is known as the Queen's Domain and is public parkland.

This large park contains reserves and grounds for cricket and athletics, as well as wide areas of native grasslands. There are good views across the river and the city from many parts of the Domain; the best are from the hilltop lookouts at the park's northern end. If walking across the park, don't try to descend the northern end to New Town, as deep road cuttings prevent pedestrian access. There are several pedestrian overpasses on the western side that provide good access to North Hobart.

On the eastern side, near Tasman Bridge, is the small but beguiling **Royal Tasmanian Botanic Gardens** *(admission free; open 8am-6.30pm daily Oct-Mar, 8am-5pm daily Apr-Sept).* Features include the largest collection of mature conifers in the southern hemisphere, an outstanding conservatory and the Sub-Antarctic Plant House, with unique specimens from chilly Macquarie Island. After wandering through the flora, you can explore their world in more detail in the interactive **Botanical Discovery Centre** *(☎ 6234 6299; admission by donation; open 9am-5pm daily Sept-May, 9am-4.30pm daily June-Aug).*

Located next door to the botanic gardens is **Government House**, the residence of the state's governor. Although it is not open to the public and not visible from the road, you can get a good view of the building's turrets and towers from high up on the hill in Queen's Domain.

MT WELLINGTON

Hobart is dominated by 1270m-high Mt Wellington, which has fine views and many walking tracks. You can walk from the city centre to the summit and back in a day, but you need to be pretty fit. The top is sometimes under cloud and in winter it often has a light cover of snow.

You can catch bus No 48 or 49 from the Macquarie St side of Franklin Square to Fern Tree, a small suburb halfway up the mountain, from where you can walk to the summit and back in about five to six hours via Fern Glade Track, Radfords Track, then the Zig Zag Track. The Organ Pipes walk from the Chalet is an impressive flat walk below these outstanding cliffs. Buy a copy of the *Mt Wellington Walks* map for details of all tracks.

A quicker but more expensive option is the **Mt Wellington Shuttle Bus Service** *(☎ 0417 341 804),* which will pick up from hotels or the travel & information centre and drive you to the summit and back ($25 per person); bookings are required. You can also get to the mountaintop by joining a bus tour: see the Organised Tours section later in this chapter for details.

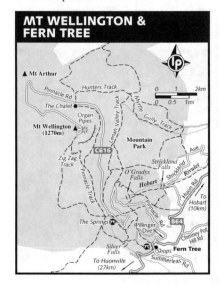

MT WELLINGTON & FERN TREE

MT NELSON

If Mt Wellington is under a cloud, the **Old Signal Station** on Mt Nelson, which is much lower, will still provide excellent views over the city. When Port Arthur was operating as a penal station, a series of semaphore stations were positioned on all the high hills and used to transmit messages across the colony. The one on Mt Nelson – first established in 1811, though the current building dates from 1910 – served as the major link between Hobart and the rest of the colony.

Beside the signal station is a restaurant (see Places to Eat later). The lookout can be accessed by a steep winding road from Sandy Bay, or via the turn-off at the Southern Outlet (the main road from Hobart to Kingston) on top of the hill. You can also walk to it via the Truganini Track (90 minutes return) which starts at Cartwright Reserve, beside the Channel Hwy between Sandy Bay and Taroona. From the Macquarie St side of Franklin Square, catch bus No 57 or 58 to the lookout.

RISDON COVE

Often acknowledged only as the site of Tasmania's first European settlement in 1803, Risdon Cove was unfortunately also where the first massacre of the land's traditional owners – the Tasmanian Aborigines – took place. It was one of a dozen sites returned to the Aboriginal community by the state government in 1995. Found north of the centre, it now has a grouping of unoccupied buildings initially intended as an information centre, some picnic and barbecue facilities, and a meditative stillness. Across the creek at Landing Stage is a stone memorial unveiled in 1904, which marks the centenary of Lieutenant Bowen's landing here.

WHAT'S FREE

Hobart is so walker-friendly that just strolling around the docks and Battery Point is probably the best free activity possible. The natural and cultural treats of the Botanic Gardens and the Tasmanian Museum & Art Gallery are also free. No park fees apply to Mt Wellington, which is a fantastic place for bushwalks, and swimming at Kingston Beach or Blackmans Bay is great if the weather is warm enough. Kids might enjoy watching the clockwork nursery rhyme characters that appear on the hour on the wall next to the clock in the Cat and Fiddle Arcade. Salamanca Market, held every Saturday morning along Salamanca Place, is free as long as you don't indulge yourself and actually buy something – there are usually buskers about to keep you entertained, and you can also browse in the nearby galleries and speciality shops.

SAILING

The Derwent River and D'Entrecasteaux Channel are wonderful sailing waters; see the Sailing section of the Activities chapter for details.

SEA KAYAKING

Kayaking around the docks in Hobart, particularly at twilight, is a popular activity. **Blackaby's** (☎ 6267 1508; ⓦ www.blackaby seakayaks.com.au) organises morning, afternoon and sunset paddles for $43 per person. A day trip involving transport to Port Arthur and a kayak journey around the peninsula costs $175 per person (minimum two people).

CYCLING

There's a cycle route from central Hobart to the northern suburb of Glenorchy, part of which follows the banks of the Derwent River. Bikes can be hired at **Derwent Bike Hire** (☎ 0407 342 918; open 10am-5pm Sat & Sun), at the Cenotaph in the Regatta Grounds, from $7/20 per hour/day (includes helmets). It is open longer in summer. You can also take a $45 organised ride from the top of Mt Wellington with **Brake Out Cycling Tours** (☎ 6239 1080; 683 Summerleas Rd, Fern Tree).

ORGANISED TOURS
Walking Tours

There's a wealth of detailed historic walks literature available at the travel & information centre to guide you around the docks and streets of the CBD and Battery Point with ease. These include *Hobart's Historic* ne *Battery Point & Sullivan's Discovery*.

nformative two-hour **Hobart Historic Walk** departs from the travel & information centre at 10am daily October to May and costs $17/15 per adult/concession; children under 12 are free. Those unconventional souls who don't like to walk in straight lines may want to try the **Hobart Historic Pub Tour**, organised via the travel & information centre (tours on demand Thursday to Sunday; adult $17) and taking in four watering holes with historic ambience or surrounds: the Hope & Anchor Hotel, Brooke St Bar & Cafe, Irish Murphy's and Knopwood's Retreat.

For a look at Hobart from the basement up, take a tour of the **Hobart Rivulet**, which runs beneath the CBD. Tours are run by the **city council** *(☎ 6238 2711; cnr Davey & Elizabeth Sts)*, cost $15/10 per adult/concession and leave from the council offices at 4pm on Thursday (also 4pm Tuesday during January and February).

√ Cruises

Several cruise companies operate from the Brooke St Pier and Franklin Wharf, offering a variety of cruises in and around the harbour. Note that timetables can be unreliable. Some cruises have advertised running times but only operate if there are enough passengers; if you arrive to book just before it leaves, you may find that day's tour has already been cancelled.

One of the most popular cruises is the four-hour Cadbury Cruise (adult/child $38/18.50) run by **The Cruise Company** *(☎ 6234 9294)*. The boat leaves at 10am on weekdays and takes you on a slow return cruise to the Cadbury factory in Claremont, where you disembark and tour the premises.

The sailings offered by **Roche O'May Cruises** *(☎ 6223 1914)* include a four-hour trip north taking in the Cadbury factory and the Moorilla Wine Centre (adult/child $45/24), departing Brooke St Pier at 11am Monday to Friday (except public holidays). Its MV *Cartela* runs morning cruises ($17.50/9), lunch cruises ($28/14), afternoon tea cruises ($15/7.50) and 2½-hour dinner

cruises ($30/15), while Friday sees a counter lunch cruise for a bargain $15.

Captain Fell's Historic Ferries *(☎ 6223 5893; Franklin Wharf)* runs 90-minute harbour cruises (adult/family $12/30) and 2½-hour lunch ($23/55) and dinner ($26/68) jaunts.

Port Arthur Cruises *(☎ 6231 2655, 1300 134 561; Brooke St Pier)* offers several cruises to and around the Tasman Peninsula, including two that drop you off at Port Arthur – the cruise to the historic site combined with a return trip to Hobart by coach is $120/85 per adult/child, while a one-way cruise to Port Arthur is $85/55.

Cadbury Chocolate Factory Tour

You can go direct to this factory *(☎ 6249 0333, 1800 627 367; Cadbury Rd, Claremont; adult/child $12.50/6.50)* yourself and explore it without boarding a boat. Tours are run weekdays at 9am, 10am, 10.30am, 11am, noon, 12.30pm and 1.30pm (extra tours are held between 8am and 9am, and 2.30pm and 3.30pm on demand). The factory is closed on public holidays and also shuts down a few days before Christmas for at least the following two weeks. Bookings are essential. Take bus No 37, 38 or 39 to Claremont from stop E on Elizabeth St. See the boxed text 'Sweet Dreams' for some historical background to the factory.

Bus Tours

Day and half-day bus tours in and around Hobart are operated by **Tigerline** *(☎ 6272 6611, 1300 653 633; ⓦ www.tigerline.com .au)*, usually running only if there are bookings. Its half-day trips include jaunts to Mt Wellington and various city sights (adult/child $34/21), the Cadbury factory ($35/22) and Richmond ($39/27). Full-day destinations include Port Arthur ($60/38), the Huon Valley ($100/60) and the Tahune Forest Airwalk ($60/40). Tours usually depart from the information centre and/or Roche O'May Cruises at Pier One. Tigerline also runs open-topped bus tours combined with a Derwent cruise ($20/15).

Another company offering coach tours of and from Hobart is **Experience Tasmania**

Sweet Dreams

Anyone who thinks making chocolate is just about sugary confection and not spiritual conviction has obviously never heard of George Cadbury. Born in 1839 and the son of John Cadbury, founder of the all-things-sweet Cadbury empire, George became well versed in the Quaker ideology practised by his family. Quakers belong to the nonconformist Religious Society of Friends, which was established in the 17th century and preaches notions of equality and social change based on morality overriding individual differences.

George applied these reformist beliefs to the transformation of Bournville, the Cadbury factory near Brighton in England, into a 'garden city', with bucolic surrounds, recreational facilities and nice, affordable housing for workers. It was a place designed to reject the health and spirit-sapping industrialisation of the time, while ensuring the highest productivity by having 'happier' workers and strict moral codes such as the segregation of males and females. The Cadbury factory in Hobart was built in 1922 along the same lines, being outfitted as a mini-village that included sports facilities, with the Claremont site chosen because it was outside the city.

The Cadbury family's direct involvement in what has become a market-hungry multinational ended in the 1940s, but Quaker involvement in Tasmanian society continues through The Friends' School, a well-respected educational facility in North Hobart that began its teachings in 1887.

(☎ 6234 3336; W www.experiencetas.com .au; 129 Liverpool St), which has free hotel pick-ups. It has half-day tours to Mt Wellington (adult/child $22/11); Mt Wellington and the Salamanca Market ($25/17); Bonorong Wildlife Park and Richmond ($35/18); and Mt Field National Park and the Bonorong Wildlife Park ($45/22). Its full-day tours include trips to Port Arthur ($55/35); Cadbury's, Bonorong Wildlife Park and Richmond ($70/40); and Huon Valley and

Tahune Airwalk ($95/50). It also has a coach disguised as a tram offering three-hour city tours ($26/18), departing from the travel & information centre.

Other local operators include **City Sights Under Lights** (☎ 6235 4353; W www.city sights.com.au) and the double-decker **Gregory Omnibuses** (☎ 6224 6169).

Car Tours

You can take two- to six-hour tours with the cruisy cabs of **United Taxis** (☎ 6278 2244), which visit most of the places the bus tours go to – a three-hour tour of Richmond, for example, will cost you $150. A wheelchair-accessible vehicle is also available; however, it's in demand and should be booked well in advance.

Scenic Flights

Par Avion (☎ 6248 5390; W www.paravion .com.au) and **Tasair** (☎ 6248 5088; W www .tasair.com.au) offer scenic flights from Cambridge aerodrome, 15km from the city. **Tasmanian Seaplanes** (☎ 6227 8808, 0419 147 755; W www.tas-seaplane.com) flies as far as Lake St Clair and Port Arthur from a pontoon at Wrest Point. See the Scenic Flights section of the Activities chapter for details.

SPECIAL EVENTS

In 2001, Hobart was the focus of celebrations to launch Tasmania's first major cultural festival, **Ten Days on the Island** (W www.tendaysontheisland.org). This biennial event, held from late March until early April, is a creative acknowledgement of the state's island culture and of other water-bound cultures around the world, and comprises statewide performances by local and international artists. The annual **Mountain Festival**, a combined artistic and scientific acknowledgement of Mt Wellington, runs in conjunction with Ten Days on the Island, and includes concerts, exhibitions, guided walks and environmental seminars.

The Tasmanian capital's own premier festival, comprising sports events, outdoor banquets, concerts and street performances, is the **Hobart Summer Festival**, held from late December to late February. It kicks off with the Taste of Tasmania, a week-long waterfront food and drink extravaganza. Another of its key events is the completion of the annual Sydney to Hobart Yacht Race, usually on December 29, when Hobart's waterfront swarms with celebrating yachties and their groupies. A simultaneous yacht race, the Melbourne to Hobart, takes contestants down Tassie's wilder west coast and usually hits Hobart on December 31. Other summer festival highlights include a New Year's Eve party for revelling sailors, locals and visitors alike; the Tasmanian Women's International Tennis tournament in early January; the Royal Hobart Regatta, a major three-day aquatic carnival in early February; and the horse-racing spectacle of the Hobart Cup Carnival in early February.

Hobart has a thriving literary scene and hosts the annual **Tasmanian Readers and Writers Festival** (March), enlisting the creative services of many local, national and international writers – for details, contact the **Tasmanian Writers' Centre** (☎ 6224 0029; W www.fearless.org.au/taswriters). The **Royal Hobart Show**, an agricultural festival held at the showgrounds in Glenorchy, bookends the year's festivities in late October.

PLACES TO STAY

Hobart has a wide variety of accommodation catering to all tastes and price brackets. The main areas for budget accommodation are the city centre and the suburbs to the immediate north and south. Mid-range and upper-end accommodation is spread all over town. One of the most popular suburbs in which to stay is historic Battery Point – almost all prices here are in the middle to upper range.

PLACES TO STAY – BUDGET
Camping & Cabins

All the camping grounds listed here are out of walking distance of the city centre except the Sandy Bay Caravan Park.

North Eight kilometres from town is **Elwick Cabin & Tourist Park** (☎ 6272 7115, fax 6272 6923; 19 Goodwood Rd, Glenorchy;

unpowered/powered site doubles $11/15, cabin doubles from $50), next to the road leading across Bowen Bridge.

Treasure Island Caravan Park (☎ 6249 2379; 671 Main Rd, Berriedale; unpowered/powered site doubles $16/18, cabin doubles $65-72), 14km out, provides some pleasant camping on a small chunk of land jutting into the Derwent.

South The large, bushy **Sandy Bay Caravan Park** (☎ 6225 1264, fax 6225 1265; 1 Peel St; unpowered/powered site doubles $18/19, on-site van doubles $44, cabin doubles $70) is a 40-minute walk along Sandy Bay Rd from the city centre, or you can catch bus No 54, 55 or 56 from the Macquarie St side of Franklin Square.

East On the Derwent's eastern shore, near Risdon Cove, is **Bowen Park** (☎ 6243 9879; W www.cosycabins.com/bowen; 673 East Derwent Hwy; doubles from $65), with standard self-contained cabins.

Mornington Park (☎ 6244 7070, fax 6244 7199; 346 Cambridge Rd, Mornington; doubles from $65), in the first suburb you reach when approaching the city from the airport, is another large cabin park. Airport transport can be organised.

Hostels

Hobart has a few good hostels and a couple of budget hotels with 'backpacker' accommodation.

City At the rambling **Central City Backpackers** (☎ 6224 2404, 1800 811 507; W www.centralbackpackers.com.au; 138 Collins St; dorm beds/singles/doubles $18/35/45), space is not at a premium, be it in the kitchen or communal areas. The staff are helpful and there are convenient distractions like a pool table and a bar.

Montgomery's (Monty's; ☎ 6231 2660; e engel@southcom.com.au; 9 Argyle St; dorm beds/singles/doubles $20/65/90) is a small hotel with an upstairs YHA hostel. It's centrally located, very clean and modern, but the dorms are a bit squeezy and the 1st-floor common room is inadequate.

Transit Centre Backpackers (☎/fax 6231 2400; 199 Collins St; dorm beds from $17) is a hospitable, functional place upstairs in the Transit Centre. Book ahead if you're arriving late at night to make sure a bed is available and to arrange access (reception closes 11pm).

The Pickled Frog (☎ 6234 7977; w www .thepickledfrog.com; 281 Liverpool St; dorm beds from $17) is one of Hobart's newest hostels, a sunburnt, unselfconscious and cheerfully threadbare place behind the Transit Centre. It has a good, friendly vibe and an in-house bar/café.

Narrara Backpackers (☎ 6231 3191; 88 Goulburn St; dorm beds/doubles $17/44) is a well-maintained backpackers with the feel of a large, friendly group house.

New Sydney Hotel (☎ 6234 4516, fax 6236 9965; 87 Bathurst St; dorm beds/doubles from $16/43) is a laidback, shamrock-green hotel with cooking facilities, 24-hour access, serviceable rooms and small, basic dorms. They get a lot of live music and spirited patrons here, so don't expect a monastic retreat.

Ocean Child Hotel (☎ 6234 6730; 86 Argyle St; dorm beds/doubles $16/32) sometimes looks a bit shabby, but you could do a lot worse for budget accommodation.

North The long-serving, well-equipped YHA hostel **Adelphi Court** (☎ 6228 4829, fax 6278 2047; 17 Stoke St, New Town; dorm beds YHA members/nonmembers $20/23.50, singles with/without bathroom $60/50, doubles with/without bathroom $65/55) has a tired, world-weary look and is surprisingly overpriced considering the old rooms. Take bus No 15 from stop H in Elizabeth St to stop 8, or any bus leaving stop E to stop 13, which is close to Stoke St.

Allport's (☎ 6231 5464; 432 Elizabeth St; w www.tassie.net.au/~allports; dorm beds/ singles/doubles $20/35/50) has come along nicely since setting itself up in an impressive two-storey Italianate mansion just north of the State Cinema. The atmosphere is relaxed and the facilities first-rate, including a spacious kitchen, off-street parking and decent beds. You can also book yourself continental breakfast ($5) or dinner ($10).

Waterfront Lodge Motel (☎ 6228 4748; e waterfrontlodge@bigpond.com; 153 Risdon Rd, New Town Bay; dorm beds $15) is basically a motel but also has a lodge with great-value four-bunk dorms with fridge and microwave. Also an excellent deal for groups is the upstairs two-bedroom apartment in the motel that sleeps six (room $135).

Colleges
During the longer school and university holiday periods you can stay in the hostels and halls of residence used by students.

City The cheapest, most convenient university hostel is **Hollydene House** (☎ 6234 6434; 55 Campbell St; B&B per person $30).

South Next to the university is **Christ College** (☎ 6221 4567; College Rd, Sandy Bay; singles per 1/2/3+ nights $50/40/30), with single rooms and shared facilities; rates include breakfast.

Jane Franklin Hall (☎ 6223 2000; 6 Elboden St, Sth Hobart; singles/doubles $39/50), bordering Davey St, also offers B&B in rooms with shared facilities.

PLACES TO STAY – MID-RANGE
Guesthouses & B&Bs
These are often housed in historic buildings, with facilities that vary widely but are usually of a high standard. Price is a decent guide to quality, except around Battery Point where you inevitably pay. Check-in times for guesthouses and B&Bs are often early afternoon; ask about this when you make your booking if you expect to be arriving in the morning. Guesthouse owners/managers usually live on-site, but there are plenty of exceptions, particularly in Battery Point.

City Splashed with bright colours and attempting an ultra-modern ambience, **Harringtons of Hobart** (☎ 6234 9240; 102 Harrington St; rooms $70-120) has good prices for its location.

Battery Point The two-storey **Barton Cottage** (☎ 6224 1606, 0418 138 849; w www .bartoncottage.com.au; 72 Hampden Rd;

singles/doubles from $120/140) is a National Trust building dating from 1837. It has a few rooms and full cooked breakfasts.

Cromwell Cottage (☎ 6223 6734, 0418 138 849; 6 Cromwell St; singles/doubles $110/130) is a steep-roofed townhouse with dated furnishings, in a beautiful position overlooking the Derwent River.

Colville Cottage (☎ 6223 6968; w www .colvillecottage.com.au; 32 Mona St; singles/ doubles $130/155) is a garden-enclosed B&B, full of colonial heritage but without the clutter. The hosts live on-site.

Tantallon Lodge (☎ 6224 1724; w www .view.com.au/tantallon; 8 Mona St; singles/ doubles $95/130) is the place for those who like an Edwardian feel to their accommodation, and Scottish kippers, smoked cod or pancakes for breakfast. Try for an east-facing room with water views.

North Next to Queen's Domain in the small suburb of Glebe is **Wellington Lodge** (☎ 6231 0614; w www.wwt.com.au/welling tonlodge; 7 Scott St; singles/doubles from $80/ 100), with comfortable B&B in a restored Victorian townhouse.

South Located on the chicane that winds up from Sandy Bay to Mt Nelson, **Crawfords B&B** (☎ 6225 3751; w www.users.big pond.com/msn/waynecrawford; 178 Nelson Rd; singles/doubles from $80/90) offers leisurely accommodation in a homely self-contained unit, with reduced rates for longer stays.

Lapoinya Lodge (☎/fax 6239 1005; 9 Lapoinya Rd, Fern Tree; rooms $90-120) has a special mountain location amid one hectare of gardens, yielding serene views of the city and the D'Entrecasteaux Channel. Its two in-house rooms come with a hearty continental breakfast. To get there, drive towards Mt Wellington but go past the turn-off to the mountain and turn left at Fern Tree Tavern.

East Just across the Tasman Bridge are the walled gardens of **Roseneath** (☎ 6243 6530, fax 6243 0518; 20 Kaoota Rd, Rose Bay; singles $80-95, doubles $95-120), a homely B&B with fine views across the river and a choice of in-house or self-contained rooms.

Orana House (☎ 6243 0404, 1800 622 598; w www.oranahouse.com; 20 Lowelly Rd, Lindisfarne; singles from $80, doubles $110-145) is a stately, well-preserved and hospitable Federation home that squares off to Mt Wellington across the Derwent. It has 10 rooms, including three with spa.

West Perched up in the hills of West Hobart is the aptly named **Crows Nest B&B** (☎/fax 6234 9853; w www.wwt.com.au/crowsnest; 2 Liverpool Crescent; doubles $85-100). It offers distant harbour views and two apartments, the larger one with a kitchenette. Prices include full breakfast provisions.

Hotels

Hobart has a large number of old hotels built from sandstone or brick and usually two to four storeys in height. Most were erected last century and are close to the city centre. The cheaper ones generally offer rooms with shared bathroom and vary in standard depending on how long ago the last major renovation was done. Often the downstairs area is classy while the upstairs rooms are fairly plain. The more expensive hotels have en suite rooms similar to motel rooms.

City Dating from 1927, the central **Brunswick Hotel** (☎ 6234 4981, fax 6298 1206; 67 Liverpool St; singles/doubles $35/50) promises guests an end-of-week sleep undisturbed by loud bands, as it closes early on Friday and Saturday nights.

Alabama Hotel (☎ 6234 3737; 72 Liverpool St; singles/doubles from $35/50), across the road from the Brunswick Hotel, is another decent mid-range hotel option in the inner city, with recently revamped rooms.

Hotel Astor (☎ 6234 6611; w www.astor privatehotel.com.au; 157 Macquarie St; singles/doubles from $60/70) is an excellent downtown deal. This small, atmospheric hotel offers rooms with shared facilities, plus some four- or five-bunk rooms that can be booked by groups ($35 per person). At the time of research, some en suite rooms were also being prepared.

Welcome Stranger Hotel (☎ 6223 6655, fax 6224 1093; cnr Harrington & Davey Sts; singles/doubles $65/80) has very clean en suite rooms, though they grow them small out here.

Theatre Royal Hotel (☎ 6234 6925, fax 6234 6356; 31 Campbell St; singles $45-60, doubles $65-100), located in the vicinity of the hospital, is a gracious old hotel, which has a handful of refurbished rooms. The cheaper rates are for rooms with shared facilities.

Royal Exchange Hotel (☎ 6231 4444; cnr Campbell & Bathurst Sts; singles/doubles $50/65), just down from the Theatre Royal Hotel, has B&B in rooms with their own basic facilities.

Hobart Macquarie Motor Inn (☎ 6234 4422, 1800 802 090, fax 6234 4273; 167 Macquarie St; singles/doubles $85/105) has dated but centrally located rooms.

Hobart Mid City Hotel (☎ 6234 6333, fax 6231 0898; 96 Bathurst St; rooms $120-150) is a similar multistorey deal to the Hobart Macquarie.

Hadleys Hotel (☎ 6223 4355; ⓦ www.do hertyhotels.com.au; 34 Murray St; rooms with/ without buffet breakfast from $140/125) is a sumptuous place that has clocked up over 150 years of hospitality and gained plenty of modern embellishments since its colonial beginnings.

Customs House Hotel (☎ 6234 6645; ⓦ www.view.com.au/customs; 1 Murray St; singles/doubles from $55/75) is an old place with good waterfront views from some of its rooms.

Battery Point Known locally as Shippies, the **Shipwrights Arms Hotel** (☎ 6223 5551; ⓔ shippies@southcom.com.au; 29 Trumpeter St; singles/doubles $45/65) is a cosy landmark pub with basic rooms with shared facilities, plus a two-bedroom option for $150 per double.

Prince of Wales Hotel (☎ 6223 6355, fax 6223 2311; 55 Hampden Rd; singles/doubles from $60/70) has straightforward, well-priced en suite rooms, with rates including breakfast. There are also free laundry facilities available.

North There are several reasonable hotels just out of the inner city.

Waratah Hotel (☎ 6234 3685, fax 6231 2365; 272 Murray St; singles $55-70, doubles $65-80) is a boxy structure where rooms come with continental breakfast. There's a small lounge with coffee-making facilities on each floor.

Claremont Hotel (☎ 6249 1119; 1 Main Rd, Claremont; singles/doubles from $30/55) is a plain outer-city hotel close to the Cadbury factory.

South The grammatically correct **Dr Syntax Hotel** (☎ 6223 6258, fax 6224 0132; 139 Sandy Bay Rd; singles/doubles $50/65) is a lively local pub with small but cheap rooms.

Cascade Hotel (☎ 6223 6385; 22 Cascade Rd, Sth Hobart; singles/doubles from $65/80) is 3km from town on the continuation of Macquarie St and has several self-contained brick units around the back.

West In the heights of West Hobart, 1km from the centre, is the **Marquis of Hastings Hotel** (☎ 6234 3541; 209 Brisbane St; singles/ doubles $70/80), which has plain motel-style rooms with city views.

Globe Hotel (☎ 6223 5800; 178 Davey St; singles/doubles $40/50) is more basic than the Marquis; rooms come with shared facilities and breakfast.

Motels

There are plenty of motels in Hobart, but the majority are typically a long way out and you'll need your own transport to reach them. Some are attached to licensed hotels and often have their own restaurants.

City The name of the **Fountainside Motor Inn** (☎ 6234 2911; ⓦ www.bestwestern.com .au; 40 Brooker Ave; rooms $100-129) is a little misleading, as its actually beside a large roundabout on the northern edge of town, not a fountain. The dowdy rooms are serviced by a 24-hour reception.

Battery Point Two good central motels on Sandy Bay Rd, within walking distance of the city and docks, are **Blue Hills Motel**

(☎ 6223 1777, 1800 030 776; W www.best western.com.au; 96a Sandy Bay Rd; singles/doubles $100/110), which is plain but with a nice feel, and **St Ives Motel** (☎ 6224 1044; 86 Sandy Bay Rd; doubles $89).

North No prizes for guessing that most of the cheaper motels are all on the outskirts of town.

Highway Village Motor Inn (☎ 6272 6721, fax 6273 1061; 897 Brooker Hwy, Berriedale; singles/doubles from $53/64) is a well-managed place with budget rooms and also bigger, more expensive river-view singles/doubles ($77/90).

Waterfront Lodge Motel (☎ 6228 4748; e waterfrontlodge@bigpond.com; 153 Risdon Rd, Lutana; singles/doubles from $55/65) has been nicely spruced up over the last couple of years and offers good-value motel accommodation.

Hobart Tower Motel (☎ 6228 0166; e hobtower@southcom.com.au; 300 Park St, New Town; singles/doubles from $70/75) has numerous well-maintained motel units beside the busy Brooker Hwy.

Argyle Motor Lodge (☎ 6234 2488, 1800 811 504, fax 6234 2292; cnr Lewis & Argyle Sts; doubles from $80) has a range of units and suites, including some with spa.

South Directly opposite the waters of Sandy Bay is the well-equipped, comfortable **Sandy Bay Motor Inn** (☎ 6225 2511; W www.view.com.au/sbmotorin; 429 Sandy Bay Rd; singles/doubles $90/100), which has a frontage colour scheme imported direct from Miami.

East Conveniently located in Montagu Bay, next to the highway near the Tasman Bridge, is **City View Motel** (☎ 6243 8388, fax 6243 8155; 30 Tasman Hwy; doubles from $85). The rooms aren't yet old enough to seem too staid, and come with continental breakfast.

Lindisfarne Motor Inn (☎ 6243 8666, fax 6243 5820; 101-105 East Derwent Hwy, Lindisfarne; singles/doubles from $65/70) is also near the Tasman Bridge, with a crop of unusual-looking units.

West Immerse yourself in colonial decor at friendly **Motel Mayfair** (☎ 6231 1188, fax 6231 2554; 17-19 Cavell St, West Hobart; rooms from $95). There's so much floral carpet, wallpaper and bedspreads that they could almost prompt a hay fever sniffle.

Self-Contained Units

Hobart has a number of self-contained flats and units with fully equipped kitchens. Prices vary, as does what's on offer – the cheaper units are normally flats in apartment blocks while the dearest are historic cottages.

Battery Point Bookings for the one- and two-bedroom units of **Crelin Lodge** (☎ 6223 1777, fax 6223 3995; 1 Crelin St; doubles $100-120) are handled by the nearby Blue Hills Motel (see Motels earlier).

Portsea Terrace (☎ 6234 1616; 62 Montpelier Retreat; singles/doubles from $85/105), close to Hampden Rd, offers 'Accommodation for Gentlefolk' according to a sign in the window, specifically apartments in a two-storey, red-brick 1850s terrace; rates include breakfast.

North The best self-contained bargains are out of the city, like **Graham Court Apartments** (☎ 6278 1333, 1800 811 915, fax 6278 1087; 15 Pirie St, New Town; doubles from $80), which has lots of quality one- to three-bedroom units, some with wheelchair-access.

Northside Holiday Villas (☎ 6272 4472; 9b McGough St, Glenorchy; units $60-115) is another accommodation option in this mould, located beside the Brooker Hwy 8km from Hobart.

South Sandy Bay is a convenient location, as it's close to town and has some good shops and units.

Grosvenor Court (☎ 6223 3422; W www.view.com.au/grosvenor; 42 Grosvenor St; singles/doubles from $90/100) has modest, back-street motel units and self-contained apartments.

Bay Arcade Holiday Units (☎ 6223 2457, fax 6224 1153; 163 Sandy Bay Rd; singles/doubles from $60/80) has large, inexpensive units. Stow away in dark downstairs rooms or grab a balcony-laden room upstairs.

East On the eastern shore of the Derwent you'll find the cheap **Silwood Park Holiday Unit** (☎ 6244 4278; 7 Silwood Ave, Howrah; singles/doubles $65/70), which can sleep five and is close to Howrah Beach.

West Two kilometres from the city centre, with facilities for disabled and elderly travellers, a games room and an indoor pool, is **Bay View Villas** (☎ 6234 7611; 34 Poets Rd, West Hobart; doubles from $110). Its two-and three-bedroom units – the east-facing ones with bay views and thus more expensive – get booked out well in advance at peak times.

PLACES TO STAY – TOP END

Compared with other Australian capital cities, the top-end accommodation in Hobart is cheap, generally starting at around $120 a double. Outside the peak season and holidays, many of the plush hotels offer special weekend accommodation/dinner deals and walk-in rates, while luxury B&Bs can also reduce their prices.

Guesthouses & B&Bs

The restoration work on many of Hobart's older mansions has resulted in some fine accommodation.

City Plush, high-ceilinged heritage rooms and cooked breakfasts are the order of the day at the well-groomed, Regency-style **Macquarie Manor** (☎ 6224 4999, 1800 243 044; W www.macmanor.com.au; 172 Macquarie St; singles/doubles from $125/160).

Battery Point Built circa 1834, **Battery Point Manor** (☎ 6224 0888, fax 6224 2254; 13-15 Cromwell St; doubles $125-200) has a wide range of in-house rooms, most with king-size beds and views over the Derwent, plus a two-bedroom cottage. Prices include buffet-style breakfast.

Ascot of Battery Point (☎ 6224 2434; W www.view.com.au/ascot; 6 Colville St; singles/doubles from $115/150) has expan-

sive, well-outfitted rooms; the downs[...] rooms have higher ceilings. Rooms co[...] with cooked breakfast.

Battery Point Guest House (Mandalay; ☎ 6224 2111, fax 6224 3648; 7 McGregor St; singles/doubles from $120/150), located close to Salamanca Place, was originally the coach house and stables for the nearby Lenna of Hobart. Rooms come with cooked breakfast.

Jarem Waterfront B&B (☎ 6223 8216; e jarem@bigpond.com; 8 Clarke Ave; singles/doubles from $110/150) is a modern guesthouse with bright rooms in an excellent waterfront location.

Gattonside (☎ 6224 1200, 1800 223 410, fax 6224 0207; 51-53 Sandy Bay Rd; doubles $150-200) is an appealing Victorian manor. Its grand rooms, one equipped for disabled travellers, come with a hearty continental breakfast.

North The compact Georgian **Lodge on Elizabeth** (☎ 6231 3830; W www.thelodge .com.au; 249 Elizabeth St; singles/doubles from $105/130) presents its rooms in serious yesteryear style.

Elms of Hobart (☎ 6231 3277; W www .theelmsofhobart.com; 452 Elizabeth St; doubles $160-230) is a WWI-era mansion featuring lovely gardens, luxurious rooms and cooked breakfasts. Dinners can also be arranged on some weeknights.

Wendover (☎ 6278 2066, fax 6278 2329; 10 Wendover Place, New Town; doubles $150-200), 4km north of the city centre in a leafy little street, is one of the city's original mansions, built in 1815. This National Trust–classified accommodation includes several spacious apartments.

Thirlmere Manor (☎ 6228 1777; W www .thirlmere-manor.com.au; 92 Pedder St, New Town; doubles $125-190) is an 1890s homestead that merges colonial decor and old gardens with modern conveniences like a heated pool and aromatherapy treatments; a place to indulge the senses.

South Close to the Sandy Bay shopping area is **Merre Be's** (☎ 6224 2900; W www .merrebes.com.au; 17 Gregory St; B&B doubles

ART

l house in a quiet street, sformed into a boutique gourmet breakfasts. *(☎ 6225 1005; W www .....erley; 391 Sandy Bay Rd; singles $108-124, doubles $118-136)*, opposite the casino, is an elegant, high-ceilinged Victorian house with a scattering of antiques and old-fashioned rooms. Double-glazing negates noise from the adjacent main road. Breakfast is available from $6 extra per person.

Hotels & Motels

There are a couple of luxury lofts in the city centre.

City International-standard indulgence is available at the waterfront monolith known as the **Hotel Grand Chancellor** *(☎ 6235 4535, 1800 625 138; W www.grandchancellor .com; 1 Davey St; rooms $150-400)*.

Corus Hotel Hobart *(☎ 6232 2225, 1800 030 003; e reservations.hobart@corushotels .com.au; 156 Bathurst St; rooms $140-250)* has very comfortable rooms and significantly reduced walk-in rates during slow times.

Savoy Hobart *(☎ 6220 2300; W www .savoyhobart.com.au; 38 Elizabeth St; suites $140-320)* has superb modern suites – including barrier-free rooms – in the heart of downtown, making it ideal for meeting-plagued businesspeople. It advertises undercover parking, but this is off-site at the nearby Grand Chancellor.

Battery Point Foregoing the heritage look for the ultra-contemporary is the exceptionally well-catered **Salamanca Inn** *(☎ 6223 3300; W www.salamancainn.com.au; 10 Gladstone St; doubles $200-270)*, just behind Salamanca Place. Walk-in rates can be much lower, depending on the season.

Lenna of Hobart *(☎ 6232 3900, 1800 030 633; W www.lenna.com.au; 20 Runnymede St; doubles $170-245)* is ostensibly a grand Italianate mansion, but all the accommodation is in a newer concrete wing. The rooms are huge and the facilities are also very good, though the decor is starting to look a little dated.

North The 63-suite **Rydges Hobart** *(☎ 6231 1588, 1800 801 703; W www.rydges.com; cnr Argyle & Lewis Sts; rooms $140-280)* is in a restored set of heritage-listed buildings and offers standard hotel rooms and antique-dotted suites. Discount packages are frequently available.

South Three kilometres south of the city centre is **Wrest Point** *(☎ 6225 0112, 1800 030 611; W www.wrestpoint.com.au; 410 Sandy Bay Rd; motel/hotel doubles from $120/240)*, a conspicuous waterfront accommodation complex based around a flashy, well-established casino. Package deals regularly give attractive discounts for the more expensive rooms in the hotel's luxury-stuffed tower.

Mayfair Plaza Motel *(☎ 6220 9900; W www.mayfairplaza.com.au; 236-244 Sandy Bay Rd; rooms from $130)* has cavernous modern rooms that are lined up along an indoor court at Sandy Bay. There are business conveniences like Internet access and a secretarial service available. One room has wheelchair-access.

Apartments

Quite a few inner-city apartments have opened in Hobart over the past few years.

Quest Waterfront *(☎ 6224 8630; W www .questapartments.com.au; 3 Brooke St; doubles $125-205)* has top-end suites and apartments, plus some cheaper motel-style rooms that are great value considering the location.

Trinity House *(☎ 6236 9656; W www .questapartments.com.au; 149 Brooker Ave; apartments $130-240)* is another Quest complex, this one just north of the centre in Glebe. It has spacious serviced apartments with a long list of mod-cons, including data points.

Oakford on the Pier *(☎ 6220 6600, 1800 620 462; W www.the-ascott.com; suites $170-200)* is a complex at the end of Elizabeth St Pier that is absolutely riddled with self-contained luxury accommodation.

The Old Woolstore *(☎ 6235 5355; W www.oldwoolstore.com.au; 1 Macquarie St; rooms $160-220)* is a lavishly equipped hotel and apartment complex that has retained the facade of the original Sullivans Cove building.

Salamanca Terraces (☎ 6232 3900, 1800 030 633; W www.lenna.com.au; 93 Salamanca Place; doubles $175-275) is one of Hobart's newest and best-situated luxury developments, a gathering of serviced studios and apartments (which include two-bedroom versions) overlooking Salamanca Place. The complex is managed by neighbouring Lenna of Hobart.

Oakford on Salamanca (☎ 6220 6600, 1800 620 462; W www.the-ascott.com; 8 Salamanca Place; doubles $175-275) has a similar upmarket pedigree to nearby Salamanca Terraces, with modern and well-equipped apartments. It's managed by its sibling hotel on Elizabeth St Pier: everything from inquiries to check-in should be directed there.

Battery Point Boutique Accommodation (☎ 6224 2244, 0407 503 676, fax 6224 2243; 27-29 Hampden Rd; doubles $135-155) is a block of four stylishly modern serviced apartments in the heart of Battery Point; direct inquiries to unit No 1.

Self-Contained Units & Cottages

There's a more-than-reasonable selection of units and cottages in this price bracket.

Battery Point With mostly two-bedroom units and a sandstone facade that's only 25 years young, **Avon Court Holiday Apartments** (☎ 6223 4837, 1800 807 257; W www.view.com.au/avon; 4 Colville St; doubles $95-140) makes for good, modern family accommodation in the area.

The Grand Old Duke (☎ 6224 1606; W www.bartoncottage.com.au; 31 Hampden Rd; doubles $165) is a self-contained apartment with polished floorboards, on the ground floor of a historic building smack in the centre of Battery Point.

Coopers Cottage (☎ 6224 0355; W www.cooperscottage.com.au; 44a Hampden Rd; doubles from $135), hemmed in behind a shopfront on Hampden Rd, is a cosy self-contained place to stay. If you're looking for a motor yacht to hire, ask the owners.

North Located beside the greenery of Queen's Domain and a short walk from the city is **Corinda's Cottages** (☎ 6234 1590; W www.corindascottages.com.au; 17 Glebe St, Glebe; doubles $160-220), with accommodation in the sumptuously renovated outbuildings of an old mansion.

South Fairly close to town is **Woolmers Inn** (☎ 6223 7355, 1800 030 780; e woolmersinn@bigpond.com.au; 123-127 Sandy Bay Rd; doubles $100-130), with very accommodating studio and two-bedroom units.

East Otago Cottage (☎ 6273 3922; W www.tassie.net.au/otagocottage; 19 Restdown Dr, Otago; doubles $160, extra guests $33) has three bedrooms, lots of warm timber, a lovely riverside aspect and privacy – a great place to base family explorations or to just mellow.

Southeast of Hobart airport, a full 18km from town but close to a good swimming beach, is **Pines Resort** (☎ 6248 6222; Surf Rd, Seven Mile Beach; doubles from $130), which has its own tavern.

West On the northwestern edge of the centre is **Warwick Cottages** (☎ 6254 1264; 119 Warwick St, West Hobart; doubles $170), comprising two units that can each take four guests; breakfast is provided.

PLACES TO EAT
Restaurants

Hobart's waterfront streets, docks and piers are the collective epicentre of the city's restaurant scene, though there are also plenty of fine eateries in the landlocked urban blocks.

Seafood Tucked away in a weathered pavilion on the foreshore at Sandy Bay Point is **Prosser's on the Beach** (☎ 6225 2276; Beach Rd; mains $12-25; open lunch & from 6pm Wed-Fri, from 6pm Mon, Tues & Sat), one of Hobart's most highly rated seafood eateries. You can get a rather large, tiered seafood platter for $35 per person.

Drunken Admiral (☎ 6234 1903; 17-19 Hunter St; mains $18-26; open from 6pm daily), opposite the Grand Chancellor, serves up a bit of everything on its Deck-hand's Platter for two ($65).

Upper Deck (☎ 6231 2121; Victoria Dock; open daily), nearby in Mures Fish Centre, is a popular wooden parlour with a boat suspended from the ceiling and a great selection of fishfood.

Squid Roe (☎ 6234 7978; 144 Harrington St; mains $10-22; open from 6pm Tues-Thur & Sat, lunch & from 6pm Fri) is a very good BYO restaurant with the freshest of plated seafood offerings.

Kelleys Seafood Restaurant (☎ 6224 7225; cnr James & Knopwood Sts; mains $20-34; open noon-3pm & from 6pm Mon-Fri, from 6pm Sat & Sun) is located in an 1849 sailmaker's cottage in the back streets of Battery Point. The menu favours Atlantic salmon, sea trout and blue eye.

Poseidon's (☎ 6223 5977; 54 King St, Sandy Bay; mains $13-22; open from 6.30pm Wed-Sat) does marine cooking with Greek style – its speciality is BBQ octopus. Plenty of non-seafood Greek standards are also available.

Italian A popular place for pasta, gourmet pizzas and seafood is **Trattoria Casablanca** (☎ 6234 9900; 213 Elizabeth St; mains $11-22; open 5.15pm-late Wed-Mon).

Rozzini's (☎ 6234 1366; 201 Elizabeth St; mains $16-20; open 5pm-11pm Mon-Sat) has a nice modern atmosphere and lots of pasta and pan-fried meats.

Gusto Italiano (☎ 6234 9100; 186 Collins St; mains $7-16; open noon-2.30pm & 5pm-late Mon-Fri, 5pm-late Sat) has good, fresh-made pasta at very reasonable prices, plus pizzas, grills and ice cream.

Da Angelo Ristorante (☎ 6223 7011; 47 Hampden Rd, Battery Point; mains $9-15; open 5pm-11pm daily) is a bustling establishment specialising in fundamental Italian cuisine. Try the macaroni Siciliana for something with zing.

Other solid Italian restaurants include the licensed **Maldini** (☎ 6223 4460; 47 Salamanca Place; mains $10-24; open 8am-late daily) and the laid-back **Riviera Ristorante Italiano** (☎ 6234 3230; 15 Hunter St; mains $13-19; open 6pm-late Tues-Sat).

Indian Some outstanding Indian curries are available at the **Tandoor & Curry House** (☎ 6234 6905; 101 Harrington St; mains $10-15.50; open noon-2.30pm & 5.30pm-10.30pm Mon-Fri, 5.30pm-10.30pm Sat).

Flavour of India (☎ 6223 5733; 196 Macquarie St; mains $11-16; open 11.30am-3pm & 5.30pm-11pm Mon-Fri, 5.30pm-11pm Sat & Sun) has similarly fine Indian food, with plenty of spiced-up meat and vegetarian dishes.

Annapurna (☎ 6236 9500; 305 Elizabeth St, Nth Hobart; mains $10-15; open noon-3pm & 5.30pm-10pm daily) is another worthwhile curry choice, and it has a delicious variety of both northern and southern Indian cuisine.

Magic Curries (☎ 6223 4500; 41 Hampden Rd; mains $11-15; open from 5.30pm daily), on Battery Point's main drag, has a good variety of dine-in or takeaway food, including some nice vegetarian options.

Asian In the middle of town is **Thai Hut** (☎ 6234 4914; 80 Elizabeth St; mains $8-15; open 11am-3pm & 6pm-9.30pm Mon-Fri, 6pm-9.30pm Sat), with lots of meaty mains and a half-dozen vegie meals like pad thai (vegie stir-fry with spicy noodles).

Vanidol's (☎ 6234 9307; 353 Elizabeth St; mains $11-17; open 6pm-late Tues-Sun), in the Elizabeth St restaurant strip in North Hobart, has a handful of Indian and Indonesian dishes, but predominantly Thai curries and stir-fries. It also serves reasonably priced seafood and plenty of vegetarian.

Dede (☎ 6231 1068; 369 Elizabeth St, Nth Hobart; mains $10-18; open from 5.30pm daily), on the same strip as Vanidol's, is a BYO eatery with a menu featuring a triad of Thai, Indonesian and vegetarian choices.

Sen's Asian Sensation (☎ 6236 9345; 345 Elizabeth St; mains $9-20; open 11am-10pm daily) is a delicious yum cha and noodle bar, to dine in or takeaway.

A few Chinese restaurants worth trying are **Golden Bamboo** (☎ 6234 2282; 116 Elizabeth St) and **Flourishing Court** (☎ 6223 2559; 252 Macquarie St). There's also an extensive choice of Chinese dishes, among other Asian options, at Wrest Point's **The**

HOBART

Asian Restaurant *(☎ 6225 0112; 410 Sandy Bay Rd)*.

The Sushi Bar *(☎ 6231 1790; Victoria Dock; mains $10-25; open noon-2.30pm & 6pm-9pm Mon-Sat)*, in Mures Fish Centre, serves reasonable Japanese meals.

Mikaku *(☎ 6224 0882; 87 Salamanca Place; mains from $16; open noon-2.30pm & from 6pm Mon-Sat, from 6pm Sun)* also prepares decent Japanese food.

Tea House Restaurant *(☎ 6224 8700; The Galleria, 33 Salamanca Place; mains $13-21; open 5.30pm-late daily)* is a long-established and highly reputable emporium of Singaporean and Malaysian food. From the laksa to the spicy Asian soups, you can't go wrong.

Mexican In North Hobart you can fill up on tasty burritos, enchiladas and other stomach-bulging Mexican food at **Amigo's** *(☎ 6234 6115; 329 Elizabeth St; mains from $12; open dinner daily)*.

Turkish Serving fine Turkish dinners is **Anatolia** *(☎ 6231 1770; 321 Elizabeth St, Nth Hobart; mains $12-17; open 6pm-late Tues-Sun)*, which often celebrates Saturday with a belly dance or two.

Pashas *(☎ 6231 9822; Elizabeth St Pier; mains $16-25; open noon-late Mon-Sat, 9am-5pm Sun)* is awash with the tempting aromas of Kurdish-influenced Turkish dishes.

French The suburban BYO **Le Provencal** *(☎ 6224 2526; 417 Macquarie St, Sth Hobart; mains from $13; open dinner Tues-Sat)*, on the corner of Macquarie and Weld Sts, has wonderful, hearty French fare.

A Splash of Paris *(☎ 6224 2200; Elizabeth St Pier; mains $20-25; open noon-3pm & from 6.30pm daily)* is an ultra-modern though geographically misplaced eatery with a great waterside ambience. Its cuisine is French-influenced rather than French-dominated, so expect stylised international cooking.

Other Cuisine Set in the flamboyantly renovated confines of the old city mill is **Rockerfellers** *(☎ 6234 3490; 11 Morrison St; mains $17-22; open lunch & dinner daily)*, a semi-formal eatery serving *confit* duck and

seared lamb. Jazz and tapas are on the menu from 6pm Sunday and Monday.

Sisco's *(☎ 6223 2059; Murray St Pier; mains $18-25; open nightly Tues-Sat)*, with good water views from upstairs, cooks up seafood like Moreton Bay bugs with Mediterranean flair – the paella is very good.

Blue Skies *(☎ 6224 3747; Murray St Pier; mains $15-25; open from 11am-late daily)*, earthbound beneath Sisco's, is an enormous waterfront eatery with a big range of pastas, risottos and light meals. Grab an outside table if you can.

Mummaluka *(☎ 6224 2929; 89 Salamanca Place; mains $15-22; open 11.30am-2.30pm & from 5.30pm Mon-Fri, from 5.30pm Sat & Sun)* has adopted a tenuous African theme for its decor and then embarked on a light-hearted romp through international cookery. If you don't like the sound of a 'Bucket of Sea Trash' or 'Mumbo Jumbo Gumbo', sit at the bar and sink a Guinness and a half-dozen oysters for $13.

Mr Wooby's *(☎ 6234 3466; Wooby's Lane; mains $25; open from 6pm daily)*, in a lane between Salamanca Place and Salamanca Square, and named after a well-known 19th-century local stallholder, likes meat: from quail and salmon to beef tapenade.

Elbow Room *(☎ 6224 4254; 9-11 Murray St; mains $22-28; open lunch & dinner Tues-Fri, dinner Sat)* is an intimate restaurant in an old stone basement. The menu focuses on Tassie produce, hence the home-made gnocchi with King Island blue cheese, and is highly recommended.

Ball & Chain Grill *(☎ 6223 2655; 87 Salamanca Place; mains $17-24; open noon-2.30pm & from 6pm Mon-Fri, from 6pm Sat & Sun)* does your meat any way you like it on a charcoal grill and should be avoided by committed vegetarians.

Astor Grill *(☎ 6234 3809; 157 Macquarie St; mains $20-30; open lunch & dinner Mon-Fri, dinner Sat & Sun)* features lots of beef char-grilled to order, and also seafood.

Restaurant Gondwana *(☎ 6224 9900; cnr Hampden Rd & Francis St; dinner mains $10-28; open noon-2.30pm & 6pm-9.30pm Tues-Fri, 6pm-9.30pm Sat)* has moved on nicely from its ancient-continent origins and now serves contemporary nouveau-Aussie fare like twice-roasted duck, eucalyptus-smoked kangaroo and polenta-crusted Fremantle sardines. It also has some great blackboard desserts.

Mount Nelson Signal Station Restaurant (☎ 6223 3407; 700 Nelson Rd; mains $12-22; open 9.30am-4.30pm daily), set in Mt Nelson's historic chief signalman's house, is an elegant semi-formal restaurant with a panoramic view. It serves morning/afternoon teas and light/full lunches, and also has a good selection of desserts.

Cornelian Bay Boathouse (☎ 6228 9289; Queen's Walk; mains $18-22; open noon-3pm & from 6.30pm Mon-Sat, noon-3pm Sun) is a popular, stylish restaurant-bar in a great location on Cornelian Bay, just north of Queen's Domain. It serves contemporary cuisine like vegetable pilaf and red anise, and Sichuan pepper-braised lamb.

Most of Hobart's expensive hotels have expensive restaurants, including Lenna of Hobart's **Alexander's Restaurant** (☎ 6232 3900; 20 Runnymede St, Battery Point), Wrest Point's **The Point Revolving Restaurant** (☎ 6225 0112; 410 Sandy Bay Rd) and the Hotel Grand Chancellor's **Meehan's Restaurant** (☎ 6235 4535; 1 Davey St). The nightly $44 buffet dinner at **The Cove**, also at the Grand Chancellor, is literally a feast and includes a ton of fresh seafood.

Cafés & Wine Bars

Located in a former hotel (now private apartments) 2km south of Wrest Point is the **Beach House Hotel Cafe Bar** (☎ 6225 4644; 646 Sandy Bay Rd; mains $14-18; open from 9am daily), a laidback café/bar with beachy decor and creative seafood and pasta.

Cumquat (☎ 6234 5858; 10 Criterion St; meals $5-15; open from 8am Mon-Fri) is a vibrant café that serves up creative fare for breakfast, lunch and dinner. It caters amply to vegetarians, vegans and coeliac sufferers.

Cafe Toulouse (☎ 6234 3806; 79 Harrington St; open 7.30am-6pm Mon-Fri, 8am-4pm Sat) sells an abundance of croissants, danishes, quiche and gateaux.

Noobar (☎ 6234 6669; upstairs, 37a Elizabeth St; mains $10-12; open 11am-5pm Mon-Thur, 11am-late Fri, 11am-4pm Sat) is an innovative café/bar making full use of the slender noodle, which you can have wok-style (ramen noodles) or soup-style (udon noodles). Cocktails and plenty of other booze are also available.

Afterword Cafe (☎ 6224 2488; 140 Collins St; open 9am-5.30pm Mon-Fri, 9am-5pm Sat, 10am-4pm Sun), upstairs at Fullers Bookshop, is good for browsing your latest purchase (note: that's purchase, not pre-purchase) over a bagel, frittata or cup of java.

Kaos Cafe (☎ 6231 5699; 237 Elizabeth St; mains $10-15; open noon-8pm Mon, noon-midnight Tues-Fri, 10am-10pm Sat) busies itself with a fine assortment of meat and vegie dishes, including upmarket burgers and salads.

Mummy's (☎ 6224 0124; 38 Waterloo Crescent, Battery Point; mains $7-15; open 10am-late daily), a long-serving, late-night licensed café with a bright interior and a small courtyard, has a regular menu of vegie burgers and focaccias, and daily specials like stir-fry and fish.

Z's (☎ 6224 7124; 60 Hampden Rd; mains $12-23; open 10am-late daily) is a café/wine bar adding a distinctive cosmopolitan flavour to Battery Point, with food ranging from omelettes to tapas and Moroccan vegetable couscous, plus heart-starting coffee.

Retro Cafe (☎ 6223 3073; 31 Salamanca Place; mains $8-12; open 8am-6pm Mon-Sat, 8.30am-6pm Sun) is a hip, brisk café usually crowded with people vying for one of the blackboard specials, like spinach roti or a beef or vegie burger.

Zum Cafe (☎ 6223 7511; 27 Salamanca Place; mains $7-18; open 7am-6pm Mon-Fri, 7am-5pm Sat & Sun) is a café/bakery with good breakfast choices like pancakes and eggs Benedict or Florentine, and plenty of risottos, pastas and pastries to plug further holes in your stomach.

Foyer Espresso Bar (☎ 6223 7228; dishes $3-8; open 8.30am-5pm Tues-Sat) is an artsy place for a caffeine fix, not surprising considering it's set up outside the doors to the Peacock Theatre within the Salamanca Arts Centre. It also serves scrambled eggs, Welsh rarebit and various smoothies.

Sugo (☎ 6224 5690; 9 Salamanca Square; lunch $7-12; open 8am-5pm Mon-Thur, 8am-9pm Fri, 9am-5pm Sat & Sun) has tasty pasta, pizza, focaccias and salads.

Sal's (☎ 6224 3667; 55 Salamanca Square; mains $11-24; open 7am-late daily) is a large, perpetually busy eatery/bar that spills out into Salamanca Square. The broad menu includes salads, pastas, grills, burgers and seafood; there's also a carvery, salad bar and takeaway section fronting Salamanca Place.

Bar Celona (☎ 6224 7557; 24 Salamanca Square; mains $10-15; lunch 11am-3pm daily), a few doors down from Sal's, has a wine-bar menu featuring wood-fired pizzas.

T-42° (☎ 6224 7742; Elizabeth St Pier; mains $11-22; open 9.30am-late daily) has upmarket fare like chilli cuttlefish and char-grilled kangaroo, and views to both sides of the pier; it also does a good weekend brunch from 10am to 3pm.

Sticky Fingers (☎ 6223 1077; Murray St Pier; open from 11am daily), a few piers south, will drown you in sundaes, spiders (the edible kind) and bubblegum-flavoured ice cream.

Golden Tulip Patisserie (☎ 6224 3122; 15 Magnet Court, Sandy Bay; open 7.30am-6pm Mon-Fri, 7.30am-2pm Sat) is favoured by an older clientele for its fine cakes and pastries, like sour cherry flan.

Tonic (☎ 6224 4444; 217 Sandy Bay Rd; mains $12-24; open from 11am Mon-Fri, from 10am Sat & Sun) feeds a mainly corporate crowd in its fashionably sparse interior and on its big outside deck with a limited menu that includes baby squid and quail. The wine list, however, is mammoth.

Tasmanian Coffee Roasters (☎ 6223 5822; 14 Gregory St; meals $4-8; open 9.30am-5pm Mon-Fri, 10.30am-2pm Sat) is a linoleum-floored coffee-grinding favourite of local bean-lovers, selling roasts and blends from New Guinea, Colombia and Ethiopia. It also serves light food like cheese platters and salads.

Machine Laundry Café (☎ 6224 9922; 12 Salamanca Square; open 8am-6pm daily) is a laundry with a twist. Here you can munch all-day breakfasts or polenta pizza and sip serious coffee while your cl spin; meals end at 3pm.

Pub Meals

Hobart's pubs dish out dependable, if so what predictable counter and bistro meals Lunch hours are usually from noon to 2.30pm and dinner is from 6pm to 8pm daily, though a few places have declared that Monday and/or Tuesday are cookery-free zones.

In the city, is the **Brunswick Hotel** (☎ 6234 4981; 67 Liverpool St; mains from $10). The **New Sydney Hotel** (☎ 6234 4516; 87 Bathurst St; mains from $10) is popular for its tasty, filling grills and seafood. **Montgomery's** (☎ 6231 2660; cnr Argyle & Macquarie Sts), which has bowed out of the credibility stakes by declaring itself 'Hobart's home of karaoke', has good mains and cheaper counter meals like Guinness casserole. The **Hope & Anchor Tavern** (☎ 6236 9982; 65 Macquarie St), dating from 1807, has a great, antiquated upstairs dining room and decent bar snacks.

Other commendable pubs in the city include the **Customs House Hotel** (☎ 6234 6645; 1 Murray St), serving schnitzel, laksa and cheap counter meals; the lively **Brooke Street Bar & Cafe** (☎ 6234 6254; 19 Morrison St); **Irish Murphy's** (☎ 6223 1119; 21 Salamanca Place; mains $10-16); the ever-popular **Knopwood's Retreat** (☎ 6223 5808; 39 Salamanca Place); and the **Theatre Royal Hotel** (☎ 6234 6925; 31 Campbell St).

In North Hobart, give the good food at the **Republic Bar & Cafe** (☎ 6234 6954; 299 Elizabeth St) a try. In Battery Point, the **Shipwright's Arms** (☎ 6223 5551; 29 Trumpeter St) is popular with locals for its seafood and appealing beer garden, and is also well worth a visit.

Takeaways & Light Meals

The following places all have food for under $10 and most are open for lunch and dinner daily.

Banjo's (☎ 6230 887; 201 Sandy Bay Rd), the ubiquitous Tasmanian chain-bakery, serves a variety of baked snacks and light meals from breakfast time onwards (but

ns stomaching

...9 Murray St; open ...lament House, is a ...asserie serving home- ...and warm octopus salad. ...cRoss (☎ 6223 3186; 57-59 ...is a bakery/café serving mini-pizza, friattas and an array of great cakes. Being in the middle of Battery Point, it gets jammed at lunchtime, so be early if you want a table.

Little India (☎ 6231 1167; 75 Harrington St), a tandoori-coloured place, has two-dish curry and vegetarian lunch specials for $6.

Little Bali (☎ 6234 3426; 84a Harrington St) has mouth-watering Indonesian takeaway, while next door is **Little Salama** (☎ 6234 9383; 82a Harrington St), selling Mediterranean kebabs and Asian grills.

Vanny's (☎ 6234 1457; 181 Liverpool St), near Little Salama, is a Cambodian place with numerous curries, including egg and bean curd.

Fortune Court (☎ 6231 3327; 131 Collins St; open Mon-Sat) is a Chinese takeaway that avoids the use of MSG.

Dave's Noodle Box (☎ 6234 2868; 346 Elizabeth St), in North Hobart, unloads boxes of tasty tom yam, Malaysian curries and Japanese and Singaporean noodles.

Bangkok Wok (☎ 6224 7400; Shop 6-8, 236-244 Sandy Bay Rd), in Sandy Bay, dishes out a good range of simple Thai, including plenty of vegetarian with either steamed rice or noodles.

There are a number of takeaways at Salamanca Place, most with outdoor tables, such as the cheap **Vietnamese Kitchen** (☎ 6223 2188; 61 Salamanca Place), where you can get two courses plus rice or noodles for $7. In Salamanca Square you'll find **Toshi's Kitchen** (☎ 6223 1230; 8 Salamanca Square; mains $9-15), an excellent Japanese takeaway with sushi for $3 per two pieces; and **Salamanca Bakehouse** (☎ 6224 6300; 5 Salamanca Square), its ovens disgorging pies, pastries and rolls 24 hours around the clock.

In the Elizabeth St Pier complex is **Fish Frenzy** (☎ 6231 2134; Elizabeth St Pier), its takeaway servings including fish burgers and fresh oysters. Across the bridge, on Constitution Dock, are a couple of permanently moored barges that serve as **floating takeaway seafood stalls**. Close by is Mures Fish Centre, where you can get excellent fresh fish and chips and other seafood at the **Lower Deck** (☎ 6231 2121; Victoria Dock). Another place that sells good fish and chips is **The Fish Bar** (☎ 6234 5691; 50 King St, Sandy Bay). For even cheaper takeaway seafood and all manner of fried and battered fare in Sandy Bay, try **Mykonos** (☎ 6223 2072; 165 Sandy Bay Rd; open until late).

You can get takeaway pizzas at many places around town, including **Marti Zucco** (☎ 6234 9611; 364 Elizabeth St), **La Porchetta** (☎ 6231 6777; 315 Elizabeth St) and **Concettas** (☎ 6234 4624; 340 Elizabeth St), all of which are on North Hobart's Elizabeth St eatery/shopping strip; **Da Angelo Ristorante** (☎ 6223 7011; 47 Hampden Rd) in Battery Point; and **La Bella Pizza** (☎ 6224 2425; 163 Sandy Bay Rd) and **Solo Pasta** (☎ 6234 9898; 50b King St) in Sandy Bay. All the aforementioned places have Italian restaurants on-site.

Self-Catering

On the northern edge of the centre is a **Woolworths Supermarket** (189 Campbell St), while in Sandy Bay there's a **Coles Supermarket** (246 Sandy Bay Rd).

ENTERTAINMENT

The Mercury newspaper, published daily, lists the details of Hobart's main entertainment venues.

Bars & Pubs

See Cafés & Wine Bars in the Places to Eat section for a few café-bars that are fine for an intoxicating late afternoon or evening. The list includes **Bar Celona** (☎ 6224 7557; 24 Salamanca Square; open 11am-late daily), a wine bar with the interior of an upmarket saloon, attracting mainly suited types late in the weekday. There's an excellent choice of wine by the glass/bottle, $9 cocktails and some free laidback music on the weekend.

T-42° (☎ 6224 7742; Elizabeth St Pier; open 9.30am-late daily) seems to draw a mass of barflies to its minimalist interior after dinner with plenty of booze and funky background music.

Isobar (☎ 6231 6600; 11 Franklin Wharf; open noon-late Mon-Sat) is one of Hobart's more colourful, cool and popular hang-outs, with free live music in the downstairs bar/café most nights. It also has an upstairs club (see the Clubs section following).

Knopwood's Retreat (☎ 6223 5808; 39 Salamanca Place; open 10am-late daily) is a perennial Hobart pub favourite, usually hidden behind a solid mass of sidewalk drinkers on Friday night.

Bakers (☎ 6223 5206; cnr Barrack & Macquarie Sts; open 11am-late Mon-Fri, noon-late Sat) is a good place for a drink, be it wine, beer or cocktails. Food is available all day.

Cow (☎ 6231 1200; 112 Murray St; open noon-11pm Mon-Fri, 6.30pm-midnight Sat), formerly the old Tattersalls (Tatts) Hotel, is now a loungy meeting point for upwardly mobile ranch-hands, with plenty of space around the bar to strike a casual pose.

For details of more bars and pubs, see the upcoming Folk, Rock, Blues & Jazz section.

Clubs

A great place for late-night drinks and a mixture of live music and DJs playing to the techno/house crowd is **Round Midnight** (☎ 6224 8249; 39 Salamanca Place; admission Wed free, Thur $5, Fri & Sat $7; open from 8pm Wed-Sat), above Knopwood's Retreat. Sharing the premises is the also-popular bar/club **Syrup** (admission Wed free, Thur $5, Fri & Sat $7; open from 8pm Wed-Sat).

Regines Nite Club (☎ 6225 0112; 410 Sandy Bay Rd; admission $4/6 Fri/Sat, free other nights; open 10pm-4am Mon & Wed-Sat) is another local mainstay (albeit a poorly spelt one) in the towering Wrest Point complex.

Isobar the club (admission $6; open 10pm-5am Fri & Sat), upstairs at Isobar the bar, was originally launched to great fanfare as Carbon and proved rampantly popular for a while, but since its name change and the adoption of a more commercial musical agenda, it's struggled to pull the original crowds. Check it out and see what you think.

lalaland (☎ 6224 9531; 192 ... adult/concession $8/5) is a ga... located above Bakers bar/caf... opens its clubbing borders from 9pm to 4am on the second and fourth Saturdays of each month.

Folk, Rock, Blues & Jazz

Mostly free, low-key Irish folk, jazz and blues plays nightly from Tuesday to Saturday at the **New Sydney Hotel** (☎ 6234 4516; 87 Bathurst St), but the occasional pub-rock outfit and end-of-week crowds add a few decibels. It has a dozen beers on tap and is a sociable place for a drink.

Irish Murphy's (☎ 6223 1119; 21 Salamanca Place) has fake, prehistoric-looking earthenware walls that were perhaps built by a Guinness-soused Fred Flintstone, but it's nonetheless a popular pub with free live bands from 10pm Thursday to Sunday.

Sal's (☎ 6224 3667; 55 Salamanca Square), around the corner from Murphy's, amplifies some relaxed chords from Friday to Sunday nights (free), and stages the occasional bit of live theatre.

Republic Bar & Cafe (☎ 6234 6954; 299 Elizabeth St, Nth Hobart) is a fine, raucous Deco bar with usually (not always) free live music and the occasional comedy gig, available most nights from around 8pm.

Other bar/pub gig options (all free) include the **Prince of Wales Hotel** (☎ 6223 6355; 55 Hampden Rd), with bands on Wednesday and Sunday nights; **Brooke St Bar & Cafe** (☎ 6234 6254; 19 Morrison St), with gigs from Wednesday to Saturday; **Bridie O'Reilly's** (☎ 6224 9494; 124 Davey St), which has bands Friday, Saturday and Monday nights; and the **Customs House Hotel** (☎ 6234 6645; 1 Murray St), where live music usually plays Friday and Saturday nights.

Temple Place (☎ 6223 2883; 121 Macquarie St), like all decent jazz places, hides its marquee entry in a dead-end laneway and has a separate cigar lounge. Prior to its excellent jazz programme (from 9pm Tuesday to Thursday, from 10.30pm Friday and Saturday, 4.30pm to 9pm Sunday; usually free), it does a good dinner trade from 6pm.

Cla~~...~~Ho~

Trapped inside the large, graceless metal cylinder welded to the Hotel Grand Chancellor is the **Federation Concert Hall** (☎ 6235 3633, 1800 001 190; W *www.tso.com.au; 1 Davey St; box office open 9.30am-4.30pm Mon-Fri*). The hall is home to the Tasmanian Symphony Orchestra and is also used to stage other classical performances. The box office is open before all performances and tickets start at $40.

Conservatorium Recital Hall (☎ 6226 7306; 5-7 Sandy Bay Rd, Sandy Bay Rd) presents concerts by performers attending the Tasmanian Conservatorium of Music, at the University of Tasmania.

Cinemas

For a selection of mainly independent local and international flicks, head for the **State Cinema** (☎ 6234 6318; 375 Elizabeth St, Nth Hobart).

Village Cinemas (☎ 6234 7288; 181 Collins St; adult/child/concession $12/8.50/ 10) is a large inner-city complex that fishes for mainstream releases.

Theatre

Live theatre can be enjoyed at a number of venues around town, including the venerable **Theatre Royal** (☎ 6233 2026; 29 Campbell St). At the back of the Royal, down Sackville St, is the smaller **Backspace Theatre**, staging innovative, more artistically alternative productions. There's also the **Peacock Theatre** (☎ 6234 8414), in the Salamanca Arts Centre; the evangelical **Odeon Theatre** (☎ 6234 3358; 167 Liverpool), which is sometimes rented out to local theatre groups by its church owners; and the University of Tasmania's **Stanley Burbury Theatre** (☎ 6226 2799).

Other Distractions

There is a maze of late-night, often lurid bars, lounges and clubs to be found at **Wrest Point** (☎ 6225 0112; 410 Sandy Bay Rd), but its centrepiece is the main **casino** (open from 2pm daily), which is augmented by several early-bird **gaming lounges** (open from 10am).

Savoy Baths (☎ 6224 1586; W *www .savoybaths.com.au; 38 Elizabeth St; open 7am-9pm Mon-Fri, 9am-9pm Sat, 9am-6pm Sun*), in the hygienic depths of the Savoy Hobart hotel, is the place to go to buff the once-healthy gleam tarnished by late nights at the aforementioned bars. Choose from a range of massages ($55 per hour), pedicure/ manicure ($30 to $50) or whole-body treatments ($40 to $80), or just hit the spa, sauna and saltwater pool for $15 per visit; children under 16 are not admitted.

SHOPPING

Most of Hobart's speciality shops and services are in the city centre. The main shopping area extends west from the mall on Elizabeth St and shopping arcades dot the inner-city blocks. There are also shopping centres to the south at Sandy Bay, to the north at Glenorchy and on the eastern side of the river at Bellerive – these are fairly generic consumer rallying points, but they have been known to yield the odd interesting shop. There are also numerous shops and galleries on Salamanca Place selling fine Tasmanian arts and crafts.

At Salamanca, visit **Despard Gallery** (☎ 6223 8266; 15 Castray Esplanade; open daily), exhibiting and selling top-quality contemporary Tasmanian artworks. For woollen wear, try the **Tasmanian Woollen Co** (☎ 6234 1711; 69 Salamanca Place).

For a broad selection of Tasmanian goodies, visit **The Tasmania Shop** (☎ 6231 5200; 120a Liverpool St), which sells edible fare from cheese to chutney and vino, plus knitwear and wood, glass and ceramic crafts. Speaking of edibles, **Say Cheese** (☎ 6224 2888; 7 Salamanca Square) sells a great range of Tasmanian cheeses and wines daily – cheese platters can be sampled for between $9 to $15 and there's also a separate lunch menu.

Mundy & Sons (☎ 6234 8266; 222-228 Elizabeth St), in North Hobart, is a fine-food showcase, with lots of specialty cheeses, meats and coffee. And don't forget the sweet, melt-in-your mouth stuff sold courtesy of Island Produce Tasmania's **fudge factory** (☎ 6223 3233; 16 Degraves St, Sth

Hobart) at the female factory site (see the Cascade Brewery & Female Factory section earlier in this chapter).

For a huge range of the state's wines, head for **The Tasmanian Wine Centre** (☎ *6234 9995; 201 Collins St),* which also organises winery tours and tutored wine tasting.

If you need bushwalking or outdoor equipment, try **Paddy Pallin** (☎ *6231 0777; 119 Elizabeth St)* or **Snowgum** (☎ *6234 7877; 104 Elizabeth St).* Another good shop for all your bushwalking requirements is **Mountain Designs** (☎ *6234 3900; 111 Elizabeth St).* A few doors down is **Jolly Swagman's** (☎ *6234 3999; 107 Elizabeth St),* where you can stock up on camping equipment and items necessary for outdoor activities, like canoeing and rock climbing. Blundstone boots can be bought in the city from **Tradewear** (☎ *6234 5167; 135 Elizabeth St).* For fishing supplies, head to **Spot On Fishing Tackle** (☎ *6234 4880; 89 Harrington St).*

The Antiques Market (☎ *6236 9905; 11 Elizabeth St; open 10am-5pm Mon-Sat, noon-4pm Sun),* on the ground floor of the building next to the main post office, displays china, jewellery and furniture from over a dozen antiques dealers; pick up some Royal Winton crockery or perhaps a stand-up 1940s console radio with an upholstered speaker. There are more old knick-knack and collectibles businesses to browse on the building's other floors.

Auto Miniatures (☎ *6231 4533; 61 Liverpool St)* is the place to go when you can't afford to buy your dream set of wheels and are prepared to settle for the Lilliputian model. This unique model car shop has a world-class collection of new and old dye-cast collectables.

For some more ideas about what to buy in Tasmania, see the Shopping section in the Facts for the Visitor chapter.

GETTING THERE & AWAY
Air
For information on domestic flights to and from Hobart, see the Getting There & Away chapter. **Qantas** (☎ *13 13 13;* W *www.qantas .com.au)* has an office in the Elizabeth St Mall.

Bus
The main bus companies opera Hobart are **Redline Coaches** (☎ *6336 1446, 1300 360 000;* W *www.tasredline.com.au)* and **TassieLink** (☎ *6272 7300, 1300 300 520;* W *www.tigerline.com.au).* Both companies were running out of the **Transit Centre** *(199 Collins St)* at the time of writing, but Tassie-Link had unveiled plans to outfit a new depot for itself in Brisbane St. Also based in the capital is **Hobart Coaches** (☎ *6233 4232, 13 22 01; 9 Elizabeth St),* owned and operated by Metro city buses. See the Bus section in the Getting Around chapter for general information on the services offered by these companies, then turn to the section in this book relating to the specific destination you wish to travel to for more information on services from Hobart.

Car
There are a large number of car-rental firms in Hobart. The bigger, more expensive companies represented locally include **Budget** (☎ *6234 5222, 1800 030 035; 96 Harrington St),* **AutoRent-Hertz** (☎ *6335 1111, 1800 067 222; Harrington St)* and **Europcar** (☎ *1800 030 118; Goulburn St).* Some of the cheaper ones are **Rent-a-Bug** (☎ *6231 0300; 105 Murray St),* **Lo-Cost Auto Rent** (☎ *6231 0550; 30 Barrack St)* and **Selective Car Rentals** (☎ *6234 3311; 47 Bathurst St).* See the Car section of the Getting Around chapter for more details.

Hitching
To start hitching north, take a Bridgewater or Brighton bus from the Elizabeth St bus station. To hitch along the east coast, take a bus to Sorell first. However, with the regular and reasonably priced bus routes traversing the state, we don't recommend hitching. Lifts on some roads are few and far between and there is always the chance of a potentially dangerous situation.

GETTING AROUND
To/From the Airport
The airport is 16km east of the centre. The **Airporter shuttle** (☎ *0419 382 240)* runs between the CBD and the airport (via various

places to stay) for $8.40/4.20 per adult/child. A taxi to/from the airport should cost around $25.

Bus

The local bus service is run by **Metro**. Its main office (☎ 13 22 01; 9 Elizabeth St) is inside the post office. Most buses leave from this area of Elizabeth St, which is known as the Metro city bus station, or from around the edges of nearby Franklin Square.

If you're planning to bus around Hobart it's worth buying Metro's user-friendly timetable (50c). For $3.40 ($9.60 per family), you can get an unlimited-travel Day Rover ticket that can be used after 9am Monday to Friday, and all day Saturday, Sunday and public holidays. If you're staying in Hobart for a while, you should get a Day Rover pass for $26.50, which is valid for any 10 days (not necessarily consecutive) and has the same restrictions on peak-hour travel. An alternative is to buy a book of 10 discounted tickets that can be used at any time of day.

Taxi

Try **City Cabs** (☎ 13 10 08) or **Taxi Combined** (☎ 13 22 27). **Hobart & Southern Maxi-Taxis** (☎ 6227 9577, 0418 126 515) can provide vehicles accommodating disabled persons.

Bicycle

At the time of writing, due to spiralling insurance costs, **Derwent Bike Hire** (☎ 0407 342 918; open 10am-5pm Sat & Sun) was one of the few places still renting out bicycles, at a cost of $20 per day. It's open longer in summer.

Boat

The *Wanderer* ferry, operated by **Roche O'May Cruises** (☎ 6223 1914), departs the Brooke St Pier from Monday to Friday at 11am, 1.30pm and 3pm to visit the Botanic Gardens ($3), Bellerive ($6) and Wrest Point ($9), with the round trip costing $12/6 per adult/child ($13/6.50 with afternoon tea); you can get on and off as many times as you like. On weekdays there's also a 10.30am service that goes direct to Wrest Point ($3). On Saturday and Sunday, the service departs at 90-minute intervals from 10.30am to 3pm. The same boat also operates a Bellerive service, run primarily to transport residents to and from work on weekdays.

Around Hobart

When you've had your fill of cosmopolitan treats and bumping elbows with your fellow humans, you won't have to travel too far from Hobart to swap the cityscape for great natural scenery and some popular historical sites. The lush countryside and water views between the capital and its satellite suburbs/towns are attractions in themselves, and the historic penal settlement of Port Arthur and the stunning cliffs of the Tasman Peninsula make for a good day trip. You can immerse yourself in convict history by visiting Richmond, which has a fascinating old jail and a noteworthy convict-built bridge.

South of Hobart

The Channel Hwy is the continuation of Sandy Bay Rd and hugs the coastline as it heads south. It became a pleasant tourist drive after the construction of the Southern Outlet from Hobart to Kingston and beyond removed most of the traffic. This winding road is benched into the lower slopes of Mt Nelson, so drive slowly.

TAROONA
☎ 03 • postcode 7053
Ten kilometres from Hobart on the Channel Hwy is the peripheral town of Taroona, its name derived from an Aboriginal word meaning 'seashell'.

Shot Tower
Just south of Taroona is the landmark Shot Tower (☎ 6227 8885; adult/child $4.50/2; open 9am-6pm daily). Completed in 1870, the 48m-high tower is made from sandstone, with every block curved and tapered. From the top are fine views over the Derwent River estuary. Lead shot for use in guns was once produced in high towers like this by dropping molten lead from the top, which formed a perfect sphere on its way down.

Take care if you're climbing the tower with small children, as the railing around

Highlights

- Climbing the shot tower near Taroona
- Experiencing the beautiful, winding riverside drive from Taroona to Tinderbox
- Doing absolutely nothing on Kingston Beach
- Tracing your fingers over Port Arthur's old stonework
- Walking on the sea cliffs of the Tasman Peninsula

the deep stairwell is less than fall-proof. The tower is surrounded by leafy grounds and contains a small museum, a craft shop and a **tearoom** (light meals $4-6.50); if it's sunny, gobble one of their 'convictshire' teas on the stone rampart outside.

To get here, take bus No 56, 60 or 61 from the Macquarie St side of Franklin Square to stop 45. The tower closes earlier in winter.

Alum Cliffs
The Alum Cliffs Track extends 4.5km from Taroona Beach to Kingston Beach. However, due to as-yet-unrectified landslip at its northern end, it should now be accessed

from Taronga Rd – the turn-off is 1km down the highway from the shot tower. At some points the track runs close to rock cliffs and you can get good views of the Derwent River. Allow around two hours each way.

Places to Stay & Eat

Taroona Hotel (☎ *6227 8748; singles/doubles from $35/50)*, a wayside place 1km north of the Shot Tower, had cheap accommodation and bistro meals at the time of research. However, the hotel was about to undergo redevelopment.

Hillgrove (☎ *6227 9043, fax 6227 8337; 269 Channel Hwy; B&B doubles $110, extra adults $20)*, with its mansard roof, on the hill opposite the Shot Tower, is a salubrious 19th-century Georgian brick cottage which received stone and Baltic pine extensions. Guests get the run of the two-bedroom, self-contained ground floor, plus a large veranda and a garden to gaze at.

KINGSTON
☎ 03 • postcode 7050 • pop 13,750

Kingston, 11km south of Hobart and basically a sprawling outer suburb of the city, expanded rapidly once the Southern Outlet provided fast access to the town. The beach here is a superb spot to laze and study the contours of your belly-button.

Kingston Beach

As you branch off from the Southern Outlet and approach Kingston, continue straight ahead at the first set of lights instead of turning right onto the Channel Hwy; this road takes you all the way to the beach. If coming down the Channel Hwy from Taroona, follow the arrow to Blackmans Bay. Kingston Beach is a popular swimming and sailing spot, with attractive wooded cliffs hemming in a long arc of white sand.

There's a good picnic area at the northern end, accessed by a pedestrian bridge over the

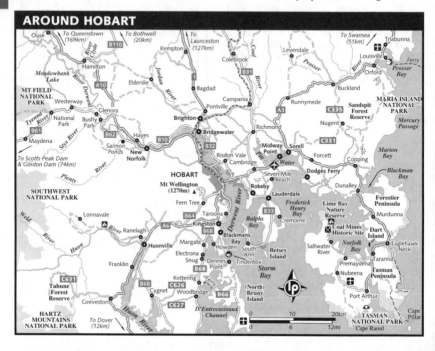

AROUND HOBART

reputedly pollution-prone, non-swimmable (and therefore aptly named) Browns River.

Located behind the sailing clubhouse at the southern end is the start of a track to a beautiful secluded beach called **Boronia**, which has a deep rock pool – note, though, that sections of this walk are heavily eroded and council-signposted as 'dangerous'. An alternative route to Boronia is to head toward Blackmans Bay, turn left on Roslyn Ave at the roundabout and go through the first gate to the steep beach trail on the right. **Blackmans Bay** has another good beach and a blowhole (down Blowhole Rd). The water at these beaches is usually quite cold, and there's rarely any surf.

Many Hobart abseiling and rock-climbing companies offer abseiling instruction on the cliffs and in the blowhole at Blackmans Bay (see the Activities chapter).

Tinderbox

Make time to drive through Blackmans Bay to Tinderbox. The views along the way are gorgeous and at Tinderbox itself is a small beach bordering a marine reserve – here you can snorkel along an underwater trail that runs alongside a sandstone reef and is marked with submerged information plates. Bruny Island is just across the water and locals often launch their outboards here to skim over to Dennes Point.

From Tinderbox, you can continue around the peninsula to Howden and return to Kingston along the Channel Hwy.

Antarctic Division

Beside the Channel Hwy south of Kingston is the headquarters of the Australian Antarctic Division (☎ 6232 3209; Ⓦ www.antdiv .gov.au; Channel Hwy; admission free; open 9am-5pm Mon-Fri), the department administering Australia's 42% portion of the frozen continent. Australia has had a long history of exploration and scientific study of Antarctica and is one of the original 12 nations that set up the Antarctic Treaty in 1961. Downstairs from reception is a fine **display** (admission free), which features authentic equipment like signalling pistols and transports, plus ecology information. The centre's

cafeteria (open 8.30am-4.30pm) is open to the public and sells souvenirs.

Places to Stay

Beachside Hotel (☎ 6229 6185, fax 6229 7668; 2 Beach Rd; singles/doubles $45/55) has plainly refurbished motel-style rooms on the well-trafficked beachside thoroughfare.

Kingston Beach Motel (☎/fax 6229 8969; 31 Osborne Esplanade; singles/doubles $75/ 95) has a row of simple, lemon-meringue units opposite the beach.

Tranquilla (☎ 6229 6282; 30 Osborne Esplanade; B&B singles/doubles $75/85) is a nice, garden-variety guesthouse (as in there's plenty of garden), close to the corner of Osborne Esplanade and Beach Rd.

On the Beach (☎/fax 6229 3096; 38 Osborne Esplanade; doubles $80) offers one well-equipped beachfront unit attached to the front of the owners' weatherboard cottage.

Welcome Inn (☎ 6229 4800; Kingston View Dr; doubles $80-100) is a large complex 2km west of Kingston, near the Southern Outlet as it heads towards Huonville. The inn's more expensive units have spas. Continental breakfast is provided and there's a reasonably priced bistro (mains $12.50 to $15.50), which is open from 6pm to 8pm daily. There's also a sports centre nearby.

Places to Eat

There are plenty of low-cost eating options around town, from counter meals to Chinese restaurants and takeaways in Kingston's Channel Court and Blackmans Bay's shopping centre.

Kingston Hotel (☎ 6229 6116; Channel Hwy; mains $10-20; open noon-2pm & 5.30pm-8pm Mon-Sat, noon-2pm Sun), known locally as Darcy's, has a huge bistro with everything from rissoles and gravy to a fisherman's platter.

Kingston Beach Brasserie (☎ 6229 1670; 39 Beach Rd; mains $10-22; open from 6pm Wed-Sat, noon-2pm & from 6pm Sun) has a pastel-swathed interior yielding seafood like crayfish pâté and tiger prawns.

Citrus Moon Cafe (☎ 6229 2388; 23 Beach Rd; mains $4-9; open 9am-late Mon-Sat, 10am-late Sun) is a vibrant café with a

AROUND HOBART

predominantly vegetarian menu concocted from mainly organic produce. Demolish pancakes for breakfast, bagels or laksa for lunch, and then lunge into the side room for an ice cream.

Getting There & Away
Hobart Coaches (☎ 6233 4232, 13 22 01) runs a regular service from Hobart to Kingston (a 15-minute ride) and Blackmans Bay throughout the day on weekdays (note there can be a few hours between services) but only twice on Saturday. Buses leave Hobart from either Murray St between Davey and Macquarie Sts, or from Franklin Square.

MARGATE
☎ 03 • postcode 7054 • pop 1050
Eight kilometres south of Kingston is the small town of Margate. Train buffs can examine the last **passenger train** to be used in Tasmania. It stands on a piece of railway track beside the highway on the northern side of town and houses bric-a-brac shops and a **café** serving pancakes and other light meals for around $8; there's also a Sunday **boot market**.

On weekdays, Hobart Coaches runs several buses from Hobart through Margate to Kettering. On Saturday there's a morning and evening service in both directions, but only as far as Margate.

Derwent Valley

NEW NORFOLK
☎ 03 • postcode 7140 • pop 5300
Set in the lush, rolling countryside of the Derwent Valley is the interesting historical town of New Norfolk. The area was first visited by Europeans in 1793 and began taking on the hallmarks of a town in 1808, when an Irish convict built the first house. By the 1860s the valley had become an important hop-growing centre, which is why the area is dotted with old oast houses (used for drying the plant). Hops, which give beer its characteristic bitterness, are sensitive to wind and so trees were planted as a natural barrier – today, distinctive rows of tall

poplars mark the boundaries of former hop fields.

Originally called Elizabeth Town, New Norfolk was renamed after the arrival of settlers (from 1808 onwards) from the abandoned Pacific Ocean colony on Norfolk Island. Today the town is a mixture of colonial remnants and more contemporary sights and activities.

Information
The **Derwent Valley Visitors Information Centre** (☎ 6261 3700; Circle St; open 10am-4pm daily) is behind the courthouse.

Oast House
The eye-catching Oast House (☎ 6261 2830), on the perimeter of Tynwald Park, off the highway on the Hobart side of town, was built in the 1820s and served as a piggery before devoting itself to hops from 1867 to 1969. The timber building's kilns were used to dry and package hops for delivery to breweries. You can go on a self-guided tour of its **museum** (adult/child $4/3; open 10am-6pm daily), following the story of how hops were processed. There's also a local crafts, vegies and bric-a-brac **market** (open 10am-3pm Sat & Sun) in the house grounds every weekend.

Historic Buildings
St Matthew's Church (Bathurst St), built in 1823, is Tasmania's oldest Anglican church. It's been extensively altered since it first rose from the ground and its best features today are the excellent stained-glass windows. In the adjacent St Matthew's Close is a craft/souvenir shop that raises money for the church's ongoing restoration – on one wall is an enormous clockface from the clocktower (long demolished) of the Royal Derwent Hospital, the asylum around which the town was based in the 1850s.

The **Bush Inn** (49 Montagu St), built in 1815, claims to be the oldest continuously licensed hotel in Australia, though the Hope & Anchor Tavern in Hobart reckons it beat this place to it by eight years.

Old Colony Inn (☎ 6261 2731; 21 Montagu St; adult/child $2/50c; open daily) is a

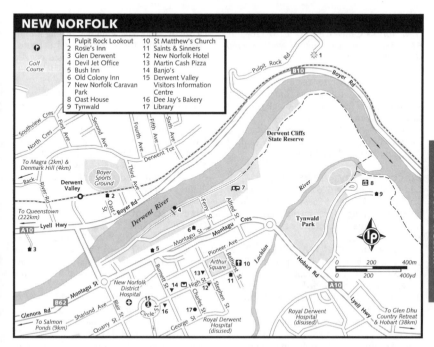

NEW NORFOLK

1 Pulpit Rock Lookout
2 Rosie's Inn
3 Glen Derwent
4 Devil Jet Office
5 Bush Inn
6 Old Colony Inn
7 New Norfolk Caravan Park
8 Oast House
9 Tynwald
10 St Matthew's Church
11 Saints & Sinners
12 New Norfolk Hotel
13 Martin Cash Pizza
14 Banjo's
15 Derwent Valley Visitors Information Centre
16 Dee Jay's Bakery
17 Library

AROUND HOBART

distinctive, magpie-coloured museum of colonial furnishings and artefacts, built in 1815 as a hop shed. It's on a one-way street, so prepare to make a tight U-turn at the top end of the road division on Montagu St if you're approaching from Hobart. The owners live here so the inn is open most times, just rattle the chain, or ring ahead.

Salmon Ponds
In 1864, rainbow and brown trout were bred for the first time in the southern hemisphere in Salmon Ponds (☎ 6261 1076; 70 Salmon Ponds Rd, Plenty; adult/ child $5.50/3.50; open 9am-5pm daily), 9km west of New Norfolk. You can feed fish in six display ponds, visit the hatchery and investigate an angling museum. You can also eat in the on-site restaurant (see Places to Eat later).

Lookout
Get a fine view over New Norfolk by following the road along the northern side of the river eastward for 1km, then up a steep side road to **Pulpit Rock**. From here you can overlook a sweeping bend of the Derwent River.

Jet-Boat Rides
Devil Jet (☎ 6261 3460; Esplanade) whisks you 10km upriver and back in a jet boat, taking 30 foam-filled minutes. The 'jets' take off on the hour between 9am and 4pm daily, and cost $48/24 per adult/child; bookings are recommended in summer.

Train Rides
The **Derwent Valley Railway** (☎ 6261 1946) runs a train from New Norfolk to Westerway at 10.30am (returning 3.15pm) on the second Sunday of each month, costing $25/15 per adult/child. A much shorter rail journey is the one between New Norfolk and Hayes ($6/4), with trains leaving on the hour from 10am to 3pm on the first and third Saturday of each month.

Places to Stay – Budget

New Norfolk Caravan Park (☎ 6261 1268, fax 6261 5868; Esplanade; unpowered/powered site doubles $9/14, on-site van doubles $35, cabin doubles $50), on the Derwent's south bank, is a great place for fishing enthusiasts. Cabins come with toilets but the only showers are in the amenities block (20c per three minutes).

Bush Inn (☎ 6261 2256; 49 Montagu St; singles/doubles $23/55) has plain budget rooms with shared facilities.

Places to Stay – Mid-Range

Old Colony Inn (☎ 6261 2731; 21 Montagu St; singles/doubles $55/80) has a single charming cottage for romantic types who like the intimate character of small doors and low ceilings.

Rosie's Inn (☎ 6261 1171, fax 6261 3872; 5 Oast St; doubles $90-130) applies the floral theme vigorously, with some fittings overgrown with garden motifs. The rooms in this hospitable B&B come with home-cooked breakfasts.

Saints & Sinners (☎ 6261 1877, fax 6261 2955; 93 High St; singles/doubles $90/110) has a handful of B&B rooms in a renovated mid-19th-century building near the town centre, plus a café utilising organic produce and serving sinful cakes.

Denmark Hill (☎/fax 6261 3313; 43 Black Hills Rd; singles/doubles $90/100), in the countryside 4km north of town at Magra, offers a single en suite room and hearty breakfast.

Glen Dhu Country Retreat (☎/fax 6261 4443; W www.ozemail.com.au/~glenhops; 8237 Glen Dhu Rd; doubles $95-120), on a rural plot east of New Norfolk off the Lyell Hwy, has two late-19th-century hop-pickers' cottages, both self-contained and with breakfast provisions.

Places to Stay – Top End

Tynwald (☎ 6261 2667; e tynwald@trump .net.au; Tynwald St; doubles $135-190) is a striking three-storey, 1830s mansion overlooking the river. For many years it was the residence of the operators of nearby Oast House and was then given architectural adjustments in the 1890s like wide verandas, lace-work and bay windows. It has a half-dozen antique-furnished rooms, a heated swimming pool, a tennis court and cooked breakfasts. It also has a highly palatable restaurant (see Places to Eat).

Glen Derwent (☎ 6261 3244; W www .glenderwent.com.au; 44 Hamilton Rd; rooms $125-180) is hidden behind a hawthorn hedge in extensive grounds beside the Lyell Hwy, just west of the bridge over the Derwent River. This luxurious, circa 1820 mansion has several in-house B&B rooms and two self-contained cottages; three-course dinners can be arranged.

Places to Eat

Dee Jay's Bakery (☎ 6261 5552; 9 High St; open 7am-6pm daily) and **Banjo's** (☎ 6261 8766; 16 High St; open 6am-6pm daily) are two bakeries in town where you can get your fill of doughy or sweet treats from early morn to dusk.

Martin Cash Pizza (☎ 6261 2150; 15 Stephen St; open from 5pm Tues-Sun) serves Italian-style meals and takeaway.

New Norfolk Hotel (☎ 6261 2166; 79 High St; mains $11-16; open lunch daily, dinner Mon-Sat) serves lots of steak and also basic seafood.

Bush Inn (☎ 6261 2256; 49 Montagu St; mains $12-16) is a similar culinary deal to the New Norfolk Hotel.

Oast House (☎ 6261 2830; Tynwald Park; meals $10-12; open 10am-6pm daily) has a licensed tearoom specialising in sweet and savoury European-style pancakes.

Old Colony Inn (☎ 6261 2731; 21 Montagu St; open daily) also has a tearoom; lunch and dinner are available but only by prior arrangement.

Tynwald (☎ 6261 2667; Tynwald St; mains $25; open from 6.30pm daily) has an excellent, regularly changing à la carte menu, the mainstay of which is gammon steak (double-smoked ham) with plum sauce.

The Ponds Restaurant (☎ 6261 1614; 70 Salmon Ponds Rd, Plenty; open 9am-5pm daily) is a restaurant at the Salmon Ponds where you can eat reasonably priced, home-grown trout and salmon, plus Tassie cheeses.

Getting There & Away

Hobart Coaches (☎ 6233 4232, 13 22 01) is the main operator between Hobart and New Norfolk (50 minutes), and provides six services a day in both directions on weekdays, and three on Saturday. A one-way/return adult fare costs $5.10/8.20. In New Norfolk, the buses leave from Circle St, while in Hobart they depart from stop F on Elizabeth St.

BUSHY PARK TO WESTERWAY

As you head west from New Norfolk towards Mt Field, you leave the Derwent River and follow the narrow valley of the Tyenna River. In the three historic rural communities of Bushy Park, Glenora and Westerway you can see old barns, a water wheel and extensive hop fields. The many shingled buildings exemplify the way in which 19th-century farms were built.

Hop growing has vanished from much of Tasmania but it is still pursued commercially by the company Bushy Park Estates. In late summer and autumn you can see the hops growing up the thin leader strings.

Westerway is a substantial town with a general store and petrol station. A few hundred metres down the road to Mt Field, you can stay at **Tyenna Retreat** (☎ 6288 1552, fax 6288 1478; 1587 Gordon River Rd; doubles $95), a private, self-contained space at one end of a modern home surrounded by lovely gardens. Guided trout-fishing and wildlife-spotting tours can also be organised here.

For food, head further down the road to the cheerful confines of **The Possum Shed** (☎ 6288 1477; meals $10-12; open 10.30am-6pm daily Dec-Feb), where you can sit beside a platypus-inhabited stream (visitations are not guaranteed, though) to eat great light lunches. The owners here have backgrounds in Australian natural history and conduct knowledgeable Mt Field tours. The Possum Shed has reduced opening hours during winter.

For transport information, see Getting There & Away in the Mt Field National Park section of the Mt Field & The Southwest chapter.

North of the Derwent

PONTVILLE & BRIGHTON
☎ 03 • postcode 7030 • pop 1425

Twenty-five kilometres north of Hobart on the Midland Hwy is Brighton, and just north of it the historic town of Pontville. Both were once considered possible capitals of Van Diemen's Land and have some interesting buildings dating from the 1830s. Much of the freestone used in Tasmania's early buildings was supplied from quarries at Pontville and the town boasts some sandstone buildings of its own. The Pontville and Brighton area is used by the Australian military, which has some large bases nearby.

In Pontville, up on top of the hill, is **St Mark's Anglican Church** (Midland Hwy), where there's an excellent view of Mt Wellington. The church was built in 1841 and is one of several sandstone buildings in the area.

Sheiling (☎ 6268 1951; Rifle Range Rd; singles $85-110, doubles $120-145), just north of the church, is a two-storey ivy-cloaked house, built in 1819 and one of the oldest in the state. It was undergoing impressive renovations at the time of research and had been adorned with antique Victorian furniture.

Lythgo's Row (☎ 6268 1665; Midland Hwy; doubles from $120) is a Georgian sandstone building that originally housed soldiers and now provides B&B in the erstwhile barracks.

Brighton is of less interest than Pontville, being composed mostly of houses recently built to serve the military. You can stay at the gaming-dominated **Brighton Hotel** (☎ 6268 1201; Midland Hwy; singles/doubles $50/70); rates include continental breakfast, and counter meals (mains $13 to $16.50) are served daily.

Nearby, 3km down well-signposted side roads, is **Bonorong Wildlife Park** (☎ 6268 1184; Briggs Rd; adult/child $10/5; open 9am-5pm daily). 'Bonorong' comes from an Aboriginal word that means 'native companion' and there are plenty of native companions here that receive regular feeding, like devils, koalas, echidnas and quolls. Besides its well-inhabited outdoor spaces, the park also has a **café** serving light lunches, teas and 'bush damper'. You can get to Bonorong by bus: from Hobart take any service to Glenorchy bus station, where you catch bus No 125 or 126.

RICHMOND
☎ 03 • postcode 7025 • pop 770

Richmond is just 24km from Hobart and, with more than 50 19th-century buildings, is arguably Tasmania's premier historic town. Straddling the Coal River and on the old route between Hobart and Port Arthur, Richmond was once a strategic military post and convict station. The much-photographed Richmond Bridge is the town's historical centrepiece.

With the completion of the Sorell Causeway in 1872, traffic travelling to the Tasman Peninsula and the east coast bypassed Richmond. The town remained the focus of a farming community but ceased to grow – in fact, for more than a century it changed very little. It has since transformed into a tourist destination and is a delightful spot to visit.

Information

There's no information centre as such, but plenty of brochures are available from the **kiosk** in front of the model village.

Things to See & Do

Famous **Richmond Bridge** still funnels traffic across the Coal River. You can walk under and around it, and there are good views on both sides. Built by convicts in 1823, and hence the oldest road bridge in Australia, it formed a vital link for the young colony and encouraged construction of the many old buildings seen today.

The northern wing of the remarkably well-preserved **Richmond Gaol** (*☎ 6260 2127; Forth St; adult/child/family $4.50/2/ 11.50; open 9am-5pm daily*) was built in

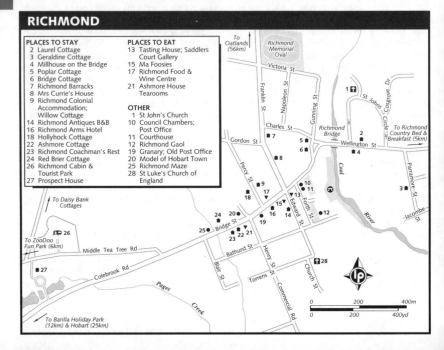

RICHMOND

PLACES TO STAY	PLACES TO EAT
2 Laurel Cottage	13 Tasting House; Saddlers Court Gallery
3 Geraldine Cottage	15 Ma Foosies
4 Millhouse on the Bridge	17 Richmond Food & Wine Centre
5 Poplar Cottage	21 Ashmore House Tearooms
6 Bridge Cottage	
7 Richmond Barracks	
8 Mrs Currie's House	**OTHER**
9 Richmond Colonial Accommodation; Willow Cottage	1 St John's Church
14 Richmond Antiques B&B	10 Council Chambers; Post Office
16 Richmond Arms Hotel	11 Courthouse
18 Hollyhock Cottage	12 Richmond Gaol
22 Ashmore Cottage	19 Granary; Old Post Office
23 Richmond Coachman's Rest	20 Model of Hobart Town
24 Red Brier Cottage	25 Richmond Maze
26 Richmond Cabin & Tourist Park	28 St Luke's Church of England
27 Prospect House	

1825, five years before the penitentiary [at] Port Arthur. Its locks and punishment a[nd] solitary confinement cells have not be[en] modified. The various displays describe t[he] old penal system.

Other places of historical interest inclu[de] the 1837 **St John's Church** (off Wellington S[t]), the first Catholic church in Australia; t[he] 1834 **St Luke's Church of England** (Edwar[d] St); the 1825 **courthouse** (Forth St); the o[ld] **post office** (Bridge St), built in 1826; t[he] 1817 **Bridge Inn** (Forth St); the **grana**[ry] (Bridge St), constructed in 1829; and t[he] 1888 **Richmond Arms Hotel** (Bridge St).

There's also an interesting **model villa**[ge] (☎ 6260 2502; laneway off Bridge St; adu[lt/] child $7.50/3.50; open 9am-5pm daily) of Hobart Town in the 1820s, re-created from the city's original plans. The detail of the 60-plus miniature buildings and Hobart's shrunken population is excellent.

Herd the kids into the wooden-walled **Richmond Maze** (☎ 6260 2451; 13 Bridge St; adult/child $5/3; open 8am-5pm daily). They'll be safe, as the resident Minotaur has taken long-service leave. The maze has reduced opening hours in the low season.

There are several arts and crafts places around town selling paintings, carved bowls and trinkets, leather goods, books and furniture, much of it locally made. Prices aren't particularly cheap but many items are of good quality. **Saddlers Court Gallery** (☎ 6260 2132; Bridge St; open 9.30am-5.30pm daily Oct-Apr, 10am-5pm daily May-Sept) has some exceptional items for sale.

ZooDoo Fun Park (☎ 6260 2444; 620 Middle Tea Tree Rd; adult/child $10/9; open 9am-5pm daily), 6km west of Richmond on the road to Brighton, has steam train rides, a model village, playgrounds and enough captive wildlife – from miniature horses to emus and ducklings – to keep the kids absorbed.

Places to Stay – Budget

Richmond Cabin & Tourist Park (☎ 6260 2192, fax 6260 2652; 48 Middle Tea Tree Rd; unpowered/powered site doubles $15/18, on-site van doubles $38, cabin doubles from $55), opposite Prospect House, has extensive facilities and neat, inexpensive vans

Red Brier Cottage (☎ 6260 2349[...] 2782; 15 Bridge St; doubles $14[...] cious, fully equipped cedar [...] private, almost secretive f[...]

Mrs Currie's Hous[e] www.mrscurrieshou[...] B&B rooms $100-1[...] storey Georgia[n] 1850s. It was[...] for most of [...] get here[...] nishe[d]

House. Recharge yourself in this warm, laid-back and peaceful farmhouse environment.

Richmond Arms Hotel (☎ 6260 2109; 42 Bridge St; doubles from $99) has rooms in the adjacent, snug former stables.

Richmond Antiques B&B (☎ 6260 2601; 25 Edward St; doubles $85) is one of the cheapest places in town, with plain but comfortable rooms above an antique shop in a private brick residence.

Richmond Coachman's Rest (☎/fax 6260 2630; 30 Bridge St; doubles $75) is a basic motel-style unit that probably hasn't rested any real coachmen.

Places to Stay – Top End

Prospect House (☎ 6260 2207, 13 24 00; w www.prospect-house.com.au; 1348 Richmond Rd; doubles $145-160), immediately west of Richmond on the Hobart road, is a superb Georgian mansion offering well-appointed rooms and continental breakfast; full breakfast costs $15 extra.

Richmond Colonial Accommodation (☎/fax 6260 2570; e cottages@bigpond.com; 4 Percy St; doubles $120-135) manages four well-catered historic cottages in town, namely **Ashmore** (32 Bridge St), **Bridge** (47 Bridge St), **Poplar** (49 Bridge St) and **Willow** (4 Percy St). All cottages are self-contained and have a roll call of colonial touches.

Laurel Cottage (☎ 6260 2397, fax 6260 2536; 9 Wellington St; doubles from $120) is in a similar old-fashioned vein and is in the centre beside the bridge.

*fax 6260
...) is a spa-
...cottage with a
...el.

... (☎ 6260 2766;
...se.com; 4 Franklin St;
...) is a beautiful, double-
... place dating from the
...the abode of one Alma Currie
... a century. The welcome you'll
...is exemplified by the nicely fur-
...rooms and gourmet breakfasts.

...ollyhock Cottage (☎/fax 6260 1079; 3 ...ercy St; doubles $135) is a relaxing, National Trust–listed brick-and-timber cottage modernised with a double spa; rates include cooked breakfast. Inquire here about **Geraldine Cottage** (12 Parramore St; doubles $125).

Richmond Barracks (☎ 6260 2453, fax 6260 2373; 16 Franklin St; B&B singles/doubles from $90/120) is an attractive low-slung 1830s building with en suite units.

Daisy Bank Cottages (☎ 6260 2390, 0419 103 081, fax 6260 2635; Daisy Bank; doubles from $130), off Middle Tea Tree Rd, is a real treat, with lovely rooms in a converted 1840s sandstone barn, well away from the main house. There are plenty of distractions for the kids on this working property.

Millhouse on the Bridge (☎ 6260 2428; W www.millhouse.com.au; 2 Wellington St; rooms from $130) is a masterfully restored, antique-filled 1853 flour mill abutting Richmond Bridge. It has four highly polished rooms, and cooked breakfasts.

Places to Eat
Richmond Food & Wine Centre (☎ 6260 2619; 27 Bridge St; mains $9.50-19.50; open 8am-5pm Sun-Wed, 8am-5pm & from 6pm Thur-Sat) is an exemplary eatery, set back from the main street, where Tassie produce reigns supreme. Consume numerous wines, cheese or antipasto platters or dishes like veal terrine, either indoors or out. Tastings and sales are available.

Tasting House (☎ 6260 2050; Shop 4, 50 Bridge St; open 10am-5.30pm daily), in the back of the Bridge Inn & Mews complex, also offers local wines and cheeses for sampling (cheese platters $6.50). There's a small wine-tasting fee (refundable on purchase) and Coal River Valley wine tours can be organised here.

Ashmore House Tearooms (☎ 6260 2146; 34 Bridge St; dishes $4-12; open 9.30am-5pm daily) cooks burgers, nachos, sandwiches and an all-day breakfast amid lace and ribbons.

Ma Foosies (☎ 6260 2412; 46 Bridge St; dishes $4-8; open 10.30am-5pm daily) is another cosy tearoom that does ploughman's lunches and zucchini slices.

Richmond Arms Hotel (☎ 6260 2109; 42 Bridge St; mains $13.50-21.50; open lunch & dinner daily) has various counter meals to choose from.

Prospect House (☎ 6260 2207; mains $17.50-25.50; open daily) has a restaurant where the staples include duck, venison and *boeuf*; other dishes change seasonally. Light lunches are available over summer.

Getting There & Away
If you have your own transport, you'll find that Richmond is an easy day trip from Hobart. If not, you can take a bus tour from Hobart with **Tigerline** (☎ 6272 6611, 1300 653 633; W www.tigerline.com.au), costing $39/27 per adult/child. **Hobart Coaches** (☎ 6233 4232, 13 22 01) runs four buses a day to and from Richmond on weekdays only (one way/return $5/8, 30 minutes).

The **Richmond Tourist Bus** (☎ 0408 341 804) runs a twice-daily service from Hobart ($25 return, 9.15am and 12.15pm, minimum two people) that gives you three hours to explore Richmond before returning.

Tasman Peninsula

The Arthur Hwy runs 100km from Hobart through Sorell to the Tasman Peninsula, one of the state's most popular tourist regions. Sited here is Port Arthur, the infamous and allegedly 'escape-proof' prison of the mid-19th century. Yet the region is also famous for its 300m-high cliffs, which, together with its delightful beaches and beautiful bays, make this a fantastic place for bushwalking, diving, sea kayaking and rock climbing.

Much of the best bushwalking on the Tasman Peninsula is in **Tasman National Park**, a coastal enclave of spectacularly high cliffs and other towering rock formations, chunky offshore islands, magical underwater kelp forests, and heaths containing rare plants. The cliffs are favoured by numerous seabirds and wedge-tailed eagle nests, while the waters far below are occupied by seals, dolphins and whales. The usual national park entry fees apply. (See the Bushwalking, Diving & Fishing and Nature Tour entries in the Eaglehawk Neck section later for more information.)

TASMAN PENINSULA

Information
The main information centre for the region is the **Eaglehawk Neck visitors information centre** (☎ 6250 3722; 443 Pirates Bay Dr; open 9am-5.30pm daily), at the Officers Mess café and store. Information is also available at Know-How Travel (see Sorell on this page) and the Copping Colonial & Convict Collection (see the Copping section).

The *Convict Trail* booklet ($5.50), available from the information centre, covers the peninsula's key historic sites.

Three-In-One Pass You can save around 10% of the combined entry cost of Port Arthur Historic Site, Bush Mill and Tasmanian Devil Park passes by purchasing a Three-In-One Pass (adult/child/family $48/23/115) at any of those sites.

Getting There & Around
TassieLink (☎ 6272 7300, 1300 300 520; W www.tigerline.com.au) runs buses from Hobart's **Transit Centre** (199 Collins St) down the Tasman Peninsula to Port Arthur, stopping at all the main towns along the way. The service departs Hobart at 4pm Monday to Friday, with an extra 10am service scheduled three times a week over summer, and costs $17 for the full 2¼-hour one-way trip.

Another way you can visit the area is via a **Tigerline** (☎ 6272 6611, 1300 653 633; W www.tigerline.com.au) coach tour.

Take care if driving down the peninsula to Port Arthur. Plenty of bad accidents have occurred on the Arthur Hwy in recent years due to its winding nature, road exits being hidden behind hills and around corners, and idiots with lead feet.

Organised Tours From Hobart, you can take a two-hour cruise around the peninsula's cliffs and capes with **Port Arthur Cruises** (☎ 6231 2655, 1300 134 561; W www.portarthurcruises.com.au; Brooke St Pier, Hobart). The tour costs $49/35 per adult/child.

SORELL
☎ 03 • postcode 7172 • pop 3600
This is one of Tasmania's oldest towns, settled in 1808 primarily to supply locally processed wheat and flour to the rest of the colony, but its aura of history has diminished somewhat over time. Visitors information is available at **Know-How Travel** (☎ 6265 3370; 23 Gordon St; open 9am-5pm Mon-Fri).

AROUND HOBART

Things to See

A few 19th-century buildings have survived near the centre of town and are worth a look. The 1841 **Scots Uniting Church** is behind the high school. Also near the school are the **barracks** and the **Blue Bell Inn** (c. 1829). In the main street is **St George's Anglican Church** and next door is an interesting **graveyard** with headstones marking early settlers' plots.

At the friendly, accoladed **Sorell Fruit Farm** (☎ 6265 2744; W www.sorellfruitfarm.com; 174 Pawleena Rd; open 8.30am-5pm daily late-Oct–Feb, 8.30am-5pm Tues-Sun Mar-May), on the road to Pawleena, you can pick your own fruit – from tayberries to cherries and nectarines, with choice dependent on the season – or nibble the exceptional produce in the relaxing tearooms. The farm also produces sweet Thornlea fruit wines.

Places to Stay & Eat

Blue Bell Inn (☎ 6265 2804; fax 6265 3880; W www.rcat.asn.au/bluebell; 26 Somerville St; singles/doubles $95/110) is a welcoming, two-storey sandstone place offering fine en suite rooms and a choice of cooked breakfasts in its plum-washed interior. The **dining room** (mains $19-23; open from 6.30pm Thur-Tues) serves meals with a Polish bent to both guests and visitors, and will cater to vegans and coeliacs with prior notice; book ahead.

Cherry Park Estate (☎ 6265 2271; W www .cherryparkestate.com; 114 Pawleena Rd; doubles $85-95), down from Sorell Fruit Farm, has comfortable rooms in a modern house, lots of surrounding open spaces, homegrown apricots and creative flourishes like an old phone booth in the front yard.

Sorell is a **takeaway** town, evidenced by the wide range of reasonable takeaways along the main street.

Getting There & Away

The TassieLink service down the Tasman Peninsula from Hobart is the only bus option for reaching Sorell ($5, 40 minutes).

COPPING

☎ 03 • postcode 7174

This tiny town's singular tourist attraction is the **Copping Colonial & Convict Collection**

(☎ 6253 5373; Arthur Hwy; adult/child $5/ free; open 9am-5pm daily), an oddball bric-a-brac collection that includes a church pump organ, old typewriters, antique pistols, an unselfconscious mermaid in a washtub and a horse-drawn potato planter. The items were accumulated over 50 years by a self-confessed local 'tip rat'.

DUNALLEY

☎ 03 • postcode 7177 • pop 290

The well-timbered Forestier Peninsula is connected to Tasmania by an isthmus known as Dunalley. A canal complete with a raiseable bridge cuts across the isthmus, providing a short-cut for small boats.

Places to Stay & Eat

Potters Croft (☎ 6253 5469; W www.view .com.au/croft; Arthur Hwy; singles/doubles from $75/106), at Dunalley's northern end, is a combination craft gallery, Bream Creek wine outlet and provider of cosy, exceedingly well-catered accommodation in loft rooms and a cottage. You can practise Zen-like stares at the coastal horizon from the adjacent field.

Waterfront Cafe (☎ 6253 5122; Imlay St; dishes $5-16; open 9am-5pm daily) is a hybrid antique store and pleasant café with an outdoor deck, serving lunch fare from sandwiches to seafood.

Cactus Cafe (☎ 6253 5527; 166 Arthur Hwy; dishes $3-6.50; open 10am-4.30pm Tues-Fri, 10am-2.30pm Sat & Sun), located in the Canal Central shopping centre, serves light meals like vegie or venison burgers in its south-of-the-border interior; it accepts cash only.

Getting There & Away

TassieLink's Tasman Peninsula service will take you to Dunalley from Hobart ($12, one hour).

EAGLEHAWK NECK

☎ 03 • postcode 7179 • pop 210

Eaglehawk Neck is another isthmus, this one connecting the Tasman Peninsula to the Forestier Peninsula. In the days of convict occupation, the 100m-wide neck had a row of unsociable dogs chained across it to prevent escape. Dog platforms were also placed in narrow Eaglehawk Bay to the west to prevent convicts from wading around the barrier. Rumours were circulated that the waters were shark-infested (not true) to discourage swimming. Remarkably, despite the authorities' precautions, a few convicts did escape.

Information

There's a **visitors information centre** (☎ 6250 3722; 443 Pirates Bay Dr; open 9am-5.30pm daily) at the Officers Mess café and store, which sells national park and Port Arthur passes.

Things to See

As you drive down from the north, turn east onto Pirates Bay Dr to the **lookout** – there's a wonderful view of Pirates Bay and the rugged coastline beyond.

The only remaining structure from the convict days is the 1832 **Officers Quarters**, the oldest wooden military building in Australia. Sitting diagonally opposite the Officers Mess, its interior is fitted out with information boards on the history of the building and Eaglehawk Neck.

At the northern end of Pirates Bay is **Tessellated Pavement**, a rocky terrace that has eroded into what looks like tiled paving. At low tide you can walk along the foreshore to **Clydes Island**, where there are fine views of the coastline (you can see as far south as Cape Hauy) and several graves on top.

Follow the side roads to **The Blowhole** and **Tasmans Arch** for some famous close-up views of spectacular coastal cliffs. Take care around The Blowhole, as several people have died here, and keep behind the fences at the other features, as the cliff edges are prone to crumbling.

On the road to The Blowhole is the signposted turn-off to the 4km gravel road leading to **Waterfall Bay**, which has more great views (see the following Bushwalking section). For something more gentile, drive further towards The Blowhole to catch a glimpse of the self-titled **Doo Town**, whose inhabitants have nominated their homes quaint doo-goody names like Doo-Little,

Wee-Doo, This-Will-Doo, Love-Me-Doo and the cryptic Yickle-Doo.

Bushwalking

Waterfall Bluff From the car park at Waterfall Bay, take the 1½-hour return walk to Waterfall Bluff. While much of the walk is through a forest of tall, slender trees that somewhat obscure the view, the track stays close to the bay and there are plenty of places to stop and admire the magnificent scenery from the clifftops, which are unfenced except at the car park. Make sure you continue to the bluff itself before returning to the part of the walk that takes you down past the falls, as the vista from here is breathtaking.

Tasman Trail Waterfall Bay is also the start of the Tasman Trail, which climbs over Tatnells Hill then follows the coast to Fortescue Bay. This is a full day's walk, with some camp sites along the way. If you need to return to your car, walk only as far as Tatnells Hill, where you can enjoy a wonderful view all the way from Eaglehawk Neck to the stunning rock formations of Cape Hauy (7km, one day return). Track notes to this walk and many others in the area are detailed in *Peninsula Tracks* by Peter & Shirley Storey, available from the information centre.

Diving & Fishing

The erosion that has caused the impressive cliff faces has also created some amazing caves and canyons, which are mainly underwater. To see these, go diving with **Eaglehawk Dive Centre** (☎ 6250 3566; w www.eaglehawkdive.com.au; 178 Pirates Bay Dr). Regular dive sites include caves, kelp forests, a sea lion colony and shipwrecks. The cost per dive ranges from $35 to $55; full equipment hire for a day is $70. Diving tickets are required for diving in Australia and full instruction is provided here. A one-day scuba-diving course for those without a certificate is $190.

Personalised Sea Charters (☎ 6250 3370; e seachart@southcom.com.au; 322 Blowhole Rd) takes groups of up to four people on fishing and sight-seeing tours (group charge $80/480 per hour/day).

Nature Tours

Tasmanian Nature Guiding (☎ 6250 3268; W www.tasnatureguiding.com.au; 70 Old Jetty Rd) runs knowledgeable, customised flora- and ornithology-focused excursions on the peninsula (including Tasman National Park; park fee is not included in the tour price) for small groups.

Places to Stay

While there's not a lot of accommodation around the Neck, it's varied enough to suit most people's needs. The advantages of staying here are that it's far more scenic than Port Arthur, relatively uncrowded and close to all the peninsula's major features.

Eaglehawk Neck Backpackers (☎ 6250 3248; 94 Old Jetty Rd; camp sites/dorm beds $6/15) is a simple, endearing hostel located down Old Jetty Rd to the west of the isthmus. Apart from bunks, it also has a small camping area and bicycle hire is available for guests ($5).

Lufra Country Hotel (☎ 6250 3262, 1800 639 532, fax 6250 3460; Pirates Bay Dr; singles/doubles from $60/70) sits above Tessellated Pavement and has great views from the water-facing rooms.

Wunnamurra (☎/fax 6250 3145; 21 Osprey Rd; B&B doubles $100-120) has two nature-surrounded rooms, the larger one with a private veranda, and is only a short amble from the beach.

Osprey Lodge (☎ 6250 3629; W www.view.com.au/osprey; 14 Osprey Rd; doubles from $180) has a great beachfront location, a comfortable bedroom or self-contained cabin to choose from, pre-dinner cheese platters and an unbeatable lounge to lounge in.

Penzance's Pirates Bay Motel (☎ 6250 3272, fax 6250 3519; 210 Blowhole Rd; singles/doubles $65/80) is a no-frills place in a good, near-beach location. It was being sold at the time of writing.

The Treasure Box (☎ 6250 3050; 439 Pirates Bay Dr; doubles $100), though not literally bejewelled, is a large, accommodating unit bookable through the Officers Mess. It has many holiday mod-cons such as a video player, and a long yard sloping down to the beach.

The Neck Beach House (☎ 6250 3541; 423 Pirates Bay Dr; doubles from $90, extra guests $15) is a two-bedroom place next door to The Treasure Box.

Places to Eat

Officers Mess (☎ 6250 3635; mains $9-16; open lunch 11.30am-2.30pm) is a licensed café favouring seafood, with takeaway options too.

Lufra Country Hotel (☎ 6250 3262; mains $17.50-24.50; open 6pm-8pm daily) has a bistro chock-full of scotch fillets and roasts; cheaper counter meals are also available.

Eaglehawk Cafe (☎ 6250 3331; Arthur Hwy; mains $8.50-20; open 9am-late daily) is a licensed, social and refreshing place that hosts the odd gig and poetry reading. There are usually plenty of vegetarian options on the excellent menu, and the old pizza oven out back gets fired up on Friday night.

Getting There & Away

TassieLink can bus you from Hobart to Eaglehawk Neck in 1½ hours; the one-way fare is $14.

TARANNA

☎ 03 • postcode 7180

Taranna is a small town stretched along the shores of Norfolk Bay about 10km north of Port Arthur, its name coming from an Aboriginal word meaning 'Hunting Ground'. It is a historically important village as it was the terminus for Australia's first **tramway**, which ran from Long Bay near Port Arthur to here. This public transport was powered by convicts, who pushed the carriages uphill, then jumped on for the ride down. In those days Taranna was called Old Norfolk.

Dart Island was used as a semaphore station to relay messages from Port Arthur to Hobart. Today, the waters near the island are used for oyster farming.

Taranna's main attraction is the **Tasmanian Devil Park** (☎ 6250 3230; adult/child $14/7; open 9am-5pm daily), which displays the little devils (feedings 10am, 11am and 1.30pm daily year-round, and 5pm daily October to May) and a sea eagle (shows 11.15am and 3.30pm daily). It plays a key role in local wildlife rescue and conservation, and is a breeding centre for endangered birds of prey.

Places to Stay & Eat

Taranna Tavern (☎ 6250 3800; 977 Arthur Hwy; dorm beds $22.50) has tiny, very clean, almost hermetically-sealed bunk rooms on the edge of a now-defunct fishing village (though there has been talk of rehabilitating the village for tourists). Tavern food (mains $9.50 to $19.50) includes a Sunday two-course roast for $15.

Mason's Cottages (☎/fax 6250 3323; 5741 Arthur Hwy; doubles from $80), on the northern edge of town, has a huddle of modern, brick-lined units available for your self-contained pleasure.

Teraki Cottages (☎ 6250 3436, fax 6250 3736; 996 Arthur Hwy; B&B doubles $66) keeps to itself in quiet bushland off the highway and has simple, one-bedroom cabins equipped with fireplaces.

Norfolk Bay Convict Station (☎ 6250 3487; [W] www.convictstation.com; 5862 Arthur Hwy; doubles $120) was built in 1838 and was the tramway's port station. It's now an excellent waterfront B&B where the eclectic rooms come with a hearty cooked breakfast that includes home-made preserves. It also takes bookings for the fully self-contained, Federation-style **Taranna House** (10 Annie St; house per 1/2/3 couples $100/160/220), up on the hill opposite the convict station; you get full run of the house and fantastic views.

The Mussel Boys (☎ 6250 3088; 5927 Arthur Hwy; open dinner Thur-Sat), diagonally opposite Taranna Tavern, is a marine bivalve dispenser and all-purpose seafood café set in a modern cottage.

FORTESCUE BAY

Hidden 12km down a gravel road from the highway is this remote and captivating bay, with a sweeping sandy beach backed by thick forests. Apart from swimming and lazing on the beach, the main activity here is walking. Excellent tracks lead to some of the best coastal scenery in the state, with the cliffs taller and more impressive than those around Eaglehawk Neck. For those with their own boats, this is an excellent base for fishing; it has a boat ramp and calm waters.

The sheltered bay was one of the semaphore station sites used during the convict period to relay messages to Eaglehawk Neck. Early last century a timber mill was in operation and the boilers and jetty ruins are still visible near Mill Creek, as are the remains of some of the timber tramways used to collect the timber. The mill closed in 1952. A fish factory was also in operation in the 1940s in Canoe Bay. Fortescue Bay is part of the Tasman National Park; the usual park entry fees apply.

The bay's **camping ground** (☎ 6250 2433; camp sites per 1 person/2-6 people $5.50/11) lacks powered sites, but firewood is available and there are gas BBQs; there are also plans for hot showers. Bookings are advised at major holiday periods and rates don't include the national park entry fee. There are no shops here so bring in all your own food. There's also no public transport to the bay; it's a 12km walk to the highway, from where buses run to Port Arthur.

Bushwalking

Several walking tracks start from the bay. The best walk is to **Cape Hauy** (four hours return) – a well-used path leads out to sensational sea stacks like **The Candlestick** and **Totem Pole**. To see rainforest, follow the same track towards Cape Hauy and then take the side track to **Mt Fortescue**, which takes six to seven hours return. To the north, a good track follows the shoreline to **Canoe Bay** (two hours return) and **Bivouac Bay** (four hours return). The tracks extend all the way to **Cape Pillar**, where the sea cliffs are 300m high; this requires around three days to visit. For track notes, see Lonely Planet's *Walking in Australia*.

PORT ARTHUR

☎ 03 • postcode 7182

Port Arthur is the name of the small settlement in which the Port Arthur Historic Site is situated. In 1830, Governor Arthur chose the Tasman Peninsula as the place where prisoners who had committed further crimes in the colony would be confined. He called the peninsula a 'natural penitentiary' because it was connected to the mainland only by a strip of land less than 100m wide: Eaglehawk Neck.

Between 1830 and 1877, about 12,500 convicts served sentences at Port Arthur and for many it was a living hell, though convicts who behaved well often lived in better conditions than those they'd experienced back home. The soldiers who guarded them lived in similar conditions and they too were often imprisoned for what would today be regarded as minor offences.

The penal establishment of Port Arthur became the centre of a network of penal stations on the peninsula, but transcended its role as a prison town. It had fine buildings and thriving industries, including timber milling, shipbuilding, coal mining, shoemaking and brick and nail production.

A semaphore telegraph system allowed instant communication between Port Arthur, the penal out-stations and Hobart. Convict farms provided fresh vegetables, a boys prison was built at Point Puer to re-form and educate juvenile convicts, and a church was erected.

Port Arthur was reintroduced to tragedy in April 1996 when a gunman opened fire on visitors and staff at the site, killing 35 people, either there or close by, and injuring several others. The gunman was finally captured after burning down a local guesthouse and was subsequently imprisoned.

Historic Site

Port Arthur's well-preserved historic site (☎ 6251 2310, 1800 659 101; **w** *www.port arthur.org.au; open 8.30am-dusk daily*) is one of Tasmania's prime tourist attractions.

Information The large visitor and interpretation centre includes a regional **information counter** (☎ 6251 2371; open 10.30am-7pm daily Dec-Apr, 10.30am-4pm daily May-Nov). Some of the centre's other facilities (toilets, ticket counter, Felons Restaurant) are accessible until later in the evening. There is no fee for accessing the visitors centre.

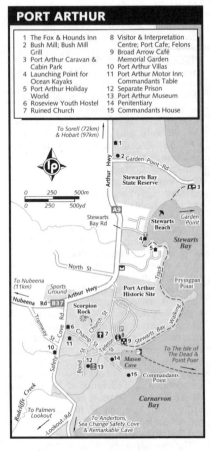

PORT ARTHUR

1 The Fox & Hounds Inn
2 Bush Mill; Bush Mill Grill
3 Port Arthur Caravan & Cabin Park
4 Launching Point for Ocean Kayaks
5 Port Arthur Holiday World
6 Roseview Youth Hostel
7 Ruined Church
8 Visitor & Interpretation Centre; Port Cafe; Felons
9 Broad Arrow Café Memorial Garden
10 Port Arthur Villas
11 Port Arthur Motor Inn; Commandants Table
12 Separate Prison
13 Port Arthur Museum
14 Penitentiary
15 Commandants House

Buggy transport around the site can be arranged for people with restricted mobility; ask at the information counter. The new ferry plying the harbour is wheelchair-accessible.

Prices For a fee of $22/10/48 per adult/child/family you can visit all of the site's 30-plus restored buildings and ruins, including the Asylum (now the Port Arthur Museum) and the Separate (or Model) Prison. The ticket, valid for the day of purchase and the following day, also entitles you to a guided tour of the settlement and a short harbour cruise (cruise not available during August). Tickets can be converted into two-year passes for an extra $3.30/6.60 per person/family. If you arrive late in the day, you should be offered a half-price Twilight Ticket, valid only on the day of purchase. Also available is a Three-In-One Pass (see Information at the beginning of the Tasman Peninsula section).

Penal Settlement To learn about the history of the site and its buildings, take the informative free guided tour and check out the visitor centre's bookshop for a range of publications on the subject. The **Port Arthur Museum**, containing numerous displays and a café, was originally the Asylum, housing patients from throughout the colony. The **Separate Prison** was built as a place of punishment for difficult prisoners, following a decision to 'reform' prisoners by isolation and sensory deprivation rather than by flogging. The **church** was built in 1836 but was destroyed by fire in 1884, while the **Penitentiary**, converted from a granary in 1857, was also eaten by fire in 1897.

Broad Arrow Café The Broad Arrow Café, scene of many of the 1996 shootings, was gutted following the massacre. Today, the shell of the building has been preserved and a Memorial Garden established around it.

Organised Tours Free, 40-minute **guided tours** of the historic site leave hourly from the visitors centre between 9.30am and 3.30pm, plus at 4pm.

Ghostly apparitions, poltergeists and unexplained happenings have apparently been recorded at Port Arthur since the 1870s, as explained during the popular lantern-lit, 90-minute **Ghost Tour**; the tour costs $14/8.60/36.30 per adult/child/family and departs from the visitors centre nightly at dusk. The **Isle of the Dead Landing Cruise & Tour**, which costs $6.60/5.50 per adult/ child and is conducted daily (no cruises during August), comprises a guided tour of Port Arthur's old burial ground in the harbour. Both of these tours should be booked well in advance.

Tasmanian Seaplanes (☎ 6227 8808; W *www.tas-seaplane.com)* takes off along the spectacular local coastline. Prices range from $80/40 per adult/child for a 20-minute flight, to $160/85 for 40 minutes of air time.

See the Getting There & Away section later for details on tours from Hobart.

The Bush Mill
The Bush Mill (☎ 6250 2221; W *www.bush mill.com.au; Arthur Hwy; adult/child $15/ 6.50 including train ride; open 9am-5pm daily),* north of the historic site, has a popular steam train undertaking a 4km ride over hill and dale (departs 10.15am, 11.15am and 2.30pm daily; extra trips require a minimum of six adults). The site takes a pioneering approach, with sawmill, blacksmith and bush doctor exhibits illustrating what life was like in the Australian bushland around 1890.

Sea Kayaking
Blackaby's (☎ 6267 1508; W *www.blackaby seakayaks.com.au)* offers a full-day tour of Port Arthur's immediate coastline by sea kayak, conducted on demand and costing $175 per person.

Places to Stay
Port Arthur Caravan & Cabin Park (☎ 6250 2340, 1800 620 708, fax 6250 2509; Garden Point Rd; dorm beds per adult/child $15/10, unpowered/powered site doubles $16/18, cabin doubles $75-85) is located 2km north of Port Arthur in quiet bushland. It is well looked after and has a cooking shelter, games area and lots of trees. You can pay historic site entry fees at reception and follow a track around the shoreline from here to Port Arthur.

Roseview Youth Hostel (☎/fax 6250 2311; Champ St; dorm beds $18, doubles per person $20), at the edge of the historic site, has brightened considerably in recent times and has an appealing rough-around-the-edges charm. To get here, continue 500m past the Port Arthur turn-off and turn left at the sign for the hostel into Safety Cove Rd. You can buy your historic site entry ticket here.

Port Arthur Motor Inn (☎ 6250 2101, 1800 030 747, fax 6250 2417; 29 Safety Cove Rd; doubles from $116), near the youth hostel, has flashy views over the historic site and non-flashy motel accommodation.

Port Arthur Villas (☎ 6250 2239, 1800 815 775; W www.wwt.com.au/portarthurvillas; 52 Safety Cove Rd; doubles $114-135) adjoins the former penal settlement and has older-style self-contained units.

Andertons (☎ 6250 2378; 239 Safety Cove Rd; doubles $65-75) is right on Carnarvon Bay, not far from a beach. It has B&B in the large weatherboard main house and there is cheaper accommodation in functional self-contained units.

Port Arthur Holiday World (☎ 6250 2262; W www.ontas.com.au/portarthur_holiday _world; Arthur Hwy; 1-bedroom cabin per single/ double from $109/132) is ruled by self-contained log cabins, one of them wheelchair-accessible. It sits peacefully above the swimming beach of Stewarts Bay.

The Fox & Hounds Inn (☎ 6250 2217, 1800 635 840; W www.foxtas.com; Arthur Hwy; motel singles/doubles from $90/100, unit doubles from $120) is a mock-Tudor complex near the Bush Mill, where you can choose between motel rooms and two-bedroom self-contained units. Despite their quaint appearance, all the rooms here have modern interiors.

Sea Change Safety Cove (☎ 6250 2719; W www.safetycove.com; 425 Safety Cove Rd; doubles from $110) is 5km south of Port Arthur, just off the sandy sweep of Safety Cove Beach. It has both B&B and self-contained rooms, and fantastic views of peninsula cliffs off the balcony.

Places to Eat

Port Cafe (☎ 6251 2310; open from 8.30am daily), in the visitors centre, is an overpriced cafeteria with standard eat-in or takeaway meals.

Felons (☎ 1800 659 101; mains $17-24; open from 5pm daily), also in the visitors centre, is a licensed restaurant with upmarket, mainly meat-based dishes.

Bush Mill Grill (☎ 6250 2221; mains $16-22; open 6pm-9pm daily), in the complex of the same name, lets you dine close to the surrounding bush on the outdoor deck. It serves seafood, but it's the porterhouse and

eye fillets that jump off the plates here. The Bush Mill also has a light-lunching café.

Commandants Table (☎ 6250 2101; mains $15.50-25.50; open from 6pm daily), at the Port Arthur Motor Inn, has a selective menu featuring fare like locally farmed wallaby; alternatively, rest your weary teeth on some chicken and spinach 'pillows' (filo pastry).

The Fox & Hounds Inn (☎ 6250 2217; mains $18.50-24.50) does reputable à la carte lunches and dinners daily; it also has a kiddies' menu.

Getting There & Away

TassieLink (☎ 6272 7300, 1300 300 520; W www.tigerline.com.au) journeys once every weekday from Hobart (departing 4pm, with extra services three days a week at 10am over summer) to Port Arthur; the 2¼-hour one-way trip costs $17.

Tigerline (☎ 6272 6611, 1300 653 633; W www.tigerline.com.au) runs day tours from Hobart to Port Arthur for $60/38 per adult/child.

Port Arthur Cruises (☎ 6231 2655, 1300 134 561; Brooke St Pier, Hobart) offers a cruise from Hobart to Port Arthur via Cape Raoul and Tasman Island, with the trip back to Hobart conducted by coach. The tour costs $120/85 per adult/child. You can also take a one-way trip to Port Arthur for $85/55.

REMARKABLE CAVE

South of Port Arthur is Remarkable Cave, a series of arches eroded into shape by the sea. A boardwalk provides access to a metal viewing platform. From the car park you can follow the coast east to **Maingon Blowhole** (two hours return) or farther on to **Mt Brown** (five hours return), where there are excellent views.

On the return it's worth deviating to **Palmers Lookout**, which also provides good views of the entire Port Arthur and Safety Cove area.

NUBEENA

☎ 03 • postcode 7184 • pop 265

This is the largest town on the peninsula, fanned out along the shore, yet it's much quieter than Port Arthur. It's really just a holiday destination for locals. Nubeena is an Aboriginal word for 'Crayfish'.

The main activities here are swimming and relaxing on **White Beach**, or fishing from the jetty or foreshore. Down a side road is some energetic walking to **Tunnel Bay** (five hours return), **Raoul Bay Lookout** (two hours return) and **Cape Raoul** (five hours return). To the north is **Roaring Beach**, which gets good surf but isn't safe for swimming.

Places to Stay & Eat

White Beach Caravan & Cabin Park (☎ 6250 2142; ☒ www.whitebeachcp.com .au; unpowered/powered site doubles $16/18, on-site van doubles $45, cabin doubles $74-84) is in quiet, ghost gum–dotted surrounds south of Nubeena and has a kiosk.

White Beach Holiday Village (☎ 6250 2152; ☒ www.whitebeachholidayvillas.com .au; doubles $82-115), at the other end of the beach, has self-contained villas (one with spa); the units furthest up the hill are newer.

Fairway Resort (☎ 6250 2171; ☒ www .fairwayresort.com; doubles from $100) has a nine-hole golf course, pool, spa and restaurant, though accommodation is in cinderblock motel units with dark interiors.

A Food Affaire (☎ 6250 2749; 1625 Main Rd; open 9am-8pm daily) is a milk bar/takeaway with a separate Chinese food menu ($6 to $7) and pizzas nightly from 5pm.

Nubeena Tavern (☎ 6250 2250; Main Rd; mains $12.50-20; open 6pm-8pm daily), up a hill near Farway Resort, calls itself a 'Reef 'n' Beef Restaurant', which means plenty of meaty meals.

Getting There & Away

TassieLink's Tasman Peninsula service will take you to Nubeena from Hobart in two hours and costs $16 one way.

SALTWATER RIVER

The restored ruins at the **Coal Mines Historic Site** are powerful reminders of the colonial past. Dug in 1833, the coal mines were used to punish the worst of the convicts, who worked in terrible conditions. The poorly managed mining operation was not economic. In 1848 it was sold to private enter-

Windgrove

Windgrove, near Nubeena on the Tasman Peninsula, is an isolated coastal property owned by Peter Adams, a creator of beautiful Huon-pine and myrtle benches that sell for upwards of $12,000. Peter sets out to produce works that express a link between art, ecology and theology, and in November and May each year displays them in 40 hectares of revegetated coastal heath as part of the Australian Open Garden Scheme.

In the aftermath of the events of September 11, Peter also developed an eight-hectare Peace Garden on the property, which incorporates a contemporary communal 'midden', a 2km bench-lined clifftop walk, and a number of large, reflective sculptures that include a 6m-high spiral-carved blue-gum log and a split 6-tonne piece of dolerite. His latest project is the development of the peaceful Windgrove Centre, a combination sanctuary, retreat, art studio and multi-purpose hall for writers, dancers, musicians, meditators, ecologists and like-minded souls.

You can find Windgrove on the Internet (☒ www.windgrove.com) or in 3D reality (when the property is open to the public) by following the road to Roaring Beach from Nubeena for 5km, then heading left at the 'Windgrove' signage.

prise and within 10 years it was abandoned. Some buildings were demolished, while fire and weather took a toll on the rest.

Things to See & Do

The old mines site is interesting to wander around and provides a dramatic contrast to Port Arthur. Don't enter any mine shafts, because they haven't been stabilised and could be dangerous. You can, however, enter some well-preserved solitary-confinement cells, which are torturously small and dark.

Apart from the mines, the area's main attractions are **rare birds** and **butterflies**, and easy **walks** across gentle coastal country. From Lime Bay, the 2½-hour return journey to Lagoon Beach is the most popular walk.

Organised Tours
Seaview Lodge (☎ *6250 2766;* W *www .tassie.net.au/~seaview; Nubeena Back Rd, Koonya)* offers a variety of guided tours taking in the coal mines and other significant local features. Half-day tours cost $30/25 per adult/child, and full-day tours $50/40.

Places to Stay
Lime Bay Nature Reserve (*camp sites per adult/child $3.30/1.65*) is a beautiful area where bush camping is allowed north along a sandy track. Camping is very basic, with pit toilets and fireplaces. Water must be taken in, as there's no permanent fresh water.

KOONYA
☎ 03 • postcode 7187
There's little for visitors at this tiny settlement apart from some nice accommodation.

Seaview Lodge (☎*/fax 6250 2766; Nubeena Back Rd; dorm beds/doubles $16.50/ 35)* is a rambling establishment with basic bunks, fantastic views and a peaceful location. School groups often visit in winter. Linen is an extra $5.

Norfolk Bayview (☎*/fax 6250 3855;* e *norfolkbayviewbb@bigpond.com; 111 Nubeena Back Rd; doubles from $70)* is a modern B&B, with rates including a full cooked breakfast and far-fetched views from the front porch over Norfolk Bay.

Cascades (☎ *6250 3873, fax 6250 3013; 533 Main Rd; B&B singles/doubles from $100/110)* was originally an out-station of Port Arthur, with around 400 convicts working there at one time. Some of the buildings have now been restored in impressive period style to accommodate wannabe chaingangers. Continental breakfast and entry to a private museum are also thrown in.

Getting There & Away
TassieLink's Tasman Peninsula service will take you from Hobart to Koonya in 2½ to three hours; the one-way fare is $15.

Southeast Coast

This slice of the state has much to offer, particularly if you have your own transport and enjoy driving through idyllic countryside and browsing through roadside produce stores. Water views from the peninsula's mountain passes and the serenity of Bruny Island add to the region's laid-back character. The more energetic can also find fulfilment, with Hartz Peak, Hastings Cave and the South Coast Track that unravels from magnificent Recherche Bay being just a few of the southeast coast's physically enlivening features.

The wide Huon River dominates the region, carving the hills into deep valleys. Synonymous with this river is the famous Huon pine, a unique tree that can exceed 2000 years in age. Sadly, the oldest trees were logged out of existence many years ago and only a few young specimens remain. The area is also known for its spectacular rainbows, which are probably due to a combination of southern latitude and prolific waterways.

In the 1960s, Huon Valley apple growing put Tasmania on the international export map. At one stage there were over 2000 orchards exporting eight million boxes of apples, mainly to the UK. When demand from Europe declined, so did the orchards.

Farmers have since diversified into other fruit crops, and have also turned their attention to Atlantic salmon, wine and tourism. Tasmania's reputation for clean air and low pollution has led to these new products finding markets in Asia. The abundance of high-quality local produce is a bonus for the region's restaurateurs, many of whom feature it in their menus.

Fruit-picking work is available in the region from late December until April or May, though it can be difficult to obtain. See the Work section in the Facts for the Visitor chapter for more information.

Getting There & Around

Bus The company **Hobart Coaches** (☎ 6233 4232, 13 22 01) runs several buses each

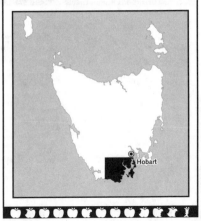

weekday from Hobart south through Margate, Snug and Kettering to Woodbridge. A bus also runs three times each weekday from Hobart to Snug and inland across to Cygnet.

TassieLink (☎ 6272 7300, 1300 300 520; **w** www.tigerline.com.au) runs buses along the Huon Hwy from Hobart through Huonville and Geeveston to Dover; there are up to five services a day from Monday to Friday, and one each on Saturday and Sunday. At 9am on Monday, Wednesday and Friday from December through March, a Tassie-Link bus departs Hobart and continues south all the way to the end of the road at Cockle Creek (bookings essential).

Car The views from the highway between Hobart and Woodbridge are especially lovely, particularly on sunny days during seasons of decent rainfall. At such times, the contrast between the lush green pastures and the deep-blue channel waters can be dazzling. If you then take the road from Woodbridge to Gardeners Bay on the way to Cygnet, you'll be rewarded with stunning water views on both sides of the ridge. Another road across the peninsula to Cygnet leaves the highway just before Kettering, but it is less scenic. You can also follow the coast around from Woodbridge through Verona Sands to Cygnet on a road that occasionally passes very close to the channel, making it an impressive detour if the water is choppy.

Further south, some sections of the side route from Surges Bay through Police Point and on to Dover are gravel, but the road is in good condition and the views are great. The 19km road from Lune River to Cockle Creek has been surfaced with very coarse gravel, which roughens the ride in an older vehicle. Check your tyres before you start out and make sure your spare is in good condition.

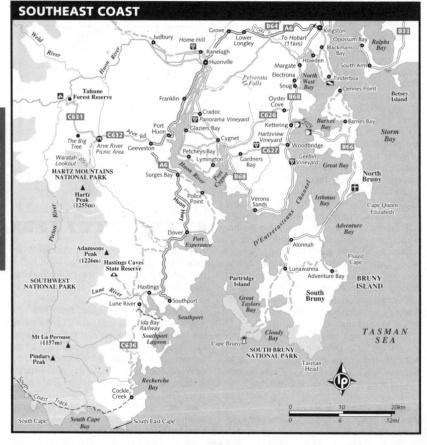

SOUTHEAST COAST

Organised Tours The **Bottom Bits Bus**
(☎ *6234 5093, 1800 777 103;* W *www.bot
tombitsbus.com*) offers a day-long tour of
the area from Hobart for $80, covering
transport and all entry fees.

SNUG
☎ 03 • postcode 7054 • pop 800

Early European explorers decided this area
provided a safe, sheltered anchorage for
their ships, hence the name Snug. The town
was devastated in the 1967 bushfires, when
80 houses burnt down. A temporary caravan
village was established beside the oval,
which eventually became the current-day
caravan park. After being rebuilt, the town
became a popular holiday spot due to its
calm waters and good boating facilities.

Things to See & Do

Oyster Cove, accessed via Manuka Rd 5km
south of Snug, was an important traditional
camp for Indigenous people (who called it
Mena Loongana, Mannina), but in 1847 it
became the next destination for the Tasmanian Aborigines who survived Wybalenna on
Flinders Island (see the History section in
the Facts about Tasmania chapter). In 1995,
Oyster Cove was returned to the Tasmanian
Aboriginal community and can now be
visited independently.

Every year on the Saturday closest to 16
January (the date in 1984 that Aboriginal
activists began their campaign to reclaim
the site), the **Oyster Cove Festival** (*admission free*) is held. It is the state's largest
Indigenous celebration and features musicians, artists and the sale of Aboriginal food
and arts and crafts.

Nearby **Snug Falls** are located 3.5km off
the highway. An easy 90-minute return walk,
complete with seats and picnic shelters, leads
to the foot of the falls. Just south of Snug at
Conningham is a good swimming beach.

Beside the highway 1km south of the town
is the **Channel Historical & Folk Museum**
(☎ *6267 9169; 2361 Channel Hwy; adult/
concession $3/2; open 10am-4pm Thur-Tues*),
a historical showcase of the local timber, fishing and ship-building industries that also has
information on the destructive 1967 fires.

Places to Stay & Eat

Snug Beach Cabin & Caravan Park (☎ *6267
9138, fax 6267 9128; 16 Beach Rd; powered/
unpowered site doubles $20/15, on-site van
doubles $40, cabin doubles $65-84*) has
grass-sprung, tree-sheltered sites beside the
beach, and man-made distractions like a
tennis court and playground.

Snug Tavern (☎ *6267 9238; 2236 Channel
Hwy; mains $11-18.50; open for meals noon-
2pm & 6pm-8pm Thur-Sat, noon-2pm Wed*)
has counter meals; its three-course special
is $15.50.

KETTERING
☎ 03 • postcode 7155 • pop 315

The small port of Kettering lies at the head
of scenic Little Oyster Cove. This bay shelters a marina for fishing boats and yachts, as
well as the Bruny Island car ferry terminal.
It's a reasonable place to base yourself for
regional explorations.

Information

The **Bruny D'Entrecasteaux visitors centre**
(☎ *6267 4494;* W *www.tasmaniaholiday.com;
81 Ferry Rd; open 9am-5pm daily*) is located
at the ferry terminal and provides heaps of
information on Bruny Island and the surrounding district.

Sea Kayaking

Among the numerous offerings of **The
Roaring 40°s Ocean Kayaking Company**
(☎ *6267 5000;* W *www.roaring40skayaking
.com.au; Ferry Rd*) are classes in the basics of
sea kayaking ($65 to $75), day tours across
the channel to Bruny Island suitable for
first-timers and including lunch (adult/child
$115/65, minimum age 12), and sea-kayak
rental (single/double kayaks $15/20 per
hour and $45/65 per day).

Places to Stay & Eat

Oyster Cove Inn (☎ *6267 4446;* W *www
.view.com.au/oyster; Ferry Rd; singles/doubles
from $40/65*) has a mixture of budget singles
and bigger rooms with views over the boat-
cluttered harbour. The on-site restaurant
(mains from $10) serves good lunches and
dinners daily. Eat or drink on the outside

deck and check out some of the many wooden sculptures decorating the landscape.

The Old Kettering Inn (☎ 6267 4426, fax 6267 4884; 58 Ferry Rd; B&B doubles $100), on the road to the ferry terminal, has one comfortable suite with a private entrance, and a lounge affording marina views.

Herons Rise Vineyard (☎ 6267 4339; W www.heronsrise.com.au; Saddle Rd; B&B doubles from $120), north of town, has two grevillea-decorated luxury cottages to retreat into. Three-course dinners and some of the vineyard's fine white pinot can be supplied by prior arrangement.

Mermaid Cafe (☎ 6267 4494; 81 Ferry Rd; meals $6-12.50; open 9am-4.30pm daily), at the visitors centre, is a relaxed licensed café where you can enjoy light meals such as salads and pan-fried salmon burgers on Kettering's waterfront.

Getting There & Away

Hobart Coaches runs four buses each weekday from Hobart to Kettering ($6.50/10.40 one way/return, one hour). They stop in the vicinity of the two service stations on the main street in the town's north.

BRUNY ISLAND
☎ 03 • postcode 7150

Beautiful, sparsely populated Bruny Island is two lumps of land joined by a sandy isthmus less than 100m wide. However, locals refer to the two different sections as North and South Bruny. North Bruny has rolling hills that are extensively farmed, while South Bruny is more scenic, with steeper, forested hills and the varied wildlife of South Bruny National Park. In-between is the narrow 5km isthmus, home to mutton birds and other waterfowl.

The island's coastal scenery is superb and there are plenty of fine swimming and surf beaches, plus good sea and freshwater fishing. There are also several signposted walking tracks within the national park and reserves, especially on the southern Labillardiere Peninsula and at Fluted Cape.

The island was sighted by Abel Tasman in 1642 and later visited by Furneaux, Cook, Bligh and Cox between 1770 and 1790. It

was eventually named after Rear-Admiral Bruni D'Entrecasteaux, who explored and surveyed the area in 1792. Strangely, confusion reigned about the spelling and in 1918 it was changed from Bruni to Bruny.

Tasmanian Aborigines belonging to the Nuennone band originally called the island Lunawanna-Alonnah, a name given contemporary recognition by being broken up and used to identify two of the island's settlements. Among their numbers was Truganini, daughter of Mangana, chief of the Nuennone band – she left Bruny Island in the 1830s to accompany George Robinson on his infamous statewide journey to win the trust of all the Tasmanian Aborigines (see the boxed text 'Truganini' in the Facts About Tasmania chapter). Many of Bruny Island's landmarks, including Mt Mangana, are named after Indigenous individuals.

The island has experienced several commercial ventures. Sandstone was mined from a rocky point and used in prominent buildings such as the post office and Houses of Parliament in Melbourne, and coal was also locally mined. But these industries gradually declined due to high transportation costs. Only farming and forestry had long-term viability.

Tourism is becoming increasingly important to the island's economy but at the moment remains fairly low-key. There are (as yet) no homogenised resorts, just plenty of interesting cottages and houses, most self-contained. Too many visitors try unsuccessfully to cram their experience of Bruny into a day or less. If you can, stay for a few days and really begin exploring the island's striking coastal environment and at least some of the walking tracks within its stunning national park.

Information

The **Bruny D'Entrecasteaux visitors centre** (☎ 6267 4494; W www.tasmaniaholiday.com; 81 Ferry Rd; open 9am-5pm daily), at the ferry terminal in Kettering, can help you out with ferry tickets, accommodation bookings, books, souvenirs and tourist information. It's a good idea to pick up the free handouts on the local fauna, walks and camping, and the self-drive tour; while

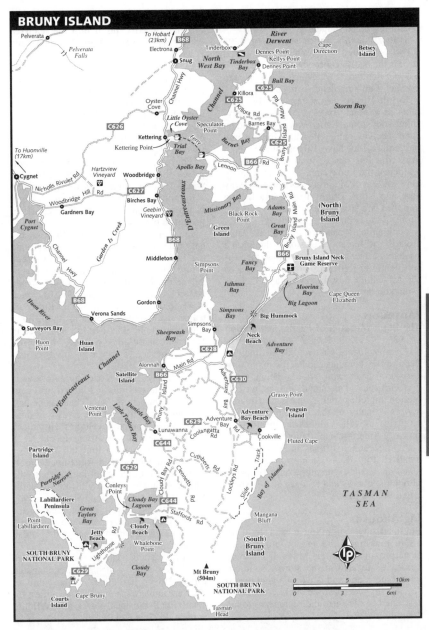

SOUTHEAST COAST

you're at it, grab some of the delicious island-produced fudge too.

Bruny Island's **police station** (☎ 6293 2090) is located in Alonnah. Also found here is the **health centre** (☎ 6293 1143; open 8.30am-4.30pm daily), which is the place to contact if an ambulance is needed.

South Bruny has several fairly well-stocked **general stores**, though not everything your stomach desires will be found on their shelves. The ones at Alonnah and Adventure Bay have Eftpos and are both Australia Post and Commonwealth Bank agencies; the Lunawanna store, on Cloudy Bay Rd, has basic groceries and takeaway fare. On North Bruny, Eftpos and fishing supplies are available at Kelly's Village Store, Dennes Point.

National park passes should be available from the aforementioned stores, though it's probably easier to purchase them at the visitors centre in Kettering. For petrol, stick to the Adventure Bay, Lunawanna or Dennes Point stores.

Museums

The **Bligh Museum of Pacific Exploration** (☎ 6293 1117; 876 Main Rd; adult/child $4/2; open 10am-3pm daily) details the Adventure Bay landings and Pacific exploits of early European explorers like Bligh, Cook and Furneaux. This small, interesting collection includes maps, charts and manuscripts – many of them originals or first editions – as well as globes and information on early Antarctic explorations.

At the council offices in Alonnah is a small **History Room** (admission free; open 10am-4pm daily), with numerous newspaper clippings, photos and records of the island community's past.

Lighthouse

South Bruny's lighthouse was built in 1836, making it the second-oldest such structure in Australia. Made from local stone, it's located at the stormy southern end of the island and is worth a visit just to see the rugged coastline. Public access is restricted to the surrounding **reserve** (open 10am-4pm daily).

National Park & Reserve

Popular **Fluted Cape**, one of the scattered extremities of **South Bruny National Park**, is east of the small township of Adventure Bay. The trail leading here from the main beach passes **Grassy Point** (one to 1½ hours return), a great breakfast spot on a sunny morning. From here you can walk along the shore to **Penguin Island**, accessible at low tide, or complete a more difficult circuit and climb the cape for some glorious views (two to 2½ hours return).

The park's southwestern portion comprises the large **Labillardiere Peninsula**, which features rugged coastal scenery and a lighthouse. Walks range from leisurely beach explorations to a 4½-hour circuit of the entire peninsula.

For descriptions of walks through the national park, as well as other walks around the island, like the easy **Mavista Creek** nature trail (30 minutes return) southwest of Adventure Bay, consult the booklet *Bruny Island: A Guide for Walkers* ($6.50), which is available from the Bruny D'Entrecasteaux visitors centre. Bear in mind, however, that the booklet was last published in 1998 and many changes have since taken place. The centre can also supply a free leaflet on local trails.

The **Bruny Island Neck Game Reserve** is home to mutton birds and little (fairy) penguins that nest in the sand dunes. The best time and place to see these birds is at dusk in the warmer months at **Highest Hummock Lookout** (park at the Bruny Island Neck Game Reserve sign). Climb the 273 timber steps to the lookout and **Truganini Memorial** for sweeping views of both parts of the island. A timber walkway also crosses the Neck to the other beach. Make sure you keep to the boardwalk in this area, as the mutton birds dig deep holes into the sand – the holes can be hard to see and you can break an ankle in them.

Bird-watchers visit the island to catch glimpses of species such as the endangered forty-spotted pardalote. Over summer there are numerous ranger-led activities; for details, call the local **Parks and Wildlife Service** (PWS; ☎ 6293 1419).

SOUTHEAST COAST

Camel Rides

For a novel, four-footed touring option, try a camel ride with **Camel Tracks Tasmania** (☎ *6260 6335; 2125 Main Rd, Great Bay*), located just north of the isthmus beside the island's main north-south road. Short rides start at $8/6 per adult/child, one hour is $30/22 and a 2½-hour beach trek is $65/50; longer rides are also available.

Organised Tours

Bruny Island Ventures (☎ *6229 7465, 1300 653 633*) conducts day tours of the island that cost $115/85 per adult/child. Tours depart from and return to Hobart and take in the island's prime features.

The highly recommended **Bruny Island Charters** (☎ *6293 1465;* W *www.bruny charters.com*) departs from the jetty at Adventure Bay for tours of the island's glorious southern coastline, taking in rookeries, seal colonies and towering sea cliffs. These tours cost from $85 per person and bookings are essential.

Places to Stay

Bruny Island is a popular Tasmanian holiday destination, as evidenced by the multitude of self-contained cottages for hire, most suitable for medium-sized groups and offering economic rates for one-week rentals. Bookings are essential, as owners/managers and their keys are not always easily located – the visitors centre at Kettering is a good place to start, though keep in mind it doesn't list all the available accommodation.

The township of Adventure Bay on South Bruny's east coast is the main accommodation area, but there are plenty of other places around the island. Alonnah is the other main settlement on South Bruny, and Dennes Point and Barnes Bay on North Bruny both have places to stay.

Places to Stay – Budget

National Park & Reserve If you have a vehicle and a tent, the cheapest accommodation is at one of the free designated **bush camp sites** – camping on Bruny is restricted to these places to prevent the island's foreshores being damaged by indiscriminate tent

placement. The site places; BYO firew

There are sites (national park pa **Beach**, a beautiful of the lighthouse, There is also a can tional park at **Neck Beach**, at the southern end of The Neck.

Adventure Bay The **Captain James Cook Memorial Caravan Park** (☎*/fax 6293 1128; Main Rd; unpowered/powered site doubles $10/14, on-site van doubles $32-40*) has a great beachside location with a mountainous backdrop, plus welcoming owners and good facilities. Fishing charters are also available here, with all equipment provided (half-day charters from $65 per person, minimum two people).

Adventure Bay Holiday Village & Caravan Park (☎ *6293 1270, fax 6293 1485; Main Rd; unpowered/powered site doubles $12/ 14, dorm beds per adult/child $18/10, on-site van doubles from $32, cabin doubles $50- 95*), beside the beach at the end of Adventure Bay Rd, has dorm beds and cabins to suit all budgets. Those in a loud or celebratory mood should be warned that disruptions to the status quo could result in a request to move on.

Lumeah (☎ *6293 1265;* e *lumeah@tassie .net.au; Main Rd; doubles from $50*), a 115-year-old sawmiller's cottage, offers several comfortable rooms, continental breakfast and a very cosy communal area. Formerly the island's hostel, it still supplies sound advice on what to see and do here. Transport to walking tracks can be provided and you can also arrange to be picked up from Hobart ($40 return; service is available Monday, Wednesday, Friday and occasionally Saturday).

Places to Stay – Mid-Range

South Bruny The two main settlements on the western side of South Bruny, Lunawanna and Alonnah, are small villages that aren't as attractive as the Adventure Bay area.

Hotel Bruny (☎ *6293 1148; Alonnah; singles/doubles $65/75*) offers two squat units, though an effort has been to brighten the interiors.

ayaree Estate (☎ 6293 1088; 4391 Main d; doubles $80, extra adult/child $15/5), midway between Alonnah and Lunawanna, is a rustic three-bedroom farmhouse on a vineyard estate, complete with log fire.

Bruny Island Explorers' Cottages (☎ 6293 1271; Lighthouse Rd; doubles from $85) are in a secluded location south of Lunawanna on the road to the lighthouse and offer good-value, self-contained habitats for up to six people.

Inala (☎ 6293 1217; W www.inalabruny .com.au; Cloudy Bay Rd; doubles $120), on the road to Cloudy Bay, has isolated, comfortably furnished timber environs. Guided nature tours can be arranged here.

North Bruny Barnes Bay was once the ferry terminal but is now pleasantly lacking in noisy activity. A clutch of accommodation has popped up here in recent times.

Barnes Bay Villa (☎ 6260 6287; e kdunc@ netspace.net.au; doubles $80) has a large, well-equipped brick unit with old-style aesthetics.

Lennonville Cottage (☎ 6260 6205; W www.lennonvillecottage.com.au; Lennon Rd; doubles $130) is on a working sheep-and-cherry farm overlooking Barnes Bay and has water views from the large back deck. To get there, travel 2.5km from the ferry terminal, turn left through the stone gate and the cottage is 1km on the right.

Lennon Farm Retreat (☎ 6260 6258; Wisbys Rd; doubles $80, extra guests $10), on nearby Quarantine Bay, is a fully self-contained two-bedroom place near a swimmable beach. The route there is a little complicated so get directions from the owners when booking.

Places to Stay – Top End

South Bruny On the road to the lighthouse is **St Clairs** (☎ 6293 1300; W www.stclairs .com; Lighthouse Rd; doubles $165), a plush getaway cottage surrounded by bushland. Rental nets you a spa and cooked breakfast.

The Tree House (☎ 0405 192 892; e the treehouse@iprimus.com.au; Alonnah; doubles $150) is a lofty, attractively designed timber place overlooking the unattractively named Sheep Wash Bay. It has all the mod-cons and superb views. The price drops to $130 per double for stays of two nights or more.

Mavista Cottages (☎/fax 6293 1347; W www.storyshare.com.au/mavista; 120 Resolution Rd, Adventure Bay; doubles $120-145) is fenced in by tea trees and lots of shrubbery, and the cottages have loft rooms. The property was for sale at the time of writing.

Morella Island Retreats (☎ 6293 1131; W www.morella-island.com.au; 46 Adventure Bay Rd; B&B doubles from $130), just north of Adventure Bay, has a couple of beautifully imagined cottages, great for a romantic interlude. Non-guests can still peruse the surrounding **gardens** (admission $4; open 10am-5pm daily) with their sizeable rhododendrons, best enjoyed in August and September.

North Bruny Overlooking splendid Bull Bay on the northern tip of North Bruny is **Kelly's Lookout** (☎ 6260 6466; e kellys lookout@aol.com; 212 Main Rd, Dennes Point; doubles from $130). Its loquacious host has created a jack-of-all-trades guesthouse, with comfortable en suite rooms, a seafood-specialising café/restaurant, tourist information and beer from the old country.

Swanhaven B&B (☎ 6260 6428; W www .bruny.tco.asn.au/swanhaven; 150 Power Rd, Barnes Bay; doubles from $110) is a homely bushland retreat with upstairs B&B rooms, full cooked breakfasts and a deepwater dock for the boat-equipped; three-course dinners can be arranged from $25 per person. You'll need directions from the hosts to find this place.

Places to Eat

Provisions and takeaways are available at the island's **general stores**. (See Information earlier in this section.)

Penguin Tearoom & Craft Shop (☎ 6293 1352; Adventure Bay; meals $6-12.50; open 9am-5pm daily Oct-Apr, 9am-5pm Wed-Mon May-Sept), located beside the Adventure Bay Shop, serves Devonshire teas, ploughman's lunches and salmon burgers.

Hotel Bruny (☎ *6293 1148; Alonnah; mains $10-15; open lunch & dinner Mon-Sat, dinner Sun*) has decently priced counter meals.

Hothouse Cafe (☎ *6293 1131; 46 Adventure Bay Rd; meals $6-20; open from 10am daily*), at Morella Island Retreats, has an impressive view of The Neck. Besides wine and strong coffee, it also serves good breakfasts, salads and seafood until late; bookings are preferred after 5.30pm.

Rao's (☎ *6260 6444; 360 Lennon Rd; mains $7.50-14.50; open 10am-late daily Oct-Apr, 10am-late Wed-Sun May-Sept*) is a pleasingly modern eatery not far from the ferry terminal, with an ever-changing menu of tasty Italian meals; slump into the old club lounge on the slate-floored porch and take your pick. Rao's also sells Tasmanian wine to take away.

Getting There & Away

Access to the island is via a **car ferry** (☎ *6272 3277*) that motors from Kettering to Roberts Point on North Bruny in 20 minutes. The ferry can carry 75 cars and is propelled by unusual Voith Schneider propellers, which look like vertical paddle wheels and provide excellent manoeuvrability.

There are 10 services a day from Monday to Thursday and on Saturday, 11 services on Friday, and eight on Sunday. The first ferry to Bruny departs Kettering at 6.50am (8am on Sunday), while the last ferry to Kettering departs Roberts Point at 7pm (7.50pm on Friday). The timetable may vary, however, so double-check departure times.

The following quoted fares are for return trips: a car costs $21 ($28 on public holidays and public holiday weekends); motorcycles $11 ($14 on public holidays and public holiday weekends); bicycles $3; there's no charge for passengers.

At least two buses a day from Hobart to Kettering, run by **Hobart Coaches** (☎ *6233 4232, 13 22 01*), will stop, on request, at the ferry terminal but the Roberts Point terminal on Bruny is a long way from anywhere.

Getting Around

You'll need a vehicle to get around, as there are no buses; a bicycle is another option,

though be prepared for long rides between destinations. Bruny Island has some narrow, winding gravel roads – the slippery, logging truck-infested road over Mt Mangana being the prime case in point – and speed-related accidents are not uncommon. Drive carefully and, if possible, schedule at least a few days for a full exploration of the island.

WOODBRIDGE
☎ 03 • postcode 7162 • pop 250

Established in 1874 and originally called Peppermint Bay due to the area's peppermint gums, Woodbridge was eventually renamed by a landowner nostalgic for his old home in England. It's a quiet town with a tranquil waterfront setting, worth prising your hands from the steering wheel for a quick stop.

Hartzview Vineyard (☎ *6295 1623;* W *www.hartzview.com.au; 70 Dillons Rd; open 9am-5pm daily July-May, 9am-5pm Sat & Sun June*) is located 7km from Woodbridge, off the road to Gardners Bay. It has a fine range of fortified wines (tastings $2) and also sells drops from a dozen other Tasmanian vineyards.

Also on the road to Gardners Bay but closer to Woodbridge is **Woodbridge Hill Handweaving Studio & Gardens** (☎ *6267 4430; Gardners Bay Rd; admission to gardens $3.50; open 9.30am-1pm & 2pm-5.30pm daily Oct-Apr*). It offers a range of handwoven items, from the decorative to the sartorial. The 1.2-hectare gardens allow good channel views. It is open only by appointment from May to September.

Geebin Vineyard (☎ *6267 4750;* W *www .geebin.alltasmanian.com; 3729 Channel Hwy; open daily*), 3km south of Woodbridge, is a good place to sample some distinctive chardonnay, riesling or cabernet sauvignon.

Places to Stay & Eat

Woodbridge Hotel (☎ *6267 4604; Channel Hwy; singles/doubles $35/65*) has standard rooms with shared facilities; continental breakfast is available at a steep extra charge. Its **Cliffs Restaurant** (*mains $9-22; open dinner Mon-Sat Oct-Apr, dinner Thur-Sat May-Sept*) has excellent views over the

SOUTHEAST COAST

channel and specialises in slow-cooked beef and seafood. Cheaper counter meals are also available.

The Old Woodbridge Rectory (☎ 6267 4742; e rectory@southcom.com.au; 15 Woodbridge Hill Rd; doubles $80), at the start of the Gardners Bay road, is a friendly place with large en suite rooms (one wheelchair-accessible). Continental/cooked breakfast is an extra $5/10 per person.

Hartzview Vineyard (☎ 6295 1623; 70 Dillons Rd; B&B doubles $130) has a cottage endowed with antiques, a log fire, complimentary wines and views over Gardners Bay. You can also take limbering bushwalks around the property (or lumbering walks, depending on how much wine you've had).

Geebin Vineyard (☎ 6267 4750; 3729 Channel Hwy; doubles from $95) is the place to come for tranquillity, hospitality and great channel views. Greet the morn with a cooked breakfast; dinners can also be arranged.

There are a couple of accommodation options on Pullens Rd, which intersects with the Channel Hwy on the northern outskirts of Woodbridge.

Telopea (☎/fax 6267 4565; e cartb@ozemail.com.au; 144 Pullens Rd; doubles $90) comprises two self-contained brick units with good views of the tree line.

Honeywood Cottage (☎/fax 6267 4654; e fiddy@bigpond.com; 72 Pullens Rd; doubles from $70) is a timber cottage on a discreet seven-hectare block adjacent to a working farm; inquire at 66 Pullens Rd.

Getting There & Away
Hobart Coaches arrive at and depart from the general store; the trip from Hobart takes one hour ($6.60/10.60 one way/return).

CYGNET
☎ 03 • postcode 7112 • pop 850
This small township was originally named Port de Cygne Noir (Port of the Black Swan) by Rear-Admiral D'Entrecasteaux because of the many swans seen on the bay. Youthfully reincarnated as Cygnet (a young swan), the town and surrounding area now have many apple and other fruit orchards, and offer excellent fishing, bushwalking,

flat-water canoeing and some fine beaches, particularly farther south at Randalls Bay and Verona Sands.

It's the largest town on the peninsula, with all the requisite services. Travellers interested in antiques will enjoy browsing in the various old furniture stores.

Things to See & Do
After heavy rain, **Pelverata Falls**, 12km north of town, are well worth visiting. A 4km walk leads to the base of the 81m-high waterfall; allow three to four hours for the return walk.

The popular **Cygnet Folk Festival** (☎ 6295 0280; w www.cygnetfolkfest.southcom.com.au) is held annually in January. You can check out the programme on the festival website.

To learn about the history of the town and its inhabitants, visit the small, photo-filled **Cygnet Living History Museum** (☎ 6295 1602; admission by donation; open 11am-3pm daily Oct-Apr; 11am-3pm Fri, 10am-3pm Sat, 12.30pm-3pm Sun Sept-May), next to the church on the main street. The opening hours sometimes vary, but if the museum is closed you can call and make an appointment to be shown through.

Places to Stay
Huon Valley (Balfes Hill) Backpackers (☎ 6295 1551, fax 6295 0875; 4 Sandhill Rd, Cradoc; dorm beds/doubles $17.50/50), located off the Channel Hwy 5km north of town, has serviceable rooms (some wheelchair-accessible) and facilities, and a great view from the large communal area. The host may be able to help you find seasonal fruit-picking work.

Cygnet Hotel (☎ 6295 1267, fax 6295 0636; Mary St; singles/doubles from $25/50) has clean, decent-value rooms and a spacious lounge.

Cygnet Holiday Park (☎ 6295 1869; 3 Mary St; unpowered/powered site doubles $8/12) is basic, cheap and accessed via the side road next to the Cygnet RSL.

Howard's Cygnet Central Hotel (☎ 6295 1244; Mary St; singles/doubles $45/55), at the northern end of the main street, has an array of motel-style units.

Cygnet Guest House (☎ 6295 0080, fax 6295 1905; 89 Mary St; singles/doubles from $85/95) is a colourful and very comfy place, offering attractive upstairs rooms and a cooked breakfast.

Leumeah Lodge (☎ 6295 0980, fax 6295 0998; Lot 22, Crooked Tree Point; B&B doubles $90-110) has five nice upstairs rooms with shared facilities in the pastel-swabbed, red-carpeted main house, as well as a self-contained two-bedroom unit. Rates include a country-style breakfast.

Places to Eat

School House Coffee Shop (☎ 6295 0237; Mary St; meals $4-10; open 9am-5pm daily) makes its own hearty pies and soups, and tempting cakes.

The Red Velvet Lounge (☎ 6295 0466; 24 Mary St; meals $6.50-12; open 9am-6pm Mon-Fri, 10am-6pm Sat & Sun) is an eclectic wholefood café serving deliciously healthy light meals like filled potatoes, laksa, and roast pumpkin and ricotta lasagne. In the back is an organic/health food shop where you can stock up on pecan halves, organic buckwheat flour and herbal teas.

Old Bank Teashop (☎ 6295 0080; dishes $5-6; open 10.30am-5pm Wed-Mon Sept-May), adjacent to Cygnet Guest House, has scones, soups and nachos. As if handling cooking and accommodation isn't enough, they also do ceiling frescos.

Howard's Cygnet Central Hotel (☎ 6295 1244; mains $10.50-15; open lunch & dinner daily) is popular with locals, serving lots of seafood and grilled meats.

Getting There & Away

Hobart Coaches travel to Cygnet via Snug three times each weekday, utilising several stops along Mary St; the trip takes one hour and costs $8/12.80 one way/return.

CYGNET COAST ROAD

To take the scenic route to Cradoc (on the way to Huonville) past Petcheys Bay and Glaziers Bay, follow the sign on Cygnet's main street pointing south to Lymington. In January and February, you may be able to pick your own fruit at one of the **blueberry** farms along the way, but these farms are also worth seeing in autumn, when the bushes turn a spectacular shade of red.

Further around the coast is **The Scented Rose** (☎ 6295 1816; e scentedrose@optusnet .com.au; 1338 Cygnet Coast Rd, Glaziers Bay; adult/child $6.50/3; open 10am-5pm Sat & Sun Nov-Mar), a display garden and nursery nurturing specialist David Austin roses. It is open by appointment at other times.

One kilometre from Cradoc junction, is **Panorama Vineyard** (☎ 6266 3409; 297 Lower Wattle Grove, Cradoc; open 10am-5pm daily Aug-May, 10am-5pm Thur-Mon June & July), where you can sample several wine types (tastings free), including a very well-regarded pinot noir, in impressive surroundings.

HUONVILLE & AROUND
☎ 03 • postcode 7109 • pop 1720

Huonville straddles the banks of the Huon River and is only a short drive from some lovely vineyards, interesting small towns and other attractions. The town was originally sited beside the river's first rapid and served as an important crossing point; a modern bridge now spans the water, enabling access to the south.

The Huon and Kermandie Rivers were named after Huon D'Kermandec, second-in-command to the explorer D'Entrecasteaux. Prior to that, the area was known by Tasmanian Aborigines as Tahune-Linah. The region was originally covered in tall forests and so timber milling quickly became a major industry; the commercially coveted softwood Huon pine was first discovered here. The initial plundering of Huon pine groves nearly wiped the tree out because it is extremely slow-growing. Today, only immature trees survive along the river. Once the forest was levelled, apple trees were planted and thus began the orchard industry, still the region's primary agricultural activity.

Information

The **Huon visitors centre** (☎ 6264 1838; Esplanade; open 9am-5pm daily) is in the Huon River Jet Boats office.

The **Huon Valley Environment Centre** (☎ 6264 1286; 6/17 Wilmot St; open 9.30am-4.30pm Tues-Thur, 8.30am-6.30pm Fri, 10am-3pm Sat) is an excellent resource for anyone interested in the environmental issues facing the valley (and Tasmania).

Things to See & Do

Take a frenetic, 40-minute jet-boat ride through the local rapids with **Huon River Jet Boats** (☎ 6264 1838; Esplanade; adult/child $50/32; open 9am-5pm daily); bookings are recommended at peak times. Those seeking a less-aggressive water sport can opt for pedal boat or canoe hire, or book a slow **cruise** on the MV *Southern Contessa*; 2½-hour cruises depart at 10am from Monday to Friday and cost $30/20 per adult/child, while two-hour night cruises depart at 6.30pm on Friday (minimum 10 people) and cost $40/30 per adult/child.

Near the township of Ranelagh are the beautiful vine-surrounded environs of **Home Hill** (☎ 6264 1200; 38 Nairn St; open 10am-5pm daily), producers of pinot noir, chardonnay and dessert wines. Tastings are free.

If you find hooking fish problematic, visit the **Snowy Range Trout Fishery** (☎ 6266 0243; adult/child $4/2; open 9am-dusk daily Jan, 9am-dusk Wed-Sun Feb-June & Aug-Dec) for a guaranteed catch. It's 15km west of Huonville, signposted off the road to Judbury. Besides the admission fee, you also pay by weight for any salmon, rainbow or brown trout you catch.

The **Apple Valley Centre** (☎ 6264 1844; adult/child $7/3.50; open 9am-5.30pm daily) has a room devoted to the detailed Tudor Court Model Village, which took polio sufferer John Palotta 12 years to build, and a German 'Model Train World' (it's a rather small world). Considering the entry price, it's probably only really worthwhile for true model enthusiasts.

Grove, a small settlement 6km north of Huonville, has become the tourist centre of the region's apple industry. Beside the highway in an old packing shed is the **Huon Apple & Heritage Museum** (☎ 6266 4345; 2064 Main Rd; adult/child $4.50/2; open 9am-5pm daily Sept-May, 10am-4pm daily

June-Aug), filled with restored machines, plus displays on 500 types of apple and 19th-century apple-picking life.

Also in Grove is Australia's oldest jam company, **Doran's** (☎ 6266 4377; ⊠ www.doransjams.com; Pages Rd; open 10am-4pm daily). Here, you can see tasteful jams and juices being readied for distribution (and sample some), and peer at old labelling and bottle-making machines.

Not everything in Grove is apple-oriented, however. At the back of the heritage museum is **Tahune Pottery** (☎ 6266 4109; open 8.30am-4pm Mon-Fri, 9.30am-4pm Sat & Sun), where you can watch artisans pottering, buy their work or have something clay-baked to order.

Places to Stay

Though Huonville is the region's commercial centre, it isn't a typical overnight stop for visitors.

Grand Hotel (☎ 6264 1004; 2 Main St; singles/doubles $30/40) is a friendly old brick pub beside the bridge, with plenty of basic rooms.

Constables (☎ 6264 1691, fax 6264 2002; 12 Crofton Crt; singles/doubles $75/110) is a well-established B&B set up in the old police residence.

Matilda's of Ranelagh (☎ 6264 3493; ⊠ www.matildasofranelagh.com.au; 44 Louisa St; doubles from $150), 2km from Huonville at Ranelagh, offers luxurious B&B in an attractive Victorian house with its own colony of golden retrievers.

Places to Eat

Cafe Moto (☎ 6264 1496; 2 Wilmot St; meals $4-10; open 9am-5pm Wed-Mon) is a cool minimalist place with fresh, tasty fare and good coffee. The menu changes regularly but has included roast vegetable lasagne, and chicken and camembert pies.

Huon Manor Bistro (☎ 6264 1311; Short St; mains $10-19; open lunch daily, dinner Mon, Tues & Thur-Sat), located opposite the Grand Hotel, has very good country-style fare – highlights include seafood, venison and baked apples in wine – and numerous Tassie wines.

Apple Valley Centre (☎ 6264 1844; open 7am-5pm daily) has a teahouse that is a cosy place for tasty specialty pies, Devonshire teas and a $7.50 big breakfast.

JJ Cafe (☎ 6266 4377; meals $3.50-9.50; open 10am-4pm daily), in Doran's, can serve you pancake stacks or apple pie with spiced apple butter; or alternatively you can just smear your face with a plum and port jam–topped muffin.

Home Hill (☎ 6264 1200; 38 Nairn St; mains $8.50-22; open noon-3pm Wed-Sun, 6pm-late Fri & Sat) has a stylishly modern à la carte restaurant. The excellent seasonal menu relies on Tassie produce like Bothwell goats cheese, Huon Valley mushrooms and Bruny Island oysters; eat your way through it.

Getting There & Away

TassieLink buses arrive at and depart from outside the newsagency on the main street in the town's south, and from opposite the other main newsagency in the town's north. The trip from Hobart takes one hour and costs $6.30.

FRANKLIN

☎ 03 • postcode 7113 • pop 455

The highway follows the Huon River south for a long way, passing through the tiny settlements of Franklin, Castle Forbes Bay and Port Huon. These were once important shipping ports for apples but nowadays the wharves and packing sheds are rarely used.

Franklin is the oldest town in the Huon area and the wide, peaceful river it sits beside comprises one of Australia's best rowing courses. The town is fairly large considering its small population and there has been little change to many of its buildings in the last century, particularly the main street's Federation architecture.

An excellent example is the **Palais Theatre**, begun in 1911 and ultimately an amalgamation of Federation and Art Deco styles, now with a superbly renovated interior thanks to dedicated members of the local community. Local events are now being held here, with proceeds going to the theatre's continued revitalisation.

The Shipwright's Point **School of Wooden Boatbuilding** (☎ 6266 3586; Main Rd), established in 1992, runs accredited courses in traditional wooden boatbuilding using some of Tasmania's sturdiest timbers, including Huon and King Billy pine. Depending on what stage the course is at, you may be able to see a boat under construction; ring to check.

Terry's Crafted Wooden Toys (☎ 6266 3489; open 9am-5pm Mon-Fri) sells wooden trucks, dollhouse furniture and rocking horses. Browse other local crafts at the **Huon Showcase** (☎ 6266 3260; Castle Forbes Bay; open 9am-5.30pm daily), on the highway south of town.

If you're thirsty, sidle in to the **Franklin Tavern** (☎ 6266 3205; Main Rd; open 11am-late daily), a stonewalled place built in 1853 and uniquely renovated since by an abalone diver. It has a slouchy bar feel, with plenty of stools to perch on and some pool tables, and has been in operation for 30 years. Talk to the barkeeper about the bar's history over a brew or three.

Places to Stay & Eat

Franklin Lodge (☎ 6266 3506; W www .franklinlodge.com.au; Main Rd; doubles $126-162) is a lovely two-storey building begun in the 1850s and eventually extended into the current grand Federation structure. It has four en suite rooms, one with spa; a hearty continental breakfast is provided.

Camellia Cottage (☎ 6297 1528; W www .vision.net.au/~maplehill; 119 Crowthers Rd, Castle Forbes Bay; B&B doubles $90) has a bucolic location on a hobby farm. It's signposted off the highway around 15km south of Huonville.

Castle Forbes Bay House (☎ 6297 1995; Meredith Rd; singles/doubles $50/75), near Camellia, is a former schoolhouse with an apple orchard for company. It provides accommodation and a cooked breakfast at a reasonable rate; an extra $20 per double gets you the entire cottage.

Cafe Purple (☎ 6266 3522; Main Rd; mains $9-15; open from 5pm Wed-Sun) makes creative, plate-licking pizzas in a unique corrugated-iron, concrete-floored

SOUTHEAST COAST

oven. Take the food away or stuff your face out on the small deck; the café is BYO.

Franklin Grill *(☎ 6266 3645; Main Rd; mains $13-25; open from 6pm Wed-Sun)* has an inviting atmosphere and a menu dominated by char-grilled meat, from small porterhouse to large eye fillet portions; seafood and chicken are available too.

Getting There & Away
TassieLink buses do the one-hour trip from Hobart for $9; they arrive at and depart from Arthur's Takeaway on the main street.

PORT HUON
☎ 03 • postcode 7116

For visitors to Port Huon, once the biggest export port for the local apple industry, the riverside **Shipwright Reserve** picnic ground is a good spot to enjoy the view.

Kermandie Lodge *(☎ 6297 1110;* w *www .kermandielodge.com.au; Main Rd; motel singles/doubles $80/88, unit singles/doubles $90/106)* offers plain motel rooms, two-bedroom units and a café (open from 8am to 8pm daily), plus a swimming pool and tennis courts.

Huon River Cruises operates from Kermandie Lodge. A 90-minute cruise visiting Atlantic salmon farms runs at 11am and 2pm daily, costing $18/9 per adult/child.

GEEVESTON
☎ 03 • postcode 7116 • pop 780

Located 31km south of Huonville, this is the administrative centre for Australia's most southerly municipality and the gateway to the Hartz Mountains National Park. While most towns declined as apple sales dropped, this town reversed the trend and grew. It is an important timber industry base, with an economy encouraged by forestry operations and the tourists who come to see both the forests and nearby wilderness. That said, the town has a bit of a dour feel, with little to keep you here overnight.

Geeveston was founded in the mid-19th century by the Geeves family, whose descendants are still active in local affairs. In the 1980s the town was the epicentre of an intense battle over the future of the forests

of Farmhouse Creek. At the height of the controversy, some conservationists spent weeks living in the tops of 80m-tall eucalypts to prevent them from being cut down. The conservation movement ultimately won – Farmhouse Creek is now protected from logging.

On the main street is a **post office** that is also a Commonwealth Bank agency.

Things to See
In the centre of town is the **Forest & Heritage Centre** *(☎ 6297 1836; Church St; open 9am-5pm daily)*. Its **Forest Room** *(adult/child $5/3)* has comprehensive displays on all aspects of forestry, such as logging practices and land management, and regularly hosts wood turners who displays their craft; lessons in how to turn wood can also be arranged. Upstairs is the **Hartz Gallery** *(admission by gold coin donation)*, which displays the artistic abilities of a number of the craftspeople.

The complex includes a **visitors centre** *(admission free)* where you can pick up national park passes, maps and descriptions of walks in the Hartz Mountains, and buy tickets for the Tahune Forest Airwalk – a combined Airwalk/Forest Room ticket costs $11.50/8 per adult/child.

The grandiose gateway to the town, with its swamp gum logs, has an adjacent reserve where a short **walking track** highlights the range of forest plants. There are also picnic tables and barbecues.

Places to Stay
Forest House *(☎ 6297 1102; Arve Rd; dorm beds/doubles $14/28)* has ultra-simple dorms and a couple of just-as-simple doubles. It's in town at the start of the Hartz Mountains road. If no one's at the house, inquire at the post office.

Lightwood House *(☎ 6297 1336, fax 6297 1866; Arve Rd; singles/doubles $30/50, extra guests $10)*, just a bit further down the road leading to the Hartz Mountains, is a suburban-looking three-bedroom house that is administered by the adjacent high school. It doesn't look too flash from the outside, but it's very cheap.

SOUTHEAST COAST

Cambridge House (☎ 6297 1561; e dv_po tter@southcom.com.au; Huon Hwy; singles/ doubles $70/90), overlooking Kermandie River, offers upstairs accommodation in three bedrooms with shared facilities, plus continental breakfast.

Getting There & Away

TassieLink buses arrive at and depart from opposite the visitors centre. The 1½-hour trip from Hobart costs $11.50.

ARVE ROAD

The Arve Rd, constructed to extract timber from the extensive forests, and now sealed thanks to the new Tahune Airwalk, heads west from Geeveston through rugged, timbered country to the Hartz Mountains and the Tahune Forest Reserve.

Follow the road to the **Arve River Picnic Area**, which also has a short forest walk.

Just past here you can turn left for the climb to Hartz Mountains. If you stay on Arve Rd, it will take you over the next ridge to the Tahune Forest Reserve and Airwalk beside the Huon River, which you can visit without a park pass.

Along the road to Tahune are several short tracks (about 10 minutes each) that are worth walking. **Keogh's Creek Walk** is a short circuit with an all-weather covered bridge for viewing the forest. The **Big Tree Walk** leads to a timber platform beside a giant 87m-high swamp gum. The **West Creek Lookout** provides views from a bridge extending out onto the top of an old tree stump.

TAHUNE FOREST RESERVE

The name of this reserve is derived from Tahune-Linah, which was the Aboriginal name for the area around the Huon and

---

Tahune Forest Airwalk

Forestry Tasmania's grandly realised initiative for the Tahune Forest Reserve is the Airwalk (☎ 6297 0068; w www.forestrytas.com.au; adult/child/family $8/5.50/25; open 9am-9pm daily Dec-Mar, 9am-5pm daily Apr-Nov), nearly 600m of horizontal steelwork suspended at an average height of 20m above the forest floor. The floor of the catwalk is see-through metal mesh, allowing views right past your feet to the ground. There's also a 24m cantilevered section designed to have a disconcerting sway and bounce to it, caused by vibrations from approaching footsteps.

The Airwalk has an indisputably great view from its walkways, especially from the cantilever towards Mt Picton. But what has been disputed is why it was placed here among modest specimens of myrtle and sassafras, rather than among the towering old-growth forests of the Styx Valley to the north. Some conservationists have speculated that Forestry Tasmania's plans for the ongoing logging of valuable hardwoods in the Styx dictated the Airwalk's position at Tahune, as opposed to a desire to let the public experience a fundamentally significant wilderness. The irony of this is that according to organisations like the Wilderness Society, the long-term tourism (and therefore economic) potential of the Styx Valley would likely be much greater than that of the current Tahune facility. (For more information on the Styx, see the boxed text 'Valley of the Giants' in the Mt Field & The Southwest chapter.)

Facilities at the visitors centre were somewhat slim during the Airwalk's first season of business, apparently because the scheme's architects underestimated the number of people who would be accessing it. The basic café (meals $4-12) here serves quiches, smoked trout pate and 'strudels' with Atlantic salmon. At the time of writing, night-time visits to the Airwalk accompanied by a four-course dinner were being advertised for $50 per person; bookings through the visitors centre are essential.

Getting to the beginning of the Airwalk from the visitors centre involves a short trot across a bridge over the Huon River and a climb up a significant number of steps embedded in the hillside. Transportation to the start of the steelwork for disabled visitors can be arranged, just ask at reception. When we visited, the only way to get out to the Airwalk from Geeveston was by car.

Kermandie Rivers. The picnic ground has tables, toilets and a shelter (it often rains here). There are a couple of signposted walks, the most popular a 20-minute riverside stroll through young stands of Huon pine. But the reason most people come here is to stroll along the Airwalk (see the boxed text 'Tahune Forest Airwalk' earlier).

HARTZ MOUNTAINS NATIONAL PARK

A century ago, the Hartz plateau was receiving the attention of loggers, and local stocks of small varnished gums were being harvested for eucalyptus oil, which ended up being distilled in Hobart for medicinal applications. But eventually an area of nearly 65 sq km was declared a national park and in 1989 this area was made a part of the Tasmanian Wilderness World Heritage Area.

Hartz Mountains National Park is regularly visited by weekend walkers and daytrippers as it's only 84km from Hobart. The park is renowned for rugged mountains, glacial lakes, gorges and dense rainforest, not to mention wonderful alpine moorlands where fragile cushion-plant communities grow in cold, misty climes. Being on the edge of the Southwest National Park, the region is subject to rapid changes in weather, so take waterproof gear and warm clothing even on a day walk. The usual park entry fee applies.

There are some excellent isolated viewpoints and walks in Hartz Mountains National Park. **Waratah Lookout** is only 24km from Geeveston and is an easy five-minute walk from the road; look for the jagged peaks of the Snowy Range and the Devils Backbone. Other shortish walks on well-surfaced tracks include **Arve Falls** (20 minutes return) and **Lake Osborne** (40 minutes return). The easy walk to **Lake Esperance** (90 minutes return) takes you through some truly magnificent high country. You'll need to be fairly fit and experienced, however, to tackle the steep, rougher track that leads to **Hartz Peak** (four to five hours return), which is poorly marked beyond **Hartz Pass** (3½ hours return).

POLICE POINT

☎ 03 • postcode 7116

The main road from Geeveston to Dover heads inland at Surges Bay and makes for an uninteresting but quick route to Dover. The more scenic alternative is to leave the highway at Surges Bay and follow the Esperance Coast Rd through Police Point and Surveyors Bay. Some of this road is unsealed but has a firm gravel surface. The road allows fine views over the wide Huon River and passes many scenic places like **Desolation Bay** and **Roaring Bay**. Along the way you'll get close-ups of the waterlogged pens of commercial salmon farms.

Places to Stay & Eat

Huon Charm Waterfront Cottage (☎ 6297 6314; 525 Esperance Coast Rd; doubles from $90, extra guests $20), a rustic two-bedroom place, is much more aptly named than its location, Desolation Bay (actually a delightful, secluded little bay).

Huon Delight (☎/fax 6297 6336; w www .tassie.net.au/huondelight; 582 Esperance Coast Rd; singles/doubles $85/95), just around the next point, is a modern brick unit with fine self-contained views over the river.

Emma's Choice (☎ 6297 6309), further down the road from Huon Delight, offers glimpses of the process that converts local fruit into several varieties of jam. Devonshire teas can be supped in **Emma's Tearoom** (open 9am-5pm daily Oct-Apr). The tearoom is open reduced hours between May and September.

DOVER

☎ 03 • postcode 7117 • pop 480

This picturesque fishing port, 21km south of Geeveston, is a good spot to bunk down while you're exploring the area. Originally it was called Port Esperance after one of the ships in Rear-Admiral D'Entrecasteaux's fleet, but that name is now only applied to the bay. The bay's three small islands are known as Faith, Hope and Charity.

In the late 19th century, the processing and exporting of timber was Dover's major industry. Timber was milled and shipped from here and also the nearby towns of

Strathblane and Raminea. While much of it was Huon pine, hardwoods were also harvested and sent to countries like China, India and Germany for use as railway sleepers. Today the major industries are fruit growing, fishing and aquaculture. Fish factories near the town employ many local workers to harvest Atlantic salmon, which is exported throughout Asia.

The town has reasonable services, including supermarkets and bank agents. If you have your own car and are heading further south, buy petrol and food supplies here.

Yacht Cruises

From September to May, cruises can be arranged on the historic *Olive May* (☎ 6298 1062; W *www.dover.tco.asn.au/olivem.htm*), a 42-foot, 120-year-old Huon pine vessel. The vessel's Dover office is next to Dover Bayside Lodge.

Places to Stay

Dover is the region's main tourist base, with accommodation for all budgets.

Dover Beachside Caravan Park (☎ 6298 1301; Kent Beach Rd; unpowered/powered site doubles $12/16, on-site van doubles $35, cabin doubles $60) has claimed an attractive, tree-encircled chunk of flat turf opposite the picturesque bay. It includes a basic two-room bunkhouse ($15 per person).

Dover Hotel (☎ 6298 1210, fax 6298 1504; Main Rd; dorm beds $15, singles/doubles from $40/70, unit doubles $110) has a range of accommodation, including upstairs rooms (the more expensive with en suites) with continental breakfast, an adjacent large unit with beach views, and four-bed budget dorms at the hotel's rear. When bands are playing downstairs, some of the upper-level rooms can be disquieting.

Dover Bayside Lodge (☎/fax 6298 1788; Bay View Rd; B&B doubles $75-100) has fine waterfront views and decent rooms, one wheelchair-accessible.

Anne's Old Rectory (☎/fax 6298 1222; Huon Hwy; doubles from $70) has two rooms with shared facilities in a character-filled, late-19th-century building. À la carte dining can be prearranged.

Smuggler's Rest (☎/fax 6298 1396; Station Rd; doubles from $60) has an external marquee look reminiscent of an old nightclub, self-contained motel-style units, and no smugglers.

Driftwood Holiday Cottages (☎ 6298 1441; W *www.farsouth.com.au/driftwood*; Bay View Rd; doubles $130) has several decidedly modern, self-contained brick units; balconies provide the requisite water view. The owners also manage nearby **Beach House**, which has a cedar hot tub, and the three-bedroom **Cove House** (doubles $170).

Riseley Cottage (☎ 6298 1630, fax 6298 1815; 170 Narrows Rd, Strathblane; singles/doubles from $70/95), signposted off the highway south of Dover, is perched glamorously on a hill with views over Esperance Bay. Unwind over full cooked breakfasts; three-course dinners can be prearranged.

Places to Eat

Dover Hotel (☎ 6298 1210; Main Rd; mains $12-18) serves meals daily in its bistro. Opt for a cheaper counter meal if you'd prefer a double cheeseburger and fries to a parmigiana. There's a separate kids' menu.

Dover Woodfired Pizza & Eatery (☎ 6298 1905; Main Rd; mains $9-18; open 4pm-9pm Wed, Thur & Sun, 4pm-10pm Fri & Sat) churns out a tasty range of pizzas in its inviting weatherboard premises. It also has a small takeaway pasta menu.

Gingerbreadhouse Bakery (☎ 6298 1502; Main Rd; lunch $3-11; open 8.30am-5pm daily), on the main bend as you enter town, dishes out tasty baked goods.

Getting There & Away

TassieLink buses arrive at and depart from the Dover Store on the main street; the trip from Hobart takes 1¾ hours and costs $15. Note there are only two services each weekday from Hobart, except from December through to March when an extra two services run every Monday, Wednesday and Friday.

SOUTHPORT

☎ 03 • postcode 7109

Originally, Southport was called Baie des Moules (Bay of Mussels) and it has been known by several other names during its history. Its current name is fairly descriptive as it's located at the southern end of the sealed highway. Many travellers don't visit the town, as there's a major road junction 2km to the north, but it's worth a detour to stay in some of the B&Bs now making good use of the appealing local landscape.

The bluff south of town is called **Burying Ground Point** because it was a convict cemetery; it's now a public reserve. There's also a memorial to an early shipwreck in which 35 people perished.

Far South Charters (☎ 6298 3216; Southport Wharf) does three- to four-hour scenic cruises from $40 per person, and personalised tours with fishing, diving or surfing.

Places to Stay & Eat

Southport Tavern (☎ 6298 3144; Main Rd) is a pub, general store and caravan park. The road-weary can stop for the night in the caravan paddock (unpowered/powered site doubles $5/15, on-site van doubles $30), while the hungry can eat well-prepared dishes like chicken roulade for lunch and dinner in the bistro (mains $12 to $17) or try one of the cheaper bar meals.

Jetty House (☎ 6298 3139; e rosandcarl @bigpond.com; Main Rd; singles/doubles from $60/85), down near the wharf, is a lovely, gardened abode built in 1875 and now tailor-made for relaxation. Rates include full cooked breakfast.

Southern Forest B&B (☎/fax 6298 3306; e souforest2@bigpond.com; Kent St; doubles from $85, extra guests $30), up the hill opposite Southport Tavern, is equally lovely and hospitable. This warm, wooden-floored hideaway is set on 12 mostly forested hectares and offers homegrown fare.

HASTINGS
☎ 03 • postcode 7109

The spectacular **Hastings Cave & Thermal Springs** (☎ 6298 3209; 754 Hastings Caves Rd; adult/child $13.20/6.60; open 9am-5pm daily Mar, Apr & Sept-Dec, 9am-6pm daily Jan & Feb, 10am-4pm daily May-Aug), now supplemented by a new visitors centre and café, attracts visitors to the vicinity of this

once-thriving logging and wharf town, 21km south of Dover. The admission includes entry to the thermal pool.

Though the main cave is called Hastings, this name is informally derived from the surrounding **Hastings Caves State Reserve**, which is riddled with karst formations – the official name of the cave is actually Newdegate. A computer-controlled, low-wattage lighting system was recently installed in Newdegate to give visitors a crisper, more focused view of the formations.

The cave is 10km inland from Hastings and 5km beyond the visitors centre. To get there from the town centre, allow for a 10-minute drive, then a five-minute walk through rainforest to the cave entrance. Cave tours leave on the hour, the first an hour after the visitors centre opens and the last an hour before it closes.

Next to the visitors centre is a **thermal swimming pool** (adult/child $4.40/2.20), filled daily with warm water from a thermal spring. The wheelchair-accessible **Hot Springs Trail** does a big loop from the pool area, taking 20 minutes to navigate.

Organised Tours

The visitors centre organises guided tours of the lesser-known **King George V Cave**, a dolomite marvel reached via a forest walk. Three-hour tours cost $69 per person and six-hour tours (including a BBQ and entry to the pool) cost $135 per person. Tours need to be booked at least a day in advance and a minimum of two people is required. No caving experience is necessary and all equipment is provided.

At the time of research, the centre was also considering starting tours of the wild **Mystery Creek Cave**, known for its significant glow-worm population.

LUNE RIVER
☎ 03 • postcode 7109

A few kilometres southwest of Hastings is the tiny enclave of Lune River. From here you can take a scenic 6km, 1½-hour ride on **Fell's Ida Bay Railway** (☎ 6298 3110; adult/child $20/10), a narrow-gauge affair that works its way through scrub and light bush to the beach at Deep Hole Bay. Trains run at 12.30pm and 2.30pm from Wednesday to Monday over summer (2.30pm only on Tuesday) and at 12.30pm and 2.30pm Wednesday and Sunday over winter. The trip includes some wandering time along Elliot Beach.

The Lune River Youth Hostel burnt down a few months before this book was researched and it was unclear as to whether it would be resurrected; check at your nearest YHA hostel.

Lune River Cottage (☎ 6298 3107, 6298 3273; Lot 2, Lune River Rd; singles/doubles $40/70), fronted by the settlement's post office, offers B&B and can rustle up evening meals with advance notice.

COCKLE CREEK

The most southerly drive you can make in Australia is along the secondary gravel road from Lune River to Cockle Creek and beautiful **Recherche Bay**. This is an area of spectacular mountain peaks and endless beaches, ideal for camping and bushwalking. It's also the start (or end) of the challenging **South Coast Track**, which, with the right preparation and a week or so to spare, will take you all the way to Port Davey and beyond in the southwest. See Lonely Planet's *Walking in Australia* for detailed track notes.

Cockle Creek, which clings to the edge of the enormous **Southwest National Park**, provides a naturally decorous base for several walks. You can follow the shoreline northeast to the lighthouse at **Fishers Point** (three hours return), passing a sculpture of a baby southern right whale along the way. The South Coast Track can also be followed to **South Cape Bay** (four hours return), a popular short hike. National park entry fees apply to these walks; self-register at Cockle Creek.

Places to Stay

There are several great free places to **camp** at Recherche Bay, including at Gilhams Beach, just before Catamaran. You can also camp for free at Cockle Creek itself, but national park fees apply as soon as you cross the bridge. Bring all your own provisions, including firewood – there are pit toilets and some tank water, but it's recommended you bring your own supplies.

Getting There & Away

TassieLink buses arrive at and depart from the Cockle Creek PWS station; the 3½-hour trip to Hobart costs $51.60.

SOUTHEAST COAST

Midlands & Lake Country

Parts of Tasmania's inland region have a definite pseudo-English atmosphere, due to the diligent efforts of early settlers who nostalgically planted English trees and hedgerows. Agricultural exploitation of the area contributed to Tasmania's rapid settlement, and coach stations, garrison towns, stone villages and pastoral properties soon raised themselves up from the dirt.

This diamond-shaped region extends from the Midland Hwy in the east to the Derwent River in the southwest, and north to the edge of Launceston. At its centre is an elevated, sparsely populated region known as the Lake Country. Three major highways traverse the region: the Lyell Hwy, running between Hobart and Queenstown; the Lake Hwy, which climbs onto the high Central Plateau; and the Midland Hwy, connecting Hobart to Launceston.

Midland (Heritage) Highway

Hobart was founded in 1804 and Launceston in 1805. By 1807, the need for a land link between the two prompted surveyor Charles Grimes to map out an appropriate route. The road was constructed by convict gangs and by 1821 was suitable for horses and carriages. Two years later a mail cart operated between the two towns and this became the first coach service, as it sometimes carried passengers. The main towns along this road were all established in the 1820s as garrisons for prisoners and guards.

The Midlands is a fairly dry area that yields fine wool, beef cattle and timber, products that made the region economically important, though today tourism is another prime source of income.

If you're interested in antiques and other old wares, you'll find plenty of browsing opportunities along the Midland Hwy.

Highlights

- Dropping the Central Plateau a long (fishing) line
- Watching the mist descend on Great Lake in winter
- Viewing the formidable hydroelectricity equipment at Waddamana
- Seeing first-hand the detailed, convict-era carvings on Ross Bridge
- Seeking an antique bargain along the Heritage Hwy

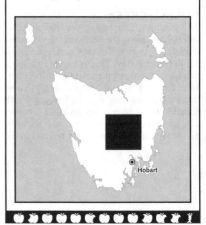

There are antique shops in most of the towns mentioned in this section and also in **Kempton**, signposted off the highway north of Brighton.

The course of the Midland Hwy has wavered slightly from its original route and many of the historic towns are now bypassed – this has been good news for motorists who want to travel between the state's two biggest cities as speedily as possible, but has isolated some of the smaller towns from the through-traffic that was their contemporary lifeblood. It's definitely worth making a few detours to see these quiet old towns. The route is now marketed as the Heritage Hwy and you can pick up a free tourist map of it and the surrounding region at information centres around the state.

Getting There & Around

Redline Coaches (☎ 6336 1446, 1300 360 000; **W** www.tasredline.com.au) runs along the Midland Hwy several times a day; you can disembark at any of the main towns – like Brighton, Oatlands, Ross, Campbell Town and Perth – provided you're not on an express service. It's best to pre-book

pick-ups/drop-offs in these towns. The fare from Hobart to Launceston is $23.50.

OATLANDS

☎ 03 • postcode 7120 • pop 540

Oatlands has Australia's largest collection of Georgian architecture and so has an interesting streetscape. On the main street alone, there are 87 historic buildings, the oldest being the 1829 convict-built **courthouse**.

Much of the sandstone for these early buildings came from the shores of adjacent **Lake Dulverton**. After enduring a long drought and being kept afloat with pumped

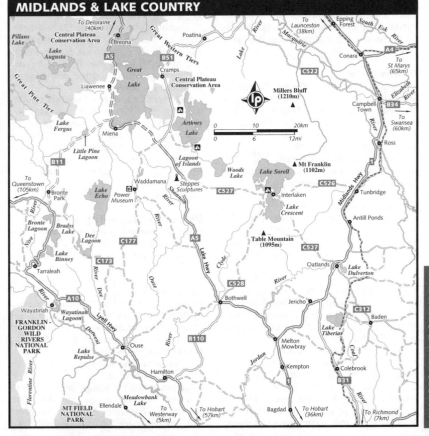

MIDLANDS & LAKE COUNTRY

bore water, the lake was recently full again thanks to a long wet winter. The lake area is a designated reserve that sustains nearly 80 types of birds.

The town's site was chosen in 1821 as one of four military posts on the road from Hobart to George Town, but was slow to develop. In 1832 a proper survey of the town was made and, in a spurt of optimism, the surveyor marked out 50 miles (80km) of streets on the assumption it would become the Midlands capital. Many people certainly made it their new home in the 1830s, erecting numerous solid buildings with the help of former convicts and soldiers who were skilled carpenters and stonemasons. But alas, the town never grew into the hoped-for capital. Today, Oatlands is a charming small town, with many historic properties now privately occupied.

Information

The highly informative **Central Tasmanian Tourism Centre** (☎ 6254 1212; e oatlands@ tasvisinfo.com.au; 85 High St; open 9am-5pm daily) has a free handout called *Welcome to Historic Oatlands*, which includes directions for a self-guided tour of town.

The **post office**, **ANZ Bank** and **Commonwealth Bank** are on the main street; the banks have restricted opening hours.

Things to See & Do

Callington Mill (☎ 6254 0039; Mill Lane; admission free; open 9am-4pm daily), off High St, was built in 1837 and used until 1891. Restoration work was begun after a century of neglect, but for the past few years the project has moved in fits and starts. There's not really a lot to do except for a vigorous climb of the fantail-capped, 15m-high mill tower, and a browse of **Dolls at the Mill** (admission $2), a collection of over 2000 dolls from all over the world.

Fielding's Oatlands Tours (☎ 6254 1135) offers a one-hour town tour ($5) that departs from 7 Gay St on demand from 9am to 5pm Saturday and Sunday. It also offers the long-running 90-minute ghost tour ($8), which starts at 8pm most nights from May to September, and at 9pm from October to

April. This is a candle-lit excursion that takes in the old gaol, courthouse and other spirited convict sites.

Places to Stay – Budget

Free **camping** is permitted for up to three nights in the picnic area beside Lake Dulverton, at the northern end of the Esplanade.

Midlands Hotel (☎ 6254 1103; 91 High St; singles/doubles $35/45) has decent budget rooms with shared facilities.

Places to Stay – Mid-Range

Oatlands Lodge (☎/fax 6254 1444; 92 High St; singles/doubles $75/95) has a couple of dandy en suite rooms that come with a full English-style breakfast.

Thimble Cottage (☎ 6254 1372; 101 High St; singles/doubles $70/90), beside the White Horse Inn, sleeps up to six people in attic and ground-floor rooms. Breakfast provisions are provided and the downstairs is wheelchair accessible.

Ellesmere Cottage (☎ 6254 4140, fax 6254 4134; doubles $90, extra guests $15) is a timber cottage on a large sheep farm 2km along a gravel road from the highway – 13km south of Oatlands is the Jericho turn-off, where there's also a signpost to Ellesmere. The cottage sleeps up to five people and guests have access to a pool and a trout-stocked lake.

Places to Stay – Top End

Oatlands' upper-end accommodation is of the colonial type, where 'convict-built' is regarded as a mark of historical excellence.

Waverley Cottages (☎ 6254 1264, fax 6254 1527; singles/doubles $130/148) manages a collective of fully equipped, thoroughly colonial local cottages: **Amelia Cottage** (104 High St), opposite the hotel; **Forget-me-not Cottage** (17 Dulverton St), directly behind Amelia; and **Waverley Cottage** and **Waverley Croft**, both 7km west of town. The stand-by rates are often significantly reduced.

Commandant's Cottage (☎ 6254 4115; w www.vision.net.au/~jtsalmon; Park Farm, Jericho; B&B doubles $110, extra guests $33), between Jericho and Oatlands, is a

Georgian sandstone cottage that sleeps 12 people, perfect for a *Brady Bunch* reunion.

Places to Eat

Midlands Hotel (☎ *6254 1103; 91 High St; mains $11.50-13.50)* has a huge meat-stuffed menu available at lunch and dinner daily.

Blossom's Georgian Tea Rooms (☎ *6254 1516; 116 High St; open 10am-4pm Wed-Mon),* at the northern end of the main street, exudes an old-fashioned warmth and is a nice place for a cuppa.

White Horse Inn Tearooms (☎ *6254 1155; 99 High St; open 9.30am-5pm daily)* specialises in the home-made, from cinnamon rolls to lasagne and quiches. Breakfast is available until 10.30am.

Getting There & Away

Redline Coaches (☎ *6336 1446, 1300 360 000;* W *www.tasredline.com.au)* services Oatlands, with buses arriving at and departing from near Blossom's Georgian Tea Rooms on the main street. From Oatlands, the 1½-hour trip to Launceston costs $17, and the one-hour trip to Hobart costs $13.10.

ROSS

☎ 03 • postcode 7209 • pop 275

This ex-garrison town, 120km from Hobart, is steeped in colonial history, with most of its buildings constructed from sandstone between 1820 and 1870. Ross has now added a peaceful charm to its resume – there are strict rules on development, thankfully usurping the possibility of overcommercialism.

Ross was established in 1812 as a protective shelter 'for highway travellers and was the crossing point for the Macquarie River. Originally the crossing was a ford, but in 1821 a low-level bridge was made with logs laid on stone buttresses. In 1836 this rough structure was replaced with the current stone bridge.

In the days of horse and carriage, Ross became important as a staging post. It consolidated its position at the centre of the wool industry, but ceased to grow in size. The historic value of Ross' buildings was eventually realised and development along the main street was rejected, further preserving its

'village' feel. Soak up this ambience by exploring the town on foot.

Information

The **visitors centre** is in the **Tasmanian Wool Centre** (☎ *6381 5466; Church St; open 9am-5.30pm daily);* there's a free brochure detailing the town's historical buildings.

Ross Bridge

The town is famous for the much-photographed, convict-built Ross Bridge, one of the oldest and most beautiful bridges in Australia, boasting unique, decorative

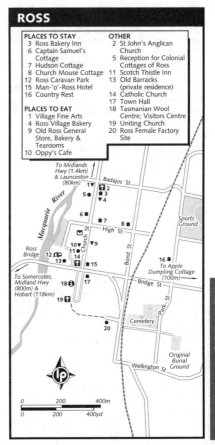

ROSS

PLACES TO STAY	OTHER
3 Ross Bakery Inn	2 St John's Anglican
6 Captain Samuel's	Church
Cottage	5 Reception for Colonial
7 Hudson Cottage	Cottages of Ross
8 Church Mouse Cottage	11 Scotch Thistle Inn
12 Ross Caravan Park	13 Old Barracks
15 Man-'o'-Ross Hotel	(private residence)
16 Country Rest	14 Catholic Church
	17 Town Hall
PLACES TO EAT	18 Tasmanian Wool
1 Village Fine Arts	Centre; Visitors Centre
4 Ross Village Bakery	19 Uniting Church
9 Old Ross General	20 Ross Female Factory
Store, Bakery &	Site
Tearooms	
10 Oppy's Cafe	

To Midlands Hwy (1.4km) & Launceston (80km)

Badajos St

River

Macquarie

Ross Bridge

High St

Church St

Bond St

Sports Ground

16

To Apple Dumpling Cottage (100m)

To Somercotes, Midland Hwy (800m) & Hobart (118km)

Bridge St

Park St

Cemetery

20

Original Burial Ground

Wellington St

0   200   400m
0   200   400yd

MIDLANDS & LAKE COUNTRY

carvings. Its graceful proportions were designed by John Archer and it was built by two convict stonemasons, Colbeck and Herbert, who were granted freedom for their work. Herbert has also been credited with the intricate work on the 184 panels that decorate the arches. Each panel is different, with Celtic symbols, animals and the faces of notable people all carved into the sandstone. At night the bridge is lit up and the carvings really stand out.

Historic Buildings

In the heart of town is a crossroads that can lead you in one of four directions – 'temptation' (represented by the Man-'o'-Ross Hotel), 'salvation' (the Catholic church), 'recreation' (the town hall) and 'damnation' (the old gaol).

Other interesting old buildings include the 1832 **Scotch Thistle Inn** (Church St); the **old barracks** (Bridge St), restored by the National Trust and now a private residence; the 1885 **Uniting Church** (Church St); **St John's Anglican Church** (cnr Church & Badajos Sts), built in 1868; and the still gainfully employed **post office** (26 Church St), constructed in 1896. The town's three churches are all floodlit at night.

Tasmanian Wool Centre

The Tasmanian Wool Centre (☎ 6381 5466; W www.taswoolcentre.com.au; Church St; admission by donation; open 9am-5.30pm daily) is a museum, wool exhibition and craft shop. It has displays on the convict era, including mouldings of some Ross Bridge carvings, and on the Australian wool industry – there are bales of wool you can touch and an audiovisual display on the fibre. The wool centre also runs a guided tour of itself and another of the town proper (both tours adult/child $4/2.50), and a combined wool centre/Ross jaunt (adult/child $7/4); bookings are essential.

Ross Female Factory Site

The Ross Female Factory (admission free; open 9am-5pm daily) was one of only two female prisons in the convict period, with one building still standing. Although there's

little to see inside, the husk of this weathered edifice is evocative and a few descriptive signs and a model of the prison give you an idea of what it was like. Get a copy of the *Ross Female Factory* brochure, available from the visitors centre.

To walk to the site, follow the sign at the top of Church St, near the Uniting Church. Up the hill on the other side of the site is Ross' original **burial ground** with its carved headstones; these were done by the same stonemasons who worked on the bridge.

Places to Stay – Budget

Ross Caravan Park (☎ 6381 5224; unpowered/powered sites $8/12, cabin singles/doubles $25/30) is an appealing little council-run patch of green adjacent to Ross Bridge, which includes a row of simple conjoined cabins. Inquire at the post office; the phone number given above is also applicable after hours.

Places to Stay – Mid-Range

Man-'o'-Ross Hotel (☎ 6381 5240, fax 6381 5423; cnr Church & Bridge Sts; singles/doubles $40/80) offers OK rooms (some are a bit dim) accompanied by continental breakfast. The vertically unchallenged should watch out for some low lintels.

Ross Bakery Inn (☎ 6381 5246; e ross bakery@vision.net.au; Church St; singles/doubles $70/110), originally a coaching inn built in 1832, offers small cosy rooms, freshly baked breakfasts and a good story about a fictional Japanese witch.

Country Rest (☎ 6381 5118; 22 Park St; B&B singles/doubles $45/90), east over the railway tracks, has a plainly modern self-contained brick unit, for when colonialism underwhelms you.

Places to Stay – Top End

Colonial Cottages of Ross (☎ 6381 5354, fax 6381 5408; 12 Church St; doubles $90-120) manages the following carefully restored, self-contained abodes: **Apple Dumpling Cottage** (Bridge St); **Captain Samuel's Cottage** (Church St); **Hudson Cottage** (High St); and **Church Mouse Cottage** (cnr High & Bond Sts). Continental breakfast is included.

A stream cascading over rocks on the southeast coast of Tasmania near Franklin

Wildflowers at Hartz Mountains National Park, part of the World Heritage Area

View of the Australian bush, Bruny Island

Old mill, Campbell Town

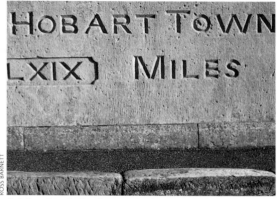

Detail on Ross Bridge showing the distance to Hobart Town

Virginia creeper–covered exterior of Monds Roller Mills, built in 1846, Carrick

Historic church at Oatlands, in the Midlands, illuminated by moonlight

Somercotes (☎ 6381 5231; e somercotes@ bigpond.com.au; doubles $150), off Mona Vale Rd 4km south of Ross, is a splendid estate with a Georgian homestead and B&B in 1820s outbuildings. Guided tours of the homestead can be arranged.

Places to Eat

Oppy's Cafe (☎ 6381 5413; 32-34 Church St; dishes under $5; open 8am-7pm daily Oct-Apr, 8am-5pm daily May-Sept) has burgers, sandwiches and breakfasts.

Old Ross General Store, Bakery & Tearooms (☎ 6381 5422; Church St) has slightly more varied fare than Oppy's Cafe.

Ross Village Bakery (☎ 6381 5246; Church St; open 9am-5pm daily) has a 100-year-old wood-fired oven and good coffee.

Village Fine Arts (☎ 6381 5251; 6 Church St; open 10am-4pm Thur-Sun) is partly a small tearoom with 100 types of tea, but is predominantly a gallery presenting a range of artists; it's one of the few authentic Pro Hart stockists around.

Getting There & Away

Redline Coaches (☎ 6336 1446, 1300 360 000; w www.tasredline.com.au) services Ross, with buses arriving at and departing from Ross Newsagency. The 1½-hour trip to Hobart costs $17.60 and the one-hour journey to Launceston costs $12.

CAMPBELL TOWN

☎ 03 • postcode 7210 • pop 820

Campbell Town, 12km north of Ross, is another former garrison settlement on the Midland Hwy. Today it's the commercial centre of a cattle and sheep farming area and has reasonable services, with a couple of hotels, a supermarket and general stores.

Information

The attentive **information centre** is in the **Heritage Highway Museum** (☎/fax 6381 1353; High St; open 9am-4.30pm Mon-Fri, 9.30am-3pm Sat), located beside the post office in the courthouse, a 1905 building still used several times a year for judicial proceedings. There's a brochure here detailing a self-guided tour of the town.

The interesting museum (admission free) has potted histories of figures like John Batman and Martin Cash, and artefacts like a 1930s film projector, old toys, coins and books.

Things to See & Do

The town has many buildings over 100 years old; they're scattered and display a variety of architectural styles. Most historic buildings can be seen by travelling along High St and returning along Bridge St. They include **The Grange** (High St), built in 1847; **St Luke's Church of England** (High St), constructed in 1835; the 1840 **Campbell Town Inn** (100 High St); the 1834 **Fox Hunters Return** (132 High St); and the 1878 **old school** (Hamilton St), in the current school's grounds.

The main bridge across the Elizabeth River was completed in 1838, making it almost as old as Ross Bridge. The 'Red Bridge' was convict-built from bricks made on-site and is the subject of a comprehensive booklet available from the visitors centre.

Visit one of the oldest farms in the area, **Winton** (☎ 6381 1221), founded in 1835 as a merino sheep stud and still operating today. Ninety-minute tours of the original buildings and gardens, located 13km northwest of town, are conducted by arrangement (minimum four people) and cost $8.80/6.60 per adult/child.

The showgrounds, behind the high school, host the annual **Campbell Town Show** (also called the Midlands Agricultural Show) in early June. Held every year since 1839, this is the oldest continuous show in Australia.

The annual **Campbell Town Summer Festival of Art** is a week-long event taking place in mid-January, during which invited artists complete and exhibit plein-air paintings (works painted outdoors, emphasising natural light).

Places to Stay & Eat

Campbell Town Motel (☎ 6381 1158, fax 6381 1494; 118 High St; singles/doubles $45/55) has basic but clean motel rooms. It seems unlikely from the outside, but part of the building predates all the other hotels in town. Reasonably priced meals are served in the **Caledonia Bistro** *(mains $12-17; open noon-2pm & 6pm-8pm daily)*; if you don't feel like a chicken stack or surf 'n' turf, there's a separate menu of light meals.

The Grange *(☎ 6381 1686; ⓦ www.the grangecampbelltown.com.au; Midland Hwy; singles $65-100, doubles $80-132)*, down the laneway beside the Caltex service station, is a grand old manor with B&B in five en suite rooms (the east-facing ones have mountain views). There is also a two-bedroom cottage. You can have continental breakfast in the sun-filled conservatory.

Fox Hunters Return *(☎ 6381 1602; ⓦ www.classicallytasmania.com.au/foxret .htm; 132 High St; singles/doubles $110/145)*, on the left as you enter the town from Hobart, was built with convict labour in the 1830s as a coaching inn. It has great old spacious rooms within the main house, most with private bathroom and all with continental breakfast. Also here is a formal **restaurant** *(mains $19.50-24; open dinner daily)* with tempting dishes like coconut and peppercorn poached chicken; vegetarian meals are easily arranged with prior notice.

The Gables *(☎/fax 6381 1347; 35 High St; house/cottage doubles from $95/105)*, beside the highway on the northern side of town, has three in-house rooms with shared facilities and continental breakfast, and three cottages with breakfast provisions.

Eliza's Cottage *(☎ 6381 1221, fax 6381 1407; doubles $120)*, at the aforementioned Winton farm, comes with breakfast provisions and tours of the historic property.

Zeps *(☎ 6381 1344; 92 High St; meals $5-13.50; open 8.30am-9pm daily)* is an inexpensive, high-quality licensed eatery on the main street, with good breakfast fodder and lots of pasta, panini and pizzas (the latter served from 5pm).

St Andrews Inn *(☎/fax 6391 5525; Midland Hwy; singles/doubles from $70/100)* is 15km north of Campbell Town at Cleveland. Built in 1845, this National Trust–classified coaching inn has comfortable B&B in two well-outfitted rooms. Its licensed **restaurant** *(mains $14.50-18.50; open lunch Wed-Sat, dinner Tues-Sat)* has a small menu featuring Cleveland country pie and Thai prawns.

Getting There & Away

Redline Coaches *(☎ 6336 1446, 1300 360 000; ⓦ www.tasredline.com.au)* runs to Campbell Town, arriving at and departing from outside Fishers Milkbar, next to the police station. The 1¾-hour trip to Hobart costs $20 and the 45-minute journey to Launceston costs $10.20.

There is a secondary road from Campbell Town heading through the excellent fishing and bushwalking area around **Lake Leake** (32km) to Swansea (67km) on the east coast. Redline buses travel this route once a day from Monday to Friday and drop you at the Lake Leake turn-off, 4km from the lake. Another highway, the A4, runs from Conara Junction, 11km north of Campbell Town, east to St Marys. Redline buses running from Hobart and Launceston to St Helens follow the A4.

Lake Country

The sparsely populated lake country of Tasmania's Central Plateau is a region of breathtaking scenery, comprising steep mountains, glacial lakes, waterfalls, various wildlife and remarkable flora like the ancient pencil pine. The plateau's northwestern portion, roughly one-third of its total area, has been incorporated into the Tasmanian Wilderness World Heritage Area. It's also known for its fine trout fishing and for its controversially ambitious hydroelectric schemes, which have seen the damming of rivers, the creation of artificial lakes, the building of power stations (both above and below ground) and the construction of massive pipelines over rough terrain.

Tasmania has the largest hydroelectric power system in Australia. The first dam was constructed on Great Lake in 1911 and subsequently the Derwent, Mersey, South Esk, Forth, Gordon, King, Anthony and Pieman Rivers were also dammed. If you want to see the developments firsthand, go to the active Tungatinah, Tarraleah and Liapootah power stations on the extensive Derwent scheme between Queenstown and Hobart.

There's excellent fishing all over the Central Plateau, with good access to most of the larger lakes. Great Lake, Lake Sorell, Arthurs Lake and Little Pine Lagoon are popular spots. The plateau itself actually contains thousands of lakes; many are tiny but most still contain trout. You'll have to walk to many of the smaller lakes, which means getting some lightweight camping gear, as the region is prone to snowfalls.

On the western edge of the Central Plateau is Walls of Jerusalem National Park, a favourite of mountaineers, bushwalkers and cross-country skiers (see the Walls of Jerusalem National Park section in The North chapter). Well-equipped hikers can walk across the plateau into this national park and also into Cradle Mountain-Lake St Clair National Park.

BOTHWELL

☎ 03 • postcode 7030 • pop 360

Bothwell is a sleepy historic town in the beautiful Clyde River valley, decorated with over 50 National Trust–acknowledged buildings. Stand-outs include the beautifully restored **Slate Cottage** (☎ 6259 5649; High St), built in 1835 and open for viewing by appointment; an old **bootmaker's shop** (☎ 6259 5649; High St), also open by appointment; the 1820s **Thorpe Mill** (Dennistoun Rd); the lovely 1831 **St Luke's Church** (Dennistoun Rd); and the **Castle Hotel** (Patrick St), first licensed in 1821.

The **visitors information centre** (☎ 6259 4033; Market Place) is in the Australasian Golf Museum. The leaflet Let's Browse in Bothwell has a map marked with the locations of all the historic buildings.

Although Bothwell is best known for its great trout fishing, it also has Australia's oldest golf course, created by the Scottish settlers who established the town in the 1820s. The course is still in use today and is open to members of any golf club.

Maintaining the golfing theme is the **Australasian Golf Museum** (☎ 6259 4033; W www.ausgolfmuseum.com; Market Place; admission $3; open 10am-4pm daily Sept-May, 11am-3pm daily June-Aug), set up in Bothwell's **old School House** (1887).

A little-known but nevertheless prestigious Bothwell event, taking place in early March biennially, is the **International Highland Spin-In**, a three-day wool-spinning festival that includes the 'longest thread' competition, where contestants must spin and ply a continuous thread from a specified amount of raw wool.

Places to Stay & Eat

Bothwell Caravan Park (☎ 6259 5503; Market Place; unpowered/powered sites $5/10) isn't exactly a park, more a small patch of dirt behind the visitors centre, with a graveyard next door for company no less. Check in at the council chambers (Alexander St) or after hours at 5 Queen St (opposite the park).

Park House (☎/fax 6259 5676; 25 Alexander St; doubles $65, extra guests $20) is a self-contained house sleeping up to six people; inquire at 28 Elizabeth St.

Bothwell Grange (☎ 6259 5556, fax 6259 5788; Alexander St; B&B singles/doubles from $85/105), built as a hotel in 1836, is understandably popular for its hospitality and charmingly Georgian atmosphere.

Nant Highland House (☎/fax 6259 5506; cottage doubles $85, extra guests $30), privately located off Dennistoun Rd on a working farm 3km east of Bothwell, is an attractive self-contained cottage that sleeps up to five people; breakfast provisions are included. Nant is Welsh for 'Brook'.

Castle Hotel (☎ 6259 5502; Patrick St) has typical pub counter meals on offer.

Getting There & Away

Hobart's **Metro** (☎ 6233 4232, 13 22 01) has a bus (No 140) departing stop F on Elizabeth St at 4pm each weekday for the 1½-hour trip to Bothwell; the one-way fare is $11.20.

BOTHWELL TO GREAT LAKE

At Waddamana, on the dirt road that loops off the Lake Hwy between Bothwell and Great Lake, is the **Waddamana Power Station Museum** (☎ 6259 6175; admission free; open 10am-4pm daily), a hydroelectric station constructed between 1910 and 1916. Originally a private venture, financial difficulties resulted in the government taking over and creating a Hydro-Electric Department, which today is Hydro Tasmania. The power station has a display on the state's early hydro history and operational turbines; the machinery's scale is particularly impressive.

Signposted off the highway 26km south of Miena is the **Steppes Sculptures**, a ring of mini-menhirs with affixed iron representations of Midlands life – there's assorted wildlife, cattle drovers and Tasmanian Aborigines. They are the work of sculptor Stephen Walker, who created them in 1992 as a Midlands tribute. There's also a 900m track leading north from the stones to the remnants of a **historic homestead** that was the preserve of the locally notable Wilson family for 112 years from 1863.

LAKES
Information
For information on the area and the activities possible within it, try the **PWS visitors centre** at Liawenee (☎ 6259 8148), 10km north of Miena on the western side of Great Lake.

Great Lake
Located 1050m above sea level on the Central Plateau, Great Lake is the largest natural freshwater lake in Australia. The first European to visit the lake was John Beaumont in 1817; he sent a servant to circumnavigate it, which took three days. In 1870 brown trout were released into the lake and it soon became famous for its fishing. Rainbow trout were added to the waters in 1910 and they also thrived. Attempts were subsequently made to introduce salmon, but this time the fish simply refused to multiply. The trout have now penetrated most of the streams across the plateau, with some of the best fishing in the smaller streams and lakes west of Great Lake.

In the early days of the hydroelectric schemes, a small dam was constructed on Great Lake to raise the water level near Miena. The lake is linked to nearby Arthurs Lake by canals and a pumping station, and supplies water to the Poatina Power Station located on its northeastern shore.

Other Lakes
Lake Crescent, **Lake Sorell** and **Arthurs Lake** have also established themselves as popular fishing spots. Unfortunately, Lake Crescent has been closed indefinitely as a result of carp infestation.

Fishing
A wide variety of regulations apply to fishing in this area, aimed at ensuring fish continue to breed and their stocks aren't depleted. On some parts of Great Lake, for instance, you can use only artificial lures, and you're not allowed to fish in any streams flowing into the lake. On the Central Plateau, some waters are reserved for fly-fishing, and bag, size and seasonal limits apply to all areas. See the Fishing section in the Activities chapter for more information, including details of professional guided-fishing outfits who can tell you the difference between claret dabblers, brown bead head buggers and yum-yum emergers (all local trout flies).

Places to Stay & Eat
Campers can try the basic camping ground at **Dago Point** (camping per adult/child $3.30/1.65), beside Lake Sorell, which has toilets and drinking water. A better bet for a family is the camping ground on Arthurs Lake at **Pumphouse Bay** (camping per adult/child $3.30/1.65), which has better facilities including hot showers. Another camping option is **Jonah Bay** (camping per adult $2.20), also on Arthurs Lake, where sites are a little cheaper. Campers self-register at all of the aforementioned and fee payments rely on an honour system. Note that at Great Lake there are no PWS-sanctioned camping places selling food.

Central Highlands Lodge (☎ 6259 8179, fax 6259 8163; Haddens Bay; singles/doubles from $90/110), on the outskirts of Miena, used to offer its comfortable cabins from October to April only, but at the time of writing there were plans to keep the lodge open from August until at least May. The lodge **restaurant** (mains $17-25; open lunch & dinner daily) offers a game pie that usually has bits of deer, rabbit and possum in it – be game and try it, it's delicious.

Hooked on Trout

It should be easy to catch a trout in Tasmania, as most of the state's rivers and lakes have been well stocked with the brown and rainbow varieties. But you still need to organise your fishing gear and be in the right place at the right time. There are also restrictions on the types of tackle that can be used in various areas at different times of the year.

The use of live bait is one tried-and-true fishing technique, requiring a grasshopper, grub or worm to be attached to the hook. However, this form of fishing is banned in most inland waters.

Artificial lures, which come in many different shapes, sizes, weights and colours, are a more acceptable way to fish. You cast the lure from a riverbank or boat and (hopefully) reel your catch in. Depending on the season, you might find that a 'Cobra' wobbler or Devon-type 'spinner' works well in lakes, while one of the most effective accessories in streams is the 'Celta'-type lure.

One of the most challenging forms of this activity is fly-fishing. Many keen anglers make their own artificial flies, but you can purchase a large variety. There are many areas in Tasmania specifically reserved for fly-fishing, which most often involves wading shallow rivers and lake shores in the early morning.

When fishing in the Lake Country, remember to always come prepared for Tasmania's notoriously changeable weather with warm and waterproof clothing, even in the middle of summer.

MARTIN HARRIS

Great Lake Hotel (☎ 6259 8163, fax 6259 8147; Swan Bay; singles/doubles $66/77) is a few hundred metres down the road to Bronte Park. Besides self-contained cabins, you can also bunk down in ultra-basic anglers' cabins for $25; counter meals (mains $12.50 to $17) are available daily.

Getting There & Away

From December through March, **TassieLink** (☎ 6272 7300, 1300 300 520; **W** www.tiger line.com.au) runs a service between Launceston and Lake St Clair via Miena. Buses leave Launceston at 9.30am on Monday, Wednesday and Saturday for the two-hour trip to Miena ($33); bookings are essential.

Derwent Valley

The Derwent Valley Hwy follows the farmlands and valley of the Derwent River from New Norfolk to the Central Plateau, past Derwent Bridge to Queenstown.

HAMILTON
☎ 03 • postcode 7140

This National Trust–classified town was originally laid out on a grand scale to be a major centre, but never developed beyond a small, sleepy village. Hamilton's historic buildings are spread out and surrounded by farms, and there are excellent views of mountain ranges and peaks farther west.

The area was settled in 1808 when New Norfolk was established, and by 1835 had a population of 800, served by 11 hotels and two breweries. Many streets were surveyed, but the rich, yet dry, soils near town defeated many farmers, the town stagnated, and a number of buildings were eventually removed. The remaining structures are a reminder of what was a boom town during the mid-19th century; the major buildings are nicely floodlit at night.

The town's history is documented in the **Hamilton Heritage Centre** (Tarleton St; admission by donation), set up in the 1840 Warders Cottage; keys are available from

MIDLANDS & LAKE COUNTRY

ncil chambers or Glen
Places to Stay & Eat).

' & Eat

...milton Inn (☎ 6286 3204; Tarleton St; singles/doubles $50/80), off the highway, has an elderly, deteriorating facade, questionable angles on some floors and walls, and gruff service, but it's inexpensive and you get a continental breakfast. Counter meals (mains $12 to $18) are served for lunch and dinner daily except on Sunday night. The hotel bottles and exports mineral water from an underground spring beneath its foundations.

McCauley's Cottage (Main Rd) and **Overington's** (Arthur St) are two historic sandstone-and-blackwood cottages managed by **Jackson's Emporium** (☎ 6286 3258; Main Rd; doubles from $160). Their meticulously renovated, olde-worlde interiors come at a premium.

Emma's, **George's**, **Victoria's** and **Edward's** comprise another collective of old sandstone cottages with authentic furnishings, strung out beside the main road in the town centre. They're managed from **Uralla House** (☎ 6286 3270; cnr Main Rd & Clyde St; doubles $120, extra adult/child $35/25).

The Old School House (☎ 6286 3292; W www.schoolhouse.southcom.com.au; Main Rd; doubles from $130), a block south of McCauley's Cottage along the main highway, was built in 1856 and served as the school until 1935. Its very English B&B rooms aren't equipped for young children. Home-cooked meals can be arranged.

Over the Back (☎ 6286 3332, fax 6286 3350; doubles $135, extra adult/child $20/15), off the highway 4km west of the town, has a luxurious, secluded cottage (sleeps seven people) beside a fish-stocked lake, 3km from the main house on a 3.2-sq-km sheep farm. Credit cards are not accepted and breakfast is available for $7 per person.

Glen Clyde House (☎ 6286 3276; Franklin Place; dishes $5-13; open 9.30am-5pm daily), on a sharp bend at the town's northern end, is part licensed tearoom (Devonshire teas to chicken casserole) and part craft gallery, with lots of Huon pine necessities like teaspoon caddies.

Getting There & Away

TassieLink (☎ 6272 7300, 1300 300 520; W www.tigerline.com.au) runs once daily from Tuesday to Friday and on Sunday between Hobart and Queenstown via Hamilton and Ouse. The 1¼-hour trip from Hobart to Hamilton costs $10; buses arrive at and depart from Hamilton newsagency.

ELLENDALE
☎ 03 • postcode 7140

This tiny village is on a quiet, narrow (but sealed) link road joining the Lyell Hwy with Westerway. It's a convenient shortcut to Mt Field if you're heading south by car; the route isn't serviced by bus. Shortly after turning on to the signposted Ellendale Rd, which leaves the Lyell Hwy about midway between Hamilton and Ouse, you cross **Meadowbank Lake**, part of the Derwent River hydroelectric power scheme. It's pretty on a calm day and you can see the piers of the original Dunrobin Bridge next to the current bridge crossing. The original bridge was built in 1850 and marked the start of Dawsons Rd, which led to Gordon Bend in the southwest. It was intended to continue to Port Davey but was abandoned after settlers decided the area was too rugged to farm.

Ellendale was once a hop-growing area, though few remnants of the industry remain. There's little in town apart from a picnic shelter beside the creek, a general store and some accommodation, making it a quiet base for day trips to the nearby national park. Just north of the town centre is an attractive sandstone **church** and **graveyard**.

Places to Stay & Eat

Hopfield Cottages (☎ 6288 1223, fax 6288 1207; Main Rd; doubles $100-120) offers two self-contained abodes under the one conjoined roof, including country breakfast and lots of quaint touches.

Old Macdonald's Farm (☎ 6288 1199; 263 Dillons Rd; doubles $65, extra guests $10) has cheap self-contained cabins. Even if you're not staying here, you can visit the property (admission $3.30; open 10am-5pm Fri-Mon Oct-May) to let your kids feed the chooks and play in the farmyard, and to see giant tree ferns on the **rainforest walk** (one hour return).

Hamlet Downs *(☎ 6288 1212, fax 6288 1258; 50 Gully Rd; doubles $120)*, 6km south of Ellendale at Fentonbury, has plainly modern B&B rooms in a century-old house on a permaculture farm. You can take long, relaxing walks around the well-gardened property and order fresh, healthy á la carte dinners (mains $18).

OUSE
☎ 03 • postcode 7140

This area was settled early in the saga of colonialism, but for a long time there was no town and Ouse (pronounced ooz) was little more than a river crossing; most of its ordinary weatherboard buildings were erected in the last 100 years. The Ouse River was once known as Big River, a name taken by the once-resident Big River Tribe, sometimes called the Larmairremener people.

Ouse is a popular highway food-stop, with several **cafés** and **takeaways**; the riverside picnic ground is great for alfresco dining. The **Lachlan Hotel** *(☎ 6287 1215; Lyell Hwy; singles/doubles $32/55)* has rooms with continental breakfast and counter meals Tuesday to Sunday. **Rosecot** *(☎ 6287 1222; Victoria Valley Rd; singles/ doubles $80/110)*, north of town, has B&B in a self-contained cottage. Another self-contained option is **Sassa-del-Gallo** *(☎ 6287 1289; singles/doubles $50/70)*, opposite the Lachlan Hotel.

Getting There & Away
See the Hamilton Getting There & Away section earlier in this chapter for details. The fare for the 1½-hour trip from Hobart is $12; buses pull up at the Ouse Roadhouse on the main street.

WAYATINAH
☎ 03 • postcode 7140

Wayatinah is the permanent village from which Hydro Tasmania runs the power stations of the Lower Derwent Power Scheme. It's 1km off the Lyell Hwy; buses travelling the highway don't deviate into this town. There's a shop open weekdays and a tavern open daily except Monday. The only place to stay is the pleasant **Wayatinah Camping Ground & Caravan Park** *(☎ 6289 3317; unpowered/powered site doubles $9/12)*, beside Wayatinah Lagoon. The camping fee admits you to the local **swimming pool** (open November to April).

TARRALEAH
☎ 03 • postcode 7140

Tarraleah was built as a residential village for staff at the nearby hydroelectric power stations and dams. But in 1998 much of the town was sold off and today it's just a scruffy collection of prefabricated houses.

The main features of interest are the Tarraleah and Tungatinah **power stations** in the bottom of the gorge north of the town; these are side-by-side yet receive water from different catchments. The huge pipelines feeding the stations are major features – the one running past the town has two tall surge tanks that dominate the settlement.

The only place to stay is the rambling **Tarraleah Chalet** *(☎ 6289 3128; Oldina Dr; singles/doubles $45/75)*, which looks a little spooky at twilight but is haunted only by smallish rooms; counter meals are available in its tavern. Buses don't service Tarraleah.

East Coast

Tasmania's scenic east coast, known as the 'sun coast' because of its mild climate and above-average exposure (by Tasmanian standards) to the great yellow orb, devotes itself to long sandy beaches, fine fishing and that special sort of tranquillity that occurs only by the ocean. The light-hued granite peaks and glorious bays of Freycinet Peninsula are among the state's most attractive features, but even from the highway the water views are often magnificent. And if you have a yen for seaside towns, this is the place to fulfil it.

Settlement of the region, which was suitable for grazing, proceeded rapidly after Hobart was established in 1803. Fishing, whaling, tin mining and timber cutting became particularly important. Many convicts who served out their terms stayed to help establish the fishing, wool, beef and grain industries that are still prominent today.

The major towns along the coast are Orford, Triabunna, Swansea and Bicheno. There are also three national parks: Maria Island National Park has been reserved as much for its interesting history as its natural beauty; the large, dramatic peninsula of Freycinet National Park is an excellent walking venue; and Douglas-Apsley National Park has waterfalls, rainforest and remnants of the dry eucalypt forests that once blanketed the region.

There's plenty of accommodation, for which you'll pay 50% more over summer and public holidays. As this coast is a first-choice holiday destination for many Tasmanians, it crowds out at Easter, and during the last week of December and most of January. If you plan to cruise the coast at these times, book well ahead.

East-coast banking facilities are improving but can be limited; in some towns, banks are open only one or two days a week. There are agencies for the Commonwealth Bank at all post offices, though many have restricted opening hours. Eftpos is available at many places frequented by tourists.

Highlights

- Getting white sand in your shorts at Scamander
- Navigating Freycinet Peninsula's red-granite Hazards
- Snorkelling off Maria Island
- Knocking on some east-coast cellar doors
- Cooling down in the Apsley Waterhole

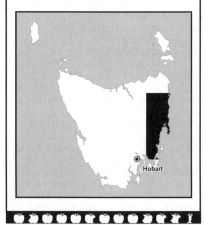

Getting There & Around

Bus The main east-coast bus companies are **Redline Coaches** (☎ 6336 1446, 1300 360 000; Ⓦ www.tasredline.com.au) and **TassieLink** (☎ 6272 7300, 1300 300 520; Ⓦ www.tigerline.com.au).

Redline runs at least one service each weekday from Hobart to Swansea, the Coles Bay turn-off, Bicheno and return via the Midland Hwy and the inland B34 linking road, with a similar run that travels from/to Launceston. You change buses in Campbell Town, where you'll have to wait anything from five minutes to three hours depending on your particular service.

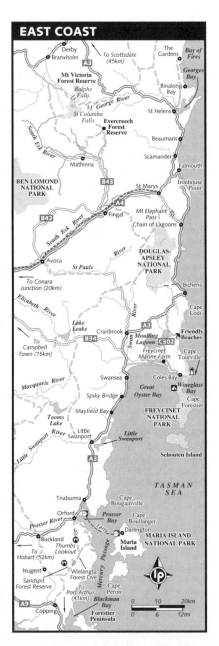

EAST COAST

Derby
Branxholm
To Scottsdale
(45km)
The Gardens
Bay of Fires
Georges Bay
A3
Mt Victoria
Forest Reserve
Ralphs Falls
George River
St Columba Falls
Evercreech Forest Reserve
South Esk River
Mathinna
BEN LOMOND NATIONAL PARK
B43
B42
South Esk River
Fingal
River
DOUGLAS-APSLEY NATIONAL PARK
Avoca
St Pauls
To Conara Junction (20km)
Elizabeth River
Lake Leake
Cranbrook
B34
To Campbell Town (15km)
Macquarie River
Swansea
Spiky Bridge
Tooms Lake
Mayfield Bay
Little Swanport River
Little Swanport
A3
Triabunna
Prosser River
Orford
Buckland
To Hobart (52km)
Thumbs Lookout
Nugent
Sandspit Forest Reserve
A9
Copping
Binalong Bay
St Helens
Beaumaris
Scamander
Falmouth
Ironhouse Point
St Marys
Mt Elephant Pass
Chain of Lagoons
Bicheno
Cape Lodi
Moulting Lagoon
C302
Freycinet Marine Farm
Friendly Beaches
Cape Tourville
Coles Bay
Great Oyster Bay
Wineglass Bay
Cape Forestier
FREYCINET NATIONAL PARK
Schouten Island
TASMAN SEA
Cape Bougainville
Prosser Bay
Cape Boullanger
Darlington
MARIA ISLAND NATIONAL PARK
Maria Island
Wielangta Forest Dve
To Port Arthur (41km)
Cape Peron
Blackman Bay
Forestier Peninsula
Mercury Passage
Ferry
0   10   20km
0   6   12mi

Redline also runs daily services (except Saturday) from Hobart and Launceston to St Helens and then return via Fingal and St Marys.

On Wednesday, Friday and Sunday (and Monday in summer), TassieLink runs between Hobart and Bicheno via Buckland, Orford and the Coles Bay turn-off, with a similar service from/to Launceston (Wednesday summer only) via Fingal and St Marys. TassieLink also runs one bus each weekday (Tuesday, Thursday and Saturday only during school holidays) from Hobart to Swansea via Richmond and Buckland.

Bicheno Coach Service (☎ 6257 0293, 0419 570 293) is the only bus company servicing Freycinet Peninsula. See the Coles Bay & Freycinet National Park section for more details.

Bicycle Arguably the most popular cycle route in Tasmania, a trip along the east coast makes for a wonderfully varied ride. Traffic in the area is usually light and the hills are not too steep, particularly if you follow the coastal highway from Chain of Lagoons to Falmouth. For details of an extensive cycle trip down this coastline, see Lonely Planet's *Cycling in Australia*.

For those cycling between Swansea and Coles Bay, there's an informal **boat service** (☎ 6257 0239) that costs $12 per person including bikes, from Point Bagot to Swanwick, 6km north of Coles Bay, which will save you 65km. The approximate cycling time from Swansea to Point Bagot is one hour. The service operates October to late April, weather permitting; ring first.

BUCKLAND
☎ 03 • postcode 7190

This tiny township, 63km from Hobart, was once a staging post for coaches heading to the east coast.

Ye Olde Buckland Inn (☎ 6257 5114; 5 Kent St; mains $9.50-14; open noon-1.30pm Sun-Thur, noon-1.30pm & dinner Fri & Sat) has been the refuge of coach drivers and travellers for over a century. It's now a fair-dinkum locals' pub with Aussie gourmet meals such as meatballs and gravy. Light meals are also available in the **roadhouse** on the highway.

The large east-facing window behind the altar of the 1846 sandstone **Church of St John the Baptist** (*admission free, donations welcome*) has an interesting though disputed history. A leaflet available in the church (60c) argues that the beautifully stained glass dates from the late 14th century and that it also has a legendary link with William the Conqueror and once sat in Battle Abbey, making its mysterious way to Buckland around 1850. But it's been claimed elsewhere that the window is in fact of Victorian descent and was probably made by a London-based artisan in the mid-19th century.

ORFORD

☎ 03 • postcode 7190 • pop 460

The highway approaches this reserved township from the west by following the Prosser River through the rock-lined, emphatically named **Paradise Gorge**. Within the gorge, close to town on the northern side of the river, are the remains of an incomplete **convict-built road**, now a pleasant riverside walk.

Orford was once an important sea port which served whalers and the local Maria Island garrison. The **Prosser River** was named after an escaped prisoner was caught on its banks. The area has really good fishing and diving, and swimming at the sheltered beaches near town. Idyllic **Spring Beach**, 4km south of town, is a good surfing location.

A 2km **walking track** leads from Shelly Beach around the cliffs of Luther Point to Spring Beach, passing the site of an old quarry which was the primary source of sandstone for many of the older buildings in Melbourne and Hobart.

Signposted off the highway opposite the Ampol service station is **Darlington Vineyard** (*☎ 6257 1630; Holkham Court; open 10am-5pm Thurs-Mon*), a small family affair which has reasonably priced wines (tastings free); the 2001 sauvignon blanc is a splendid drop.

Places to Stay – Budget

Raspins Beach Camping Park (*☎ 6257 1771; Tasman Hwy; unpowered/powered site doubles $11/13*) is small with minimal man-made aesthetics, but has a great sandy location on the water. Hot showers cost $1 for five minutes.

Island View Motel (*☎ 6257 1114, fax 6257 1534; Tasman Hwy; singles/doubles $62/75*) has an odd marshmallow-like look and ordinary rooms with good views.

Blue Waters Motor Inn (*☎ 6257 1102, fax 6257 1621; Tasman Hwy; singles/doubles $44/66*) has large, basic rooms that get the odd bit of traffic noise off the adjacent highway; they're good value for the price though.

Places to Stay – Mid-Range

Shalom Waterfront (*☎ 6257 1175; 50 Tasman Hwy; singles from $45, doubles $65-95*) is imprinted with the owners' personal tastes and has a green yard to laze in. Prices include continental breakfast; cooked breakfasts cost $7.50 extra per person.

Holkham House (*☎ 6257 1248, 6225 1248; Tasman Hwy; doubles $95, extra adult/child $25/15*) is a well-preserved, self-contained 1908 house surrounded by mostly empty pasture; you can squeeze as many as 14 people in here. On the same block is the newer **Miranda Cottage** (sleeps four). Inquire at the house diagonally opposite the roadside 'Holkham House' signage.

Places to Stay – Top End

Spring Beach Holiday Villas (*☎/fax 6257 1440; e springbv@southcom.com.au; Rheban Rd; doubles $125*) is 4km south of town on the road to Rheban, facing the beckoning waters of Spring Beach and the offshore silhouette of Maria Island. Kids will remain happily occupied here.

Eastcoaster Resort (*☎ 6257 1172; W www.eastcoaster.com.au; Louisville Point Rd; motel singles/doubles $88/110, cabin doubles $110-160*), just north of Orford, was once a kelp-harvesting factory and is now a sprawling place with large motel-style rooms and one-to three-bedroom cabins. The Maria Island ferry leaves from the wharf opposite the resort (see the Maria Island section later).

Orford Riverside Cottages (☎/fax 6257 1655; W www.riversidecottages.com.au; Old Convict Rd; B&B doubles $110-160) has four luxurious spa cottages beside the Prosser River. Guests also get continental breakfasts, free dinghy use and a video library to ransack.

Places to Eat

Just Hooked (☎ 6257 1549; Tasman Hwy; mains $10-23; open lunch & dinner Tues-Sat) is a small, licensed eatery serving full-on seafood like baked stripey trumpeter topped with prawns, scallops and calamari. It also has a popular takeaway section.

Blue Waters Motor Inn (☎ 6257 1102; Tasman Hwy; dinner mains $15.50-22; open 6pm-8pm Mon-Thur, noon-2pm & 6pm-8pm Fri-Sun) has a restaurant with big windows looking out on the river, and serves nicely presented seafood chowder and chicken breast with brie.

Blue Marlin (☎ 6257 1172; Louisville Point Rd; mains $12.50-17; open dinner daily Nov-Apr), at the Eastcoaster Resort, is a licensed restaurant specialising in seafood, but with encrusted lamb (French rack) and other meat dishes also on offer. It's open fewer nights from May to October. Also at the resort is the **Bayside Tavern** (mains $10.50-14; open for meals noon-2.30pm & 5.30pm-7pm daily).

Getting There & Away

TassieLink (☎ 6272 7300, 1300 300 520; W www.tigerline.com.au) coaches stop at the Orford Roadhouse; the 1½-hour trip from Hobart costs $13.10. See the Getting There & Around section at the start of this chapter for more information.

WIELANGTA FOREST

There's a direct link from the Tasman Peninsula to Orford, a road leaving the Tasman Hwy at Copping and following 35km of gravel north through Wielangta Forest, which is managed for timber harvesting. Significant portions of the forest have been reserved for recreational use and contain a couple of walking tracks.

About halfway between Copping and Orford is **Sandspit River Reserve**, with a picnic shelter and a 20-minute rainforest walk beginning at an impressive bridge constructed of massive logs and passing rock formations once used as shelters by Tasmanian Aborigines. There's also a longer track (90 minutes return) called the **Wielangta Walk**, which follows the river valley. Just south of the reserve is a **viewing platform** revealing the reserve's wet and dry eucalypt forests.

Thumbs Lookout is only 6km from Orford. A rough side road leads to a picnic ground and lookout giving good views of Maria Island. The two-hour return walk to the open, rocky summit of the highest 'thumb' rewards you with even better panoramic views of the coast.

There are no bus services along this road. If you've driven from Orford, you'll reach a give-way sign at the southern end of the forest road – turn right and head past nearby Kellevie to reach the turn-off to either Buckland or Copping. The route makes an invigorating run for cyclists, though there's the occasional logging truck and tour bus passing through.

MARIA ISLAND NATIONAL PARK

This peaceful island was declared a national park in 1972. It features some magnificent natural scenery: forests, fern gullies, fossil-studded sandstone and limestone cliffs, and beautiful white beaches. It has some invigorating walks for hikers, while mountain bikers have plenty of great trails to ride, bird-watchers have plenty to look at, and snorkellers and divers are in for a treat in the waters of the island's marine reserve.

On a day trip to Maria Island, you can see many of its restored buildings and a variety of wildlife. But it's well worth staying here for longer.

History

At various times, Maria Island has been a penal settlement, a factory site and a farming district. The island was originally occupied by the Oyster Bay Tribe of Tasmanian Aborigines, who called it Toarra Marra Monah. They lived primarily on shellfish and crossed to the mainland in canoes, resting on tiny Lachlan Island.

In 1642 Abel Tasman bumped into the island and gave it a European name in honour of Anthony Van Diemen's wife.

The island was selected as Tasmania's second penal settlement in 1821; four years later the first convicts arrived and began work on Darlington.

Over the next seven years many major buildings, including the Commissariat Store (1825) and the Penitentiary (1830), were built from locally made bricks. A water race, mill pond and jetty were also built. In 1832 it was decided that the costs involved in running three penal settlements outside Hobart were too great, and the convicts were moved. For the next 10 years, whalers, farmers and smugglers used the island.

Darlington reopened in 1842 (after renovations) to once again be used by the penal system, this time as a probation station. In 1845 a second settlement was established

at **Long Point** and by 1850 a road connected the two sites. The road allowed ready access to the island and extra land was cleared for sheep grazing. At one stage there were more than 600 convicts at Darlington. However, the flow of convicts to Tasmania slowed and in 1850 Darlington closed. Long Point followed suite the next year and the island was leased for grazing.

In 1884 an enterprising businessman, Signor Bernacchi, leased the island to develop silk and wine-making industries. Darlington's buildings were again renovated and structures like the coffee palace added (1888), and the town of 260 was renamed San Diego. Over the next 40 years there were various other industries here, the most notable being the cement plant established in 1922. The plant soon closed due to the Great Depression, however, and the island reverted to a farming district.

In the 1960s the government gradually bought the properties on the island. Since

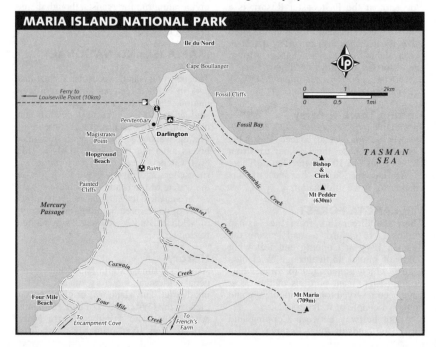

European occupation, none of the larger animals or birds had survived on the island, so in the late 1960s, Forester kangaroos, Bennett's wallabies, Cape Barren geese and emus were introduced; the kangaroos and geese have since thrived. In 1971 the island was declared a wildlife sanctuary and a year later became a national park.

Information

Various brochures are available from the **information centre** in the old Commissariat Store (close to where the ferry docks), including information on the Bishop & Clerk peaks walk, the Fossil Cliffs and tips for enjoying the island by bike. There's a public telephone close to the centre of Darlington.

Things to See & Do

The old township of **Darlington** is worth wandering around. The best short walk (1½ hours return) is to **Painted Cliffs** at the southern end of Hopground Beach. The sandstone here has been stained with iron oxide, forming intricate, colourful patterns.

There's a good circuit walk of 1½ hours, which takes in **Cape Boullanger**, the **Fossil Cliffs** and the old brickworks. If the peaks are clear, you'll be rewarded with great views by climbing **Bishop & Clerk**; a good track leads to the summit and takes about four hours return from Darlington. A walk of six hours return takes you to **Mt Maria**, the island's highest point.

The coastline from Return Point to Bishop & Clerk is a marine reserve, which means no fishing is allowed, including in the Darlington area. The reserve, together with the giant kelp forests and caves around **Fossil Bay**, has some fantastic scuba diving and snorkelling – two of the best underwater spots are at the ferry pier and further south at Painted Cliffs. The water is chilly and wetsuits are essential.

Feather fanciers can see 11 of the state's native bird species here, including the endangered forty-spotted pardalote.

Places to Stay

Penitentiary Accommodation Units (☎ 6257 1420, fax 6257 1482; dorm beds/6-bunk rooms $8.80/22) are rooms in the old penitentiary which have been converted into bunkhouses. The cells have mattresses only, bedding is not supplied and there are no cooking facilities or electricity. You will have to bring your own stove to cook on. The units are very popular (with school groups as well as travellers) and it's essential to book ahead.

Camping (sites per adult/child/family $4.40/2.20/11) is possible by the creek to the east of Darlington. Fires are allowed only in designated fireplaces and during summer these are often banned; portable stoves are therefore recommended. Hot showers are available behind the BBQ shelter and are activated by a $1 coin.

For those keen to walk or cycle, the camp sites at **French's Farm** and **Encampment Cove** are three to four hours away, while **Robey's Farm** is six to seven hours away. All three have limited rainwater supplies; French's Farm and Robey's Farm are fire-free areas where you'll need a portable stove, but fireplaces and wood are provided at Encampment Cove. There are no camping fees at these grounds.

You'll need to bring all your food, as the island has no shops. You'll also need clothing suitable for cool, wet weather, but remember the hat and sunscreen too. A current national park pass is also required.

Getting There & Away

The **Eastcoaster Express** (☎ 6257 1589) operates from the wharf next to the Eastcoaster Resort on Louisville Point Rd, a few kilometres north of Orford. It departs Louisville Point at 10.30am, 1pm and 3.30pm, and returns from Darlington 30 minutes later. An extra service heads out to Maria Island at 9am from Boxing Day right through to April, and extra return services from the island are scheduled during the summer period.

The 10km crossing takes 25 minutes each way. The return fare per adult/child is $19/11 for day visitors and $22/14 for campers; bikes, kayaks and dive tanks incur an extra $3 charge. Tickets can be bought at the kiosk opposite the Bayside Tavern.

The ferry service was up for sale at the time of research and as a result, prices and timetables may eventually change.

TassieLink (☎ 6272 7300, 1300 300 520; Ⓦ www.tigerline.com.au) east-coast services will stop at the Eastcoaster Resort provided you book ahead (see the Getting There & Around section at the start of this chapter for service details).

It is also possible to land on the airstrip near Darlington by light plane. These can be chartered from either Triabunna, Hobart or Launceston.

TRIABUNNA
☎ 03 • postcode 7190 • pop 770
Eight kilometres north of Orford is the larger community of Triabunna; its name is derived from an Aboriginal word for a species of native hen. Located at the head of the attractive sheltered inlet of Spring Bay, it was originally a whaling station, then a military base during the area's penal era, and is now the region's commercial centre. Triabunna handles woodchip processing and is the port of call for scallop and cray-fishing boats.

Down at the Triabunna docks is the **Tasmanian Seafarers' Memorial**, a modest fish-shaped monument that is dedicated to Tasmanians who have died at sea, and to those who have died in the state's waters. One of the more recent plaques commemorates the six sailors who died during the storm-tossed 1998 Sydney to Hobart yacht race.

Girraween Gardens & Tearooms (☎ 6257 3458; 4 Henry St; meals $2-9; open 9.30am-4.30pm daily) has a hectare of pleasant, rigorously manicured private gardens and a tearoom serving regulation Devonshire teas, club sandwiches and milkshakes. Garden access costs $2/5 per person/family (free for tearoom diners).

Information
The well-stocked **visitors information centre** (☎ 6257 4090; Ⓔ triabunna@tasvisinfo .com.au; cnr Esplanade & Charles St) can provide information on chartering boats for fishing or cruising.

Organised Tours
East Coast Eco Tours (☎ 6257 3453; Ⓦ www .springbay.tco.asn.au/ecotours) conducts customised tours of the local coastline from the wharf by the information centre, including trips out to a seal colony and Maria Island.

Places to Stay & Eat
Triabunna Caravan Park (☎ 6257 3575; 6 Vicary St; unpowered/powered site doubles $12/14, on-site van doubles $33-44, cabin doubles $66) is a friendly, low-key compound with cheap camp sites.

The Udda Backpackers (☎/fax 6257 3439; Ⓔ udda@southcom.com.au; 12 Spencer St; dorm beds/doubles $16/36) will give you a warm rural welcome. It has spotless budget accommodation, home-grown vegies for cheap sale, and a licence to sell alcohol to parched travellers. Also available is free transport to/from the Triabunna bus stop and to the 9am Eastcoaster Express (return transport at 4pm provided by the boat operator). The Udda is in 'east' Triabunna; head over the bridge and keep left, following the signs.

Spring Bay Hotel (☎ 6257 3115; 1 Charles St; singles/doubles $35/55) has waterfront rooms with shared facilities and serves counter meals.

Tandara Motor Inn (☎ 6257 3333; Tasman Hwy; singles/doubles $55/66) is a large brick place beside the highway, with plenty of units and a restaurant.

Sufi's (☎ 6257 3212; cnr Charles & Vicary Sts; open 10am-5pm daily Oct-Apr, 10am-4pm daily May-Sept) has Devonshire teas and assorted snacks, plus crafts and haberdashery for sale.

Getting There & Away
TassieLink (☎ 6272 7300, 1300 300 520; Ⓦ www.tigerline.com.au) coaches stop at the Shell service station; the 1½-hour trip from Hobart costs $14. See the Getting There & Around section at the start of this chapter for more information.

LITTLE SWANPORT
☎ 03 • postcode 7190
The hamlet of Little Swanport is arranged around its namesake river, which flows into

a large lagoon. Its attractions are its natural beauty, lack of development and easy coast-line access. The area has some fine beaches, such as Mayfield Bay, Kelvedon, Raspins and Cressy, all accessible by side roads.

The bushy **Gum Leaves** (☎ 6244 8147, fax 6244 7560; Swanston Rd; dorm beds $22, cabins from $90) is 2km down a side road to the south of town. It has cabins of various sizes and plenty of recreational facilities to keep the most restless of families occupied.

SWANSEA
☎ 03 • postcode 7190 • pop 495
Swansea lies on the western shore of Great Oyster Bay and is popular with visitors for the local camping, boating, fishing and surf-ing, not to mention the superb views across to Freycinet Peninsula. Originally known as Great Swanport, the town also has some interesting historic buildings.

European settlers arrived in the 1820s and the town eventually became the admin-istrative centre for Glamorgan. It's Aus-tralia's oldest rural municipality. In 1993 it merged with Spring Bay and the adminis-tration moved to Triabunna.

Because it's a holiday-maker magnet, food and accommodation prices are gener-ally higher here than in most other coastal towns. Another consequence of its popular-ity is that several modern accommodation blocks now dominate part of the old water-front. Regardless, Swansea has retained a laid-back friendliness and still ranks as one of the nicest towns on the east coast.

Information
The **Swansea Wine & Wool Centre** (☎ 6257 8677; 96 Tasman Hwy; open 9am-5pm daily) contains the local **visitors information centre**. There's a multi-card ATM in the **Swansea Corner Store** (Franklin St).

Bikes can be hired for $22 a day from the Caltex service station, opposite the Swansea Corner Store.

Historic Buildings
Conduct a self-guided tour of the town's prime buildings using the *Swansea Heri-tage Walk* booklet ($2), available from the

SWANSEA

PLACES TO STAY & EAT	
1	Swansea Holiday Park
2	Swansea Cottages & Sherbourne Lodge
4	The Left Bank
5	Amos House & Swansea Ocean Villas; Viewpoint Restaurant
8	Tubby & Padman
10	Meredith Mews
11	Meredith House
12	Scarecrow Cottage
13	Freycinet Waters
14	Oyster Bay Guesthouse; Shy Albatross Restaurant
16	Swansea Youth Hostel
17	Swansea Motor Inn
18	The Swan Inn
19	Swansea Waterloo Inn
20	Schouten House
21	Swansea-Kenmore Cabin & Tourist Park
22	Braeside
23	Lester Cottages
24	Wagners Cottages

OTHER	
3	Swansea Bark Mill & East Coast Museum; Swansea Wine & Wool Centre
6	Morris' General Store
7	Glamorgan Community Centre; Museum of Local History
9	Council Chambers; History Room
15	Swansea Corner Store; Bus Arrivals & Departures

information centre. Many of these buildings are located along Franklin and Noyes Sts, including the 1838 **Morris' General Store** *(13 Franklin St)*, still trading and with a small roomful of artefacts and visitor information, and the 1860 **council chambers** *(Noyes St)*.

Most of Swansea's historic buildings are privately owned but the **Glamorgan Community Centre** *(☎ 6257 8215; Franklin St)*, dating from the 1860s, houses a **museum of local history** *(adult/child $3/50c; open 9am-5pm Mon-Sat)*. The major feature here is an impressive oversized billiard table, bought from Hadleys Hotel in Hobart. When it was being made, the builders didn't want to trim the four pieces of slate so instead made the table larger. It's possible to play on the table after 5pm for a small fee if you book. The museum also contains Aboriginal artefacts and early settlers' possessions. There's also a war memorial and an interesting display of old local photographs. Ring the bell for entry.

Swansea Bark Mill & East Coast Museum

In the front section of this museum *(☎ 6257 8382; 96 Tasman Hwy; adult/child/family $5.50/3.25/13.50; open 9am-5pm daily)*, the processing of black-wattle bark is demonstrated on restored machinery. This bark produces tannic acid, a basic ingredient used in the tanning of heavy leathers. The mill was made from scavenged materials and what you see today is how it actually operated. The bark mill was one of the few local industries that remained in operation throughout the Great Depression and it helped keep Swansea alive. The adjoining museum features displays of Swansea's early history, including some superb old photographs.

Other Attractions

Duncombes Lookout, 3km south of town, provides panoramic views of Oyster Bay and Freycinet Peninsula. A further 4km south is **Spiky Bridge**, which was convict-built in 1843 using thousands of local fieldstones but no mortar. The nearby beach and headland are popular for picnics and rock fishing.

Running between Waterloo Beach and the Esplanade is the 45-minute return **Loon.tite.ter.mair.re.le.hoin.er.** walk, named after the Tasmanian Aboriginal tribe that originally lived here. The walk allows great ocean views and passes through the short-tailed shearwater rookery on Waterloo Point; during the breeding season, which runs from September/October to April, you can see the inhabitants return to their burrows at dusk.

Wine Tasting

At the Bark Mill is the **Swansea Wine & Wool Centre** *(☎ 6257 8382; 96 Tasman Hwy; admission free; open 9am-5pm daily)*. It sells Tasmanian wines from around 50 vineyards; you can sample four types of wine for $2. The centre also has a sheepish side, stocking a variety of woollen products: $45 buys you sheepskin/lambswool 'SkinSox', the ugh boot for the new millennium.

There are several wineries off the Tasman Hwy to the north of town, all with free tastings. **Freycinet Vineyard** *(☎ 6257 8574; open 9am-5pm Mon-Fri, 10am-4pm Sat & Sun Aug-May; 9am-4.30pm Mon-Fri June & July)* produces some wonderful pinot noir; the 1998 release is particularly renowned. Next door is **Coombend Estate** *(☎ 6257 8881; open 9am-5pm daily)*, which produces some excellent riesling and sauvignon blanc – you can stay overnight here (see Places to Stay).

Spring Vale Vineyards *(☎ 6257 8208; ⓦ www.springvalewines.com; 130 Spring Vale Rd; open 10am-5pm Sat & Sun)*, 15km north of Swansea, produces some great chardonnay and pinot noir. It opens other times by prior arrangement.

Places to Stay – Budget

Swansea Holiday Park *(☎ 6257 8177; ⓦ www.swansea-holiday.com.au; Shaw St; unpowered/powered sites $14/18, unit doubles $55-80)* has a nice position by the beach on the northern edge of town. The units range from bare-bones budget to more expensive en suite models.

Swansea-Kenmore Cabin & Tourist Park *(☎ 6257 8148, fax 6257 8554; unpowered/powered site doubles $15/17.50,*

Fishing trawlers in Waubs Bay, Bicheno, heading out to try their luck

One of Tasmania's most profitable exports to Asia is crayfish. Delicious!

Granite peaks of The Hazards at sunset, Coles Bay

Historic hotel in Evandale

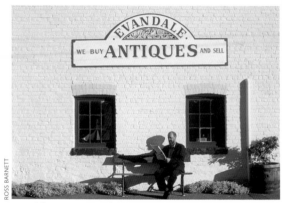

Evandale Antiques was first built as the Royal Oak Stables

Brisbane St, the main drag in Launceston

Rows of sweet-smelling lavender at the Bridestowe Estate Lavender Farm, Nabowla

on-site van doubles $40, cabin doubles from $70) is a flat, fairly characterless cabin park, though it has good facilities like a playground and barbecues.

Swansea Youth Hostel (☎ 6257 8367; 5 Franklin St; YHA members/nonmembers $16/19.50) is a clash of old-fashioned floor coverings and laminate, but is well-outfitted and has a good seaside location.

Places to Stay – Mid-Range
Guesthouses & B&Bs Swansea has a plethora of high-standard B&Bs.

Freycinet Waters (☎ 6257 8080; W www .freycinetwaters.com.au; 16 Franklin St; singles $95-115, doubles $110-130) is a fresh, bright B&B with an exemplary seaside ambience. There are standard or spa rooms, all with cooked breakfast.

Oyster Bay Guesthouse (☎ 6257 8110, fax 6257 8703; 10 Franklin St; singles/ doubles $60/110) is a friendly, colonial-style place dating from 1836. It looks a bit scuffed from the outside but inside it's well maintained.

Braeside (☎ 6257 8008; W www.tassie .net.au/braeside; 21 Julia St; singles $85-110, doubles $105-132), which means 'Side of the Hill', is a good-humoured Scottish enclave south of the centre, where you'll be spoiled with cooked breakfasts, lots of places to lounge and a solar-heated pool.

Hotels & Motels Smack on the beach you'll find **The Swan Inn** (☎ 6257 8899, fax 6257 8073; 1 Franklin St; doubles $55), which has cheap rooms.

Swansea Motor Inn (☎ 6257 8102; 1 Franklin St; singles $55-77, doubles $66-88), next door to the Swan, has cheap standard rooms and more expensive ones with water views.

Amos House & Swansea Ocean Villas (☎ 6257 8656; e abetts@tassie.net.au; 3 Maria St; doubles $90-110) has small but pleasant motel rooms above a very busy restaurant.

Places to Stay – Top End
Guesthouses & B&Bs A short, brisk walk uphill from the main street is the National Trust–classified **Mered** (☎ 6257 8119, fax 6257 8123; 15 singles/doubles $110/160), a renov... 1853 home offering rose-coloured B&B. Hearty three-course dinners can be arranged.

Schouten House (☎ 6257 8564, fax 6257 8767; 1 Waterloo Rd; singles/doubles from $80/110) is a large Georgian house with an earthenware facade and good B&B in en suite rooms.

Redcliffe House (☎ 6257 8557, 1800 638 677; 13569 Tasman Hwy; singles/doubles from $90/100), charmingly situated 1km north of town on a garden-enhanced block beside the Meredith River, has large en suite rooms with hearty breakfasts.

Tubby & Padman (☎/fax 6257 8901; W www.tubbyandpadman.com.au; 20 Franklin St; B&B doubles $120-155) is definitely the place to reinvigorate yourself. It's a well-appointed B&B set in a renovated 1840s cottage, with a mixture of modern and heritage accommodation.

Kabuki by the Sea (☎/fax 6257 8588; W www.kabukibythesea.com.au; Tasman Hwy; singles $75-100, doubles $95-135), astride some cliffs 12km south of town, is a self-labelled *ryokan* (Japanese inn) with comfortable units and stupendous ocean views. You can choose room-only lodgings or opt for a package that includes continental breakfast and a three-course lunch or dinner ($195 per double), courtesy of the on-site Japanese restaurant (see Places to Eat).

Motels The higher prices you pay for the bay-facing rooms at the **Swansea Waterloo Inn** (☎ 6257 8577, fax 6257 8397; 1a Franklin St; doubles $70-150) are explained by the water views afforded from their balconies, but there's no explanation for why the inn's several dozen rooms begin at number 729.

Self-Contained Units & Cottages
Amos House & Swansea Ocean Villas (☎ 6257 8656; W www.swanseaoceanvillas .com.au; 3 Maria St; doubles $150-180) has attractive, two-storey self-contained villas close to the beachfront.

Meredith Mews (☎ 6257 8119, fax 6257 8123; 15 Noyes St; doubles $180) is a row of luxury spa apartments next door to Meredith House, which come with breakfast and small back verandas overlooking some gardens.

Scarecrow Cottage (☎ 6343 6340; 22 Noyes St; doubles from $130) is a quiet, inviting 1860 weatherboard abode with a small back garden.

Wagners Cottages (☎ 6257 8494; W www .wagnerscottages.com.au; doubles from $110) is in gardens beside the highway, 3km south of town. Of its four cottages, two were built in the 1860s – the living room in one has a ceiling composed of slight lengths of wood that were hand-split and planed with a drawing knife.

Lester Cottages (☎ 6257 8105, fax 6257 8425; 42 Gordon St; doubles from $125) has a clutch of appealingly colonial self-contained cottages. One of the two-bedroom cottages has wheelchair access.

Swansea Cottages & Sherbourne Lodge (☎ 6257 8328, fax 6257 8502; 43 Franklin St; lodge/cottage doubles from $132/165) has a colonial-style lodge and a half-dozen plush cottages, all immaculate and set in spacious grounds. Breakfasts are also available.

Coombend Cottages (☎ 6257 8256; e coombendest@vision.net.au; Tasman Hwy; doubles from $120), at the vineyard of the same name north of Swansea, has two self-contained cottages set in rolling farmland close to Great Oyster Bay; rates include breakfast provisions.

Piermont Retreat (☎ 6257 8131; W www.piermont.com.au; Tasman Hwy; doubles $195-225), 3km south of town, is a collection of luxurious stone-walled cottages overlooking a quiet beach.

Places to Eat

The Left Bank (☎ 6257 8896; cnr Main & Maria Sts; lunch $6-12; open 8am-5pm Wed-Mon) is a colourful, eclectic café with simply excellent breakfasts and lunches, plus fresh juices and good coffee. It's identifiable by its blazing-red front door.

The Swan Inn (☎ 6257 8899; 1 Franklin St; mains $14.50-19) has an à la carte restaurant that's open daily. It serves standard bistro fare for lunch, but has a more varied dinner menu (Hokkien lamb noodles, ossa bucco).

Schouten House (☎ 6257 8564; 1 Waterloo Rd; mains $19-24; open nightly Tues-Sun) offers a simple menu of mainly meat dishes, though it has a couple of appealing vegie entrees.

Shy Albatross Restaurant (☎ 6257 8110; 10 Franklin St; mains $9-15.50; open from 6pm daily), in the Oyster Bay Guesthouse, serves a selection of pastas, crepes and a smattering of seafood, plus desserts like Mississippi mud cake.

Viewpoint Restaurant (☎ 6257 8656; 3 Maria St; mains $9-20; open from 6pm daily) often has all of its 40 seats occupied by diners enjoying the seafood selections, so book well ahead.

Kabuki by the Sea (☎ 6257 8588; dinner mains $20; open lunch & dinner Tues-Sat, lunch Sun & Mon Dec-Apr) has a licensed restaurant serving simple Japanese-influenced dishes, and morning and afternoon teas. Bookings are recommended.

Kate's Berry Farm (☎ 6257 8428; Addison St; open 9am-6pm daily), 3km south of Swansea with a nice vantage over the bay, offers tastings and sales of its berries, jams, sauces, ice cream and wine.

Getting There & Away

Buses arrive at and depart from the Swansea Corner Store. The fare for the 2¼-hour **TassieLink** (☎ 6272 7300, 1300 300 520; W www.tigerline.com.au) bus ride to/from Hobart is $20; the **Redline Coaches** (☎ 6336 1446, 1300 360 000; W www.tas redline.com.au) fare from Hobart/Launceston is $25/21. See the Getting There & Around section at the start of this chapter for more about bus and cycle routes.

COLES BAY & FREYCINET NATIONAL PARK
☎ 03 • postcode 7215

The township of Coles Bay is both dominated and sheltered by the spectacular 300m-high pink-granite outcrops known as The Hazards. This formation marks the northern boundary of the beautiful Freycinet National Park, noted for its magnificent scenery, coastal heaths, orchids and other wildflowers. Local fauna includes black cockatoos, yellow wattlebirds, yellow-throated honey-eaters and Bennett's wallabies.

History

The Oyster Bay Tribe of Tasmanian Aborigines inhabited the Freycinet area, living off the abundant shellfish – there are some large shell middens along Richardsons Beach.

The first European to visit this area was Abel Tasman in 1642, who identified and named Schouten Island, but also mistook Freycinet for another island. In 1802, Baudin's French expedition discovered that Freycinet was actually a peninsula and named it and many other nearby features. When other expeditions noted the high numbers of seals, sealers arrived from Sydney and quickly wiped most of their number out.

In 1824 a whaling station was established at Parsons Cove, but by the 1840s the whales had been slaughtered and the station had closed. Coles Bay was named after Silas Cole, who arrived in the 1830s and burnt some of the midden shells to produce lime. Mortar made from this lime was used in the construction of many of Swansea's older buildings.

Schouten Island was mined for coal from 1840 to 1880, and also for tin. Both Freycinet and Schouten Island were also farmed. In 1906, both areas were declared game reserves to stop the over-hunting of animals. In 1916 Freycinet shared the honours with Mt Field in becoming Tasmania's first national park; Schouten Island was added in 1977. To complete protection of the coastal regions, the Friendly Beaches were added to the national park in 1992.

Information

Coles Bay is 31km down a sealed side road from the Tasman Hwy and has reasonable amenities. It's the man-made gateway to the glorious beaches, coves and cliffs of the Freycinet Peninsula.

Park information is available from the new **East Coast Interpretation Centre** (☎ 6256 7000, e freycinet@dpiwe.tas.gov.au; open 8am-5pm daily) at the park entrance. The centre should be open longer hours during summer.

The **post office/store** (☎ 6257 0109; 1 Garnet Ave, Coles Bay; open 8am-6.30pm daily) sells groceries, basic supplies and petrol; it also serves as a newsagency. The **Iluka Holiday Centre** (☎ 6257 0115; Coles Bay Esplanade), off Muir's Beach, has takeaway food, a bistro and petrol, plus a **mini-supermarket** (open 8am-8pm daily) which also dispenses basic tourist information.

You can hire tents, sleeping bags, fishing rods, boats and more at **Freycinet Rentals** (☎ 6257 0320; 5 Garnet Ave, Coles Bay).

Beaches & Lagoons

The signposted turn-off to the **Friendly Beaches** is 22km north of Coles Bay. From the car park at Isaacs Point, a five-minute walk leads to a vantage point for uninterrupted views of pristine sand and water.

The road connecting the Tasman Hwy with Coles Bay skirts around the edge of the large **Moulting Lagoon Game Reserve,**

COLES BAY

To Freycinet Caravan Park &
Freycinet Backpackers, Freycinet
Marine Farm, Friendly Beaches,
Churinga Farm Cottages &
Edge of the Bay

C302

Muirs Beach

Harold St

Esplanade Esplanade

FREYCINET NATIONAL PARK

Coles
Bay

Richardsons

Freycinet Dr

0   0.5   1km
0   0.25   0.5mi

Bradley Dr

1 Freycinet Adventures
2 Freycinet Cafe & Bakery
3 Iluka Tavern
4 Iluka Holiday Centre;
   Iluka Backpackers
5 Gum Nut Cottage
6 Freycinet Villas
7 Three Peaks Holiday Units;
   Royle Retreat
8 Oyster Bar
9 Jessie's Cottage
10 Freycinet Rentals
11 Post Office & General
   Store; Madge Malloys
12 Boat Ramp
13 East Coast Interpretation
   Centre
14 Freycinet Camping Ground
15 Freycinet Lodge;
   Richardsons Bistro;
   Bay Restaurant
16 Coles Bay Youth Hostel

Parsons
Cove

Honeymoon
Bay

Cape Tourville Rd
To Cape
Tourville (6km)

The Fisheries
Start of Walking Tracks to
Wineglass Bay, Hazards Beach
& Cooks Beach

a protected breeding ground for birdlife that includes black swans and wild ducks.

Freycinet Marine Farm

Off the road to Coles Bay is Freycinet Marine Farm (☎ 6257 0140; 88 Flacks Rd), which conducts 90-minute guided tours of its oyster-cultivating operation, including a barge trip to the cages and oyster tastings. The tours must be pre-booked, take place at 10am daily and cost $25 per person. You can also buy your fill of top-quality Pacific and Tasmanian oysters. The turn-off to the farm is 8km north of Coles Bay.

Cape Tourville Lighthouse

The best short drive is to follow the 6km road out to Cape Tourville lighthouse. The road enters the park (so national park fees apply) and is in reasonable condition, but care must be taken in places. The cape has a new short walk and extensive coastal views.

Fishing

There's excellent fishing around the bay; charter a boat or hire a dinghy and go catch your own dinner.

From March to May, Coles Bay is a fantastic base for big-game fishing, especially when the giant bluefin tuna run. Freycinet Sea Charters (☎ 6257 0355) can take you to the best spots. The bay is also famous for crayfish.

Water Sports & Cruises

Coles Bay is at the head of the large, sheltered Great Oyster Bay, where you can swim, windsurf and water ski (or learn these activities) in safe ocean waters.

Freycinet Sea Charters (☎ 6257 0355) offers peninsula cruises where you may see dolphins, seals, sea eagles, albatrosses, penguins (in flat conditions) and/or whales (in winter). A two-hour trip down the peninsula's west coast leaves at 3pm and costs $55 per person, while a four-hour chug taking in Schouten Island departs at 10am and costs $88 per person (lunch included). Another option is a six-hour cruise, costing $132 per person with a light lunch, or from $180 to $200 per person for gourmet tucker.

The sea kayaking in this area is superb. Freycinet Adventures (☎ 6257 0500; W www.freycinetadventures.com; cnr Coles Bay Esplanade & Freycinet Dr) offers everything from twilight paddles ($45) to full-day tours including lunch ($130); multi-day tours can also be organised.

Abseiling & Rock Climbing

Freycinet Peninsula is regarded as one of the best abseiling and rock-climbing spots in Australia. The tempting granite peaks of The Hazards and other cliffs in the area attract both experienced climbers and novices. Freycinet Adventures (☎ 6257 0500; W www.freycinetadventures.com; cnr Coles Bay Esplanade & Freycinet Dr) runs half-day abseiling trips for $80 per person.

Bushwalking

Roads penetrate only a small way into the park, so exploring the lay of the land means hitting some much-plodded tracks.

One of the most beautiful walks in Tasmania is to Wineglass Bay (2½ to three hours return). Alternatively, walk along the same track only as far as Wineglass Bay Lookout (one hour return), with its inspired, postcard-captured view. Another superb walk, if you're fit, is the trek to the spectacular views from the summit of Mt Amos (three hours return). Instead of driving from Coles Bay to the start of the main walking tracks, you can follow the shoreline on foot via Honeymoon Bay (1½ hours one way).

There are also plenty of worthy shorter walks, like Sleepy Bay, just off the Cape Tourville Road, and the hilltop lookout in Coles Bay. An easy wheelchair-accessible track was recently created at Cape Tourville, yielding great views along its 30-minute path. For details of a two-day, 31km circuit of the peninsula, see Lonely Planet's Walking in Australia.

For all national park walks, remember to get a parks pass and to sign in (and out) at the car park registration booth.

Between October and April, Freycinet Experience (☎ 6223 7565, 1800 506 003; W www.freycinet.com.au; 2 Macquarie St, Hobart) guide a four-day peninsula walk.

Accommodation, food, wine, boat trips and transport from Hobart are provided for around $1350 per person. The walk's final night is spent at the cosy Friendly Beaches Lodge.

Other Activities

If you feel like **cycling**, hire a bike from the post office/store on Garnet Ave for $11/17 per half/full day. Thirty-minute **scenic flights** over the area are available for $80 (minimum two people) from **Freycinet Air** (☎ 6375 1694; W www.freycinetair.com.au).

Places to Stay – Budget

Camp sites worth walking to for their scenery include **Wineglass Bay** (one to 1½ hours), **Hazards Beach** (two to three hours) and **Cooks Beach** (4½ hours). Farther north, at **Friendly Beaches**, are two extremely basic camp sites with pit toilets. While there are no camping fees at the aforementioned sites, national park entry fees apply.

Bush camping can be done for free outside the national park at the **River & Rocks site** at Moulting Lagoon; drive 8km north of Coles Bay, turn left onto the unsealed River & Rocks Rd, then turn left at the T-junction. Note there's no permanent drinking water at any of the free camp sites. There's a water tank at Cooks Beach, but this can run dry (ask about its current status at the interpretation centre). It's better to carry your own water.

Richardsons Beach (unpowered/powered sites per double $11/13) is the main camping ground. Its series of dune sites, located at the national park entrance, can be booked at the **visitor centre** (☎ 6257 0107). Book well in advance during peak holiday periods, when sites are allocated using a ballot system; a national park pass is required to camp here. You'll need to lock food away, as the possums will break into tents and packs to get a feed. The general rule is avoid feeding the wildlife.

Iluka Holiday Centre (☎ 6257 0115; e iluka@trump.net.au; Coles Bay Esplanade; unpowered/powered site doubles $17/19, on-site van doubles $50, cabin doubles $60-110) has plenty of camp sites and

old/new-style cabins in its l... maintained grounds. Also on-si... YHA **Iluka Backpackers** (dorm beds/a... per YHA member $16.50/44, nonmem... $20/51), light on for character but ver... clean and with a large kitchen.

Coles Bay Youth Hostel is another YHA facility, this one at scenic Parsons Cove in the national park. It comprises two basic five-person cabins, equipped with a fridge and stove but pit toilets and no running hot water. Bunks are $9 per person (minimum two people per booking) and cabins can be rented for $45 via a ballot system from mid-December to mid-February and at Easter. Bookings are essential and must be made through the **YHA** head office in Hobart (☎ 6234 9617; e yhatas@yhatas.org.au; 1st floor, 28 Criterion St); keys are obtained from the Iluka Holiday Centre.

Coles Bay Caravan Park & Freycinet Backpackers (☎ 6257 0100, fax 6257 0270; 2352 Coles Bay Rd; unpowered/powered sites $9/11, dorm beds $16.50) is 3km by road from Coles Bay, at the western end of Muir's Beach. This park has lots of bushland tent sites and gloomy, twin-bunk backpacker rooms. At the time of research it was on the market.

Places to Stay – Mid-Range

Freycinet Rentals (☎/fax 6257 0320; 5 Garnet Ave, Coles Bay) manage three self-contained properties: **Freycinet Villas** (2 Bradley Dr; doubles $120), a pair of three-bedroom brick units; the cosy **Gum Nut Cottage** (50 Freycinet Dr; doubles from $95); and **Three Peaks Holiday Units** (doubles $115-135), a foursome of buildings, all but one on Freycinet Dr – 'The Views', at 2 Florence St, naturally has the best views.

Churinga Farm Cottages (☎ 6257 0190, fax 6257 0397; Coles Bay Rd; singles/doubles from $75/90) are set on 50 bushy hectares, secluded yet only a 10-minute drive from the town centre.

Royle Retreat (☎ 6257 1104; 2 Royle Ave; singles/doubles from $65/85) offers two rooms in a private residence; rates include a full cooked breakfast.

End

7 0143; e jessies
Esplanade East,
60) is actually two
at views to The
de verandas.
57 0101; W www
cabins $185-257),
situated within the national park at the southern end of Richardsons Beach, has dozens of
free-standing, bush-surrounded cabins, including two that are barrier-free. From
Christmas until the end of March, a minimum
stay of two nights applies. Lodge guests still
need to buy their own national park pass.

Edge of the Bay (☎ 6257 0102; W www
.edgeofthebay.com.au; 2308 Main Rd; doubles
$155-210), 4km north of Coles Bay, has
snazzy modern suites and spread out, well-
equipped cottages with requisite Hazardous
views. Over summer, there's a two-night
minimum-stay requirement for waterfront
rooms, which come with a $20 dinner voucher
for the on-site restaurant (see Places to Eat).

Places to Eat
Iluka Tavern (☎ 6257 0429; Coles Bay
Esplanade; mains from $10), serves pub
lunches and dinners daily.

Freycinet Cafe & Bakery (☎ 6257 0272;
Shop 2, Coles Bay Esplanade; lunch $3-10;
open from 8am daily) is the place for freshly
baked vegan pies, all-day breakfasts, or
pizza (served after 5pm).

Madge Malloys (☎ 6257 0399; 7 Garnet
Ave, Coles Bay; mains $20-25; open 6pm-
late Tues-Sat) has a huge wine list and a
great reputation for seafood. It also does the
odd drunken Irish chicken, plus desserts
like sticky-date pudding.

Oyster Bar (dishes $6-16; open until
7pm daily) serves up food of the freshly
shucked variety.

The Edge (☎ 6257 0102; mains $14-26;
open for lunch & dinner daily), Edge of the
Bay's view-blessed restaurant, serves great
seafood. And just try declining desserts like
baked white-chocolate cheesecake or honey-
glazed apple and mascarpone tart.

Richardsons Bistro (☎ 6257 0101; mains
$7-22; open 7.30am-9pm daily Nov-Apr,
lunch May-Oct) is at Freycinet Lodge, as is
the more expensive **Bay Restaurant** (mains
$18-28.50; open from 6.30pm daily). Book-
ings are essential for Bay Restaurant, where
the seasonal menu has included the world's
most adjective-plagued mollusc: the three-
seared Swansea black-lipped baby abalone.

Getting There & Away
Bus Bicheno Coach Service (☎ 6257 0293,
0419 570 293) runs buses between Bicheno,
Coles Bay and the national park, connecting
with **TassieLink** (☎ 6272 7300, 1300 300
520; W www.tigerline.com.au) and **Redline
Coaches** (☎ 6336 1446, 1300 360 000;
W www.tasredline.com.au) services at the
Coles Bay turn-off; the Redline/TassieLink
fare from Hobart to the turn-off is
$25/23.50. From May to November there
are up to four services on weekdays and at
least one on Saturday and Sunday. Extra
services are scheduled on demand from
December to April.

Many services run only if bookings exist,
so book at least the night before. The one-way/
return fare from Bicheno to Coles Bay is
$7.50/14 ($8.80/16 from Bicheno to the
walking tracks car park; $6.30/12 from the
highway turn-off to Coles Bay). The bus
picks up from accommodation if requested.
Buses depart Bicheno from the Bicheno
Takeaway (52 Burgess St) and in Coles Bay
from the post office/store (1 Garnet Ave).

It's more than 5km from the town to the
national park walking tracks car park.
Bicheno Coach Service (☎ 6257 0293, 0419
570 293) does the trip up to four times each
weekday and once on Saturday and Sunday;
bookings are essential. The one-way/return
cost is $4/6. Park entry fees apply.

BICHENO
☎ 03 • postcode 7215 • pop 700
Bicheno has all the attributes of a successful
holiday resort, including soporific water
views, a mild climate and abundant sunshine.
That said, the town has had an unstable time
of late, with a number of businesses opening
and closing their doors in rapid succession.

Fishing is the community's mainstay and
the local fleet shelters in a tiny, picturesque

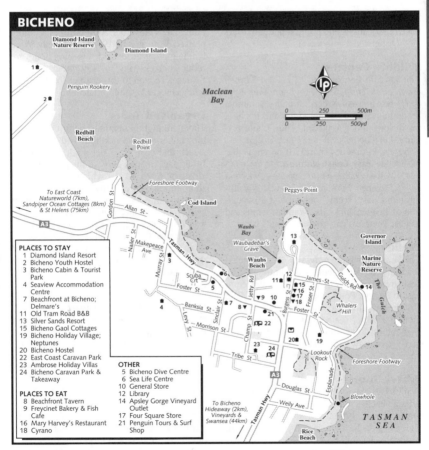

BICHENO

Diamond Island
Nature Reserve

Diamond Island

Penguin Rookery

Maclean
Bay

Redbill
Beach

Redbill
Point

Foreshore Footway

Peggys Point

To East Coast
Natureworld (7km),
Sandpiper Ocean Cottages (8km)
& St Helens (75km)

Allan St

Cod Island

Waubs
Bay

Waubadebar's
Grave

Governor
Island

Waubs
Beach

Marine
Nature
Reserve

The
Gulch

James St

Gulch Rd

Whalers
Hill

Lookout
Rock

Foreshore Footway

Douglas St

Blowhole

To Bicheno
Hideaway (2km),
Vineyards &
Swansea (44km)

Weily Ave

TASMAN
SEA

Rice
Beach

PLACES TO STAY
1 Diamond Island Resort
2 Bicheno Youth Hostel
3 Bicheno Cabin & Tourist
 Park
4 Seaview Accommodation
 Centre
7 Beachfront at Bicheno;
 Delmare's
11 Old Tram Road B&B
13 Silver Sands Resort
15 Bicheno Gaol Cottages
19 Bicheno Holiday Village;
 Neptunes
20 Bicheno Hostel
22 East Coast Caravan Park
23 Ambrose Holiday Villas
24 Bicheno Caravan Park &
 Takeaway

PLACES TO EAT
8 Beachfront Tavern
9 Freycinet Bakery & Fish
 Cafe
16 Mary Harvey's Restaurant
18 Cyrano

OTHER
5 Bicheno Dive Centre
6 Sea Life Centre
10 General Store
12 Library
14 Apsley Gorge Vineyard
 Outlet
17 Four Square Store
21 Penguin Tours & Surf
 Shop

harbour called The Gulch. With reasonable prices for food and accommodation, it's a good place to stay for a few days.

History

The town began as a sealers' port and was called Waubs Bay Harbour after an Aboriginal woman, Waubadebar, who was enslaved by sealers in the early 19th century. A strong swimmer, she became famous for rescuing two sealers when their boat was wrecked 1km offshore. Years after her death, the town honoured her by constructing a grave off the main beach. Bicheno was renamed after James

Ebenezer Bicheno, colonial secretary of Van Diemen's Land in the 1840s.

In 1854 the town became a coal-mining port, but a year later most of the miners left and joined the Victorian gold rush. The town shrank drastically, which is why so few historic buildings remain. Around the 1940s, the town's fortunes changed as it started developing into the holiday destination it is today.

Information

The local information centre was defunct at the time of research, having metamorphosed into a surf shop. But the proprietor still handles bookings for a couple of Bicheno-based tours, including popular penguin tours (see Organised Tours later).

Wildlife Centres

The **Sea Life Centre** (☎ 6375 1121; 1 Tasman Hwy; adult/child $5/2.50; open 9am-5pm daily) has a small aquarium and a scramble around a restored trading ketch, but it's all a bit forlorn and overpriced. The on-site restaurant is a better deal (see Places to Eat).

Seven kilometres north of town is the 32-hectare **East Coast Natureworld** (☎ 6375 1311; w www.natureworld.com.au; adult/child $11/5.50; open 9am-5pm daily), with a walk-through aviary, scenic lookout and a population of Tasmanian devils, wombats, emus and eagles. There's plenty to occupy kids here.

Walks

The 3km **Foreshore Footway** was constructed for the 1988 Bicentennial celebrations. The best stretch extends from the Sea Life Centre east to **Peggys Point**, taking you through The Gulch and along to the **Blowhole**, where there's a large, sea-rocked granite boulder. You return along footpaths with panoramic views over town. In whaling days, passing whales were spotted from **Whalers Hill**.

Water Sports

Waubs Beach and Rice Beach are fairly safe ocean beaches for swimming. For warmer water, the sheltered and shallow Denison River, beside the highway 8km north of town, is popular. Redbill Point often has good surfing breaks and water skiing is also popular.

The **Bicheno Dive Centre** (☎ 6375 1138; e bichenodive@tasadventures.com; 2 Scuba Court; open 9am-5pm daily) hires diving equipment and organises underwater trips. One-day charters including all equipment and two boat dives cost from $140.

Wine Tasting

The tiny outlet of the nearby **Apsley Gorge Vineyard** (AGV; ☎ 6375 1221; The Gulch; open 10am-5pm daily Oct-Apr) offers wine tastings (free) and freshly cooked crayfish ($40 for two people) from a nondescript room at Bicheno Winery – people have been known to sit outside for hours indulging in both. The vineyard's 2000 pinot is a highly praised drop, as is its 1998 chardonnay. Wine by the glass is around $5. Opening hours are reduced from May to September. See the Swansea section of this chapter for details of other vineyards south of Bicheno.

Organised Tours

There are nightly one-hour **penguin tours** of the rookery at the northern end of Redbill Beach that cost $15/7 per adult/child. Tours fill up fast so book early at the **penguin tour kiosk** (☎ 6375 1333), which is also a surf shop, in the centre of town – this is also the place to book 45-minute **glass-bottom boat** trips around the local marine park (adult/child $15/7) and **4WD tours** ($35 per person).

Bicheno Coach Service (☎ 6257 0293, 0419 570 293) links up with guided tours of the oyster-harvesting **Freycinet Marine Farm** on demand. (See the Coles Bay & Freycinet National Park section.)

Places to Stay – Budget

Camping & Cabins The **Bicheno Caravan Park & Takeaway** (☎ 6375 1280; 52 Burgess St; unpowered/powered site doubles $12/13, on-site van doubles $30) is a plain-living park with a few vans on offer, for which you'll need your own linen.

Bicheno Cabin & Tourist Park (☎/fax 6375 1117; 30 Tasman Hwy; cabin doubles $66-89) eschews the greenery of a standard 'park' for concrete and gravel, but its range of cabins are new and mod con–filled.

East Coast Caravan Park (☎ 6375 1999; 4 Champ St; unpowered/powered sites $14/16, cabin doubles from $65) is a well-maintained place not far from Waubs Beach. Its laundry facilities are open to the public.

Hostels The compact **Bicheno Hostel** (☎/fax 6375 1651; 11 Morrison St; dorm beds $15) has the cosy layout of a large, inviting bunkhouse and comfortable beds.

Bicheno Youth Hostel (☎ 6375 1293; 47 Tasman Hwy) was closed at the time of writing, but there was a strong possibility this formerly ramshackle beachside place would reopen its doors.

Seaview Accommodation Centre (☎ 6375 1247; W www.users.bigpond.com/seaview _accom; 29 Banksia St; dorm beds $15, family units with/without linen from $50/60) is another option for hostel accommodation. Cheap family units are also available; rates cover two adults and two children. It often caters to large school groups, though, so ring ahead.

Places to Stay – Mid-Range
Motels The spic-and-span but generic **Beachfront at Bicheno** (☎ 6375 1111; e beachfront_bicheno@bigpond.com; Tasman Hwy; doubles $85-130) is opposite the beach, but you can opt for a man-made watery environment by hanging around the pool.

Silver Sands Resort (☎ 6375 1266, fax 6375 1168; Burgess St; doubles $65-90) is less a resort and more a wagon-train of motel units encircling a pool. It has variously priced rooms, the most expensive with ocean views.

Self-Contained Units There are a dozen timber-panelled, parquetry-floored units at **Ambrose Holiday Villas** (☎ 6375 1288, fax 6375 1512; cnr Tribe & Champ Sts; doubles $90), available in one- to three-bedroom forms.

Places to Stay – Top End
B&Bs At the **Old Tram Road B&B** (☎/fax 6375 1555; e oldtrambb@tassie.net.au; 3 Old Tram Rd; B&B doubles $95-105) are two very comfortable rooms only 100m from the beach, accessed via a private track from the back garden. Adding to your relaxed stay are gourmet breakfasts and a convivial host.

Resorts The **Diamond Island Resort** (☎ 6375 1161, 1800 030 299; e diambich@fc-hotels .com.au; 69 Tasman Hwy; singles $80-155, doubles $90-165) doesn't have gemstones littering the driveway but it does have well-appointed double-storey Tudor units, a well-stocked bar and a tidy licensed restaurant.

Self-Contained Units & Cottages The impressive **Bicheno Hideaway** (☎ 6375 1312; W www.bichenohideaway.com; 179 Harveys Farm Rd; singles/doubles $75/120) is 2km south of town. It's a tranquil spot with several striking arc-shaped units with ocean views.

Bicheno Gaol Cottages (☎ 6375 1430; W www.bichenogaolcottages.com; cnr Burgess & James Sts; B&B doubles $120-140), offers good old colonial accommodation in either the 1845 gaol (Bicheno's oldest building), the old school house (has a barrier-free room) or the stables. Inquire at Mary Harvey's Restaurant next door.

Bicheno Holiday Village (☎ 6375 1171, fax 6375 1144; cnr Foster & Fraser Sts; doubles $150-260) has one- to four-bedroom A-frame units spread out in private bushland between the town's two lookouts. Also planted in the undergrowth are tennis courts, a pool and a small lake. The western-most units with ocean views are recommended.

Sandpiper Ocean Cottages (☎/fax 6375 1122; e reeflawn@vision.net.au; Tasman Hwy; B&B doubles $125) are 8km north of Bicheno, but only a short walk from a pristine beach.

Places to Eat
Freycinet Bakery & Fish Cafe (☎ 6375 1972; 44-46 Foster St; meals $4-14; bakery open from 8am, café open from 11am daily) serves all-day breakfasts, pies, focaccias and pizzas to people clustered around its outside tables; it's also a qualified fish and chippery.

Sea Life Centre Restaurant (☎ 6375 1121; 1 Tasman Hwy; mains $7-22; open lunch & dinner daily) offers a variety of sea morsels and other meaty options, plus fine bay views. Meals are served less frequently over winter.

Beachfront at Bicheno (☎ 6375 1111; Tasman Hwy) has two eateries: **Delmare's** (mains $10-19), usually open for lunch and dinner, with a modish tiled floor and a mixture of pasta, pizza, salads and meat dishes; and the laid-back **Beachfront Tavern** (mains from $10), which serves counter meals daily.

Silver Sands Resort (☎ 6375 1266; Burgess St; mains $14-18.50) has OK, seafood-slanted bistro meals.

Neptunes (☎ 6375 1762; cnr Foster & Fraser Sts; mains $14.50-18.50; open evening daily Apr-Oct) is a seafood restaurant in the grounds of Bicheno Holiday Village. For a taste of oyster, prawns, mussels, calamari and fish at one sitting, throw your face into a banquet platter ($55/98 for one/two people). It has reduced opening hours from May to September.

Cyrano (*☎ 6375 1137; 77 Burgess St; mains $17.50-22.50; open from 5.30pm daily*) is a BYO restaurant specialising in seafood and French cuisine, including a sweet crepe suzette.

Mary Harvey's Restaurant (*☎ 6375 1430; cnr Burgess & James Sts; mains $16-18; open from 6pm daily Sept-June, light lunch daily late-Dec–mid-Apr*), in the grounds of the old gaol, uses Tasmanian produce to delicious effect: try the game-and-Guinness pie. Hours vary at other times.

Getting There & Away

TassieLink (*☎ 6272 7300, 1300 300 520;* w *www.tigerline.com.au*) and **Redline Coaches** (*☎ 6336 1446, 1300 360 000;* w *www.tasredline.com.au*) stop at the Four Square Store on Burgess St. **Bicheno Coach Service** (*☎ 6257 0293, 0419 570 293*) stops at Bicheno Takeaway, also on Burgess St. For service details see the Coles Bay & Freycinet National Park section.

TassieLink's 2½- to three-hour trip from Launceston/Hobart costs $23/24.20. Redline fares from Launceston/Hobart are $26/25. **Bicheno Coach Service** (*☎ 6257 0293, 0419 570 293*) runs from Bicheno to Coles Bay ($7.50/14 one way/return; $8.80/16 to the national park). For all services, book ahead if you have a bicycle or you might find there's no room for it.

DOUGLAS-APSLEY NATIONAL PARK

This is a large area of undisturbed dry eucalypt forest, typical of much of the original east-coast land cover. It was declared a national park in 1989 after public concern was expressed over local wood chipping and the large-scale clearing of old-growth forests. The park's significant features include rocky peaks, river gorges, beautiful waterfalls and prolific bird and animal life.

Access to the park is by gravel roads. To reach the southern end, turn west off the highway 5km north of Bicheno and follow the signposted road for 7km to the car park. A basic camping ground with a pit toilet is provided and you can throw yourself into the **Apsley Waterhole** for refreshment. To access the northern end, at **Thompsons Marches**, turn west off the highway 24km north of Bicheno onto the rough 'E' Rd. This is a private road, so obey any signs as you follow it to the car park and boom gate at the park border. You won't find suitable places to camp near the car park. National park entry fees apply. Open fires are not permitted here from October to April, when cooking is only allowed on fuel stoves.

Bushwalking

At the Apsley Waterhole is a five-minute, wheelchair-standard track leading to a lookout with a great view over the river. A two- to three-hour return walk leads to **Apsley Gorge**.

At the park's northern end is the walk to **Heritage Falls**, which takes five to six hours return. There's good camping near the falls.

The major walk in the park is along the **Leeaberra Track**, which takes three days. The walk should be done from north to south to prevent the spread of a plant disease present in the south.

IRONHOUSE POINT

The road following the coast from Chain of Lagoons to Falmouth, then Scamander, passes through some excellent coastal scenery and avoids the slow climb over two passes to St Marys. Much of the coastline is rocky and the best place to stop along it is at Ironhouse Point and **Four Mile Creek**, where the beaches begin. Ironhouse Point is named after the first house in the region to have an iron roof.

White Sands Resort (*☎ 6372 2228;* w *www.white-sands.com.au; 21554 Tasman Hwy; doubles from $75*), formerly Cray Drop-In Holiday Village, has numerous well-outfitted, porch-fronted cabins sprawled around tennis courts, a pool and a nine-hole golf course. It also has a **bar/café** (*meals $4-14.50; opening times vary seasonally*).

SCAMANDER & BEAUMARIS
☎ 03 • postcode 7215 • pop 435

The low-key townships of Scamander and Beaumaris stretch languidly along white-sand beaches in a coastal reserve. You can take long walks along the beach, fish for bream from the old bridge over the Scamander River, or try catching trout farther upstream.

Their wide ocean beaches are great for swimming, while water-skiers head for the lagoons north of Beaumaris. There are good surfing spots as far south as Four Mile Creek; local surfers congregate just north of here.

For a fine view of the area, a 5km drive along gravel forestry roads takes you to the start of a steep five-minute walk to **Skyline Tier Scenic Lookout**; follow Campbell St from beside the BP service station in Scamander.

Eureka Farm *(☎ 6372 5500; 89 Upper Scamander Rd; open 8am-6pm daily Nov-May, café open 10am-5pm)* is a fruit-lover's paradise, and we're not just saying that because they fed us some exquisite summer pudding and a ladle of strawberry moonshine. They take their apricots, plums, peaches, figs and assorted berries and turn them into jams and authentic, tongue-smacking fruit ice cream. Sample these efforts and an array of light lunches in the café.

Places to Stay & Eat
Kookaburra Caravan Park *(☎/fax 6372 5121; unpowered/powered site doubles $12/13.50, on-site van doubles $35, cabin doubles $50)*, close to the beach, has nice hillside sites and helpful managers.

Carmens Inn *(☎/fax 6372 5160; 4 Pringle St; doubles from $65)* has good-value, self-contained units only a short roll to the sand.

Blue Seas *(☎ 6372 5211; e blue.seas@ tassie.net.au; units $85-190)*, up on the hill on the northern side of the river, has pleasant self-contained units of varying sizes and an indoor pool if you get sick of the sun and salt. Fishing tackle is available for guests.

Pelican Sands *(☎ 6372 5231; w www.peli cansandsscamander.com.au; singles/doubles from $75/85)*, immediately north of the bridge in Scamander, presents a low-profile exterior but lies right on the beach and has attentive owners. Besides one- and two-bedroom units, they also have cheap bunks in eight-bed dorms ($19) and take breakfast orders.

The well-managed **Surfside Motor Inn** *(☎ 6372 5177, fax 6372 5322; Tasman Hwy; singles/doubles $65/80)*, on the northern outskirts of Beaumaris, offers decent rooms with cooked breakfast. The **bistro** *(mains $12-19; open daily)* has ultra-fresh seafood

and dabbles in the odd Thai curry. Their 'boardroom' is a decent place for a drink.

Scamander Beach Resort Hotel *(☎ 6372 5255; doubles $50-75)* does little for the look of the foreshore, but the facilities (including a playground) are first-rate and the views pretty good from the topmost storey. Bistro meals are available.

Bensons *(☎ 6372 5587; w www.bensonsb -andb.com.au; 8 Freshwater St, Beaumaris; B&B doubles from $145)* is a stylish and very hospitable getaway, offering full cooked breakfasts and en suites that are the antithesis of dinky. Set three-course gourmet dinners (from $44 per person) can be arranged and Bensons is licensed to serve tipple to guests.

Green Peacock *(☎ 6372 5148; 62 Riverview Rd; mains $17-27; open from 6pm Mon-Sat)* is a BYO restaurant signposted off the highway, a great place to enjoy a variety of fresh, local produce.

ST MARYS
☎ 03 • postcode 7215 • pop 590
St Marys is a serene little town near the Mt Nicholas range, 10km inland of the Tasman Sea. A visit here entails peaceful countryside wanderings that take in waterfalls, state forest and hilly heights.

The rocky hills around town have good views and are worth climbing. The top of **South Sister**, towering over German Town Rd 6km north of town, is a 10-minute walk from the car park. Just east of town, turn south down Irish Town Rd to get to **St Patricks Head**, where you'll be confronted by a long, steep 90-minute climb (one way) complete with some cables and a ladder; the top has some of the best views around, 360° around that is.

Places to Stay & Eat
St Marys Seaview Farm *(☎ 6372 2341; w www.seaviewfarm.com.au; 686 German Town Rd; cottage bunks/singles/doubles $16.50/33/44)* is a working farm that doubles as a fine rural hostel. It's surrounded by state forest and crisp air, and commands blissful views of the coastline and mountains. You'll find it at the end of a dirt track 8km from St Marys – take Franks St

opposite St Marys Hotel, which becomes German Town Rd. Bring your own supplies.

St Marys Hotel (☎ *6372 2181; 48 Main Rd; singles/doubles $25/45*) has low-key, good-standard accommodation. Continental breakfast is provided and counter meals are also available.

Addlestone House (☎ *6372 2783;* [e] *addlestone@bigpond.com; 19 Gray Rd; doubles from $77*), on the road to Bicheno, has two charming en suite rooms, and nourishes guests with a full English breakfast.

Todd's Hall Café & Theatre (☎ *6372 2066; 1 Story St; dishes $5.50-15; café open 10am-5pm Mon-Sat*) is a lively, satisfying place for an all-day breakfast or good lunch fodder. Ask about upcoming events in the adjoining hall, which usually hosts film screenings each Wednesday night and a wide variety of live music and theatre.

Mt Elephant Pancake Barn (☎ *6372 2263; Mt Elephant Pass; mains $14-18.50; open 8am-6pm Sat-Thur, 8am-8pm Fri*), south of town off the highway to Bicheno, serves tasty but expensive savoury and sweet pancakes in a high-mountain setting. Devotees really hype it up, but ultimately we're still just talking about pancakes.

Getting There & Away

Redline Coaches (☎ *6336 1446, 1300 360 000;* [w] *www.tasredline.com.au*) stops at the newsagent (Story St), and **TassieLink** (☎ *6272 7300, 1300 300 520;* [w] *www.tigerline.com .au*) coaches stop outside the Coach House Restaurant (34 Main St).

Redline's two-hour run from Launceston costs $19. The Redline service from Hobart requires a change of coach en route, meaning the trip can take anywhere from three to 6½ hours; the one-way fare is $35.50. TassieLink's Launceston to St Marys service costs $16.50.

Broadby's (☎ *6376 3488*) buses between St Helens and St Marys on weekdays. A bus departs the BP service station in St Helens between 7.30am and 7.45am, and returns from the post office in St Marys at 8.45am; the fare is $5 each way ($10 with a bicycle).

See the Getting There & Around section at the start of this chapter for more details.

Warning Cyclists riding Elephant Pass must be extremely careful. The road is steep, narrow and winding, and it's difficult for vehicles (particularly trucks) to negotiate their way around bicycles.

FINGAL

☎ 03 • postcode 7214 • pop 380

Landlocked Fingal is 21km west of St Marys. Its main attraction is the annual Fingal Valley Festival, held in early March, which includes World Roof Bolting and World Coal Shovelling Championships – for the record, the fastest time for shovelling half a ton of coal stands at 26.59 seconds.

The surrounding valley contains several abandoned mining-era towns – Mangana, Rossarden and Storys Creek display piles of tailings, mine machinery and deserted cottages. If you prefer something verdant, visit **Evercreech Forest Reserve**, to the north near Mathinna. A 20-minute circuit walk through blackwood and myrtle takes you to the White Knights, a grouping of the world's highest white gums (*Eucalyptus viminalis*); the tallest tree reaches 91.3m.

Fingal Hotel (☎ *6374 2121; 4 Talbot St; singles/doubles $33/45*) has small basic rooms and serves counter meals daily. While you're here, check out the attractive **St Peters Anglican church** (1867) next door.

Glenesk (☎*/fax 6374 2195;* [w] *www.fingal .tco.asn.au/glenesk; 9 Talbot St; B&B singles/ doubles $50/90*) is an old-fashioned cottage with lots of personal touches. It's behind the post office, which is where you should direct any inquiries.

Getting There & Away

TassieLink (☎ *6272 7300, 1300 300 520;* [w] *www.tigerline.com.au*) and **Redline Coaches** (☎ *6336 1446, 1300 360 000;* [w] *www.tasred line.com.au*) stop at the service station. The 1¾-hour trip from Launceston with Redline costs $16. The Redline service from Hobart requires a change of coach en route, meaning at worst the trip can take 6½ hours; the one-way fare is $32. TassieLink's Launceston to Fingal service costs $14. See the Getting There & Around section at the start of this chapter for more information.

The Northeast

Tasmania's northeast is a beautifully secluded, untrammelled part of the state. Most visitors have heard of the nearby wineries of Pipers Brook and Pipers River, the pretty seaside town of St Helens, the historic mining town of Derby and the big splash made by St Columba Falls, but may overlook remote Mt William National Park and the superb beaches of the Bay of Fires and the northern coast. The sparse landscape here is memorably different to what you'll find elsewhere in the state.

The area is bypassed by the main route from Launceston to the east coast but if you take the Tasman Hwy (A3) from Launceston to Scottsdale, you can head out in several directions from here: north to the holiday town of Bridport, with fine vineyards not far west (see the Around Launceston section of the Launceston & Around chapter later) and the Waterhouse Protected Area to the east; east to Derby, then northeast to Mt William National Park, Ansons Bay and the Bay of Fires; or southeast from Derby to the waterfalls around Ringarooma and Pyengana, with St Helens just beyond.

Getting There & Around

Bus The main bus company servicing Tasmania's northeast is **Redline Coaches** (☎ 6336 1446, 1300 360 000; Ⓦ www.tasredline.com.au), which runs from Launceston to Conara Junction, then through Fingal ($16, 1¾ hours) and St Marys ($19, two hours) to St Helens ($23.10, 2¾ hours). Redline also runs coaches from Launceston to Scottsdale ($11.10), Derby ($16) and then Winnaleah ($18), where you can catch the Broadby's (Suncoast) bus to St Helens (see the following section). Redline fares from Hobart are Fingal ($32), St Marys ($35.50) and St Helens ($38.20); the trip varies in duration due to the change of coaches en route.

Broadby's (☎ 6376 3488), also operating as Suncoast, runs between St Helens and

Highlights

- Camping on the serene Bay of Fires
- Taking in the region's remote arcs of white sand and turquoise water
- Falling for St Columba and Ralph
- Engaging in some rafting rivalry in the Derby River Derby
- Marvelling at the strange dazzle of Blue Lake

THE NORTH EAST

St Marys each weekday, departing the BP service station in St Helens between 7.30am and 7.45am, and leaving St Marys post office at 8.45am; the fare is $5 each way ($10 with a bicycle). Broadby's also runs a bus from St Helens to Derby, then on to Winnaleah, then direct to St Helens, which connects with Redline's northeast service at Winnaleah. This bus departs St Helens post office weekdays at 10.15am, leaves Derby at 12.15pm and leaves Winnaleah around 12.45pm; the fare is $7 one way to/from either Derby or Winnaleah.

TassieLink (☎ 6272 7300, 1300 300 520; Ⓦ www.tigerline.com.au) has a service from

Hobart to St Helens via the east coast on Friday and Sunday; the trip takes 4¾ hours and the fare is $35.20.

Stan's Coach Service (☎ 6356 1662 after 6.30pm) runs a service on weekdays between Scottsdale and Bridport ($3 one way), connecting with Redline's Launceston to Scottsdale service.

Bicycle The Tasman Hwy (A3) is a winding, narrow road that crosses two major passes as it heads west through the towns of Weldborough and Scottsdale – it demands vigilance from cyclists. An alterna-

tive is to follow the secondary roads around the coast, where there's little traffic and fewer hills to climb. Pack a tent to take advantage of the camping areas at both ends of Mt William National Park and at Tomahawk en route from St Helens to Bridport; there's also some accommodation at Gladstone.

Organised Tours If you're looking for someone to do the hard work for you, **Beach to Bush Adventures** (☎ 6372 5468, 0417 377 803; 137 Tasman Hwy, Beaumaris) offers catered 4WD and bushwalking tours of the

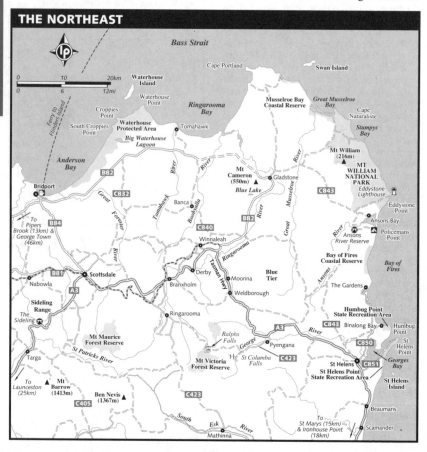

THE NORTHEAST

northeast. A full-day excursion costs from $165/33 per adult/child.

Pepper Bush Peaks 4WD Adventure Tours (☎ 6352 2263, 0419 570 887; 65 King St, Scottsdale) knowledgeably roams the topography of the northeast in comfortable 4WDs looking for natural splendour and local fauna, some of which (eg, kangaroo) is presented on a plate at mealtime. This is not roughing it – day tours cost in the vicinity of $260/130 per adult/child.

ST HELENS
☎ 03 • postcode 7216 • pop 1780

St Helens, on Georges Bay, was occupied in 1830 by sealers and whalers, but by the 1850s farmers had created a permanent settlement. In 1874 rich inland tin deposits were discovered and many arrived to try their mining luck; St Helens, with its sheltered bay, became the port for shipping the metal. Despite the eventual closure of the mines, St Helens continued to grow and today is the largest town on the east coast. It's also Tasmania's largest fishing port, with a big fleet afloat in the bay.

Information
St Helens' interesting past is recorded in the **History Room** (☎ 6376 1744; 61 Cecilia St; adult/child $2/1; open 9am-5pm Mon-Fri, 9am-noon Sat, 10am-2pm Sun Jan-Apr), which shares its space with the town's helpful **visitor information centre**.

The post office and banks are on Cecilia St; both Westpac and Commonwealth banks have ATMs. Eftpos facilities are available at the town's petrol stations and supermarkets.

Things to See & Do
Both sides of the wide entrance to Georges Bay are designated state recreation areas and provide some easy walking. A good track circles around **St Helens Point** (one hour return). On the north side, **Skeleton Bay** (10km north) and **Dora Point** (11km north) are good places from which to explore the coastline.

Ask at the information centre for details of the half-dozen walks (one wheelchair-accessible) and old tin mine sites on the nearby **Blue Tier** plateau.

While the town's beaches aren't particularly good for swimming, there are excellent scenic beaches at **Cosy Corner** (12km north), **Binalong Bay** (10km north) and **Stieglitz** (7km east on St Helens Point), as well as at **Humbug Point**. Out on St Helens Point are the spectacular **Peron Dunes** (7km east).

The flat, clear waters of Georges Bay are excellent for canoeing, windsurfing and diving. **East Lines** (☎ 6376 1720, 6376 8368; 28 Cecilia St) hires equipment and organises dive charters. They also hire bikes ($5/15/25 per one hour/four hours/day) and at the time of writing were hoping to establish backpacker accommodation at Binalong Bay (124 Binalong Bay Rd).

Boats can be chartered from **Professional Charters** (☎ 6376 3083), which provides gear for reef, game, deep-sea and bay fishing. Prices vary considerably according to group numbers and the type of fishing.

For overnight fishing, try the 53-foot cruiser **Norseman III** (☎ 6424 6900). It takes a maximum of six passengers (12 for day trips) and can be hired from $1100 per day; BYO food.

Places to Stay – Budget
Camping, Cabins & Hostels There are free **camping** sites north of St Helens at Humbug Point and south at Diana's Beach (8.5km south).

St Helens Caravan Park (☎ 6376 1290, fax 6376 1514; Penelope St; unpowered/powered site doubles $17/22, on-site van doubles from $40, cabin doubles $68-80) has a pleasant bushland setting to the south of town. The playground and games room may help occupy the kids.

Hillcrest Caravan Park (☎ 6376 3298, fax 6376 3055; Chimney Heights; unpowered/powered sites $12/15, cabin doubles $60-71) is 7km along the side road to St Helens Point, near some very swimmable beaches. The park has good facilities, including a small shop.

St Helens Youth Hostel (☎ 6376 1661; 5 Cameron St; YHA members/nonmembers $16/19.50, doubles $36) lacks character but has a peaceful location near the water and is close to a supermarket.

THE NORTHEAST

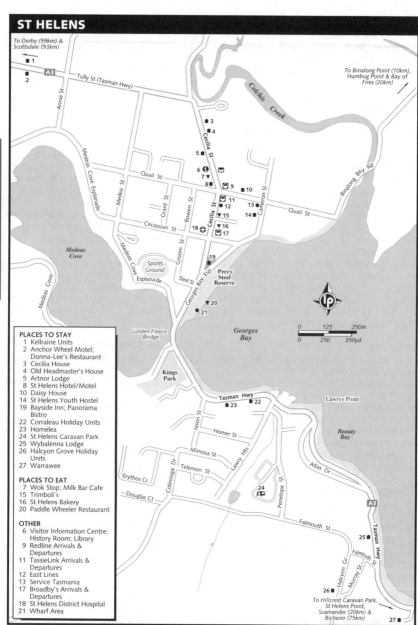

ST HELENS

To Derby (59km) &
Scottsdale (93km)

■ 1

■ 2

A3

Tully St (Tasman Hwy)

Annie St

To Binalong Point (10km),
Humbug Point & Bay of
Fires (20km)

Colchis Creek

Cecilia St

■ 3

□ 4

5 ■

Quail St

Medeas Cove Esplanade

Medea St

6 ℹ
7 ▼
8 ■

✉

□ 9

■ 10

Cameron St

Grant St

Bowen St

Cecilia St

□ 11
● 12
▼ 15
□ 16
□ 17

13 ●
14 ■

Quail St

Binalong Bay Rd

Circassian St

18 ✚

Groom St

Medeas
Cove

Sports
Ground

Medeas Cove

Medeas
Cove

Esplanade

Steel St

19 ◉

Georges Bay Esp

Percy
Steel
Reserve

▼ 20
● 21

Golden Fleece
Bridge

Georges
Bay

0   125   250m
0   250   250yd

Kings
Park

Tasman Hwy

Jason St

■ 23

● 22

Homer St

Lawrys Point

Beauty
Bay

Mimosa St

Lawry Hts

Cobrooga Dr

Telemon St

Atlas Dr

Erythos Cr

24
⚑

Penelope St

Douglas Ct

Falmouth St

A3

Falmouth St

25 ■

Halcyon Gr

Murray St

Falmouth St

Tasman Hwy

26 ■

To Hillcrest Caravan Park,
St Helens Point,
Scamander (20km) &
Bicheno (75km)

27 ■

PLACES TO STAY
1 Kellraine Units
2 Anchor Wheel Motel;
   Donna-Lee's Restaurant
3 Cecilia House
4 Old Headmaster's House
5 Artnor Lodge
8 St Helens Hotel/Motel
10 Daisy House
14 St Helens Youth Hostel
19 Bayside Inn; Panorama
   Bistro
22 Corraleau Holiday Units
23 Homelea
24 St Helens Caravan Park
25 Wybalenna Lodge
26 Halcyon Grove Holiday
   Units
27 Warrawee

PLACES TO EAT
7 Wok Stop; Milk Bar Cafe
15 Trimboli's
16 St Helens Bakery
20 Paddle Wheeler Restaurant

OTHER
6 Visitor Information Centre;
   History Room; Library
9 Redline Arrivals &
   Departures
11 TassieLink Arrivals &
   Departures
12 East Lines
13 Service Tasmania
17 Broadby's Arrivals &
   Departures
18 St Helens District Hospital
21 Wharf Area

Motels The Anchor Wheel Motel (☎ 6376 1358; e anchorwheel@vision.net.au; 59 Tully St; singles/doubles $45/55), beside the highway on the western side of town, has a raft of clean budget rooms.

St Helens Hotel/Motel (☎ 6376 1133; 49 Cecilia St; singles $40-50, doubles $45-55) is cheerfully down-to-earth. The rooms are small and have humble aesthetics, but the cheap prices are attractive. The **restaurant** (mains $10-17) has daily counter meals.

Self-Contained Units Bordering the highway to the west of the town centre is **Kellraine Units** (☎/fax 6376 1169; 72 Tully St; doubles from $40), a mini-suburb of one- to three-bedroom self-contained units, one with wheelchair access. It's a ways from the water, but inexpensive.

Daisy House (☎ 6376 1371; Quail St; doubles $50-60), behind the Kodak shop, has two self-contained cottages with plain facades but big, comfortable interiors.

Corraleau Holiday Units (☎/fax 6376 1363; 22 Tasman Hwy; doubles $44-60) has older-style conjoined units with a mixture of open fireplaces, wood and electric heaters. The adjacent small park has a couple of playground swings.

Places to Stay – Mid-Range
Guesthouses & B&Bs The guesthouse **Artnor Lodge** (☎/fax 6376 1234; 71 Cecilia St; doubles with/without en suite $70/55) is a fastidious place on the main street, with an excess of peace and quiet.

Cecilia House (☎ 6376 1723, fax 6376 2355; 78 Cecilia St; singles/doubles $83/108) is a Federation-style house with a pair of simple, homely en suite rooms. Prices include a home-made breakfast.

Old Headmaster's House (☎/fax 6376 1125; 74 Cecilia St; rooms $85-100) is a quaint B&B cottage set back from the main street, and without a blackboard in sight.

Motels Opposite the wharf, **Bayside Inn** (☎ 6376 1466; e bayside_inn@vision.net.au; 2 Cecilia St; rooms $60-102) is a slightly creaky motel with a heated pool, where rooms are priced from budget to 'ocean-view'. Early-to-bed folk won't like the muted sounds of live bands on Friday night.

Self-Contained Units The hillside **Halcyon Grove Holiday Units** (☎/fax 6376 1424; 16 Halcyon Grove; doubles $60-80) has a double-storey, motel-style frontage and rooms looking out to the distant water.

Homelea (☎ 6376 1601; e jlefevre@ vision.net.au; 16-18 Tasman Hwy; doubles $105), on a hillside south of the town centre, currently has one very comfortable, self-contained spa cottage in a corner of its yard; a second cottage was on the drawing board when we visited.

Places to Stay – Top End
Wybalenna Lodge (☎ 6376 1611; e wyba lenna@a1.com.au; 56 Tasman Hwy; singles/ doubles from $130/160) is an Edwardian guesthouse with luxurious rooms, a couple of cottages and fantastic bay views; it's very English, down to the surrounding garden. Sumptuous in-house dinners featuring dishes like orange duck and chilli prawns can be arranged with reasonable notice. It also serves oysters and crayfish to the public between noon and 2pm daily.

Warrawee (☎ 6376 1987; w www.vision .net.au/~warrawee; Kirwans Beach; doubles $98-198) is a colonial homestead retreat in the south of town, with restful acreage looking down on the nearby water and a choice of cooked or continental breakfast. All the rooms are nice, but try for one opening onto the veranda.

Places To Eat
St Helens Bakery (☎ 6376 1260; 8 Cecilia St; open 7am-5pm daily; breakfast $7) has a breakfast menu with straightforward options like eggs or baked beans on toast, plus sweets and lots of tasty pies.

Milk Bar Cafe (☎ 6376 2700; 57b Cecilia St; meals $5.50-10; open 9am-5pm Mon-Fri, 10am-3pm Sat & Sun) is a vivacious place in a courtyard opposite the post office, serving stomach-fillers like eggs Benedict and heaps of fresh vegetarian meals.

Wok Stop (☎ 6376 2665; 57a Cecilia St; mains $6.50-11.50; open 11.30am-9pm daily

Nov-Apr, reduced hours May-Oct), across the courtyard from Milk Bar Cafe, has its own fair share of foodie exuberance and outdoor tables. Try a tomato or spinach dhal, or one of the other delicious curries.

Trimboli's *(☎ 6376 1429; 1 Pendrigh Place; mains $8.50-17; open 7.30am-10pm Mon-Thur, 7.30am-11pm Fri, 6am-11pm Sat, 6am-9.30pm Sun)* has an all-day breakfast and a huge range of pizzas (around 25 varieties) and pastas. The marine-minded should try the seafood pizza, topped with garlic scallops, pan-fried squid and honey prawns.

Paddle Wheeler Restaurant *(☎ 6376 1208; Marine Parade; mains $15-19; open from 6pm Tues-Sun),* onboard the wharf-moored *Lady Annie Elizabeth,* plates up fresh seafood nightly. They do a good seafood platter for two ($39); credit cards are not accepted.

Panorama Bistro *(☎ 6376 1466; 2 Cecilia St; mains $14-22.50; open noon-2pm & 6pm-8pm Mon-Sat, noon-2pm Sun)* at the Bayside Inn serves good lunches and dinners daily except Sunday night, like grilled, pesto-lathered fish in pastry (Bermuda triangle) and pork stuffed with apple and pine nuts.

Donna-Lee's Restaurant *(☎ 6376 1358; 59 Tully St; mains $12-19.50; open 6.30pm-8.30pm Mon-Sat),* at the Anchor Wheel Motel, has a huge seafood, chook and steak menu. Thursday is Mexican night, with $10 all-you-can-gulp chilli.

Getting There & Away

See the Getting There & Around section at the start of this chapter for details of Redline, TassieLink and Broadby's bus services. Redline buses stop outside the newsagency on Cecilia St, while TassieLink buses stop on Quail St, opposite the newsagency. Broadby's depart from the BP service station or from the post office, depending on the route.

BAY OF FIRES
☎ 03

A minor road heads northeast from St Helens to meet the coast at the start of the Bay of Fires, and then continues up to The Gardens. The bay's northern end is reached

via C843, the road to the settlement of Ansons Bay and Mt William National Park.

This captivating bay, also a coastal reserve, is a series of sweeping beaches, rocky headlands, heathlands and lagoons. The ocean beaches provide some good surfing but aren't safe for swimming due to the numerous offshore rips – instead, plunge into the calmer waters of a lagoon.

South of Ansons Bay, the road crosses the **Ansons River Reserve**. Just before the floodway, on the left as you drive towards Ansons Bay, is a tiny, overgrown picnic area with a lovely outlook upriver. Ansons River is good for a relaxed paddle and you can launch a boat at the picnic area. There are no petrol stations or shops at Ansons Bay, so fill up at either St Helens or Gladstone.

Places to Stay

There are some deliriously beautiful free **camping** spots along the bay, which come *au natural* (without toilets or fresh water). Particularly recommended are the sheltered beachfront sites at **Policemans Point**, reached by a turn-off before Ansons Bay.

Bay of Fires Character Cottages *(☎ 6376 8262, fax 6376 8261; Binalong Bay; doubles $110)* is a welcoming enclave of modern one- to three-bedroom cottages. The breezy hilltop vistas should be enjoyed from the veranda while clutching a glass of something appropriately refreshing. Plentiful breakfasts are available at extra cost.

PYENGANA & ST COLUMBA FALLS
☎ 03 • postcode 7216

The settlement of Pyengana sits reclusively up in the hills, its name derived from an Aboriginal word describing the meeting of two rivers in the valley in which it's situated.

A century ago, European pioneers recognised that this beautiful green spot was ideal dairy country. Exporting milk from the isolated valley was impractical, but when converted into cheese and butter the produce was able to survive the slow journey to the markets. Today, cheddar cheese is still produced using the old methods at the **Pyengana Cheese Factory** *(☎ 6373 6157;*

Fire Walking

Stretching south of Mt William National Park is the Bay of Fires, a long sweep of white sand named by early European explorers after the Aboriginal fires they spotted along the coastline. Middens (piles of discarded mollusc shells) are mute evidence of those age-old feasts.

From October to early June, **Cradle Huts** (☎ 6331 2006; W www.bayoffires.com.au; 22 Brisbane St, Launceston) conducts a four-day, three-night Bay of Fires experience, where a maximum of 10 people embark on an extremely well-catered journey of natural discovery, at a cost of $1365 per person.

Perched on a ridgetop high above the bay's blue waters is the stunning Bay of Fires Lodge. Architecturally it's good enough to grace the title page of Australian Architecture Now, a weighty coffee-table book featuring some of the 1990s' most noteworthy Australian buildings. But the resort is far more than simply a beautiful design. It's also built according to the very best ecological principles, right down to composting toilets, and showers for which water has to be hand-pumped up to a holding tank.

To ensure prospective guests really appreciate the environmentally sensitive luxury, the superb views and the fine food and wine, they have to pass a test before reaching the check-in desk: they have to walk for two days.

After a bus trip down from Launceston, the first day sees a 12km walk to a permanent camp hidden in dunes behind the beach. The second day's exertions alternate between beachside and inland walks, and include fording Deep Creek, a lunch break near Eddystone lighthouse, and, finally, crossing a series of headlands and dramatic little coves before climbing up to the lodge.

The next morning, guests can do a spot of kayaking on Ansons River or simply laze around enjoying the views and working up an appetite for dinner. The final day comprises a short walk out to a waiting minibus, which whisks you back to Launceston, stopping at Ninth Island winery on the way.

Tony Wheeler

St Columba Falls Rd; open 9am-6pm daily Sept-May, 10am-4pm daily Jun-Aug), open daily for tastings and sales. Besides mature clothbound cheese, you can purchase seven different flavoured cheddars (eg, chilli, peppercorn, caraway), as well as milkshakes and ice creams.

The nearby **Pub in the Paddock** (☎ 6373 6121; singles/doubles $35/45) has been plying its trade as a hotel for well over a century and has good rooms with clean, shared facilities; continental breakfast costs an extra $5.50 per person. The counter meals here ($10 to $19; lunch and dinner daily except Sunday night) are on the larger side of big.

The best-known feature of the valley is St Columba Falls, 6km past the pub and 24km from St Helens. At around 90m high, they are among the state's highest falls. Although you can see them from the road, you get a much more impressive view from the platform at their base, an easy 10-minute walk from the car park. The rivers in the valley also provide good trout fishing.

MT VICTORIA FOREST RESERVE & RALPHS FALLS

It's possible to drive a scenic, rugged loop from St Columba Falls into the wild Mt Victoria Forest Reserve and visit magnificent Ralphs Falls before continuing north to **Ringarooma**, thanks to the dedicated efforts of members of this small community. Construction of the road began during the Depression but wasn't finished until 1998, after years of laborious vegetation clearing and earth moving by locals. Major sections of this very rough gravel byway were slated for extensive grading at the time of research, which will save visitors a jittery ride on a stony, shallow-rutted one-lane road. Ralphs Falls, a 20-minute return walk from the car park, is a spectacular sight, a thin pipe of water snaking its way down tall curving cliffs. From the same car park there's also a 45-minute return walk via scenic Cash's Gorge. For more information on the road and the surrounding forest, drop into the 'White House' in Ringarooma and have a long conversation with local historians Norm and Sonia.

WELDBOROUGH

☎ 03 • postcode 7264

As the Tasman Hwy approaches the **Weldborough Pass**, an arabesque cutting famously popular with motorcyclists, it follows a high ridge with spectacular glimpses of surrounding mountains. As you ascend to the north, stop at the **Weldborough Pass Rainforest Walk** for a 15-minute interpretive-signed circuit through attractive myrtle rainforest.

Weldborough boomed last century when tin was discovered nearby, but today its inhabitants are few in number. At one stage the town had 800 Chinese inhabitants, mostly miners, who brought many examples of their own culture, including an ornate joss house now on display in Launceston's Queen Victoria Museum & Art Gallery. Other mining towns in the area also had a Chinese contingent – at **Moorina** to the north is a cemetery (off Amos Rd) with a memorial dedicated to the Chinese who lived and worked there.

Weldborough Hotel (☎ 6354 2223, fax 6354 1011; Tasman Hwy; unpowered/ powered sites $6/8, rooms $20) has camp sites in the small, sheltered grounds behind it and a handful of budget rooms inside. The hotel serves up good grub (mains $9 to $15.50) daily for lunch and dinner (except Sunday night), including plenty of hearty steaks and generic pub seafood, plus a kids' menu.

GLADSTONE

☎ 03 • postcode 7264

About 25km north of Weldborough, off the Tasman Hwy between St Helens and Scottsdale, is the tiny town of Gladstone. It was one of the last tin-mining centres in northeastern Tasmania, up until the mine closed in 1982 and forced the inhabitants to look for new ways to eke out a living. The surrounding area also held a number of mining communities and a large Chinese population, though today many are just ghost towns.

Gladstone Hotel (☎ 6357 2143; singles/ doubles $30/45) provides accommodation with shared facilities; prices include cooked breakfast.

On the road between the Tasman Hwy and Gladstone is the unnaturally hued **Blue Lake**, the copper sulphate–saturated legacy of an old tin mine. While you're there, look for **Cube Rock**, perched incongruously on the ridge of **South Mt Cameron**, which you can observe close up by taking the two-hour return walk to the mountain's summit; the trail starts just north of the lake.

MT WILLIAM NATIONAL PARK

This marvellous park consists of long sandy beaches, low ridges and coastal heathlands. The highest point, Mt William, is only 216m high yet allows some fine views. The area was declared a national park in 1973 primarily to protect the endangered Forester kangaroo – an animal that prefers open grassy areas, the very lands also preferred by farmers. Thankfully, the kangaroos have flourished here and can now be seen throughout the park.

It's best to visit during spring and early summer, when the heathland wildflowers are at their colourful best. Mt William provides good views of the Furneaux Group of islands, including Flinders Island. When sea levels were lower, these formed part of a land bridge to what we now call the mainland. This bridge was used by Aborigines to migrate to Tasmania. Aboriginal habitation of the area is exemplified by the very large midden at **Musselroe Point**.

The main activities in the national park include bird- and animal-watching, fishing, swimming, surfing at Picnic Rocks, and diving around Stumpys Bay and Cape Naturaliste. Horse riding is only allowed under permit, so first contact the **ranger** (☎ 0428 572 108), based in Bridport. Spotlighting is also permitted, but the ranger must be advised well in advance.

The easy climb to the rocky summit of **Mt William** takes around one hour return. The view extends from St Marys in the south to Flinders Island in the north. Farther south at Eddystone Point is the impressive **Eddystone lighthouse**, assembled by the Galloway brothers in 1889 using granite blocks; if you follow the fence line at the car park down to the beach, you'll find the quarry from which the granite was cut, plus huge stone remnants of the quarrying process. There's a small picnic spot here overlooking a beach of red-granite outcrops. A short drive away is the idyllic, free camping ground of **Deep Creek**, beside a lovely tannin-stained creek and yet another magnificent arc of white sand and aqua water.

Camping is allowed at four spots at Stumpys Bay, and also at Musselroe Top Camp and in the south at Deep Creek. You can also camp at several reserves to the north of the national park, namely Great Musselroe Bay, Little Musselroe Bay and Petal Point. Facilities are very basic, with only pit toilets, bore water for washing (at Stumpys Bay and Deep Creek) and fireplaces provided; there's no power and you'll need to bring your own water. Fires are allowed only in established fireplaces and it's advisable to bring your own wood (available from Gladstone) or, preferably, a portable stove. On days of total fire ban, only gas cookers are permitted. All rubbish needs to be taken back out as there's no refuse disposal here.

National park entry fees apply. If you're arriving via the northern access road, you can formalise your visit at the self-registration kiosk. If approaching from the south, you can buy a pass from the St Helens office of **Service Tasmania** (☎ 6376 2431; 23 Quail St; open 8.30am-4.30pm Mon-Fri).

Getting There & Around
You can enter the park, which is well off the main roads, from the north or the south. The northern end is 12km from Gladstone and the southern end is 50km from St Helens. From Bridport, take the road towards Tomahawk and continue on to Gladstone. Don't forget to get petrol at Gladstone or St Helens, as there's no petrol station at Ansons Bay. And try to avoid driving here at night, as that's when animals are most active.

DERBY
☎ 03 • postcode 7264
In 1874 tin was discovered in Derby (pronounced der-bee, not dar-bee) and the little

township flourished. Several mines soon operated in the area and these eventually amalgamated into one large mining company, which supported a town of 3000 people. Operations continued until 1929 when the local dam burst, flooding the town and drowning many residents. The mines closed for five years, reopened, then closed for good in 1940, causing an exodus. Derby has since leveraged its hard-working past in the form of a museum to attract the tourist dollar, but is struggling to reinvigorate itself.

Information
Derby's butcher leads a poorly disguised double life as the local tourist information provider. You can consult him on the area's attractions and browse the assorted displays in his shop during business hours weekdays.

Things to See & Do
Some of Derby's historic old mine buildings form part of the informative **Derby Tin Mine Centre** (☎ 6354 2262; Main St; adult/child $4.50/2; open 9am-5pm daily Sept-May, 10am-4pm daily Jun-Aug). The museum, which is in the old schoolhouse, displays old photographs and mining implements. Outside is a modest re-creation of an old mining shanty town, with shops and cottages, and a re-creation of a 1938 radio station.

Derby gets inundated by thousands of visitors in late October for its annual **Derby River Derby**. The derby sees around 500 competitors in all sorts of inflatable craft, including the distinctly home-made, racing down a 5km river course. The primary goal in this enthusiastically good-humoured contest is not so much to reach the finish line, however, but to sabotage your neighbours' vessels and be the last one floating. As a free-for-all spectacle, it's hard to beat.

At the nearby town of **Branxholm**, the Imperial Hotel (built 1909) has an impressive facade worth checking out; it's also a good place for a drink.

Places to Stay
Free **camping** (short term) is permitted at the riverside picnic area at the western end of town.

Merlinkei (☎ 6354 2152; e mervync@
vision.net.au; 524 Racecourse Rd, Winnaleah;
dorm beds/doubles $17/40) is an authenti-
cally rural YHA hostel on a commercial
dairy farm 10km from Derby. Besides letting you get up close and personal with
the property's 240 cows (overalls and gum
boots provided), it also has terrific views of
the Blue Tier plateau, decent bunks and
a pool table. To get here, drive 2km north of
Derby on the Tasman Hwy and take the
turn-off to the township of Winnaleah. Head
out of Winnaleah towards Banca, turn
right on Racecourse Rd and follow it for
about 5km; alternatively, ring from Winnaleah or Derby and the manager will pick
you up.

Cobbler's (Main St; singles/doubles $40/
80) is a self-contained cottage managed by
the nearby **Federal Hotel** (☎ 6354 2482). It
doesn't look like much from the outside and
parts of the floor slope a little, but
it's private, roomy, very comfortable and
meticulously cared for.

Winnaleah Hotel (☎ 6354 2331, fax 6354
1003; Main St; singles/doubles from $30/40)
is located in Winnaleah, north of Derby.
It has good budget accommodation and a
restaurant, **Jan's** (open lunch Sun & Mon,
lunch & dinner Tues-Sat), serving fresh
country-style lunches and dinners.

Places to Eat

Berries (☎ 6354 2520; 72 Main St; meals
$7.50-10.50; open 9am-5pm daily) exuber-
antly serves tasty muffins (berry flavoured,
of course), hearty ploughman's lunches and
Caesar salads, plus daily specials like
savoury meat loaf. There's a good selection
of teas and flavoured coffees too. Three-
course dinners ($35 per person) can be
arranged by booking before 3pm on the day
in question.

Crib Shed Tearooms (☎ 6354 2262; Main
St), in the tin mine centre, is a homely place
serving tasty soups, scones and cakes.

Getting There & Away

See the Getting There & Around section at
the start of this chapter for buses servicing
Derby. If you're driving, as you cross the

bridge into Derby from the north, check out
the mutant rockfish stranded on the cliffs
across the river.

SCOTTSDALE
☎ 03 • postcode 7260 • pop 1925
Scottsdale, the largest town in the northeast, was named after a surveyor called
Scott, who opened the area for European
settlement. The rich, fertile valleys were
conducive to farming and Scottsdale grew
into the region's business centre. Farming is
still important to the town.

In January and February, poppies provide
a blaze of colour and there are extensive
hop fields that are used in beer production.
In town, the frozen-vegetable factory produces mountains of frozen peas and french
fries. The Department of Defence keeps
its food laboratories here, manufacturing
rations for the armed services.

The area also has several huge pine
plantations. The trees are processed by two
large sawmills just outside town, which also
digest felled hardwoods.

Information

Opened with great fanfare in early 2002, the
Forest Eco-Centre (☎ 6352 6466; King St;
admission free; open 10am-5pm daily), run
by Forestry Tasmania, is shaped like part
of a giant shuttlecock and contains Scottsdale's **visitor information centre** (open
until 3pm). Ostensibly a public-relations
presentation by the state's timber industry,
and a rather insipid 'Animal Walk', the
centre is nonetheless interesting for the
energy-efficient design of its main building, which has a separate outer casing that
regulates the climate inside through a
system of sensor-equipped louvres and a
downdraught fan. At the time of research,
a small licensed café was planned to be
built at the centre.

There's an ANZ bank and a Westpac
ATM in the town centre.

Things to See & Do

Near Nabowla, 21km west of Scottsdale,
is the turn-off to the **Bridestowe Estate
Lavender Farm** (☎ 6352 8182; 296 Gillespies

Rd; open 9am-5pm daily Nov-Apr, 10am-4pm Mon-Fri May, Sept & Oct, by appointment Jun-Aug), the largest lavender oil-producing farm in the southern hemisphere and the only source of perfumed lavender outside Europe. During the lavender's spectacular flowering season, from around mid-December to late January, admission is $4 per adult (children free), which covers a guided tour; at other times admission is free. The farm has a kiosk and toilets, and visitors can avail themselves of the barbecues in the picnic area.

The road from Scottsdale to Launceston crosses a pass called **The Sideling**. Outfitted with toilets, picnic tables, a shelter and outstanding views stretching as far as Flinders Island on a clear day, it makes a great respite from the winding road. For even better views, take the road on the other side of the pass to **Mt Barrow**; a walk of about one hour return provides panoramic views over a third of Tasmania.

Places to Stay & Eat

North-East Park (Tasman Hwy; unpowered/powered sites $7.50/10) squeezes camping spots between a small river-fronted wildlife sanctuary and the road to Derby. Fees are payable at the house opposite the entry to the park (knock between 6pm and 7pm only). At the time of research there was uncertainty over the camping ground's future, due to possible tourist development of the parkland.

Lords Hotel (☎ 6352 2391; cnr George & King Sts; singles/doubles $22/35) has plain, value-for-budget rooms with shared facilities. An extra $5 gets you continental breakfast in the upstairs eating area, which has expansive rural views. It also serves counter meals daily ($9 to $16).

Scottsdale Hotel/Motel (Kendall's; ☎ 6352 2510, fax 6352 3545; 18-24 George St; singles/doubles $43/54) is a distinctive custard-and-clay-coloured place with no-fuss motel rooms, that serves lunch and dinner daily (dinner only Saturday).

Anabel's of Scottsdale (☎ 6352 3277; 46 King St; singles/doubles $90/100) is an endearing National Trust–classified abode

with spacious modern rooms spilling out into a beautiful garden. It also handles bookings for **Belle Cottage** (☎ 6352 3277; 80 King St; doubles $130), two doors down from the Eco-Centre. Anabel's salubrious **restaurant** (mains $20; open noon-2pm & 6.30-8pm Wed-Fri, 6.30pm-8pm Tues & Sat) indulges you with quality Tassie wine and game; bookings are essential.

Beulah (☎ 6352 3723, fax 6352 3077; 9 King St; singles $90-110, doubles $110-150), around the corner from Lords Hotel, is an elegant cottage built in 1878, that offers three rooms, full cooked breakfast, a wandering garden and a congenial atmosphere, due in large part to the congenial hosts. Those who have recently endured physical activity might choose to recover in the room equipped with a private spa and sauna.

Kames Cottage (☎ 6352 2760; 461 Bridport Rd; singles/doubles from $75/85) is another B&B option, set on a small, garden-enhanced acreage 2.5km from town on the road to Bridport.

Getting There & Away

See the Getting There & Around section at the start of this chapter for information on getting to/from Scottsdale.

TOMAHAWK

☎ 03 • postcode 7262

The small holiday settlement of Tomahawk is out on an isolated bit of the north coast 40km from Bridport on a sealed road. For most of the year its beaches are largely devoid of humanity, so it's a good place to get away from your travelling peers. It has excellent fishing for keen anglers; particularly good is the trout fishing at **Blackman's Lagoon** in the Waterhouse Protected Area, 20km west of Tomahawk.

The sole place to stay is **Tomahawk Caravan & Tourist Park** (Wanyeke; ☎ 6355 2268; Main Rd; unpowered/powered site doubles $12/14, on-site van doubles $45, cabin doubles $50). At the park entry are petrol bowsers, a café and a small shop, although the selection of foodstuffs is limited. You'll also need your own linen.

BRIDPORT
☎ 03 • postcode 7262 • pop 1235

This well-entrenched holiday resort is on the shore of Anderson Bay. Just 85km from Launceston, it's popular with leisure-seeking Tasmanians and there are plenty of holiday houses lazing about town.

Bridport has safe **swimming beaches** and its sheltered waters are also ideal for **water skiing**. Sea, lake and river **fishing** are also popular here. The area is renowned for its **native orchids**, which flower from September to December, and for its spectacular, abundant **birdlife**.

Places to Stay & Eat
Bridport Caravan Park & Camping Ground (☎ 6356 1227; Bently St; unpowered/powered sites $10.50/14.50) is strung out along Bridport's sheltered beachfront. It fills up quickly during summer's tourist high tide.

Bridport Seaside Lodge (☎/fax 6356 1585; e seasidelodge@bigpond.com; 47 Main St; dorm beds/doubles from $16/42) is a relaxing YHA hostel-cum-beachhouse. The front porch offers tempting views of the nearby water.

Bridport Hotel (☎ 6356 1114; Main Rd; singles/doubles $23/45) has modest rooms with shared bathroom. Meals from breakfast through dinner (mains $11 to $19) are available in the huge auditorium-like dining area.

Bridairre B&B (☎ 6356 1438; 22 Frances St; singles $40-50, doubles $65-80) is a somewhat suburban place clinging to a hillside, with mostly en suite rooms with continental breakfast. It's friendly and the guest lounge has long views.

Bridport Bay Inn (☎ 6356 1238; 105 Main St; singles/doubles from $70/80) has motel-style rooms around the back and satisfying meals within. Don't expect an early night's sleep on Friday, when you'll likely hear the muffled sounds of visiting bands and their fans.

Indra (☎ 6356 1196; e indra@vision.net.au; 53 Westwood St; singles $60-70, doubles $65-80) has brick-corralled units with standard facilities, plus some green bits outside to flop on. It's at the western end of town, 1km from the main shops.

Platypus Park Country Retreat (☎ 6356 1873; w www.bridport.tco.asn.au/platypus; Ada St; singles $50-90, doubles $70-140), just out of town beside the Brid River, has conjoined units and a double-spa cottage situated on a peaceful expanse of land. The accommodation (choice of room-only or with breakfast) is enhanced by porch views and there are trout-stocked dams nearby.

Bridport Resort (☎ 6356 1789; w www.bridport-resort.com.au; 35 Main St; villas $135-195) has bred an architecturally cloned crop of roomy, well-equipped timber villas, sized from one to three bedrooms. Extras include a heated indoor pool and tennis courts.

Joseph's (☎ 6356 1789; mains $18-24; open from 6.30pm Tues-Sat), at Bridport Resort, is a licensed restaurant that cooks Creole-spiced quail and baby barramundi for discerning carnivores.

Getting There & Away
See the Getting There & Around section at the start of this chapter for details of the bus service running between Bridport and Scottsdale. Also see the Sea section of the Getting There & Away chapter for details of the ferry service from Bridport to Port Welshpool in Victoria, via Flinders Island.

Launceston & Around

Launceston

☎ 03 • postcode 7250 • pop 67,800

Officially founded in 1805, making it the third-oldest city in Australia and the second-oldest in Tasmania, Launceston now ranks as the commercial centre of northern Tasmania. It's a sheltered city, situated among steep hills 64km inland from Bass Strait, at the end of the deepwater channel of the Tamar River where the South Esk and North Esk Rivers merge.

The area's Tasmanian Aboriginal inhabitants were part of the North Midlands Tribe, who knew the Tamar River as 'Ponrabbel'. They sustained themselves primarily by hunting animals on the region's open plains, plains that ultimately attracted European sheep farmers. The Europeans fought the land's traditional owners to control the property, and Aboriginal women and children were also kidnapped by sealers and whalers.

The first Europeans to visit the Tamar River were Bass and Flinders in 1798, who were attempting to circumnavigate Van Diemen's Land to show that it wasn't joined to the rest of Australia. A large swell south of Point Hicks in Victoria had long encouraged the belief that Tasmania was an island. Demonstrating that this was true meant that thereafter the passage from Europe to Sydney, which previously had involved rounding the coast of southern Tasmania, was shorter and less hazardous.

Around the same time, the French were also exploring the coast. Out of fear that they would establish a colony, Colonel William Paterson set up camp near the mouth of the Tamar River in 1804, though unfortunately the choice of site proved to be a poor one.

Launceston was the third attempt at a permanent settlement on the Tamar River and was originally given the swollen title of Patersonia, after its founder. In 1907, the city was renamed in honour of Governor King,

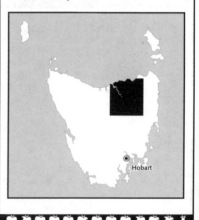

who was born in Launceston, England, a town settled a full millennium before, on the Tamar River in Cornwall county.

A notable event in Launceston's history occurred in 1835 when John Batman sailed from Launceston to Victoria and founded the town of Melbourne.

Though a wander around town on a weeknight will reveal few signs of life, Launceston has in recent years undergone plenty of social invigoration, with new eateries, leisure and tourist facilities trying to utilise the city's scattering of aged but unintimidating architecture and its refreshingly open, greenery-dotted layout.

ORIENTATION

The compact Launceston city centre is arranged in a grid pattern centred on The Mall, on Brisbane St, between Charles and St John Sts. The main shopping centre is based around this mall and the nearby Quadrant Mall, which is a semicircular side street. Two blocks north, on Cameron St, there's another pedestrian mall in the centre of a block called the Civic Square, around which many public buildings, such as the library, the town hall and the police station, are to be found. Two blocks to the east of Civic Square is the small Yorktown Square,

a charming not-really-square-shaped area of restored buildings that have been spruced up and converted into an array of shops and restaurants.

Launceston has plenty of attractive greenery and relaxing open spaces. Close to the city centre are the formal gardens of City Park, the wide sweeping lawns of Royal Park and the more intimate open spaces of Princes Square and Brickfields Reserve. To the west of the city centre is Cataract Gorge, a magnificent, naturally rugged ravine that is one of the city's major tourist drawcards.

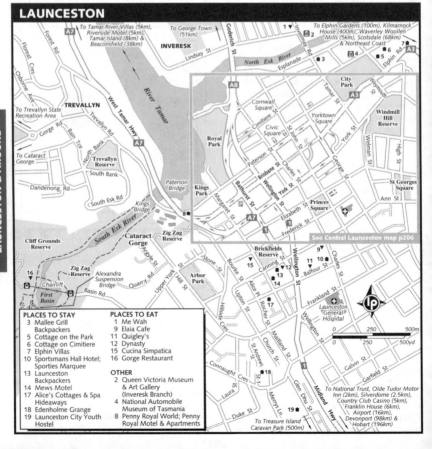

LAUNCESTON

PLACES TO STAY
3 Mallee Grill Backpackers
5 Cottage on the Park
6 Cottage on Cimitiere
7 Elphin Villas
10 Sportsmans Hall Hotel; Sporties Marquee
13 Launceston Backpackers
14 Mews Motel
17 Alice's Cottages & Spa Hideaways
18 Edenholme Grange
19 Launceston City Youth Hostel

PLACES TO EAT
1 Me Wah
9 Elaia Cafe
11 Quigley's
12 Dynasty
15 Cucina Simpatica
16 Gorge Restaurant

OTHER
2 Queen Victoria Museum & Art Gallery (Inveresk Branch)
4 National Automobile Museum of Tasmania
8 Penny Royal World; Penny Royal Motel & Apartments

INFORMATION

The **Gateway Tasmania Travel & Information Centre** (☎ 6336 3133, 1800 651 827; w www.gatewaytas.com.au; cnr St John & Paterson Sts; open 9am-5pm Mon-Fri, 9am-3pm Sat, 9am-noon Sun & public holidays) is helpful. Besides racks of pamphlets, the centre also handles state-wide accommodation, tour and transport bookings.

The **post office** (107 Brisbane St; open 9am-5.30pm Mon-Fri, 9.30am-1pm Sat) is near Quadrant Mall.

Banks are open for business from 9am or 9.30am to 4pm Monday to Thursday, and to 5pm on Friday. ATMs are installed at most banks in the city centre – the branches are mainly on St John St or Brisbane St near the mall.

The **Royal Automobile Club of Tasmania** (RACT; ☎ 6335 5633, 13 11 11 for roadside assistance; cnr George & York Sts) is affiliated with the automobile clubs of other Australian states and supplies road maps and motoring information.

Paddy Pallin (☎ 6331 4240; 110 George St) sells (and hires) camping gear, maps and travel accessories, as does **Allgoods** (☎ 6331 3644; cnr York & St John Sts). Bookish types have a number of shops to choose from, including **Angus & Robertson Bookworld** (☎ 6334 0811; 80-82 St John St) and **Birchall's** (☎ 6331 3011; The Mall).

If you're in a market mood, there are **craft markets** every weekend at Yorktown Square (open 9am-2pm Sun) and in the Exhibition Centre (or large shed) at Inveresk (open 10am-3pm Sun).

For speedy email and Internet access, try: **iCaf Internet Cafe** (☎ 6334 6815; e icaf@tassie.net.au; Quadrant Mall; open 9am-5.30pm Mon-Fri, 10am-2pm Sat), which charges $2 per 15 minutes; **Cyber King** (☎ 0417 393 540; e jwking@vision .net.au; 113 George St; open 9am-8pm Mon-Fri, 9am-6pm Sat, 10am-6pm Sun), which charges 17c per minute; or **Central City Computers** (☎ 6334 9226; e info@centcity .com.au; 173 Charles St; $2/4/6 per 10/30/60min; open 9am-6pm Mon-Fri, 9am-4pm Sat), which charges $2/4/6 per 10/30/60 minutes.

CATARACT GORGE

A mere 10-minute walk west of the city centre is the magnificent Cataract Gorge. Here, near-vertical cliffs crowd the banks of the South Esk River as it enters the Tamar. The area around the gorge is a wildlife reserve and one of Launceston's most popular tourist attractions.

Two walking tracks, one on either side of the gorge, lead from Kings Bridge up to First Basin, where you'll find a concrete **swimming pool** (admission free; open Nov-Mar), picnic grounds, an à la carte restaurant with sociable peacocks loitering outside, and trails leading up to the vista-packed Cataract and Eagle Eyrie **Lookouts**. The gorge walk takes about 30 minutes; the northern trail is the easier, while the southern Zig Zag Track has some steep climbs as it passes along the clifftops. The gorge is well worth visiting at night when it's lit up.

You don't have to walk to First Basin, however. To drive to the main car park, follow the signs from York St to Hillside Crescent, Brougham St, then Basin Rd.

A **chairlift** (adult/child $6.60/4.40; open 9am-4.30pm daily) crosses the waters of the First Basin; upstream, also spanning the water, is the swingin' **Alexandra Suspension Bridge**. A good walking track (45 minutes one way) leads farther up the gorge to Second Basin and the site of the first municipal hydroelectric power station in Australia (established 1895) at Duck Reach.

QUEEN VICTORIA MUSEUM & ART GALLERY

The Queen Victoria Museum & Art Gallery (☎ 6323 3777; w www.qvmag.tased.edu.au; adult/child $10/free; open 10am-5pm daily) has two branches, one at a site purpose-built for the museum in the late 19th century at Royal Park (Wellington St) and the other at the revamped Inveresk railyards. Both have cafés and wheelchair access – ask at reception for a mobility map. The one-off admission fee allows access to both sites.

The Royal Park branch includes exhibitions on the island's Aboriginal inhabitants and Tasmanian fauna, a splendid **joss house** donated by the descendants of Chinese settlers, and a **planetarium** *(adult/child $3.30/2.20)* with shows at 3pm daily Tuesday to Friday, and at 2pm and 3pm Saturday.

The Inveresk site houses an **art gallery** in the Stone Building (named after engineer Edward Stone), which has a significant collection of colonial and contemporary Tasmania-related sculpture and painting – one of the largest brushstrokes is Robert Dowling's culturally white-washed *Aborigines of Australia* (1859). Also at Inveresk are displays of aboriginal shell necklaces and Asian artworks, and railway history exhibitions including the 'Blacksmith Shop'.

The historic 1842 **Johnstone & Wilmot warehouse** *(☎ 6323 3726; 45 St John St; admission free; open 10am-4pm Tues & Wed)* houses the museum's community history branch and a genealogy service.

BOAG'S BREWERY

The ubiquitous Boag's beer has been brewed in a monolithic building on William St since 1881, though other beers were produced here 50 years prior. Contrary to Boag's expensive advertising, it's just beer, not a lifestyle, but it's definitely worth a taste test (or two). If you want to see the kilns, filters and kettles in action, take one of the 90-minute guided **tours** *(☎ 6331 9311; W www.boags.com.au; 21 Shields St)*. Tours depart at 9am, 11.45am and 2.30pm daily Monday to Thursday, and at 9am and 11.45am Friday. The cost is $12/8 adult/concession; no children under 10 years.

PENNY ROYAL WORLD

The Penny Royal complex *(☎ 6331 6699; 147 Paterson St; adult/child $16/6.50; open 9am-4.30pm daily)* is a historical re-creation that includes functional 19th-century wind and gunpowder mills, and a 'sloop-of-war' that bobs around a small lake. You can also take a ride on a barge or a restored city tram. A paddle steamer called the *Lady Stelfox* used to embark on 45-minute cruises part-way up Cataract Gorge, but at the time of writing its future was in doubt. Parts of the complex are interesting, but overall it's a bit tired and struggles to justify the full admission price – you can, however, just

pay to see single attractions (eg, gunpowder mill $12, corn mill/windmill $5).

TREVALLYN STATE RECREATION AREA

Farther upstream from Duck Reach is Trevallyn Dam, which constricts the flow of Lake Trevallyn. Here you can view a 90m-long elver ladder, constructed to help young eels negotiate the dam wall during their annual 3500km migration.

Beside the lake is a **reserve** *(open 8am-dusk daily)* comprising 4.5 sq km of natural forest and bushlands just waiting to be exploited for recreational use. There are picnic grounds and a motorcycle track, and archery, horse riding and bushwalking are the main activities catered for. Water-skiing is allowed on the lake, as is general boating, windsurfing and canoeing.

At the Trevallyn Dam quarry you can have a go at simulated **hang-gliding** *(☎ 0419 311 198; open 10am-5pm daily Dec-Apr, 10am-5pm Sat & Sun May-Nov)*, which involves swooping down a 200m-long cable – great fun until you hurtle over the lip of the quarry and your stomach tries to turn around and go back. Adults are $15, children $10 and tandem glides $20.

To get to the reserve, follow Paterson St west (after crossing Kings Bridge it becomes Trevallyn Rd and then Gorge Rd), then turn right into Bald Hill Rd, left into Veulalee Ave and veer left into Reatta Rd to the reserve. Access is restricted when the river is in flood, and camping is not allowed here.

HISTORIC BUILDINGS

Launceston's architectural heritage is less significant than that of Hobart and other towns in Tasmania. The older buildings that still stand, however, are more varied than those seen elsewhere because they date from several architectural periods. In response to the local availability of materials there has also been a greater use of brick.

In Civic Square is **Macquarie House**, built in 1830 as a warehouse but later used as a military barracks and office building, and the **Town Hall**, an imposing building built in 1864 in a Victorian Italianate style.

Opposite the Town Hall is the **old post office** (Cameron St) with its unique round clocktower.

One block away is the **Batman Fawkner Inn** (35 Cameron St), built in 1822 and known as the Cornwall Hotel until 20 years ago. It was on this site that John Batman and John Fawkner got together to plan what is now the city of Melbourne.

One corner of City Park contains **Albert Hall**, erected in 1891 for a trade fair. The hall features the unusual Brindley water organ and is now used as a convention centre.

The National Trust–classified **Old Umbrella Shop** (☎ 6331 9248; 60 George St; admission free; open 9am-5pm Mon-Fri, 9am-noon Sat) was built from Tasmanian blackwood in the 1860s and still displays old umbrellas, but most of the shelf space is now devoted to various National Trust and Tasmanian goods.

Many of Launceston's churches were constructed between 1830 and 1860. The wide range of religions and denominations represented reflect the influence of the 1837 Church Act, which, in addition to acknowledging the existence of all religions, exempted places of worship from many taxes. By 1860 there were 12 churches. On the Civic Square block are the **Pilgrim Uniting** and **St Andrews Presbyterian** churches, and opposite Princes Square is **St Johns Anglican Church**.

Six kilometres south of the city is **Franklin House** (☎ 6344 7824; 413 Hobart Rd; adult/concession $7.70/5.50; open 9am-5pm daily Sept-May, 9am-4pm daily June & Aug), one of Launceston's most attractive Georgian homes. Built in 1838, it has been beautifully restored and furnished by the National Trust. An outstanding feature of its interior is the woodwork, which has been carved from New South Wales red cedar. To get there by bus, take Metro bus No 21 or 25 from St John St near The Mall.

PARKS & GARDENS

Launceston is sometimes referred to as 'the garden city', and with so many beautiful public squares, parks and reserves, it's easy to understand why.

City Park is a relaxing Victorian garden that features an elegant fountain, a bandstand, a revamped monkey enclosure and a conservatory. It also has a tiny **radio museum** (☎ 6326 8640; admission by gold-coin donation; open 10am-3pm Tues & Thur, 10am-3pm Sat Dec-Feb), sharing the premises of Launceston's community radio station. **Princes Square**, between Charles and St John Sts, features a bronze fountain bought at the 1855 Paris Exhibition.

Other public parks and gardens include **Royal Park**, at the junction of the North Esk and Tamar Rivers; **Punchbowl Reserve** in the city's southeast, with its magnificent rhododendron garden; and **Windmill Hill Reserve**.

A 10-minute drive north of the city is **Tamar Island** (☎ 6327 3964; West Tamar Hwy; adult/child $2/1; open 9am-dusk daily), where you'll find a 2km wheelchair-friendly boardwalk through a significant wetlands reserve, teeming with birdlife.

OTHER ATTRACTIONS

On the edge of City Park is the **Design Centre of Tasmania** (☎ 6331 5506; cnr Brisbane & Tamar Sts; open 9am-5.30pm daily), a retail outlet displaying high-quality work by Tasmanian craftspeople. The **Wood Design Collection** (adult/child $2.20/1.10) was recently incorporated into the centre.

The oxymoronic **National Automobile Museum of Tasmania** (☎ 6334 8888; 86 Cimitiere St; adult/child $8.50/4.50; open 9am-5pm daily Sept-May, 10am-4pm daily June-Aug) will please motor enthusiasts, with a ground floor devoted to four-wheelers – from old Bentleys to a '69 Monaro – and a loft full of classic motorbikes, including a 1927 Harley Davidson.

The **Waverley Woollen Mills** (☎ 6339 1106; Waverley Rd; tours adult/child $4/2; open 9am-4pm daily, shop open 9am-5pm daily), 5km east of the city centre, were established in 1874 and are the oldest such mills still operating in Australia. The 20-minute guided tours, which depart on demand, used to take in the mill's hydro-electric station, built in 1889 and possibly the first hydro plant in the southern hemisphere, but now concentrate solely on the looms.

LAUNCESTON & AROUND

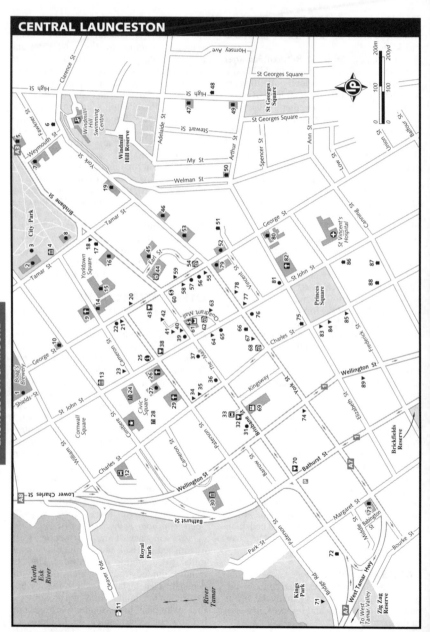

CENTRAL LAUNCESTON

LAUNCESTON & AROUND

CENTRAL LAUNCESTON

PLACES TO STAY
5 Sandor's on the Park
6 Waratah on York
7 Parklane Motel
10 Lloyds Hotel
14 Batman Fawkner Inn;
   La Porchetta
15 Launceston International
   Hotel
16 The Maldon
17 Metro Backpackers
19 Adina Place
45 Great Northern Hotel
46 York Mansions
47 Windmill Hill Tourist Lodge
48 Hatherley House
49 Ashton Gate
50 Highfield House
51 Fiona's B&B
53 Balmoral Motor Inn
66 New St James Hotel
72 Rose Lodge
73 Old Bakery Inn
75 Launceston Saloon
80 Colonial Motor Inn;
   Quill & Cane;
   Three Steps on George
86 Airlie
87 Canning Cottages
88 The Edwardian

PLACES TO EAT
18 Royal Oak Hotel
20 La Cantina
21 Vegiemania
23 Postreos Cafe-Restaurant;
   Old Post Office
34 Arpar's Thai Restaurant
35 Star Bar Cafe
40 Banjo's
41 Red Peppers Coffee Shop
42 Croplines Coffee
55 O'Keefe's Hotel
58 Konditorei Cafe Manfred
59 Pepperberry Cafe
63 Pasta Resistance Too
64 Cafi Centrö
67 Sushi Shack
71 Stillwater
74 Jailhouse Grill
77 The Metz
78 Fu Wah
83 Cafe Elm
84 Fresh
85 Fee & Me
89 Calabrisella Restaurant

OTHER
1 Boag's Brewery Tours
2 Albert Hall
3 Monkey Enclosure
4 Radio Museum
8 Design Centre of Tasmania;
   Wood Design Collection
9 Holy Trinity Anglican Church
11 Tamar River Cruises
12 Redline Coaches
13 Community History Museum
22 Old Umbrella Shop
24 Town Hall
25 Gateway Tasmania Travel &
   Information Centre
26 St Andrews Presbyterian
   Church
27 Library
28 Macquarie House
29 Pilgrim Uniting Church
30 Queen Victoria Museum & Art
   Gallery (Royal Park Branch)
31 Low Cost Auto Rent
32 Jacks Bus Service
33 Tamar Valley Coaches
36 Qantas
37 Birchall's
38 The Lounge Bar
39 Teague's
43 Royal on George
44 Princess Theatre
52 Aquarius Roman Baths
54 Cyber King
56 Europcar
57 Paddy Pallin
60 ANZ Bank ATM
61 Commonwealth Bank &
   ATM; Post Office
62 iCaf Internet Cafe
65 Angus & Robertson
   Bookworld
68 Central City Computers
69 Village Cinemas
70 Irish Murphy's
76 Allgoods
79 RACT
81 Thrifty
82 St Johns Anglican Church

LAUNCESTON & AROUND

SKYDIVING
For those who prefer freefall, **Tandemania** (☎ 0418 550 859; Hangar 14, Launceston airport) will strap you to an instructor and then throw you both out of a plane at 10,000 feet. The cost of this experience, which involves 15 minutes of flight time and around five minutes of plummeting, is $335 per person; those under 14 years of age or weighing over 95kg need not apply.

WALKING TOUR
One-hour guided strolls with **Launceston Historic Walks** (☎ 6331 3679; adult/concession/child $15/11/free) around the city centre's architecture begin at 9.45am daily from Monday to Friday; tours depart from the travel & information centre.

ORGANISED TOURS
The Coach Tram Tour Company (☎ 6336 3133, 0419 004 802) operates three tours, all of which depart from outside the travel & information centre: a three-hour tour of Launceston's key sights at 10am and 2pm daily January to April, and at 10am daily May to December, costing $26/18 per adult/child; a half-day excursion around the Tamar Valley at 1.30pm daily, costing $48/39 per adult/child (extra charge for visiting Seahorse World at Beauty Point); and an evening tour of the countryside around Launceston at 6pm Tuesday, Thursday and Saturday, costing $55/48 per adult/child (dinner included).

Tigerline (☎ 6272 6611, 1300 653 633; w www.tigerline.com.au) conducts a number of half/full-day tours year-round that include the following: Launceston's attractions (adult/child $39/23); Tamar Valley vineyards (adult/child $84/45); Tamar Valley attractions, such as Seahorse World (adult/child $69/42); and a jaunt through Sheffield to the exceptional short walks at Cradle Mountain (adult/child $89/55). Pick-up for the tours is from the travel & information centre.

Tamar River Cruises (☎ 6334 9900; w www.tamar-river-cruises.com.au; Home Point), based at Home Point in Royal Park, conducts river cruises of between 2½ and four hours' duration from September to May. The cost per adult ranges from $30 to $60, and per child from $15 to $30.

SPECIAL EVENTS

Three days in mid-February are feverishly devoted to Launceston's **Festivale** (adult/child $8/free), an eating, drinking, arts and entertainment indulgence that takes place in City Park. The event involves over 70 Tasmanian food and wine stalls, dancing, theatre and bands doing electric and acoustic gigs.

Also in February, horses race for the **Launceston Cup**, while over Easter the trotting track gets pounded during the **Easter Pacing Cup**. October sees the staging of the **Royal Launceston Show**.

PLACES TO STAY – BUDGET
Camping & Cabins

Treasure Island Caravan Park (☎ 6344 2600, fax 6344 1764; 94 Glen Dhu St; unpowered/powered site doubles $16/18, on-site van doubles $40, cabin doubles $65-72) is two kilometres south of the city, with all the requisite facilities. You'll have to like counting cars in your sleep, though, as it's beside the busy Midland Hwy.

Hostels

Launceston Backpackers (☎ 6334 2327; w www.launcestonbackpackers.com.au; 103 Canning St; dorm beds/doubles $15.50/18.50), behind its plain exterior, is a well-managed interior with plenty of dorm beds on offer. It also has off-street parking.

Mallee Grill Backpackers (☎ 6334 9288, fax 6334 6830; 1 Tamar St; dorm beds/singles/doubles $16/30/40), above the Mallee Grill eatery, has decent bunks but they're in small, dingy dorms, and the communal area needs sprucing up.

Launceston City Youth Hostel (☎/fax 6344 9779; 36 Thistle St; dorm beds/singles $15/20) is a private hostel 2km south of the city centre, set up in the former canteen of the nearby Coats Patons Woollen Mill. It's a friendly, helpful place with plenty of mountain bikes and camping/hiking equipment for hire.

Metro Backpackers (☎ 6334 4505; w www.backpackersmetro.com.au; 16 Brisbane St; dorm beds/doubles $23/55) is a newish YHA hostel that offers a bright upbeat interior, tours and good facilities that include Internet access and a rooftop outdoor terrace.

Hotels & Pubs

Sportsmans Hall Hotel (☎ 6331 3968; 252 Charles St; singles/doubles $35/45) is located in a relatively peaceful part of town, with tidy but no-frills rooms.

Lloyds Hotel (☎ 6331 4966, fax 6331 5589; 23 George St; singles/doubles $35/55) has centrally located budget accommodation that has the feel of an inviting old dormitory.

New St James Hotel (☎ 6334 7231; fax 6334 7631; 122 York St; singles/doubles $45/60) has Darth Vader rooms (they're on the dark side) but they're clean and cheap. Note that the hotel's nightclub fires up late on Friday and Saturday nights.

Batman Fawkner Inn (☎ 6331 7222, fax 6331 7158; 35 Cameron St; singles $40-70, doubles $80) has a historic, eye-catching facade that fronts a rabbit warren of plain, comfortable budget rooms. Brady's, the bar downstairs, attracts some vocal patrons on the weekend.

Irish Murphy's (☎ 6331 4440; 211 Brisbane St; dorm beds/doubles $16/35) has good cheap bunks, an appealing common room and a balcony to pose on. It also has a downstairs bar that becomes particularly lively when bands are on.

historically themed apartments in the Georgian, National Trust–classified **York Mansions** (☎ 6334 2933; W www.yorkmansions .com.au; 9 York St; apartments $190-225). Besides old-era luxury, rates include provisions for a full cooked breakfast.

Elphin Villas (☎ 6334 2233; W www .elphinvillas.com.au; 29a Elphin Rd; villas $130-185) has spacious two- and three-bedroom villas (some spa-equipped), or less-spacious motel rooms for the agoraphobic. They also run the nearby **Elphin Gardens** luxury apartments (47-49 Elphin Rd; apartments $190-230).

Cottages

A total of 11 prim and enthusiastically romanticised B&B cottages are managed by **Alice's Cottages & Spa Hideaways** (☎ 6334 2231; e alices.cottages@bigpond.com; 129 Balfour St; singles/doubles from $120/160), including 'Aphrodites' and 'The French Boudoir'. Most are located in the Balfour/Margaret St area.

Cottage on the Park (☎ 6334 2238; 29 Lawrence St; singles/doubles from $110/145) is a two-bedroom abode sleeping five people off City Park, as is **Cottage on Cimitiere** (☎ 6334 2238; 33 Cimitiere St; singles/doubles from $110/145). For both cottages, inquire at 27 Lawrence St; rates include breakfast.

PLACES TO EAT
Restaurants

Calabrisella Restaurant (☎ 6331 1958; 56 Wellington St; mains $14-20; open 5pm-late Wed-Mon) has been in business for two decades, probably due to the fact that it serves simply good Italian food for the whole family.

Jailhouse Grill (☎ 6331 0466; 32 Wellington St; mains $15-20; open from 6pm Sat-Thur, lunch & from 6pm Fri) dabbles in chook and seafood, but this is primarily a world of steak, where you choose your cut (eye fillet, scotch, rump or porterhouse), how well it's cooked, and the sauce. For the record, the building, which dates from the mid-1800s, was convict-made but was an inn, not a jail.

Konditorei Cafe Manfred (☎ 6334 2490; 106 George St; mains $10-16; open 8.30am-5pm daily) allows you to gorge yourself on really good baked goods (gourmet breads, tarts, tortes) and plenty of creative vegetarian dishes at either a downstairs table or upstairs on the weather-proofed terrace.

Pepperberry Cafe (☎ 6334 4589; 91 George St; lunch under $10, dinner mains $5-15; open 7.30am-5pm Mon-Wed, 7.30am-late Thur-Sat) is an enthusiastically run place encouraging healthy eating with delicious muffins, baguettes and Asian-influenced dishes. They'll happily cater to vegans and the coeliac-affected – just let them know.

Vegiemania (☎ 6331 2535; 64 George St; mains $10-19; open noon-2pm & from 5pm Mon-Fri, from 5pm Sat & Sun) is an excellent Asian culinary celebration for vegetarians and vegans; start with seaweed soup and eat your way through the menu to the highly satisfying 'Heavenly Four Delicious'.

Cucina Simpatica (☎ 6334 3177; 57 Frederick St; lunch $6-15, dinner $18-28; open 11am-late Tues-Sun, 11am-5pm Mon) has decor carefully designed to look like not a lot of care was taken. It's fairly expensive (most dish ingredients are accompanied by an adjective: wilted spinach, carmelised pumpkin, grass-fed eye fillet) but the food is excellent.

La Cantina (☎ 6331 7835; 61-63 George St; mains $10-20; open 11.30am-2pm & 6pm-late Mon-Sat, 6pm-late Sun) serves all the Italian standards, including the saucer-shaped ones baked in the associated pizza house next door; wash it all down with a glass of Frascati, Lambrusco or Chianti.

Arpar's Thai Restaurant (☎ 6331 2786; cnr Charles & Paterson Sts; mains $7-17; open from 6pm Sat-Thur, lunch & from 6pm Fri) is a well-patronised Thai eatery giving both meat-eaters and vegetarians plenty of tasty choices.

Fu Wah (☎ 6331 6368; 63-65 York St; open noon-2pm & 5pm-9pm Mon, noon-2pm & 5pm-10pm Tues-Thur, noon-2pm & 5pm-11pm Fri & Sat, 5pm-9pm Sun; mains $8-17), has been putting its enormous Chinese menu to the consumer taste-test for 15

LAUNCESTON & AROUND

years – you'll doubtless find something satisfying here.

Dynasty (☎ 6334 7000; 95 Canning St; mains $10-19; open noon-2.30pm & 5pm-late Mon-Sat, 5pm-late Sun) serves up competent Chinese cuisine amongst some elaborately stylised decor; try the Mongolian lamb.

Me Wah Restaurant (☎ 6331 1308; 39 Invermay Rd; mains $15-22; open 11.30am-2.30pm & from 5pm Tues-Sun, from 5pm Mon), opposite the Inveresk railyards, is a long-established Chinese restaurant with an impressive motif-festooned ceiling. Specialities like Peking duck and abalone are available for around $50.

Gorge Restaurant (☎ 6331 3330; Cliff Grounds Reserve; lunch $8-15, dinner $20-25; open noon-2.30pm & 6.30pm-late Tues-Sat, noon-3pm Sun) has its views a bit obscured by surrounding trees, but the setting is nonetheless undeniably grand. Feast on quail, duck breast and BBQ calamari.

Three Steps on George (☎ 6334 2084; 158 George St; mains $11-21; open 4pm-late daily) is next to (and part of) the Colonial Motor Inn. It dishes out all manner of meats, including a beefed-up burger for an equally beefed-up $14.

Quigley's (☎ 6331 6971; 96 Balfour St; mains $20-22; open lunch & from 7pm Tues-Fri, from 7pm Mon-Sat), set in a quaint 1860s terrace, makes a meal of game like Lenah wallaby and venison. If you want to impress, order the chateaubriand for two, which is silver-served direct to your plate.

Fee & Me (☎ 6331 3195; cnr Charles & Frederick Sts; 4-course dinner $60; open from 7pm Mon-Sat) does outstanding, innovative, upmarket cuisine that's received more than a few accolades over the years. Set in a charming old building, it remains one of Launceston's finer restaurants.

Stillwater (☎ 6331 4153; 2 Bridge Rd; dinner mains $20-30; open 9am-late daily) is a much-praised café/restaurant set in the stylishly renovated 1830s Ritchies flour mill beside the Tamar. The exceptional fare includes all manner of seafood and meat dishes, a separate vegetarian menu and a comprehensive wine list.

Cafés & Takeaways

Wake up your nerve endings with a consummate brew at **Croplines Coffee** (☎ 6331 4023; Brisbane Court; open 7.30am-5.30pm Mon-Fri, 7.30am-12.30pm Sat); pull out your sweet tooth before exploring 'confectionary corner'.

Red Peppers Coffee Shop (☎ 6334 9449; Centreway Arcade, 82 Brisbane St; lunch $5-10; open 8am-4.30pm Mon-Fri, 9am-2pm Sat) is a good-health place serving freshly made gourmet rolls, quiche and other light meals, plus coffee could-a-beens like soy-cino and caro-cino.

Cafí Centrö (☎ 6331 3605; 76 St John St; mains $8-19; open 8am-6pm Sat-Thur, 8am-late Fri) is a two-level, awkwardly arty café with good service and a big, varied menu – try the seafood-topped veal followed by some gluten-free lemon cake.

Elaia Cafe (☎ 6331 3307; 238-240 Charles St; mains $10-20; open 9am-9.30pm Mon-Sat, 9am-5pm Sun) is a breezy place with outdoor tables. Sample its gourmet salads, pidas, pastas and sweets, and something from the sizeable Australian wine list.

Postreos Cafe-Restaurant (☎ 6331 9962; 68 Cameron St; mains $7-19; open 8am-5pm Mon-Thur, 8am-5pm & dinner Fri) is a licensed eatery in the skylit interior of the old Launceston post office; it's a great spot for that morning omelette or afternoon Caesar salad.

Star Bar Cafe (☎ 6331 9659; 113 Charles St; mains $10-20; open 11am-late Mon-Sat, noon-late Sun) has the spacious feel of a large indoor patio, though unfortunately surrounded by Ken Done walls. The good food ranges from burgers so trendily large you can't bite into them, to curried lentil stew and wok-fried calamari.

Fresh (☎ 6331 4299; 178 Charles St; lunch $8-16; open 8.30am-5pm Mon-Sat), opposite the attractive Princes Square, is a retro-style vegetarian café with just-squeezed juices and tasty bruschettas, gado gado and a plug-your-stomach brekkie 'with the works'.

Cafe Elm (☎ 6333 0600; 168 Charles St; mains $8-22; open 8am-9pm Tues-Sat, 9am-5pm Sun-Mon), a few doors down from Fresh, is a licensed, rustic eatery with a handy all-day cooked breakfast, pan-fried pizzas and freshly shucked Bruny Island oysters.

The Metz (☎ *6331 7277; 119 St John St; mains $8-20; open 10am-midnight Mon-Wed, 10am-2am Thur-Sun)* is a cruisy café/bar which foregoes upmarket sterility for a comfortable, well-worn feel. The varied menu includes wood-fired pizzas and a vegetarian wrap with chickpea-battered eggplant, goat's cheese and basil tapenade.

Pasta Resistance Too (☎ *6334 3081; 23 Quadrant Mall; lunch $4.50-6; open 8.30am-6pm Mon-Fri, 9am-3pm Sat)* is a tiny place with wonderfully fresh pasta and sauces. You can bulk-buy pasta at $8/kg and sauces (bolognaise, marinara, mushroom) at $10/kg.

Sushi Shack (☎ *6331 4455; 134 York St; sushi $4.50-8; open 11am-late daily)* does mouth-watering flat and rolled sushi to eat in or run away with, plus Japanese mains like tempura and teppanyaki for around $17.

Banjo's (☎ *6334 2130; 98 Brisbane St; open 6am-7pm daily)* is an inevitably crowded bakery/café with fresh mounds of croissants, quiches and sticky-fingered Boston buns.

Pub Meals

Most hotels serve meals from noon to 2pm and from 6pm to 8pm daily.

Sporties Marquee (☎ *6331 3968; 252 Charles St; mains $10-19)*, in the Sportsmans Hall Hotel, does a good trade in non-typical pub fare like spiced venison medallions on couscous.

Other pub options include **O'Keefe's Hotel** (☎ *6331 4015; 124 George St; mains $11-21)*, where you can get good chargrilled steak done any way you like it; the cheap **Launceston Saloon** (☎ *6331 7355; 191 Charles St; mains $5-12)*; and the **Royal Oak Hotel** (☎ *6331 5346; 14 Brisbane St; mains $11-18)*, which does a popular sideline in Greek food.

La Porchetta (☎ *6331 7464; 35 Cameron St; mains $8-16; open from 11am daily)*, in what looks like an old auditorium at the back of the Batman Fawkner Inn, is part of an efficient pizza, pasta and parmigiana franchise that migrated to Launceston from Melbourne.

ENTERTAINMENT

Most of Launceston's entertainment options are advertised in the daily newspaper *The Examiner*.

Launceston Saloon (☎ *6331 7355; 191 Charles St; open noon-midnight Sun-Tues, noon-3am Wed-Sat)* has *Bonanza* decor that's a mixture of *The Good, The Bad and The Ugly*, but it does have serviceable pool tables, as well as a mixture of DJs and mainly cover bands Wednesday through Saturday nights. If a cover charge applies, it's usually in the order of $5.

Micky D's (☎ *6334 7231; 122 York St; hotel guests/nonguests free/$5; open 10pm-5am Fri & Sat)* is a nightclub in the New St James Hotel that juggles regular drag shows with techno.

Irish Murphy's (☎ *6331 4440; 211 Brisbane St; admission free; open noon-midnight Sun-Wed, noon-2am Thur-Sat)*, the popular local branch of a ubiquitous franchise, is stuffed full of Emerald Isle paraphernalia and has live bands Wednesday through Sunday.

Royal on George (☎ *6331 2526; 90 George St; open 7.30am-late daily)* is a great refurbished 1852 pub that packs out when live bands play on Friday and Saturday nights (sometimes Wednesday too), and when jazz hits the air on Sunday. It's also worth getting a sidewalk table and a plate of the Royal's excellent food.

The Lounge Bar (☎ *6334 6622; 63 St John St; admission after 9pm Fri & Sat $5; open 4pm-late Sun-Tues, 3pm-late Wed & Thur, noon-late Fri, 2pm-late Sat)* is one of the city's newest late-night venues. It's inside a cavernous, atmospheric 1907 ex-bank building and is fitted out with a veritable warehouse of old lounges, chairs and tables, plus hanging lampshades and lanterns. Watch the bands who play regularly upstairs or investigate the cool confines of the downstairs vodka bar, in the old bank vault. Light meals, cakes and coffee are also available.

Princess Theatre (☎ *6323 3666; 57 Brisbane St)*, built 1911 and including the smaller Earl Arts Centre, stages a mixture of significant local and interstate drama, dance and comedy.

Village Cinemas (☎ 6331 5066; 163 Brisbane St; adult/child $12/8.50) is for fans of the big-budget silver screen.

Country Club Casino (☎ 6335 5707; Country Club Ave, Prospect Vale; open noon-midnight Sun-Wed, noon-3am Thur-Sat), south of the city centre, is a large brassy hall with various games tables and rows of slot machines beckoning gamblers with one arm. After 7.30pm, you'll need to swap any shorts, T-shirts or runners for more formal wear, like 'smart dress jeans'.

Aquarius Roman Baths (☎ 6331 2255; 127-133 George St; open 8.30am-9pm Mon-Fri, 9am-6pm Sat & Sun) is the place to go for a more salubrious form of self-indulgence, with its luxurious, colonnaded warm baths and hot rooms ($20), massages ($38/55 per 30/60 minutes) and beauty clinic (treatments from $55). It caters to females and males over 16 years of age.

GETTING THERE & AWAY
Air
There are regular flights between Launceston and both Melbourne and Sydney, with connections onward to other Australian capital cities, plus a flight from Traralgon in Victoria via Flinders Island. For information see the Getting There & Away chapter. **Qantas** (☎ 6332 9911; 140a The Mall) is on the corner of Brisbane and Charles Sts.

For details of the daily flights from Launceston to Flinders Island, see the Getting Around chapter. Charter flights with the smaller airlines can also be arranged.

Bus
The main bus companies operating out of Launceston are **Redline Coaches** (☎ 6336 1446, 1300 360 000; Ⓦ www.tasredline .com.au; 16-18 Charles St), **TassieLink** (☎ 6272 7300, 1300 300 520; Ⓦ www.tiger line.com.au; departs Gateway Tasmania Travel & Information Centre) and **Tamar Valley Coaches** (☎ 6334 0828; 4 Cuisine Lane). At the time of writing a new depot for all intrastate buses was being built at Cornwall Square.

Redline runs several buses each day from Hobart to Launceston ($23.50 one way,

2½ hours), which usually connect with a service running along the north coast through Devonport ($16.50, one to 1½ hours) to Burnie ($22, two to 2½ hours). From Burnie, Redline runs northwest to Wynyard ($3.10, 20 minutes) and Stanley ($13, one hour). It also services Deloraine ($8.20, 45 minutes).

Redline also runs buses from Launceston to Conara Junction, then through St Marys ($19, two hours) to St Helens ($23.10, 2¾ hours) on the east coast. Another of its services runs northeast to Scottsdale ($11.10), Derby ($16) and Winnaleah ($18), from where **Broadby's** (Suncoast; ☎ 6376 3488) runs a connecting service to St Helens (see the Getting There & Around section at the start of The Northeast chapter).

On weekdays, Tamar Valley Coaches runs three to five buses a day up and down the West Tamar Valley; there are no services on weekends or public holidays. Destinations from Launceston include Legana ($3), Exeter ($4), Beaconsfield ($6.50) and Beauty Point ($7.20, one hour).

Redline runs three buses every weekday (no weekend services) along the eastern side of the Tamar River from Launceston to Dilston, Hillwood and George Town ($8.60, 45 minutes).

Jack's bus service runs from Launceston to Longford ($3.70, 30 minutes), departing Brisbane St (near the corner of Wellington St) at 8.45am, 10.45am, 3pm and 5.40pm from Monday to Friday.

TassieLink runs a daily express service between the Bass Strait ferry terminal in Devonport and Launceston ($16.50, 1¼ hours) – the morning service from Devonport to Launceston continues south to Hobart ($24, 2¾ hours). TassieLink also drives from Launceston to Sheffield ($19, 2½ hours), Gowrie Park ($22.20), Cradle Mountain ($43.60, 3½ hours), Rosebery ($39.50, five hours), Zeehan ($45.50, 5½ hours), Queenstown ($53, 6½ hours) and Strahan ($60, eight hours) year-round on Monday, Tuesday, Thursday and Saturday. On Friday and Sunday (plus Monday and Wednesday over summer), TassieLink also runs from Launceston east to Bicheno ($23, 2½ hours), via St Marys ($16.50).

Car

There are plenty of car-rental firms in Launceston. The bigger ones include **Europcar** (☎ 6331 8200, 1800 030 118; 112 George St) and **Thrifty** (☎ 6333 0911, 1800 030 730; 151 St John St), while smaller, cheaper operators include **Low Cost Auto Rent** (☎ 6334 3437, 1800 647 060; 174 Brisbane St). Prices range from $40 to $80 per day, depending on the time of year, length of rental and car model; see the Car section in the Getting Around chapter for more information.

GETTING AROUND
To/From the Airport

Launceston airport is 16km south of the city. **Tasmanian Shuttle Bus Services** (☎ 0500 512 009) runs a door-to-door airport service costing $10 per passenger. The shuttle runs between 8.30am and 5.30pm (except in summer, when it usually services flights up until around 8.30pm).

A taxi to the city costs about $25.

Bus

The local bus service is run by **Metro** (☎ 13 22 01); the main departure points are on the two blocks of St John St between Paterson and York Sts. For $3.40 you can buy an unlimited-travel Day Rover ticket that can be used after 9am Monday to Friday and all day Saturday, Sunday and public holidays. Most routes, however, do not operate in the evenings and Sunday services are limited.

Between mid-January and early April, the **City-Go-Round Bus** (☎ 6336 3133) does an hourly, 21-stop loop around Launceston's main attractions from 9.15am to 5.15pm. Tickets (adult/concession $6/3) are valid for 24 hours and can be purchased from the travel & information centre, Teague's tobacconist or from the driver. The service was trialled in 2002 and was expected to continue due to its popularity.

Bicycle

At the Launceston City Youth Hostel is **Rent-A-Cycle** (☎ 6344 9779), with a good range of bikes for hire (touring bikes $10/70 per day/week, mountain bikes $15/110 per

day/week). Hire prices include a helmet and panniers; the longer you hire, the cheaper it gets.

Metro Backpackers (☎ 6334 4505) has a handful of mountain bikes for hire. Half/full-day tours cost $10/15 and prices include helmets etc.

Around Launceston

The Tamar Valley funnels the river of the same name north from Launceston to Bass Strait. Tidal for this 64km stretch, the Tamar River separates the east and west Tamar districts and links Launceston with its ocean port of Bell Bay. Crossing the river near Deviot is Batman Bridge, a unique single-tower structure that is the only bridge on the lower reaches of the Tamar. The Tamar Valley area is growing quickly in tourist stature, due partly to the serene nature of its many waterside orchards, pastures and forests, the good local fishing and the pontoons that have been set up to accommodate the sport, and new drawcards such as the seahorse-rearing facility at Beauty Point. The accommodation and eating options in the area also remain pretty good value.

The Tamar Valley and nearby Pipers River are among Tasmania's main wine-producing areas, and the dry premium wines produced here have achieved international recognition.

European history in the region dates from 1798, when Bass and Flinders discovered the Tamar estuary. The valley slowly developed from its initial settlement in 1804, first becoming a port of call for sailors and sealers from the Bass Strait islands, and then a sanctuary for some of the desperate characters who took to the bush during the convict days. By the mid-19th century, the Tasmanian Aborigines had been violently forced from their traditional hunting grounds by the Europeans slowly spreading across the plains, turning the forested land into farming country.

In the late 1870s, gold was discovered by William and John Dally at Cabbage

Tree Hill, just west of present-day Beaconsfield, and the fortunes of the north took a new turn. The region boomed and for a time – until the mines closed in 1914 – this was one of the biggest towns in Tasmania. Further gold deposits have subsequently been discovered in the Beaconsfield area.

Scattered to the south of Launceston are a number of historic homesteads, such as the impressive Clarendon and Woolmers, and small towns littered with interesting 19th-century buildings, gardens and waterfalls.

Getting There & Around

Bus On weekdays (no services weekends), **Tamar Valley Coaches** (☎ 6334 0828) runs three to five buses a day from Launceston up and down the West Tamar Valley. Destinations from Launceston are Legana ($3), Rosevears ($3.20), Exeter ($4), Gravelly Beach ($4.70), Sidmouth ($5), Beaconsfield ($6.50) and Beauty Point ($7.20, one hour).

Redline Coaches (☎ 6336 1446, 1300 360 000; **W** www.tasredline.com.au) runs three buses every weekday (no weekend services) along the eastern side of the Tamar from Launceston to Hillwood ($5.50), the

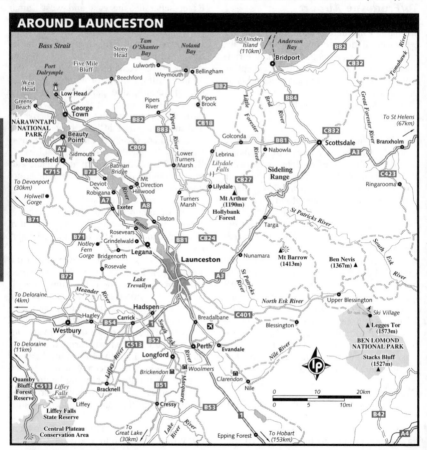

Batman Bridge turn-off ($6.60) and George Town ($8.60, 45 minutes).

Four times each weekday, Redline runs between Launceston and Deloraine ($8.20, 45 minutes), via Hadspen ($2.70), Carrick ($3.50) and Westbury ($5).

Jack's bus service runs from Launceston to Longford ($3.70, 30 minutes), departing Brisbane St (near the corner of Wellington St) at 8.45am, 10.45am, 3pm and 5.40pm from Monday to Friday.

Bicycle The ride north along the Tamar River is an absolute gem. On the west bank, it's possible to avoid most of the highway and follow quiet roads with few hills through the small settlements. On the eastern shore, follow the minor roads inland to Lilydale – there are plenty of hills but the varied landscape more than compensates for the work.

LEGANA
☎ 03 • postcode 7277 • pop 1990

Just 12km north of Launceston, Legana is fast becoming a satellite suburb of its larger neighbour. The area originally consisted of orchards, but these days it's new houses that are taking seed.

A conspicuous and somewhat incongruous feature of the area is **Grindelwald** (☎ 6330 0400; Waldhorn Dr), a Swiss 'village' that inexplicably emigrated to Tasmania to start a new life as a residential suburb, shopping centre and resort.

At the intersection of the highway and Grindelwald's northern access road are the sizeable hilltop headquarters of **Rosevears Estate** (☎ 6330 1800; 1A Waldhorn Dr; open 10am-5pm daily), a wine-maker that incorporates three local vineyards. Winery tours ($3.30 per person) take place at 11.30am daily. Also here is a stylish **restaurant** (mains $20-23; lunch Sun-Wed, lunch & dinner Thur-Sat Nov-Mar) with a tasty upmarket menu – the seafood linguini is recommended.

The authentically overgrown **Notley Fern Gorge** is hidden in the hills 14km west of Legana and, while only small, is the last remnant of the original forest that once covered the region. The big hollow tree in the park was reputedly the hiding place of Matthew

Brady, a famous 19th-century bushranger. It's a nice cool place on a warm day and the circuit walk takes about 45 minutes.

Places to Stay & Eat
Launceston Holiday Park (☎ 6330 1714; 711 West Tamar Hwy; unpowered/powered site doubles $7/13, on-site van doubles $40, cabin doubles $50-75) has a range of cabins, from basic stuffy versions to deluxe spa units.

Freshwater Point (☎ 6330 2200, fax 6330 2030; 56 Nobelius Dr; B&B doubles $145-165), well off the highway, is a charming riverside homestead (built in 1824) with lovely grounds and a pool.

Grindelwald Resort (☎ 6330 0400, 1800 817 595; W www.grindelwaldresort.com.au; Waldhorn Dr; doubles $150-225) has both hotel rooms and chalets to yodel in. Foodwise, you can try **Edelweiss Restaurant** (☎ 6330 1440; mains $17-22; open 11am-late Tues-Sat, lunch Sun), but only if you can successfully order 'Züri Geschnelzelle's'.

ROSEVEARS
☎ 03 • postcode 7277

On the western side of the Tamar, it's worth leaving the highway and following the narrow sealed road that winds along the river and passes through the tiny town of Rosevears. This was the place where the *Rebecca*, John Batman's ship, was constructed; he sailed across Bass Strait in it to settle Melbourne.

Rosevears Waterfront Tavern (☎ 6394 4074; 215 Rosevears Dr; mains $15-20; open 11am-late daily) first opened in 1831 and still serves pub fare today, though the food is now a tad more upmarket. The outdoor terrace is a great spot for a beer and a daydream.

Near the hotel is the nonprofit **Waterbird Haven Trust** (☎ 6394 4087; Rosevears Dr; adult/child $4/2; open 9am-dusk daily), a marine bird sanctuary that does an admirable job of harbouring a huge variety of duck, pheasant, ibis and teal, among others. **Haven House** (singles/doubles $30/50) has B&B accommodation beside the sanctuary, and also does light lunches and Devonshire teas on a scenic deck. Prices include admission to the haven.

Guzzle some vino at **Strathlynn** (☎ 6330 2388; W www.pbv.com.au; 95 Rosevears Dr; open 10am-5pm daily), an outlet for the Pipers Brook Vineyard. Tastings are $3. Also here is a highly polished **restaurant** (mains $18-28; meals noon-3pm daily) featuring Tasmanian produce.

Nearby **St Matthias Vineyard** (☎ 6330 1700; 113 Rosevears Dr; open 10am-5pm daily) has free wine tastings, cheese and antipasto platters, and Sunday jazz BBQs over summer.

Just north of St Matthias is the fully self-contained **Conmel Cottage** (☎/fax 6330 1466; 125 Rosevears Dr; singles/doubles from $95/105); prices include breakfast.

Farther north is **Tamar House** (☎ 6330 1744; W www.tamarhouse.com.au; 85 Rosevears Dr; doubles from $116), where a night's sleep is enhanced by a cooked breakfast, a spa and lots of nature in which to spread out.

When you join the highway, follow the signs to the nearby **Brady's Lookout State Reserve**. The well-known bushranger Brady used this rocky outcrop to spy on travellers on the road below.

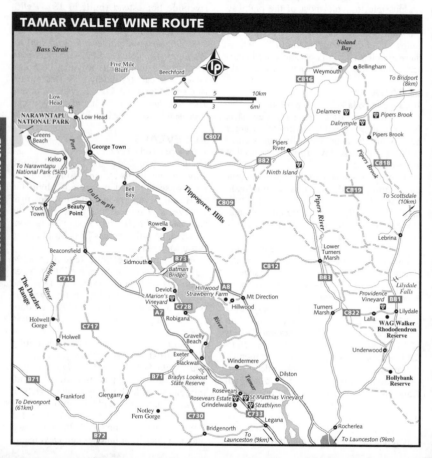

TAMAR VALLEY WINE ROUTE

EXETER

☎ 03 • postcode 7275 • pop 400

The **Tamar Visitor Centre** (☎ *6394 4454;* **W** *www.wtc.tas.gov.au; West Tamar Hwy; open 10am-4pm daily May-Nov, 9am-5pm daily Dec-Apr),* on the main street, is well stocked with regional information and travel brochures.

For budget accommodation, try the large, dirt-cheap rooms at the **Exeter Hotel** (☎ *6394 4216; Main Rd; singles/doubles $15/ 30).* Counter meals are served here from Wednesday to Saturday.

Another food option is the **Exeter Bakery** (☎ *6394 4226; Main Rd; open 6am-6pm daily; coffee house open 9am-3pm Wed-Fri, 9am-5pm Sat & Sun).* Its wood-fired oven produces all manner of pies, from wallaby to lambs fry and bacon.

On the second Sunday of every month, a **market** *(open 10am-3pm)* is held in the show hall.

ROBIGANA & DEVIOT

☎ 03 • postcode 7275

An alternative to following the highway from Exeter to Beaconsfield is to take the more scenic minor road beside the Tamar River. Turn off just south of Exeter and you'll end up passing through Gravelly Beach, Robigana and Deviot.

Robigana – derived from the Aboriginal word for 'swans' – is the spot where the road crosses the Supply River. From here there's a marked walking track beside the Tamar River to **Paper Beach**, which takes one hour return. If you prefer a shorter walk, it's a pleasant 400m along the Supply River to the meagre ruins of the first water-driven **flour mill** in Australia.

Farther upstream on the Supply River is **Norfolk Reach** (☎ *6396 3325; Motor Rd; doubles $90),* a wonderfully isolated homestead surrounded by bird-stocked bushland. It's nearly 5km up Motor Rd, but ring ahead as the manager doesn't live on-site.

Back on the main road is **Lynton** (☎ *6394 4680; 64 Deviot Rd; open 9.30am-6pm Mon-Fri, 9.30am-5pm Sat & Sun),* a predominantly organic-produce farm with fruit and vegetables for sale, a commercial kitchen

churning out fine jams and sauces, and a café serving light meals.

At Deviot, **Marion's Vineyard** (☎ *6394 7434;* **W** *www.netspace.net.au/~marions; Foreshore Dr; open 10am-5pm daily),* charges a $3 fee for wine tastings, refundable if you purchase some wine – their limited output includes the Swiss-variety Müller Thurgau and a reliable chardonnay. There's also accommodation in the form of an attractively rustic upstairs loft (singles/ doubles $88/106).

BATMAN BRIDGE

An important link between the two banks of the Tamar River, Batman Bridge has an eye-catching design that resulted not so much from creative inspiration as from foundation problems. The east bank offered poor support for a large bridge, so it just upholds a minor part of the span. Most of the bridge is actually supported by the 100m-tall west tower that leans out over the river. It opened in 1968, one of the world's first cable-stayed truss bridges. Try the river's east bank for good views and toilets.

Passing underneath the bridge on the western bank is a gravel road leading to **Sidmouth** and the long-worshipped local institution of Auld Kirk.

BEACONSFIELD

☎ 03 • postcode 7270 • pop 1015

The once-thriving but now somewhat subdued gold-mining town of Beaconsfield is still dominated by the facades of its three original mine buildings. Two of these house the **Grubb Shaft Gold & Heritage Museum** (☎ *6383 1473;* **e** *museum@courier.tas.gov .au; West St; adult/concession $8/5; open 9.30am-4.30pm daily Oct-Apr, 10am-4pm daily May-Sept).* This was once Tasmania's largest gold mine, as exemplified by the size of the equipment and the depth of the mine. The museum's hands-on interactive exhibits, including a noisy waterwheel-powered battery, are a must-see if you're travelling with children. Opposite the mine buildings is a reconstruction of a miner's cottage and old school (admission free). Beaconsfield Gold has opened up the old

Hart shaft beside the museum and gold mining is again under way here.

There's no accommodation in town.

The **Club Hotel** (☎ 6383 1191; 145-147 Weld St; mains $10-15) serves counter meals daily; Thursday's 'steak night' (6pm to 8pm) is decidedly popular.

Red Ruby Restaurant (☎ 6383 1608; 102 Weld St; mains $12-18; open from 5pm Mon-Thur, noon-2pm & from 5pm Fri-Sun) serves up the gamut of tasty Chinese cuisine, including a half-dozen mixed-vegetable dishes.

HOLWELL GORGE

In the hills 9km south of Beaconsfield is the small Holwell Gorge reserve, which contains secluded sections of original forest. There are some giant trees reaching 60m, a tangle of ferns and three waterfalls. The walking track linking the southern and northern entrances of the gorge (4.5km apart by road) was recently upgraded and takes around two hours one way.

BEAUTY POINT

☎ 03 • postcode 7270 • pop 1200

Initially the port for the nearby Beaconsfield gold mine, this town still has a wharf and ship-loading facilities. Though the surrounding landscape is certainly attractive, the town's name actually derives from a bullock called Beauty (no relation to Sandra).

Beauty Point's main attraction is **Seahorse World** (☎ 6383 4111; ⓦ www.seahorseworld.com.au; Beauty Point Wharf; adult/child $15/8; open 9.30am-4.30pm daily), based around a seahorse farm where the tiny critters are grown to supply aquariums worldwide and, eventually it's hoped, the Chinese medicine market. The facility incorporates an aquarium with a touch pool and displays on the local marine ecology, plus a café (mains $10 to $18) with a wine centre and outstanding views over the Tamar. Admission includes an interesting one-hour tour where you get right up close to the fascinating *hippocampus abdominalis* (pot-bellied seahorse). See Organised Tours in the Launceston section for details of Tigerline's half-day excursion to Seahorse World from Launceston.

Beauty Point is also home to a campus of the **Australian Maritime College**, which conducts training in fisheries, navigation and other maritime skills.

Places to Stay & Eat

Redbill Point Caravan Park (☎ 6383 4536; Redbill Point; unpowered/powered sites $12/16, on-site van doubles $35, cabin doubles $60) has some of its comfortable cabins overlooking the boat-favoured waters behind the point.

Riviera Hotel (☎ 6383 4153, fax 6383 4315; Lenborough St; singles/doubles $40/50), in the throes of significant renovation when we visited, offers comfortable budget rooms with continental breakfast, plus daily counter meals.

Pomona B&B (☎ 6383 4073; ⓦ www.pomonabandb.com.au; 77 Flinders St; homestead/cottage doubles $120/160) is a Federation abode at the southern end of town, where rooms come with full cooked breakfasts and porch-front river views. Pomona also has two hideaway spa cottages.

Tamar Cove (☎ 6383 4375; Main Rd; mains $12-21) attracts hungry crowds to its bright interior and al-fresco terrace with designer-tastebud fare such as orange marmalade–glazed quail and scallops in a shiraz-and-cream sauce. Lunch and dinner are served daily.

If you want to stay somewhere more removed, the nearby holiday settlements of **Kelso** and **Greens Beach** might appeal.

Kelso Sands Caravan Park (☎ 6383 9130, 1800 039 139; ⓔ kelsocaravanpark@tassie.net.au; Paranaple Rd; unpowered/powered sites $14/18, on-site van doubles $45, cabin doubles $70) is only 100m from the beach but has nonetheless installed a swimming pool.

Greens Beach Caravan Park (☎ 6383 9222; Main Rd; unpowered/powered sites $11/14) is adjacent to a calm ocean beach and – perhaps alarmingly on windy days – a golf course.

Holiday Lodge (☎ 6383 4188; ⓔ hollodge@southcom.com.au; Clarence Point Rd; doubles $65) is a rambling older-style B&B hotel in a rest-inducing location south of

Kelso. Besides rooms, the lodge also offers a spa, massages and counter meals.

NARAWNTAPU NATIONAL PARK

Located 25km east of Devonport, this national park used to be called Asbestos Range, a name bestowed on it in dubious honour of a particular nasty mineral once mined in the area. But several years ago authorities decided that asbestos had too many negative associations and the park was renamed Narawntapu, which is the Tasmanian Aboriginal name for the area.

The scenery here is not as sensational or as rugged as in many other parks; it's a much more gentle landscape. The park's primary purpose is to provide a habitat for Tasmania's larger animals, particularly the Forester kangaroo. Around dusk you'll also see foraging wombats, wallabies and pademelons.

Park entry fees apply and permits are available from the **rangers** (☎ 6428 6277) at Narawntapu's western end. Rangers also provide guided walks, talks and activities over summer. Horse riding is allowed and the park has corrals and a 26km trail; bookings with the ranger are required, as facilities are limited. **Bakers Beach** is the safest swimming area and water-skiing is permitted here in summer.

There are some engaging walking trails in the park. **Badger Head** can be circumnavigated in around four hours, while the **Archers Knob** walk (also around four hours return) has good views of Bakers Beach. The one-hour **Springlawn Nature Trail** includes a boardwalk over wetlands to a bird hide. Meanwhile, the beach from Griffiths Point to Bakers Point is good for beachcombing and sunset-watching; try the **West Head Lookout** for great views over Bass Strait.

The park has four **camp sites** (adult/child $4/2), each with bore water and some firewood provided; sites must be pre-booked through the ranger. The old pit toilets were recently upgraded, as was the local road network. Fees are additional to the national park fees. The park can be reached from the Beaconsfield area or Greens Beach, or from Port Sorell near Devonport.

LOW HEAD

☎ 03 • postcode 7253 • pop 465

Located on the eastern side of the Tamar River where it enters Bass Strait, this scattered settlement doesn't have a 'town centre' as such – its inhabitants rely on the shops and eateries of nearby George Town, only 5km away.

Low Head's historic **Pilot Station** was established in 1805, with the current buildings erected between 1835 and 1962. Here you'll find the interesting **Pilot Station Maritime Museum** (☎ 6382 1143; Low Head Rd; adult/concession $3/2; open 8am-8pm daily), which has 10 rooms cluttered with historical items and displays.

At the head itself, the grounds of the 1888 **lighthouse** (grounds open to 6pm daily) provide great views over the river mouth and surrounding area. There are also several navigational leading lights (mini-lighthouses) around town dating from 1881.

Penguins return to their burrows near the lighthouse at dusk and can be viewed via **Nocturnal Tours** (☎ 0418 361 860; w www.thepenguin.homestead.com). Tours cost $10/6 per adult/child and take place nightly (ring the operator in winter to double-check the penguins are still appearing), departing from a signposted spot beside the main road just south of the lighthouse. Pick-up from the George Town visitor centre can be arranged.

There's good surf at **East Beach** on Bass Strait and safe swimming in calm river water at **Lagoon Bay**.

Places to Stay

Low Head Beachfront Holiday Village (☎ 6382 1000, fax 6382 1555; 192 Gunns Parade; unpowered/powered site doubles $15/19, cabin doubles $75), formerly called Golden Beach Pines, has claimed a good location on East Beach for its multitude of sites and pine-drenched cabins.

Low Head Caravan Park (☎ 6382 1573; 136 Low Head Rd; unpowered/powered site doubles $12/15, on-site van doubles $40, cabin doubles from $55) has an unappealing location midway between George Town and Low Head.

Pilot Station (*☎/fax 6382 1143, 0417 503 292; Low Head Rd; B&B singles/doubles from $55/77, extra adults $33*) has pleasant, self-contained, waterfront accommodation for up to eight people.

Belfont Cottages (*☎ 6382 1399, fax 6382 1304; 178 Low Head Rd; doubles $120*), built to house the caretakers of the leading light next door, now offers B&B in well-equipped, period-style interiors.

GEORGE TOWN
☎ 03 • postcode 7253 • pop 4525

George Town, on the eastern shore of the Tamar River, close to the heads, grew up on the site occupied by Lieutenant-Colonel Paterson in 1804 to stave off a feared French occupation, leading to the European occupation of northern Tasmania. In 1811 the town was officially named after King George. It might have become the island's northern capital but for its lack of fresh water, which prompted Paterson to move south in 1825 and establish Launceston. Some of the older buildings in town date from the 1830s and 1840s, when it prospered as the port linking Tasmania with Victoria.

The opening of the aluminium smelter at nearby Bell Bay in 1949 revived the town, and today Bell Bay's industries continue to provide employment. The recent discontinuation of the fast catamaran service between George Town and Melbourne, however, has hit the town hard and local businesses are feeling the pinch.

Information
The **visitor information centre** (*☎ 6382 1700; Low Head Main Rd; open 10am-4pm daily*) is on the main road as you enter from the south – if you're interested in a self-guided tour of town and of nearby Low Head, pick up the *George Town Heritage Trail* brochure. There is also a **post office** (*Macquarie St*) and an ATM-equipped **Commonwealth Bank** (*Macquarie St*).

Things to See
The Grove (*☎ 6382 1336; ⓦ www.tas.quik .com.au/thegrove; 25 Cimitiere St; adult/ child $5.50/2.50; open 10am-5pm daily*) is

an extensively restored Georgian bluestone residence, classified by the National Trust and well worth a look. You can also eat and stay overnight here (see Places to Stay & Eat later).

Another historical stalwart is the **old watch house** (*Macquarie St*), built in 1843. It has served in recent years as a community arts centre but at the time of writing was closed and awaiting a new assignment. On the northern edge of town is a mural-daubed **water tower** (*cnr Arnold & Agnes Sts*), the paintjob an innovative way of improving what would otherwise be a prominent eyesore.

On nearby **Mt George**, play spot-the-restored-semaphore-mast-and-flagstaff amidst a litter of newer communication towers, or just enjoy the view. There's a wheelchair-accessible ramp from the car park to the mountaintop.

Organised Tours
The nearby industrial area of Bell Bay has Tasmania's only thermal power station, along with several other unattractive heavy industries, all clearly seen from the highway. In recent years these factories have been reducing their output of pollutants and improving their image. **TEMCO** (*☎ 6382 0200*) has a free one-hour tour of its ferro-alloy plant on the first Wednesday of every month at 11am. Make sure you wear closed-in shoes, long sleeves and pants for protection.

Seal & Sea Adventure Tours (*☎/fax 6382 3452, 0419 357 028; ⓦ www.sealandsea .com*) offers three- to four-hour trips out to the seal colony at Tenth Island in a glass-bottom boat, with an enthusiastic and knowledgeable guide at the helm; trips cost $121 per person for two people, $94 per person for groups of three to six. Tamar River cruises and fishing and dive charters can also be arranged.

North of town at the airport (follow the road to Low Head and turn right down North St) you can take 20-minute ultralight plane flights over the hills with **Ultralight Aviation** (*☎ 6382 4700*). Flights cost from $55 per person and should be booked a couple of days in advance.

Places to Stay & Eat

For camping and caravan parks in the area, see the Low Head section previously.

Travellers Lodge (*☎/fax 6382 3261; 4 Elizabeth St; tent sites/dorm beds/doubles $10/18/50*) is a bright, uplifting YHA hostel in a restored late-Victorian house dating back to 1891. The atmosphere here could hardly be better.

George Town Motor Inn (*☎ 6382 1042; 100 Agnes St; singles/doubles $55/65*) has basic units on the edge of town.

Central Court Motel (*☎ 6382 2155, fax 6382 2177; 30 Main Rd; singles/doubles from $55/65*), is in the same mould as the motor inn and is signposted off Main Rd.

Gray's (*George Town Hotel; ☎ 6382 2655; e grayshotel@vision.net.au; 75-77 Macquarie St; doubles $80*) has large but dated en suite rooms and decent bistro meals (mains $12 to $20). It also has a back-room gallery where you can buy local tapestries, watercolours or $300 acrylic-painted ostrich eggs.

The Pier Hotel Motel (*☎ 6382 1300, 13 24 00; e pierhotl@vision.net.au; 5 Elizabeth St; hotel singles/doubles $45/55, motel singles or doubles $110, villa singles or doubles $130*) offers modern riverside lodgings. Some rooms are bedecked in startling shades and florals, but all are good-sized and comfortable. The popular **bistro** (*mains $12-20; open noon-2.30pm & from 6pm daily*) satisfies meat-eaters with seafood and scotch fillets, but vegetarians will find only a few uninspired choices.

Nanna's Cottage (*☎ 6382 1336, fax 6382 3352; 25 Cimitiere St; singles/doubles $75/85*) at The Grove provides cosy B&B; BYO nanna. Light lunches and teas are also available at The Grove, served in the spirit of the past by staff in period costume.

MeJo's Cafe (*☎ 6382 1748; 48 Macquarie St; lunch $6-9; open 8am-5pm Mon-Fri*) is a cheerful place with a good range of light meals like focaccias and salads.

Red Dragon (*☎ 6382 2833; 94-96 Macquarie St; mains $8-15; open 5pm-10pm Mon, noon-10pm Tues-Sun*) serves Chinese favourites from a pink penthouse at the eastern end of Macquarie St. No truth to the rumour it's Thomas Harris' favourite eatery.

Mario's (*☎ 6382 1479; 20 Macquarie St; mains $10-13; open 11am-2pm & from 5pm Mon-Sat*) has a range of pastas and Italian meat dishes, plus a takeaway 'pasta bar'.

Getting There & Away

See Getting There & Around at the start of the Around Launceston section. The George Town agent for Redline is Pino's Gift & Hardware at 21 Elizabeth St.

HILLWOOD

☎ 03 • postcode 7252

Beside the Tamar River south of George Town is the attractive rural area of Hillwood, noted for its fishing and lovely river views.

In the rose-scented environs of the **Hillwood Strawberry Farm** (*☎ 6394 8180; w www.tassie.net.au/~pbrowett; East Tamar Hwy; open 8am-5.30pm daily*), you can pick strawberries, raspberries, apples and cherries, buy berry-fruit vinegars, and sample fruit wines and cheese. Most of the fruit is in season from December to March, while strawberries hang around from November to April.

PIPERS RIVER REGION

☎ 03 • postcode 7252

This northerly rural region plays a pivotal role in the Tasmanian wine industry. Its vintage enterprises started in 1974 with Pipers Brook and today the area produces nearly half of the state's wines – nine vineyards have made themselves at home here. The countryside through which you drive to visit the vineyards is unremarkable, but some of the vineyards themselves are quite attractive.

The most famous local grape-squeezer is **Pipers Brook** (*☎ 6382 7527; w www.pbv.com.au; 1216 Pipers Brook Rd; open 10am-5pm daily*), which was started in the wake of an academic exercise by Dr Andrew Pirie, who compared the famous wine regions of France with Australian regions. The architecturally innovative main building includes the **Winery Café** (*mains $20*), which serves a changing menu of mains and a Tasmanian cheese platter ($11). Informative 20-minute winery tours take place daily at 11am and 3pm, and cost $5 per adult (kids under 14 years free); due to safety issues, the tours are temporarily suspended during the frenetic two-month harvest (usually March to April). Tastings are $3 and are refunded on purchase.

Tall Poppies

Wine making is a well-known and lucrative Tasmanian industry, but less well known is the fact that this small island is also one of the world's most successful opium poppy entrepreneurs. Since the first commercial poppy-growing season began in 1970, after six years of intensive government-supervised agronomic trials, Tasmania has cornered 40% of the international poppy market – it's the only place in the southern hemisphere where this farming activity is legal, and the industry currently involves around 1200 growers who cultivate 200 sq km of the plant every year.

Tasmanian poppies are raised in the healthy soils along the state's north and east coasts, in the southeast and in the midlands. Using a method developed by Hungarian chemist Janos Kabay in the early 1930s, opiate alkaloids are extracted direct from the dry poppy straw, rather than from poppy juice (in the non-sanctioned opium businesses conducted elsewhere in the world, this juice is dried and condensed before being distributed as an illegal narcotic). The extracted alkaloids, primarily codeine, are then used in the production of pain killers and other medicines.

Predictably, the growing and harvesting of poppies in Tasmania is strictly controlled by the state government, which established the Poppy Advisory and Control Board to manage the licensing of the crops. But as poppies are grown in conjunction with a range of rotated farm crops, accidents can happen. A local horse trainer was recently surprised to learn that some of his steeds had ingested poppy seeds that had stowed away in horse feed – in the space of one week, three of his horses were disqualified from racing after testing positive for opium 'use'.

For those who don't like to sip and drive, the winery has **B&B** (☎ 6332 4425; e cottage@pbv.com.au; doubles $135) in a single, quaint, mezzanine-equipped cottage.

Pipers Brook also runs **Ninth Island** (☎ 6382 7622; 40 Baxters Rd, Pipers River; open 10am-5pm daily), located south of Pipers River, which has a restaurant (lunch $13 to $22) serving good Tasmanian produce on a vine-covered terrace – chow down on hollandaise-covered free-range chook breast, accompanied by a glass of the fine rose-gold-coloured Pinot Grigio. Tastings are free.

Other local vineyards worth dropping into for a tasty drop include **Delamere** (☎ 6382 7190; Bridport Rd, Pipers Brook) and **Dalrymple** (☎ 6382 7222; 1337 Pipers Brook Rd, Pipers Brook).

LILYDALE
☎ 03 • postcode 7268 • pop 345

The small town of Lilydale is 25km north of Launceston, in the centre of a region popular with visitors for its walks, wineries and gardens. The town's landmark building is **Bardenhagen's General Store** (Main Rd), operating since 1888 and still serving a few Bardenhagen kinfolk who remain in the area – the paintings on the walls are replicas of the images painted on various telephone poles in town, a colourful gimmick reminiscent of Sheffield's murals.

On the road to Lalla is the **WAG Walker Rhododendron Reserve** (admission per vehicle $2; open 9am-6pm daily Apr, May & Sept–mid-Dec, 9am-6pm Sat & Sun mid-Dec–Mar), a fine swathe of greenery that includes exotic trees, endless slopes and a distinct lack of noise; it has wonderful floral displays between September and December.

Nearby is **Providence Vineyard** (☎ 6395 1290; w www.providence-vineyards.com.au; 236 Lalla Rd; open 10am-5pm daily), Tasmania's oldest working vineyard, planted in 1956. Providence makes available around 40 wines from across the state and is the sort of place where people regularly utter enigmatic assessments like 'Goodness, what about the nose on that one?'. Tastings are free.

Three kilometres north of Lilydale is the pretty **Lilydale Falls & Reserve**, which has an easy 10-minute walk to two waterfalls. About 10km south of Lilydale, accessed via Hollybank Rd, is **Hollybank Forest**, one of Tasmania's busy 'working' forests, which means it's subjected to a continuous logging and then replanting cycle. The forest has some good picnic areas, easy walking tracks ranging from 15 to 40 minutes return, and a Forestry Training Centre – don't bother dropping in here for information, though, as what leaflets exist are several years old.

More energetic walkers may feel the urge to tackle the hike up **Mt Arthur**, which towers dramatically above Lilydale. To get to the summit of the mountain and back again takes between five and seven hours. To drive to the walk's starting point, follow Mountain Rd at the southern extremity of town.

Places to Stay & Eat

Camping is possible for $6 at Lilydale Falls Reserve. Head for the distinctive red building housing **Lilydale Takeaway** (☎ 6395 1156; Main Rd), where you'll pay a $20 deposit for a key to the amenities block; $14 is refunded on return of the key. The maximum stay is two nights.

Lilydale Tavern (☎ 6395 1230; Main Rd; doubles $65, extra guests $10) has a budget motel-style room that can squeeze in up to five people. Counter meals are available here daily.

Falls Farm (☎/fax 6395 1598; 231 Golconda Rd; B&B singles/doubles $70/90), near the falls reserve, dedicates a wing of its main house to a nice, self-contained suite (limited cooking facilities) that opens onto its own private back porch.

Plovers Ridge Host Farm (☎/fax 6395 1102; Lalla Rd; singles/doubles from $95/ 125) is a highly recommended place offering accommodation with full breakfast in two snug, timber-lined units with great valley views. Other meals (both vego and meaty) that utilise as much organic produce as possible are also available ($25 per person for two courses).

HADSPEN
☎ 03 • postcode 7290 • pop 1730

The popular residential suburb of Hadspen is 15km southwest of Launceston and has some attractive 19th-century Georgian buildings, like the **Red Feather Inn** (42 Main St), built in 1844. Down the street, the bluestone Anglican **Church of the Good Shepherd**, built in 1868, is also worth a reverent gaze.

Two kilometres west of Hadspen, beyond the South Esk River, off Old Bass Hwy, is the National Trust–run **Entally House** (☎ 6393 6201; adult/child/family $7.70/ 5.50/15.40; open 10am-12.30pm & 1pm-5pm daily), one of Tasmania's best-known historic homes. Built in 1819 by shipping entrepreneur Thomas Haydock Reibey and named after a Calcutta suburb, it's set in beautiful grounds and offers a vivid period picture of rural affluence, from the coach house and stables down to the abundance of fine furniture and silverware.

Places to Stay & Eat

Launceston Cabin & Tourist Park (☎ 6393 6391; [w] www.cosycabins.com/launceston; cnr Bass Hwy & Main Rd; unpowered/ powered sites $15/18, cabin doubles $64) is a large, well-maintained park with good facilities and fully equipped cabins.

Rutherglen Holiday Village (☎ 6393 6307; [e] rutherglentas@bigpond.com; Old Bass Hwy; singles/doubles from $72/84), immediately west of Hadspen, has decent, if slightly rustic motel rooms, as well as a bistro (open from 6pm to 8pm daily), tavern, pool and spa.

Red Feather Inn (☎ 6393 6331; 42 Main St; mains from $17; bar open from 4pm daily, restaurant open from 6.30pm daily) is a historic pub with a restaurant serving Oz cuisine staples like steak and seafood, plus a vegetarian menu; it also has a wine bar.

CARRICK
☎ 03 • postcode 7291 • pop 335

The region around Carrick, 19km southwest of Launceston on the old highway to Deloraine, was a major grain-growing area in the 19th century. Its most prominent feature nowadays is the four-storey, ivy-smothered

Carrick Mill *(67 Bass Hwy)*, built in 1846. It was most recently a convention centre but at the time of writing was up for sale.

Behind the mill is the dramatically crumbled 1860 ruin known as **Archers Folly** *(Bishopsbourne Rd)*, twice burnt down. Next door, in a building seemingly assembled by an inebriated fisherman, is the **Tasmanian Copper & Metal Art Gallery** *(☎ 6393 6440;* W *www.tascoppermetalart.com; 1 Church St; open 9.30am-6pm daily)*, where you'll find an Aladdin's Cave of imaginative metalwork for sale.

Hawthorn Villa *(☎ 6393 6150, 6393 1610; cnr Bass Hwy & Bishopsbourne Rd; B&B singles/doubles $60/95)* provides cosy B&B in the renovated main house or in an attractively old self-contained cottage.

Carrick Inn *(☎ 6393 6143; Bass Hwy; mains $12-17; open noon-2pm & 6pm-8pm daily)* has been licensed since 1833 and so is well-versed in cooking meat-dominated pub fare.

WESTBURY
☎ 03 • postcode 7303 • pop 1280
The historic town of Westbury, 32km west of Launceston, is best known for its **White House** *(☎ 6393 1171; King St; adult/child $7.70/3; open 10am-4pm Tues-Sun)*, a property built in 1841 as a general store. Now managed by the National Trust, it features collections of colonial furniture, vintage cars and 19th-century toys, including the wonderfully intricate, 1.8m-high, 20-room Pendle Hall doll's house. In front of the White House is the **village green**, a narrow park that includes a maypole and war memorial.

For a splendidly fragrant experience, visit the **Culzean Gardens** *(☎ 6393 2648; 1 William St; admission $5; open 10am-5pm daily Oct-May)*. Pronounced cull-**ayn**, this grand English floral display includes rhododendrons, azaleas, wood anemones, roses, mature oaks and numerous conifers, all planted around a large, landscaped lake.

Pearn's Steam World *(☎ 6397 3313; 65 Bass Hwy; adult/child $5/2; open 9am-4pm daily)* comprises two huge sheds filled with antique steam engines and will appeal most to old machinery enthusiasts.

Westbury Maze *(☎ 6393 1840, 10 Bass Hwy; adult/child $5/4; open 10am-5pm daily Sept-July)* is a 3000-bush walk-in puzzle with a tearoom serving dozens of brews.

See Getting There & Around at the start of the Around Launceston section for information on getting to/from Westbury.

Places to Stay
Westbury Hotel *(☎ 6393 1151; 107 Bass Hwy; singles/doubles from $35/55)* has basic hotel rooms with continental breakfast.

The Olde Coaching Inn *(☎/fax 6393 2100; 54 William St; singles/doubles $75/85)* offers pleasant, slow-paced B&B in a building dating to 1833.

Egmont *(☎ 6393 1164; 415 Birralee Rd; doubles from $90)* provides fully self-contained accommodation overlooking the Meander River.

Gingerbread Cottage *(☎ 6393 1140; 52 William St; doubles $125)* lives up to its name by being the size and colour of a hefty gingerbread loaf. It's filled with quaint and quirky touches and has a dense garden out back.

Places to Eat
White House Bakery *(☎ 6393 1066; King St; open 8am-4.30pm Tues-Sun)* sells tasty fresh pies, scones and biscuits.

Andy's *(☎ 6393 1846; 45 Bass Hwy; meals $4-10; open 9am-6pm Mon-Sat, 9am-4.30pm Sun)* has an attractive café/bakery interior and serves focaccias and other light meals.

Westbury Hotel *(☎ 6393 1151; 107 Bass Hwy; mains $9-15)* serves light meals ($5) and pub mains daily.

Hobnobs Cafe Restaurant *(☎ 6393 2007; 47 William St; meals $6-18; open 10am-5pm Tues, Wed & Sun, 10am-late Thur-Sat)* is a conversational, licensed affair set in a National Trust–listed building. It serves Devonshire teas, lasagne, grills and desserts, and has plans for an outdoor eating area.

LIFFEY VALLEY
This valley is in the Liffey Falls State Reserve at the foot of the Great Western Tiers. It has served as the site of a holiday home belonging to Dr Bob Brown, the well-known

conservationist turned politician (see the boxed text 'Bob Brown' in the Facts about Tasmania chapter) – it's no coincidence that the Tasmanian Wilderness World Heritage Area starts at the back fence of that property.

The natural centrepiece of this beautiful rainforested valley is the **Liffey Forest Reserve**, in which lies the impressive Liffey Falls. There are two approaches to the falls, which are actually four separate cascades. From the upstream car park – accessed by an often steep and winding road, and where there's a rather intimidating 50m-high browntop stringybark – it's a 45-minute return walk on a well-marked track. You can also follow the river upstream through forest to the Gulf Rd picnic area; allow two to three hours return. The area has some fine fishing.

Hidden in the undergrowth 15km before the falls car park is **Liffey Gardens & Retreat** (☎/fax 6397 3213; 40 Gulf Rd; doubles $100). Here, amongst serene gardens, you'll find a handful of compact, self-contained chalets with mind-emptying views of Drys Bluff – at 1297m it's the highest peak of the Great Western Tiers. You can also grab muffins or quiche in the **tearooms** (open 9am-6pm daily).

Another place to stay is the very hospitable **Liffey Falls Lodge** (☎/fax 6369 5363; W www.liffeyfallslodge.com.au; 1363 Bogan Rd; rooms $100-110), which has two rooms with private access and a full cooked brekkie that includes home-made bread; further meals and drinks are easily arranged.

Liffey is 34km south of Carrick and is a good day trip from Launceston.

LONGFORD
☎ 03 • postcode 7301 • pop 2830

Longford is 27km south of Launceston and is classified as a historic town due to its abundance of colonial buildings. The surrounding region is a rich pastoral area watered by the South Esk and Macquarie Rivers and is dotted with historic farmhouses and grand estates.

The Europeans initially called the area Norfolk Plains because of land grants given in 1812 to settlers from the abandoned colony on Norfolk Island. The current site

of Longford was originally called Latour. The road connecting it with Launceston was built in 1813 and, with such a reliable transportation route established, the site quickly grew into a town. It was one of the few towns in the state established by free settlers rather than convicts, and by 1823 over 500 people lived here.

Nowadays, Longford is a pretty quiet place that isn't particularly interested in picking up its pace of life. See Getting There & Around at the start of the Around Launceston section for information on getting to/from Longford.

Things to See & Do
Spread out around **Memorial Park**, the town is best known for its Georgian architecture. Buildings worth seeing include the bluestone **Anglican Church** (Goderich St), the **Town Hall** (Smith St), the **library** (Wellington St) and the **Queens Arms Hotel** (Wellington St).

From the 1950s to the early 1960s, the streets of Longford regularly doubled as a racetrack for motor car races, including three Australian Grand Prix. The **Country Club Hotel** (Wellington St) is a veritable shrine to this period in the town's history, with numerous motor racing photos and other paraphernalia arranged around the bar. Nowadays the town's main event is the **Blessing of the Harvest Festival** in March, with a street parade and country-fare stalls.

Two prime, well-aged estates in the Longford area are **Woolmers** (☎ 6391 2230; W www.woolmers.com.au; Woolmers Lane; adult/child $10/2.50; open 10am-4.30pm daily), a grandly furnished 1819 homestead with beautiful surrounds that include the flourishing National Rose Garden, and **Brickendon** (☎ 6391 1383; W www.brick endon.com.au; Woolmers Lane; adult/child $8.50/3.50; open 9.30am-5pm Tues-Sun), a combination of gardens and a historical farming village with heaps of rural-type activities – both were established by William Thomas Archer. There are tours of Woolmers daily at 11am, 12.30pm, 2pm and 3.30pm (guided inside the house, self-guided outside). The properties are south of Longford; just follow the signs from Wellington St.

Places to Stay & Eat

Longford Riverside Caravan Park (☎ 6391 1470; Archer St; unpowered/powered sites $12/14, on-site van doubles $38-55, cabin doubles $40) meanders along the quiet banks of the Macquarie River, close to the town centre. It also has a couple of cheap bunks in two small cabins ($14) and allows dogs on the premises as long as they're kept on leads.

Country Club Hotel (☎ 6391 1155; 19 Wellington St; singles/doubles $25/40) is a welcoming, often busy pub offering good-value budget rooms with shared bathroom. Hearty counter meals are dished out daily.

Kingsley House (☎ 6391 2318; Wellington St; B&B doubles $100, extra adult/child $30/10), on the northern side of town beside the railway line, is a positively old-fashioned place with cheerful suites ranging from the large to the enormous.

Racecourse Inn (☎ 6391 2352; W www.racecourseinn.com; 114 Marlborough St; singles/doubles from $130/165) is a plush, restored Georgian inn on the southern side of town. It has five antique-decorated rooms, one with a spa, and provides a full cooked breakfast.

The Old Rosary (☎ 6391 1662, fax 6391 1077; Malcombe St; singles/doubles $130/160) is at the resplendent Longford Hall, west of town and signposted off Marlborough St. The hall, planted amidst some lovely gardens, was at one time a school, then a Carmelite monastery, and is now a private residence that offers spacious accommodation (including breakfast provisions) in what were the old stables.

Brickendon (☎ 6391 1383, fax 6391 2073; Woolmers Lane; B&B doubles $144-176) has two well-equipped, early-19th-century cottages (one each for 'Coachman' and 'Gardener' wannabes), plus three much newer self-contained cottages with old-style trimmings.

Woolmers (☎ 6391 2230, fax 6391 2270; Woolmers Lane; B&B doubles from $140) also has self-contained colonial cottages; prices include breakfast provisions and a tour of the main house.

JJ's Bakery & Old Mill Cafe (☎ 6391 2364; 52 Wellington St; lunch $10-17; open 7am-5.30pm Mon-Fri, 7am-5pm Sat & Sun), in the restored Old Emerald flour mill, produces a wide variety of delicious baked goods, and serves wood-fired pizzas and daily specials in its licensed café. There's live jazz most Sundays.

Chinese Big Wok (☎ 6391 1288; 33 Marlborough St; mains $7-8.50; open 4.30pm-9.30pm Fri & Sat, 4.30pm-9pm Tues-Thur & Sun) is a speedy dispenser of good Chinese takeaway staples like sweet chilli chicken and banana fritters.

EVANDALE

☎ 03 • postcode 7212 • pop 1035

Evandale is 22km south of Launceston in the South Esk Valley, near Launceston's airport, and is yet another National Trust–classified town. Many of its 19th-century buildings are in excellent condition.

Information

The volunteer-staffed **Tourism & History Centre** (☎ 6391 8128; 18 High St; open 10am-3pm daily) has lots of written information and loquacious attendants. Pick up the pamphlet *Evandale Heritage Walk* ($2.20), which will guide you around the town's historic features.

Historic Buildings

Places worth seeing around town include the brick **water tower** (High St), two photogenic **churches** (High St), opposite each other, and historic houses such as **Solomon House** (High St), **Ingleside** (Russell St) and **Fallgrove** (Logan Rd).

The **Clarendon Arms Hotel** (11 Russell St) has been licensed since 1847. The mural-coated walls paint a few pictures of the town's early days, though they were daubed in 1978.

Eight kilometres south of Evandale is the National Trust property of **Clarendon** (☎ 6398 6220; Nile Rd; adult/concession $7.70/5.50; open 10am-5pm daily Sept-May, 10am-4pm daily June-Aug), which has been impressing visitors with its designer Georgian architecture since 1838.

Local Produce

A sizeable **market** (Logan Rd) is held every Sunday morning in Evandale. Kiddies should still be able to get their fix of train rides here. Many of the wares available are generic country market inclusions, but there's usually something authentically creative to stumble across.

Gourmet foodies will want to visit the **Tasmanian Gourmet Sauce Co** (☎ 6391 8437; 174 Leighlands Rd; open 10am-5pm Wed-Sun), 3km west of Evandale, where you can sample and buy fine relishes, jams, mustards and dessert sauces – the Thai chilli sauce will clear a path through the most stubborn sinus.

Special Events

Every February, Evandale dresses itself up in old-fashioned splendour for the **Evandale Village Fair & National Penny Farthing Championships** (W www.evandalevillagefair.com; adult/child $7/free), where national and international competitors wrestle these asymmetrical two-wheelers around a mile-long town circuit.

If you want to try this unwieldy device for yourself, **Penny Farthing Cycle Tours** (☎ 6391 9101; W www.pennyfarthingtours.com.au) offers two pricey half-day tours ($75 per person), one a circuit of Evandale and the other a ride out to historic Clarendon. Bookings are essential.

Places to Stay

Clarendon Arms Hotel (☎ 6391 8181; 11 Russell St; singles/doubles $30/60) has decent budget rooms with shared facilities.

Prince of Wales Hotel (☎ 6391 8381; cnr High & Collins Sts; singles/doubles $30/60) is similar to the Clarendon Arms.

Arndell Cottage (☎ 6391 8994; e arndellcottage@vision.net.au; 26 Russell St; rooms $110) got its name via a fishy homage to the bloke who introduced salmon and trout into Tasmanian rivers. It's a nicely outfitted B&B with a backyard to lounge in; keep your forehead on alert for the low bedroom lintels.

The Stables (☎ 6391 8048; W www.vision.net.au/~thestables; 5 Russell St; B&B singles/doubles $90/120) has three comfortable self-contained units (in the old stables) for you to flop in, and laundry facilities. Inquire at Browns Village Store.

Greg and Gill's Place (☎/fax 6391 8248; 35 Collins St; B&B singles/doubles $50/75) has eclectic surrounds that are real child-pleasers. Kiddies will find inspiration in the host family's camera displays, model plane and car collections, paintings and a great garden.

Solomon Cottage (☎ 6391 8331; 1 High St; singles/doubles $80/110) was originally built as a bakery. Its constructors most probably would never have envisaged their oven eventually being taken up by a queen-size bed. The cottage, next to Solomon House, has two bedrooms and the price includes a cooked breakfast.

Harland Rise (☎ 6391 8283; Dalness Rd; B&B singles/doubles $65/90), 3km northeast of town and only a 10-minute drive from Launceston airport, has two rooms available in a friendly farmhouse dating from 1857, surrounded by beautiful grounds. The upstairs abode has an en suite; the downstairs space is smaller and without an external window, though it does come with its own bathroom (upstairs).

Places to Eat

The Dalmeny (☎ 6391 8988; 14 Russell St; mains $8-19; open lunch & dinner Wed-Sun) is a classy BYO eatery with excellent food. It has everything from New York–style pizzas (after 6pm) to seafood platters and drool-worthy desserts such as summerberry flan.

Ingleside Bakery Café (☎ 6391 8682; 4 Russell St; lunch $7-13; open 9am-5pm daily), set in the atmospheric former council chambers, has good pies, quiches, focaccias and sweets.

Clarendon Arms Hotel (☎ 6391 8181; 11 Russell St; mains $13-17) serves meaty counter meals daily and has a outdoor beer garden.

Prince of Wales Hotel (☎ 6391 8381; cnr High & Collins Sts; mains $12-16) serves up substantial pub meals daily; it has a kids menu too.

BEN LOMOND NATIONAL PARK

This 165-sq-km park, 50km southeast of Launceston, includes the entire Ben Lomond Range and is best known for its skiing, though snow has been notoriously shy here over recent seasons. The range does not have any dramatic peaks but rather is an elevated plateau roughly 14km long by 6km wide. The plateau is around 1300m high, with its gentle hills stretching to 1500m. The highest point is Legges Tor (1573m), the second-highest peak in Tasmania and well worth climbing in good weather for its panoramic views.

The scenery at Ben Lomond is magnificent year-round. The park is particularly noted for its alpine wildflowers, which run riot in spring and summer.

Ben Lomond was named after its Scottish namesake by the founder of Launceston, Colonel Paterson, in 1804. From 1805 to 1806 Colonel Legge explored the plateau and named most of the major features after explorers of the Nile River in Africa and members of the fledgling Van Diemen's Land colony.

Things to See & Do

In summer, the plateau provides some easy walking. The most popular place to visit is the highest point, **Legges Tor**. It can be reached via a good walking track from Carr Villa, about halfway up the mountain, and takes about two hours each way. You can also climb to the top from the alpine village on the plateau, which takes about 30 minutes each way on marked tracks.

You can walk across the plateau in almost any direction, but there are no marked tracks and navigation is difficult in mist. Unless you're well equipped, walking south of the ski village is not advised.

During the ski season (which officially runs from early July to late September), a kiosk, tavern and restaurant are open in the alpine village, and there's accommodation year-round at **Creek Inn** (☎ 6390 6199; 1 High St; dorm beds $35, unit doubles summer/winter $110/150). Rates include continental breakfast.

There are eight tows for skiers and a heated day-visitor shelter. To check conditions for downhill or cross-country skiing, phone ☎ 190 229 0530. Lift tickets and ski equipment hire cost considerably less than they do on the mainland. There are three T-bars and five Poma lifts.

Getting There & Away

When it's snowing, **Starline** (☎ 6331 1411) runs a service daily at around 8am from the Launceston travel & information centre to the top of the mountain (adult/concession $22/17). The bus remains at Ben Lomond to shuttle people up and down the mountain ($11 per person each way) before returning to Launceston around 4pm.

Outside the ski season, driving is your only transport option. The route up to the alpine village from the mountain's base includes Jacob's Ladder, a very steep climb on an unsealed road with six hairpin bends and no safety barriers; in winter, chains are standard equipment for the final climb.

The North

The northern plains are actually rolling farmlands and hill country that extend from the Tamar River valley north of Launceston west to the Great Western Tiers that rise up to Tasmania's Central Plateau.

The area's original Tasmanian Aboriginal residents were members of the North Tribe, who worked some significant ochre mines at Mt Vandyke, Mt Housetop and St Valentines Peak, and left middens and rock carvings around Devonport. Closer to Launceston were the traditional hunting grounds of the North Midlands Tribe.

Heading west from Launceston, the main highway skirts the foot of the Great Western Tiers, running through Deloraine before heading north to Devonport. The state's third-largest city, Devonport is the terminal for the dual ferry services plying Bass Strait to and from Melbourne, and is also the gateway to Cradle Mountain-Lake St Clair National Park. Hidden in the hills between Devonport and Cradle Mountain are a series of small towns that are well worth discovering.

Getting There & Around

Bus The bus company **Redline Coaches** (☎ *6336 1446, 1300 360 000;* W *www.tasredline.com.au*) has several services daily from Launceston to Devonport ($16.50, one to 1½ hours), Ulverstone ($21), Penguin ($22.50) and Burnie ($22, two to 2½ hours); bookings are required for all stops. Redline also runs services four times each weekday from Launceston to Deloraine ($8.20, 45 minutes) – one afternoon service each day continues to Mole Creek ($11.70, 1¼ hours).

TassieLink (☎ *6272 7300, 1300 300 520;* W *www.tigerline.com.au*) runs a daily express service that picks up passengers who have disembarked from the Bass Strait ferry terminal in Devonport in the morning and then heads to Launceston ($16.50, 1¼ hours) and Hobart ($40.50, four hours); this service also runs daily in reverse from Ho-

Highlights

- Being surrounded by the Walls of Jerusalem
- Visiting the Tasmanian Aboriginal cultural keep of Tiagarra in Devonport
- Discovering that they're not called the *Great* Western Tiers for nothing
- Taking in the hop fields and lush countryside of Gunns Plains
- Exploring the wild caves of Mole Creek Karst National Park

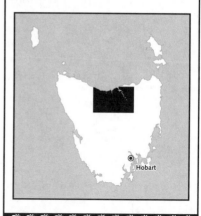

Hobart

bart, reaching Devonport in time for the nightly ferry sailing. Also connecting with the morning ferry arrival in Devonport every Wednesday and Friday is a service that heads west to Burnie, with onward connections to Tullah ($22.20, 2¼ hours), Rosebery ($23.80, 2½ hours), Zeehan ($30, three hours), Queenstown ($37.10, 3¾ hours) and Strahan ($44.10, 4¾ hours) – the route is also run in reverse on the same days. On Monday, Tuesday, Thursday and Saturday, TassieLink also has a service from Launceston to Strahan which passes through Devonport (no drop offs, pick-up

THE NORTH

only), Sheffield ($19, 2½ hours), Gowrie Park ($22.20) and Cradle Mountain ($43.60, 3½ hours).

Bicycle The old highway between Launceston and Deloraine is a good cycling route, as most vehicles follow a newer thoroughfare. It's slower and climbs more hills than the more recent highway, but it's far more interesting, passing through all the small towns. From Deloraine, the rebuilt highway that heads directly to Devonport through Latrobe is best avoided by travelling through the more subdued towns of Railton or Sheffield.

DELORAINE
☎ 03 • postcode 7304 • pop 2170

With its lovely riverside picnic area, superb setting at the foot of the Great Western Tiers and good amenities, Deloraine is a great inland alternative to nearby Launceston or Devonport, both of which could be enjoyed in a series of day trips. It's close to Cradle Mountain and a number of impressive waterfalls, caves and short walks, and although it may not always be the most convenient stopover for travellers heading for the Overland Track, it has much to offer bushwalkers as a base for exploring the central north.

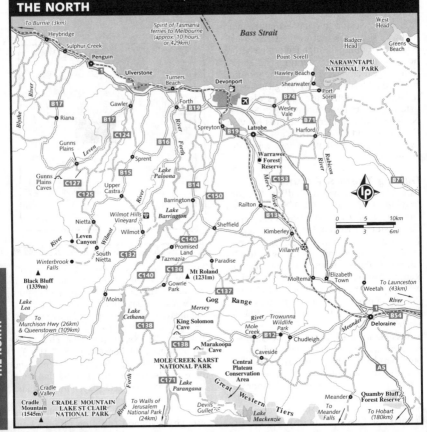

THE NORTH

Deloraine owes a good deal of its charm to its Georgian and Victorian buildings, many of which have been faithfully restored. It was first settled by Europeans in the 1820s and the older buildings date mainly from the following two decades. Cattle grazing and wheat growing were the initial mainstays of the region, but competition and disease closed the wheat mills. The farms have since diversified and now cultivate a wide variety of crops and livestock.

Most people come to Deloraine to bushwalk and explore the nearby caves of the Mole Creek Karst National Park, but another attraction is the large number of arts, antique and second-hand shops in town.

If you're travelling in this area during spring, it's worth noting that Deloraine's annual craft fair (see Special Events later) draws tens of thousands of visitors in late October and/or early November, when accommodation can book out from Launceston to Devonport.

Information

The **Deloraine visitors centre** (☎ 6362 3471; 98 Emu Bay Rd; open 9.30am-4pm Mon-Fri, 1pm-3.30pm Sat, 2pm-4pm Sun) is set in the National Trust–listed Family & Commercial Inn, which dates from the 1860s. It shares its premises with the Deloraine Folk Museum (see Museums & Galleries following). If you're a keen shopper, pick up information on Deloraine's sundry arts and crafts outlets here.

Internet access is available at the **Online Access Centre** (☎ 6362 3537; West Parade).

There are branches of Commonwealth and ANZ Banks in town, the latter with an ATM. Eftpos withdrawals can be made at the **newsagent** (30 Emu Bay Rd; open 5.30am-6pm Mon-Sat, 6am-1pm Sun) for a small transaction fee. The newsagent also contains a travel agent.

Bushwalkers can pick up basic supplies in Deloraine, but for specialised gear you'll have to travel to Devonport or Launceston

Museums & Galleries

The **Deloraine Folk Museum** (☎ 6362 3471; 98 Emu Bay Rd; adult/child $2/50c; open

9.30am-4pm Mon-Fri, 1pm-3.30pm Sat, 2pm-4pm Sun) was undergoing expansion at the time of writing. This means more room for its interesting local-history exhibits and probably extended opening hours. **Yarns: Artwork in Silk** (admission $3), a four-panel, hand-dyed silk depiction of the Meander Valley through a year's worth of seasonal change, will be relocated to the folk museum once renovations are complete.

For assorted arts and crafts, jewellery and second-hand books, check out **Gallery 9** (☎ 6362 2911; 2 West Barrack St; open 10.30am-5pm Tues-Sat, 1pm-4.30pm Sun Sept-May, 10.30am-5pm Tues, Thur & Sat, 1pm-4.30pm Sun June-Aug).

Two kilometres east of Deloraine, on the road to Launceston, is **Bowerbank Mill**. This former corn mill, built in 1853 and classified by the National Trust, now houses an **art gallery** (☎ 6362 2628; 4455 Bass Hwy; open 10am-5.30pm daily) and also provides accommodation (see Places to Stay later).

St Mark's Church

This church, which is floodlit at night, is situated on high ground on the eastern side of the river and can be seen from most parts of town. It's open to the public daily except school holidays, though you may have to find someone to let you in. The main part of the church was built in 1859, while the chancel and sanctuary were added in 1878. A detailed guide is available inside. Visitors are asked not to enter the sanctuary.

Farms & Gardens

Ten kilometres north of Deloraine you'll find **Ashgrove Farm Cheese** (☎ 6368 1105; 6173 Bass Hwy; open 9am-5pm daily), where you can see award-winning cheeses like rubicon red, smoked cheddar and creamy Lancashire being processed, and taste the fine results.

The beautiful four-hectare, sculpture-embedded gardens at **Villarett**, along a side road that departs the highway a further 8km past Elizabeth Town, are worth visiting even if you don't intend to eat or sleep there (see the Places to Stay and Places to Eat sections later). There's also an art gallery here.

Bushwalking

Dominating the southern skyline are the Great Western Tiers, which provide some excellent walking. Their Tasmanian Aboriginal name is Kooparoona Niara (Mountain of the Spirits) and they feature waterfalls, exceptional forest and some long climbs. The **Meander Forest Reserve** is the most popular starting point. From here **Split Rock Falls** can be visited in three hours, or you can walk to **Meander Falls**, which are four to five hours return. Camping is allowed in the area.

Other good walks on the Great Western Tiers include to **Projection Bluff** (two hours), **Quamby Bluff** (five hours) and **Mother Cummings Peak** (three hours); ask at the visitors centre for details. Note that several tracks on the tiers that require the crossing of private land were closed at the time of writing due to public liability issues (see the boxed text 'Public Liability' in the Activities chapter), including Montana Falls, Westmoreland Falls and the South Mole Creek Track.

Special Events

The impressive **Tasmanian Craft Fair**, held in Deloraine in late October and/or early November (the event always ends on the first Monday in November), is an enormous working craft fair. There are 200 stalls at 10 venues around town, the main one being the Deloraine Community Complex.

Places to Stay – Budget

Apex Caravan Park (☎ 6362 2345; West Parade; unpowered/powered site doubles $11/15) has an appealing location beside the Meander River, except during winter when the river is prone to flooding.

Highview Lodge Youth Hostel (☎ 6362 2996; 8 Blake St; dorm beds/doubles from $18/45) is a welcoming hillside hostel with warm, timber-floored confines. It's a steep walk from town, but the compensation includes some magnificent views of the Great Western Tiers, even from the toilets.

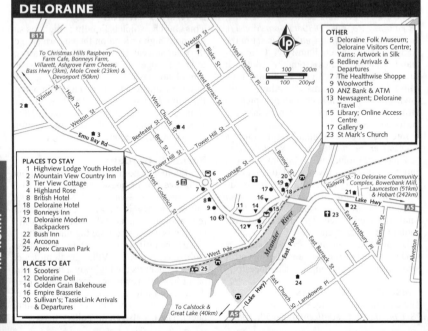

DELORAINE

To Christmas Hills Raspberry Farm Cafe, Bonneys Farm, Villarett, Ashgrove Farm Cheese, Bass Hwy (3km), Mole Creek (23km) & Devonport (50km)

To Deloraine Community Complex, Bowerbank Mill, Launceston (51km) & Hobart (242km)

To Calstock & Great Lake (40km)

OTHER
5   Deloraine Folk Museum; Deloraine Visitors Centre; Yarns; Artwork in Silk
6   Redline Arrivals & Departures
7   The Healthwise Shoppe
9   Woolworths
10 ANZ Bank & ATM
13 Newsagent; Deloraine Travel
15 Library; Online Access Centre
17 Gallery 9
23 St Mark's Church

PLACES TO STAY
1   Highview Lodge Youth Hostel
2   Mountain View Country Inn
3   Tier View Cottage
4   Highland Rose
8   British Hotel
18 Deloraine Hotel
19 Bonneys Inn
21 Deloraine Modern Backpackers
22 Bush Inn
24 Arcoona
25 Apex Caravan Park

PLACES TO EAT
11 Scooters
12 Deloraine Deli
14 Golden Grain Bakehouse
16 Empire Brasserie
20 Sullivan's; TassieLink Arrivals & Departures

THE NORTH

Deloraine Modern Backpackers (☎ 6362 2250; 24 Bass Hwy; dorm beds first night $18, per subsequent night $16) is a functional, well-managed hostel with one large dorm each for males/females, a kitchen and washing machines ($3 per load), but no communal lounge. Linen is supplied.

Bush Inn (☎ 6362 2365, fax 6362 2329; 7 Bass Hwy; single or doubles per person $15) has simple pub accommodation at hostel prices. An extra $5 per person gets you continental breakfast.

Deloraine Hotel (☎ 6362 2022, fax 6362 2354; Emu Bay Rd; singles/doubles $28/55) is a freshened-up, 150-year-old place with both en suite rooms and rooms with shared facilities, all with continental breakfast.

British Hotel (☎ 6362 2016; 80 Emu Bay Rd; singles/doubles $30/50) is a good budget deal, offering well-maintained rooms with cooked breakfast.

Places to Stay – Mid-Range

Bonneys Farm (☎ 6362 2122; 76 Archer St; doubles from $70, extra guests $12), 4km out of town, has three self-contained units and a guesthouse; breakfast is included in the guesthouse, but costs extra for the other units. To get there, head towards Devonport and take the turn-off to Weetah.

Villarett (☎/fax 6368 1214; Moltema; doubles $90, extra adults $25), on a side road that leaves the highway 8km north of Elizabeth Town, has a spacious modern unit overlooking lush, undulating countryside. Rates includes cooked breakfast.

Bonneys Inn (☎ 6362 2974; w www .bonneys-inn.com; 19 West Parade; doubles $110, extra guests $33) claims questionable historical kudos as Deloraine's first brick building (c. 1830). Originally a coaching inn, it has comfortably upgraded colonial-style en suite rooms with full breakfasts, plus its own bar and dining room.

Tier View Cottage (☎ 6362 2377; 125 Emu Bay Rd; doubles $85, extra guests $17) is a little out of the city centre but is still a pleasant place to stay. Inquire at the service station opposite the cottage.

Highland Rose (☎ 6362 2634; e highland rose.bb@bigpond.com; 47 West Church St; singles/doubles from $90/95) is a very hospitable B&B in a garden setting at the quiet end of West Church St. The comfortable rooms come with a hearty cooked breakfast.

Mountain View Country Inn (☎ 6362 2633; 144 Emu Bay Rd; rooms $80-95) has cheaper, older rooms with views of the Tiers, or more expensive rooms that lack the scenery. It also has a licensed restaurant but was up for sale at the time of writing.

Places to Stay – Top End

Arcoona (☎ 6362 3443; e arcoona@vision .net.au; East Barrack St; singles $135, doubles $170-205) is a grand old hilltop home on the eastern side of the river. Originally the town doctor's residence and then the district hospital, its credentials as a luxury B&B now include king-size beds and a billiards room.

Bowerbank Mill (☎ 6362 2628; w www .view.com.au/bowerbank; 4455 Bass Hwy; doubles from $150), 2km east of the city centre, has a pair of comfortable, double-storey, stone-walled cottages, filled with colonial character. Three-course dinners are available for $38 per person.

Calstock (☎ 6362 2642; w www.calstock .net; Lake Hwy; doubles $220-295) is an 80-hectare property south of Deloraine on which sits a marvellous mid-19th-century manor – the builder, John Field, bred highly successful racehorses. There are seven bedrooms (one wheelchair accessible), grand lounges, full breakfasts, and dinners by arrangement.

Places to Eat

Christmas Hills Raspberry Farm Cafe (☎ 6362 2186; Christmas Hills Rd; meals $7-17; open 9am-5pm daily), 8km north of town, is wildly popular for its raspberry sorbets, ice cream, waffles and crepes. It also serves a variety of gourmet sandwiches, salads and burgers, and food to take away.

Sullivan's (☎ 6362 3264; West Parade; mains $9-20; open 9am-7.30pm Mon-Wed, 9am-8pm Thur-Sun) is a brisk restaurant/takeaway that serves everything from sandwiches, vegie burgers and fish and chips to scotch fillet, plus pizzas from noon daily. It's opposite the riverside Apex Train Park, a picnic area with a little 1907 locomotive.

British Hotel (☎ 6362 2016; 80 Emu Bay Rd; mains $11-15) serves counter meals, plus cheap daily specials and snacks for under $6.

The Healthwise Shoppe (☎ 6362 2515; 86 Emu Bay Rd; open 9am-5pm Tues-Fri, 9am-noon Sat) is where healthy self-caterers should head to stock up on vitamins and organic grains, juices and bottled goods.

Woolworths Supermarket (Emu Bay Rd; open 8am-9pm Thur & Fri, 8am-6pm Mon-Wed & Sat) is for those who prefer more-processed goods.

Deloraine Deli (☎ 6362 2127; 36 Emu Bay Rd; lunch $5-10; open 9am-5pm Mon-Fri, 9am-2.30pm Sat) is a fine place for late-morning baguettes, bagels and focaccias, with a variety of tasty fillings. It can also do dairy- and gluten-free meals.

Empire Brasserie (☎ 6362 2075; 19 Emu Bay Rd; mains $7-21; open 11am-3pm & from 6pm daily), in the Empire Hotel, has a good menu selection that ranges from 'farinaceous' dishes (eg, pumpkin gnocchi) to Atlantic salmon cutlets, all at rather upmarket prices.

Golden Grain Bakehouse (☎ 6362 2157; 39 Emu Bay Rd; open 8am-5pm Mon-Fri, 8am-2.30pm Sun) has old-style biscuits and other fresh, traditional bakery fare.

Scooters (☎ 6362 3882; 53-55 Emu Bay Rd; mains $13.50-18; open 11am-late daily) sounds like a small-town US soda fountain, but in fact it's a recently opened licensed restaurant with a bright, modern feel and an excellent seasonal menu that includes venison sausages, char grills and mushroom risotto; it also has a kids menu.

Villarett (☎ 6368 1214; Moltema; mains from $13.50; open 10.30am-5.30pm Sat-Thur), north of town, has a garden-surrounded teahouse that serves Devonshire teas, tasty focaccias, hearty mains and great desserts.

Getting There & Away

See the Getting There & Around section at the start of this chapter for details of the Redline service from Launceston to Deloraine and then to Mole Creek. Redline Coaches arrive at and depart from outside Cashworks, which sells bus tickets.

Over summer, **TassieLink** (☎ 6272 7300, 1300 300 520; ⓦ www.tigerline.com.au) has special 'Wilderness' services departing at 9.30am on Monday, Wednesday and Saturday from Launceston and running to Lake St Clair via Deloraine ($14.50, 45 minutes); there's a connecting service to Hobart from Lake St Clair. Bookings are essential for these services as minimum numbers of passengers are required. TassieLink services stop outside Sullivan's (see Places to Eat).

CHUDLEIGH

Those who like sticky fingers will want to make a beeline (sorry…) for Chudleigh's **Honey Farm** (☎ 6363 6160; 39 Sorell St; open 9am-5pm Sun-Fri), where there's free Leatherwood honey tasting, audiovisual displays on honeybees, honey ice cream and lots of other sweet merchandise. There's also a small, glass-enclosed apiary containing thousands of bees. For more on Tassie honey, see the boxed text 'Leatherwood Honey' later in this chapter.

Two kilometres west of Chudleigh is the **Trowunna Wildlife Park** (☎ 6363 6162; adult/child $12.50/6; open 9am-5pm daily Feb-Dec, 9am-8pm daily Jan), which specialises in Tasmanian devils, wombats and koalas, but not (as implied by the billboard out front) Tasmanian tigers. Trowunna also features many birds, including white goshawks and wedge-tailed eagles, and has a nocturnal animal house.

MOLE CREEK

☎ 03 • postcode 7304 • pop 260

About 25km west of Deloraine is Mole Creek, in the vicinity of which you'll find spectacular limestone caves and Leatherwood honey. The town is tiny, with very few services, but has excellent views of the Great Western Tiers and is a handy access point for caving and bushwalking.

Mole Creek Karst National Park

The word 'karst' refers to the scenery characteristic of a limestone region, including caves and underground streams. Of the 200 caves in the Mole Creek area, about 50 have been included in the Mole Creek Karst National Park, declared in 1996. The park itself is in a number of small segments and entry fees are incorporated into the prices of admission to public caves and fees for wild cave tours.

Public Caves There are two public caves in the national park: **Marakoopa** (its name derived from an Aboriginal word meaning 'handsome'), a wet cave 15km from Mole Creek featuring two underground streams and an incredible glow-worm display; and **King Solomon**, a dry cave with amazing light-reflecting calcite crystals (and very few steps). In the high season there are at least five tours daily of each cave, except on Christmas Day when both are closed. The earliest tour of Marakoopa is usually at 10am, while the first King Solomon tour usually departs at 10.30am; the last tour for the day at both caves is usually at 4pm. A tour of one cave costs $9/4.50/22 per adult/child/family, or you can visit both for $13/7/33. It's a 15-minute drive between the two caves. For bookings and other information, ring the Mole Creek **ranger** (☎ 6363 5182).

Wild Caves Among the better known caves in the Mole Creek area that are without steps or ladders are Cyclops, Wet, Honeycomb and the magnificent Baldocks. If you're an experienced caver who wants to take on some vertical rope work, you'll need to make arrangements with a caving club. Everyone else can take one of the excursions offered by **Wild Cave Tours** (☎ 6367 8142; 165 Fern-lea Rd, Caveside), which provides tours for $75/150 per half/full day, including caving gear and guides. Tours must be pre-booked and the minimum age for attendees is 14 years. Take spare clothing and a towel, as you'll get wet.

Stephens Leatherwood Honey Factory

At this factory (☎ 6363 1170; 25 Pioneer Dr; admission free; open 9am-4pm Mon-Fri Jan-Apr), you can watch the honey extraction and bottling plant in operation for the few months at the beginning of each year when local honeybees do their thing (see the boxed text 'Leatherwood Honey'). There are also honey sales here and you might be able to arrange a guided tour of the factory.

Devils Gullet

In fine weather, those with transport should head for the Western Tiers. The only road that actually reaches the top of the plateau is the one to Lake Mackenzie. Follow this road to Devils Gullet, where there's a 15-minute walk leading to a platform bolted to the top of a dramatic gorge: looking over the edge is not for the faint-hearted.

Leatherwood Honey

Under the canopy of the magnificent, tall rainforest trees in the wet, western half of Tasmania, endemic leatherwood trees (Eucryphia lucida and Eucryphia milligani) grow to heights of between 20m and 35m. The name 'Leatherwood' originates from the leathery nature of the tree's timber, and from December to March the tree is covered in small, white, waxy flowers that contain very pale pink stamens.

Leatherwood honey was first produced commercially in the early 1920s, but it was not until after WWII that Tasmanian beekeepers began taking large numbers of hives into the leatherwood areas. Today, many thousands of hives are transported by truck annually.

Apiarists visit their sites several times during the flowering season to remove full boxes, known as 'supers', and replace them with empty boxes for the bees to work on. At the end of the flowering period, all the hives are transported back to their home sites and the delicious honey is extracted from the full supers.

Honey is extracted from the 'combs' inside the supers by spinning and is then packaged for sale and export. The resulting product is a distinctive, aromatic honey that is bound to tempt your taste buds.

THE NORTH

Bushwalking

There are a number of popular short walks in the area, including **Alum Cliffs Gorge** (one hour return). For information about the Walls of Jerusalem National Park, see the following section.

Places to Stay & Eat

Mole Creek Caravan Park (☎ 6363 1150; cnr Mole Creek & Union Bridge Rds; unpowered/powered site doubles $10/12) is a thin sliver of a park 2km west of town beside Sassafras Creek, at the turn-off to the caves and Cradle Mountain.

Mole Creek Hotel (☎ 6363 1102; e tiger bar69@hotmail.com; Main Rd; singles $35, doubles $55-65) has bright upstairs rooms, all except one with shared facilities; rates include continental breakfast. Downstairs in the **Tiger Lair Cafe-Bar** (mains $9-15; open lunch & dinner daily), you can get roasts, burgers and flame-grilled chicken, or just sip on an ale in the large beer garden.

Mole Creek Guest House & Restaurant (☎ 6363 1399, fax 6363 1420; 100 Pioneer Dr; singles from $85, doubles $110-130) is a friendly, comfy place to stay, with nicely presented rooms. The more-expensive rooms are larger and have en suites; rates include cooked breakfast. It also rents out **Engadine** (doubles $80), a self-contained place near Rosewick Cottage, while its **Laurelberry Restaurant** (☎ 6363 1102; mains $16-20; open 8am-8pm Wed-Sun, 8am-5pm Mon & Tues) serves good food from breakfast through to dinner, the latter including dishes such as chicken almondine and vegetarian stacks.

Mole Creek Holiday Village (☎ 6363 6124, fax 6363 6166; 1876 Mole Creek Rd; singles/doubles from $70/90) has large, self-contained timber units with great mountain views from their front porches. Also on-site is the **Wotaview Restaurant/Tearooms** (mains $10-16; open from 5.30pm daily Mar-Nov, lunch & from 5.30pm Dec-Feb), serving pasta, meat/vegie dishes and home-made soups and desserts.

Blackwood Park (☎ 6363 1208; 445 Mersey Hill Rd; cottages $96-110, extra adult/child $28/22), off a side road between Mole Creek and the aforementioned Holiday Village, has two very nice self-contained cottages with excellent crafted furniture, heated floors, home-made muffins and good facilities.

Rosewick Cottage (☎ 6363 1354; Alum Cliff Rd; singles/doubles $60/70, extra adult/child $15/5), off the same side road as Blackwood Park, can take up to five guests in a three-bedroom cottage.

Blue Wren Hideaway (☎ 6363 1393; e bluewren@tassie.net.au; 36 South Mole Creek Rd; singles/doubles $75/90) looks like a beach house marooned in the hills. This relaxing place has several en suite rooms and great views, and dinner can be arranged. Take the turn-off in town south to Caveside and follow it for 4km.

Mole Creek Cafe (☎ 6363 1200; 76 Pioneer Dr; mains $8-14; open 8am-7pm Mon-Fri, 10am-7pm Sat & Sun) serves fish and chips, steak sandwiches and various burgers (including vegetarian).

Getting There & Away

See the Getting There & Around section at the start of this chapter.

WALLS OF JERUSALEM NATIONAL PARK

This remote national park comprises a series of glacial valleys and lakes on top of the Central Plateau and is part of the Tasmanian Wilderness World Heritage Area. It has wild alpine flora and rugged dolerite peaks, and is famously appealing to bushwalkers who prefer an isolated and spectacular hiking challenge.

The most popular walk in the park is the full-day trek to the 'Walls' themselves, with the quickest, easiest route being the trail from the car park off Mersey Forest Rd (near Lake Rowallan) to Trappers Hut, Solomon's Jewels, through Herod's Gate to Lake Salome (six to eight hours return). If you have the time and equipment, it's really worth camping in the park. The area is a water catchment and a very delicate area, so if you camp within the Walls, take all of your waste out with you. The park is also exposed and subject to extremely harsh weather conditions, so you must be prepared for strong winds and snowfalls, even in summer. Walks across the park are described in *Cradle Mountain Lake St Clair and Walls of Jerusalem National Parks* by John Chapman & John Siseman, and in Lonely Planet's *Walking in Australia*.

If you prefer a guided walk, contact **Taswalks** *(☎ 6363 6112; Sorell St, Chudleigh)*, which varies the places it visits rather than running set trips. **Tasmanian Expeditions** *(☎ 6334 3477, 1800 030 230; W www.tas-ex.com)* has multi-day guided walks combining trips to the Walls of Jerusalem and Cradle Mountain.

Getting There & Away

Bus For buses on demand contact **Maxwells** *(☎ 6492 1431)*, who runs from Devonport to the Walls of Jerusalem ($40) and from Launceston to Cradle Mountain via the Walls of Jerusalem ($55). Prices quoted are per person for five or more passengers.

Car The quickest access to the Walls is from Sheffield or Mole Creek. From Mole Creek take the B12, then the C138 and finally the C171 (Mersey Forest Rd) to Lake Rowallan; remain on this road, following the 'C171' and/or 'Walls of Jerusalem' signs to the start of the track.

MOLE CREEK TO SHEFFIELD

From Mole Creek you'll pass through Paradise before arriving at a major T-intersection at which you must turn right to Sheffield or left to Gowrie Park and Cradle Mountain. If you have the time and don't intend travelling this way to Cradle Mountain later on, consider a loop through Gowrie Park and back along the eastern shore of Lake Barrington to Sheffield, instead of taking the more direct route suggested by the road sign. The views of Mt Roland alone make it a worthwhile detour, but there are also a number of attractions along the way that may be of interest to children.

Gowrie Park

Gowrie Park, 14km southwest of Sheffield, is a good place to stay if you intend to climb Mt Roland. It's also the site of a huge 94m-long mural on a Hydro Tasmania maintenance shed. There are walks to the summits of both Mt Roland and Mt Vandyke, and to Minnow Falls, as well as shorter walks in the cool, shady forests of the lower slopes.

Mt Roland This mountain looks like it would be extremely difficult to climb but is, in fact, graded as medium; that said, don't climb it in winter.

There are two access points. The first is at a place called Claude Rd, a short distance towards Gowrie Park from the T-junction at Paradise. To use this access, turn off at Kings Rd and head south for about 1.5km to the start of the Mt Roland Track, which is 6.5km long and takes 3½ hours. The other access point is at Gowrie Park itself, where you turn off the main road just near the sports ground and travel 2km to a gate, which is the start of a 10km track that takes four hours.

Places to Stay & Eat Well signposted off the main road is the very basic hostel-style accommodation at **Mt Roland Budget Backpackers** *(☎ 6491 1385, fax 6491 1848; 1447 Claude Rd; dorm beds $10)*. Adjacent to the backpackers and run by the same people are the four self-contained **Gowrie Park Wilderness Cabins** *(doubles $66)* and the rustic restaurant **Weindorfers** *(mains $10-23; open 10am-late daily Oct-May)*, which serves excellent hearty fare at reasonable prices and can cater to vegetarians and those with special diets (ring ahead to discuss your needs). Dinner bookings are essential.

Silver Ridge Retreat *(☎ 6491 1727, fax 6491 1925; Rysavy Rd, off C136; units $110-195, extra guests $20)*, 3km north of Gowrie Park, has wonderful Mt Roland views, a licensed restaurant and a heated indoor pool. It also has comfortable two-bedroom abodes, and activities such as bushwalking and bird-watching can be arranged.

Getting There & Away See the Getting There & Around section at the start of this chapter for details of the TassieLink service from Launceston to Gowrie Park.

THE NORTH

C140 & Lake Barrington

Approximately 6km down the road from Gowrie Park to Cradle Mountain, turn off onto the C140, which will take you north back towards Sheffield. From the southern end of this road, there are great views of Mt Roland, and 2km along the way you'll pass **Highland Trails Horse Riding** (☎ 6491 1533).

A further 1km north is **Cradle Vista** (☎ 6491 1129; W www.cradlevista.com.au; 978 Staverton Rd; singles $95, doubles $130-150), a 21-hectare farm offering B&B in a couple of en suite rooms in the main house and a large, open-plan unit. Besides hospitable, bright lodgings, this place also has fantastic views of the surrounding peaks, namely Mts Roland, Claude and Vandyke.

The Granary (☎ 6491 1689; W www.granary.com.au; 575 Staverton Rd; doubles $90-115, extra adults $30) has one- to four-bedroom self-contained timber cottages featuring windows produced in an on-site **stained-glass workshop**, which is open to the public when the owner feels like it. The kids will stay well amused in the enormous treehouse and by generally scampering around the property.

Down the road at Promised Land is the turn-off to Lake Barrington. Right beside the turn-off is **Tazmazia** (☎ 6491 1934; 500 Staverton Rd; adult/child $8/5; open 9am-5pm daily Sept-July), a complex of seven mazes that the owners claim is the largest of its kind in the world. The mazes vary in complexity and are entertaining, as is an extensive miniature village called Lower Crackpot. There's also a lavender farm and a large **pancake parlour** (pancakes $7-20; food service ends 4.30pm) with a huge range of sweet and savoury crepes – the biggest is called 'Wild Boar Loose in the Feedshed'.

On either side of **Lake Barrington** are steep, thickly forested slopes, which make this an attractive recreation area. The approach road from the turn-off near the maze leads to the section of the lake that has been marked out for international, national and state rowing championships. Other access roads lead to picnic areas and boat ramps.

Farther along the road is **Carinya Farm Accommodation** (☎ 6491 1593, fax 6491 1256; 63 Staverton Rd; singles/doubles $85/92), where you can get B&B (breakfast provisions) in one of two conjoined, pine-lined units, and lovely views of Mt Roland.

Wilmot

☎ 03 • postcode 7310

Wilmot, on the western side of Lake Barrington, is worth staying at if you're visiting Cradle Mountain and don't mind a drive.

Five kilometres north of Wilmot is the turn-off to **The Lake Tea Gardens** (☎ 6492 1394; Lake Barrington Rd; meals $6-9; open noon-4pm Sat-Thur Oct-Apr), a further 3km down a gravel side road in a highly scenic, garden-studded location beside Lake Barrington. Indulge in some home-made soup or milkshakes while sitting outside and gazing across at Mt Roland.

Also north of Wilmot is **Wilmot Hills Vineyard** (☎ 6492 1193; 407 Back Rd; open 9am-7pm daily), where you can taste fruit and table wines, and a dry cider.

Jaquie's (☎ 6492 1117; Cradle Mountain Rd; doubles $88), set in the 1893 Wilmot bakery, offers five nice rooms and a full cooked breakfast. It also has a **restaurant** (mains $15) with home-made Thai soups, chicken and desserts like sticky date pudding. Bookings are essential.

SHEFFIELD

☎ 03 • postcode 7306 • pop 1020

Sheffield became a tourist attraction over 15 years ago, when the first of the township's large, colourful murals was completed. This mural was so well received by visitors that another 29 have been daubed in town and a dozen in the surrounding district. (See the boxed text 'Alfresco Art', later, for more information.)

Information

The **visitors information centre** (☎ 6491 1036; Pioneer Crescent; open 10am-4pm daily) supplies information on the whole Sheffield region.

There's a multi-bank ATM in Slater's Country Store.

Kentish Museum

The Kentish Museum (☎ 6491 1861; 93 Main St; adult/child $4/1; open 10am-noon & 1pm-4pm Mon & Wed, 1pm-3pm Tues, Thur & Fri) has an interesting array of artefacts from the municipality's past, such as a 1948 Rural Automatic (telephone) Exchange, old organs, typewriters, photos and military and sports paraphernalia, much of it accompanied by posing mannequins. There's also a display on Gustav Weindorfer, the founder of Waldheim, near Cradle Mountain.

Steam Train

At the eastern end of town is **Redwater Creek Steam Rail** (☎ 6491 1613), which usually has locomotives running on a narrow track from 11am to 4pm over the first weekend of each month. At the time of writing it was being repaired, but was expected to be operational again by the beginning of 2003.

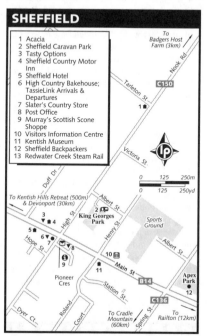

SHEFFIELD

1 Acacia
2 Sheffield Caravan Park
3 Tasty Options
4 Sheffield Country Motor Inn
5 Sheffield Hotel
6 High Country Bakehouse; TassieLink Arrivals & Departures
7 Slater's Country Store
8 Post Office
9 Murray's Scottish Scone Shoppe
10 Visitors Information Centre
11 Kentish Museum
12 Sheffield Backpackers
13 Redwater Creek Steam Rail

To Badgers Host Farm (3km)

Nook Rd

Tarleton St

C150

Victoria St

0   125   250m
0   125   250yd

To Kentish Hills Retreat (500m) & Devonport (30km)

Duff Dr

Albert St

High St

King Georges Park

Sports Ground

Henry St

Albert St

Hope St

Main St

Pioneer Cres

Apex Park

Station St

B14

Roland Court

Dyer Ct

Spring St

To Cradle Mountain (60km)

To Railton (12km)

C136

Special Events

On the Tasmanian Labor Day weekend (early March) each year Sheffield hosts a **Steamfest**, which includes displays of steam equipment, heritage games for children and stalls.

Places to Stay

Sheffield Caravan Park (unpowered/powered site doubles $11/16, on-site van doubles $35) is a small, patchy park behind the old town hall on Albert St. Bookings are made through Sheffield Backpackers.

Sheffield Backpackers (☎ 6491 2611; W www.sheffieldbackpackers.com.au; 82 Main St; dorm beds/twins $18/40) makes for great budget accommodation, with well-designed bunks, central heating, a large lounge and good kitchen facilities, plus a very relaxed atmosphere.

Sheffield Hotel (☎ 6491 1130; 38 Main St; singles/doubles from $35/45) has basic rooms with shared facilities and a nice feel. The hotel has counter lunches and dinners daily (mains $12 to $16), plus bar meals for around $6.

Sheffield Country Motor Inn (☎ 6491 1800, fax 6491 1966; 51-53 Main St; motel singles/doubles $65/70, unit doubles $85) has standard motel rooms and two self-contained units (one of them a large three-bedroom place).

Kentish Hills Retreat (☎ 6491 2484; e kentishhills@vision.net.au; 2 West Nook Rd; singles $75-100, doubles $90-140) has excellent accommodation in spacious modern units on the peaceful western edge of town.

Acacia (☎/fax 6491 2482; 113 High St; singles from $50, doubles $70-100), north of the town centre, is a 1910 home with three bedrooms and cooked breakfast; dinners can also be arranged.

There are a number of enticing rural accommodation options in the area around Sheffield – ask for details at the visitors information centre.

Badgers Host Farm (☎ 6491 1816, fax 6491 2488; 226 Nook Rd; doubles $110, extra adult/child $55/28) is a view-struck property with a three-bedroom suite, all meals and complementary farm animals. Follow High St northeast past Acacia for 3km and look for the gate on the right after Golf Course Rd.

Places to Eat

Murray's Scottish Scone Shoppe (☎ 6491 1077; 60 Main St; light meals $4-11; open 9am-5pm daily) sells home-made scones and other light fare, but it's also a shrine to Australian right-wing politics. It was established by former Queensland senator Flo Bjelke-Petersen, whose husband, Sir Joh, was for many years Queensland's highly controversial premier. It's now run by a former National Party politician who has adorned the walls with pictures of various political figures, such as the infamously anti-immigrant Pauline Hanson.

High Country Bakehouse (☎ 6491 1298; 44 Main St; open 6am-8pm Mon-Fri, 7am-8pm Sat & Sun) has lots of specialty pastries, cakes and bread.

Tasty Options (☎ 6491 1346; 47 Main St) is a modest, relaxed café open daily and selling lasagne, schnitzel, fish and chips and cheese platters, and breakfasts for less than $5. It also displays some local crafts.

Getting There & Away

See the Getting There & Around section at the start of this chapter for details of the TassieLink service to Sheffield from Launceston. TassieLink buses stop outside the bakery on the main street.

LATROBE

☎ 03 • postcode 7307 • pop 2770

Just 10km from Devonport, this historic town is often overlooked in favour of its larger neighbour, yet is of considerable interest. Founded in the 1830s, Latrobe was originally the region's port, with ships sailing up the Mersey River to its docks. It was also the location of the first ford across the river, and the discovery of coal nearby assured its development. It was named after Charles La Trobe, the first Lieutenant Governor of the state of Victoria. By 1889, when a railway line was established and the first hospital was opened, Latrobe was one of the state's largest towns.

The extension of the railway line and construction of a deep-water port at Devonport moved shipping business from Latrobe, though the town remained the business centre for the farming community. Today it's becoming subsumed by Devonport.

Alfresco Art

In the 1980s, a group of local townspeople got together to figure out a way of improving Sheffield's dour economic prospects, a meeting that led to the formation of the Kentish Association for Tourism Inc (KAT). One member of KAT had heard about a Canadian town called Chemainus that had painted itself with murals and thus begun to attract tourists, and suggested Sheffield adopt the same tactic. The association agreed and it hired artist John Lendis to paint Sheffield's first mural.

In December 1986, a mural called 'Stillness and Warmth', featuring Gustav Weindorfer of Cradle Mountain fame, was unveiled. It got the desired attention and so became the start of an endeavour by KAT to retell the history of the town through these colourful works of art.

Some murals, such as 'The Smithy at Work' and 'Early Trading at the Skin Shed', depict the early settlers, while others, such as 'Cradle Mountain Beauty' and 'Forth Falls', highlight the natural beauty that envelops the town. Murals also depict events, such as 'Mountain Rescue', which is a snapshot of Snr Constable Harry Clark's efforts to organise a helicopter rescue at Cradle Mountain in 1971. Still others are more esoteric, such as 'Masonic Lodge Symbols', a geometrically complicated image that only furtive Freemasons can understand.

More than 10 artists have been involved in the local mural painting, some taking their handiwork outside Sheffield to the sides of sheds and shops at nearby locales such as Railton, Gowrie Park, Roland and Moina. Sheffield has realised it's onto a good thing and now efficiently promotes itself as the 'town of murals', or Tasmania's 'outdoor art gallery'.

Information

The **Latrobe visitor information centre** (☎ 6426 2693; 70 Gilbert St) is in the Barclays Building. As it's volunteer-staffed, its opening hours are unpredictable.

Things to See

Warrawee Forest Reserve (gates open 9am-dusk) is a fantastic Mersey-side recreational area, its 2.3 sq km prepared by a local land-care group over a decade. It has public toilets and leisurely walks that include a 10-minute, wheelchair-accessible Pond Circuit, a 20-minute walk downstream to Farrell Park, and a one-hour return Forest Circuit. But the area's star attractions are its native flora and fauna, in particular the resident platypuses. **Platypus-spotting tours**, led by resident guides, are organised through Carnation Connection (☎ 6426 2877, after hours 6426 1774; 153 Gilbert St); bookings for the 1½- to two-hour tours should be made a day or two in advance, and usually cost around $10 per adult. Warrawee is 4.5km south of town down Hamilton St; turn off Gilbert St at the ANZ bank.

The town's history is depicted through the 600 prints and original architectural drawings on display in the **Court House Museum** (Gilbert St; adult/child $2/1; open 2pm-5pm Fri & Sun), next to the post office in the centre of town.

The **Australian Axeman's Hall of Fame** (Bells Parade) was the subject of ongoing development at the time of writing, and is ultimately intended to record (or perhaps create) legendary Australian woodchoppers.

Special Events

On Boxing Day, the town stages an annual bicycle race, the **Latrobe Wheel Race**, which attracts professional riders from all over Australia. Latrobe also hosts the **Henley-on-the-Mersey carnival**, held on Australia Day at Bells Parade, site of the town's former docks.

Places to Stay & Eat

Latrobe Motel (☎ 6426 2030; e latrobe motel@southcom.com.au; 1 Palmers Rd; singles/doubles $60/70) has roomy brick lodgings just off the Bass Hwy roundabout, opposite the hospital.

Lucas' Hotel (☎ 6426 1101, fax 6426 2546; 46 Gilbert St; doubles $90-110), a restored pub at the western end of Gilbert St, has very comfortable and well-maintained rooms; price includes continental breakfast, or a cooked breakfast for $10 extra per person. Its brasserie-style bistro (mains $11 to $20) is open for lunch and dinner daily, cooking up chicken stir-fry and polenta & vegetable stacks.

Lucinda (☎ 6426 2285; e lucindabnb@ ozemail.com.au; 17 Forth St; doubles $85-120) provides very nice B&B accommodation, including cooked breakfast. A couple of its heritage rooms have spectacular plasterwork, such as grand ceiling roses, or pressed-metal ceilings; one room has a spa.

Glo Glo's (☎ 6426 2120; 78 Gilbert St; mains $20-28; open from 6pm Mon-Sat) is a fine-dining establishment serving roast duck, marinated Lenah wallaby and various vegetarian selections; menu items are accompanied by wine suggestions.

Antonio's (☎ 6426 1069; 143 Gilbert St; meals $5-13; open 10.30am-3.30pm Thur, Fri & Sun-Tues, 10.30am-3.30pm & 6.30pm-9.30pm Sat) is a licensed café serving tapas, bruschetta, gourmet pies and desserts like Russian-baked cheesecake, in an invitingly bright interior. It was freshly opened at the time of research and its opening hours and menu were expected to change significantly once it had established itself.

PORT SORELL

☎ 03 • postcode 7307 • pop 1820

Just east of Devonport is the leisure conglomerate of Port Sorell, Shearwater and Hawley Beach, a triad of well-established holiday retreats and retirement villages on the shallow estuary of the Rubicon River. Named First Western River in 1805, this was the first area to be settled by Europeans on the northwest coast. In 1822 it was renamed Port Sorell, after the governor of the day. By the 1840s, it was the largest town on the coast and home to the region's police headquarters. However, with the development of

Latrobe, then later Devonport, the port declined and bush conquered much of the town.

The township is split into two sections by the flats of Poyston Creek. At Port Sorell are several islands in the estuary that can be reached at low tide – the flats are pretty muddy, so you'd be best to return before the tide rises. An alternative walk is to follow the track along the shoreline 6km north to Point Sorell, which takes around two hours return. Hawley Beach has sandy, sheltered swimming beaches.

Places to Stay & Eat

Port Sorell Lions Club Caravan Park (☎ 6428 7267, fax 6428 7269; 44 Meredith St; unpowered/powered site doubles $11/15) is a friendly camping ground with sites sprawled along the enticing waterfront.

Moomba Holiday & Caravan Park (☎ 6428 6140; 24 Kermode St; unpowered/powered site doubles $10/14, cabin doubles with/without en suite $46/30), is a friendly establishment with basic, well-kept cabins.

Appleby Creek Lodge (☎ 6428 7222; 55 Springfield Park; doubles $60) offers several cosy rooms, plus continental breakfast, in dreamily tranquil bush surrounds. Take the Appleby Rd turn-off 3km west of Port Sorell and then take the left turn to Springfield.

Shearwater Cottages (☎ 6428 6895, fax 6428 6895; 7-9 The Boulevard, Shearwater; singles/doubles $80/90) has a handful of self-contained suites that are eerily clean; this place is dirt's Bermuda Triangle.

Hawley House (☎ 6428 6221; ⓦ www .view.com.au/hawley; Hawley Esplanade; doubles from $155) is a nicely landscaped, peacock-laden retreat opposite a calm beach. It offers luxury accommodation in a white Gothic mansion – four-course gourmet dinners can be arranged from $45 per person.

The area's other digestive options are restricted to the various takeaways around town and the busy bistro at the **Shearwater Country Club** (☎ 6428 6205; Club Drive, Shearwater; mains $9-16; open noon-1.30pm & from 6pm daily).

DEVONPORT
☎ 03 • postcode 7310 • pop 22,300
Devonport is Tasmania's third-largest city. Originally there were two separate towns on either side of the Mersey River: Formby on the western side and Torquay to the east. But in 1890 they merged to become Devonport, although the old town of Torquay is still referred to by locals as East Devonport.

Following the name change and the extension of the railway to the town, Devonport took over from Latrobe as the region's port. Its flat land (a Tasmanian rarity) aided the town's growth. The dominant feature of the town is the lighthouse-topped Mersey Bluff, from where there are fine views of the coastline. The compact lighthouse was built in 1889 to aid navigation for the expanding port, which is still important today, handling much of the produce from northern Tasmania's agricultural areas.

For many visitors, the city is simply that bit of urbanity around the terminal for the two vehicular ferries that operate between Victoria and Tasmania, but in recent years the town has made much more of an effort to catch the attention of disembarkees, and it has a tempting array of waterside parks and reserves.

Information

The **Devonport visitors centre** (☎ 6424 8176; 92 Formby Rd) is open from 9am to 5pm daily.

For more information about Devonport and Tasmania in general, particularly on bushwalking and tours, head for the **Backpacker's Barn** (☎ 6424 3628; 10-12 Edward St; open 9am-6pm Mon-Fri, 9am-noon Sat). It has an excellent bushwalking shop with plenty of gear for sale or hire, and also handles accommodation, tour, car rental and bus bookings.

Most banks have branches and ATMs in or near the Rooke St Mall.

The **Online Access Centre** (☎ 6424 9413; 21 Oldaker St) is in the library. You can also get online at **Store 44** (☎ 6424 2131; 6 Stewart St) for $2/3 per 15/30 minutes, and at **Café Natur** (see Places to Eat later).

DEVONPORT

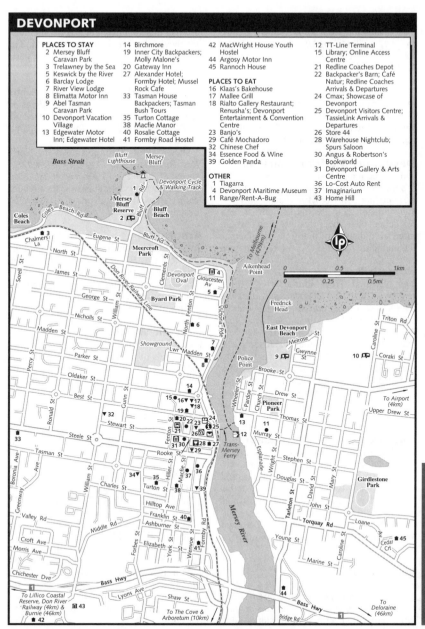

PLACES TO STAY
2 Mersey Bluff Caravan Park
3 Trelawney by the Sea
5 Keswick by the River
6 Barclay Lodge
7 River View Lodge
8 Elimatta Motor Inn
9 Abel Tasman Caravan Park
10 Devonport Vacation Village
13 Edgewater Motor Inn; Edgewater Hotel
14 Birchmore
19 Inner City Backpackers; Molly Malone's
20 Gateway Inn
27 Alexander Hotel; Formby Hotel; Mussel Rock Cafe
33 Tasman House Backpackers; Tasman Bush Tours
35 Turton Cottage
38 Macfie Manor
40 Rosalie Cottage
41 Formby Road Hostel
42 MacWright House Youth Hostel
44 Argosy Motor Inn
45 Rannoch House

PLACES TO EAT
16 Klaas's Bakehouse
17 Mallee Grill
18 Rialto Gallery Restaurant; Renusha's; Devonport Entertainment & Convention Centre
23 Banjo's
29 Café Mochadoro
32 Chinese Chef
34 Essence Food & Wine
39 Golden Panda

OTHER
1 Tiagarra
4 Devonport Maritime Museum
11 Range/Rent-A-Bug
12 TT-Line Terminal
15 Library; Online Access Centre
21 Redline Coaches Depot
22 Backpacker's Barn; Café Natur; Redline Coaches Arrivals & Departures
24 Cmax; Showcase of Devonport
25 Devonport Visitors Centre; TassieLink Arrivals & Departures
26 Store 44
28 Warehouse Nightclub; Spurs Saloon
30 Angus & Robertson's Bookworld
31 Devonport Gallery & Arts Centre
36 Lo-Cost Auto Rent
37 Imaginarium
43 Home Hill

Tiagarra

The **Tasmanian Aboriginal Culture Centre** (☎ 6424 8250; Bluff Rd; adult/child $3.30/2.20; open 9am-5pm daily), on the road to the lighthouse, is known as 'Tiagarra', the Tasmanian Aboriginal word for 'keep'. Set up to preserve the art and culture of Indigenous people, it has a rare collection of more than 250 rock engravings, some of which can be seen by following the marked trail on Mersey Bluff.

Devonport Maritime Museum

This excellent museum (☎ 6424 7100; Gloucester Ave; adult/child $3/1; open 10am-4.30pm Tues-Sun Oct-Mar, 10am-4pm Tues-Sun Apr-Sept) is in the old harbourmaster's residence near the foreshore and has an interesting display of maritime paraphernalia, including model ships both old and new.

Home Hill

The National Trust–administered Home Hill (☎ 6424 3028; 77 Middle Rd; adult/child $7.50/5.50; open noon-4pm Tues, Thur & Sat, 2pm-4pm Wed & Sun Jan-Apr; 2pm-4pm Tues-Thur & Sun, noon-4pm Sat May-Dec) was the former residence of Joseph and Dame Enid Lyons. Joseph Lyons is the only Australian to have been both a state premier and prime minister of Australia, and Dame Enid Lyons was the first woman to become a member of the House of Representatives and a cabinet minister.

Don River Railway & Museum

The Don River Railway (☎ 6424 6335; Bass Hwy; adult/child $8/5), 4km west of town, has lots of brightly coloured engines and carriages for kids to climb on. Diesel trains run Monday to Saturday and steam trains run on Sunday and public holidays – the trains leave on the hour between 10am and 4pm inclusive for 30-minute round trips alongside the Don River.

Imaginarium

The Imaginarium (☎ 6423 1466; 19-23 Macfie St; adult/child $7.50/5; open 10am-4pm Mon-Thur, noon-5pm Sat & Sun) is a large hall filled with simple, stand-alone interactive exhibits. It should occupy younger kids, but may not leave adults feeling they've had their money's worth. The main entrance is off the Wenvoe St car park.

Arts & Crafts

The **Devonport Gallery & Arts Centre** (☎ 6424 8296; 45-47 Stewart St; admission free; open 10am-5pm Mon-Sat, 2pm-5pm Sun) has a collection of Tasmanian paintings, ceramics and glasswork.

Showcase of Devonport hosts the North West Regional Craft Centre (☎ 6424 1287; 11 Best St; open 9am-5.30pm Mon-Sat, 2pm-6pm Sun), where you can browse the timbers, leathers, jewellery and prints of over 250 local artists.

Arboretum

Ten kilometres south of the city, beside the Don River at Eugenana, is the Tasmanian Arboretum (admission by donation; open 9am-dusk daily), founded 20 years ago and featuring various native and exotic trees and shrubs.

Penguin-Watching

From December to February, the comings and goings of a local fairy penguin colony can be observed at dusk from a special viewing area at Lillico Coastal Reserve, just off the Bass Hwy on the western edge of town.

Organised Tours

Tasman Bush Tours (☎ 6423 2335; W www .tasmanbushtours.com; 114 Tasman St), operating out of Tasman House Backpackers, offers guided walks along the Overland Track (see the Cradle Mountain-Lake St Clair section of The West chapter for details).

Sheffield Minibus Charters (☎ 6491 2530, 0409 208 134) conducts day tours taking in destinations like Sheffield, Mole Creek and Cradle Mountain. A minimum of three people is required and the per-head costs starts at $55 (entry fees not included).

You can charter a plane from **Tasair** (☎ 6427 9777; W www.tasair.com.au) for flights from Devonport over Cradle Mountain and the surrounding areas for $250 per hour.

Places to Stay – Budget

Camping & Cabins The **Mersey Bluff Caravan Park** (☎ 6424 8655, fax 6424 8657; Bluff Rd; unpowered/powered site doubles $14/17, on-site van doubles $40, cabin doubles $55) is a pleasant park with some good beaches nearby.

Abel Tasman Caravan Park (☎ 6427 8794, fax 6428 2687; 6 Wright St; unpowered/powered site doubles $12/16, on-site van doubles $39, cabin doubles $65) has a good beachfront location in East Devonport.

Devonport Vacation Village (☎ 6427 8886, fax 6427 8388; 20-24 Nth Caroline St; unpowered/powered site doubles $14/18, cabin doubles $50-75) is another budget East Devonport option.

Hostels Above Molly Malone's Irish pub is **Inner City Backpackers** (☎ 6424 1898, fax 6424 7720; 34 Best St; dorm beds $14), centrally located and with clean, basic four-bed dorms, a lounge and laundry facilities.

MacWright House (☎ 6424 5696; 115 Middle Rd; dorm beds/singles $13/19) is Devonport's YHA hostel, with simple, clean accommodation. It's 3km from the city centre, about a 40-minute walk or a five-minute bus ride (No 40).

Tasman House Backpackers (☎ 6423 2335; W www.tasmanhouse.com; 114 Tasman St; dorm beds/doubles $12/30) is a sprawling independent hostel in the converted nurses quarters of the old regional hospital. It's a 15-minute walk from town or transport can be arranged when booking.

Formby Road Hostel (☎ 6423 6563; 16 Formby Rd; dorm beds/doubles $16/36) is set in a classic, century-old, high-ceilinged house several blocks from the highway, and offers decent facilities, tour information and a peaceful atmosphere. Double rooms have a TV and fridge.

Hotels A good central place is **Alexander Hotel** (☎ 6424 2252; 78 Formby Rd; singles/doubles $30/40), which has rooms with shared facilities plus continental breakfast (a cooked breakfast is $8 extra).

Formby Hotel (☎ 6424 1601, fax 6424 8123; 82 Formby Rd; singles/doubles $30/55)

has straightforward singles with shared facilities and doubles with en suites; continental breakfast is just $10.

Places to Stay – Mid-Range

B&Bs The foreshore-situated **River View Lodge** (☎ 6424 7357; e riverviewlodge@ microtech.com.au; 18 Victoria Parade; singles with/without bathroom $65/50, doubles with/without bathroom $85/60) is a friendly, old-fashioned timber place opposite a strip of picnic table–dotted greenery.

Motels There are quite a number of ultra-plain motels in the city centre and East Devonport.

Elimatta Motor Inn (☎ 6424 6555; 15 Victoria Parade; singles/doubles $55/65) has ordinary but cheap motel-style rooms and is an easy walk from the city centre.

Barclay Lodge (☎ 6424 4722, 1800 809 340; 112 Nth Fenton St; rooms $75-130) is a scattering of brick motel suites and apartments with odd-looking roofs; one unit is equipped for disabled travellers.

Edgewater Motor Inn (☎ 6427 8441, fax 6427 8290; 2 Thomas St; singles/doubles $50/60) eschews an attractive appearance for a convenient location near the ferry terminal.

Argosy Motor Inn (☎ 6427 8872, 1800 657 068; Tarleton St; singles $80-110, doubles $85-116) has a dowdy exterior and rooms ranging from standard to 'executive' suites with spa.

Places to Stay – Top End

Guesthouses & B&Bs Offering B&B close to the city centre is **Macfie Manor** (☎ 6424 1719, fax 6424 8766; 44 Macfie St; singles $85, doubles $95-110), a beautiful two-storey Federation building.

Birchmore (☎ 6423 1336; 8-10 Oldaker St; singles/doubles from $100/105) is an attractive, double-storey red-brick place on the edge of the town centre; rooms come with cooked breakfast.

Keswick by the River (☎ 6424 3745; e elaine@southcom.com.au; 2 James St; rooms $100-110) looks a tad suburban but it has a great garden and a fully self-contained unit with breakfast provisions.

Trelawney by the Sea *(☎/fax 6424 3263; 6 Chalmers Lane; rooms $90-110)* has an overdose of timber panelling, but also has great views beyond Coles Beach and use of an outdoor spa.

Rannoch House *(☎ 6427 9818; W www .heritagebandb.com/rannoch/entry.html; 5 Cedar Court; singles/doubles $90/110)* is a peaceful Federation-style place on landscaped grounds in East Devonport. Rates include cooked breakfast.

Motels There are very well-appointed rooms at the tidy, efficient **Gateway Inn** *(☎ 6424 4922; 16 Fenton St; rooms $100-150)*, located right in the city centre.

Cottages Both **Rosalie Cottage** *(66 Wenvoe St)* and **Turton Cottage** *(28 Turton St)* are managed by **Devonport Historic Cottages** *(☎ 6424 1560, fax 6424 2090)* and can be rented for between $140 and $150 per double, with breakfast provisions and log fires to doze in front of. Extra touches include an old gramophone in Rosalie and hand-stencilled walls in Turton.

Places to Eat

Restaurants For prompt platefuls of pasta, try the **Rialto Gallery Restaurant** *(☎ 6424 6793; 159 Rooke St; mains from $15; open noon-2pm & from 6pm Mon-Fri, from 6pm Sat & Sun)*.

Chinese Chef *(☎ 6424 7306; 132 William St; mains around $8; open noon-2pm & 5pm-10pm Mon-Thur, noon-2pm & 5pm-11pm Fri & Sat, 5pm-10pm Sun)* serves cheap Chinese meals, like a $6 two-course lunch special.

Golden Panda *(☎ 6424 9066; 38-39 Formby Rd; mains $10-17; open noon-2pm & from 5pm Tues-Fri, from 5pm Sat-Mon)* has Chinese dishes like chilli calamari, and braised broccoli with crab-meat sauce.

Renusha's *(☎ 6424 2293; 153 Rooke St; mains from $15; open from 5.30pm daily)* is a BYO Indian restaurant with eat-in or takeaway food, including chicken, lamb and vegetarian choices.

Mallee Grill *(☎ 6424 4477; 161 Rooke St; mains $12-24; open noon-2pm & from 6pm* *Mon-Fri, from 6pm Sat & Sun)* has some seafood and gourmet sausages, but steak claims most of the menu; the biggest feed is the mixed charcoal grill.

Essence Food & Wine *(☎ 6424 6431; 28 Forbes St; mains $18-23; open noon-2.30pm & from 6pm Tues-Fri, from 6pm Sat)* is a licensed restaurant and wine bar (bar open 5.30pm) with upmarket contemporary cuisine.

The Cove *(☎ 6424 6200; 17 Devonport Rd; mains $14-29; open noon-late daily)*, south of town off the road to Spreyton, is a modern waterfront restaurant with great, varied meals like sushi and sashimi plates and thyme venison with Guinness compote. There's a glossary of terms on the dinner menu if you don't know your wasabi from your tapanade.

Cafés & Takeaways A large selection of breakfasts, burgers, focaccias and meaty mains, plus tapas, is available at the licensed, roomy **Café Mochadoro** *(☎ 6424 2932; 12-14 Rooke St; lunch $8-15; open 8.30am-5.30pm Mon-Thur, 8.30am-8pm Fri)*. It also stages art exhibitions and live music.

Café Natur *(☎ 6424 1917; 10-12 Edward St; lunch $5-8; open 9.30am-4.30pm Mon-Fri, 9.30am-2pm Sat)*, at the front of the Backpacker's Barn, does fresh, healthy burgers, salads, focaccias and soups, including vegan and gluten-free meals. There's also a selection of organic and biodynamic fruit, vegetables and grains.

Banjo's *(☎ 6421 6466; 40 Rooke St; open 6am-6pm daily)* has plenty of mass-produced bakery fare.

Klaas's Bakehouse *(☎ 6424 8866; 11 Oldaker St; open Mon-Fri)* has excellent cakes and pastries.

Pub Meals Most hotels have good counter meals for between $10 and $20, such as **Alexander Hotel** *(☎ 6424 2252; 78 Formby Rd)*, which mixes pub standards with turkey filo, and roast vegetable lasagne.

Mussel Rock Cafe *(☎ 6424 1601; 82 Formby Rd; mains $11-19)*, in the Formby Hotel, piles on grills, roasts and pasta.

Edgewater Hotel *(☎ 6427 8443; 4 Thomas St; mains $9-17; open lunch & dinner daily)* serves cheap counter meals like seafood kebabs and 'volcano steak'.

Molly Malone's (☎ 6424 1898; 34 Best St; mains $10-18; open daily) has a bistro, with plenty of fish, roasts, stews and grills.

Entertainment

Check the *Advocate* newspaper for entertainment listings. Most pubs have free bands one or two nights a week, usually rock and blues.

Warehouse Nightclub (☎ 6424 7851; 18 King St; admission $6-10; open 10pm-late Fri & Sat) is one of the local clubbing hangouts; King St hosts a couple of these venues.

Spurs Saloon (☎ 6424 7851; 18 King St; open 5pm-late Wed-Sat) fronts the Warehouse and, judging by its name, hankers for another era on another continent, but it will still quench your thirst.

Molly Malone's (☎ 6424 1898; 34 Best St) is an expansive, wood-panelled Irish pub that gets big crowds guzzling its beer and watching free bands on Friday and Saturday nights.

Cmax cinema (☎ 6420 2111; 5-7 Best St; adult/child $11.50/8.50) hosts blockbusters and teen flicks.

Devonport Entertainment & Convention Centre (☎ 6420 2900; 145-151 Rooke St; box office open 10am-4pm Mon-Fri) stages everything from children's concerts to ABBA impersonators.

Getting There & Away

Air For information on domestic flights to/from Devonport, see the Getting There & Away and Getting Around chapters earlier in this book. There are regular flights to/from Melbourne with Qantas and Regional Express, while Tasair flies between Devonport and King Island via Burnie/Wynyard.

Bus See the Getting There & Around section at the start of this chapter for details of Redline services from Launceston to Devonport and on to Burnie (for details of a route further west from Burnie to Smithton, see the Getting There & Around section at the start of The Northwest chapter). Also see this section for details of the TassieLink

services that run disembarked ferry passengers to Launceston, Hobart and Burnie, and that deliver embarking passengers from Strahan/Queenstown and Hobart. TassieLink also runs from Launceston to Devonport (drop-off only) and then via Sheffield to Cradle Mountain (for details of a route further west from Cradle Mountain to Strahan, see the Getting There & Around section at the start of The West chapter).

Redline buses arrive at and depart from opposite the Backpacker's Barn, while TassieLink coaches pull up outside the Devonport visitors centre.

If none of the scheduled services suit your particular bushwalking needs, charter a minibus from **Maxwells** (☎ 6492 1431) or the Backpacker's Barn. For example, if you hire a Maxwells bus from Devonport to Cradle Mountain, it will cost $140 for one to four people and $35 for each extra person.

Car Devonport has plenty of cheap car-rental firms, such as **Range/Rent-a-Bug** (☎ 6427 9034; 5 Murray St) and **Lo-Cost Auto Rent** (☎ 6424 9922, 1800 802 724; Formby Rd), where high-season rates for older cars start at $35. **Budget** (☎ 6427 0650, 13 27 27) and **Thrifty** (☎ 6427 9119, 1800 030 730) have representatives at the airport and ferry terminal, and hire out everything from new cars to old petrol guzzlers.

Boat See the Getting There & Away chapter at the beginning of this book for details of the *Spirit of Tasmania* ferry services between Melbourne and Devonport. A high-speed ferry leaves Devonport at 9pm nightly year-round, while another arrives daily at 7am; extra services are scheduled over summer. The **TT-Line ferry terminal** (☎ 13 20 10) is on the Esplanade in East Devonport.

Getting Around

The airport is 5km east of town. **Topline Coaches** (☎ 6424 6333) runs a twice-daily airport shuttle on weekdays only (not on public holidays) for $10, with stops at the Devonport visitors centre and the Backpacker's Barn. Alternatively, a **taxi** (☎ 6424 1431) will cost $12 to $15.

Local buses operated by **Merseylink** (☎ 1300 367 590) run from Monday to Saturday. Merseylink also runs a **shuttle** (☎ 0409 006 013) between hostels and ferry.

A small ferry departs from opposite the post office, docking on the eastern side of the river beside the ferry terminal. It runs on demand from around 9am to 5pm Monday to Saturday ($1.70 one way).

FORTH
☎ 03 • postcode 7310 • pop 345

This tiny town off the highway 10km west of Devonport, self-titled the 'Village by the River', is worth driving through just because it's so pretty. It also has a fine up-market B&B called **Ochill Manor** (☎ 6428 2660, fax 6428 2330; 27 Old Kindred Rd; singles/doubles from $110/140) – this fine Victorian place is on a hill at the northern edge of town and has its extensive gardens, plus a grand view to the mouth of the Forth.

ULVERSTONE
☎ 03 • postcode 7315 • pop 9780

Ulverstone, at the mouth of the River Leven, is a relaxed, uncommercial base from which to explore the surrounding area. The town's main features are spacious parklands and several war memorials, the most impressive being the clock-topped **Shrine of Remembrance**, built in 1953 and incorporating an older WWI memorial.

The **visitors information centre** (☎ 6425 2839; Car Park Lane; open 9.15am-3.30pm Mon-Fri, 10am-3pm Sat & Sun) can be reached via an arcade from Reibey St. As it's staffed by volunteers, its weekend opening hours can vary. Inside are some public toilets, and there are public telephones nearby. Public Internet access is available at the **Online Access Centre** (☎ 6425 7579; 15 King Edward St), in the local library.

The **Ulverstone Local History Museum** (☎ 6425 3835; 50 Main St; entry by gold-coin donation; open 1.30pm-4.30pm Tues, Thur, Sat & Sun) concentrates on the area's early farmers, displaying their tools, manuscripts and assorted artefacts behind its mock-pioneer facade.

See the Burnie Rail entry in the Burnie section of The Northwest chapter for details of a **historic train** service running between Burnie, Penguin and Ulverstone.

Places to Stay – Budget
Camping Right off Picnic Point Beach on the western side of the Leven River mouth is **Apex Caravan Park** (☎ 6425 2935; Queen St; unpowered/powered site doubles $11/14).

Ulverstone Caravan Park (☎ 6425 2624, fax 6425 4654; 57 Water St; unpowered/powered site doubles $14/16, on-site van doubles $40, 3-bunk cabins $60, units from $65), near the water and the town centre, has playgrounds and adjoining parkland.

Places to Stay – Mid-Range
Hotels & Motels You'll find decent-standard en suite rooms at **Furners Hotel** (☎ 6425 1488, fax 6425 5933; 42 Reibey St; singles/doubles $60/80).

Bass & Flinders Motor Inn (☎ 6425 3011; 49-51 Eastland Dr; doubles from $100, extra guests $12) has one- to three-bedroom brick units, some with kitchen facilities.

Beachway Motel (☎ 6425 2342, fax 6425 5798; Heathcote St; singles/doubles from $55/62) has lots of motel rooms around a large, foliage-filled court.

Waterfront Inn (☎ 6425 1599; Tasma Parade; singles $55, doubles $55-95), across the River Leven from the town centre, has a crowd of economical waterfront rooms.

Self-Contained Units The collection of generic modern units at **Willaway Motel Apartments** (☎ 6425 2018; ⒲ www.will away.southcom.com.au; 2 Tucker St; singles $70-90, doubles $80-100) are opposite a nice stretch of lawn with barbecue facilities.

Places to Stay – Top End
Hotels There are large and comfortable rooms at **Lighthouse Hotel** (☎ 6425 1197; 33 Victoria St; doubles from $95-205), which has a good feel to it, due in part to its large atrium space.

Guesthouses & B&Bs If you're looking for well-appointed, heritage-style rooms (one suite is equipped for disabled travellers) try **Ocean View Guesthouse** (☎/fax 6425 5401; 1-3 Victoria St; singles $75-130, doubles $100-150), which is 100m from the beach and an easy walk from the town centre. You can choose a standard en suite room or pay a bit more for a spa suite; prices include cooked breakfast.

Boscobel (☎/fax 6425 1727; W www .boscobel.com.au; 27 South Rd; doubles $110-160) supplies luxurious accommodation in the formal surroundings of a 19th-century home. Prices include cooked breakfast and use of a heated indoor pool.

Westella House (☎ 6425 6222; e westella@westella.com; 68 Westella Dr; singles/doubles from $90/125), close to the highway towards the east of town, is a spacious, National Trust–listed and colonially furnished house with a distinctive Gothic roof. The very comfortable rooms come with cooked breakfast.

Places to Eat
Pedro's the Restaurant (☎ 6425 6663; Wharf Rd; mains $18-25; open noon-2.30pm & from 6pm daily) is an appealing waterfront restaurant specialising in upmarket seafood

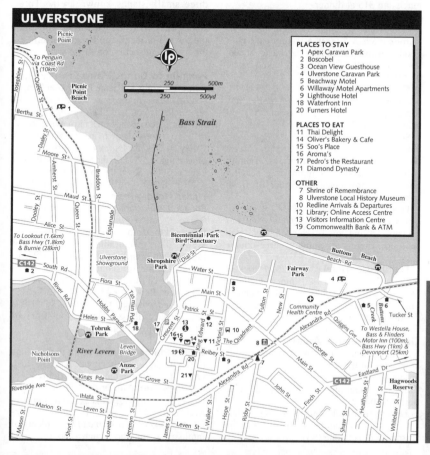

ULVERSTONE

PLACES TO STAY
1 Apex Caravan Park
2 Boscobel
3 Ocean View Guesthouse
4 Ulverstone Caravan Park
5 Beachway Motel
6 Willaway Motel Apartments
1 Lighthouse Hotel
18 Waterfront Inn
20 Furners Hotel

PLACES TO EAT
11 Thai Delight
14 Oliver's Bakery & Cafe
15 Soo's Place
16 Aroma's
17 Pedro's the Restaurant
21 Diamond Dynasty

OTHER
7 Shrine of Remembrance
8 Ulverstone Local History Museum
10 Redline Arrivals & Departures
12 Library; Online Access Centre
13 Visitors Information Centre
19 Commonwealth Bank & ATM

THE NORTH

dishes, but with other meat and vegetarian meals too. Next door is **Pedro's Takeaway** (☎ 6425 5181; open 11am-8pm daily).

Thai Delight (☎ 6425 3055; 25 King Edward St; mains from $9; open 11.30am-2pm & 5pm-9.30pm Wed-Fri, 5pm-9.30pm Sat & Sun) is a BYO restaurant/takeaway that serves great soups and vegetarian versions of most of the meaty mains. It's highly recommended.

Diamond Dynasty (☎ 6425 4045; 48-52 King Edward St; open noon-2pm & 5pm-late Tues-Fri, 5pm-late Sat-Mon) has all-you-can-munch Chinese smorgasbords for $7.50 at lunch and $15 at dinner.

Aroma's (☎ 6425 2051; 23 Reibey St; light meals $5-9; open 8am-5pm Mon-Fri, 8am-4pm Sat & Sun) is a bakery/café with good, cheap light meals and basic breakfasts such as the fundamental baked beans on toast.

Oliver's Bakery & Cafe (☎ 6425 4118; 41 Reibey St; open 6am-6pm daily) has focaccias and croissants for around $5, and heaps of other baked fare.

Soo's Place (☎ 6425 6619; 31 Reibey St; lunch $5-11; open 9.30am-4pm Mon & Tues, 9am-4.30pm Wed-Fri) is a bright, friendly café on Ulverstone's main drag serving gourmet sandwiches, a variety of fresh salads and lots more.

Furners Hotel (☎ 6425 1488; 42 Reibey St; mains $13-19; open lunch & dinner daily) has a bistro serving lots of chicken, steak and seafood; there's a Sunday three-course carvery for $15.

Lighthouse Hotel (☎ 6425 1197; 33 Victoria St; mains $16-20; lunch & dinner Mon-Sat, lunch Sun) has a similar menu to Furners Hotel, but with additional pasta and risotto selections.

Getting There & Away

See the Getting There & Around section at the start of this chapter. Redline Coaches arrive at and depart from outside Victoria St Collectibles, where you can also purchase tickets.

During the week, **Metro** (☎ 6431 3822, 13 22 01) has regular local buses from Burnie to Ulverstone ($3).

AROUND ULVERSTONE
Gunns Plains Scenic Circuit (B17)

☎ 03 • postcode (Gunns Plains) 7315

If you're staying in Ulverstone for a couple of days and have your own transport, consider spending a day doing this circuit, particularly if you have children with you. Or better still, stay overnight at one of the many accommodation options along the way.

Begin by driving to Penguin along the **Old Bass Hwy**, a narrow, winding road that follows the coast and offers attractive views of the shores around Penguin Point. The three small islands known as the **Three Sisters** are particularly scenic, and there are some pretty roadside gardens as you enter the town. For details on Penguin itself, see the upcoming section on the town.

Penguin to Gunns Plains From Penguin, follow the signs to Riana. In the **Dial Range**, behind the town, there are some good walking tracks. If you feel like overnighting in a self-contained cottage on a farm, with breakfast provisions thrown in, try **Watercress Valley** (☎ 6437 1145, fax 6437 1308; Browns Lane; doubles $70-80); the turn-off to Browns Lane is 500m down the road to Riana.

Near Riana you'll see the turn-off to **Pindari Holiday Farm** (☎ 6437 6171; Wyllies Rd; adult/child/family $4/3/10; open 10am-5pm Sat, Sun & public holidays), a hilltop farm 17km from Penguin with sweeping views. The restaurant here serves light lunches and dinners by appointment. There are also some self-contained, wheelchair-accessible cabins (doubles $115 to $135).

Pioneer Park (☎ 6437 6137, 6437 6129; unpowered/powered site doubles $6/9) is a large, peaceful park on the outskirts of Riana, towards Gunns Plains.

Gunns Plains The drive down to the plains is picturesque, with views over the lush valley and some extensive hop fields.

Wing's Farm Park (☎ 6429 1335; e wfp@tassie.net.au; 137 Winduss St; admission farm adult/child $4/3, farm & reptile centre $8.50/5; open 10am-4pm daily) has plenty of family rural attractions such as domesticated deer and ostriches, bushwalks, trout in the nearby Leven River, and an animal nursery. A reptile centre features some tortoises and snakes, and pretend reptiles in the shapes of quolls, bandicoots and a confiscated axolotl. **Accommodation** *(camping adult/child $4.40/ 3.30, backpackers singles/doubles $14/20, cabins $60-75)* is also available, as are light meals at Nan's Tearooms.

Gunns Plains Caves *(☎ 6439 1388; adult/child $8/4; open 10am-4pm daily)*, 32km from Penguin and 25km from Ulverstone, are captivating limestone caves that make for an entertaining guided exploration.

From the caves, return to the turn-off on the main road. From here continue the circuit back to Ulverstone or take the C127 to the C125, which will lead you to Leven Canyon. On the C127 you'll find **Moonrakers** *(☎ 6429 1186; 321 Raymond Rd; open 9am-5pm daily)*, a small, commendable vineyard producing pinot noir and a fruity chardonnay, and displaying woodturning, pottery and prints from a triad of local artists.

Leven Canyon

On the southern side of Gunns Plains, the River Leven emerges from a deep gorge. To view the gorge, follow roads through Nietta to the **Leven Canyon Lookout**, 41km from Ulverstone. A 15-minute track leads to the sensational gorge-top lookout – driving beyond the car park turn-off takes you to the canyon floor. You can walk through the gorge but this takes at least 10 hours and is not recommended. Better nearby day walks lead to **Winterbrook Falls** (four hours return) or to **Black Bluff** (six hours return).

There are several smaller waterfalls around Upper Castra and Nietta, and Cradle Mountain is only a short drive away. Be warned that the road linking Upper Castra to Wilmot crosses a deep river gorge and is very steep; don't use it in very wet weather or with low-powered vehicles.

There's B&B accommodation in garden surrounds at **Kaydale Lodge** *(☎ 6429 1293; 250 Loongana Rd, Nietta; singles/doubles $60/100)*, with rooms upstairs in a modern, timber-lined home. Teas and lunches are served here daily.

Penguin

☎ 03 • postcode 7316 • pop 3050

This is a pretty little seaside town, though the large, emphatic ferro-concrete penguin standing on the foreshore and the smaller artificial penguins adorning rubbish bins along the main street stretch the aesthetic credibility of the place.

Penguin has a well-stocked **visitor information centre** *(☎ 6437 1421; 78 Main Rd; open 9am-4pm daily Oct-Mar, 9.30am-3.30pm daily Apr-Sept)*. Here you'll find a brochure detailing a self-guided walk around this town, which was established in 1875.

Real penguins still appear around dusk each day from September to March at **Penguin Point** and can be seen via a 1½-hour **tour** *(☎ 6437 2590)* running Sunday to Friday. Tours are $10 for adults and $5 for children. **Hiscutt Park**, beside Penguin Creek, has good playground equipment and a scaled-down working **Dutch windmill** – in September, the tulip display surrounding the 'Wipmolen' mill adds a touch of brightness.

On Johnson's Beach Road, near the caravan park, is a **miniature railway** *(rides $1; open 1pm-4pm)* that operates on the second and fourth Sunday of each month, when the popular, 150-stall **Penguin Old School Market** *(open 9am-3.30pm)* takes place. For details of a life-size **historic train** that visits Penguin, see the Burnie Rail entry in the Burnie section of The Northwest chapter.

There's low-cost accommodation at **Penguin Caravan Park** *(☎ 6432 2785; Johnson's Beach Rd; unpowered/powered site doubles $11/16, cabin doubles $45)*. The beachside **Monty's** *(☎ 6437 2080; Johnson's Beach Rd; mains $9-22; open 10am-4pm daily)* serves everything from focaccias and bouillabaisse to Cajun ocean trout. Dinner is available by reservation only.

Getting There & Away See the Getting There & Around section at the start of this chapter.

During the week, **Metro** *(☎ 6431 3822, 13 22 01)* runs regular local buses from Burnie to Penguin ($3).

The Northwest

Tasmania's magnificent northwest coast is as rich in history as it is diverse in scenery. Its story stretches back 35,000 years to when giant kangaroos and wombats were not yet extinct, and Aboriginal tribes took shelter in the caves along the coast, where they left a remarkable legacy of rock engravings and middens.

Europeans quickly realised the region's potential and, after violently dispossessing its Indigenous people, built towns along the coast and inland on the many rivers. Originally heavily forested, the area was cleared and soon transformed into a vital part of the colony's developing economy. Today it's a major producer of frozen vegetables and potatoes for Australia.

Along the coast are some impressive headlands providing spectacular views. From the north across to the Queenstown region the scenery is great and there are few towns. The enormous wild area between the Arthur and Pieman Rivers is known as the Tarkine Wilderness and it was here that conservationists fought a protracted and ultimately unsuccessful battle a decade ago to prevent the upgrading of the track between Corinna and Balfour. The resulting road, the C249, now forms part of what was christened the Western Explorer (see the Western Explorer & Arthur Pieman Conservation Area section later in this chapter), a mostly rough route from the west coast to Smithton. If you're using this road, see the Corinna & Pieman River section later in this chapter for information about the vehicular ferry across the Pieman River.

The other important road in the area is the CI32 from the Murchison Hwy (A10) through to Cradle Mountain Lodge. This link road enables vehicles to travel directly from Devonport to Queenstown, thereby avoiding the northwest coast altogether. However, if you have time it's far better to follow the older, slower roads that pass through this interesting region.

Highlights

- Cruising on the wide, forested Arthur and Pieman Rivers
- Savouring the quiet charm of Stanley
- Surfing the big swells at Marrawah
- Swimming in the crystal-blue waters at Boat Harbour Beach
- Rattling through the Tarkine Wilderness on the road to nowhere

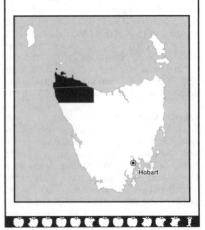

Getting There & Around

Air The airport for the region is in Wynyard, and is known as both Wynyard and Burnie airport (we refer to it as 'Burnie/Wynyard airport'). See Getting There & Away in the Wynyard section later for details of airlines servicing the northwest.

Bus Several **Redline Coaches** (☎ 6336 1446, 1300 360 000; **w** www.tasredline .com.au) run daily from Hobart to Launceston ($23.50 one way, 2½ hours) – these usually connect with a service running from Launceston along the north coast to Devonport ($16.50, one to 1½ hours) and Burnie

($22, two to 2½ hours). From Burnie, Redline runs two times each weekday (three times on Friday) to Wynyard ($3.10, 20 minutes), the Boat Harbour turn-off ($5.50, 30 minutes), the Rocky Cape turn-off ($7.50, 40 minutes), Stanley ($13, one hour) and Smithton ($13, 1½ hours). It also services Deloraine ($8.20, 45 minutes).

TassieLink (☎ *6272 7300, 1300 300 520;* W *www.tigerline.com.au)* runs a Wednesday and Friday service from Devonport's ferry terminal to Burnie (one hour), with onward connections to Tullah ($22.20, 2¼ hours), Rosebery ($23.80, 2½ hours), Zeehan ($30, three hours), Queenstown ($37.10, 3¾ hours) and Strahan ($44.10, 4¾ hours).

BURNIE
☎ 03 • postcode 7320 • pop 19,140

Burnie, Tasmania's fourth-largest city, sits on the shores of Emu Bay – its deepwater port has led to cargo shipping becoming an important part its economy. Due to decades of heavy industry, Burnie acquired (not unreasonably) a reputation as a city dominated by industrial emissions, water pollution and other unhealthy and anti-aesthetic features. But in recent years Burnie has cleaned up its act considerably, particularly along the foreshore, and, assisted by various new attractions and the odd nearby glade, has developed a much more appealing coastal atmosphere.

The town was named after William Burnie, a director of the Van Diemen's Land Company (VDL). It started life as a potato-growing centre but changed careers when tin was discovered on Mt Bischoff at Waratah 40 years later. In 1878 VDL opened a wooden tramway between the Waratah mine and the port of Burnie, the humble beginning of the important Emu Bay Railway that linked the port to the rich silver fields of Zeehan and Rosebery in the 1900s. The Emu Bay Railway still transports ore from the west coast, travelling through some wild

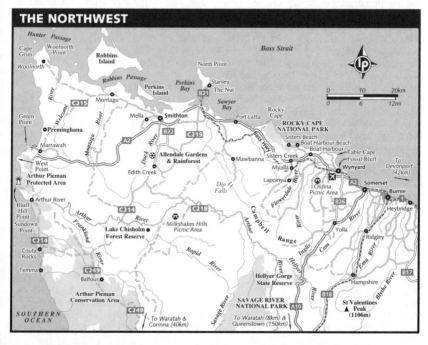

THE NORTHWEST

and impressive country on the way. Unfortunately it doesn't carry passengers, but depending how the Abt Wilderness Railway fares, that may just change down the track.

Information

The **Burnie Travel & Information Centre** (☎ 6434 6111; Little Alexander St; open 9am-5pm Mon-Fri, 1.30pm-4.30pm Sat & Sun Mar-Nov; 9am-5pm Mon-Fri, 10.30am-4.30pm Sat, 1.30pm-4.30pm Sun Dec-Feb), in the same building as the Pioneer Village Museum, has plenty of information on Tasmania's northwest and Burnie itself.

Internet access is available at the **Burnie Online Access Centre** (☎ 6431 9469; 2 Spring St). For medical treatment, you'll find **North-West Regional Hospital** (☎ 6430 6666; Brickport Rd) a few minutes west of the city centre: take Brickport Rd off the Bass Hwy just east of the suburb of Cooee. **Wilkinson's Pharmacy** (Chemmart; ☎ 6431 1233; 16 Wilson St; open 9am-9pm daily) is the main pharmacy in the city centre.

Pioneer Village Museum

This absorbing museum (☎ 6430 5746; Little Alexander St; adult/child $6/2.50; open 9am-5pm Mon-Fri, 1.30pm-4.30pm Sat & Sun), next to the Civic Plaza shopping centre, is an authentic indoor re-creation of a village street circa 1900. It includes a blacksmith, printer, wash house, stage coach depot and bootmaker, and should keep the attention of kids with over 30,000 items on display.

Burnie Regional Art Gallery

The Burnie Regional Art Gallery (☎ 6431 5918; Wilmot St; admission free; open 9am-5pm Mon-Fri, 1.30pm-4.30pm Sat, Sun & public holidays) has excellent permanent and changing exhibitions of contemporary Australian artworks, including photography, sculpture and painting, and is well worth a look.

Parks & Gardens

Burnie Park (gates open to cars sunrise-sunset) features an animal sanctuary and the oldest building in town, **Burnie Inn**. The National Trust–classified inn was built in 1847 and in 1973 moved from its original site on Marine Terrace to the park. The oval on the northern side of the park is the site of the annual Burnie Athletics Carnival, which has been held on New Year's Day for more than 100 years.

The serene **Emu Valley Rhododendron Garden** (☎ 6433 0478; Breffny Rd; adult/child $4/3; open 10am-5pm daily Aug-Feb), 8km south of Burnie via Mount St and then Cascade Rd, sprouts over 15,000 flowers on 13 colourful hectares. Nearby are the rather English **Annsleigh Gardens & Tearooms** (☎ 6435 7229; 4 Metaira Rd; adult/child $4.50/free; open 9am-5pm daily Sept-May).

In the Burnie area, there are some waterfalls and viewpoints a few kilometres from the city centre, including **Round Hill Lookout** and **Fern Glade**. Round Hill is accessed by a side road off Stowport Rd, which departs the Bass Hwy on the eastern fringe of suburban Burnie. Fern Glade is also east of the city centre – turn off the Bass Hwy into Old Surrey Rd, just past the old Australian Paper Mill, then take Fern Glade Rd to the left. There are also the impressive **Guide Falls** at Ridgley, 16km southwest of town.

Lactos Cheese Factory

Down Old Surrey Rd, which is the first part of the route to Fern Glade, you'll find the Lactos Cheese Factory (☎ 6431 2566; 145 Old Surrey Rd; open 9am-5pm Mon-Fri, 10am-4pm Sat & Sun), where you can taste and purchase sundry specialty cheeses or have a ploughman's lunch accompanied by a glass of wine.

Creative Paper Mill

Just behind the Australian Paper Mill is the **Creative Paper Mill** (☎ 6430 7717; Old Surrey Rd; open 9am-4pm Mon-Fri), where paper and paper mementos are handmade using the traditional mould-and-deckle technique. Buy some paper-thin souvenirs or the work of local artists in the showroom, or take one of the guided tours departing at 11am and 1pm daily (adult/child $6/4.50; bookings essential).

Pencil pine, Walls of Jerusalem

Grasstree detail

ROB BLAKERS

GRANT DIXON

Expansive fields of opium poppy, near Devonport

GRANT DIXON

Walls of Jerusalem Park

GLENN VAN DER KNIJFF

'The Smithy at Work' by John Lendis, one of the murals to be found in the small town of Sheffield

CHRIS KLEP

The Nut, a volcanic rock formation in Stanley

Lichen and archeria, Southwest National Park

Natural beauty of the Tarkine Coast

There is no disguising Queenstown's mining industry and its repercussions on the landscape

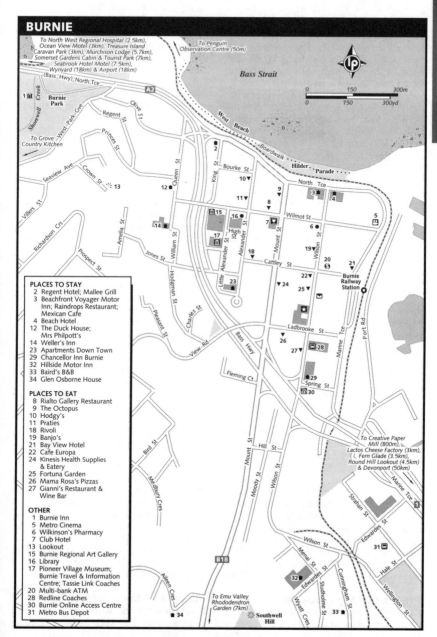

BURNIE

To North West Regional Hospital (2.5km),
Ocean View Motel (3km), Treasure Island
Caravan Park (3km), Murchison Lodge (5.7km),
Somerset Gardens Cabin & Tourist Park (7km),
Seabrook Hotel Motel (7.5km),
Wynyard (18km) & Airport (18km)
(Bass Hwy) North Tce

Bass Strait

To Penguin
Observation Centre (50m)

1 🏛 Burnie Park

Shorwell Creek

West Park Gve

To Grove
Country Kitchen

West Beach

Boardwalk

Hilder Parade

Olive St

Regent St

Princes St

Seaview Ave

Crown St

Villers St

Richardson Crs

Amelia St

Prospect St

Queen St

King St

William St

Hodgman St

Bourke St

North Tce

Wilmot St

High St

Alexander St

Little Alexander St

Cattley St

Charles St

View Rd

Jones St

Bass Hwy

Mount St

Wilson St

Ladbrooke St

Marine Tce

Port Rd

Burnie
Railway
Station

Spring St

Fleming Ct

Bird St

Medbury Crs

Hill St

Mount St

Moody St

Wilson St

To Creative Paper
Mill (800m),
Lactos Cheese Factory (3km),
Fern Glade (3.5km),
Round Hill Lookout (4.5km)
& Devonport (50km)

Strahan St

Menai St

Studholme St

Cunningham St

Edwardes St

Wilson St

Hale St

Wellington St

Aileen Crs

Wyatt Crs

To Emu Valley
Rhododendron
Garden (7km)

Southwell
Hill

PLACES TO STAY
2 Regent Hotel; Mallee Grill
3 Beachfront Voyager Motor
  Inn; Raindrops Restaurant;
  Mexican Cafe
4 Beach Hotel
12 The Duck House;
   Mrs Philpott's
14 Weller's Inn
23 Apartments Down Town
29 Chancellor Inn Burnie
32 Hillside Motor Inn
33 Baird's B&B
34 Glen Osborne House

PLACES TO EAT
8 Rialto Gallery Restaurant
9 The Octopus
10 Hodgy's
11 Praties
18 Rivoli
19 Banjo's
21 Bay View Hotel
22 Cafe Europa
24 Kinesis Health Supplies
   & Eatery
25 Fortuna Garden
26 Mama Rosa's Pizzas
27 Gianni's Restaurant &
   Wine Bar

OTHER
1 Burnie Inn
5 Metro Cinema
6 Wilkinson's Pharmacy
7 Club Hotel
13 Lookout
15 Burnie Regional Art Gallery
16 Library
17 Pioneer Village Museum;
   Burnie Travel & Information
   Centre; Tassie Link Coaches
20 Multi-bank ATM
28 Redline Coaches
30 Burnie Online Access Centre
31 Metro Bus Depot

0   150   300m
0   150   300yd

Burnie Rail

The Burnie Railway Station (☎ 6432 3400), formerly the old Emu Bay Railway Station, is the departure point for the Market Train and a Saturday Shuttle, both utilising a restored locomotive. The station is off Marine Terrace.

The *Market Train*, which coincides with the Penguin Old School Market, departs Burnie at 9am, noon and 3pm on the second and fourth Sunday of each month (September to May) to travel to Penguin, then Ulverstone, then back to Penguin and Burnie. Each individual town-to-town 'sector' involves a 25- to 35-minute ride and costs $6.50/5/15 per adult/child/family, or you can travel all four sectors for a slightly cheaper collective fare.

The *Saturday Shuttle* usually runs on the Saturday before each Market Train and on other Saturdays when there's a tie-in with a local event. Services to Wynyard and back depart Burnie at 8.30am, 11.30am and 3pm, while services to Penguin and back depart Burnie at 10am, 1.30pm and 4.30pm. Sector prices are the same as those for the Market Train.

Bookings can be made at the railway station from 8am on the day of a train service; at all other times book through the travel & information centre.

Wildlife Watching

During summer, get down to nearby Fern Glade by 6.30pm on Monday, Wednesday or Friday, when trips to spot **platypus** in Emu Creek take place. The guided excursions last up to 90 minutes.

A new boardwalk has been constructed on Burnie's foreshore, leading from Hilder Parade to the western end of West Beach, where there's a **penguin observation centre**. Over summer you can observe the shy birds at dusk if they choose to make an appearance. Wildlife guides are present to talk about the penguins and their animal habits.

For more information on both of these free council-run activities, call ☎ 6430 5794.

Places to Stay – Budget

Camping & Hostels Four kilometres west of the city centre in the suburb of Cooee is

Treasure Island Caravan Park (☎ 6431 1925, fax 6431 1753; 253 Bass Hwy; unpowered/powered site doubles $14/16, dorm beds $14, on-site van doubles $42, cabin doubles $65). It has two budget lodge rooms (four to six bunks) equipped with fridge and stove, some decent camping sites at the property's rear, vans with kitchenettes and a range of cabins. It's a friendly, well-managed park.

Somerset Gardens Cabin & Tourist Park (☎ 6435 2322, fax 6435 1431; Bass Hwy, Somerset; unpowered/powered site doubles $11/14, cabin doubles $45), 6km west of Burnie, charges a one-off fee of $3.50 per person for linen in its cabins. The park is run in conjunction with Two Oaks Nursery & Gallery, the counter of which doubles as the reception for the tourist park. Also in the nursery/gallery building is the bright, independently run Ladybugs Cafe.

Hotels Hotels comprise the budget accommodation in the town centre.

Regent Hotel (☎ 6431 1933; 26 North Terrace; singles/doubles from $25/40), overlooking West Beach, has straightforward, dirt-cheap hotel rooms.

Beach Hotel (☎ 6431 2333; 1 Wilson St; singles/doubles $50/65) also fronts West Beach, but being opposite the main waterfront car park, is a tad more central.

Seabrook Hotel Motel (☎ 6435 1209, fax 6435 2711; Bass Hwy, Somerset; singles/doubles from $40/50), west of town and ostensibly a gaming venue, has basic, dark-brown brick motel bunkers to bunk down in.

Motels Providing decent budget rooms just a short hike from town is **Hillside Motor Inn** (☎ 6431 3222, fax 6431 7055; cnr Edwardes & Menai Sts; singles/doubles $40/55).

Ocean View Motel (☎ 6431 1925, fax 6431 1753; 253 Bass Hwy; singles/doubles from $65/80) fronts Treasure Island Caravan Park, 4km west of the city centre, and has neat, serviceable rooms peering across the highway at Bass Strait.

Places to Stay – Mid-Range

Guesthouses & B&Bs Fittingly, Bill Duck's name has been immortalised at

The Duck House (☎ 6431 1712; 26 Queen St; singles/doubles $85/105), the charming two-bedroom cottage where he lived with Winnie Duck for 30 years. Managed by the same people is **Mrs Philpott's** (28 Queen St), the equally charming place next door that's enhanced by leadlight and an unusual keyhole-shaped entry. Inquiries for both should be made at 24 Queen St.

Motels It's an uphill battle to walk from the city centre to the large **Weller's Inn** (☎ 6431 1088; 36 Queen St; rooms from $100). Room rates can be flexible depending on the occupancy rate.

Murchison Lodge (☎ 6435 1106, fax 6435 2778; 9 Murchison Hwy, Somerset; rooms $105), west of Burnie, in a peaceful spot opposite the Cam River picnic ground, has ordinary motel rooms and a single two-bedroom unit (double $136). The on-site restaurant is open nightly except Sunday.

Places to Stay – Top End

Guesthouses & B&Bs It may be set in the suburban hills in Burnie's south, but there's nothing suburban about **Glen Osborne House** (☎ 6431 9866, fax 6431 4354; 9 Aileen Crescent; singles/doubles from $80/110). It provides high-standard hospitality in a lavish, National Trust–listed Victorian house with established gardens.

Baird's B&B (☎ 6431 9212, fax 6431 9797; 22 Cunningham St; singles/doubles from $90/110) has three rooms on offer in South Burnie, at the base of Southwell Hill.

Motels & Apartments Opposite the surf lifesaving club on the main section of West Beach is **Beachfront Voyager Motor Inn** (☎ 6431 4866, 1800 355 090, fax 6431 3826; 9 North Terrace). Its large, very well-equipped rooms are advertised at around $120, but cheaper walk-in rates are available. Rooms with a balcony overlooking the beach are recommended.

Chancellor Inn Burnie (☎ 6431 4455; e ciburnie@southcom.com.au; 139 Wilson St; rooms $85-120) has received a significant upgrade from its former incarnation as Burnie Town House. The rooms and

facilities are pretty good, and the downstairs bar, Maginty's, is good for a drink.

Apartments Down Town (☎ 6432 3219; 52 Alexander St; singles/doubles from $99/110) lives in a bygone era, a classic Art Deco one to be precise. Its spacious, well-equipped apartments are full of the trimmings of the 1930s and make a pleasant change from the colonial time warp offered by other guesthouses.

Places to Eat

Restaurants In the low-lit confines of **Gianni's Restaurant & Wine Bar** (☎ 6431 9393; 104 Wilson St; open from 6pm Tues-Sat) is an à la carte Italian eatery that also does a decent trade in glasses of local vintages.

Rialto Gallery Restaurant (☎ 6431 7718; 46 Wilmot St; mains $11-18; open noon-2pm & 5.30pm-late Mon-Fri, 5.30pm-late Sat, 5.30pm-9pm Sun) is one of those restaurants that looks like it's always been there, pre-dating the town itself. Some mouthwatering smells waft from its doorway, emanating from its huge range of pasta, beef and veal specialities.

Hodgy's (☎ 6431 3947; 8 Alexander St; mains $17-21; open noon-2pm Wed-Fri, 6.30pm-late Tues-Sat) is an à la carte place serving contemporary Oz food, including vegetarian options. It also has a wine bar open from 4.30pm Wednesday to Friday.

Fortuna Garden (☎ 6431 9035; 66 Wilson St; mains $9-15; open 11.30am-2.30pm & from 5pm Mon-Sat, from 5pm Sun) is a licensed and BYO Chinese restaurant/takeaway with plenty of braised prawns, fried squid and stir-fried vegetables to keep diners happy.

Raindrops Restaurant (☎ 6431 4866; 9 North Terrace; mains $17-25; open lunch & dinner daily), in the Beachfront Voyager Motor Inn, is a reasonable seafood and steak bar. Also at the Beachfront is the poncho-plagued **Mexican Cafe** (mains $10-20; open 11am-2pm & 5pm-9pm daily), where you can pig out on rich Mexican standards.

Cafés For some carefree Spanish-style ambience, try **Cafe Europa** (☎ 6431 1897;

cnr Cattley & Wilson Sts; dishes $4-12; open 8am-10pm Tues-Thur, 8am-midnight Fri, 10am-midnight Sat, 10am-6pm Sun). Within its cruisy sky-blue walls you can order liquids from coffee to wine and cocktails, and food that includes croissants, toasted Turkish bread and tapas platters.

Kinesis Health Supplies & Eatery (☎ 6431 5963; 53 Mount St; lunch $5-10; open 8.30am-6pm Tues-Thur, 8.30am-late Fri, 8.30am-4pm Sat) serves simple, vital lunches among a homely mishmash of furniture – including old club lounge chairs – that make you feel like you're eating in someone's cluttered living room.

Grove Country Kitchen (☎ 6431 9779; 63 West Park Grove; lunch $4-13; open 10am-4pm daily) is a great place for light meals, serving sweet chilli chicken and vegetarian grills in its pleasant interior or on the outdoor deck. It's at the West Park Nursery (drive up West Park Grove alongside Burnie Park) and you'll need your own transport to get there.

Pub Meals West of town on the Bass Hwy at Somerset is **Seabrook Hotel Motel** (☎ 6435 1209; mains from $10), which has a $14 all-you-can-eat Sunday carvery.

Bay View Hotel (☎ 6431 2711; 10 Marine Terrace; mains $9-17; open lunch & dinner Mon-Sat) serves pastas and roasts.

Beach Hotel (☎ 6431 2333; 1 Wilson St; mains $11-20) serves generous meals, including overloaded pub favourites like reef 'n' beef and surf 'n' turf.

Mallee Grill (☎ 6431 1933; 26 North Terrace; mains $12-18; open noon-2pm & from 6pm Mon-Fri, from 6pm Sat & Sun), in the Regent Hotel, is a meat showcase, serving gourmet sausages and seafood, but with steaks as the kitchen's centrepiece. The biggest meal is 50g of rump ($24.50).

Takeaways There's no half-baked fare at **Banjo's** (☎ 6434 4444; 38 Wilson St; open 6am-6pm daily), which feeds the masses.

Praties (☎ 6431 9144; 18 Alexander St; open 11am-9pm daily) is the Mr Potato Head of the cuisine world, part of a chain serving stuffed, sauced spud snacks.

The Octopus (☎ 6431 6478; 4 Mount St; open 9am-7pm Mon-Thur, 9am-7.30pm Fri & Sat) is the place for fish and chips.

Rivoli (☎ 6431 1971; 54 Cattley St; open 8am-7pm Mon-Fri, 10am-7pm Sat & Sun) has takeaway like souvlaki and cheap eat-in meals like steak and salad, and sausages and eggs.

Mamma Rosa's Pizzas (☎ 6431 3194; 25 Ladbrooke St; medium pizzas $10-12; open from 5pm Tues-Sun) concocts very good edible frisbees.

Entertainment

Metro Cinema (☎ 6431 5000; cnr Marine Terrace & Wilmot St; adult/concession/child $12/10/8.50) is a shiny cinema with shiny, mainly American flicks.

Club Hotel (☎ 6431 2244; 22 Mount St) was renovated a few years back and its floorboards host DJs late on Thursday, Friday and Saturday night.

Getting There & Away

Air The Burnie/Wynyard airport – known as either Burnie or Wynyard airport – is at Wynyard, 20km northwest of Burnie. See the Wynyard Getting There & Away section later in this chapter for details of services.

Bus See the Getting There & Around section at the start of this chapter for details of Redline and TassieLink services to/from Burnie.

From Monday to Friday, except on public holidays, **Metro** (☎ 6431 3822, 13 22 01; 28 Strahan St) has regular local buses to Penguin, Ulverstone and Wynyard ($3 each), which depart from bus stops on Cattley St.

WYNYARD

☎ 03 • postcode 7325 • pop 4510

Sheltered by the impressive Table Cape and Fossil Bluff, and surrounded by beautiful patchwork farmland, Wynyard sits both on the seafront and on the banks of the Inglis River.

The area was first settled by Europeans in 1841 and for most of the late 19th century Wynyard was the principal port on this section of coast. While Burnie eventually nabbed the shipping trade, Wynyard remained the centre of a rich agricultural region. Butter, cheese, milk, vegetables and speciality crops such as tulips support the town's economy.

Wynyard is also the location of the Wynyard/Burnie airport, which serves the northwest.

Information

Wynyard's volunteer-run **visitors information centre** (☎ 6442 4143; e wynyard@ tasvisinfo.com.au; Goldie St; open 9.30am-4.30pm Mon-Sat, 12.30pm-4.30pm Sun) has all the information you could desire, including the brochure *Scenic Walks of Wynyard and the Surrounding Districts*. The brochure explains how to get to Fossil Bluff on foot and gives details of walks in the Oldina Forest Reserve, to Detention Falls and in Hellyer Gorge.

There are branches of the ANZ and Commonwealth Banks, both with ATMs, on Goldie St.

Things to See & Do

You can hire scuba gear from the **Scuba Centre** (☎ 6442 2247; 62 Old Bass Hwy), diagonally opposite Leisure Ville (see Places to Stay), for dives in Wynyard Bay, Boat Harbour or at Sisters Beach. The centre also runs occasional charters to Bicheno and Eaglehawk Neck.

See the Burnie Rail entry in the Burnie section earlier in this chapter for details of a **historic train ride** between Burnie and Wynyard.

Scenic flights over Cradle Mountain ($100 per person) and the southwest ($195 per person) can be arranged with **Western Aviation** (☎ 6442 1111), located next to the airport.

Places to Stay

Wynyard Cabin/Caravan & Backpacker Park (☎ 6442 1998; 30 Old Bass Hwy; unpowered/powered site doubles $13/16, dorm beds $17, on-site van doubles $45, motel/cabin doubles $60/65), close to town right beside the beach, is on a mission to conquer dirt – all the enclosed accommodation, from the small, basic bunk rooms to the old-style vans to the bright motel rooms

lining the park's road, have been scrubbed into submission. The backpackers' lounge is well equipped.

Leisure Ville Holiday Centre (☎ 6442 2291; w www.leisureville.com.au; 145a Old Bass Hwy; unpowered/powered site doubles $16/19, on-site van doubles $45, cabin doubles $70-100) is a large, well-managed accommodation/recreation centre some distance from town. The huge range of facilities include an indoor pool/spa, tennis court and a kids playground.

Federal Hotel (☎ 6442 2056; 82 Goldie St; singles/doubles $35/55) is a central pub offering rooms with shared facilities and lots of happy barflies for company.

Inglis River Hotel/Motel (☎ 6442 2344; 10 Goldie St; singles/doubles from $35/55) has inexpensive rooms and some self-contained accommodation across from the river.

Waterfront Motor Inn (☎ 6442 2351, fax 6442 3749; 1 Goldie St; singles/doubles from $65/85) won't win any architectural or interior-design awards, but this riverside motel does have clean, good-value rooms.

Gutteridge Court (☎ 6442 2886; Unit 5, 22 Goldie St; singles/doubles $65/80, extra adult/child $15/10) is a two-bedroom red-brick unit in a court almost directly opposite the information centre, a convenient stroll from the city centre.

Alexandria (☎ 6442 4411; e alexandria@ ozemail.com.au; 1 Table Cape Rd; singles/doubles from $110/130), on the northern side of town at the start of the road to Table Cape, is a high-quality B&B in a Federation-style home beside the Inglis River. It has several rooms in-house, en suite rooms in the back garden near the pool and BBQ, and a relaxed atmosphere.

Places to Eat

Buckaneers for Seafood (☎ 6442 4104; 4 Inglis St; mains $11-23; open noon-9pm Thur-Sat, noon-7.30pm Sun-Wed) is a hugely popular and highly recommended seafood emporium – you won't ever be surrounded by more marine paraphernalia unless you're underwater. Locals and visitors sit around the clinker-built sailing boat in the middle of the dining room and chow down on a broad menu of fresh catches; steaks, pasta and takeaways are also available. Inglis St angles off Goldie St at the roundabout in the town centre. Bookings are a must for end-of-week meals.

Cafe Ricardo (☎ 6442 1755; 8A Inglis St; mains from $10; open 5pm-10pm Tues-Thur, 5pm-midnight Fri & Sat, 5pm-9pm Sun & Mon) bakes tasty pizzas and lots of other Italian mainstays.

Sea View Diner (☎ 6442 1727; 30 Old Bass Hwy; mains $11-15; open 10am-8pm Wed-Sun), at the entrance to the caravan park, has main-sized schnitzels, mixed grills and curried scallops, plus great burgers.

Inglis River Hotel/Motel (☎ 6442 2344; 10 Goldie St; mains $12-17) serves reef 'n' beef and other typical pub selections from 6pm to 9pm nightly.

Federal Hotel (☎ 6442 2056; 82 Goldie St; open lunch & dinner daily) serves a variety of good casseroles and roasts for under $10 and lots of blackboard specials.

Gumnut Gallery Restaurant (☎ 6442 1177; 43 Jackson St; lunch $5-12, dinner per adult/child $25/15; open 10.30am-3pm Mon-Fri, from 6pm Fri & Sat) serves lunch (sandwiches, Spanish omelettes, fried seafood), while dinner is chosen from a small à la carte menu.

Toysun Chinese Restaurant (☎ 6442 1101; 25 Goldie St; mains $10-16; open 11.30am-2pm & from 5pm Tues-Sat, from 5pm Sun & Mon) has a great range of meals for in-house dining or takeaway.

Waterfront Restaurant (☎ 6442 2351; 1 Goldie St; mains $13-21; open from 6pm Mon-Sat), at Waterfront Motor Inn, has efficient service and good-quality meals like duck sausage and sea-run trout.

Getting There & Away

Air The Burnie/Wynyard airport is just one block from Wynyard's main street. The airport is often listed as Burnie airport.

Both **Qantas** (☎ 13 13 13; w www.qantas .com.au) and **Regional Express** (☎ 13 17 13; w www.regionalexpress.com.au) fly to Burnie/Wynyard from Melbourne for $220 and $155 one way (14-day advance purchase) respectively.

Tasair (☎ 6248 5088, 1800 062 900; w www.tasair.com.au) flies between Devonport and King Island via Burnie/Wynyard at least once a day (advance bookings essential) – one-way flights from Burnie/Wynyard to either Devonport or King Island cost $165. Tasair also flies to Burnie/Wynyard from Hobart on weekdays for $165 one way.

Bus See the Getting There & Around section at the start of this chapter for details.

During the week, **Metro Burnie** (☎ 6431 3822) runs regular local buses from Burnie to Wynyard for $3. The main bus stop is on Jackson St.

AROUND WYNYARD
Fossil Bluff

Three kilometres from the town centre is Fossil Bluff, where the oldest marsupial fossil found in Australia was unearthed. The soft sandstone here features numerous shell fossils deposited when the level of Bass Strait was much higher, some of which are on display in the Tasmanian Museum & Art Gallery in Hobart. At low tide you can walk along the foot of the bluff, observe the different layers in the rocks and find the fossils yourself – pick up the *Looking for Fossils* brochure from the visitors centre. It's also worth walking east along the rocks to the mouth of the Inglis River, where there's a seagull rookery. If the tide is high, it's still worth climbing to the top of the bluff for the good views.

The Bluff is quite close to Wynyard on the northern side of the river, a pleasant two-hour return walk from town; by car, the route winds through several side streets, so keep your eyes peeled for the signs. It's a shame that a housing development extends all the way to the base of the bluff.

Table Cape

If you have transport, ignore the highway and follow the minor roads towards Table Cape, 4km north of Wynyard. The narrow sealed roads lead to a car park and lookout on top of the cape, 177m above the ocean. It's often windy here but the view over

Wynyard and the coast is excellent. You can also visit the nearby **lighthouse**, which began its seaside vigil in 1888.

The **Table Cape Tulip Farm** (☎ 6442 2012; 363 Lighthouse Rd; adult/child $4/2; open 10am-4.30pm daily late-Sept–mid-Oct) is worth visiting when in full flower. It's beside the road to the lighthouse, where its brightly coloured fields contrast with the rich red soils of the cape. Admission entitles you to wander around the paddocks and also view the large display of tulips in the greenhouses.

The best route from the cape to Boat Harbour is to follow Tollymore Rd northwest. There are some great views of the cliffs and rocky coast along this road.

Places to Stay There are excellent cape views from the very private, 'exclusively yours' wing of **Skyescape** (☎ 6442 1876; 282 Tollymore Rd; doubles $175-250). This lavishly modern home with its panoramic windows and private beach access provides gourmet breakfasts and (by arrangement) equally gourmet lunches and dinners.

Lapoinya

At the time of writing, there were rumours of a rock-lobster viewing and interpretation centre being set up at nearby Lapoinya – double-check this at the Wynyard visitors centre.

Oldina State Forest

Most of the hills south of Wynyard are used for timber production and form part of the Oldina State Forest. Pines were first planted here in 1920 and willows, Douglas firs and poplars, as well as native trees, are a feature of the forest.

Some sections have been reserved for recreation, with separate zones for walking, horse riding and trail-bike riding. Each forest zone has its own parking and picnic site. The walking reserve features the **Noel Jago Walk**, a short nature walk beside Blackfish Creek. Passing under man-ferns and eucalyptus trees, it takes 30 to 45 minutes to complete. There are reputed to be platypuses in the creek.

BOAT HARBOUR BEACH
☎ 03 • postcode 7321

Located just 14km northwest of Wynyard and 3km off the Bass Hwy, this holiday resort has a beautiful cliche of a bay, with white sand and crystal-blue water, and is a lovely spot for exploring rock pools and snorkelling. It was originally used in the 19th century as a port, but because the harbour isn't sheltered from easterly winds it very quickly lost maritime favour. In the 1920s holiday-makers discovered the area and now most buildings in the small village are holiday shacks.

The town consists of a single street, The Esplanade, which is the continuation of the steep access road. As you descend towards the town, a short path on the left leads to a timber platform and a panoramic view over Boat Harbour.

Places to Stay

Boat Harbour Beach Caravan Park (☎ 6445 1253, fax 6445 1248; The Esplanade; unpowered/powered site doubles $11/15.40, on-site van doubles $38, cabin doubles $71.50) is a leisurely sun-drenched sprawl opposite a short walkway to the beach, with good facilities and a laundrette open to the public. They also rent out an older-style, self-contained bungalow (doubles $100) on a nearby hillside.

Seaside Garden Motel (☎ 6445 1111, fax 6445 1705; The Esplanade; motel singles/doubles $70/75, unit doubles $104), also directly opposite the beach, has nice, compact holiday units in a large garden, including a two-bedroom structure.

Boat Harbour Beach Resort (☎ 6445 1107; W www.view.com.au/bhbr; The Esplanade; singles from $90, doubles $100-175), next door to Seaside Garden Motel, is a sociable place with accommodation ranging from tiny 'economy' motel rooms to larger rooms nearer the beach, to spa units. Also lurking enticingly on the premises are an indoor heated pool, sauna and spa.

Harbour House (☎ 6442 2135; W www.harbourhouse.com.au; The Esplanade; doubles $185-200), directly opposite the caravan park, is dressed to impress in ultra-modern style, with a price to match its upmarket intentions. It accepts cash or cheque only.

Cape View B&B (☎ 6445 1273; 64 Strawberry Lane; downstairs/upstairs doubles $95/120, extra guests $30), scenically sited on a hill overlooking the beach, has a homely two-bedroom upstairs suite with attractive views, and a smaller downstairs room.

Country Garden Cottages (☎ 6445 1233, 0419 792 663, fax 6445 1019; 15 Port Rd; singles/doubles from $80/90), back near the highway, has an arc of snug, timber-lined cottages fronting two rambling hectares of gardens.

Killynaught Cottages (☎ 6445 1041, fax 6445 1556; Bass Hwy; doubles $124), on the highway farther back towards Wynyard, has attractive, rural views to the rear. The cottages are fully self-contained and lavishly decorated in Federation style. There are open fireplaces in the lounge rooms, spas in the bathrooms and ingredients for cooked breakfasts in the kitchens.

Places to Eat

Boat Harbour General Store (☎ 6445 1253; The Esplanade; open 8am-8pm daily), at the caravan park, has a counter serving takeaway.

Jolly Rogers (☎ 6445 1710; The Esplanade; meals $10-24; open 10am-10pm daily Sept-May) is a laid-back beachside café serving focaccias and garlic tiger prawns for lunch (between 11am and 2.30pm), pasta and stuffed scotch fillets for dinner (between 6pm and 9pm) and drinks and snacks in-between. In the immediate vicinity is a fenced play area where you can stow the little ones.

Avalon Restaurant (☎ 6445 1111; The Esplanade; mains $14-24; open from 6.30pm Mon-Sat), at the Seaside Garden Motel, has the feel of a formal tearoom and serves lobster tails, scallops and other generally hearty fare; bookings are recommended.

Jacobs Restaurant (☎ 6445 1107; The Esplanade; mains $16.50-23; open lunch & from 6pm Thur-Mon, from 6pm Tues & Wed) is an à la carte eatery at the Boat Harbour Beach Resort. It has a good selection of mains; desserts include wild-berry pancakes and the somewhat intriguing bourbon and vanilla-

bean ice cream. Also here is the **Jetty Bar & Cafe** (mains $12-19; open from 10am daily), where you can eat and drink a tad more informally either inside or al fresco.

Getting There & Away

Unless you have your own transport, you'll have to hitch to get here. The twice-daily (weekdays only) Redline service from Burnie will drop you at the turn-off to Boat Harbour (3km) and Sisters Beach (8km) for $5.50.

ROCKY CAPE NATIONAL PARK

☎ 03 • postcode 7321

This small area was declared a national park in 1967. Its major features are rocky headlands, heath-covered hills and caves once occupied by Aborigines – these caves were used from 8000 years ago up until European occupation in the 19th century. The coast here is mostly rugged quartzite and the park is believed to contain the only stands of *Banksia serrata* in the state.

There are a couple of beaches within the park, the best known being **Sisters Beach**, an 8km expanse of bleached sand. The Sisters Beach village, reached by following the side road from the Bass Hwy that passes the turn-off to nearby Boat Harbour, is a popular resort surrounded by the national park.

In 1998, an intense fire started by picnickers swept through most of the park, and it's estimated that it will take 10 years for the vegetation to fully regenerate, a cause not helped by a scrub fire in early 2002 that burnt out another 3 sq km. Until the bush reestablishes itself, you may prefer to walk in the unburnt section east of Sisters Beach township. That said, the western end is arguably the more attractive, as it has a more rugged coastline, and even in the aftermath of fire, wildflowers and orchids bloom throughout the park in spring and summer.

On Rocky Cape, you can drive to a stunted **lighthouse** (more the size of an outhouse), with The Nut floating distantly on the horizon. Overnight camping is not allowed and, as with all national parks, entry fees apply.

Sisters Beach is a good place for swimming and fishing. On the eastern side of the creek there are picnic tables and a shelter; a foot-bridge crosses the creek, providing access to the beach.

Bushwalking

From Sisters Beach, the walk to **Wet Cave**, **Lee Archer Cave** and **Banksia Grove** takes 45 minutes; to reach the start of this walk, follow the signs to the boat ramp. You can continue farther along the coast to Anniversary Point (three hours return). It's also possible to follow the coast to Rocky Point and return along the **Inland Track** (eight hours return).

From the western end of the park at Rocky Cape Rd (accessed from a separate entrance off the Bass Hwy, west of the turn-off to Sisters Beach), you can visit two large Aboriginal caves, the South and North Caves, the latter off the road to the lighthouse; both caves involve a 30-minute return walk. There's also a good circuit of the cape itself; allow 2½ hours.

Places to Stay & Eat

Sisters Beach Old-style but tranquil and good-value bushy abodes are on offer at **Birdland Holiday Cottages** (☎ 6445 1471; 7 Banksia Ave; doubles $65, extra adult/child $6/4).

Tasman Buray Holiday Units (☎ 6445 1147; Kenelm Ave; doubles from $70, extra adult/child $10/5) are less secluded but nonetheless attractive timber cottages lying amidst some large Banksia serrata; inquire at the general store.

Nigel Lazenby's Fine Art Studio Gallery & Accommodation (☎/fax 6445 1428; W www.nigellazenby.com.au; 8 Elfrida Ave; doubles $90, extra guests $10) has a stylish, self-contained upstairs pad with a breezy feel and views of nature that will relax you in no time.

Holiday shacks in the area can sometimes be rented short-term, but the owners generally prefer occupancies of at least a week, so definitely do not rely on this possibility for overnight accommodation. Ask about the shacks at **Sisters Beach General Store** (☎ 6445 1147; Honeysuckle Ave; open 7.30am-8.30pm daily summer, 7.30am-7.30pm daily winter), which sells takeaway and park passes.

Western End On the highway near the entrance to the western end of the national park is **Rocky Cape Tavern & Caravan Park** (☎ 6443 4110; Bass Hwy; unpowered/powered site doubles $8/13, on-site van doubles $30, motel doubles $50). The on-site tavern serves counter meals daily.

Araluen Holiday Camp (☎ 6443 4197; units per person/family $20/40), 2km west of the park and 27km from Stanley, is a scruffy-looking roadside enclave with self-contained family units.

Rainbow Gardens & Tearooms (☎ 6443 4187; 19469 Bass Hwy; open 10am-5pm Wed-Mon) is naturally decorated with a colourful garden and birdlife. It sells a range of light meals and local arts and crafts.

AROUND ROCKY CAPE

In the hills south of the national park you can visit a number of waterfalls, including **Detention Falls**, 3km south of Myalla, and **Dip Falls**, near Mawbanna.

TARKINE WILDERNESS

The Tarkine is a 3500-sq-km wilderness between the Arthur River in the north and the Pieman River in the south.

A decade ago, conservationists tried unsuccessfully to prevent the development of what they called the 'the road to nowhere' between Corinna and Balfour, a road that now runs close to – and at times within – the eastern border of a section of the Tarkine called the Arthur Pieman Conservation Area (see the Western Explorer & Arthur Pieman Conservation Area section later). Today, conservation groups are seeking World Heritage area protection for this diverse region, beyond the small section of it declared the Savage River National Park several years ago (see the Savage River National Park section later in this chapter).

Not everyone agrees it's a wilderness area though – former Tasmanian premier Tony Rundle once said that the Tarkine 'has no more wilderness than Battery Point'. And the state's forestry industry would seem to prefer fewer restrictions on logging in order to allow the exploitation of the Tarkine's 2000 sq km of rainforest.

A leaflet published by the **Wilderness Society** (☎ 6234 9366; 130 Davey St, Hobart) details a self-guided tour of the northern reaches of what constitutes Australia's largest temperate rainforest, beginning from the highway township of Sisters Creek and heading off on a network of dirt forestry roads (suitable for two-wheel drives) until emerging onto the Murchison Hwy at Henrietta. The scenic lows and highs of the drive respectively include logging coupes and a walk to the stunningly tranquil Myrtle Reach on the Arthur River. Allow at least a half-day for the trip, fill up your car's tank before setting off, drive carefully and check road conditions after heavy rain.

For some snapshots of this profoundly beautiful region, buy the pictorial *The Tarkine: Endangered Wilderness,* published by the Wilderness Society.

PORT LATTA

This part of the coastline is a series of pretty little beaches and rocky coves marred by the heavy-industry complex at Port Latta, the terminus for the 85km iron-ore pipeline from Savage River. Fortunately there's only one factory here, and away from the busy smokestack the coast is pleasant.

Two kilometres west of Port Latta is the **Peggs Beach Conservation Area** (camp sites per adult/child $2.20/1.10), which has toilets, tables, fireplaces, water and an on-site caretaker with whom you register.

Caradale Caravan Park & Holiday Cabins (☎/fax 6443 4228; e caradale@our.net.au; 20049 Bass Hwy; unpowered/powered site doubles $10/14, on-site van doubles $30, cabin doubles $55-75) is set beside the bushland-lined Crayfish Creek 2km east of Port Latta. Besides wild secluded sites and a beach a short walk away, Caradale also has a fine multi-level 'tree house' for those who prefer lofty accommodation.

STANLEY

☎ 03 • postcode 7331 • pop 550

Nestled at the foot of the extraordinary Circular Head (better known as The Nut), Stanley is a historic village with some significant buildings and a great seascape. In 1826 it became the headquarters of the London-based Van Diemen's Land Company, which was granted a charter to settle and cultivate Circular Head and the northwestern tip of Tasmania. The company built its headquarters at Highfield, to the north of Stanley, and the town started at the same time, serving as the port.

For 30 years the company struggled with its vast land-holding and by 1858 had sold most of it. The area prospered when it began shipping large quantities of mutton, beef and potatoes to Victoria's goldfields in the 1850s and 1860s, and continued to prosper when settlers established dairying land behind Sisters Hills and found tin reserves at Mt Bischoff.

Today, even though it receives a good number of visitors, Stanley has a quiet, self-possessed air, reinforced by a dearth of tourism promotion; there were a number of local shopfronts for sale when we visited, particularly along Church St.

Information

There's a **visitors centre** (☎ 6458 1330; e stanley@tasvisinfo.com.au; 45 Main Rd; open 9am-5pm Mon-Fri, 10am-4pm Sat & Sun) on the left-hand side of the road as you head into town. A reliable place for advice on accommodation and tour options is **The Booking Centre** (☎ 1300 656 044; w www.bookings.tassie.net.au; Church St; open 8am-early evening daily), in the Town Hall.

Fishing tackle, fishing licences and film are available from **De Jonge's Country Store** (☎ 6458 1255; 15 Church St). There are no ATMs in town but Eftpos withdrawals can be made at the local **newsagency** (☎ 6458 1372; 17 Church St).

The Nut

This striking 152m-high volcanic rock formation, thought to be 12.5 million years old, can be seen for many kilometres around Stanley. It's a steep 20-minute climb to the top, but the view is definitely worth it. For the lazy, there's a **chairlift** (☎ 6458 1286; adult/child $7/5; open 9.30am-5.30pm daily Oct-May, 10am-4pm daily Jun-Sept). The best lookout is a five-minute walk to the south of the chairlift. You can also take a 35-minute walk on a path around the top.

Stanley Discovery Museum

To learn more about Stanley, visit this single-room folk museum *(Church St; adult/child $3/50c; open 10am-4pm daily)*, filled with old Circular Head photos and artefacts, including marine curios. It also runs a genealogical service.

Scenic Drive

Follow Dovecote Rd north to the **Jimmy Lane Memorial Lookout**. This is a timber platform providing a reasonable view over the cape area. The road then passes Highfield before winding back down to Stanley past some attractive scenery.

Highfield

This homestead *(☎ 6458 1100; Green Hills Rd; adult/child $5.50/3.30, grounds only $2; open 10am-4pm daily)* was built in 1835 on the high land north of Stanley to serve as the headquarters of the Van Diemen's Land Company (VDL), a wool-growing venture launched in 1824 and granted 1000 sq km of unexplored territory. The company had

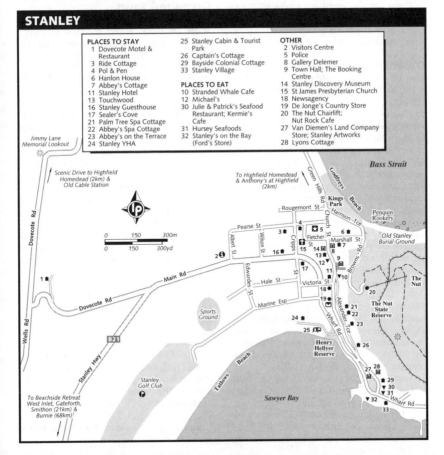

STANLEY

PLACES TO STAY
1 Dovecote Motel & Restaurant
3 Ride Cottage
4 Pol & Pen
6 Hanlon House
7 Abbey's Cottage
11 Stanley Hotel
13 Touchwood
16 Stanley Guesthouse
17 Sealer's Cove
21 Palm Tree Spa Cottage
22 Abbey's Spa Cottage
23 Abbey's on the Terrace
24 Stanley YHA
25 Stanley Cabin & Tourist Park
26 Captain's Cottage
29 Bayside Colonial Cottage
33 Stanley Village

PLACES TO EAT
10 Stranded Whale Cafe
12 Michael's
30 Julie & Patrick's Seafood Restaurant; Kermie's Cafe
31 Hursey Seafoods
32 Stanley's on the Bay (Ford's Store)

OTHER
2 Visitors Centre
5 Police
8 Gallery Delemer
9 Town Hall; The Booking Centre
14 Stanley Discovery Museum
15 St James Presbyterian Church
18 Newsagency
19 De Jonge's Country Store
20 The Nut Chairlift; Nut Rock Cafe
27 Van Diemen's Land Company Store; Stanley Artworks
28 Lyons Cottage

great difficulty developing its land, however, and in 1856 Highfield was leased, then eventually sold.

In 1982 the state government purchased Highfield and undertook restorations to establish it as a visitable historic site. The Ford family, who purchased Highfield post-VDL and lived there through two generations, recently returned around 100 pieces of original furniture to the site. Guided tours of the Regency-style house take place on weekdays; on weekends tours are self-guided. The grounds include stables, grain stores, workers' cottages and the chapel.

There are also one-hour after-dark tours of the property (adult/child/family $10/5/25) at 8.30pm daily from October to April; bookings are essential.

Other Historic Buildings

The old bluestone building on the seafront is the **Van Diemen's Land Company Store** (1844), designed by John Lee Archer, a famous colonial architect. Today it houses **Stanley Artworks** (☎ 6458 2000; 16 Wharf Rd; open 9am-6pm daily Nov-May), where a pair of artisans creatively sculpt wood into decorative pieces and furniture (such as myrtle coffee tables and blackwood cabinets), and exhibit an even wider variety of local arts and crafts. It can be visited other times by appointment. Meanwhile, for paintings that attempt to capture the Stanley area's sundry natural moods, check out **Gallery Delemer** (☎ 6458 2021; 16 Church St), usually open well into the evening.

Also near the wharf is the particularly fine old bluestone **Ford's Store** (or Customs Bond Store), first used for grain storage and then as a bacon factory. It's believed to have been built in 1859, although the plaque near its door dates it from 1885. Now the restaurant Stanley's on the Bay (see Places to Eat later), it was constructed from stones brought to Stanley as ship's ballast.

Next door to the Discovery Museum is the restored **Plough Inn** (Church St), a Georgian terrace that began its life in 1854 as a hotel.

Other buildings of historical interest include **Lyons Cottage** (☎ 6458 1145; 14 Alexander Terrace; admission by donation; open 10am-4pm daily Nov-Apr, 11am-3pm daily May-Oct), the birthplace of one-time prime minister Joseph Lyons; the **Stanley Hotel** (Church St), formerly Union Hotel, which dates from 1849; and the dazzling whitewash of **St James Presbyterian Church** (Fletcher St), which was probably Australia's first prefabricated building, bought in England and transported to Stanley in 1885.

The **Wiltshire Junction Railway Station** was saved from demolition by being transported to Stanley, where it's now part of the Stanley Village accommodation complex.

Organised Tours

Stanley-based **Wilderness to West Coast Tours** (☎ 6458 2038; W www.wilderness tasmania.com) has platypus-spotting excursions (adult/child $25/10) which are regularly successful. It also offers penguin-viewing tours (adult/child $10/5) when the birds appear at either end of Godfreys Beach from late September until February, plus half-day trout-fishing excursions (adult/child $100/ 50), half-day wilderness tours (adult/child $100/50) and an overnight trip to remote Sandy Cape that includes cabin accommodation and food and drink (adult/child $500/ 225).

To see Australian fur seals, try the 75-minute cruise provided by **Stanley Seal Cruises** (☎ 6458 1312; W www.users.bigpond .com/staffordseals). The cruises usually take place daily at 10am, 1.30pm and 4.30pm (3.30pm April to September), weather permitting, and cost $30/15 per adult/child.

Places to Stay

Town Centre Located on a great site right on Sawyer Bay, **Stanley Cabin & Tourist Park** (☎/fax 6458 1266; W www.stanleycab inpark.com.au; Wharf Rd; unpowered/ powered site doubles $14/18, on-site van doubles $35-40, cabin doubles from $55) is loaded with amenities and has well-serviced vans and cabins, plus the clean, no-frills **Stanley YHA** (dorm beds $18).

Stanley Hotel (☎ 6458 1161; 19 Church St; singles/doubles $25/50), formerly the Union Hotel, has clean, basic hotel rooms with shared facilities.

Pol & Pen (☎ 6458 1186, 1800 222 397, fax 6458 1290; 8 Pearse St; doubles $75) are neighbouring, modern two-bedroom cottages on a quiet side street.

Ride Cottage (☎ 6458 1137; 12 Pearse St; singles/doubles $75/80), near Pol & Pen, is another two-bedroom self-contained option. Inquire at 16 Pearse St.

Hanlon House (☎ 6458 1149; W www .tassie.net.au/hanlonhouse; 6 Marshall St; singles $100-130, doubles $125-170), originally a Catholic presbytery, has comfortably old-fashioned en suite rooms accompanied by generous breakfasts. Evening vittles and vino in front of the log fire can be arranged with prior notice.

Stanley Guesthouse (☎ 6458 1488; 27 Main Rd; doubles $85-110) is a pleasant, antique-furnished, Federation-style (Queen Anne) B&B; prices include full cooked breakfast.

There's a collective of 'Abbey' accommodation in town, all of which can be booked at the **Nut Rock Cafe** (☎ 6458 1186, 1800 222 397, fax 6458 1290; The Nut State Reserve): there's the period-style **Abbey's Cottage** (1 Marshall St; doubles $150, extra guests $25), across the road from Hanlon House; the more modern **Abbey's on the Terrace** (34 Alexander Terrace; doubles $150, extra guests $25); and the light and bright **Abbey's Spa Cottage** (46 Alexander Terrace; doubles $150, extra guests $25). Managed by the same people and also on Alexander Terrace – a hillside thoroughfare that yields some fine views of the water – is the plush **Palm Tree Spa Cottage** (48 Alexander Terrace; doubles $170).

Captain's Cottage (☎ 6458 3230, 0419 871 581, fax 6458 3237; 30 Alexander Terrace; doubles from $155) is another upmarket B&B possibility on Alexander Terrace, built in 1838 and with good views.

Bayside Colonial Cottage (☎/fax 6458 1209; 4 Alexander Terrace; singles/doubles from $100/110), on Marine Park near the waterfront, is a two-bedroom place dressed in period garb; prices include breakfast provisions.

Touchwood (☎/fax 6458 1348; 31 Church St; doubles $150) provides nicely upgraded, self-contained colonial accommodation in the centre of town. Breakfast provisions and extras like port and chocolate are provided; there is a minimum stay of two nights.

Sealer's Cove (☎ 6458 1414, fax 6458 2076; 2-4 Main Rd; singles/doubles $90/95) is a relatively recent B&B addition to Stanley, with two rooms (and continental breakfast) available in a modern house.

Stanley Village (☎ 6458 1404, fax 6458 1403; 15 Wharf Rd; singles/doubles downstairs $90/110, upstairs with spa $130/140) is a small village at that, comprising just eight modern units on the edge of the rock-strewn bay shore.

Out of Town The welcoming **Dovecote Motel & Restaurant** (☎ 6458 1300; W www .dovecote.com.au; 58 Dovecote Rd; singles from $70, doubles $80-130), close to town, has a selection of motel rooms and self-contained accommodation. If you go the motel option, take an upper-level room, recline on the balcony and soak up great views of The Nut. The restaurant has a satisfying menu selection.

Old Cable Station (☎ 6458 1312, fax 6458 2009; West Beach Rd; singles/doubles $85/140) upheld a telephonic link with the mainland for over 30 years from 1935 and now upholds modern B&B, though the premises were for sale at the time of writing.

Anthony's at Highfield (☎ 6458 1245; Green Hills Rd; doubles $88, extra guests $22), a large cottage built for the Van Diemen's Land Company in 1828, is directly opposite Highfield homestead and sleeps up to six people.

Beachside Retreat West Inlet (☎/fax 6458 1350, 0409 407 094; W www.smithton .tco.asn.au/westinlet; doubles $140-190), back towards the highway on The Neck, comprises a roomy spa lodge and two artful units equipped with sundecks and the odd designer porthole, all on a 70-hectare property with access to a private beach and migratory birds for company.

Gateforth (☎ 6458 3230, 0419 871 581, fax 6458 3237; Bass Hwy, Black River; doubles $155, extra guests $30) is a vegetable, cattle and sheep farm located east of town overlooking Stanley. It has three attractive self-contained cottages, two with spas and all with porches from which to look across expansive pastureland to the distant Nut. This place is private and attentive to guests, and dinners utilising farm-fresh produce can be arranged with prior notice.

Places to Eat
Hursey Seafoods (☎ 6458 1103; 2 Alexander Terrace; open 9am-6pm daily) is awash with tanks filled with live sea creatures – including fish, crayfish, crabs and eels – for the freshest of seafood takeaways. The Hursey complex includes **Kermies Cafe** (lunch $7-16; open 9am-8pm daily summer, 9am-6pm daily winter), a café/takeaway serving battered prawns, crayfish salad and abalone patties, and, upstairs, the licensed **Julie & Patrick's Seafood Restaurant** (mains $18.50-28; open from 6pm daily), where you can dine on marinated octopus and abalone 'steaks'. Both eateries have ankle-biter menus.

Stranded Whale Cafe (☎ 6458 1202; 6 Church St; lunch $3.50-8; open 9.30am-4pm daily, 9.30am-8.30pm Fri Sept-May), just down from the Town Hall, serves homemade, non-heavy meals, contrary to its bloated name. It is open shorter hours from June to August.

Touchwood (☎ 6458 1348; 31 Church St; lunch $5-13; open 10am-5pm daily) has a café serving light lunches, putting fresh seafood to use in crayfish rolls and octopus salad. While you're here, check out the array of local woodwork, pottery and glass in the adjoining gallery.

Nut Rock Cafe (☎ 6458 1186; Brown Rd; lunch $4.50-13.50; open 9.30am-5.30pm daily) is a cheery café at the base of The Nut with a good range of breakfasts and light lunches, from pancakes to smoked salmon.

Stanley's on the Bay (☎ 6458 1404; 15 Wharf Rd; mains $21-27.50; open from 6pm Mon-Sat Sept-Jun) is formally set inside the atmospheric old Ford's Store down on the wharf; it's best to book ahead.

Sealer's Cove (☎ 6458 1414; mains $10-16.50; open from 5pm Tues-Sun) is not just a B&B but also runs an Italian restaurant with a large selection of reasonably priced pasta and pizzas – herbivores should try the 'Sassafras vegetarian' pizza.

Michael's (☎ 6458 1144; 25 Church St; lunch mains $7-13, dinner mains $18.50-24.50; open 11.30am-2.30pm & from 6pm daily Nov-Apr, from 6pm Thur-Sun May-Oct) is a quality restaurant serving fresh salads, pita rolls and the odd steak for lunch, and dishes like Thai chicken and roulades for dinner. An adjoining room is conveniently devoted to sales of Tasmanian wines.

Getting There & Around
Bus See the Getting There & Around section at the start of this chapter for details.

SMITHTON
☎ 03 • postcode 7330 • pop 3320
Located 22km southwest of Stanley, Smithton serves one of Tasmania's largest forestry areas and is also the administrative centre for Circular Head.

Smithton is on Duck River, named after the wild ducks that frequent the estuary. The town started to develop in the 1850s after the Van Diemen's Land Company sold off most of its holdings. Clearing of the giant forests was the first main activity, but once this was accomplished the land was used for potato farming. The tempo picked up in the 1890s when the first sawmill opened. Soon afterwards dairy farming began and the Duck River Butter Factory came into production. In the 1940s, vegetable dehydration and fish processing added to the town's economy.

For an insight into the European history of Circular Head, visit the **Circular Head Heritage Centre** (☎ 6452 3296; cnr Nelson & King Sts; adult/child $2/1; open 10am-3pm Mon-Sat, 12.30pm-3pm Sun).

You'll find Commonwealth and Westpac Banks (both with ATMs) on Emmett St.

Woolnorth
Sprawling across the northwestern tip of Tasmania is the 220-sq-km cattle and sheep property of Woolnorth, the only remaining holding of the Van Diemen's Land Company. Managed by New Zealand company TasAg, it's now Australia's largest dairy – its 80-bail rotary operation can milk 1800 cows a day.

The property and surrounding features such as Woolnorth Point and Cape Grim can be visited on a six-hour, lunch-supplied **tour** (☎ 6452 1493), that costs $82/41 per adult/child and departs at 9.30am daily from Woolnorth's front gates (a 15-minute drive from Smithton). Pick-up from Stanley or Smithton can be arranged at an extra cost.

The road heading from Smithton towards Woolnorth passes through farmlands with views over the narrow waterways that separate Perkins and Robbins Islands.

Lacrum
Located 6km west of Smithton, this dairy (☎ 6452 2653; Hardmans Rd; adult/child $5/2.50; open 3pm-5pm daily Nov-Jun) uses non-animal rennet to produce a range of tasty cheeses, including brie, camembert and the powerful Limburger. You can visit during the milking season to see the turnstile dairy in operation and taste some cheese.

Allendale Gardens & Rainforest
To the south of Smithton on the road to Edith Creek, the Allendale estate (☎ 6456 4216; B22 Rd, Edith Creek; adult/child $7.50/ 3.50; open 9am-6pm Oct-Apr) has two hectares of bird-filled gardens, a lengthy spirit-lifting walk through temperate rainforest, and a café serving Devonshire teas.

Milkshakes Hills Forest Reserve
Temperate rainforest and buttongrass moorland can be found at this reserve, 45km south of Smithton – the perfect place for a date with a picnic hamper. There are several short walking tracks around the picnic grounds and a longer track of one hour return to the top of Milkshakes Hills.

Lake Chisholm
Even farther south of Smithton is this tranquil lake, actually a limestone sinkhole. It's located in beautiful rainforest and is a 15-minute walk from the car park. The gravel roads leading to the lake may be closed after heavy rain.

Dismal Swamp
At the time of writing, Forestry Tasmania was setting up a much-touted 'below the swamp' experience at the alluringly named Dismal Swamp 20km west of Smithton. The experience is apparently being set up in one of the state's few remaining blackwood groves – blackwood is a type of wattle that can grow up to 50m high.

Places to Stay & Eat
Montagu Camping Ground (Old Port Rd; camp sites $7; open Nov-Apr) is just east of the diminutive Montague township, which is 16km west of Smithton.

The Bridge Hotel/Motel (☎ 6452 1389, fax 6452 2709; Montagu Rd; hotel singles/ doubles $35/45, motel singles/doubles $65/ 80), on the road heading out to Montagu, has rooms with shared facilities in the hotel proper and several dozen motel units round the back. Lambs fry and seafood platters are available nightly in the bistro.

Tall Timbers Hotel/Motel (☎ 6452 2755, 1800 628 476; Ⓦ www.talltimbershotel.com .au; Scotchtown Rd; singles/doubles from $95/110), 2km south of town, has been impressively hammered together using blackwood and celery-top cuttings. It hosts live bands and has a good bistro serving plenty of grilled meat for lunch and dinner daily, but also catering to non-carnivores.

Rosebank Cottage Collection (☎ 6452 2660; Ⓦ www.tassie.net.au/~rosebank; doubles from $135) comprises two nice B&B cottages, one in Smithton (42 Goldie St) and the other (with a spa) 6km east of town at Sedgy Creek.

Woolnorth (☎/fax 6452 1493; doubles $110-250) offers accommodation on its enormous, secluded property ranging from a room with shared facilities and continental breakfast to very well-appointed lodgings with a fully cooked breakfast and dinner provided.

Allendale Gardens (☎ 6456 4216, fax 6456 4223; B22 Rd, Edith Creek) was, at the time of research, busily fitting out three large and comfy rooms in a private wing of the main house to serve as thoroughly peaceful B&B.

Getting There & Away
See the Getting There & Around section at the start of this chapter for details.

MARRAWAH
☎ 03 • postcode 7330

Marrawah, an untrammelled delight, is where the wild Southern Ocean occasionally throws up the remains of ships wrecked on the dangerous and rugged west coast. Its nearby beaches and rocky outcrops can be hauntingly beautiful, particularly at dusk, and the seas are often huge. It was at the relatively small beach of Green Point that 35 sperm whales stranded themselves and died in February 1998, and it's at this same beach that the annual West Coast Classic, a notable round of the state's surfing championships, is often held.

Marrawah General Store (☎ 6457 1122; 800 Comeback Rd) sells supplies and petrol, is an agent for Australia Post and Commonwealth Bank, and has a café. If you're planning to take the Western Explorer (see the Western Explorer & Arthur Pieman Conservation Area section later in this chapter), fill up here, as there are no other petrol outlets for around 200km.

As yet, there's no regular public transport to Marrawah.

Surfing
One of Marrawah's major attractions is its enormous surf. The **West Coast Classic**, that most excellent round of the state's surfing championships, is regularly decided here, as is a round of the state's windsurfing championships. Green Point, 2km from the city centre, has a break that's impressive in southerly conditions, and there's also good surfing farther along the road at Nettley Bay. South of Marrawah, there's good surfing in an easterly at Lighthouse Beach (at West Point) and great reef surfing in similar conditions at Bluff Hill Point. West Point surf beach is reached by taking the left-hand branches of the road from the turn-off on the C214, while Bluff Hill Point surf beach is to the right of the lighthouse at the end of another side road farther south.

Bushwalking
There's a beach walk from Bluff Hill Point to West Point that takes four hours one way, and a coastal walk from Bluff Hill Point to the mouth of the Arthur River that takes two hours one way. There's also a good walk of around three hours return north along the beach from Green Point to Preminghana. These are beautiful areas that are well worth seeing.

Fishing
The whole region is good for fishing. In winter you can catch Australian salmon at Nettley Bay or off the rocks at West Point, while in summer you can catch blackbacked salmon here and at the mouth of the Arthur River. Estuary perch can be caught in the Arthur River.

Organised Tours
Geoff King (☎ 6457 1191; e jonesking@tassie.net.au), the owner of Glendonald Cottage (see Places to Stay & Eat), conducts a range of wildlife tours in the area, including a twilight trip out to an old fishing shack on his 300-hectare property to see some voracious Tasmanian devils tuck in to a buffet dinner (devil trip $40 per person).

Places to Stay & Eat
Camping is possible for free at beautiful Green Point, 2km east of Marrawah, where there are toilets, water and an outdoor cold shower. You must pitch your tent by the toilets back from the beach, not on the foreshore.

Marrawah Beach House (☎ 6457 1285; 19 Beach Rd; singles/doubles from $70/90), on the short road to Green Point beach, has an unobstructed view to the ocean. Ring ahead, as the managers live off-site.

Ann Bay Cabins (☎/fax 6457 1361; Green Point Rd; singles/doubles $90/110) is a pair of superb, soporific, spa-equipped beach houses, both filled with handcrafted furniture and with views to the water from their front decks.

Glendonald Cottage (☎/fax 6457 1191; 79 Arthur River Rd; singles/doubles from $60/85), just down the C214 towards Arthur River, is a comfortable two-bedroom rural place with plenty of reading material on Aboriginal history and the ecology of the area.

Tasmanian Aboriginal Sites

The Marrawah area, with its isolated west-coast beaches and cliffs, has seen minimal disturbance from European development, in direct contrast to the maximal disturbances visited by Europeans upon the area's former Aboriginal inhabitants – these include the massacre of an estimated 30 Aborigines in 1827 at the aptly named Cape Grim to the north, apparently in response to the slaughter of a flock of sheep. Particular areas have now been proclaimed reserves to protect the relics, including rock carvings, middens and hut depressions.

There's a significant Aboriginal site along the road to Arthur River at West Point, and another beyond the township at Sundown Point, the latter with several dozen mudstone slabs engraved with mainly circular motifs. There are also innumerable important traditional sites in the Arthur Pieman Conservation Area farther south, and several impressive cave sites at Rocky Cape National Park (know to Indigenous people as Tang Dim Mer) to the east. But arguably the most important Aboriginal art site in the area, if not the state, is to be found 7km north of Marrawah at Preminghana (formerly known as Mt Cameron West) – drive along the gravel road north of the Marrawah General Store and take the first turn left.

Three kilometres beyond Preminghana at the northern end of the beach are low-lying slabs of rock encrusted with geometric motifs that are believed to date back at least two millennia. Also in this area are remnants of stone tools, the quarries from which these were dug, and middens. There are also natural links with Tasmanian Aboriginal culture, such as boobialla, honeysuckle and tea tree clusters, plants used to prepare food and traditional medicines.

Preminghana was returned to the Aboriginal people in 1995. If you're interested in visiting the area independently, try driving down to the access point and asking the caretaker for permission to look around. If you'd like to be authoritatively guided around this and other significant Aboriginal sites, contact the **Tasmanian Aboriginal Land Council** (TALC; ☎ 6231 0288, fax 6231 0298; 4 Lefroy St, Nth Hobart), which keeps a list of heritage officers who can accompany you to the sites for a set group fee.

Marrawah Tavern (☎ 6457 1102; Comeback Rd; mains $9-17) doesn't have accommodation but serves big, excellent counter meals for lunch and dinner daily; the steaks are a real feast.

Blue Wren Tearooms (☎ 6457 1307; meals $4.50-7.50; open 9am-5pm daily), beside the general store, has fresh home-made soups, burgers and scones. There's also a range of craftwork made by the manager, including bark pictures, Huon-pine furniture and photo-cards depicting the local landscape.

ARTHUR RIVER
☎ 03 • postcode 7330

The sleepy town of Arthur River, 14km south of Marrawah and mainly a collection of holiday houses for people who come here to fish, is unserviced by regular public transport. There's a Parks and Wildlife Service **ranger station** (☎ 6457 1225) on the northern side of

the river, where you can get camping information and permits for off-road vehicles.

Gardiner Point, signposted off the main road on the southern side of the bridge, has been christened 'The Edge of the World' by locals because the sea here stretches uninterrupted all the way to Argentina. There's a plaque at the point and a great view of some rocky coastline.

Cruises
Arthur River Cruises (☎ 6457 1158) has been operating for nearly 20 years and offers a comfortable, scenic day cruise departing at 10am and returning at 3pm, available most days as long as a minimum of eight people have booked. Its boat, the spacious MV *George Robinson*, motors upriver to the confluence of the Arthur and Frankland Rivers, where you can see birdlife like sea eagles and azure kingfishers, and enjoy a BBQ and

an interesting rainforest walk. The cost is $49/16.50 per adult/child and cruises must be booked at least a day in advance.

An alternative cruise is offered by **AR Reflections River Cruises** (☎ 6457 1288; 4 Gardiner St). Its attractive MV *Reflections* departs at 10.15am daily for a five-hour return trip to Warra Landing, where you also get a guided rainforest walk; a BBQ lunch is provided back at the kiosk. The cruise costs $55/22 per adult/child.

Canoeing

You can explore the river on your own via **Arthur River Canoe & Boat Hire** (☎ 6457 1312, 6457 1158). It hires boats for $18/110 per hour/day and canoes from $60 per day (depending on the craft). You can also be transported upriver for a 40km downriver paddle, which takes two days.

Places to Stay & Eat

Camping grounds (1-5-person camp sites $3.85) in the area include Manuka, Peppermint and Prickly Wattle, the latter on the road to Couta Rocks. All grounds have taps and toilets but no bins – take your rubbish out with you. Self-register at the Parks and Wildlife Service office.

Arthur River Holiday Units (☎/fax 6457 1288; 2 Gardiner St; doubles from $77, extra guests $22) are self-contained and range in size from one to three bedrooms; continental breakfast costs extra.

Ocean View Holiday Cottage (☎ 6452 1278; e effymac@hotmail.com; Lot 80 Gardiner St; singles/doubles from $60/75, extra guests $15) is a pleasant three-bedroom house looking out to the river mouth.

Sunset Holiday Villas (☎/fax 6457 1197; 23 Gardiner St; singles/doubles from $55/70) has two very comfortable self-contained units sharing a balcony and views of the beach, which can be stunning at sunset.

The town also has a **kiosk** with limited supplies.

WESTERN EXPLORER & ARTHUR PIEMAN CONSERVATION AREA

The Western Explorer is the name of the road linking Smithton to the Pieman River.

Because there's a barge to carry cars across the Pieman at the tiny settlement of Corinna, it's possible to use this route to the west coast as an alternative to the Murchison Hwy. More significantly, though, the road is an attraction in its own right, running through or close to the eastern boundary of the Arthur Pieman Conservation Area.

The condition of the C249 – the 53km section from the C214 to Corinna that was upgraded from a 4WD track in 1995 – varies from season to season, if not month to month. Try asking the barge operator at Corinna or a Parks and Wildlife Service ranger at Arthur River for an up-to-date assessment. Although this road is regularly negotiated by vehicles without 4WD and is promoted as a tourist route, it is remote, mostly unsealed, narrow, potholed, and has steep ascents and descents, all of which well justifies its 50km/h speed limit. The road should probably not be attempted in bad weather or at night.

Another hazard is the bleak, rugged terrain you pass at its southern end: in places it's so seductive that despite the challenging nature of the drive, you just can't help snatching the occasional glance. The northern end, however, is far less scenic and therefore not such a hazard.

Make sure you remember to fill your car's fuel tank at Zeehan, Tullah or Waratah in the south or at Marrawah in the north, because petrol is unavailable between these points. For more information about the barge across the Pieman, see the Corinna & Pieman River section later. For a map of the southern region of the Western Explorer, see the regional map in The West chapter.

The remote features of the 1000-sq-km Arthur Pieman Conservation Area, part of the outstanding Tarkine Wilderness (see the Tarkine Wilderness section earlier), include magnificent ocean beaches with some of the wildest swells in the state, **waterfalls** on the Nelson Bay River, **Rebecca Lagoon**, **Temma Harbour**, the old mining town of **Balfour**, the **Pieman River** and the **Norfolk Ranges**. Birdwatchers will relish the chance to see three rare birds in this region: the ground parrot, orange-bellied parrot and hooded plover.

A management plan for the Arthur Pieman was finally produced by the state government in early 2002, which attempts to address local commercial issues (fishing, wind farms, bull-kelp collection), recreational issues (camping, off-road driving) and the area's highly significant Aboriginal heritage.

CORINNA & PIEMAN RIVER
☎ 03

The small vehicular ferry across the Pieman River at the tiny settlement of Corinna, on the river's northern bank, makes this one-time gold-mining settlement a connector between the west and northwest coasts. The other main reason to visit Corinna's somewhat idyllic, forested surrounds is to take the **Pieman River Cruise** (☎ 6446 1170), a laidback, far more rustic alternative to the crowded, mass-produced Gordon River cruises out of Strahan. Costing $40/20 per adult/child, the tour on the MV *Arcadia II* departs daily at 10am and returns at 2pm. It's best to book 24 hours in advance, as during summer it can be booked out and in winter it only runs if there are bookings.

Places to Stay & Eat
The basically supplied concessionaire in Corinna (☎ 6446 1170) runs a small, unpowered **camping ground** (camp sites $3.85) and **Retreat Cabins** (doubles $70, extra adults $12), which are large self-contained units sleeping up to six people – these can get a bit musty but are fine for an overnight stop. There's no other accommodation here.

Getting There & Away
There is no regular public transport to Corinna. From the south, it's approximately a 45-minute drive from Zeehan and a 1½-hour drive from Strahan, while from the north it will take a three- to four-hour drive from Smithton. See the Western Explorer & Arthur Pieman Conservation Area section earlier for more details.

The *Fatman* ferry (cars $11, motorcycles/bicycles $11, $5.50 each if two or more) slides across the Pieman on demand from 9am to 5pm daily April to September, and from 9am to 7pm daily October to March.

HELLYER GORGE
Seven kilometres west of Burnie is the small town of Somerset, at the junction of the Murchison and Bass Hwys. Forty kilometres south of Somerset, the Murchison Hwy winds its way through the impressive Hellyer Gorge, which is on the banks of the Hellyer River. At the picnic area by the river are two short walks that make for a pleasant roadside repose – the River Walk takes 10 minutes return and the Old Myrtle Forest Walk is 15 minutes return.

Connecting Burnie with the Waratah area is an alternative road that's faster but less scenic. Route B18, which passes through Ridgley and Hampshire and avoids the winding road through Hellyer Gorge, has diverted traffic away from the gorge and enhanced the peacefulness of its reserves.

About 40km south of Hellyer Gorge is the CI32 turn-off to Cradle Mountain. This is a major highway that was constructed in the 1980s, providing a link from the west coast to the northern end of Cradle Mountain-Lake St Clair National Park.

WARATAH
☎ 03 • postcode 7321 • pop 230

Near Waratah is the Mt Bischoff mine. Once the world's richest tin mine, it opened in 1888 and was very profitable until 1929, when it was leased. The mine then continued as a minor operation until 1947. From a population of 4000 in the 1890s, Waratah almost vanished when the tin finally ran out. But the nearby prospecting of low-grade iron ore at Savage River in 1968 revived the town. The ore is mined by the Australian Bulk Minerals company and pumped as a slurry along an 85km pipeline to Port Latta on the north coast.

In 1983 a rich lead-zinc-silver-copper ore body was found near the junction of the Murchison Hwy and the road to Cradle Mountain, and by 1989 the Aberfoyle Hellyer Mine, now owned by Western Metals, had started operating.

The town's not-so-greatest claim to fame is that the last verifiably breathing Tasmanian tiger was trapped nearby and shipped off to die in a Hobart zoo in 1936.

Things to See & Do

Waratah is built on both sides of a narrow lake and parts of town look on to encroaching ravines and engagingly wild hillsides. To preserve assorted relics and records of the boom days, the town set up a **museum** (*☎ 6439 1252; Smith St; open 10am-4pm daily Oct-May, noon-3pm Mon-Fri Jun-Sept*). As it's staffed by volunteers, the museum's opening hours tend to vary; if you find it unmanned, inquire at the post office across the road or, if that's closed, at the nearby roadhouse.

Next door to the museum is **Philosopher Smith's Hut**, a reconstruction of the abode of one James Smith, the prospector who discovered tin at Mt Bischoff and then – true to his simple-living, philosophical nature – gave away or cheaply sold every share he'd obtained in the blue-chip Mt Bischoff Tin Mining Company before receiving a solitary dividend.

There are also some signposted **walking tracks** around town, including the recommended two-hour return journey to the Power House.

Places to Stay & Eat

Waratah Camping Ground (*☎ 6439 7100; Smith St; unpowered sites $5.50 plus amenities $3.30, powered sites including amenities $11*), behind the post office/council chambers, consists of a gravelled area for caravans and lakeside lawns for tent-pitchers. Keys to the amenities block are available at the post office or after hours at the Bischoff Hotel.

Bischoff Hotel (*☎ 6439 1188; Main St; singles/doubles from $35/55*), opposite a gully with a small waterfall, is 100 years old and the town's main remnant from the old mining days. New owners are gradually sprucing it up – try for the newer, slightly more expensive room with water views. Counter meals ($8.50 to $13) are served from 6.30pm to 7.30pm daily.

Villas on Que (*☎ 6439 1214; 54 Que St; doubles from $70, extra guests $10*) is a pair of comfortably furnished, fully self-contained two-bedroom units; the price makes it a good, cost-effective base for exploring the countryside. Direct your inquiries to 47 Que St.

SAVAGE RIVER NATIONAL PARK

In 1997, a remote area of 180 sq km in Tasmania's northwest was declared the Savage River National Park. In fact, the area is so remote that the sum total of related information appearing on the website of the Department of Primary Industries, Water and Environment, which oversees the Parks and Wildlife Service, which in turn oversees this park, is: 'A remote wilderness park in Australia's largest area of cool temperate rainforest'. This blunt description fails to acknowledge that the park also contains a swathe of buttongrass on its central Baretop Ridge, and that Savage River was initially worked over for its alluvial gold and subsequently for its iron ore. Prior to the park's creation, the Public Land Use Commission recommended it should be 350 sq km (twice its current size) and that its location within the sizeable Tarkine Wilderness – the subject of an ongoing debate/dispute between the forestry industry and environmentalists – may have affected its ultimate size.

Speaking of access, there are no roads into Savage River National Park, though highways pass by about 5km to 10km from the park's southern and eastern boundaries.

The West

Nature at its most dramatic and inspiring is the attraction of Tasmania's rugged and magnificent west. Formidable mountains, buttongrass plains, ancient rivers, tranquil lakes, dense rainforests and a treacherous coast are all compelling features of this beautiful region, much of which is now part of the Tasmanian Wilderness World Heritage Area.

For thousands of years before European invasion, the island's west was home to Tasmanian Aborigines, who lived through the last ice age in a number of caves along the Franklin River – such as the remote Kutikina Cave – and undoubtedly lived elsewhere inland. Members of the Big River Tribe (also known as the Larmairremener people) had a seasonal 'road' between Lake St Clair and Cradle Mountain, a hardy precursor to today's gentrified Overland Track.

Prior to 1932, when the Lyell Hwy from Hobart to Queenstown was built, the only way into the area was by sea, through the dangerously narrow Hells Gates into Macquarie Harbour. Despite such near-inaccessibility, early European settlement brought explorers, convicts, soldiers, loggers, prospectors, railway gangs and fishermen. The 20th century subsequently brought outdoor adventurers, naturalists, tourists and environmental crusaders.

It was over the wild rivers, beautiful lakes and serene valleys of Tasmania's southwest that battles between environmentalists and governments raged. In the 1980s, the proposed damming of the Franklin and lower Gordon Rivers caused one of the greatest, longest-running environmental debates in Australia's history (for more details, see the upcoming Franklin-Gordon Wild Rivers National Park section). The harbourside town of Strahan has subsequently profited from an ecotourism boom.

Tourism continues to develop in the west. Contemporary projects such as the reconstruction of the historic Abt Railway between Queenstown and Strahan have caught the

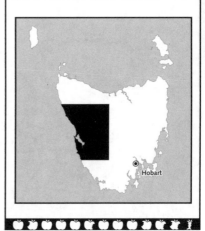

Highlights

- Rafting down the magnificent Franklin River
- Hiking overland from Cradle Mountain to Lake St Clair
- Rolling down the giant Henty Dunes
- Discovering the fascinating mining history of Queenstown and Zeehan
- Jumping on a cruise, seaplane flight or wilderness railway from Strahan

attention of west-coast residents, whose traditional faith in mining as a dependable source of employment has been sorely tested in recent times.

Getting There & Around

TassieLink (☎ 6272 7300, 1300 300 520; W www.tigerline.com.au) runs one bus a day – from Tuesday to Friday and on Sunday – from Hobart to Bronte Junction ($25.50, 2½ hours), Derwent Bridge ($30.50), Lake St Clair ($35.50, three to 3½ hours), the start of the Frenchmans Cap walk ($37, four hours), Queenstown ($45, five to 5½ hours) and Strahan ($52, 6½ to 8½ hours, times varying due to Queenstown stopover); there are return services on the same days. From Launceston, TassieLink buses run once-daily on Monday, Tuesday, Thursday and Saturday to Sheffield ($19, 2½ hours), Gowrie Park ($22.20), Cradle Mountain ($43.60, 3½ hours), Tullah ($38, 4¼ hours), Rosebery ($39.50), Zeehan ($45.50, 5½ hours), Queenstown ($53, 6½ hours) and Strahan ($60, eight hours); again, there are return services on the same days. TassieLink also has a twice-weekly service (on Wednesday and Friday) that picks up passengers disembark-

ing from the ferry terminal in Devonport in the morning and runs them to Burnie (one hour), Tullah ($22.20, 2¼ hours), Rosebery ($23.80, 2½ hours), Zeehan ($30, three hours), Queenstown ($37.10, 3¾ hours) and Strahan ($44.10, 4¾ hours) – the route is also run in reverse on the same days to bring travellers from the west to Devonport in time for the nightly ferry sailing.

For information about additional services for those walking the Overland Track, see Getting There & Away in the Cradle Mountain-Lake St Clair National Park section later.

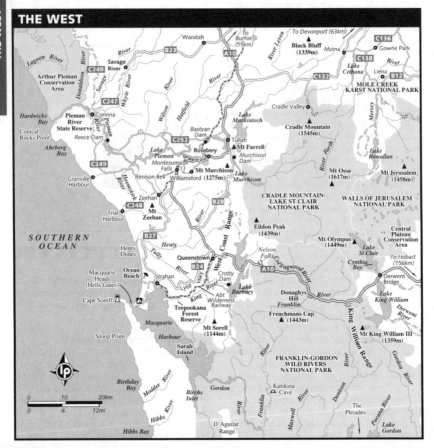

THE WEST

Drivers heading north up the Western Explorer should fill up at Zeehan, Tullah or Waratah, as there's no fuel at either Savage River or Corinna, only at distant Marrawah.

TULLAH

☎ 03 • postcode 7321 • pop 270

This old mining town has had its fair share of isolation to endure – for a long time, the only access was on foot or, later, by train. The town was established in 1892 when a lead-zinc-copper-silver-ore body was discovered on Mt Farrell, the mining of which continued until the early 1970s.

In 1962, the construction of the Murchison Hwy from Burnie to Queenstown linked Tullah with the rest of Tasmania. When the mine closed, the town probably would have imploded if it hadn't received a reprieve by being chosen as the accommodation site for hydroelectric-scheme workers. Throughout the 1970s and early 1980s, around 2000 construction workers resided here.

With the completion of the dams and power stations, the workers vanished and the town emptied; many of the buildings were also removed. The remaining residents are now trying to survive on tourism, with the biggest drawcard being the impressive trout caught in the lakes around town.

The name Tullah comes from an Aboriginal word meaning 'meeting of two rivers', a definition now muddied by the flooding of the rivers in question to form Lake Rosebery, part of a large hydroelectric scheme. The town has great views of Mt Murchison and the surrounding ranges.

Information

At the jerry-built Tullah Village is a **visitors information room** (☎ 6473 4264; Farrell St; open 10am-noon & 1pm-3pm peak holiday periods), staffed by volunteers. The café here is also an Australia Post and Commonwealth Bank agency, and has public toilets.

Things to See & Do

At the **Radford Woodcrafts** gallery and workshop (☎ 6473 4344; open 9am-5pm daily), opposite the pub, you can watch the woodturner at work on Tassie timbers, and buy good-quality lamps, clocks, bowls and wine racks, plus other souvenirs.

There are several scenic drives passing the major hydroelectric dams and lakes. Three kilometres north of town you can follow a road west for 55km to **Reece Dam**. The road crosses the dam wall and continues a farther 29km to Zeehan. The other main scenic road starts 5km south of town and heads over the flanks of Mt Murchison towards Queenstown – known as the **Anthony Rd**, it provides good views as it crosses the West Coast Range. From town, a very scenic minor road also leads to **Murchison Dam**.

The area's best **walks** include **Mt Farrell** (three hours return), which has glorious views of peaks near and far, and **Mt Murchison** (six hours return).

From 1908 until the 1960s, Tullah's only transport link with the rest of the allegedly civilised world was a train line. Eventually a road was built and train services ceased, but in 1977 local residents decided to restore *Wee Georgie Wood* (☎ 6473 2228, 0417 147 015; Murchison Hwy; adult/child/family $5/2/10), one of the engines that had operated on the train line. It's opposite Farrell Park. From September to April the train runs two or three days each month, almost always on a Sunday. Though the 20-minute rides normally take place between noon and 4pm, over daylight saving the hours of operation are sometimes between 3pm and 9pm.

One way to see the region is to go horse riding or boating with **Tullah Horse-Back & Boat Tours** (☎ 6473 4289; Mackintosh Track). Horse rides/boat tours start at $25/18 for the first hour, with rates reduced for subsequent hours. Book at least 24 hours in advance.

Places to Stay & Eat

Tullah Village Bed & Breakfast (☎ 6473 4377, after hours 6473 4136; Farrell St; beds $30) can sleep up to four people in one very large room with its own bathroom, and also handles bookings for rooms in a few houses around town. Prices include continental breakfast. Bookings are made at the café (meals under $10) in the same complex,

THE WEST

which serves breakfasts, takeaway and heavier fare (hamburgers, tuna patties, schnitzels), and kids' meals. It's open from 7am to 7.30pm daily.

Tullah Lakeside Cottage (*☎ 6473 4165, fax 6473 4177; 21 Sale St; singles/doubles $60/70, extra adult/child $15/10)* can sleep up to four people. To find it, drive past Tullah Village (towards the lake) and take the first left, then the first right.

Wombat Lodge (*☎ 6473 4252; Murchison Hwy; rooms $60)* is a quaint two-storey timber cottage that from the outside looks barely big enough to fit a wombat, but most assuredly does. Next door is **Bush Nook Tearooms** *(open 10am-4pm daily)*.

Tullah Chalet (*☎ 6473 4121, fax 6473 4130; Farrell St; backpacker/standard/chalet rooms $50/75/105)* is a recently upgraded, well-managed lakeside complex with a range of accommodation. 'Backpacker' rooms can fit two to six people, making the ones with more bunks a great deal; that said, these rooms are often completely booked out by tour groups. 'Standard' and 'chalet' rooms are all en suite and have natural touches like timber bed-heads (no phones or TVs though). The chalet can advise on canoe/boat hire and local walks. It also has an attractive restaurant (mains $10 to $25), open breakfast through to dinner, with a cheap Sunday roast, plus a wine-stocked bar.

Tullah Tavern *(Murchison Hwy; mains from $10)* has counter meals from 6pm to 8pm on Friday and Saturday only.

Getting There & Away
See the Getting There & Around section at the start of this chapter. Buses arrive at and depart from the BP service station.

ROSEBERY
☎ 03 • postcode 7470 • pop 1440
Gold was discovered in Rosebery in 1891. Further prospecting revealed rich sulphide deposits and the first mines opened here in 1896. By 1899 the Emu Bay Railway from Burnie had reached town and the multi-element ore was shipped to Zeehan for smelting. However, when the Zeehan lead smelters closed in 1913, operations also

closed in Rosebery, as did the nearby Hercules Mine on Mt Read.

In 1920 the Electrolytic Zinc Company bought both mines and, a hefty 16 years later when a mill had finally been designed and constructed, production resumed at both mines. An aerial ropeway from Mt Read transported the ore from the Hercules Mine to Rosebery. In 1986 the Hercules Mine was closed and the aerial ropeway collapsed, though it can still be seen from the highway.

Today the mine at Rosebery continues to employ several hundred people and supports the town's economy.

Information
The **post office** *(Agnes St)* is a Commonwealth Bank agent, while the **newsagency** *(Agnes St; open Mon-Fri, until 1pm Sat & Sun)* handles ANZ transactions.

Things to See & Do
Located behind the Plandome Hotel, the high school (Propsting St) has some interesting old **mine remnants** along its front fence, including a water wheel and railway carriage for steep inclines. The school also contains a small, free-entry **mining museum** that displays artefacts and old photos; ask at the school's reception.

The picnic area at the southern entrance to town is the start of a short walk along the Stitt River and over Park Rd to **Stitt Falls**, which are good after recent rainfall.

The two-day **Rosebery Festival** takes place yearly in mid-March, with heaps of live music, wood-chopping and billycart races, and kids' activities like face-painting.

Sealed roads lead to Williamsford, 8km south of Rosebery, the site of an abandoned mining town and also the start of an excellent walk to the impressively tall but not voluminous **Montezuma Falls**. These are over 100m high and among the highest falls in the state. The excellent, easy return walk along an abandoned railway line takes about three hours return. You can explore the adit at the end of the walk if you bring a torch.

If you prefer a guided walk to Montezuma Falls, **Hay's** (*☎ 6473 1247)* runs trips for $45 per person, which includes lunch and takes three to 3½ hours. Another option with Hay's is a two-hour surface tour of the **Pasminco Zinc Mine**, which departs at 12.30pm daily and costs $13/8 per adult/child. Hay's also runs trips to see an extraordinary stand of Huon pine in the Lake Johnston Nature Reserve ($77 per person, 1½ to two hours; also see the boxed text 'Lake Johnston Nature Reserve' in the Facts about Tasmania chapter). Additionally, Hay's has a boat and can take you trout fishing on any of the lakes that are part of the hydroelectric schemes.

Places to Stay & Eat

Rosebery Caravan Park (☎ 6473 1366; Park Rd; unpowered/powered site doubles $13/15, dorm beds $17, on-site van doubles $30, cabin doubles $60) is surrounded by hills and has a small, grassy camping area, a gravel caravan area and a functional budget lodge.

Miner's Cottages (☎ 6473 1796; 12 & 16 Karlson St; singles/doubles from $65/90) offers a pair of old, two-bedroom cottages with breakfast provisions; direct inquiries to the house in-between, No 14.

Mount Black Lodge (☎ 6473 1039; e mountblacklodge@hotmail.com; Hospital Rd; singles with/without en suite $77/30, doubles with/without en suite $88/40) is a great place to stay, equipped with sizeable rooms, a wood-heated lounge, a thoroughly relaxing atmosphere and fine views of Murchison Range from the en suite rooms. The excellent food at its **Blue Moon Restaurant** (mains $14-20; open from 6pm daily) includes Atlantic salmon and char-grilled Scotch fillet; vegetarians should identify themselves and will be amply catered for. It's occasionally open for lunch too.

Nancy's Guesthouse (☎ 6473 1405; Propsting St), opposite the school, is rumoured to serve regular three-course lunch and dinner buffets for a paltry $10.

There are also a number of **snack bars** and a large **bakery** on the main street.

Getting There & Away

See the Getting There & Around section at the start of this chapter. Buses arrive at and depart from Mackrill's Milkbar at 24 Agnes St.

ZEEHAN

☎ 03 • postcode 7469 • pop 1120

In 1882, rich deposits of silver and lead were discovered in the quiet little town of Zeehan, and by the century's end it had become a booming mining centre known as Silver City, with a population that peaked at nearly 10,000. In its heyday Zeehan had 26 hotels and its Gaiety Theatre seated 1000 people.

In 1908, however, the major mines began to fail. The town began a slow decline, culminating in the closure of the last significant mine in 1960. Later that decade, with the reopening and expansion of the Renison Tin Mine at Renison Bell, 17km towards Rosebery, Zeehan revived when it became the housing base for Renison Ltd.

Orientation & Information

Zeehan is a very small town, but it's worth noting that the historic part of Main St is at the northern end of town, not the bit you see when entering from Strahan or Queenstown. The town is the administrative centre for the region run by the West Coast Council and has branches of the **ANZ** and **Commonwealth Banks**, and a **library** with public Internet access. Tourist information and books on the history of the west coast can be obtained at the West Coast Pioneers Memorial Museum.

Zeehan is a convenient place to spend the night if you're planning on driving the 50km to the Pieman River to take a cruise or go boating on the beautiful watercourse (see the Corinna & Pieman River section in The Northwest chapter), or continue along the Western Explorer to the northwestern corner of the state.

West Coast Pioneers Memorial Museum

This excellent museum (☎ 6471 6225; Main St; adult/child $5.50/3.30; open 8.30am-5pm daily Apr-Sept, 8.30am-6pm daily Oct-Mar) is in the 1894 School of Mines building. The ground floor features an interesting mineral collection, a fauna display and a mining gallery set up by a local company. Upstairs are photographs of old mining towns and their inhabitants. To one side of the museum is an exhibit of steam locomotives and carriages used on the early west-coast railways, while downstairs from here is a crocoite 'cavern', filled with specimens of the rare mineral, which happens to be Tasmania's official mineral emblem.

Gaiety Grand

The Gaiety Theatre and the Grand Hotel are a single building known as the Gaiety Grand, a short distance up Main St from the museum.

The Gaiety was one of the biggest, most modern theatres in the world when it opened in February 1899, and what a bonus it must have been for the miners to be able to move between the pub and the theatre through connecting doors. In his book *The Peaks of Lyell,* historian Geoffrey Blainey notes that to mark the Gaiety's opening a Melbourne troupe of 60 was brought to town, where it played to a house of 1000 every night for a week, pulling audiences from as far afield as Queenstown, then a six-hour journey away.

Silver City Info/Tours (☎ *6471 5095, 0438 716 389; 8 Parkinson St)* can guide you around this grand old venue with a 30-minute tour of the theatre or a one-hour tour of the entire building from $6.50/4.50 per adult/concession (tour times by arrangement). It also does informative guided tours of the Pioneers Museum and of Zeehan township.

After being subjected to some appalling renovations over the years, the Gaiety Grand is slowly being restored using donations given to the Pioneers Museum, whatever government grants can be secured, and any proceeds from sales in the volunteer-run gallery at the front of the building. In time, the West Coast Heritage Authority also hopes to restore the town's other historic buildings, including the still-used post office (Main St), the old bank (Main St) and St Luke's Church (Belstead St).

Historic Walk

An excellent way to see more of Zeehan is to take the following circuit walk. Starting from the museum, follow Main St west,
turn left down Fowler St towards the golf course and walk through **Spray Tunnel**, a former railway tunnel. Turn left again to follow the Comstock track (an old tramway) south to **Florence Dam**. Follow the right track at the fork, winding around Keel Ridge, then descend to the southern end of Main St. The walk takes two to three hours and passes a lot of old mine sites.

More detailed notes on this walk and others around the mining sites of the west coast are detailed in *Historic Mines of Western Tasmania* by Duncan How, available at the museum for $10. Alternatively, take the Spray Tunnel scenic drive suggested by the museum (all the way or as far as the tunnel, from where you can continue on foot).

Other Attractions

There are plenty of old mining relics outside town. Four kilometres south of Zeehan you'll find some **old smelters** beside the highway. For panoramic views you can follow the track starting near the smelters to the top of **Mt Zeehan**; the walk takes three hours return.

At Renison Bell, 17km east of Zeehan, there's a signposted **Battery Mill Walk** starting 300m west of the mine entrance. This visits the old mill site where rock from the mine was crushed. A locomotive, railway sidings and old workings are described with the aid of photographic plaques beside the track. Allow about 45 minutes return for a visit.

Northwest of Zeehan, a quiet sealed road leads to **Reece Dam** on the Pieman River, part of the Pieman hydroelectric scheme. This road allows access to some rarely visited places like **Granville Harbour**, a small coastal holiday place down a side road where you can camp, and Corinna, the departure point for the Pieman River Cruise (see the Corinna & Pieman River section in The Northwest chapter). The road to Reece Dam also provides a view of **Heemskirk Falls**; a one-hour return walk leads to the base of the falls. For **fishing** enthusiasts, Granville Harbour is a good place for crayfish and Lake Pieman, behind Reece Dam, has some fine trout.

A gravel road heads west to **Trial Harbour**, Zeehan's original port and now a collection of holiday homes and a few permanent residences; there are no shops or other facilities. You can do a few short and long walks around here and there are some great fishing spots, plus it's a beautiful place to camp – pick up the brochure on Trial Harbour from Zeehan's Pioneers Museum. Another feature is the **local history room**, with old photos and other memorabilia. It's open most days.

To sample a bit of local entrepreneurialism, visit **Shorty's** (☎ 6471 6595; 22 Shaw St; admission by gold-coin donation; open 10am-5pm daily) for an unusual collection of minerals, mining odds and ends, and 'bushcraft oddities'. Shaw St runs off Main St at the northern end of town.

From Zeehan, you can take Henty Rd (B27) to **Henty Dunes** (see the Ocean Beach & Henty Dunes entry in the Strahan section later).

Warning If walking off marked tracks in the bush close to Zeehan or at Trial Harbour, beware of abandoned mine shafts hidden by vegetation.

Places to Stay & Eat

Treasure Island Caravan Park (☎ 6471 6633, fax 6471 6615; Hurst St; unpowered/powered site doubles $14/17, on-site van doubles $40, cabin doubles $65) is spread out alongside the Zeehan Rivulet on the northern edge of town. It has friendly management and plenty of greenery.

Hotel Cecil (☎ 6471 6221, fax 6471 6599; Main St; singles $35, doubles with/without en suite $60/50) has small but ultra-clean hotel rooms and, on an adjacent block, three very comfortable self-contained miners' cottages (doubles $80). It serves pub meals (mains $12 to 19) like rissoles and garlic prawns daily.

Heemskirk Motor Hotel (☎ 6471 6107, 1800 639 876, fax 6471 6694; Main St; rooms $74-90), at the eastern entrance to town, has decent-sized motel rooms and the **Abel Tasman Bistro** (mains $12-19; open lunch & dinner daily), which serves Mongolian lamb, chilli chicken and salmon patties, and has

the occasional mealtime floorshow to entertain the occasional coach group.

Mt Zeehan Retreat (☎ 6471 6424, fax 6471 6430; 12 Runcorn St; singles $40-50, doubles $80-90) is a friendly modern house with a couple of B&B en suite rooms, the upstairs one a room with a view. There are no credit facilities.

Zeehan Motor Inn & Lodge (☎ 6471 6107; Main St; doubles from $80) has brick motel units. It also has cheap beds in a nearby hostel, which was being done up at the time of research.

Museum Coffee Lounge, in the West Coast Pioneers Memorial Museum, has $5 light lunches like soup and savoury croissants. You don't need to pay the museum's entry fee to have a coffee here.

The Coffee Stop (☎ 6471 6709; 110 Main St; open 9am-5pm Tues-Sun) serves light meals and takeaway snacks, and has local crafts on display.

Getting There & Away

See the Getting There & Around section at the start of this chapter. Buses arrive at and depart from Marina's Coffee Shop, on the main street.

STRAHAN

☎ 03 • postcode 7468 • pop 700

Strahan is 40km southwest of Queenstown on Macquarie Harbour and is the only sizeable town on the rugged west coast.

Macquarie Harbour was discovered by sailors searching for the source of the Huon pine that frequently washed up on southern beaches at a time when the area was totally inaccessible by land and its treacherous coast made it very difficult to reach by sea. In 1821 these dubious assets prompted the establishment of a penal settlement on Sarah Island, in the middle of the harbour. Its main function was to isolate the worst of the colony's convicts and to use their muscle to harvest huge stands of Huon pine. The convicts worked upriver 12 hours a day, often in leg-irons, felling the pines and rafting them back to the island's saw-pits, where they were used to build ships and furniture.

Sarah Island, which featured in Marcus Clarke's novel about the convict experience, *For the Term of His Natural Life,* was one of Australia's most notorious penal settlements. The most dreaded punishment meted out there was confinement on tiny Grummet Island, little more than a windswept rock. Despite its brutal credentials, the island was abandoned in 1834 after the establishment of an 'escape-proof' penal settlement at Port Arthur.

Strahan prospered during the west-coast mining boom of the late 19th century, when ore was transported to its port along the Abt

Railway from Queenstown. Consequently, steamers shuttled between Strahan and Hobart, Launceston and Melbourne carrying copper, gold, silver, lead, timber and passengers. However, following the closure of many mines, the opening of the Emu Bay Railway from Zeehan to Burnie, and the construction of the Lyell Hwy between Hobart and Queenstown, the town was economically and socially anaesthetised.

Strahan unpredictably shot to fame in the 1980s as the centre for the Franklin River Blockade. The powerful state hydroelectricity authority had already constructed a

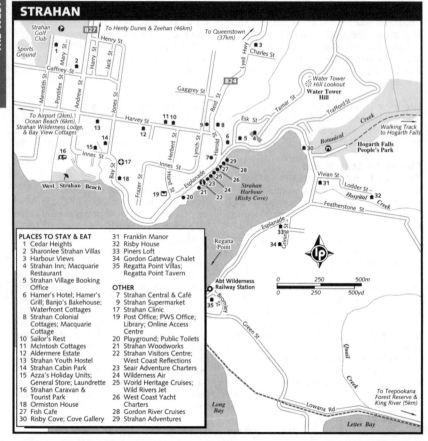

STRAHAN

PLACES TO STAY & EAT
1 Cedar Heights
2 Sharonlee Strahan Villas
3 Harbour Views
4 Strahan Inn; Macquarie Restaurant
5 Strahan Village Booking Office
6 Hamer's Hotel; Hamer's Grill; Banjo's Bakehouse; Waterfront Cottages
8 Strahan Colonial Cottages; Macquarie Cottage
10 Sailor's Rest
11 McIntosh Cottages
12 Aldermere Estate
13 Strahan Youth Hostel
14 Strahan Cabin Park
15 Azza's Holiday Units; General Store; Laundrette
16 Strahan Caravan & Tourist Park
18 Ormiston House
27 Fish Cafe
30 Risby Cove; Cove Gallery

31 Franklin Manor
32 Risby House
33 Piners Loft
34 Gordon Gateway Chalet
35 Regatta Point Villas; Regatta Point Tavern

OTHER
7 Strahan Central & Café
9 Strahan Supermarket
17 Strahan Clinic
19 Post Office; PWS Office; Library; Online Access Centre
20 Playground; Public Toilets
21 Strahan Woodworks
22 Strahan Visitors Centre; West Coast Reflections
23 Seair Adventure Charters
24 Wilderness Air
25 World Heritage Cruises; Wild Rivers Jet
26 West Coast Yacht Charters
28 Gordon River Cruises
29 Strahan Adventures

large dam on the Gordon River and flooded Lake Pedder, and was about to construct a series of dams on the Franklin and lower Gordon Rivers. Protesters set off from Strahan in rubber boats and canoes to physically prevent work from proceeding. In the summer of 1982–83, 1400 people were arrested in a widely publicised dispute. The conservationists eventually won and the Franklin River still flows free. For more details, see the Franklin-Gordon Wild Rivers National Park section of this chapter.

Strahan has since exploited its proximity to wilderness by offering a variety of tours on the Gordon River, and several developers have aggressively transformed its harbourside main street into what is now euphemistically called Strahan Village – it's more an expensive, self-aggrandising shopping centre than a true community. The town's true appeal ironically lies in the natural and historical attractions around it rather than in the town itself.

There's no denying Strahan's popularity as a tourist destination, reputedly the second most popular in the state, a statistic easily believed by anyone who has been packed into a peak-season Gordon River cruise. So if you like a bit of luxury, you may find the polish of this continuously developing commercial settlement the perfect foil for the harsh landscape and uncompromising authenticity of the surrounding mining towns.

Information

The architecturally innovative **Strahan visitors centre** (☎ 6471 7622; e strahan@tasvis info.com.au; Esplanade; open 10am-8pm daily) is almost a tourist attraction in its own right. It was substantially renovated in 1998, when the gardens were rejuvenated, activities introduced for kids, and the outside amphitheatre transformed into an all-weather venue. Its punctilious staff can find you accommodation or issue a national park pass. See the Museums & Galleries and Entertainment entries in this section for more information on the centre's diverse offerings.

There's a **Parks and Wildlife Service** office (PWS; ☎ 6471 7122; open 9am-5pm Mon-Fri) in the old Customs House, a fine

Federation structure adorning the foreshore. This building also houses a branch of the **State Library of Tasmania**, an **online access centre** and the **post office**. For banking, the post office is a Commonwealth Bank agent, the **supermarket/newsagent** (Reid St) handles ANZ accounts, and there's a multi-card ATM at **Azza's general store** (Innes St; open 6.30am to 9pm daily). For health-related matters, visit the **Strahan Clinic** (☎ 6471 7152; Bay St).

Abt Wilderness Railway

At the time of research, the Abt Wilderness Railway was only travelling the 11km from Queenstown to Rinadeena before turning back, and was yet to make its first commercial journey along the entire 34km of track between Queenstown and Strahan, despite hopes the full service would be up and running by the dawn of 2002. But regardless of the ongoing delays faced by the railway, it was still hoped that passengers would be completing the entire rail journey between the two west-coast towns – passing through a half-dozen stations and immaculate rainforest, and over numerous reconstructed bridges spanning the wild King River – by the beginning of 2003. When the Abt is finally launched in Strahan, it will depart from and arrive at the newly constructed **railway station** (☎ 6471 7999) on the Esplanade at Regatta Point. For more information, see the Abt Wilderness Railway entry in the Queenstown section, and also the boxed text 'The Abt Railway' later in this chapter.

Museums & Galleries

West Coast Reflections (Esplanade; adult/concession/child $3.50/2.50/free; open 10am-8pm daily) is the museum section of the Strahan visitors centre, installed beyond the Huon-pine reception desk. It's a creative and thought-provoking display on the history of the west coast, with a refreshingly blunt appraisal of the region's environmental disappointments and achievements, including the Franklin Blockade.

Nearby is **Strahan Woodworks** (☎ 6471 7244; 12 Esplanade; open 8.30am-5pm daily), where you can see Huon pine, sassafras and myrtle being turned and then buy the end results, mainly kitchen knick-knacks, platters and ornamental objects. For more arts and crafts, check out the **Cove Gallery** (☎ 6471 7572; Esplanade; open 8am-6pm daily summer, 10am-4pm daily winter), around the bay in the Risby Cove complex.

Ocean Beach & Henty Dunes

Six kilometres from town is the impressive Ocean Beach, a 33km stretch of sand from Trial Harbour in the north to Macquarie Heads in the south – the sunsets here have to be seen to be believed. Due to rips and undertows, swimming at this beach is not recommended. The dunes behind the beach become a mutton bird **rookery** from October, when the birds return from their 15,000km winter migration – they remain here until April, providing an evening spectacle as they return to their nests at dusk.

Fourteen kilometres along the road from Strahan to Zeehan are the spectacular Henty Dunes, a series of 30m-high white sand dunes on Ocean Beach. They're a soothing contrast to the harshness of other west-coast scenery and an irresistible sand-slide to any children. Unfortunately, the strident, peace-shattering noises of off-road vehicles are permitted here, though the beach is often claimed solely by those on foot. From the picnic area you can take a 1½-hour return walk through the dunes and out to Ocean Beach; remember to carry drinking water.

Teepookana Forest & King River

The Teepookana Forest surrounds the King River to the east of Strahan. The condition of the King River is on the improve but it has long-served as a graphic example of that other west-coast feature, environmental degradation: a fixture along each of its banks has been a band of sludge in which nothing grows, the result of pollution from mining operations in Queenstown. Yet incongruous as it sounds, the forest and the river remain beautiful. An extensive section of the Abt Railway line follows the King River and is to install a station at the now-defunct port of Teepookana and access to **Teepookana Tower**, a Forestry Tasmania–built lookout.

Other Attractions

There is a lookout over the town at **Water Tower Hill**, accessed by following Esk St beside the Strahan Village booking office; it's less than 1km from the Esplanade.

Hogarth Falls is a pleasant one hour return walk through the rainforest beside the platypus-inhabited Botanical Creek. The track starts at People's Park.

The 45m-high **Cape Sorell Lighthouse**, at the harbour's southern head, is purportedly the second-highest in Australia. A return walk of two to three hours along a vehicle track from the jetty at Macquarie Heads leads to the lighthouse. You'll need a boat to cross the heads unless you can find an accommodating fisher to take you over.

Next to the caravan park is **West Strahan Beach**, with a gently shelving sandy bottom that provides safe swimming.

Organised Tours

River & Harbour Cruises Operating a catamaran purpose-built to minimise wake and any subsequent effects on the fragile Gordon riverbanks is **Gordon River Cruises** (☎ 6471 4300, 1800 628 286; W www.strahan village.com.au). The boat advertises 5½-hour cruises at 8.30am and 2.30pm daily year-round (except Christmas Day), but note that from Easter until the end of winter, a booking through Gordon River Cruises will see you wind up on a World Heritage Cruises boat (see following) – Gordon River Cruises leases its own craft elsewhere during that period. The cost depends on where you sit and whether meals are involved: a trip with buffet lunch on the upper deck costs from $100 to $120 per person, while standard seats without food cost from $55/28 per adult/child. All trips involve a rainforest walk at Heritage Landing and a guided tour of Sarah Island.

World Heritage Cruises (☎ 6471 7174; W www.worldheritagecruises.com.au; Esplanade) also runs Gordon River cruises on purpose-built catamarans. There's a five-hour cruise departing 9am daily from October through April that costs $50/22 per adult/child, and a 6½-hour cruise setting off at 9am daily (except Christmas Day) that costs $55/25 per adult/child. A smorgasbord is available onboard (adult/child $9/6) for those who don't pack their own lunchboxes. Both cruises include a rainforest walk and views of Hells Gates (the narrow entrance to Macquarie Harbour), but only the longer trip has a one-hour stopover on Sarah Island.

West Coast Yacht Charters (☎ 6471 7422; Esplanade; open 8.30am-5pm daily Apr-Nov, 8.30am-6pm daily Dec-Mar) has a 2½-hour cruise around Macquarie Harbour including a crayfish dinner. The cruise costs $55/40 per adult/child and departs daily at 5pm (6pm over summer). It also advertises a 'two days/two nights sailing cruise' up the Gordon River for $360/180, but the description is misleading, as the first night is spent moored at Strahan Wharf; also note that dinner is provided the second night but not the first. You can also arrange three-hour fishing-only trips ($40 per adult) or get a B&B bunk on the water (see Places to Stay later).

Strahan Marine Charters (☎ 0418 135 983), at the end of Strahan Wharf, is another option for fishing or sightseeing charters, which can be arranged from $55 per person (minimum four people).

Sea Kayaking Experienced or inexperienced paddlers can take sea-kayak tours with **Strahan Adventures** (☎ 6471 7776; Esplanade), which operates from the Gordon River Cruises building. Tours from Risby Cove along the waterfront and back cost $50 per person, while twilight tours of Henty River cost $80 per person. Hardier trips to the Franklin or Gordon Rivers or to Sarah Island can also be arranged.

Jet-Boat Rides Operating from the same office as World Heritage Cruises is **Wild Rivers Jet** (☎ 6471 7174; Esplanade), which runs 50-minute jet-boat rides on the hour from 9am to 4pm up the rainforest-lined gorges of the King River. This wet experience costs $48/29/132 per adult/child/family and there is a minimum of two people per ride.

Scenic Flights The following companies offer daily flights (weather permitting); trips should be booked ahead.

Seair Adventure Charters (☎ 6471 7718; W www.seairac.com.au; Strahan Wharf; open 8.30am-5pm daily Sept-July) conducts light-plane flights over Frenchmans Cap, the Franklin and Gordon Rivers ($110 per person), Cradle Mountain and Lake St Clair ($165 per person), as well as helicopter flights over the Teepookana Forest ($130 per person) and Sarah Island ($180 per person). Fixed-wing flights take off from Strahan airport while the helicopters flutter up from a landing pad down at the wharf.

Wilderness Air (☎ 6471 7280; Strahan Wharf; open 8.30am-5pm daily) has seaplanes departing the wharf area roughly every 90 minutes from 9am until 5pm, flying upriver to land at Sir John Falls, where you get to walk in the rainforest; the 80-minute flights cost $132/73 per adult/child. Flights that include a return trip via Frenchmans Cap cost $168/89 per adult/child.

Places to Stay

Much of the accommodation in the centre of town is run by **Strahan Village**, which has its booking office (☎ 6471 4200, 1800 628 286; W www.strahanvillage.com.au; open 7am-7pm daily May-Oct, 7am-9pm daily Nov-Apr) under the clocktower on the Esplanade. Another chunk of the town's accommodation, including the hostel, is handled by the booking office of **Strahan Central** (☎ 6471 7612; e strahancentral@ trump.net.au; cnr Esplanade & Harold St; open 9am-5.30pm daily), which doubles as a café.

Strahan's popularity means it's inevitably a good idea to book ahead, definitely over summer and during school and public holidays. Outside the high season you should be able to negotiate reasonable stand-by discounts late in the day – this tactic may pay off when you want some of the more expensive waterfront accommodation at a more affordable price.

Places to Stay – Budget

Camping is possible at the basic camping ground (camp sites $5) at Macquarie Heads, 15km southwest of Strahan; follow the signs to Ocean Beach and see the caretaker.

Strahan Caravan & Tourist Park (☎ 6471 7239, fax 6471 7692; Innes St; unpowered/powered site doubles $15/18, on-site van doubles $45, cabin doubles $75) has been thoroughly spruced up in recent years and has a number of clean, well-equipped cabins.

Strahan Youth Hostel (☎ 6471 7255; 43 Harvey St; dorm beds per YHA member/non-member $18/21.50, singles/doubles from $25/50) is in a nice bush setting 10 minutes' walk from the town centre, with plain bunks and doubles, and tiny A-frame cabins with shared facilities. Bookings are also handled through Strahan Central.

Places to Stay – Mid-Range
Guesthouses & B&Bs Sleep in a floating bunk on a wharf-moored yacht belonging to **West Coast Yacht Charters** (☎ 6471 7422; e wcyc@tassie.net.au; Esplanade; adult/child $35/10). Because the yacht is used for charters, it has late check-in and early check-out. Prices include continental breakfast.

Strahan Wilderness Lodge (☎ 6471 7142; Ocean Beach Rd; singles/doubles $50/60), a kilometre or two north of town among 11 peaceful hectares of low coastal vegetation, is an old-style, laidback place with large rooms; prices include continental breakfast. The same people run the private **Bay View Cottages** (doubles from $85, extra guests $20).

Harbour Views (☎ 6471 7143, fax 6471 7766; 1 Charles St; doubles from $70), on the road into Strahan from Queenstown and a fair way from the harbour, has a pair of motel-style, self-contained B&B rooms.

Hotels Managed by Strahan Village, **Hamers Hotel** (☎ 6471 4200, 1800 628 286, fax 6471 4389; Esplanade; singles/doubles from $42/55) has unspectacular but cheap rooms with continental breakfast.

Self-Contained Units At the back of the general store are **Azza's Holiday Units** (☎ 6471 7253; 7 Innes St; doubles $77), a set of plain self-contained cubicles.

Strahan Cabin Park (☎ 6471 7442, fax 6471 7278; cnr Innes & Jones Sts; doubles from $80), has standard prefabricated cabins; pets are not allowed.

Sailor's Rest (☎ 6471 7237; e sr@sailorsrest.com.au; 14-16 Harvey St; doubles $100-125, extra guests $25), on an unassuming street a short stroll from the waterfront, has spacious, fully equipped cottages in all sizes, to suit loners and families. There's a one-bedroom unit with wheelchair access.

Cedar Heights (☎ 6471 7717; e cedarheights@vision.net.au; 7 Meredith St; singles/doubles from $75/90) has timber cabins in a quiet street next to the golf course and opposite an oval.

Places to Stay – Top End
Guesthouses & B&Bs A few doors down from Sailor's Rest is **McIntosh Cottages** (☎ 6471 7358, fax 6471 7074; Harvey St; doubles $170), two conjoined colonial places in what was once a general store. Considering the price and the off-waterfront location, you'll need to be a big fan of period decor.

Strahan Colonial Cottages (☎ 6471 7612, fax 6471 7513; Reid St; doubles $165-195), managed by Strahan Central, is a hillside row of plushly renovated old cottages; breakfast provisions are included.

Macquarie Cottage (☎/fax 6471 7028; 5 Reid St; doubles $130-160, extra adults $30) snuck unannounced into the midst of the Strahan Colonial Cottages group. It's another yesteryear-style cottage, dating from 1890 and now nicely updated with a range of modern conveniences. It sleeps up to five people.

Franklin Manor (☎ 6471 7311; w www.franklinmanor.com.au; Esplanade; doubles $180-245), on the foreshore across Risby Cove from the town centre, is an especially charming, century-old hideaway in lovely grounds. Extras you'll appreciate are king-size beds in the deluxe rooms, a formidably stocked underground cellar and a fine on-site restaurant (see Places to Eat later).

Piners Loft (☎ 6471 7036; e pinersloft@trump.net.au; Grining St; doubles from $190, extra adults $40) is a good-looking two-storey lookout atop poles of King Billy and celery-top pine. Replete with modern facilities, the whole place can be yours (sleeps seven); breakfast provisions are supplied.

Ormiston House (☎ 6471 7077; w www.ormistonhouse.com.au; Esplanade; doubles

CHRIS BELL

Aerial view of the meandering Gordon River

LINDSAY BROWN

Boats moored in Strahan harbour

SARA-JANE CLELAND

The bark on a snow gum, Cradle Mountain

KAREN TRIST

Cradle Mountain looms behind Dove Lake in Tasmania's west

Oysters for dinner, King Island

Checking cheese wheels at King Island Dairy

Cape Wickham lighthouse, King Island

The masses of Bull Kelp that wash onto King Island's shore are harvested and exported

$185-245), off West Strahan Beach, is a sumptuous but not overtly formal 1899 manor with well-appointed rooms.

Motels Also referred to as the Hilltop and now managed by Strahan Village, **Strahan Inn** (☎ 6471 4200, 1800 628 286, fax 6471 4389; Jolly St; doubles $85-95) is the large edifice on the hill above the clocktower. Many of its standard rooms have good views of the harbour, which is fortunate considering their badly aged exteriors.

Strahan Central (☎ 6471 7612, fax 6471 7513; cnr Esplanade & Harold St; doubles $145-165) has a number of modern, attractive, split-level suites above its booking office/café; continental breakfast is provided.

Risby Cove (☎ 6471 7572; [W] www .risby.com.au; Esplanade; doubles from $180) is an eye-catchingly modern complex on the foreshore, 500m east of the town centre. The main building, with a surprisingly appealing corrugated-iron look, has great one- and two-bedroom suites, some with spa. Risby Cove also manages the three-bedroom **Risby House** (Lodder St; doubles $144, extra adult/child $33/17), nearby on the inland side of the Esplanade.

Self-Contained Units There's a mass of standard brick units (15 in all) at **Sharonlee Strahan Villas** (☎ 6471 7224, fax 6471 7375; cnr Andrew & Gaffney Sts; doubles $130, extra guests $25) in the town's west, on the road that leads to Zeehan.

Regatta Point Villas (☎ 6471 7103, fax 6471 7366; Esplanade; doubles $120, extra adults $20), near the Abt Railway station at Regatta Point and managed by the local tavern, has eight units with fair views.

Gordon Gateway Chalet (☎ 6471 7165, fax 6471 7588; Grining St; doubles $100-125), in a scenic hillside location on the way to Regatta Point, has modern, well-outfitted studio units (including a barrier-free room) and several larger A-frame chalets with views out to Strahan Harbour.

Strahan Village (☎ 6471 4200, 1800 628 286, fax 6471 4389; Esplanade; doubles $150-220) conglomerate runs a group of self-contained cottages and terraces on the waterfront near the booking office, built in various colonial styles and with varying degrees of luxury.

Aldermere Estate (☎/fax 6471 7418; [e] aldermereonharvey@bigpond.com; 27 Harvey St; apartments from $200) has several stylish and luxuriously modern two-storey apartments, each with two bedrooms. They're perfect for a two-person indulgence or for two couples to share (rates from $140 per couple).

Places to Eat

Banjo's Bakehouse (☎ 6471 7794; Esplanade; open 6am-late daily) is a BYO bakery near Hamer's Hotel, with a breakfast menu and oven-baked pizzas after 6pm.

Fish Cafe (☎ 6471 4386; Esplanade; open noon-3pm & 6pm-9pm daily Sept-May) serves a variety of fish and chips, plus salmon burgers and oysters, most for under $10. The café is also licensed.

Hamer's Grill (☎ 6471 4200; Esplanade; mains $14-20; meals noon-2.30pm & 6pm-9pm daily), in Hamers Hotel, has a literal culinary emphasis, but also serves lots of fresh seafood and pasta in its busy interior.

Regatta Point Tavern (☎ 6471 7103; Esplanade; mains $16-18), near the railway terminus 2km around the bay from Strahan's centre, serves good hearty seafood and steak lunches and dinners daily in its bistro; there's also a kiddies' menu.

Strahan Central Café (☎ 6471 7612; cnr Esplanade & Harold St; open 9am-5.30pm daily) is a licensed place with smoked salmon salad, focaccias and soup for under $10, plus distinctive blackboard specials.

Macquarie Restaurant (☎ 6471 4200; Jolly St; buffet per person $33; open from 6pm daily Sept-May), with a scenic lookout from within the hilltop Strahan Inn, hosts an impressive, seafood-laden buffet.

Franklin Manor (☎ 6471 7311; Esplanade; mains $27-35; open from 6.30pm daily) makes for a deliciously grand dining space. The menu features local produce and changes seasonally, though ocean trout is a fixture, and meals for vegetarians, vegans and coeliac sufferers are easily prepared with advance notice. Wine fanciers will love the huge wine list. Bookings are recommended.

Ormiston House (☎ 6471 7077; Esplanade; mains $24; open from 7pm daily) has an excellent à la carte restaurant serving dishes such as crispy-skinned duck and salmon fillets. House guests seeking dinner are prioritised, so book ahead to make sure there's a seat available.

Risby Cove (☎ 6471 7572; Esplanade; dinner $19-27; open 10am-9pm daily) serves lunches, teas and dinners top-heavy with seafood in its licensed, innovative surrounds.

Entertainment
The Strahan visitors centre stages *The Ship That Never Was* (☎ 6471 7622; Esplanade; adult/concession/child $12/9/2) in its amphitheatre. It is the entertainingly theatrical story of some convicts who escaped from Sarah Island by building their own ship, and pleases all age groups. Performances are held at 5.30pm daily year-round, and also at 8.30pm daily in January.

Risby Cove (☎ 6471 7572; Esplanade; adult/child $8.50/5.50) regularly screens evening films in its auditorium; ring for details.

Getting There & Away
Bus See the Getting There & Around section at the start of this chapter. Buses arrive at and depart from the visitors centre.

At the time of research, **Strahan & West Coast Taxis** (☎ 0417 516 071) was trialling a weekly bus service to Burnie via Zeehan, Rosebery and Tullah.

Hitching If you're hitching, it can be a long wait between vehicles on both the Lyell and Murchison Hwys, and in winter it gets bloody cold. The bus services are a useful alternative.

Getting Around
The township adds to its coffers by charging up to $4 per day for car parking; those embarking on a cruise can park for free at the wharf car park. Spaces in front of the main shopping area have 30- to 60-minute time limits.

QUEENSTOWN
☎ 03 • postcode 7467 • pop 2630

The final, winding descent into Queenstown from the Lyell Hwy is unforgettable, with deep, eroded gullies and denuded, variegated hills testifying to the destruction of the local environment by long-term mining operations.

The discovery of alluvial gold in the Queen River valley in 1881 brought prospectors to the area. Two years later, mining began on the rich Mt Lyell deposits and for nearly a decade miners extracted a few ounces of gold a day from the Iron Blow, ignoring the mountain's rich copper reserves. In 1891 the Mt Lyell Mining Company began to concentrate on copper, but it had trouble raising financial backing. The discovery of a rich vein of silver rescued the company and in 1895 the first of the Mt Lyell smelters began operating. Copper had become the most profitable mineral on the west coast.

The initial township was at Penghana, based around the smelters, but a bushfire in 1886 wiped out this shanty settlement and the residents moved to a newly planned town on the Queen River, which became known as Queenstown. At the turn of the century, Queenstown had a population of over 5000 and was the third-largest town in Tasmania. It had 14 hotels, 28 mining companies working the Mt Lyell deposits, and 11 furnaces involved in the smelting process. The Mt Lyell Mining & Railway Company eventually acquired most of the mines or leases.

By the 1920s, after 25 years of mining, the previously rainforested hills around Queenstown had been stripped bare: three million tonnes of timber had been felled to feed the furnaces. By 1900, uncontrolled pollution from the copper smelters was already killing any vegetation that hadn't already been cut down, and bushfires – fuelled by sulphur-impregnated soil and dead stumps – raged through the hills every summer. Rains then washed away the exposed topsoil until only bare rocky hills remained.

For a long time after the smelters finally closed in 1969, there was no change to the barren hills around town. But now bits of scrub and a few small trees have started re-colonising the slopes and already the landscape is less stark than it was just a decade ago. Real environmental improvements will take a long time though, a fact reinforced by the widespread local recommendation that you boil the town's discoloured water before drinking it.

The Mt Lyell mine closed in late 1994 and the town's future looked as bleak as the surrounding hills. But a year later the Copper Mines of Tasmania company took over the mine's lease and reopened it, and, after weathering a phase of desperately low copper prices, is now extracting 8000 tons of ore-bearing rock every day.

Queenstown is beginning to occupy itself with tourism, spurred by the development (albeit one that has had its problems) of the Abt Wilderness Railway, and expectations abound for other profitable local ventures. But, at least at the time of research, Queenstown still had a somewhat inactive parochial air, like that of a community still waiting for something to happen. Regardless, the town still has much to offer those interested in social and industrial history.

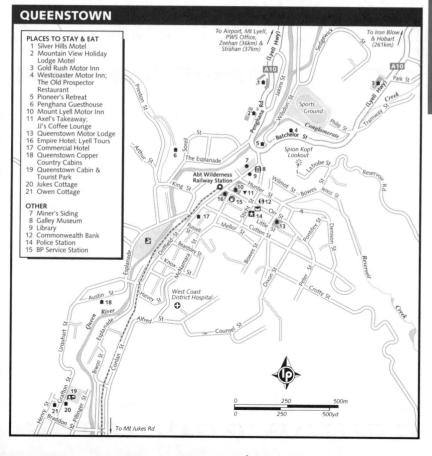

QUEENSTOWN

PLACES TO STAY & EAT
1 Silver Hills Motel
2 Mountain View Holiday Lodge Motel
3 Gold Rush Motor Inn
4 Westcoaster Motor Inn; The Old Prospector Restaurant
5 Pioneer's Retreat
6 Penghana Guesthouse
10 Mount Lyell Motor Inn
11 Axel's Takeaway; JJ's Coffee Lounge
13 Queenstown Motor Lodge
16 Empire Hotel; Lyell Tours
17 Commercial Hotel
18 Queenstown Copper Country Cabins
19 Queenstown Cabin & Tourist Park
20 Jukes Cottage
21 Owen Cottage

OTHER
7 Miner's Siding
8 Galley Museum
9 Library
12 Commonwealth Bank
14 Police Station
15 BP Service Station

THE WEST

Orientation

Orr St, which meets Driffield St almost directly opposite the Abt Railway station, is the subdued heart of the town – most shops, hotels and businesses are either on this street or very close by.

Information

Tourist information is available in the office of **Lyell Tours** (☎ 6471 2388; 2 Orr St; open 8.45am-4.30pm daily), at the front of the Empire Hotel.

The local **Parks and Wildlife Service office** (PWS; ☎ 6471 2511; Penghana Rd; open 8am-5pm Mon-Fri), next door to the Mt Lyell Museum at the mine entrance, is the place to find out about nearby walking tracks and to buy national park passes. If you intend to use the Mt McCall Rd, a controversial 4WD track from the southern end of Lake Burbury to the Franklin River, you should contact the ranger to issue you with a free permit and a key to the gate – there's an after-hours number for permit requests (☎ 6471 2533).

Abt Wilderness Railway

The Abt Wilderness Railway (☎ 6471 1700; Queenstown Station, Driffield St) is a recently restored 1896 rack-and-pinion line between Queenstown and Strahan. At the time of writing the line was still only operational to Rinadeena (11km), even though the entire track (34km) was supposed to have been hosting diesel locomotives by the beginning of 2002. A Queenstown to Rinadeena return trip costs $39/15 per adult/child. When the whole stretch of track is in service,

---

The Abt Railway

The restoration of the century-old railway line between Queenstown and Strahan, a three-hour journey through some of the state's wildest wilderness, is quite an achievement considering the patience and resources that were needed.

The rack-and-pinion line was the reason why the company that mined Mt Lyell for so long was called the Mt Lyell Mining and Railway Company. For the mining to be profitable, a railway connecting Mt Lyell with the port of Teepookana on King River, and later with Strahan, was vital. Construction began in 1894 and by its completion had cost the mining company over half its capital investment and covered 34km of rugged terrain.

Opened in 1896 and extended to Strahan in 1899, the line ran along the Queen River and up the one-in-16 Abt section to Rinadeena, before heading down the one-in-20 Abt section through magnificent rainforest to the King River. Here it crossed a stunning, curved 400m bridge high above the water, before continuing on to Teepookana and Regatta Point.

The Abt system (named after its inventor) was used to cover terrain too steep for the standard haulage of large quantities of ore. In this arrangement, a third toothed rack rail is positioned between the two conventional rails, and locomotives are equipped with geared pinion wheels that lock into the rack rail, allowing trains to climb and descend gradients they'd otherwise be unable to negotiate when fully loaded.

The railway closed in 1963 and fell into disrepair. But throughout the 1990s, members of the Mt Lyell Abt Railway Society spent incalculable hours clearing vegetation, fixing drainage and mending bridges, hoping that one day they might get enough funding to reconstruct the railway. They got their wish in 1998 in the form of a $20 million federal grant. Work on the new railway began in January 2000 and by year's end 11km of it (including 30-odd bridges) had been renovated, and refurbished locomotives were chugging to Rinadeena and back.

It's hard to predict the ultimate effect of the Abt Railway on the economy of the mid-west coast, or how much new development will accompany it, but it's easy to imagine the expectations that local communities and the tourism industry in general have for this scenic and historic project.

locomotives will chug in from both Queenstown and Strahan to meet in the heart of the rainforest at Dubbil Barrel station; passengers from one train will be able to transfer to the other to continue their journey, or just double-back. Consequently, a raft of ticket prices will ultimately be available that are dependant on the length of the journey taken. Currently, trains depart at 10am and 3pm daily over summer (at 2pm daily in winter), but this schedule is also bound to change when the last length of track is opened.

The railway is already showing signs of overcommercialisation, with stops at various stations along the way where passengers are enticed to spend more cash. But there's no denying that the railway traverses some of the west's most pristine wilderness, including stunning dense myrtle rainforest and the wild contours of the King River. For mor details, see the boxed text 'The Abt Railway'.

Galley Museum

This museum (☎ 6471 1483; 1-7 Driffield St; adult/concession $4/2.50; open 9.30am-6pm Mon-Fri, 12.30pm-6pm Sat & Sun Oct-Apr, 10am-5pm Mon-Fri, 1pm-5pm Sat & Sun May-Sept) started life as the Imperial Hotel in 1898 and features an intriguing jumble of old photographs, mining equipment, household goods and clothing from Queenstown's past. Particularly impressive are the 800-plus B&W photographs collected by local Eric Thomas and displayed on the walls of seven rooms – most date from before 1940 and have wonderfully idiosyncratic captions written by Mr Thomas.

Miner's Siding

Opposite the museum is the Miner's Siding, a public park that features an elevated length of railway track and various rock, bronze and Huon pine sculptures – up until the recommissioning of the Abt Railway, a restored Abt locomotive was parked here. This was Queenstown's centenary project and the sculptures tell the story of the Abt Railway's journey to Strahan and a hundred years of mining. Fittingly, the siding is located where the original train station used to be.

Spion Kopf Lookout

Follow Hunter St uphill, turn left onto Bowes St, then do a sharp left onto Latrobe St to a small car park, from where a short, steep track leads to the summit of Spion Kopf. The track features a rail adit near the car park and the top of the hill has a pithead on it. The panoramic views of town are excellent, particularly at sunset. If you look at the football oval you'll notice that it's cream instead of green. Queenstown's footy team is tough: it plays on gravel, not grass. (Turf quickly turns to mud underfoot in Queenstown, a result of the exceptionally high rainfall. In fact, the local golf course is said to be so sodden that members sometimes wish they could tee off in gumboots, or even waders.)

Iron Blow

On top of the pass on the Lyell Hwy, just before the final descent into Queenstown, is a sealed side road leading to a lookout over the geological wound of Iron Blow. This is the now-deserted and flooded open-cut mine where the town's illustrious mining career began in 1883.

Mt Jukes Rd

Continue south along Conlan St to Mt Jukes Rd, which will take you to side roads leading to sections of the Abt Railway. Farther along this scenic road (9km south of Queenstown) is **Newall Creek**, where a platform provides access to a patch of superb King Billy and Huon pine rainforest. The bitumen section of the road ends at **Lake Burbury**, a mountain-surrounded Hydro Tasmania lake that can be seen to magnificent effect from a lookout on the descent to its shores (also see the Lake Burbury section later). All roads past the dam wall are 4WD only – the best way to visit the places farther south is with Lyell Tours (see the following Organised Tours section).

Organised Tours

Mine Tours The open-cut section of the Mt Lyell Mine is no longer worked, but mining continues deep beneath the massive West Lyell crater. **Lyell Tours** (☎ 6471 2388;

2 Orr St), at the front of the Empire Hotel, offers both surface and underground tours. The one-hour surface tour departs the Lyell Tours office daily at 9.15am and 4.30pm (4pm daily June to August) and costs $15/7.50 per adult/child. The underground tour takes 2½ hours and costs $55 per adult (children under 12 not admitted); ring to ask about departure times. Bookings are essential and participants must wear long sleeves, long pants and enclosed shoes.

Wilderness Tours Lyell Tours also operates 4WD tours to the Bird River rainforest. The half-day tour departs at 8.30am daily from October to May, and also at 2pm in the high season (tours from June to September are on demand, with a minimum of two people required), and costs $74/44 per adult/child.

Places to Stay
If you yearn for comfort and carefully managed scenery, even if it's often starkly overpriced, make Strahan your west-coast base. But if you're made of sterner stuff, consider spending a night or two near Mt Lyell, because accommodation (and meals) here are much cheaper and generally of decent quality.

Queenstown Cabin & Tourist Park *(☎ 6471 1332, fax 6471 1125; 17 Grafton St; unpowered/powered site doubles $18/20, dorm beds $15, on-site van doubles $40, cabin doubles $50)*, about 500m south of the town centre, covers all price brackets. It has an ultra-budget lodge with basic rooms sleeping two to four people, spotless vans and cabins, and also manages the simple timber **Jukes Cottage** and **Owen Cottage** *(doubles/quads $100/150)*.

Places to Stay – Budget
Lake Burbury camping ground, a 10-minute drive from Queenstown, is a scenic alternative to accommodation in town (for details see the Lake Burbury section later).

Mountain View Holiday Lodge Motel *(☎ 6471 1163, fax 6471 1306; 1 Penghana Rd; dorm beds/singles/doubles $15/55/75)* has shared accommodation in four-bed

rooms, each with their own toilet and shower, and small motel units.

Empire Hotel *(☎ 6471 1699; e empirehotel@tassie.net.au; 2 Orr St; singles $25, doubles with/without en suite $50/40)* is a majestic, century-old hotel that dominates the town centre. Constructed from timbers that were sent to England to be wood-turned and then shipped back to Queenstown, it contains an imposing blackwood staircase classified by the National Trust, and fair budget rooms.

Places to Stay – Mid-Range
Mount Lyell Motor Inn *(☎ 6471 1888; 1 Orr St; singles/doubles $45/55)*, opposite the Empire Hotel, has basic motel suites.

Queenstown Motor Lodge *(☎ 6471 1866, fax 6471 2433; 54-58 Orr St; singles/doubles $65/80)*, down the end of Orr St, is another generic, medium-priced motel.

Commercial Hotel *(☎ 6471 1511, fax 6471 1826; Driffield St; singles $20-40, doubles $40-65)* has a choice of self-contained motel units or cheaper hotel rooms.

Silver Hills Motel *(☎ 6471 1755; Penghana Rd; singles/doubles $75/90)* has lots of very simple motel shackettes with even simpler decor, but the views from the top floors of the brick units at the back are pretty good.

Westcoaster Motor Inn *(☎ 6471 1033; e westcoaster@dohertyhotels.com.au; Batchelor St; rooms from $95)* has excellent motel rooms and facilities, all a short walk from the city centre.

Gold Rush Motor Inn *(☎ 6471 1005, fax 6471 1084; 65 Batchelor St; rooms $90)* certainly has a golden-coloured coating, but there's little rush around this laidback motel.

Pioneer's Retreat *(☎ 6471 3033, fax 6471 3011; 1 Batchelor St; doubles $90)* has a large community of plain but spacious self-contained two-bedroom units. If it looks like an old block of flats from the outside, that's because it used to be an old block of flats.

Queenstown Copper Country Cabins *(☎ 0417 398 343, fax 6471 1086; 13 Austin St; singles $55-75, doubles $65-95)* is a compact collection of modern, self-contained timber cabins, one of which is equipped for disabled travellers.

Places to Stay – Top End

Penghana Guest House (☎ 6471 2560, fax 6471 1535; 32 The Esplanade; rooms $110-135) was built in 1898 for the first general manager of the Mt Lyell Mining & Railway Company, and, as befits its managerial stature, is located on a hill above town amidst a rare number of trees. The B&B accommodation here is first-rate and includes a billiards room and a grand dining room.

Places to Eat

This is a town of takeaways, snack bars, bistros and counter meals. The main meals are pretty good value, but few rise to the challenge of a demanding palate.

Axel's Takeaway (☎ 6471 1834; 7 Orr St) will suit the undemanding palate with its cakes and big burgers.

JJ's Coffee Lounge (☎ 6471 1793; 13 Orr St; open 8.30am-5pm daily) also has plenty of burgers and other light meals like chicken Dijon salad.

The Old Prospector Restaurant (☎ 6471 1033; Batchelor St) at the Westcoaster Motor Inn usually puts on a pricey buffet ($25 per person) at dinnertime.

Empire Hotel (☎ 6471 1699; 2 Orr St; mains $12-17; open noon-2pm & 6pm-8pm daily) has an atmospheric dining room serving well-priced lamb rissoles, pasta and rogan josh.

Mount Lyell Motor Inn (☎ 6471 1888; 1 Orr St; mains $10-16) has slightly cheaper counter meals than the Empire, offering lots of steaks, grills and roasts.

Smelters Restaurant (☎ 6471 1755; Penghana Rd; mains $15-18; open 6pm-8pm daily Sept-May) may have some of the priciest à la carte in town, but that didn't prevent an undercooked chook from appearing on our plate.

Getting There & Away

See the Getting There & Around section at the start of this chapter. Buses arrive at and depart from the milkbar at 65 Orr St.

LAKE BURBURY

This is a large hydroelectric dam, the construction of which flooded 6km of the old Lyell Hwy. The scenery around the lake is magnificent, especially when there's snow on the nearby peaks. You can have a leisurely gaze at this vista from the attractive shoreline **camping ground** (unpowered sites $5) just east of Bradshaw Bridge, which has a caretaker, a public picnic area with covered electric barbecues, and a children's playground. You can also camp for free on the other side of the lake but the environment is less salubrious: dirt sites, no facilities.

FRANKLIN-GORDON WILD RIVERS NATIONAL PARK

This environmentally awesome park is part of the Tasmanian Wilderness World Heritage Area and includes the catchments of the Franklin, Olga and Gordon Rivers. The park was established in 1980 thanks to the lobbying efforts of the Tasmanian Wilderness Society (TWS), the organised conservation group that emerged in the aftermath of the failed campaign to stop the Hydro Electric Commission (HEC; now Hydro Tasmania) from flooding Lake Pedder.

The TWS, trying to prevent the HEC from building more dams on the lower Gordon and Franklin Rivers, pushed for World Heritage listing for the area, a nomination duly made in 1981 by the federal government. In the same year, the Tasmanian government held a referendum asking the public to choose between two different dam schemes – despite being told that writing 'No Dams' on their ballot papers would render their votes informal, 46% of voters did just that, a big indication of public dissatisfaction with *any* dam scheme.

While this referendum was being conducted, state parliament was in turmoil, with both the premier and the opposition party leader being dumped over the issue. A state election was forced that resulted in a change of government, but the new governing party also supported the HEC dam project. When the World Heritage Committee eventually announced the area's World Heritage listing and expressed concern over the proposed dam, the new premier attempted to have the listing withdrawn.

The TWS and other conservation groups turned their attention to federal politics. In May 1982, at a Canberra by-election, 41% of voters wrote 'No Dams' on their ballot papers, but the federal government still refused to intervene.

Dam construction began in 1982, and almost immediately, protesters set off from Strahan to stage what became known as the 'Franklin River Blockade'. They protested peacefully, but even so, the Tasmanian government passed special laws allowing protesters to be arrested, fined and jailed: in the summer of 1982–83, 1400 people were arrested in a confrontation so intense it received international news coverage.

The Franklin River became a major issue in the 1983 federal election, in which the reigning party was defeated and the country's new political supervisors stepped in to fully implement the Franklin and Gordon Rivers' World Heritage assignation. After its victory, the TWS changed its name to the Wilderness Society and remains involved in conservation issues Australiawide.

The national park's most significant peak is Frenchmans Cap, with a magnificent white-quartzite top that can be seen from the west coast and from the Lyell Hwy. The mountain was formed by glacial action and has Tasmania's tallest cliff face.

The park also contains a number of unique plant species and major Aboriginal sites. The most significant is **Kutikina Cave**, where over 50,000 artefacts have been found, dating from the cave's 5,000-year-long occupation between 14,000 and 20,000 years ago. The only way to reach the cave, which is on Aboriginal land in remote forest, is by rafting down the Franklin.

Much of the park consists of deep river gorges and impenetrable rainforest, but the Lyell Hwy traverses its northern end. Along this road are a number of signposted features of note, including a few short walks that you can take to see just what this park is all about:

Collingwood River This is the usual starting point for rafting the Franklin River, of which the Collingwood is a tributary. You can camp for free here; there are pit toilets and fireplaces.

Donaghys Hill Located 4km east of the bridge over the Collingwood River, this 40-minute return walk leads to the top of the hill above the junction of the Collingwood and Franklin Rivers. It has spectacular views of the Franklin and Frenchmans Cap.

Franklin River Nature Trail From the picnic ground where the highway crosses the river, a 25-minute return nature trail has been marked through the forest.

Frenchmans Cap Six kilometres farther east is the start of the three- to five-day walk to Frenchmans Cap, the park's best known bushwalk. It has two shelter huts along the way and lots of lovely, deep mud. Even if you don't intend doing the whole bushwalk, you'll enjoy the initial 15-minute walk along the banks of the Franklin River. You can take a TassieLink-scheduled service to the beginning of this walk – see the Getting There & Around section at the start of this chapter for details.

Nelson River Just east of Lake Burbury, at the bottom of Victoria Pass, is an easy 20-minute return walk through rainforest to the excellent, 35m-high Nelson Falls. Signs beside the track highlight common plants of the area.

Rafting the Franklin

Rafting the very wild Franklin River makes for an utterly sensational but hazardous journey. Experienced rafters can tackle it if they're fully equipped and prepared. For the inexperienced (who make up about 90% of all Franklin raftees), there are tour companies offering complete rafting packages. Whether you go with an independent group or a tour operator, you should contact the park rangers at the **Lake St Clair visitors centre** (☎ 6289 1172; *Cynthia Bay*) or the **Queenstown PWS office** (☎ 6471 2511; *Penghana Rd*) for current information on permits, regulations and environmental considerations. You should also check out the detailed Franklin rafting notes on the PWS website ⓦ www.dpiwe.tas.gov.au.

All expeditions should register at the booth at the junction of the Lyell Hwy and the Collingwood River, 49km west of Derwent Bridge. The trip down the Franklin, starting at Collingwood River and ending at Sir John Falls, takes about 14 days. From the exit point, you can be picked up by a **Wilderness Air** (☎ 6471 7280) seaplane or paddle a farther 22km downriver to a Gordon River cruise boat.

You can also just do half the river. The upper Franklin takes around eight days from Collingwood River to the Fincham Track – it passes through Irenabyss Gorge and you can scale Frenchmans Cap as a side trip. The lower Franklin takes seven days from the Fincham Track to Sir John Falls and passes through Great Ravine. These trips are really only practical for tour groups, as the Fincham Track requires a 4WD vehicle and is a long way from the main highways.

Tour companies with complete rafting packages include: **Rafting Tasmania** (☎ 6239 1080; e raftingtas@ozemail.com.au), with 4/7/10-day trips that cost $1045/1375 /1800; **Tasmanian Wild River Adventures** (☎ 0409 977 506; w www.wildrivers.com.au), with 5/11-day trips costing $1300/1900; and **Tasmanian Expeditions** (☎ 6334 3477, 1800 030 230; w www.tas-ex.com), offering 5/ 9-day trips for $1250/1900. Tours run mainly from December to March.

Maps You'll need Tasmap's 1:100,000 *Olga and Franklin* and 1:25,000 *Loddon* maps, available from the Tasmanian Map Centre and Service Tasmania in Hobart (see the Maps section in the Hobart chapter). A laminated Wilderness Guides map may also be available from outdoor-equipment shops.

Cradle Mountain-Lake St Clair National Park

☎ 03 • postcode Cradle Mountain 7306; Lake St Clair 7140

Tasmania's best-known national park is the superb 1262-sq-km World Heritage area of Cradle Mountain-Lake St Clair. Its spectacular mountain peaks, deep gorges, lakes, tarns and wild moorlands extend from the Great Western Tiers in the north to Derwent Bridge on the Lyell Hwy in the south. It was one of the most glaciated areas in Australia and includes Mt Ossa (1617m), Tasmania's highest peak, and Lake St Clair, Australia's deepest natural freshwater lake.

The preservation of this region as a national park was due in part to Gustav Weindorfer, an Austrian who fell in love with the area and claimed: 'This must be a national park for all time. It is magnificent. Everyone should know about it, and come and enjoy it.' In 1912 he built a chalet out of King Billy pine, called it Waldheim (German for 'Forest Home'), and, from 1916, lived there permanently. Today, bushwalkers huts stand near his original chalet at the northern end of the park, and the area is named Waldheim after his old home.

There are plenty of day walks in Cradle Valley and at Cynthia Bay (Lake St Clair), but it's the spectacular 80.5km Overland Track between the two that has turned this park into a bushwalkers' mecca. The Overland Track is one of the finest bushwalks in the county and in summer up to 100 people a day set off on it. The track can be walked in either direction, but most people walk from north to south.

INFORMATION

All walking tracks in the park are signposted, well defined and easy to follow, but it's still advisable to carry a map, which can be purchased at the park's visitors centres.

Cradle Valley

On the edge of rainforest at the park's northern boundary is the **Cradle Mountain visitors centre** (☎ 6492 1110; Cradle Mountain Rd; open 8am-7pm daily Dec & Jan, 8am-5.30pm daily Feb-Apr, 8am-5pm daily May-Nov). The centre is staffed by rangers who can advise you on weather conditions, walking gear, and bush safety and etiquette. The static and audiovisual displays on the region are worth spending some time on. In summer, the rangers run many free activities, which are advertised on a board at the centre – participating in some of these activities is a good way to learn what's so special about this area, the problems people have caused and how these problems are being solved.

The centre has a public telephone, toilets, drinking water and Eftpos (maximum withdrawal $50). It's also wheelchair accessible and accepts major credit cards. Dove Lake has flushing toilets but no drinking water, while Waldheim has composting toilets, drinking water and a very good day-use hut with gas heaters.

Whatever time of the year you visit, be prepared for cold, wet weather in the Cradle Valley area: it rains on seven days out of 10, is cloudy on eight days out of 10, the sun shines all day only one day in 10, and it snows on 54 days each year.

Cynthia Bay

Occupying one wing of a large building at Cynthia Bay, on the southern boundary of the park, is the **Lake St Clair visitors centre** (☎ 6289 1172; open 8am-7pm daily Dec & Jan, 8am-6pm daily Feb, 8am-5pm daily Mar-Nov). Apart from providing all the necessary information on the Cradle Mountain-Lake St Clair National Park (as well as on the Franklin-Gordon Wild Rivers National Park), the centre also has displays on the area's geology, flora and fauna, bushwalkers and Tasmanian Aborigines, the latter augmented by fibre-work from three Indigenous artists, which acknowledges the island's nine Aboriginal nations (see the Other Bushwalks section later for details of an Aboriginal cultural walk at Cynthia Bay).

At the adjacent, separately run **Lakeside St Clair Wilderness Holidays** (☎ 6289 1137; open 8.30am-8pm daily summer, 8.30am-6pm daily winter), you can book a range of accommodation, a seat on a ferry (see Getting Around later in this section), which is also available for charter, or hire dinghies.

THE OVERLAND TRACK
Information

The **Cradle Mountain visitors centre** (☎ 6492 1110; Cradle Mountain Rd) has an Overland Track Information Kit that staff will send anywhere in the world for $25. A handy pocket-sized reference for the walk is The Overland Track – A Walkers Notebook, published by the PWS and detailing all sections of the track and the flora and fauna that live there. It's also available on the DPIWE website W www.dpiwe.tas.gov.au.

Franklin's Overland Journey

In 1842 the Governor of Van Diemen's Land, Sir John Franklin, decided that, with his wife, Lady Jane Franklin, he should travel overland from Hobart to Macquarie Harbour on the west coast. At that time over half the island was still unexplored by Europeans and such a journey was a considerable risk.

The trip started in grand style with Lady Franklin being carried in a palanquin and attended to by a servant. Within three days the entourage had completed 80% of the distance and reached Lake St Clair.

The whole journey was planned to take six or seven days but, as modern bushwalkers know, the country of the Franklin River consists of deep gorges and impenetrable scrub. Heavy rains and the difficult terrain took its toll and the group took 22 days to reach Macquarie Harbour and meet their ship. Their troubles were not yet over, as winds were unfavourable and the small ship spent a further three weeks trapped in the harbour. The group almost starved to death but eventually were able to escape from the harbour and return to Hobart.

A detailed diary was kept of the entire journey and today it makes fascinating reading. The Narrative of the Overland Journey by David Burns has been reprinted and is available in many libraries, and in bookshops at the major Tasmanian museums.

The best time to walk the Overland Track is during summer, when flowering plants are most prolific, although spring and autumn also have their attractions. You can walk the track in winter, but only if you're very experienced.

Warning

In summer the weather is often fine, but snowfalls and severe storms are also regular features. You must be prepared to walk in cold, wet conditions and, if necessary, to camp in snow. A significant number of those who walk the track for the first time have inadequate clothing and equipment –

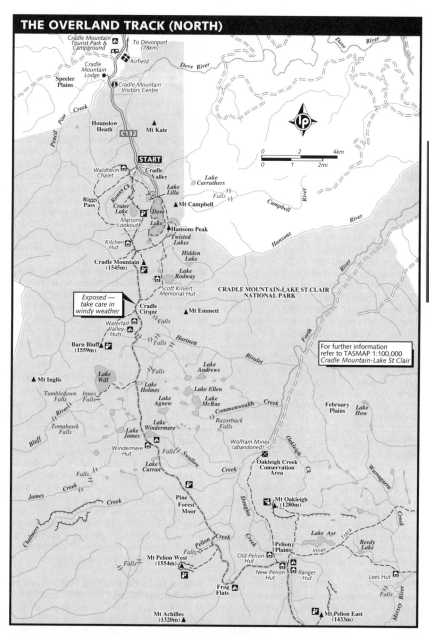

THE OVERLAND TRACK (NORTH)

THE WEST

be warned that when very cold or stormy weather occurs, the walk can transform from an adventure to, at best, a highly uncomfortable experience or, at worst, a serious health-threatening venture.

The most dangerous part of the walk is the northern half, along the exposed high plateau between Waldheim and Pelion Creek, particularly near Mt Pelion West. The southwest wind that blows across here can be dangerously cold and sometimes strong enough to knock you off your feet.

The Track

Walkers sometimes start the Overland Track at Dove Lake, but the recommended route actually begins at Ronny Creek, a walk of around 5km from the visitors centre. The start of the track was shifted here from Waldheim Chalet a few years ago, adding 500m of easy boardwalk to the route.

The trail is well marked for its entire length and, at an easy pace, takes around five or six days to walk. Along the track are numerous secondary paths leading up to features like **Mt Ossa**, so the length of time you actually take is only limited by the amount of supplies you can carry. Such is the spectacular nature of the park that you should seriously consider taking an extra couple of days to explore it more fully. Although the track takes you through wilderness, it's so well used that you can expect to meet many walkers each day – each year approximately 6000 to 7000 people hike this path.

There are unattended huts along the track that you can use for overnight accommodation, but in summer they fill up quickly so make sure you carry a tent. Camp fires are banned so you must also carry a fuel stove. You'll need a park pass to enter the park, purchasable from the visitors centres.

The walk itself is extremely varied, negotiating high alpine moors, rocky scree, gorges and tall forest. A detailed description of the walk and all major side trips is given in Lonely Planet's *Walking in Australia*. For detailed notes of all the tracks in the park, read *Cradle Mountain-Lake St Clair and Walls of Jerusalem National Parks* by John Chapman & John Siseman.

Cradle Valley to Waterfall Valley Huts (3½ to five hours; 13km) The Overland Track starts at Ronny Creek, just beyond the side road to Waldheim Chalet. Follow the signs indicating the Overland Track past Crater Falls and Crater Lake to Marions Lookout. Avoid taking the track to Lake Lilla and Dove Lake (to the left of the Overland Track) and the Horse Track (to the right of the Overland Track).

Continue on the Overland Track past Marions Lookout to Kitchen Hut, a tiny shelter permitted for use only in emergencies. Follow the track to the west of Cradle Mountain to Cradle Cirque, where there are good views of Waterfall Valley. Follow the track down into the valley and take the signposted track on your right to the two huts, which sleep a total of 28 people. Tent sites are in the forest a short distance upstream of the original hut.

Waterfall Valley Huts to Windermere Hut (three hours; 9km) Walk back to the Overland Track and follow it over an exposed ridge and down to Lake Windermere. Follow the shore to some tent sites before turning southeast to the hut, which sleeps 40 people. Note that camping around the lake is not permitted.

Windermere Hut to Pelion Huts (five hours; 14km) Follow the track across a creek to Lake Curran and continue on through Pine Forest Moor. Follow the main track to Frog Flats where there are some damp camp sites sometimes subject to flooding, the Forth River and on to Pelion Plains, where a muddy side track leads to the Old Pelion Hut. New Pelion Hut, which is indeed brand new and sleeps 60, is a little farther along the main track.

Large sections of the track before and after these huts can be heavy going following rain, when less experienced walkers may find the combination of mud, leeches and exposed roots disheartening.

Pelion Huts to Kia Ora Hut (three to four hours; 8km) Follow the track south to Pelion Gap, from where you can take side trips to Mt Pelion East (1½ hours

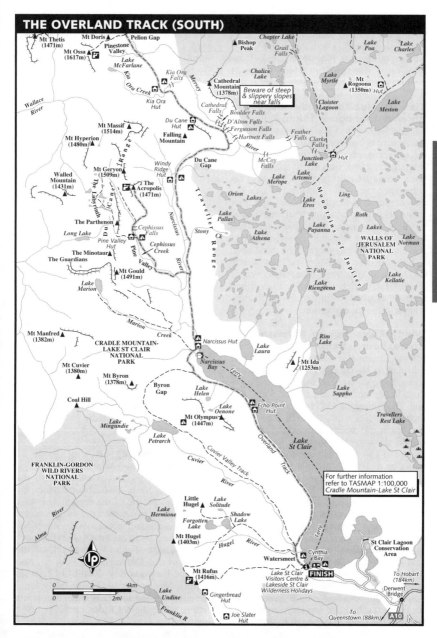

THE OVERLAND TRACK (SOUTH)

Mt Thetis (1471m)
Mt Doris
Pelion Gap
Chapter Lake
Lake Poa
Lake Charles
Mt Ossa (1617m)
Pinestone Valley
Bishop Peak
Grail Falls
Lake Myrtle
Mt Rogoona (1350m)
Lake McFarlane
Kia Ora Falls
Chalice Lake
Cathedral Mountain (1378m)
Beware of steep & slippery slopes near falls
Cloister Lagoon
Lake Meston
Kia Ora Creek
Kia Ora Falls
Cathedral Falls
Boulder Falls
D'Alton Falls
Fergusson Falls
Feather Falls
Clarke Falls
Wallace River
Du Cane Hut
Mt Massif (1514m)
Mt Hyperion (1480m)
Falling Mountain
Hartnett Falls
McCoy Falls
Junction Lake
Hut
Du Cane Gap
Feather River
Windy Ridge Hut
Walled Mountain (1431m)
Mt Geryon (1509m)
The Acropolis (1471m)
Lake Merope
Lake Artemis
Orion Lakes
Lake Eros
Ling
Roth Lakes
The Parthenon
Cephissus Falls
Lake Pallas
Lake Payanna
Long Lake
Pine Valley Hut
Cephissus Creek
Lake Athena
Lake Norman
The Minotaur
Pine Valley
WALLS OF JERUSALEM NATIONAL PARK
The Guardians
Mt Gould (1491m)
Falls
Lake Kellatie
Lake Marion
Lake Riengeena
Mt Manfred (1382m)
Marion Creek
CRADLE MOUNTAIN-LAKE ST CLAIR NATIONAL PARK
Narcissus Hut
Rim Lake
Mt Cuvier (1380m)
Mt Byron (1378m)
Narcissus Bay
Lake Laura
Mt Ida (1253m)
Coal Hill
Byron Gap
Lake Helen
Lake Oenone
Echo Point Hut
Lake Sappho
Lake Mingundie
Mt Olympus (1447m)
Travellers Rest Lake
Lake Petrarch
Lake St Clair
For further information refer to TASMAP 1:100,000 Cradle Mountain-Lake St Clair
FRANKLIN-GORDON WILD RIVERS NATIONAL PARK
Cuvier Valley Track
Cuvier River
Little Hugel
Lake Solitude
Lake Hermione
Shadow Lake
Forgotten Lake
Alma River
Mt Hugel (1403m)
Hugel River
Watersmeet
Cynthia Bay
St Clair Lagoon Conservation Area
Mt Rufus (1416m)
Lake St Clair Visitors Centre & Lakeside St Clair Wilderness Holidays
FINISH
To Hobart (184km)
Derwent Bridge
Lake Undine
Gingerbread Hut
Franklin R
Joe Slater Hut
To Queenstown (88km)
A10

0 2 4km
0 1 2mi

THE WEST

return) and Mt Ossa (three hours return), the highest point in Tasmania. From Pelion Gap, follow the track into Pinestone Valley, where you'll cross Pinestone Creek. Continue on to Kia Ora Hut, which sleeps 24 people. Limited tent sites are nearby.

Kia Ora Hut to Windy Ridge Hut (three to four hours; 11km) Follow the track across Kia Ora Creek and on to Du Cane Hut, which is National Trust–registered and no longer used, except in emergencies. Some good camp sites are available in the hut's vicinity. Continue about 2.5km to the signposted turn-off to Hartnett Falls, an excellent side trip that takes about one hour return. If you do take this track, make sure you continue from the top of the falls (where there are tent sites) down to the river and upstream to the gorge at the falls' base.

Return to the Overland Track and climb to Du Cane Gap, then descend to Windy Ridge Hut, which sleeps 24. Poor camp sites are available a little to the north, near what's left of an earlier hut.

Windy Ridge Hut to Narcissus Hut (three hours; 9km) Follow the track across substantial sections of boardwalk and a bridge to Narcissus Hut. About halfway along, there's a track on the right leading to Pine Valley and onward to The Labyrinth and The Acropolis (1471m), a highly recommended side trip – to reach Pine Valley Hut takes 1½ hours and from there you should allow another three to five hours to ascend to The Acropolis summit, where the views on a clear day are magnificent.

From Narcissus Hut, you can radio Lakeside St Clair Wilderness Holidays to get one of their ferries to come and pick you up; this will save you a five-hour (17km) walk. See the upcoming Getting Around section for details.

It can occasionally be an ordeal to get a seat on the ferry: bookings are unreliable (*always* reconfirm by radio when you arrive at the hut); seats on the ferry are limited (if you miss out on a seat, you'll have to wait for the next scheduled service); and the batteries in the radio may be flat (not unheard

of), in which case you may be stuck at Narcissus until a boat turns up of its own accord. If you want to avoid using the ferry, simply complete the track on foot via the Overland Track. A longer and more scenic route is the Cuvier Valley Track (seven hours; 19km), which branches off to the right of the main track 1km from the raised bridge at Hamilton Creek. This should only be walked in very dry conditions.

OTHER BUSHWALKS
Cradle Valley
The visitors centre features an easy but quite spectacular 10-minute circular boardwalk through the adjacent rainforest called the **Rainforest Walk**; it's more than suitable for wheelchairs and prams. There's another boarded path nearby leading to **Pencil Pine Falls** and on to **Knyvet Falls** (25 minutes return), as well as the **Enchanted Nature Walk** alongside Pencil Pine Creek (25 minutes return).

Crater Lake is a popular two-hour return walk from Ronny Creek. You can also climb **Cradle Mountain**, but this takes a full day to complete: allow seven hours.

Walks also start from **Dove Lake**. The best walk in the area is the circuit of the lake itself, which takes two to three hours to complete. All other walks involve steep climbs – the four-hour return walk to **Mt Campbell** and the **Twisted Lakes** provides great views of Cradle Mountain and nearby lakes.

Cynthia Bay Region
The **Larmairremener tabelti** is an Aboriginal culture walk that winds through the traditional lands of the Larmairremener, the Indigenous people of the region. The walk (one hour return) starts at the visitors centre and loops around through Watersmeet before leading along the lake's shoreline back to the centre. From Watersmeet, at the mouth of the Cuvier River, you can also take the **Platypus Bay Circuit** (30 minutes return). Most other walks are fairly long: the circuit of **Shadow Lake** takes four hours return, while the **Mt Rufus** circuit is seven hours return.

One way to do some good walking is to catch the ferry service to either Echo Point Hut or Narcissus Hut and walk back to Cynthia Bay along the lake shore. From Echo Point it's about three hours' walk back, and from Narcissus Hut it's about five to six hours.

ORGANISED TOURS
Bushwalking

The company most experienced at running guided bushwalking tours in this national park is **Craclair** (☎ 6424 7833; w www .southcom.com.au/~craclair; 78 Parker St, Devonport), which runs eight-day tours along the Overland Track for $1290 per person. This is a good way to walk the track because all packs, sleeping bags, tents, jackets and overtrousers are supplied. The company also runs shorter trips, like three/four-day Cradle Mountain circuits for $480/640 per person and seven days around Pine Valley for $1195 per person.

There are several other companies running similar trips. **Tasmanian Expeditions** (☎ 6334 3477, 1800 030 230; w www.tas -ex.com; 110 George St, Launceston) does an eight-day trip for $1195 (runs November to April) and a three-day trip for $540 per person (runs year-round).

Tasman Bush Tours (☎ 6423 2335; w www.tasmanbushtours.com; 169 Steele St, Devonport), operating out of Tasman House Backpackers in Devonport, offers a six-day package for $980. This includes camping gear, park pass, food, ferry tickets to Lake St Clair and transport to/from Devonport.

If camping isn't for you, then from November to May you can take a six-day guided walk in a small group (four to 10 people) along the Overland Track with **Cradle Mountain Huts** (☎ 6331 2006; w www.cradlehuts.com.au), which includes accommodation in private huts. The $1795 fee per person also includes meals, national park entry fees and transfer to/from Launceston, and you can hire bushwalking gear if you're ill-equipped for the hike.

For the much less energetic, **TigerLine** (☎ 6272 6611, 1300 653 633) offers a day tour (adult/child $89/55) to Cradle Mountain

from Launceston via Sheffield on Tuesday, Thursday and Sunday, allowing you to indulge in a number of the area's short walks.

Gentle Adventure Tours (☎ 6492 1018; w www.cradlevillage.com.au; Cradle Mountain Rd) affiliated with Cradle Mountain Wilderness Village, has numerous guided activities involving fishing, bushwalking and horse riding.

Scenic Flights

An entirely sedentary way to see the region's sights is to take a light plane or helicopter flight with **Seair Adventure Charters** (☎ 6492 1132; w www.seairac.com.au; Cradle Mountain Rd). Flights leave from the airstrip next to Cradle Wilderness Cafe, about 1.5km northeast of Cradle Mountain Lodge. Plane flights lasting 25/50/65 minutes cost $95/125/160 per person, while 45-minute helicopter spins cost $135 per person ($150 with wine and cheese).

PLACES TO STAY & EAT
Cradle Valley Region

At the time of writing, Doherty Hotels was building a $3 million resort on the road to the park entrance, with a planned opening date of summer 2003.

Cradle Mountain Tourist Park & Campground (☎ 6492 1395, 1800 068 574; w www .cosycabins.com/cradle; Cradle Mountain Rd; unpowered/powered site doubles $10/12, dorm beds $22, cabin doubles from $85) is a bushland complex situated 2.5km outside the national park. It has well-separated sites, a YHA hostel with four-bunk dorms, self-contained cabins and very good amenities.

Waldheim Cabins (☎ 6492 1110; e cra dle@dpiwe.tas.gov.au; cabin doubles $70, extra adult/child $25/10), 5km into the national park, is a bunch of basic four- to eight-bunk huts containing gas stoves, cooking utensils and wood or gas heaters; you will need to bring your own bedding and ablutions can be performed in the amenities blocks. Check-in and bookings are handled by the Cradle Mountain visitors centre.

Cradle Mountain Highlanders (☎ 6492 1116; w www.cradlehighlander.com.au; Cradle Mountain Rd; cabins $105-180) is a genuinely

THE WEST

hospitable place with a rustic collection of self-contained, different-sized timber cottages in bushland off the main road.

Cradle Mountain Wilderness Village (☎ 6492 1018; W www.cradlevillage.com.au; Cradle Mountain Rd; units $170-180, extra adult/child $30/15) is an impressive hilltop resort offering private, fully equipped units with get-away-from-it-all accessories like phones, satellite TVs and data points – chalet numbers one and 10 have the best views.

Cradle Mountain Lodge (☎ 6492 1303, 1800 737 678; e resorts.reservations@poresorts.com; Cradle Mountain Rd; doubles $200-330) should by all rights be designated a township, seeing as there are around 100 cabins surrounding the main lodge. The cabins are well appointed and spaced so you see very little, if anything, of your neighbours; an absence of phones and TVs reinforces the solitude. In the lodge proper, you can eat Caesar salad and gourmet pizzas in the informal **Tavern Bar** (mains $12-19; meals noon-3pm & 5.30pm-9pm daily) or veal loin and spinach-and-ricotta tortellini in the more formal **Highland Restaurant** (mains $19-26; open from 6pm daily). There's also a plethora of activities (guided and self-guided) to undertake in the immediate area.

Cradle Wilderness Cafe (☎ 6492 1400; Cradle Mountain Rd; mains $7-20; open 9.30am-8pm daily summer), run by the nearby Cradle Mountain Wilderness Village, has a good range of satisfying dine-in mains, including roasted vegetable risotto and chicken roulade, plus a takeaway section. It closes earlier in the off-season.

Road to Cradle Mountain

Located at Moina is **Cradle Chalet** (☎ 6492 1401; W www.cradlechalet.com.au; 1422 Cradle Mountain Rd; doubles from $170), a luxury lodge with an on-site restaurant and well-appointed chalets/suites with their own private decking.

Lemonthyme Lodge (☎ 6492 1112; W www.lemonthyme.com.au; Dolcoath Rd, Moina; lodge singles/doubles $100/110, cabins $200-300), off Cradle Mountain Rd, is a luxurious Ponderosa pine–built mountain retreat. You can stay in self-contained

cabins, some with spa, or in cheaper rooms in the main lodge, and eat in the lodge's reputable restaurant. If driving to Cradle Mountain from Devonport, turn onto the gravel Dolcoath Rd 3km south of Moina and follow it for 8km to this tranquil accommodation; it's a fair way to drive and then find out there are no spare rooms, so book ahead.

Cynthia Bay

You can choose between camp sites, spartan two- to four-bunk rooms in a budget lodge, or self-contained cabins at **Lakeside St Clair Wilderness Holidays** (☎ 6289 1137; W www.view.com.au/lakeside; unpowered sites/dorm beds per person $6/20; cabin singles/doubles $150/185, extra adult/child $35/30). It has a booking counter, a gift shop and a café (open 8.30am to 8pm daily summer, 8.30am to 6pm daily winter), serving light meals ($5 to $10) like burgers and toasted sandwiches, all under the one roof at Cynthia Bay. The camping ground has little grass cover, so pack a groundsheet. The well-maintained cabins come with continental breakfast.

You can camp for free at Fergy's Paddock, 10 minutes' walk back along the Overland Track, though bear in mind it only has pit toilets and no fires are allowed.

Derwent Bridge & Bronte Park

An impressive high-beamed roof is the centrepiece of the chalet-style **Derwent Bridge Wilderness Hotel** (☎ 6289 1144, fax 6289 1173; Derwent Bridge; dorm beds $25, doubles with/without en suite $105/85), giving the lounge bar a warm, expansive atmosphere in which many people enjoy a beer or a feed; the warmth is aided by a massive log fire. The hostel and hotel accommodation is plain but comfortable. You can also get reasonable lunches and dinners (mains $10 to 19) like ostrich and game sausages, and breakfast, every day.

Derwent Bridge Chalets (☎ 6289 1000; W www.troutwalks.com.au; Derwent Bridge; doubles $155-200, extra adult/child $35/30), beside the highway 5km from Lake St Clair, has a half-dozen roomy cabins, some with spa but all with full kitchen and laundry facilities and back-porch bush views. Two cabins have proved accessible to travellers in wheelchairs, but are not barrier-free.

Bronte Park Highland Village (☎ 6289 1126; **W** www.bronteparkhighlandvillage.com .au; unpowered/powered site doubles $12/ 14, dorm beds $20, chalet doubles $90-100, cottage doubles $80-150), just off the Lyell Hwy 30km east of Derwent Bridge, has a wide variety of budget and mid-range accommodation, plus a bar, a restaurant and large communal areas with log fireplaces. You can arrange transport from Lake St Clair with Maxwells (☎ 6492 1431).

GETTING THERE & AWAY

See the Getting There & Around section at the start of this chapter for details of year-round services to Cradle Mountain and Lake St Clair.

During summer, **TassieLink** (☎ 6272 7300, 1300 300 520; **W** www.tigerline.com.au) has additional 'Wilderness' services to Cradle Mountain (Dove Lake) from Launceston, which means there's a bus running from either end once every day ($43.60 one way, three to 3½ hours). This service runs to Cradle Mountain via the Devonport ferry terminal at least two days a week (the fare from Devonport is $28). Bookings are essential.

Over summer, TassieLink has additional 'Wilderness' services to Lake St Clair – from Hobart buses run once a day ($35.50, three hours), while from Launceston there's one bus on Monday, Wednesday and Saturday ($54, three hours).

TassieLink can also drop you off at one end of the Overland Track and pick you up at the other end. There are various options depending on where you're coming from and going to, so call TassieLink for prices; the packages must be pre-booked. While you don't have to pay to have your luggage transported, you do have to pay $5 per bag for it to be stored until you're ready to collect it.

Maxwells (☎ 6492 1431) runs services on demand from Devonport to Cradle Mountain ($35), Launceston to Cradle Mountain ($55), Devonport and Launceston to Lake St Clair ($65), and Lake St Clair to Bronte Park and Frenchmans Cap ($15). Prices quoted are per person for five or more passengers; for four or less passengers, there's a single collective price.

It's possible that you might be able to find a more convenient or cheaper transport option by talking to staff at bushwalking shops or hostels.

GETTING AROUND
Cradle Valley

A shuttle bus is run by **Maxwells** (☎ 6492 1431) from the camping ground to Cradle Mountain Lodge, the visitors centre, Waldheim and Dove Lake ($8 one way; bookings essential).

Cynthia Bay

Also run by **Maxwells** (☎ 6289 1125) is an on-demand service between Cynthia Bay and Derwent Bridge ($6 one way, minimum two people).

Lakeside St Clair Wildnerness Holidays (☎ 6289 1137) runs a ferry service – comprising two boats at peak times and one during the low season – which does one-way (adult/child $20/15) and return (adult/ child $25/20) trips from Cynthia Bay to Narcissus Hut at the northern end of Lake St Clair, taking around 45 minutes one way and departing at least three times daily; bookings are essential and you can expect to pay more if there are fewer than four people on board. You can also alight about halfway to Narcissus Hut at Echo Point (adult/child $15/12 one way). If you're using the ferry service at the end of your Overland Track hike, you *must* radio the ferry operator when you arrive at Narcissus Hut.

Mt Field & The Southwest

MT FIELD NATIONAL PARK

☎ 03 • postcode (National Park township) 7140

Mt Field, 80km northwest of Hobart, is a favourite of both locals and visitors for its spectacular mountain scenery, alpine moorlands and lakes, rainforest and waterfalls. It must be grand – this, after all, is the place that the 5cm-long Tasmanian mountain shrimp, dubbed a 'living fossil', has called home for 200 million years.

The area around Russell Falls was made a reserve in 1885 and by 1916 had become one of Australia's first national parks. To many locals it's simply known as National Park, a moniker given to the small town at its entrance. The abundance of wildlife that can be viewed at dusk makes this a great place to stay overnight with kids.

Information

The park's **visitors centre** (*☎ 6288 1149; 66 Lake Dobson Rd; open 8.30am-4.30pm Mon-Thur, 8.30am-5pm Fri-Sun*) has reams of information on the area's walks, and on the child-occupying, ranger-led activities usually held from the third week of December to the end of February. Also inside are a café and displays on the origins of the park, summarised in the pages of the booklet *Mount Field National Park: A History of Tasmania's First Nature Reserve*.

Warning If you're staying in the Lake Dobson huts, skiing on Mt Mawson or taking the Pandani Grove Nature Walk or any of the high country walks, you'll have to drive along the 15km Lake Dobson Rd. To safely navigate this unsealed road in winter, you'll need chains and antifreeze (and so will your car).

Russell Falls

The park's most promoted attraction is the magnificent 40m-high Russell Falls, which is in the valley close to the park entrance. It's an easy 10-minute walk from the car

Highlights

- Crossing the Styx (by car, not ferry) to see the earth's tallest hardwoods
- Standing at the base of Russell Falls
- Walking the South Coast Track
- Abseiling down the massive Gordon Dam wall
- Camping and bird-watching at tiny, remote Melaleuca

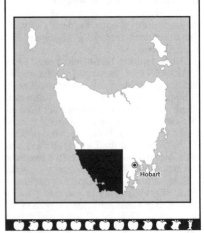

park along a wheelchair-suitable path. From Russell Falls, you can continue along the **Tall Trees Circuit** to **Horseshoe Falls** and **Lady Barron Falls**, a walk of two hours return past swamp gums, which are the world's tallest flowering plants.

Nature Walks

The 15-minute **Lyrebird Nature Walk** starts 7km up Lake Dobson Rd. It's an excellent introduction to the park's flora and fauna, particularly for children, with numbers along the track that correspond to information provided in a brochure available at the visitors centre.

For young children who don't mind a longer walk, there's the **Pandani Grove Nature Walk**, which follows the edge of Lake Dobson and passes through some magical stands of pandani (heaths resembling pandanus palms that grow up to 12m high before toppling over). This walk takes 40 minutes; park at the Lake Dobson car park, 15km from the park entrance.

High Country Walks

There are several magnificent walks at the top of the range, where glaciation has cut steep cliffs and deep valleys into what was once a continuous plateau. Attractive lakes litter the floors of these valleys, but perhaps even more beautiful are the many tarns adorning the ridge-tops.

If you intend to go walking here, take waterproof gear and warm clothing because the weather can be volatile year-round; also double-check with the visitors centre as to current track conditions. There's a good gravel road from Lake Dobson to the ski fields, but this is open only to authorised vehicles.

Tarn Shelf From the Lake Dobson car park, take the Urquhart Track to its junction with the gravel road; both track and road are steep. Continue along the road to the ski fields, at the top of which is the start of the Tarn Shelf Track. At this point the track is fairly level and the boardwalk has been laid across large sections to protect the delicate vegetation and keep walkers out of the mud. Either continue as far as you like along the track and then return by the same route, or take one of two routes that branch off at Lake Newdegate and circle back to the ski fields: if you travel east past Twisted Tarn, Twilight Tarn and Lake Webster, the walk takes five hours return from the car park, while the wonderful Rodway Range circuit to the west takes six hours return from the car park.

The Tarn Shelf is an enjoyable walk at any time of year in clear weather. In summer the temperature is pleasant, in autumn the leaves of the deciduous beeches along the way are golden, in winter you may need skis or

snowshoes, while in spring the sound of melting snow trickling beneath the boardwalk somehow seems to enhance the silence.

Other Walks The brochure you receive as you enter the park outlines many other walks in the high country. The walk of four to five hours return to **Lake Belton** and **Lake Belcher** passes some attractive scenery. It can be muddy but, on the other hand, it gives you the opportunity to combine a bit of trout fishing with your walking, if you're so inclined.

Skiing

Skiing was first attempted here in 1922 on **Mt Mawson**. A low-key resort of club huts and rope tows has developed and when nature sees fit to deposit some snow (an infrequent event in recent years) it makes a refreshing change from the highly commercial developments in the ski fields of mainland Australia.

Due to snow cover being unreliable and often patchy, there was no equipment hire in the area at the time of writing. Up-to-date snow reports are available via a **recorded message service** (☎ 6288 1319).

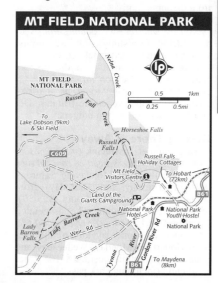

MT FIELD & THE SOUTHWEST

Places to Stay & Eat

Land of the Giants Campground (℡/fax 6288 1526; unpowered sites per adult/ child/ family $6/4/16, powered sites per adult/child/family $8.50/4/19) is a privately run, self-registration camping ground just inside the park. A park entry permit is required.

Lake Dobson Cabins (adult/child $11/ 5.50, minimum charge $22) are three very basic six-bunk cabins 15km inside the park. They're equipped with mattresses, cold water, wood heaters and firewood, and have a communal toilet block. Book well in advance at the visitors centre (℡ 6288 1149).

National Park Youth Hostel (℡ 6288 1369; Lake Dobson Hwy; dorm beds/doubles $16/36), 200m past the turn-off to Mt Field, is a dingy place with little in the way of character, though it's a lot cleaner than it was when we last visited and is no longer festooned with handwritten rules.

National Park Hotel (℡ 6288 1103; Gordon River Rd; singles/doubles $35/65) is a friendly place with reasonably priced rooms with shared facilities; prices include full cooked breakfast. The hotel also serves lots of red meat and fish (mains $10 to $15) from 6.30pm nightly.

Russell Falls Holiday Cottages (℡ 6288 1198; Lake Dobson Hwy; doubles from $80) have dated furnishings but are roomy, self-contained and extremely clean.

Café fare is available in the visitors centre (66 Lake Dobson Rd; meals $7-13; open 8.30am-4.30pm Mon-Thur, 8.30am-5pm Fri-Sun), like vegetable frittatas, Devonshire teas and salmon burgers.

Getting There & Away

During summer **TassieLink** (℡ 6272 7300, 1300 300 520; W www.tigerline.com.au) runs one bus daily from Monday to Saturday (two on Tuesday and Thursday) from Hobart to Mt Field (1½ hours, $23.50); bookings are essential. The associated **Tigerline Coaches** (℡ 6272 6611, 1300 653 633) operates a one-day tour of the area from Hobart on Monday, Wednesday and Saturday year-round, costing $110/75 per adult/child (including park pass).

THE SOUTHWEST

The southwest is a gloriously wild area covering almost one-quarter of Tasmania, with very few signs of human intervention and transformation – this is true untrammelled wilderness. A single main road penetrates as far as the hydroelectric power scheme built in the 1970s. At that stage, very little of the region was known to anyone except hardy bushwalkers and there were only two small national parks, Frenchmans Cap and Lake Pedder, the latter ultimately flooded by the power scheme despite its supposedly protected status.

Since Lake Pedder was destroyed, the regional map has changed drastically, with the whole area now contained within national parks. Every summer, thousands of bushwalkers follow the better-known wilderness tracks. While some short walks can be done from the access road, most walks require you to carry all your gear for at least a week. Across the region, the only huts are the pair at Melaleuca (bar a couple of age-worn community huts such as those at Bond Bay) and there's only one marked track.

The area's sole sealed road starts from Westerway, west of New Norfolk. It passes the entrance to Mt Field National Park before continuing to Maydena, the last fully fledged township along the thoroughfare – the Mt Field visitors centre is where park passes should be bought. From here the road becomes narrow and winding, first passing through tall forests, then traversing open country for 100km to the hydroelectricity settlement of Strathgordon; the final stretch has wonderful views of rugged mountain ranges. The road continues a short way past Strathgordon to the dam walls, which hold back the water for Lakes Pedder and Gordon. The Serpentine Dam on Lake Pedder is quite ordinary, while the mammoth curved wall of the Gordon Dam is overwhelming.

From Maydena you can detour south into the tall-timbered Styx Valley (see the boxed text 'Valley of the Giants' later). Halfway to Strathgordon is a gravel sideroad leading

40km south to Scotts Peak – at its terminus are excellent views of the major mountains of the Southwest National Park.

History

The southwest's original inhabitants were the Tasmanian Aborigines, who arrived at least 35,000 years ago. At that stage, the world was enduring an ice age and the southwest was covered with open grasslands that were ideal for hunting animals – evidence of Aboriginal habitation has been found in many local caves. Between 18,000 and 12,000 years ago, the ice retreated and, with the warmer climate, thick forests began growing across the region. The Aboriginal people regularly burned the grassy plains, but this only delayed the inexorable advance of the forests. By the time Europeans arrived, the only Indigenous people left in the area lived around the coastline.

European explorers were at first appalled by the landscape. Matthew Flinders, the first to circumnavigate Tasmania, described the southwest thus: 'The mountains are the most dismal that can be imagined. The eye ranges over these peaks with astonishment and horror.' Other reports from those who

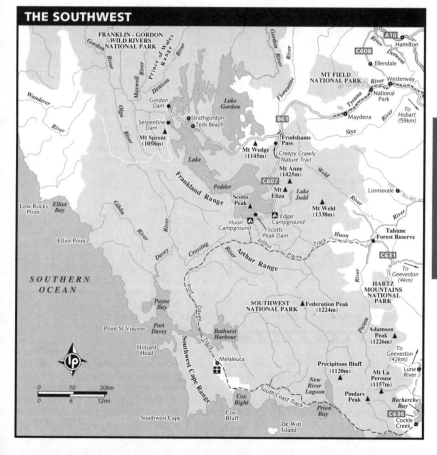

THE SOUTHWEST

The Valley of the Giants

The valley lying to the south of the Maydena Range was carved out by the Styx River on its way to joining the Derwent River. It is known evocatively as the Valley of the Giants, because it contains white-trunked specimens of eucalyptus (*Eucalyptus regnans* to be precise) that are the tallest trees in the southern hemisphere, and the highest-standing hardwoods in the world – one specimen is 92m tall.

The region, which was also one of the last-known refuges of the now-extinct Tasmanian tiger, is the subject of an ongoing tussle between the state government–managed forestry industry and conservationists. Logging companies, which are already very active in the area, appear determined to clear-fell and cable-log most of the remaining 13% of old-growth forest in the Styx (bar 10 sq km set aside in reserves) within the next few years, primarily for wood-chipping.

Conservationists, on the other hand, argue for the preservation of the upper Styx River Valley's record-breaking environment and have called for the establishment of a 150-sq-km national park, to be incorporated into the Tasmanian Wilderness World Heritage Area. The stated rationale for the Valley of the Giants National Park is not just the protection of the tall trees and the surrounding wilderness, but also the creation of an economically significant tourist attraction.

If you want to experience the Styx for yourself, including the awesome Big Tree Reserve and the magical short walk to Shingle Bend, embark on the self-drive tour detailed in Bob Brown's *Valley of the Giants,* a book that also details in text and pictures the natural significance of this area.

climbed the peaks aptly described the interior as a series of rugged ranges that extended to the horizon.

Most of the early explorers were surveyors who measured the land and cut tracks across the area under great hardship. The tracks were to provide access to the west coast and (optimistically) open the region for development. A road was eventually laid from the north to Gordon Bend and in the 1880s the government seriously considered digging a railway tunnel underneath Mt Anne or Port Davey. However, the anticipated mineral deposits and good farming lands were few and far between. Huon pine was logged around Port Davey, osmiridium was mined at Adamsfield, tin was mined at Melaleuca and a tiny farm existed at Gordonvale, but overall there was little potential for exploitation and the few tracks vanished under encroaching scrub and forest. The southwest was then left pretty much alone, with most Tasmanians regarding it as uninhabitable. The trials of early explorers make for interesting reading in *Trampled Wilderness: The History of South-West Tasmania* by Ralph & Kathleen Gowlland.

Of all the early developments, all that remains is the small-scale tin-mining operation at Melaleuca, a tiny settlement near Port Davey. But for most visitors, predominantly bushwalkers keen to set out on a long hike, Melaleuca's most important feature is its small gravel airstrip, which allows aerial access to the area by chartered plane or scenic flight.

MAYDENA
☎ 03 • postcode 7140

Maydena is on the road between Mt Field National Park and Strathgordon. North down Junee Rd, a 10-minute drive beyond the two accommodation options mentioned below, is the start of a five-minute walk to a cave-mouth of the **Junee River karst system**. This system comprises 30km of caves, including Niggly Cave, reputedly the deepest in Australia.

Tyenna Valley Lodge (☎ 6288 2293; w www.tvlodge.com; Junee Rd; lodge/cottage doubles $65/100) has comfortable B&B in a six-room lodge with shared facilities, and an array of units and cottages. Also on this 10-hectare riverside site is the very good **Cockatoo Cafe** (mains $15-18; open lunch and dinner daily), serving free-range chicken and marinated tofu and vegetable kebabs. Tours can also be arranged here.

The Wren's Nest (☎ 6288 2280; 8 Junee Rd; singles/doubles $65/100, extra guests $20), across the road from Tyenna Valley Lodge, is an excellent three-bedroom cottage with self-contained necessities (including a bath, wood heating and breakfast provisions) that you get all to yourself at a great price.

LAKE PEDDER

At the northern edge of the southwest wilderness lies Lake Pedder, once a spectacularly beautiful natural lake considered the ecological jewel of the region. The largest glacial outwash lake in the world, it covered 3 sq km and its wide, sandy beach made an ideal light-plane airstrip. The lake was considered so important that it was the first part of the southwest to be protected within its own national park, but this status ultimately failed to ensure the preservation of Lake Pedder's original, glorious environment.

In the early stages of what came to be known as 'hydro-industrialisation', the government body responsible for Tasmania's electricity production, the Hydro Electric Commission (HEC) – now Hydro Tasmania – built dams, power stations and pipelines on the Central Plateau and Derwent River. These activities went largely unchallenged until the 1960s, when the HEC proposed flooding Lake Pedder, then the only national park in the southwest, to create a much larger lake for electricity generation. There were immediate protests from people who had begun to realise the cost to Tasmania's natural environment, particularly its wilderness areas, of the HEC's all-consuming industrial agenda, inflamed by the revelation that the flooding of Lake Pedder was not even necessary for the viability of the larger scheme of which it was a part.

The protests were to no avail, however, as Lake Pedder was flooded in 1972, and the HEC turned its developmental attention to the lower Gordon and Franklin Rivers. For details of the ensuing conservation-movement struggle to prevent these new dams, which had a markedly different result to the Lake Pedder campaign, see the Franklin-Gordon Wild Rivers National Park section in The West chapter.

Together with nearby Lake Gordon, the Pedder Dam (named Lake Pedder by officialdom) now holds 27 times the volume of water in Sydney Harbour and is the largest inland freshwater catchment in Australia. The Gordon Power Station is the largest hydroelectric power station in Tasmania.

Trout fishing is popular and boats are allowed on Lake Pedder. The fish caught range from 1kg to 20kg in size. Small boats or dinghies are discouraged because the lake is 55km long and frequent storms generate sizeable, potentially dangerous waves. Boat ramps exist at Scotts Peak Dam in the south and near Strathgordon in the north. Given the scale of the controversy surrounding the inundation of Lake Pedder, you'll be surprised at just how puny the dams on this lake appear, especially when compared with the massive Gordon Dam.

There are two free camping grounds near the southern end of the lake. The **Edgar Campground** has pit toilets, water, fine views of the area and usually a fisherman or two – in wet weather it's less attractive as it's exposed to cold winds. A better place to camp is the nearby **Huon Campground**, hidden in tall forest near Scotts Peak Dam and with identical facilities to Edgar.

STRATHGORDON

☎ 03 ● postcode 7139

Built to service HEC employees during construction of the Gordon River Power Scheme, the 'township' of Strathgordon is becoming a popular bushwalking, trout fishing, boating and water-skiing destination.

A **visitors centre** (☎ 6280 1134; open 10am-5pm daily Nov-Apr, 11am-3pm daily May-Oct) is located at the 140m-high **Gordon Dam**, providing information on the scheme. At the time of writing, tours of the underground Gordon Power Station had been discontinued, but as an alternative, Hobart-based **Aardvark Adventures Tasmania** (☎ 6249 4098, 0408 127 714) organises abseils down the dam wall.

Accommodation-wise, your options are the free **Teds Beach Campground** beside

Lake Pedder (no fires permitted), or the basic motel-style units at **Lake Pedder Motor Inn** (☎ *6280 1166; rooms $50-150*), which also offers standard hotel meals daily from $15.

SOUTHWEST NATIONAL PARK

There are few places left in the world that are as isolated and untouched as Tasmania's southwest wilderness. The state's largest national park is home to some of the world's last tracts of virgin temperate rainforest, which contribute much to the grandeur and extraordinary diversity of this ancient area.

The southwest is the habitat of the endemic Huon pine, which lives for more than 3000 years, and of the swamp gum, the world's tallest hardwood and flowering plant. About 300 species of lichen, moss and fern – some very rare – festoon the dense rainforest, glacial tarns are seamless silver mirrors on the jagged mountains, and in summer the alpine meadows are picture-perfect with wildflowers and flowering shrubs. Through it all run the wild rivers, with rapids tearing through deep gorges and waterfalls plunging over cliffs.

Each year more people venture into the heart of this incredible part of the Tasmanian Wilderness World Heritage Area, in search of the peace, isolation and challenge of a region virtually untouched since the last ice age.

To walk across this region is something suggested only for fit, experienced bushwalkers. You can see a small part of it by following the gravel road from Frodshams Pass on the Strathgordon Rd to Scotts Peak. Not far from the pass, the **Creepy Crawly Nature Trail** passes through rainforest beside a creek. Farther south, the road leaves the forest near the base of towering Mt Anne, revealing wonderful views of the surrounding mountains in fine weather. To the west lies the Frankland Range, while to the south is the jagged crest of the Western Arthur Range. The road ends at Scotts Peak Dam and nearby are several free camping grounds (see the Lake Pedder section earlier in this chapter).

A whole range of escorted wilderness adventures are possible in the region, including flying, hiking, rafting, canoeing, mountaineering, caving and camping. For more information on these, contact the Mt Field office of the **Parks and Wildlife Service** (*PWS; ☎ 6288 1149*). The Mt Field visitors centre is also the place to get your national parks pass – park fees apply even if you're just driving on the Strathgordon-bound road through the park.

Day Walks

From Scotts Peak Rd you can climb to **Mt Eliza**, a steep, five-hour return walk. Using the same track, you can walk farther to climb **Mt Anne**, a trip of around eight to ten hours return. A better walk for most people skirts around Mt Anne by following the track to **Lake Judd**. The walk takes about four hours return and provides fine views of cliffs and mountains without a long, steep climb – the track starts 9km south of the car park for Mt Anne and is easily missed, as there's no large car park, only a small signpost.

From Scotts Peak, the best short walk follows the start of the **Port Davey Track** as it passes through a forest and across the buttongrass plain. You can go as far as **Junction Creek**, which takes five hours return, but the first half-hour is the most rewarding. Another short walk is the climb (one hour return) up **Red Knoll Hill**, following the road to the top.

The road to Strathgordon also provides access to some good walks, although none of them are signposted – buy maps and guidebooks for these walks. **Mt Wedge** is a popular four-hour return walk and, being located between Lake Pedder and Lake Gordon, has sweeping views. Past Strathgordon, the Serpentine Dam is the starting point for a long, steep climb on a poorly marked and muddy track to **Mt Sprent**, seven hours return. From the Gordon Dam it's possible to follow rough tracks to the **Gordon Splits** and the **Truchanas Pine Reserve** – these tracks can be very difficult to follow and are only suitable for experienced bushwalkers.

Long Bushwalks

The best-known walk in the park is the **South Coast Track** between Port Davey and Cockle Creek, near Recherche Bay. This takes about seven days and hikers should be well prepared for the often vicious weather conditions. Light planes are used to airlift bushwalkers into the southwest, landing at Melaleuca, and there's vehicle access to Cockle Creek at the park's southeastern edge. Detailed notes to the South Coast Track are available in Lonely Planet's *Walking in Australia*.

There are many other walks in the park, but you should first complete one of the better known walks. Contrary to what you might think, the South Coast Track actually makes good preparation for the more difficult walks in the area involving unmarked tracks – these require a high degree of bushwalking skill to complete safely and enjoyably. The shortest of these is the three-day circuit of the **Mt Anne Range**. Scaling **Federation Peak**, which has earned a reputation as the most difficult walk in Australia, will take a highly experienced walker around seven days. The **Western Arthur Range** is another extremely difficult traverse, for which nine to 12 days are recommended.

Getting There & Away

From December through March, **TassieLink** (☎ 6272 7300, 1300 300 520; Ⓦ *www.tiger line.com.au*) runs an early morning bus on Tuesday, Thursday and Saturday from Hobart to Mt Anne ($55, 2¾ hours), the end of the Mt Anne circuit at Red Tape Creek ($55, three hours), and Scotts Peak ($58.10, 3½ hours). TassieLink also departs Hobart for Cockle Creek (3½ hours, $51.60) at 9am on Monday, Wednesday and Friday from December through March. For both these services, bookings are essential.

If you're tackling both the Port Davey and South Coast tracks, and plan on catching TassieLink buses to/from the Scotts Peak and Cockle Creek ends, you can arrange for extra luggage to be stored at the company's Hobart depot for $5 per bag during your walk.

MELALEUCA

This is a tiny location deep in the southwest near Port Davey, where a few people mine alluvial tin on the buttongrass plain and the PWS keeps a semi-resident team. The only access to the area is by sea or light plane, or by following walking tracks for at least five days. There are no shops or any facilities apart from two walkers huts; you can also camp in a nearby tea-tree grove. The major attraction for visitors is the excellent birdhide, a substantial building from where you might see the rare orange-bellied parrot.

Flights operate to Melaleuca's gravel runway on demand from several of the state's airports. One of the most regular services is a daily flight by **Par Avion** (☎ 6248 5390; Ⓦ *www.paravion.com.au*) from Hobart to Melaleuca ($155 one way, 45 minutes).

MT FIELD & THE SOUTHWEST

Bass Strait Islands

Planted at the western and eastern ends of Bass Strait respectively are the Hunter and Furneaux groups of islands – the largest island in the Hunter Group is King Island, and the biggest piece of earth in the Furneaux Group is Flinders Island. These have served as the transient homes of prospectors, sealers and sailors, and also as a long-term destination for Tasmanian Aborigines who were 'resettled' from the Tasmanian mainland. Today, King and Flinders Islands are mainly rural communities that also offer visitors the opportunity to delve into natural coastal beauty rich in marine and other wildlife. Several islands of the Furneaux Group, including Flinders Island, also have strong, modern Tasmanian Aboriginal communities.

Fifty-five kilometres northwest of Flinders Island, roughly halfway between it and the Australian mainland, is Tasmania's newest national park, the Kent Group, a diminutive island grouping protected because of its natural and cultural heritage.

KING ISLAND
☎ 03 • postcode 7256 • pop 1765

King Island guards the western end of Bass Strait. Only 64km long and 27km across at its widest point, this small island's beautiful beaches, rocky coastline, seafood and dairy fare, and bucolic atmosphere more than compensate for its size.

Europeans encountered the island in 1798 and named it after Governor King of New South Wales. King Island quickly gained a reputation as a breeding ground for seals and sea elephants. Just as quickly, the animals were hunted close to extinction by sealers and sailors known collectively as the Straitsmen.

Over the years, the stormy seas of Bass Strait have claimed many ocean-going vessels – there are at least 57 shipwrecks in the waters around King Island. The island's worst shipwreck occurred in 1845 when the *Cataraqui,* an immigrant boat, went down with 399 people aboard; all lives were lost.

Highlights

- Indulging in the rich cheeses at the King Island Dairy
- Enjoying the Furneaux Island views from Mt Strzelecki
- Prospecting for 'diamonds' in Killiecrankie Bay
- Learning about the Indigenous community of Flinders Island
- Surfing some of Australia's best, most remote waves

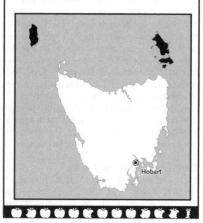

King Island is best known for its dairy produce (particularly its rich Brie cheese and cream), although kelp and large crayfish are other valuable exports. Another main industry was the production of scheelite – used in the manufacture of armaments – until the mine and factory at Grassy closed in 1990. After practising being a ghost town for several years, Grassy then began re-enlivening itself with some tourist accommodation.

There are many activities and sights to occupy your attention on the island. Short walks along beaches, around lakes and through forest will ensure you see some of the plentiful wildlife, while some of the island's more diverse features are its calcified forest, kelp industries and generally rugged coastline. You'll find that a weekend visit is barely enough to whet your appetite for all that the island has to offer.

King Island's main township is Currie, which is also the local harbour. It's close to the airport and most of the island's facilities are located here. Other notable settlements on the island are Naracoopa on the east coast and Grassy to the southeast, the latter with the only other harbour on the island.

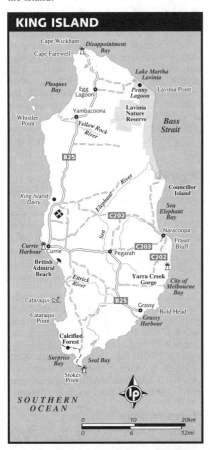

KING ISLAND

Cape Wickham
Disappointment Bay
Cape Farewell
Lake Martha Lavinia
Phoques Bay
Egg Lagoon
Penny Lagoon Lavinia Point
Yambacoona
Lavinia Nature Reserve
Bass Strait
Whistler Point
Yellow Rock River
B25
Councillor Island
Elephant River
King Island Dairy
C202
Sea Elephant Bay
Sea River
Naracoopa
Currie Harbour Currie
C203
Fraser Bluff
Pegarah C202
British Admiral Beach
Ettrick River
Yarra Creek Gorge
City of Melbourne Bay
Cataraqui
B25
Cataraqui Point
Grassy
Bold Head
Grassy Harbour
Calcified Forest
Surprise Bay
Seal Bay
Stokes Point
SOUTHERN OCEAN

0   10   20km
0   6   12mi

There's something to do on King Island almost year-round and it doesn't have the extremes of temperature that prevail in other parts of the state. However, summer is definitely the best time to visit if you're keen on water sports, while spring and autumn have numerous pleasant days.

Information

For tourist information, head for **The Trend** (☎ 6462 1360; Main St, Currie; open 9am-6.30pm daily).

Those interested in the island's maritime history should track down a copy of *The King Island Maritime Trail: Shipwrecks & Safe Havens,* a booklet with information on a dozen shipwreck sites around the island, complete with simple maps and details of the relevant coastal memorial cairns. The free booklet should be available from The Trend, or information centres intrastate.

Lighthouses

King Island has four lighthouses to guard its treacherous coasts. The one at Currie was built in 1880, while the one at Cape Wickham was built in 1861 and is the tallest in the southern hemisphere. Neither are open, but the latter is surrounded by attractive coastal scenery, and there is a cairn there to commemorate the lighthouse keepers. There's another lighthouse at Stokes Point, the most southern point of the island, while Cumberland lighthouse is south of Naracoopa on the eastern side of the island.

King Island Historical Museum

The island's volunteer-staffed museum (☎ 6462 1512; 36 Lighthouse St, Currie; admission by donation; open 2pm-4pm daily mid-Sept–June), in the cottage that once housed the chief light-keeper, features many local-history displays but is particularly fond of the remnants of maritime disasters.

Kelp Industry

Kelp Industries Pty Ltd (Netherby Rd) was established in 1975 to commercially harvest the masses of bull kelp that wash up onto the island's rocks and beaches. The factory is the only kelp-processing plant in Australia, employing 100 people to collect, dry and process the seaweed. From the roadway next to Currie Golf Course you can see the kelp being air-dried on racks. It's left on the racks for about two weeks, kiln-dried and crushed, then shipped to Scotland where it's blended with kelp from other countries to create alginates, which are used in the manufacture of a variety of products including sauces, lotions and detergents.

Calcified Forest

From Currie, head south to the Seal Rocks State Reserve (off South Rd) to visit the impressive Calcified Forest. A walk of 1km from the car park leads to a viewing platform from where the ancient petrified tree trunks can be seen. Some experts believe them to be up to 30 million years old. The place has a sombre, almost eerie feel, like a geological graveyard.

King Island Dairy

Visiting King Island inevitably entails a visit to the fromagerie of the King Island Dairy (☎ 6462 1348; North Rd, Loorana; open 9am-4.30pm Mon-Fri, 12.30pm-4pm Sun & public holidays), 8km north of Currie, just beyond the airport. Here you can watch a video detailing the local dairying activities and sample and buy some top-quality Brie, cheddar or thick cream. Renowned as a small company that became one of Australia's top gourmet cheese producers, the dairy was recently bought by the National Foods conglomerate.

Water Sports

Surf and freshwater **fishing** are popular here, as is **surfing** at the southern end of British Admiral Beach, Currie's main sandy stretch. You can **swim** at many of the island's unpopulated beaches and freshwater lagoons.

Diving among the local marine life and shipwrecks is popular. **King Island Dive Charters** (☎ 6461 1133) provides single dives for $90 and full-day diving trips for $155. Dive prices include tank, weight-belt, air per dive or, on the full-day trips, unlimited dives and lunch. The company also offers three- to seven-day packages.

Horse Riding

King Island Trail Rides (☎ 6463 1147) specialises in guided horse rides for small groups, with both novice and experienced riders catered for.

Cycling

The island's light traffic and flat roads make it straightforward for cycling. You can hire mountain bikes from **The Trend** (☎ 6462 1360; Main St, Currie).

Other Activities

Golfing is a popular pastime on the island. So is **bushwalking**, particularly in the fern gullies of Yarra Creek Gorge, where you can see some of the island's 78 bird species.

There's plenty of **wildlife** to observe, such as ducks, quails, wallabies, platypuses and seals. Tiger and brown snakes also inhabit the island, and you'll see feral pheasants and flocks of wild turkeys. In the summer months, a small colony of fairy penguins comes ashore at dusk at the end of the breakwater at Grassy – take care not to disturb them or dazzle them with bright lights.

Organised Tours

King Island Coach Tours (☎ 6462 1138, 1800 647 702; W www.kingislandgem.com.au), based at the King Island Gem Motel (see Places to Stay later) do various half/full-day island explorations ($33/65 per person), plus organised fairy penguin viewings ($33) that include port and nibbles.

Special Events

The **King Island Show** is held annually on the first Tuesday in March, while also in March, over the Victorian Labor Day weekend (second Monday of the month), is the **Queenscliff to Grassy Yacht Race** and the **Imperial 20 Coast to Coast Foot Race**. King Islanders like their equestrian events – the local **horse racing carnival** starts galloping in mid-December and pulls up in late January.

Places to Stay

Currie A few kilometres from the beach and with all the requisite facilities is **Bass**

Caravan Park (☎ 6462 1260; 100 Main St; on-site van doubles $45, cabin doubles $95).

Gulhaven (☎ 6462 1560; 11 Huxley St; doubles $70, extra adult/child $25/11) is a four-bedroom, self-contained unit that sleeps up to eight people.

King Island Colonial Lodge (☎ 6462 1066; 13 Main St; singles/doubles $60/70) offers B&B with shared facilities.

Boomerang by the Sea (☎ 6462 1288, 1800 221 288; e kiboomerang@kingisland .net.au; Golf Club Rd; singles/doubles $90/110), high on a bluff overlooking the nine-hole Currie Golf Course, has motel rooms that include continental breakfast. It has superb ocean views from all rooms and is only a short stroll into town.

King Island A-Frame Holiday Homes (☎ 6462 1260; 95 Main St; units $110) is 2km north of Currie and offers self-contained units with great sea views; each unit sleeps six.

King Island Gem Motel (☎ 6462 1260, 1800 647 702; 95 Main St; singles/doubles from $90/105) is managed by the aforementioned A-frame owners and has plain, brick motel rooms; room-service meals available.

Parers King Island Hotel (☎ 6462 1633; 7 Main St; singles $70-80, doubles $90-110), in the centre of Currie, has good motel-style suites in its double-storey structure and the main bar has a large open fireplace. The hotel provides easy access to shops, the harbour and golf course.

Devil's Gap Retreat (☎ 6462 1180; Charles St; doubles $130), on the foreshore 1km west of Currie, has two self-contained cottages with open fires, sweeping ocean views and direct beach access; price includes breakfast.

Shannon Coastal Cottages (☎/fax 6462 1370; e mrfowles@bigpond.com.au; Lot 2, Moores Dr; units $145-155) also has two well-equipped cottages to the west of Currie.

St Andrews-King Island (☎ 6462 1490; 23 Netherby Rd; doubles $110) is a well-appointed three-bedroom house, perfect for those who need to be close to a golf course.

Wave Watcher Holiday Units (☎/fax 6462 1517; 18 Beach Rd; doubles $150) has two-storey, self-contained units that come with continental breakfast.

Naracoopa For a seafront location close to the fishing jetty, try **Naracoopa Holiday Units** (☎ 6461 1326; Beach Rd; singles/ doubles $70/90). Its self-contained units are nestled in their own private gardens on Sea Elephant Bay.

Baudins (☎/fax 6461 1110; Esplanade; singles/doubles $100-160), on the beachfront at Naracoopa and with views across Sea Elephant Bay, has self-contained cedar units and lots of beach time on offer. Extra guest facilities include the use of fishing rods and mountain bikes.

Grassy Since the mine closed, Grassy has slowly been redeveloping.

King Island Holiday Village (☎ 6461 1177; e kiholiday@kingisland.net.au; 31 Blackwood St; units $130-210) has a number of houses and units in town for rent, some spa equipped; prices include breakfast.

Other Places to Stay Another accommodation option is **bush camping**, though this is permitted only at Penny Lagoon and Lake Martha Lavinia, the two large freshwater lakes at the northern end of the island. Access is by a sandy track off Haines Rd and the only facilities are bush toilets. The lakes are a favourite water-sport location with the locals and are large enough for sailing dinghies, windsurfers and water skiing. It's advisable to carry in your own fresh water and a stove, and remember to carry out all your rubbish.

Places to Eat
Currie There are many good eating places in Currie within walking distance of most accommodation.

Nautilus Coffee Lounge (☎ 6462 1868; Edward St; lunch $5-9; open daily), in a courtyard beside the roundabout, has Devonshire teas, fresh soup, burgers and other light meals, plus some local goods for sale.

King Island Bakery (☎ 6462 1337; 5 Main St; open from 6am daily) has lots of freshly baked goods like camembert-and-asparagus pies.

Boomerang By the Sea (☎ 6462 1288; Golf Club Rd; mains $21; open from 6pm daily) is a roomy restaurant featuring delicious local produce and spectacular ocean views.

Cataraqui Restaurant *(☎ 6462 1633; 7 Main St; mains $13-20; open lunch & dinner daily)*, the bistro at Parers King Island Hotel, also serves lots of the exemplary local produce and has regular, good-value lunch specials.

Naracoopa On the eastern side of the island is the colonial-style **Baudins** *(☎ 6461 1110; Esplanade; mains $20-25; open from 6.30pm daily)*, serving beef, seafood and other well-cooked local edibles in it's à la carte restaurant on the bay.

Seashells *(☎ 6461 1033; Esplanade; open daily)* is the local takeaway food specialist.

Grassy There's a **supermarket** in the town, and the **Grassy Club** *(☎ 6461 1341; Currie Rd)* has a bar and bistro.

Getting There & Away

King Island Airlines *(☎ 9580 3777)* and **Regional Express** *(☎ 13 17 13;* W *www .regionalexpress.com.au)* both fly to King Island from Melbourne (see the Getting There & Away chapter for details), while **Tasair** *(☎ 6248 5088, 1800 062 900;* W *www.tasair .com.au)* flies to King Island via Burnie/ Wynyard from both Hobart and Devonport (see the Getting Around chapter for details).

You can usually save yourself some cash through an airline package deal. King Island Airlines regularly has good low- and high-season offers, the latter usually starting at around $330 per person for two nights accommodation and air fares (car hire is extra).

Getting Around

There's no public transport on the island. However, the airlines can arrange airport transfers to Currie for around $7 per person each way and to Naracoopa or Grassy for about $30 per person each way. Hire-car companies will meet you at the airport and bookings are highly recommended.

Most of King Island's 500km of roads are not sealed, so drive carefully. If you need further convincing, some roads can be a bit rough and narrow, there are several blind corners, and there's a distinct lack of road signage. Unless you have a 4WD, take extra care choosing which roads or tracks you take, or be prepared to dig yourself out of some sandy or muddy situations.

In Currie, you can rent cars from **Cheapa Island Car Rentals** *(☎ 6462 1603; Netherby Rd)* from around $60 per day; you can reduce your excess from $750 to $300 by paying an extra $6 per day. **Howell's Auto Rent** *(☎ 6462 1282; Meech St)* has cars from $60 to $100 per day; you can reduce the excess from $1100 to $330 by paying an extra $8.80 per day.

FLINDERS ISLAND
☎ 03 • postcode 7255 • pop 1130

Flinders Island is the largest of the 52 islands that comprise the Furneaux Group. It's approximately 60km long and 20km wide, and is followed in size by Cape Barren and Clarke Islands.

First charted in 1798 by the British navigator Matthew Flinders, the Furneaux Group became a base for the Straitsmen, who not only slaughtered seals in their tens of thousands, but also indulged themselves in piracy. Of the 120 or so ships wrecked on the islands' rocks, it's thought that more than a few were purposely lured there by sealers displaying false lights.

The most tragic part of Flinders Island's history, however, was its role in the dismal treatment of Tasmanian Aborigines. Between 1829 and 1834, the Indigenous people who had survived the state's martial law (which gave soldiers the right to arrest or shoot any Aboriginal person found in a settled area) were brought to the island to be resettled. Of the 135 survivors who were transported to Wybalenna (an Aboriginal word that means 'Black Man's Houses') to be 'civilised and educated', only 47 survived to make the journey to Oyster Cove, near Hobart, in 1847. See the History section in the Facts about Tasmania chapter for more on this sorry tale.

Flinders Island has many attractions for the visitor. It has beautiful beaches, especially on the western side, and also has good

FLINDERS ISLAND

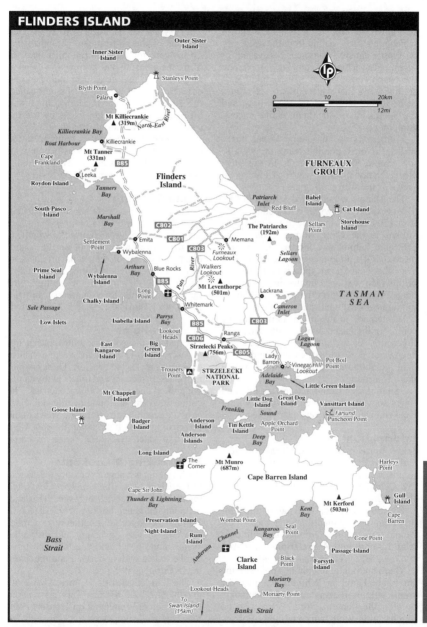

fishing and scuba diving. There's no shortage of shipwrecks around the islands, some of which are clearly visible from the shore.

A more unusual pastime is fossicking for 'diamonds' (actually fragments of topaz) on the beach and creek at Killiecrankie Bay. At one time there were plenty of stones to be found, but there are fewer now, and the locals dive for them using special equipment.

Flinders Island has some great bushwalks, the most popular being the walk to the granite Strzelecki Peaks in the Strzelecki National Park, which affords great views of the surrounding area.

The island's abundant vegetation supports a wide variety of wildlife, including more than 150 bird species. One of the most well known is the Cape Barren goose – its protected habitat and increasing numbers mean that it's no longer close to extinction. The other well-known species is the mutton bird, which was once hunted in large numbers. Drive slowly on the roads at night to hitting nocturnal wildlife.

Whitemark is the main administrative centre for the island, while Lady Barron, in the south, is the main fishing area and deepwater port. Industries on Flinders Island include farming, fishing and seasonal mutton-birding.

Summer, spring and autumn are all good times to visit. However, a sunny winter weekend can also be very enjoyable.

Information

Local tourism operators, shop managers and others on the island are the best sources of information. A good place to start is the **Gem Shop** (☎ 6359 2160; Patrick St, Whitemark).

For information on the island's Indigenous community, including the local traditional arts centre, contact the **Flinders Island Aboriginal Association Inc** (FIAAI; ☎ 6359 3532; West St, Lady Barron).

There are public telephones opposite the Interstate Hotel in Whitemark, near the wharf in Lady Barron, and at Killiecrankie outside the general store. Petrol can be purchased in Whitemark and Lady Barron.

Wybalenna Historic Site

The Wybalenna Historic Site is all that remains of this unfortunate settlement set up to 'care for' the Aboriginal people. In truth, the opposite was achieved, with most of the people sent here succumbing to disease. Because of its historical significance, this site is rated as the third most important historic site in the state. Close by are the cemetery and memorial chapel.

In 1999 Wybalenna was returned to the descendants of the Indigenous people who lived there. If you want to visit the site independently, contact the FIAAI first.

Emita Museum

The Emita Museum (adult/child $2/free; open 1pm-5pm Mon-Sun summer, 1pm-5pm Sat & Sun rest-of-year), housed in what was the first government school on the island, displays a variety of Aboriginal artefacts, as well as old sealing and sailing relics. It also has a large display on the mutton bird industry. It's run by volunteers from the Furneaux Historical Research Association.

Trousers Point

Located on the island's southwestern tip, Trousers Point is definitely worth a visit to explore its rocks and beaches. There are picnic tables, barbecues and toilets in the camping ground under the drooping sheoaks. The colourful rocks surrounding the point are easily accessible and offer great views of the Strzelecki peaks. It's a beautiful spot from which to watch the sunset.

Bushwalking & Lookouts

Bushwalking is a popular activity for visitors to the island. *The Walks of Flinders Island* (available from various shops on the island, including the general store and newsagents at Whitemark) gives information on a number of walks of varying length and difficulty. Walks along beach and coastal-heath trails can be linked with hinterland and mountain tracks throughout the island.

The 4km-long **Strzelecki Track**, a key route into the Strzelecki National Park, starts about 12km south of Whitemark on Trousers Point Rd. This well-signposted track ascends Mt

Strzelecki to spectacular views at a height of 756m. It's about a three- to five-hour return walk, and it's essential that you carry warm clothing, wet-weather gear, food and water at any time of the year. The 1½ to two hour return walk from **Trousers Point to Sarah Blanche Point** exposes you to some of the national park's coastal splendour.

There are also a number of lookouts on the island, including **Furneaux Lookout** and **Walkers Lookout**, almost in the centre of the island, plus **Vinegar Hill** in the south and **Mt Tanner** in the north.

Rock Climbing

Rock climbers will find some challenging rock stacks or granite walls on Flinders Island. Mt Killiecrankie has some very steep granite faces rising from sea level. Although there is a soak at the camp site, you'll need to take all your drinking water. The rock climbs within Strzelecki National Park and the ridge walk should be attempted only by experienced walkers and climbers.

Fossicking

Rock hounds of another variety can find various localities in which to self-fossick for the elusive Killiecrankie diamond. The **Gem Shop** (☎ 6359 2160; Patrick St, Whitemark) and **Killiecrankie Enterprises** (☎ 6359 8560; 527 Killiecrankie Bay Rd • ☎ 6359 2130; 1 Patrick St, Whitemark) can advise lapidaries where to spend some time.

Scuba Diving

There are several good scuba-diving locations on the northern and western coasts. In many places you can enter from the beach or shelving rocks. The water is warmest between January and April and coldest between June and September. Noncommercial diving licences for abalone, crayfish and scallops can be obtained from the police stations at Whitemark and Lady Barron.

Flinders Island Dive (☎ 6359 8429; e flindersdive@yahoo.com; 22 Wireless Station Rd, Emita), hires out tanks and weight-belts. It also offers full-day charters with tanks, air and weight-belts from $140 per person.

Fishing

Rock fishing along the southern, northern and northwestern coasts is good all year. Bait is easily obtained from the rocks and fishing tackle can be purchased from many stores; however, you need to bring your own rod. Beach fishing is popular on the eastern coast and from Red Bluff. The North-East River also has good fishing.

Flinders Island Adventures (☎ 6359 4507; Avondale) charters boats for fishing. A full-day charter costs $900 for a group of up to eight people, with gear and bait supplied.

Killiecrankie Enterprises (☎ 6359 8560; 527 Killiecrankie Bay Rd) charters its boat Maximum for fishing or sightseeing for $75 an hour (minimum two hours), $275 a half-day or $550 a full day for up to five people.

Organised Tours

Flinders Island Adventures (☎ 6359 4507; e jamesluddington@bigpond.com; Avondale) has full-day 4WD tours ($110 per person), cruises around the outer islands and other customisable touring options. It also runs evening tours for $30 a head (December to March) from Lady Barron to see mutton

---

Mutton Birds

Each September, mutton birds return to Flinders and other Bass Strait islands after a summer in the northern hemisphere, to clean out and re-pair their burrows from the previous year. They then head out to sea again before returning in November for the breeding season, which lasts until April. Eggs are laid in a three-day period and the parents take it in turns (two weeks at a time) to incubate the egg.

Once their single chick has hatched, both parents feed the fledgling until mid-April, when all the adult birds depart, leaving the young to fend for themselves and hopefully to follow their parents north.

Unfortunately for the well-fed little mutton birds, they are central to a local industry that commercially values their meat – once the adult birds leave their nests, the 'birders', or mutton-bird hunters, move in.

birds on the small islands in Adelaide Bay – mutton birds, or short-tailed shearwaters, fly a 15,000km migratory path from Japan to Australia (see the boxed text 'Mutton Birds').

Places to Stay

Whitemark Five kilometres north of Whitemark, next to the airport, is **Flinders Island Cabin Park** *(☎/fax 6359 2188; Bluff Rd; singles/doubles without en suite from $30/40)*. It has a handful of self-contained cabins, some with communal facilities and others with bathroom.

Interstate Hotel *(☎ 6359 2114; e inter statehotel@trump.net.au; Patrick St; singles with/without en suite $55/30, doubles with/without en suite $85/55)*, in the centre of Whitemark, was built in 1911. Renovated in heritage style, it's a comfortable hotel within easy walking distance of shops and other facilities.

Other accommodation in and around Whitemark comprises mainly holiday units and cottages.

Bulloke Holiday Home *(☎ 6359 9709; Butter Factory Rd; singles/doubles $50/80)* is a three-bedroom unit.

Seaview Farm Cottage *(☎ 6359 2011, fax 6359 2244; Ranga; doubles $70, extra guests $6)*, 5km southeast of Whitemark, is a small, modern self-contained unit on a sheep farm that sleeps up to four people.

Boat Harbour Beach House *(☎ 6359 6510; Boat Harbour; doubles $75-85, extra adults $11)*, 45km northwest of Whitemark, is a three-bedroom unit overlooking the beach.

Lady Barron Another inexpensive three-bedroom unit is on offer at **Lady Barron Holiday House** *(☎ 6359 3555; Franklin Parade; singles/doubles $55/85)*.

Bucks at Lady Barron *(☎ 6359 3535; Franklin Parade; singles/doubles from $85/95)* is also a three-bedroom unit, on the same street as Lady Barron Holiday House.

Yaringa Holiday Units *(☎ 6359 4522; Holloway St; units $85)* has three units available.

Felicity's Cottage *(☎ 6359 3641; Holloway St; singles or doubles $105)* is on the same street as Yaringa Holiday Units.

Lackrana On the island's east coast, 25km from Whitemark, is **Echo Hills Holiday Units** *(☎ 6359 6509, fax 6359 6559; Madeleys Rd; doubles $90)*. It's in a peaceful, rustic setting at the foot of the Darling Ranges.

Memana The four-bedroom unit at quiet **Carnsdale Host Farm** *(☎ 6359 9718; 1410 Fairhaven Rd, Memana; doubles $90, extra adult/child $20/11)* is 28km east of Whitemark.

Lisa's Cottage *(☎ 6359 6530; Lees Rd, Aurora; doubles $80)* is a self-contained home.

Killiecrankie There's self-contained accommodation for up to 10 people at **Killiecrankie Bay Holiday House** *(☎ 6359 8560; doubles $100, extra adult/child $15/10)*; inquire at Killiecrankie Enterprises.

Killiecrankie also has a very basic free **camping** and picnic area with barbecues, toilets and cold showers.

Places to Eat

Whitemark At the **Flinders Island Bakery** *(☎ 6359 2105; Lagoon Rd; open 7am-5.30pm Mon-Fri, 9am-1pm Sat)* you can buy an assortment of pies, bread and drinks.

Sweet Surprises *(☎ 6359 2138; 5 Lagoon Rd; open Mon-Sat)* is a popular coffee shop serving a variety of light meals.

The Interstate Hotel *(☎ 6359 2114; Patrick St; open lunch & dinner Mon-Fri, dinner Sat)*, in the centre of Whitemark, serves a range of moderately priced counter lunches and dinners in its dining room and public bar.

Flinders Island Sports Club *(☎ 6359 2220; mains from $11)* has a cosy restaurant with a quality menu; bookings are essential. Meals are also available in the bistro throughout the week in summer, and the club has its own bottleshop.

Lady Barron Selling basic supplies is **Patterson's Supermarket** *(☎ 6359 3503; 11 James St; open daily)*. It's also a post office and Commonwealth Bank agency, and sells fuel.

Killiecrankie The only place to buy food here is at the general store, **Killiecrankie**

Enterprises (☎ 6359 8560; 527 Killiecrankie Bay Rd; open 9am-5pm daily), which has snacks and various hot and cold drinks.

Shopping

Flinders Island Fleece (☎ 6359 6509; Whitemark) is where you can purchase good-quality handmade yarns and knitwear, derived from local fleece. Another good place for fleece-wear is **Carnsdale Host Farm** (see Places to Stay earlier).

Killiecrankie 'diamonds' are actually the semi-precious stone called topaz. Usually they are clear, but some have a pale blue or pink colouring. The **Gem Shop** (☎ 6359 2160; Patrick St, Whitemark) and **Killiecrankie Enterprises** (☎ 6359 8560; 527 Killiecrankie Bay Rd • ☎ 6359 2130; 1 Patrick St, Whitemark) sell cut and uncut stones. Both shops offer friendly service and fossick for their own rocks.

Getting There & Away

Air You can fly to Flinders Island with **Island Airlines Tasmania** (☎ 6359 2266, 1800 645 875) via Melbourne's Essendon airport from Traralgon in Victoria (see the Getting There & Away chapter for details). It also flies between Launceston and Flinders Island (see the Getting Around chapter for details).

Package deals could save you a good deal of money. Island Airlines Tasmania offers high-season air fare, accommodation and car-hire packages for Flinders Island starting from around $500 per person for two nights.

Ferry The **Southern Shipping Company** (☎ 6356 1753) operates a small passenger and car ferry once a week from Bridport in Tasmania's northeast to Flinders Island; once a month, the ferry continues on to Port Welshpool in Victoria. A return trip to Flinders Island from Bridport costs $80 per person ($690 for a car and its driver) – the journey sometimes takes only eight hours, but due to a refuelling stop usually takes 24 hours. The full one-way trip from Bridport to Flinders Island to Port Welshpool costs $60 per person ($580 for a car and its driver), and, including the Flinders stopover, takes about 2½ days.

Getting Around

There is no public transport on the island. Hire-car companies will meet you at the airport and bookings are highly recommended.

There are many unsealed roads on the island, so you'll need to drive carefully, particularly around the more remote areas. Unless you have a 4WD, make sure you don't end up in sandy or slippery places.

Bowman-Lees (☎ 6359 2388) is one of the car-hire firms in Whitemark, renting a mixture of early- and late-model vehicles for between $60 and $80 per day.

KENT GROUP NATIONAL PARK

In December 2001, the half-dozen tiny land masses of the Kent Group, located 55km northwest of Flinders Island, and with only Deal, Dover and Erith big enough to qualify as islands (the other three are islets), became Tasmania's 19th national park. Named by Matthew Flinders after a fellow naval officer in 1798, this 27.5-sq-km region qualified for park status partly due to its cultural heritage, which includes human occupation dating back at least 8000 years, the presence of seal hunters in the 19th century and an old lighthouse on Deal Island. It also qualified because of its outstanding wildlife, such as the sizeable fur seal colony at Judgement Rocks and roosting sea birds in the form of short-tailed shearwaters, oystercatchers, petrels and penguins.

For an innovative way of getting out to these islands, see the boxed text 'Paddling Strait'.

OTHER ISLANDS
Cape Barren Island

Cape Barren Island is around 10km to the south of Flinders Island and is the only other island in the Furneaux Group to have a permanent settlement. Kent Bay, on its southern side, was the first settlement south of Sydney.

The main settlement on Cape Barren Island, known as **The Corner**, has a small school, church and medical centre. This was the area given over for the resettlement of the Straitsmen from Flinders Island in 1881. Fishing is the main industry, although there are several cattle farms.

BASS STRAIT ISLANDS

Things to Do For experienced bushwalkers, the circuit walk of the shoreline offers great coastal views, including the wreck of the *Farsund,* lovely beaches and interesting rock formations. Mt Kerford (503m) offers quite a challenge, while a day walk to the summit of Mt Munro (687m) on a clear day provides excellent views of the surrounding area. Access is from The Corner, up to Big Grassy Hill and along the ridge to the summit.

Water is less of a problem on Cape Barren Island than on Flinders Island, with many freshwater sources available.

Getting There & Away Flights to Cape Barren Island are infrequent and it would be better to arrange a charter flight from Melbourne or Launceston if you have the numbers. Alternatively you can fly to Flinders Island and then arrange a boat charter to take you across, allowing you to cache supplies on the way to your drop-off point. You should be able to charter a boat from Flinders Island Adventures (see the Flinders Island section earlier) for this purpose.

Swan Island

There are not many islands where you can be the sole renter, and at reasonably low prices to boot. Swan Island is one of the exceptions. The owners live in one house here and rent the other house on the island.

Just 3km off the northeast coast of Tasmania, this small island is 3km long and is dominated by its lighthouse, built in 1845 and automated in 1986 when the government sold the island. The main attraction of coming here is a get-away-from-it-all experience. Many sea birds nest in its environs and you can watch the shearwaters and penguins returning to their nests around sunset. The island has several beaches and the immediate area has decent fishing and scuba diving.

Paddling Strait

Remarkably, the stormy, bitterly cold, often treacherous waters of Bass Strait have proved an irresistible attraction to occasional parties of the very hardiest sea kayakers, battling strong currents and stronger winds to cross between the mainland and Tasmania. The first successful crossing was made, it's thought, in 1971 by a trio of Victorians in slalom kayaks. Since then a number of parties have attempted the crossing, although only about 50 kayakers (so far) have successfully made it across. It's 'only' a 250km trip measured on the map, but currents, tides and wind drift mean that the kayakers travel much further than that. Bass Strait crossings involve a two-week, or longer, itinerary with entire days often lost to bad weather. Overnight, kayakers stay huddled in tents on the bleak, windswept rocks that pass for islands in the Bass Strait. After a full day's paddling through often 3m-high waves, exhausted paddlers, who just want to crawl into a tent and collapse, are sometimes required to scour rugged island coasts for a safe landing spot where their kayaks won't be dashed to pieces against the rocks. This is the Mt Everest of sea kayaking!

If you trace the usual route south on a map, kayakers run from Wilsons Promontory, the southernmost tip of the Australian mainland, to Hogan Island, the Kent Group (Erith Island), Flinders Island, Preservation Island and Clarke Island. Landfall on Tasmanian terra firma is usually at Little Musselroe Bay in Tasmania's northeast.

Obviously this is a trip attempted only by very experienced sea kayakers. If you are one yourself, and aren't put off by Bass Strait's awesome reputation (there are good historical reasons that both western and eastern Victoria claim the title 'Shipwreck Coast'), you could check out Melbourne-based **Meridian Kayak Adventures** (☎ 03-9596 8876, Ⓦ *www.meridiankayak.com.au*), who are investigating 'escorted' crossings, using a mother ship as a floating base for kayak explorations of remote islands.

Place to Stay The island's accommodation, **Swan Island Retreat** (☎ *6357 2211; singles/doubles $55/77),* is in the old lighthouse keeper's quarters and sleeps up to 11 people.

Getting There & Away There's an airstrip for light planes – discuss charter flight possibilities with the owners when making your booking.

Three Hummock Island

In a similar get-away vein to Swan Island, but at the other end of Bass Strait, is the 29-sq-km Three Hummock Island, 25km off Tasmania's northwestern tip. The sole resident family moved here in 1951 and runs the **Three Hummock Island Lodge** (☎*/fax 6452 1554, 019 330 223; singles $45-105, doubles $90-190, extra adult/child $35/20),* which sleeps up to 10 people in singles and doubles, and has some **camp sites**. Meals are included in the lodge package and basic foods can also be bought, but bring any favourite items along with you. Boat hire and guided walks are also available.

Getting There & Away Charter flights are possible from Wynyard and Smithton in Tasmania, and from Melbourne's Moorabbin airport – ask the owners when you book accommodation.

Thanks

Many thanks to the travellers who used the last edition and wrote to us with helpful hints, useful advice and interesting anecdotes:

Coral Anderson, Raymond Ang, Amy Atkinson, Lauren Atmore, Wendy Atmore, David & Dorothy Bailey, Sarah Baughn, Rick Begg, Julien Benney, David & Karen Berton, Bev Blythe, Johan G Borchert, James Boyce, Martin & Wendy Bray, Tasha Bray, A Bregman, James Brett, N & S Brew, Philip Briddon, Jeff Broadhurst, Kate van den Broek, Ann Brown, Mark Bruce, Lynda Burek, Eric & Karin Burgess, Jill Burnett, Peter Calingaert, Linda Campbell, Guy Carrier, WJ Carter, Amy Chan, J Chan, John Chaplin, Marlene Chisholm, Michael Chittick, Tan Hui Choon, Ben Clark, Patricia & Michael Clarke, Jim & Elayne Coakes, Simon Cohen, Maria Coloma, Len Cook, Katherine Cooper, J Cornelissen, Katherine Cowan, Roberta Cowdell, Vicki Cowles, Rodney Croome, Michael Cummins, Sheila Darzi, Andrew Delavere-Pawley, Phillippe Delesalle, Richard Denham, Joanne Dickinson, Leonhard Dietze, Laurie Dillon, Mildred Dumpel-Tromp, Jim Duncan, Hannah Dunleavy, Susie Dunlop, Carol Edmeades, Carolyn & Jerry Farmer, Serge Ferrier, Phyllis J Filley, Tim Fitzpatrick, Lisa Flynn, SJ Forbes, Robyn Fried, Claudia Frosch, Tony Gerber, N Gillies, Jacki Grau, David Greilach, Mardi Grimshaw, Dennis Gullan, Margaret Hall, Jo Hancock, Nick Hardy, Gloria Hawes, Martin Hayes, Alisa Hedding, Trode & Esben Henriksen, Gabi Hilgner, Roslyn Hill, Theresa Hill, Gray Hodge, Rod Holcombe, Susan Hood, Tan Howman, Jan Hyde, Elizabeth Jackson, Greg James, Dr Mike Jenkins, Petra Joho, Tom Joyce, Paul Keen, Alistair Kelly, Helen Kerslake, Alexandra King, Erica Kirby, Jan Kirkman, Diarne Kreltszheim, Audrey Leeson, Suzy & Richard Lenne, Derek Lindsay, Gert & Irmgard Ljungkvist, Kathryn Lockrey, Tang Ling Loh, Barbara Lovell, Nick Lugger, Malcolm Macdonald, Margery Maconacky, Liz Maher, Nigel Marsden, Karen McIvor, Joe McShanag, Janice Meade, Erica V Merritt, Alexandra & Beverly Meyer, Lorraine Miloro, Keith Moon, Louisa Moore, Christine Moran, Linda & Howard Moses, Roger Mueller, Dr Roderick Mundy, Laura Murphy, Lars Mygind, Sally Neil, Irene & Rupert Neudorfer, Louis Nowra, Suzanne O'Kane, Angela Odermann, Marcus Ogden, Dan O'Keefe, Richard & Susan Ord, Nicola Owen, L Paynes, Jane Penton, Michael Perring, Janet Pitt, Ian Podger, Jackie Poole, Paul Raistrick, Brian Rawding, Rebekah Ray, Nigel Reeves, Dirk Reiser, Stuart Reynolds, John Rice, William Richards, Sherry Robson, Hans Rolfsmeier, Bruce & Yarja Rollinson, Erik & Rita Ronning, Stephanie Rowatt, Todd & Amy Sattersten-Buckley, T Schamm, W Schuurman, Richard Scott, Brad Shade, Desmona Sheridan, Alice Silverberg, Matt Sisk, Krista Slade, Caroline Smith, Christine Smith, Egbert Stams, Helgar Staudinger, L Steenberg, Joel Stettner, Vinay Talwar, Andrew Tanner, John Taylor, Julie Taylor, Jol Teo, Jaap Tichler, Diane & John Tickell, Laura Tomlinson, Teresa Tripp, Marjilke van Duin, Keith Vanderstaay, Joe Varrasso, Rudiger Voberg, Stan Walerczyk, Fiona Wallace, Lorna Walsh, John Ward, Fran Wells, Annabel Westney, Anna Wilde, John Willems, P & D Williams, Vikki Williams, Petra Wink, George Woods, A Wright, Ben Wright, Cheryl Wright, John Young, Barbara Zihlman

LONELY PLANET

You already know that Lonely Planet produces more than this one guidebook, but you might not be aware of the other products we have on this region. Here is a selection of titles that you may want to check out as well:

Australia Road Atlas
ISBN 1 86450 065 4
US$14.99 • UK£8.99

Healthy Travel
Australia, NZ & the Pacific
ISBN 1 86450 052 2
US$5.95 • UK£3.99

Australian phrasebook
ISBN 0 86442 576 7
US$5.95 • UK£3.99

Australia
ISBN 1 74059 065 1
US$25.99 • UK£15.99

Victoria
ISBN 1 74059 240 9
US$19.99 • UK£12.99

Melbourne
ISBN 1 74059 181 X
US$16.99 • UK£10.99

East Coast Australia
ISBN 1 74059 012 0
US$17.99 • UK£11.99

Queensland
ISBN 0 86442 712 3
US$19.99 • UK£11.99

Aboriginal Australia
& the Torres Strait Islands
ISBN 1 86450 114 6
US$19.99 • UK£12.99

Watching Wildlife Australia
ISBN 1 86450 032 8
US$19.99 • UK£12.99

Cycling Australia
ISBN 1 86450 166 9
US$21.99 • UK£13.99

Walking in Australia
ISBN 0 86442 669 0
US$21.99 • UK£13.99

Available wherever books are sold

Lonely Planet Guides by Region

L onely Planet is known worldwide for publishing practical, reliable and no-nonsense travel information in our guides and on our Web site. The Lonely Planet list covers just about every accessible part of the world. Currently there are 16 series: Travel guides, Shoestring guides, Condensed guides, Phrasebooks, Read This First, Healthy Travel, Walking guides, Cycling guides, Watching Wildlife guides, Pisces Diving & Snorkeling guides, City Maps, Road Atlases, Out to Eat, World Food, Journeys travel literature and Pictorials.

AFRICA Africa on a shoestring • Botswana • Cairo • Cairo City Map • Cape Town • Cape Town City Map • East Africa • Egypt • Egyptian Arabic phrasebook • Ethiopia, Eritrea & Djibouti • Ethiopian Amharic phrasebook • The Gambia & Senegal • Healthy Travel Africa • Kenya • Malawi • Morocco • Moroccan Arabic phrasebook • Mozambique • Namibia • Read This First: Africa • South Africa, Lesotho & Swaziland • Southern Africa • Southern Africa Road Atlas • Swahili phrasebook • Tanzania, Zanzibar & Pemba • Trekking in East Africa • Tunisia • Watching Wildlife East Africa • Watching Wildlife Southern Africa • West Africa • World Food Morocco • Zambia • Zimbabwe, Botswana & Namibia
Travel Literature: Mali Blues: Traveling to an African Beat • The Rainbird: A Central African Journey • Songs to an African Sunset: A Zimbabwean Story

AUSTRALIA & THE PACIFIC Aboriginal Australia & the Torres Strait Islands •Auckland • Australia • Australian phrasebook • Australia Road Atlas • Cycling New Zealand • Fiji • Fijian phrasebook • Healthy Travel Australia, NZ & the Pacific • Islands of Australia's Great Barrier Reef • Melbourne • Melbourne City Map • Micronesia • New Caledonia • New South Wales • New Zealand • Northern Territory • Outback Australia • Out to Eat – Melbourne • Out to Eat – Sydney • Papua New Guinea • Pidgin phrasebook • Queensland • Rarotonga & the Cook Islands • Samoa • Solomon Islands • South Australia • South Pacific • South Pacific phrasebook • Sydney • Sydney City Map • Sydney Condensed • Tahiti & French Polynesia • Tasmania • Tonga • Tramping in New Zealand • Vanuatu • Victoria • Walking in Australia • Watching Wildlife Australia • Western Australia
Travel Literature: Islands in the Clouds: Travels in the Highlands of New Guinea • Kiwi Tracks: A New Zealand Journey • Sean & David's Long Drive

CENTRAL AMERICA & THE CARIBBEAN Bahamas, Turks & Caicos • Baja California • Belize, Guatemala & Yucatán • Bermuda • Central America on a shoestring • Costa Rica • Costa Rica Spanish phrasebook • Cuba • Cycling Cuba • Dominican Republic & Haiti • Eastern Caribbean • Guatemala • Havana • Healthy Travel Central & South America • Jamaica • Mexico • Mexico City • Panama • Puerto Rico • Read This First: Central & South America • Virgin Islands • World Food Caribbean • World Food Mexico • Yucatán
Travel Literature: Green Dreams: Travels in Central America

EUROPE Amsterdam • Amsterdam City Map • Amsterdam Condensed • Andalucía • Athens • Austria • Baltic States phrasebook • Barcelona • Barcelona City Map • Belgium & Luxembourg • Berlin • Berlin City Map • Britain • British phrasebook • Brussels, Bruges & Antwerp • Brussels City Map • Budapest • Budapest City Map • Canary Islands • Catalunya & the Costa Brava • Central Europe • Central Europe phrasebook • Copenhagen • Corfu & the Ionians • Corsica • Crete • Crete Condensed • Croatia • Cycling Britain • Cycling France • Cyprus • Czech & Slovak Republics • Czech phrasebook • Denmark • Dublin • Dublin City Map • Dublin Condensed • Eastern Europe • Eastern Europe phrasebook • Edinburgh • Edinburgh City Map • England • Estonia, Latvia & Lithuania • Europe on a shoestring • Europe phrasebook • Finland • Florence • Florence City Map • France • Frankfurt City Map • Frankfurt Condensed • French phrasebook • Georgia, Armenia & Azerbaijan • Germany • German phrasebook • Greece • Greek Islands • Greek phrasebook • Hungary • Iceland, Greenland & the Faroe Islands • Ireland • Italian phrasebook • Italy • Kraków • Lisbon • The Loire • London • London City Map • London Condensed • Madrid • Madrid City Map • Malta • Mediterranean Europe • Milan, Turin & Genoa • Moscow • Munich • Netherlands • Normandy • Norway • Out to Eat – London • Out to Eat – Paris • Paris • Paris City Map • Paris Condensed • Poland • Polish phrasebook • Portugal • Portuguese phrasebook • Prague • Prague City Map • Provence & the Côte d'Azur • Read This First: Europe • Rhodes & the Dodecanese • Romania & Moldova • Rome • Rome City Map • Rome Condensed • Russia, Ukraine & Belarus • Russian phrasebook • Scandinavian & Baltic Europe • Scandinavian phrasebook • Scotland • Sicily • Slovenia • South-West France • Spain • Spanish phrasebook • Stockholm • St Petersburg • St Petersburg City Map • Sweden • Switzerland • Tuscany • Ukrainian phrasebook • Venice • Vienna • Wales • Walking in Britain • Walking in France • Walking in Ireland • Walking in Italy • Walking in Scotland • Walking in Spain • Walking in Switzerland • Western Europe • World Food France • World Food Greece • World Food Ireland • World Food Italy • World Food Spain **Travel Literature:** After Yugoslavia • Love and War in the Apennines • The Olive Grove: Travels in Greece • On the Shores of the Mediterranean • Round Ireland in Low Gear • A Small Place in Italy

Lonely Planet Mail Order

Lonely Planet products are distributed worldwide. They are also available by mail order from Lonely Planet, so if you have difficulty finding a title please write to us. North and South American residents should write to 150 Linden St, Oakland, CA 94607, USA; European and African residents should write to 10a Spring Place, London NW5 3BH, UK; and residents of other countries to Locked Bag 1, Footscray, Victoria 3011, Australia.

INDIAN SUBCONTINENT & THE INDIAN OCEAN Bangladesh • Bengali phrasebook • Bhutan • Delhi • Goa • Healthy Travel Asia & India • Hindi & Urdu phrasebook • India • India & Bangladesh City Map • Indian Himalaya • Karakoram Highway • Kathmandu City Map • Kerala • Madagascar • Maldives • Mauritius, Réunion & Seychelles • Mumbai (Bombay) • Nepal • Nepali phrasebook • North India • Pakistan • Rajasthan • Read This First: Asia & India • South India • Sri Lanka • Sri Lanka phrasebook • Tibet • Tibetan phrasebook • Trekking in the Indian Himalaya • Trekking in the Karakoram & Hindukush • Trekking in the Nepal Himalaya • World Food India **Travel Literature:** The Age of Kali: Indian Travels and Encounters • Hello Goodnight: A Life of Goa • In Rajasthan • Maverick in Madagascar • A Season in Heaven: True Tales from the Road to Kathmandu • Shopping for Buddhas • A Short Walk in the Hindu Kush • Slowly Down the Ganges

MIDDLE EAST & CENTRAL ASIA Bahrain, Kuwait & Qatar • Central Asia • Central Asia phrasebook • Dubai • Farsi (Persian) phrasebook • Hebrew phrasebook • Iran • Israel & the Palestinian Territories • Istanbul • Istanbul City Map • Istanbul to Cairo • Istanbul to Kathmandu • Jerusalem • Jerusalem City Map • Jordan • Lebanon • Middle East • Oman & the United Arab Emirates • Syria • Turkey • Turkish phrasebook • World Food Turkey • Yemen **Travel Literature:** Black on Black: Iran Revisited • Breaking Ranks: Turbulent Travels in the Promised Land • The Gates of Damascus • Kingdom of the Film Stars: Journey into Jordan

NORTH AMERICA Alaska • Boston • Boston City Map • Boston Condensed • British Columbia • California & Nevada • California Condensed • Canada • Chicago • Chicago City Map • Chicago Condensed • Florida • Georgia & the Carolinas • Great Lakes • Hawaii • Hiking in Alaska • Hiking in the USA • Honolulu & Oahu City Map • Las Vegas • Los Angeles • Los Angeles City Map • Louisiana & the Deep South • Miami • Miami City Map • Montreal • New England • New Orleans • New Orleans City Map • New York City • New York City City Map • New York City Condensed • New York, New Jersey & Pennsylvania • Oahu • Out to Eat – San Francisco • Pacific Northwest • Rocky Mountains • San Diego & Tijuana • San Francisco • San Francisco City Map • Seattle • Seattle City Map • Southwest • Texas • Toronto • USA • USA phrasebook • Vancouver • Vancouver City Map • Virginia & the Capital Region • Washington, DC • Washington, DC City Map • World Food New Orleans **Travel Literature:** Caught Inside: A Surfer's Year on the California Coast • Drive Thru America

NORTH-EAST ASIA Beijing • Beijing City Map • Cantonese phrasebook • China • Hiking in Japan • Hong Kong & Macau • Hong Kong City Map • Hong Kong Condensed • Japan • Japanese phrasebook • Korea • Korean phrasebook • Kyoto • Mandarin phrasebook • Mongolia • Mongolian phrasebook • Seoul • Shanghai • South-West China • Taiwan • Tokyo • Tokyo Condensed • World Food Hong Kong • World Food Japan **Travel Literature:** In Xanadu: A Quest • Lost Japan

SOUTH AMERICA Argentina, Uruguay & Paraguay • Bolivia • Brazil • Brazilian phrasebook • Buenos Aires • Buenos Aires City Map • Chile & Easter Island • Colombia • Ecuador & the Galapagos Islands • Healthy Travel Central & South America • Latin American Spanish phrasebook • Peru • Quechua phrasebook • Read This First: Central & South America • Rio de Janeiro • Rio de Janeiro City Map • Santiago de Chile • South America on a shoestring • Trekking in the Patagonian Andes • Venezuela **Travel Literature:** Full Circle: A South American Journey

SOUTH-EAST ASIA Bali & Lombok • Bangkok • Bangkok City Map • Burmese phrasebook • Cambodia • Cycling Vietnam, Laos & Cambodia • East Timor phrasebook • Hanoi • Healthy Travel Asia & India • Hill Tribes phrasebook • Ho Chi Minh City (Saigon) • Indonesia • Indonesian phrasebook • Indonesia's Eastern Islands • Java • Lao phrasebook • Laos • Malay phrasebook • Malaysia, Singapore & Brunei • Myanmar (Burma) • Philippines • Pilipino (Tagalog) phrasebook • Read This First: Asia & India • Singapore • Singapore City Map • South-East Asia on a shoestring • South-East Asia phrasebook • Thailand • Thailand's Islands & Beaches • Thailand, Vietnam, Laos & Cambodia Road Atlas • Thai phrasebook • Vietnam • Vietnamese phrasebook • World Food Indonesia • World Food Thailand • World Food Vietnam

ALSO AVAILABLE: Antarctica • The Arctic • The Blue Man: Tales of Travel, Love and Coffee • Brief Encounters: Stories of Love, Sex & Travel • Buddhist Stupas in Asia: The Shape of Perfection • Chasing Rickshaws • The Last Grain Race • Lonely Planet ... On the Edge: Adventurous Escapades from Around the World • Lonely Planet Unpacked • Lonely Planet Unpacked Again • Not the Only Planet: Science Fiction Travel Stories • Ports of Call: A Journey by Sea • Sacred India • Travel Photography: A Guide to Taking Better Pictures • Travel with Children • Tuvalu: Portrait of an Island Nation

Index

Text

Bold indicates maps.

Bold indicates maps.

Boxed Text

MAP LEGEND

BOUNDARIES

---·--·-- State
--- --- Disputed
-·-■-·-■- International
+-+-+-+-+ Cliff

REGIONAL ROUTES

Tollway, Freeway
Primary Road
Secondary Road
Minor Road

CITY ROUTES

Fwy — Freeway
Hwy — Primary Road
Rd — Secondary Road
St — Street
La — Lane
On/Off Ramp
Unsealed Road
One Way Street
Pedestrian Mall
Tunnel
Footbridge

POPULATION SYMBOLS

✪ **Capital** National Capital
◉ **Capital** State Capital
● **City** City
● Town Town
● Village Village

AREA FEATURES

Aboriginal Land
Beach
Building
Campus
Cemetery
Mall
Park, Gardens, Path
Urban Area

TRANSPORT ROUTES & STATIONS

Train
Underground Train
Metro
Tramway
Monorail
Cable Car, Chairlift
Ferry
Walking Trail, Head
Walking Tour
Pier or Jetty

HYDROGRAPHY

Coastline
River, Creek
Dry River, Creek
Lake
Dry Lake; Salt Lake
Spring; Rapids
Waterfalls
Swamp

MAP SYMBOLS

■ Place to Stay
▼ Place to Eat
● Point of Interest

⊠ ✈ Airport, Airfield
☄ Airplane Wreck
⊖ Bank/ATM
🚌 Bus Stop, Terminal
↘ Bird Sanctuary/Park
⌂ Camping
⊕ Caravan
⌂ Cave
Church
Cinema
♿ Disabled Access

⬛ Dive Site
Embassy/Consulate
Golf Course
Hospital/Clinic
Internet Cafe
Lighthouse
Lookout
Monument
Mountain/Range
Museum/Gallery
National Park

Parking
Petrol Station
Picnic Area
Police Station
Post Office
Pub or Bar
Ruins
Shipwreck
Shopping Centre
Snorkelling
Surfing

Stately Home
Swimming Pool
Taxi
Telephone
Theatre
Transport
Toilets
Tourist Information
Windsurfing
Winery
Zoo/Wildlife Park

Note: not all symbols displayed above appear in this book

LONELY PLANET OFFICES

Australia
Locked Bag 1, Footscray, Victoria 3011
☎ 03 8379 8000 fax 03 8379 8111
email: talk2us@lonelyplanet.com.au

USA
150 Linden St, Oakland, CA 94607
☎ 510 893 8555 TOLL FREE: 800 275 8555
fax 510 893 8572
email: info@lonelyplanet.com

UK
10a Spring Place, London NW5 3BH
☎ 020 7428 4800 fax 020 7428 4828
email: go@lonelyplanet.co.uk

France
1 rue du Dahomey, 75011 Paris
☎ 01 55 25 33 00 fax 01 55 25 33 01
email: bip@lonelyplanet.fr
www.lonelyplanet.fr

World Wide Web: www.lonelyplanet.com *or* AOL keyword: lp
Lonely Planet Images: lpi@lonelyplanet.com.au